P9-CBX-558

SOCIOLOGY

SOCIOLOGY

Second edition

PAUL B. HORTON   CHESTER L. HUNT

WESTERN MICHIGAN UNIVERSITY

McGRAW-HILL BOOK COMPANY   NEW YORK ST. LOUIS SAN FRANCISCO TORONTO LONDON SYDNEY

Sociology

Library of Congress Catalog Card Number 68–11609

30423

3 4 5 6 7 8 9 0 K R K R 7 5 4 3 2 1 0 6 9

WHAT should an introductory sociology textbook try to do? First and most important, we believe it should capture the interest of the student and demonstrate both the process and challenge of scientific observation and analysis of social behavior in a readable and interesting way.

Second, an introductory sociology textbook should seek to cultivate in the student the habit of scientific analysis of social data. Unless the student gains a sophisticated awareness of his own ethnocentrism and some ability to objectify his observations, his sociology course has failed in one of its major objectives.

Third, an introductory sociology textbook should present the basic concepts and descriptive materials of sociology clearly and intelligibly. These should be illustrated so vividly that they "come alive" and become part of the student's thinking vocabulary. Concepts should not be learned simply as definitions to be memorized, but as accurate, descriptive names for the ways people act and the things people build. Concepts are far more than a professional vocabulary to be used in advanced studies: They are even more important as tools for identifying and understanding a process or idea. Many sociology students will find that the introductory course is a terminal course as well, and the basic concepts should be tools for continuing social observation and analysis.

In this textbook we have tried to do these things. Whether we have succeeded is for the reader to judge. We have generally avoided esoteric sources in favor of others more easily available to most students. We have often used literary and popular sources for purposes of illustration. We have done this to emphasize the fact that sociology is the disciplined observation and analysis of everyday life and that the concepts and insights of sociology are applicable to all that goes on around the student.

We have sought to minimize the overlap with other courses. This textbook is not a capsule summary of the entire sociology curriculum. We have intentionally excluded "social problem" material in favor of a more comprehensive treatment of principles and concepts.

We owe a debt of appreciation to many people, and especially to a number of our colleagues for their helpful criticisms and suggestions, to our wives for their forbearance, and to Frederick J. Ashby for his imaginative informal line drawings.

PAUL B. HORTON
CHESTER L. HUNT

Contents

One SOCIOLOGY AND SOCIETY

For centuries man has pondered the societies he has developed. Some of our oldest documents, going back five thousand years or more, record men's efforts to analyze and understand their social order. In this search men have sought truth from many sources and have used many methods, some highly successful, some less so.

Some of the sources of truth are described in Chapter 1, "Science Studies Society." This chapter shows that although each source of truth has its uses, only through scientific investigation can reliable knowledge about human society be discovered. Chapter 2, "Fields and Methods of Sociology," tells how scientific methods are used in sociological investigation. All phenomena can be studied scientifically, but the techniques of study must be fitted to the materials studied. Just how sociologists try to make this adaptation is described in Chapter 2.

1

SCIENCE STUDIES SOCIETY

No civilized society, since the first cities arose in Mesopotamia five thousand years ago, has ever, until very recently, had a way to measure the wants and feelings of the people with reasonable accuracy. History might be a very different story if a technique had been available to Pericles, say, or Caesar, George III, Louis XIV, Woodrow Wilson, or Nicholas II. . . .

Many critics distrust and discount the effort to measure public opinion scientifically. Often enough, the same skeptics who downgrade opinion polls do not hesitate to generalize about national character and desires with dogmatic finality, their tools being intuition, random observation, and projection of their own necessarily limited experience. "The American people will never consent," they say. Or, to quote a prominent commentator in the Berlin crisis of 1961: "The vast majority of U.S. citizens remain resolved to face the Communist pressure without yielding an inch." How does he know? (Stuart Chase, American Credos, Harper & Row, Publishers, Incorporated, New York, 1962, pp. 1–2.)

PATHOLOGIST after elaborate preparation places a slide under the microscope and adjusts the lens carefully. A Purari war party watch carefully as they place their canoe in the water, for unless it rocks the raid will not be successful. A man steps from a new station wagon, cuts a forked twig, and carries it around holding it above the ground, while a well-drilling crew stands by, waiting to drill where the twig tells them water will be found. A woman in Peoria, anxious over her teen-age daughter, prays to God for guidance. A physician leafs through the pages of a parasitology textbook as he tries to identify the puzzling skin rash of his latest patient. A senator scans the latest public opinion poll as he wonders how to vote on the farm bill.

Each of these persons is seeking guidance. Their problems vary, and their sources of truth are different. Where shall man find truth? How can he know where he has found it? In the million years, more or less, of man's life on this earth, he has sought truth in many places. But the sources are not all reliable, nor is any one equally useful for all kinds of problems.

SOME SOURCES OF TRUTH

Intuition Galen, a famous Greek physician of the second century, prepared an elaborate chart of the human body, showing exactly where it might be pierced without fatal injury. How did he know the vulnerable spots? He just *knew* them. True, he had learned a good deal of human anatomy through his observations and those of his associates; but beyond this, he relied upon his intuition to tell him which zones were fatal. *Intuition is any flash of insight (true or mistaken) whose source the receiver cannot fully identify or explain.* Hitler relied heavily upon his intuition, much to the distress of his generals. His intuition told him that France would not fight for the Rhineland, that England would not fight for Czechoslovakia, that England and France would not fight for Poland, and that England and France would quit when he attacked Russia. He was right on the first two insights and wrong on the last two.

Intuition is responsible for many brilliant hypotheses, which can later be tested through other methods. Perhaps intuition's greatest value is in the forming of hypotheses. As a source of knowledge, of conclusions, intuition is less satisfactory. True, sometimes intuition takes the form of a shrewd leap to a sound conclusion, based upon a mass of half-remembered experience and information. But how can such intuitive knowledge be tested and verified? Often it can't be. Anaximander propounded a theory of evolution in the sixth century B.C., but not until the nineteenth century A.D. were the facts available to determine that his theory was essentially correct. Intuitive knowledge often can't be tested at the time it is offered. Sometimes it can't be tested at all, or at least not until it is too late to make any difference, as Hitler eventually discovered.

Authority Two thousand years ago, Galen knew more about human anatomy than any other mortal; as recently as 1800, physicians were still quoting him as an authority. Aristotle stated that a barrel of water could be added to a barrel of ashes without overflowing, and for two thousand years thereafter, a student who might suggest trying it out would be scolded for his impertinence. For many centuries, creative thought was stifled by Aristotelian authority, for since an authority is *right,* any conflicting ideas must be wrong. Authority does not discover new truths, but it can prevent new truth from being discovered or accepted.

Dangerous though authority may be, we can't get along without it. Our accumulation of knowledge is too great for anyone to absorb, so we must rely upon specialists who have collected the reliable knowledge in a particular field. An authority is a necessary and useful source of knowledge—*in the field in which he is an authority.* Science recognizes no authorities on "things in general."

Authority is of several sorts. *Sacred* authority rests upon the faith that a certain tradition or document—the Bible, the Koran, the Vedas—is of supernatural origin. Or it is a faith that a certain group or institution—the medicine men, the priests, the church—is constantly receiving supernatural guidance. *Secular* authority arises not from divine revelation but from human perception. It is of two kinds: *secular scientific* authority, which rests upon empirical investigation, and *secular humanistic* authority, which rests upon the belief that certain "great men" have had remarkable insight into human behavior and the nature of the universe. The search for truth by consulting the "great books" is an example of the appeal to secular humanistic authority.

Some fields—counseling and psychological services, space travel, health and diet, for example—are cluttered with many self-styled "authorities" without professional training in these fields. The most reputable of authorities is likely to become a foolish incompetent when he strays beyond his specialty. The general who pontificates on crime prevention, the business executive who endorses a food fad, the physician who gives prescriptions for labor-management problems—each of these may be making a fool of himself. He may also be making fools of his listeners.

The layman (and everyone is a layman in all fields except that of his specialty) has no choice; he *must* rely upon authority since he cannot become an expert on everything. For the layman to disagree with the qualified experts on a question of fact is presumptuous. The layman's problem is how to find and recognize a professionally qualified authority on the matter which concerns him.

No scientific authority, however, has the final word on human knowledge. The scientist respects the qualified authority, but still questions his basic assumptions and verifies his conclusions. A man who is considered an expert in a given field deserves to have his views considered seriously, but the weight of authority does not close the door upon further investigation. Today's scientific authority becomes the springboard to tomorrow's research. Thus knowledge grows, relentlessly converting today's "final" pronouncements into tomorrow's midpoints and side streets along the road to expanding knowledge.

Tradition   Of all sources of truth, tradition is one of the most reassuring. Here is the accumulated wisdom of the ages, and he who disregards it may expect denunciation as a scoundrel or a fool. If a pattern has "worked" in the past, why not keep on using it?

Tradition, however, preserves both the accumulated wisdom and the accumulated bunkum of the ages. Tradition is society's attic, crammed with all sorts of useful tools and useless relics. A great deal of "practical experience" consists in repeating the mistakes of our predecessors. A task of social science is to sort out our folklore into the true and the merely ancient.

Tradition says:	Scientific investigation finds that:
Men are intellectually superior to women.	Neither sex is superior in inherited intellectual abilities.
Colds are caused by chills and wet feet.	Colds are caused by viruses, although exposure may lower resistance.
One's character shows in his face.	There is no dependable association between facial features and personality characteristics.
Revealing dress leads to immoral behavior.	There is no relation between nudity and moral behavior as is shown in comparing different societies.
A man who cheats at cards will cheat in business.	Honesty in one situation tells relatively little about one's behavior in a different situation.
Spare the rod and spoil the child.	Serious delinquents usually have been punished more severely than most nondelinquents.
The genius or near genius is generally delicate, impractical, unstable, and unsuccessful.	The genius and near-genius group is above average in health, emotional adjustment, and income.

Common Sense For thousands of years people's common sense told them that the earth was flat, that big objects fell faster than small ones, that stone and iron were perfectly solid materials, and that a person's true character was betrayed by his facial features; yet today we know that none of these statements is true.

When we don't know where our ideas come from or what they are based on, we sometimes call them "common sense." If we call them common sense, we don't have to prove them, for then others will join us in the collective self-deception of assuming that they have already been proved. If one presses for proof, he is told that the idea has been proved by experience. The term, common sense, puts a respectable front on all sorts of notions for which there is no systematic body of evidence that can be cited.

What often passes for common sense consists of a group's accumulation of collective guesses, hunches, and haphazard trial-and-error learnings. Many common-sense propositions are sound, earthy, useful bits of knowledge. "A soft answer turneth away wrath," and "Birds of a feather flock together," are practical observations on social life. But many common-sense conclusions are based on ignorance, prejudice, and mistaken in-

Tradition is society's attic.

terpretation. When medieval Europeans noticed that feverish patients were free of lice while most healthy people were lousy, they made the common-sense conclusion that lice would cure fever and therefore sprinkled lice over feverish patients. Not until the fever subsided would the lice remain. Common sense, like tradition, preserves both folk wisdom and folk nonsense, and to sort them out one from the other is a task for science.

Science   Only within the last two or three hundred years has the scientific method become a common way of seeking answers about the natural world. Science has become a source of knowledge about man's *social* world even more recently; yet in the brief period since man began to rely upon the scientific method, he has learned more about his world than he learned in the preceding ten thousand years. The spectacular explosion of knowledge in the modern world parallels man's use of the scientific method. What makes the scientific method so productive? How does it differ from other methods of seeking truth?

CHARACTERISTICS OF SCIENTIFIC KNOWLEDGE

Verifiable evidence   Scientific knowledge is based on verifiable evidence. By evidence we mean concrete factual observations which other observers can see, weigh, measure, count, or check for accuracy. We may think the definition too obvious to mention; most of us have some awareness of the scientific method. Yet only a few centuries ago medieval scholars held long debates on how many teeth a horse had, without bothering to look into a horse's mouth to count them.

At this point we raise the troublesome methodological question, "What is a fact?" While the word looks deceptively simple, it is not easy to distinguish a fact from a widely shared illusion. Suppose we define a fact as a *descriptive statement upon which all qualified observers are in agreement*. By this definition, medieval ghosts were a fact, since all medieval observers agreed that ghosts were real. There is, therefore, no way to be *sure* that a fact is an accurate description and not a mistaken impression. Research would be easier if facts were dependable, unshakable certainties. Since they are not, the best we can do is to recognize that a fact is *a descriptive statement of reality which scientists, after careful examination and cross-checking, agree in believing to be accurate*.

Since science is based on verifiable evidence, science can deal only with questions about which verifiable evidence can be found. Questions like, "Is there a God?" "What is the purpose and destiny of man?" or "What makes a thing beautiful?" are not scientific questions because they cannot be treated factually. Such questions may be terribly important, but the scientific method has no tools for handling them. Scientists can study human *beliefs* about God, or man's destiny, or beauty, or anything else, and they may study the *personal and social consequences* of such beliefs; but these are studies of human behavior, with no attempt to settle the truth or error of the beliefs themselves.

Science then does not have answers for everything, and many important questions are not scientific questions. The scientific method is our most reliable source of factual knowledge about human behavior and the natural universe, but science with its dependence upon verifiable factual evidence cannot answer questions about value, or esthetics, or purpose and ultimate meaning, or supernatural phenomena. Answers to such questions must be sought in philosophy, metaphysics, or religion.

Each scientific conclusion represents the most reasonable interpretation of all the available evidence—but new evidence may appear tomorrow. Therefore *science has no absolute truths.* An absolute truth is one which will hold true for all times, places, or circumstances. All scientific truth is tentative, subject to revision in the light of new evidence. Some scientific conclusions (e.g., that the earth is a spheroid; or that innate drives are culturally conditioned) are based upon such a large and consistent body of evidence that scientists doubt that they will ever be overturned by new evidence. Yet the scientific method requires that *all* conclusions be open to reexamination whenever new evidence is found to challenge them.

This receptivity to new evidence is easy to state but not always easy to maintain. Scientists are also human beings, and despite their commitment to scientific detachment, they sometimes refuse to examine new evidence if it conflicts with established scientific traditions. Galileo's colleagues refused to look through his telescope and see the moons of Jupiter; Lavoisier insisted that stones (meteorites) could not fall from the air because there were none up there; all the scientists of the Paris Academy pronounced Edison's phonograph a humbug because they knew that the human voice could not be reproduced from a disk. Harvey's circulation of the blood, Pasteur's microbes, and Simmelweis's discovery that childbed fever was carried by physicians were all rejected for many years after their discovery. A more recent survey [Warner, 1938][1] found that many of the psychologists who rejected Rhine's findings on extrasensory perception had read none of his published research. To maintain an open-minded willingness to examine new evidence is so difficult a task that even scientists do not always succeed.

Ethical neutrality Science is knowledge, and knowledge can be put to differing uses. Atomic fission can be used to power a city, excavate a harbor, or incinerate a nation. Every use of scientific knowledge involves a choice between values. Our values define what is most important to us. Science tells us that overeating and cigarette smoking will shorten our expectation of life. But can science tell us which we should choose—a longer life or a more indulgent one? Science can answer questions of fact, but has no way to prove that one value is better than another.

Science, then, is ethically neutral. Science seeks knowledge, while society's values determine how this knowledge is to be used. Knowledge about bacteria can be used to preserve health or to wage germ warfare. Knowledge about group organization can be used to preserve a democracy or to establish a dictatorship.

Since science is ethically neutral, no field of inquiry is too sacred to explore. Scientific discoveries sometimes destroy revered myths, undermine established institutions, and challenge cherished values. Vesalius laid the foundations of medical science by robbing graves to get corpses to dissect; the human body was too "sacred" to cut up. Kinsey's studies of human sexual behavior a

Evidence consists of verifiable facts.

few years ago and Masters and Johnson's more recent studies [1966][1] have aroused a chorus of protest from those who feel that human sexual behavior is "too intimate" for scientific inquiry. But science recognizes no "improper" questions. *Any* question on which verifiable evidence can be secured is a proper question for science. Science acts on the belief that, if scientific knowledge undermines established beliefs, institutions, and practices, then these beliefs, institutions, and practices need to be revised.

Science is ethically neutral, but scientists are not. The scientist has his own value system which may be very important to him. The scientist's values affect the questions which he chooses to study. He is unlikely to start counting the leaves on trees or measuring the duration of kisses unless he believes that this will add something *significant* to our body of knowledge. It is true that sheer intellectual curiosity, undirected by any thought of possible uses, often discovers useful knowledge. Yet most research is an effort to discover something the scientist believes will be important in some way. Ethical neutrality, then, does not mean that the scientist has no values; it means that he must not let his values distort the design and conduct of his research. A sociologist studying the effects of divorce upon children, for example, must design and conduct his research in such a way that his own values concerning divorce do not affect his findings. Since this sociologist almost certainly believes that well-adjusted personality is a worthy value, he may follow up his published research with a popular magazine article on how divorced parents should treat their children. The roles of the sociologist, as an ethically neutral pure scientist and as a responsibly involved applied scientist, are discussed in the following chapter.

OBSERVATION—THE BASIC TECHNIQUE OF SCIENTIFIC METHOD

The word "evidence" keeps popping up in discussions of scientific method. What is evidence and where is it found? Evidence consists of verifiable facts of all kinds and is found through scientific observation. But scientific observation is not the same as looking at things. Each of us has been looking at things all his life, but this activity does not make him a scientific observer, any more than a lifetime of swatting flies makes him an entomologist. Wherein does scientific observation differ from just looking at things?

Accuracy   Scientific observation is *accurate*. The scientific observer is extremely careful to make certain that things are as he describes them. The statement, "My

---

[1] Bracketed references in the text are to sources described in full in the Bibliography at the end of the book.

backyard is full of dead trees," is of uncertain accuracy unless the trees have been examined by an expert to be sure they are dead and not merely dormant. Or the statement, "Families are larger than they used to be," is of low accuracy. *What* size families, and *where*, are more numerous than they were *when*? If we say, "The proportion of American families with four or more children has grown substantially in the past decade," the statement is more accurate. Painstaking checking, rechecking, and cross-checking to produce carefully stated propositions are the price of scientific accuracy.

Precision   Scientific observation is *precise*. The statement, "My backyard is full of dead trees," is not precise, even though it may be accurate. What is meant by "full of" dead trees? If the sentence reads, "All the trees in my yard are dead," or "There are twenty dead trees in my yard," the statement gains in precision. While accuracy refers to the truth or correctness of a statement, *precision refers to degree or measurement.* If the above statement about family size is revised to read, "The proportion of American families with four or more children increased from 6.6 per cent of all families in 1948 to 11.1 per cent in 1965," the statement is more precise.

In a laboratory experiment the scientist weighs, measures, counts, or times each development with great care. A report which read, "I took some hot salt water, added a pinch of copper sulfate and a little nitric acid, let it cool for a while . . ." would be almost useless. How much water? How hot? How much salt, copper sulfate, and acid? Cooled for how long, and to what temperature? Unless quite precise, an observation is of limited value to science.

Since scientific writing seeks precision, science avoids colorful or extravagant language. Whereas literature aims to arouse the feelings of the reader, science aims to convey accurate information. Tennyson's lines, "Every moment dies a man; every moment one is born," is good literature. To be good science, it should be written, "In the entire world, according to 1960 figures, every 11⅛ seconds, on the average, dies a man, woman, or child; every 4⅞ seconds, on the average, an infant is born." Literary writing may be intentionally vague, imprecise, and fanciful, stimulating the reader to wonder what is meant (e.g., whether Hamlet was really insane). The dramatic sweep of the novelist and the provocative imagery of the poet have no place in scientific writing. Yet good scientific writing need not be dull, and should never plod through an insufferable mass of ill-arranged detail. Good scientific writing is clear, is easily understood by a qualified reader, and gets its suspense from a readable procession of significant facts and interpretations.

How much precision is needed? This depends upon what we are studying. In measuring atoms, a millionth of an inch may be too large an error, whereas at an agricultural experiment station, a variation of several feet may be unimportant. A social scientist might observe the behavior of a mob of "several hundred" persons without counting them, just as an entomologist can describe a "large" swarm of bees without counting them. Science, however, always seeks *as much precision as the particular problem requires.* If the conditions of observation make this degree of precision impossible, the scientist must suspend judgment until more precise observations can be collected.

System   Scientific observation is *systematic*. A scientific investigation defines a problem, then draws up an organized plan for collecting facts about it. Suppose the question is, "How does the drop-out rate of college students who marry while in college compare with the drop-out rate of unmarried students?" One might try to answer the question by simply recalling the students he has known; but this sample would be small; it might not be typical; and one's memory is imperfect. Conclusions based on casual recollections are not very reliable. If our research plan calls for a systematic check on the college records of several thousand students, then our drop-out rates for single and married students are based on dependable factual data. Unless these data have been collected as part of an organized systematic program of scientific observation, they are likely to be spotty and incomplete. Anecdotes, personal recollections, offhand opinions, and travelogue impressions may suggest an hypothesis which is worth testing; but no scientist would base a conclusion upon such data.

Records Scientific observation is *recorded.* Man's memory is notoriously fallible. Data which are not recorded are not dependable. No laboratory scientist would attempt to memorize a detailed experiment. He writes it out completely, recording each operation and reaction, so that his procedures and findings can be accurately known and verified by other scientists.

In the field of human behavior, the need for recorded observation is less fully realized. Suppose a professor were to say, "A number of women students have majored in this field, and while some do excellent work, on the average they don't quite measure up to the men students in this field." What, exactly, is this professor saying? Unless he has actually recorded and computed average scores for both groups, he is in effect saying, "I have mentally recalled the grades of hundreds of my students, and have mentally added the scores and mentally computed averages for male and female students; and I have found the female average to be lower." Such a feat of memory would be impossible. All conclusions based on recalling a mass of unrecorded data are untrustworthy.

In fact, such conclusions based on informal recollection may be worse than useless, for they generally express the prejudices of the observer, masquerading as a scientific conclusion. Since memory is imperfect, we often "remember" things the way we prefer them to have been rather than as they actually were. Prejudice, wishful thinking, and habitual attitude all operate to twist our observations to fit our preferences. It is important, therefore, that evidence be recorded as quickly as possible; the longer we wait the more greatly our prejudices, preferences, and afterthoughts may have distorted it. The following accounts of a disaster as reported by one of the survivors show the progressive changes made by time:

Man's memories of themselves aren't accurate. One month after the sinking of the Litch I questioned the survivors for a second time. The stories had altered—in some cases radically. When the ship blew up it was honorable and acceptable to save one's own skin. Later, as we got closer to civilization and normal society, many men remembered something new, how they had struggled to save others at the risk of their own lives.

My notes on a signalman, made ten minutes after he was rescued, read, "After I jumped over, I swam as fast as I could, I swam upwind like you always told us. I had no life jacket and got scared. I saw someone floating with his head under water. It was Mr. —. His back was broken; I could tell by the funny way it angled just below the neck. I said to myself if he's dead there's no use in his wasting the life jacket. I took the jacket from him and held on to it. I don't know what happened to Mr. —'s body."

When I interviewed the same man a month later he told me this: "I swam from the ship as fast as I could. I swam upwind just like you always told us. I saw someone floating with his head under water. It was Mr. —. Although his back was broken and his head had been submerged, I figured maybe the doctor could do something for him. I pulled his head out of the water and tied the jacket tie under his chin so that his head'd stay in the air. I trod water for about an hour, just holding onto Mr. —'s life jacket for a rest occasionally. I saw a raft about five hundred yards away. I thought maybe the doctor or a hospital corpsman might be on it. I swam over to it. The doctor wasn't there. We paddled over where Mr. — had been, but there was no sign of him."

I met the signalman on the street in Washington a couple of months ago—five years after the Litch sank. His story had changed more. Now it was he, the signalman, who had the life jacket. When he saw that Mr. — had a broken back, the signalman removed his life jacket and gave it to the injured officer. "I knew he was dead, but figured maybe there was a chance in a thousand he might be saved. It was my duty to try to help him, so I gave him my jacket."

From William J. Lederer, *All the Ships at Sea,* William Morrow and Company, Inc., New York, 1950, pp. 203–204. Reprinted by permission of William Sloane Associates.

Objectivity   Scientific observation is *objective*. This means that, in so far as is humanly possible, the observation is unaffected by the observer's own beliefs, preferences, wishes, or values. In other words, *objectivity means the ability to see and accept facts as they are, not as one might wish them to be.* It is fairly easy to be objective when observing something about which we have no preferences or values. It is fairly easy to study objectively the mating practices of the fruit fly, but less easy to view the mating practices of the human being with objective detachment. On any matter where our emotions, beliefs, habits, and values are involved, we are likely to see whatever agrees with our emotional needs and values. Few Americans, for example, could record a detailed description of the workings of the polygamous family system without including many words and phrases which would betray their disapproval. If a set of scientific observations is reported objectively, the reader will be unable to know whether the observer likes or dislikes what he has reported. Yet many experiments have shown that even our simplest observations are affected by our feelings and expectations. For example, in one investigation [Harvey, 1953] most observers judged a white disk imprinted with the name "Eisenhower" to be larger than disks of the same size with random names from the phone book; poor children generally estimated the size of coins to be larger than children from prosperous homes; and a leaf-shaped piece of green cloth was judged to be greener than a donkey-shaped piece of the same cloth.

Many questions which should be clear-cut scientific questions arouse violent controversy because we find it hard to be objective or even to be sure *when we are* being objective. The question, "Does cigarette smoking promote lung cancer?" is not an impossibly difficult scientific question; yet each new study provokes bitter emotional reaction. The data are now quite conclusive, but this conclusion is displeasing to many people. The tobacco industry, which can draw a mountain of conclusion from a molehill of scientific evidence when preparing advertising claims, insists that we need more evidence before drawing conclusions on *this* question. Cigarette smokers with an appetite to defend are also practicing their newly discovered habit of withholding judgment until more data are available. Some ardent battlers against the cigarette "knew" the answer long before any studies were conducted. On this question few are disinterested and few can be fully objective.

To be objective is perhaps the most taxing of all scientific obligations. It is not enough to be willing to see facts as they are. One must also know what his biases are if he is to guard against them. A bias is simply a tendency, usually unconscious, to see facts in a certain way because of our wishes, interests, and values. Thus, in a racial incident one observer sees a white person insulting or abusing a Negro while another observer sees a Negro acting presumptuously and provocatively. One observer sees American Negroes courageously asserting their democratic rights, while another sees them foolishly "asking for trouble."

Seldom are "the facts" so undebatable that bias does not distort them. Our perception is selective; we see and remember those facts which support our beliefs and overlook the others. Many experiments have shown that most people who observe a social situation will see and hear only what they expect to see and hear. If what we expect to see isn't there, we see it anyway! This is dramatically shown in a famous experiment [Allport and Postman, 1945] in which observers were shown a picture of a roughly dressed white man holding an open razor and arguing violently with a well-dressed Negro who was shown in an apologetic, conciliatory posture; then the observers were asked to describe the scene. Some of them "saw" the razor in the Negro's hand, where they expected it to be. Then, in passing on a description of the scene (A described it to B, who described it to C, and so on), the observers soon had the razor in the Negro's hand, where it "belonged." Even though they were not emotionally involved in the situation, had ample time to study it, and were making a conscious effort to be accurate in what they saw and reported or heard, the observers' unconscious biases still led many of them to "see" or "hear" a fact that wasn't there.

If the student is inclined to doubt that people often see and hear what they expect to see and hear, let him try a simple experiment. At a party, greet each arriving guest with a broad smile, a hearty handshake, and a murmured, "Pity to see you here this evening," and speed each departing guest with, "Glad you must leave so early!" Many will hear what they expect to hear, not what was actually spoken. This is why, if one's biases tell him that Negroes are lazy, Jews are pushy, businessmen are crooked, and musicians are temperamental, he will seldom see anything that conflicts with these expectations. Bias is like a sieve which allows to pass through it only what is supposed to pass through. Bias screens out our perceptions, generally admitting to our consciousness only those perceptions which agree with the biases.

Some common threats to objectivity, then, are vested interest, habit, and bias. Objectivity does not come easily to an observer, but it can be learned. One can become more objective as he becomes aware of his biases and makes allowance for them. Through rigorous training in scientific methodology, through studying many experiments and noting many examples of objective and nonobjective uses of data, an observer may eventually develop some ability to cut through many layers of self-deception and to perceive facts with a greater degree of scientific objectivity. The scientist also has another powerful ally—the criticism of his fellows. The scientist publishes his work so that it may be checked by other scientists who may not share his biases and who come to the problem with a different point of view. This process of publication and criticism means that shoddy work is soon exposed, and the scientist who lets his bias dictate his uses of data is pilloried by his fellows.

In writing his observations, the scientist uses objective language. For example, consider these statements:

The increasing American military commitment in Vietnam was accompanied by more frequent "peace" demonstrations and by increasing public debate over the wisdom of this policy.

Increasing American aggression in Vietnam aroused a mounting chorus of public indignation at our arrogant and brutal denial of self-government to the Vietnamese people.

Our rising determination to prevent the Communist enslavement of Vietnam was harassed by the mounting frenzy of our own Communist sympathizers and peace-at-any-price appeasers.

The first of these statements is written in the neutral, descriptive language of the social scientist, while the other two are fiercely partisan. Polemical writing may be appropriate in debate, but not in science.

Trained observation   Scientific observations are made by *trained observers.* A billion people watch the sun and the moon sweep across the sky, but more sophisticated observers possess certain knowledge which tells them that is not exactly what happens. The untrained observer does not know what to look for or how to interpret it. He does not know the pitfalls which lead to inaccurate observation, nor is he fully aware of the tricks his own limitations and biases may play on him. Startling reports of weird phenomena generally come from uneducated, unsophisticated persons, and are discounted by the experts. When some remarkable observations are reported, the scientist will want to know: (1) What is the observer's general level of education and sophistication? Is he a member of a superstition-ridden folk group, or of a well-informed and somewhat skeptical population? Ghosts, spells, magic, and other supernatural happenings are very real to some groups, but are an amusing absurdity to others. (2) What is his special knowledge or training in this particular field? Does he have the knowledge to know whether this event has a perfectly natural explanation? Thus the biologist among the ship's passengers is less likely to see a sea monster than are the members of the crew, and the meteorologist sees fewer flying saucers than people with no special knowledge of atmospheric phenomena.

The Bridey Murphy case of a few years ago shows the fruits of amateur investigation. A Colorado businessman who dabbled in hypnotism drew from a hypnotized housewife a fascinating account of her earlier life as Bridey Murphy in Ireland over a hundred years ago. This tale aroused great interest, became a best-selling book [Bernstein, 1956] which was syndicated in over 40 newspapers, and stimulated a rash of books and articles on hypnotism, reincarnation, and occult topics. If this businessman had been a trained psychologist, he would have known that almost any hypnotized subject in a deep trance will babble freely about earlier incarnations (or future incarnations) if asked about them. A trained observer would have checked the childhood experiences and associations of this housewife to see whether she might be dredging up childhood recollections while in a trance. When the checking was done by less gullible observers, the Bridey Murphy affair promptly collapsed [Gardner, 1957, chap. 26]. Most sensational tales of weird phenomena would be discredited by naturalistic explanations if a scientifically trained observer were present.

Many events happen without any scientific observer on the sidelines. If each sea monster broke water before a panel of ichthyologists, each ghost materialized before the searching gaze of psychologists, and each revolution were staged before a team of visiting sociologists, our knowledge would be far more complete. But for many phenomena, the only reports we have are the casual impressions of untrained observers who happened to be there; these reports may be interesting and possibly useful, but must be interpreted most cautiously by scientists.

Controlled conditions Scientific observation is conducted under *controlled conditions*. Laboratories are popular with scientists because they are handy places to control heat, light, pressure, time intervals, or whatever is important. We have a scientific experiment when we *control all important variables except one,* then see what happens when that one is varied. Unless all variables except one have been controlled, we cannot be sure which variable has produced the results. For example, if we wish to study the effects of phosphates on plant growth, all other factors—seed, soil, water, sunlight, temperature, humidity—must be the same for all the sample plots; then the varying amounts of phosphates on different test plots can be held responsible for different growth rates. This is the basic technique in all scientific experimentation—allow one variable to vary while holding all other variables constant.

Failure to control all variables is a most common error in scientific method and accounts for most false conclusions. For example, the promotion of antihistamines as a cold cure a few years ago was based on several experiments in which half the patients reporting with cold symptoms were given an antihistamine pill, while the other half were given a blank pill which contained no medicine. This latter half were the "control group," used as a base for measuring the effectiveness of the new pill upon the test group. The findings were encouraging, with many more of the test group reporting that their colds had gone away. These findings were enthusiastically and uncritically reported in popular magazines, and dozens of "cold-stopper" manufacturers climbed on the gold-filled band wagon.

These experiments were honestly conducted, but further research disclosed a serious error in method. Although the men reporting for treatment believed they were all getting the same pill, the physician knew which pill each man received. Thus when the man made his before-and-after reports to the physician, the unconscious bias of the physician apparently led him to shade the reports in the direction which would support the findings he hoped to get. When a national test of the Salk polio vaccine was arranged some time later, safeguards were erected to guard against the unconscious bias of the persons conducting the experiment. Using the "double-blind" technique, identical-appearing doses of vaccine and of blanks were numbered and recorded in a secret code book, so that neither the patients nor the physicians giving the injections and reporting each case had any way of knowing which way to shade their reports. This meant that we could *know* that the findings were due to the vaccine and not due to unconscious bias. Deliberate dishonesty is exceedingly rare among serious scientists, but unconscious bias is a constant hazard, requiring research controls which make it more difficult for bias to operate.

Since laboratories are such convenient places to control the conditions of observation, scientists use them whenever possible. But much that is important cannot be dragged into a laboratory. Volcanoes and earthquakes cannot be staged in a test tube, nor can we study the courtship process very realistically by herding some couples into a laboratory. Both physical and social scientists frequently must observe phenomena in their natural setting. Techniques may range from lowering a bathysphere to the ocean floor to giving a questionnaire to a group of army recruits. If we remember that the basic scientific procedure is the conducting of accurate observations, while laboratories, instruments, and IBM cards are merely *tools* of observation, this difference in technique will not confuse us.

As many phenomena must be observed in their natural setting and are often reported by untrained observers, the scientist is especially interested in knowing the conditions under which the event was observed. Was the observer an interested bystander or an emotionally involved participant? Was the observer calm, relaxed, and comfortable, or was he excited, terrified, exhausted, hunger-crazed, or otherwise incapable of accurate observation? What were the lighting conditions and other visual circumstances? It is not surprising that sailors, traditionally a highly superstitious group who often suffered prolonged isolation, danger, hunger, thirst, and exhaustion, should have peered through ocean spray or evening haze and seen enticing mermaids and terrifying monsters which other observers have been unable to verify.

The scientific critic will trust a reported observation only in so far as the conditions of observation have been controlled. On this basis, science is skeptical of the claims of spiritualism and mind reading. A spiritualist can conduct a very convincing seance in his own stage setting, but spirtualists are loath to attempt a seance where the room, furnishings, and lighting are controlled by the scientist. The professional mind reader is very convincing in a theater setting, but unwilling to attempt a reading under scientifically controlled conditions. Until spiritualists and mind readers will make demonstrations under conditions which preclude the possibility of deception, scientists will dismiss the one as a fraud and the other as entertainment.

In these several respects, then, scientific observation differs from looking at things. We spend our lives looking at things, and this activity brings us much information, many impressions, and numerous conclusions. But these conclusions are clouded by accident of coincidence, by selective memory, and by personal bias. Therefore, before accepting any generalization as true, the critical observer wants to know what it is based upon. Is this conclusion based upon a systematically collected body of scientific evidence, or is it an offhand reaction to haphazard observation?

STEPS IN SCIENTIFIC RESEARCH

The scientific method (some would prefer to say scientific methods) includes a great deal. The scientist must accumulate considerable background information on the problem. Then he formulates an *hypothesis.* This is a carefully considered theoretical statement which seeks to relate all the *known* facts to one another in a logical manner. The hypothesis is then tested by scientific research. For example, the hypothesis that cancer is a virus disease is based upon a great deal of observation; it relates known facts in a logical manner; and it is now being tested through many research projects. Eventually an hypothesis is confirmed, rejected, or revised, and in this manner a science grows.

There are several steps in scientific research. They are easy to list but not always easy to follow.

1. *Formulate the problem,* that is, find a problem of some apparent scientific importance and define it so that it can be studied scientifically. Suppose the question arises as to whether fraternity membership is a hindrance to academic success. Our hypothesis might be, "Fraternity members receive lower grades than comparable nonmembers."

2. *Plan the research design,* outlining just what is to be studied, what data will be sought, where and how they will be collected, processed, and analyzed. In the above example, we should need to decide how to select and match the samples of fraternity members and nonmembers, where to secure data on the grades, and what mechanical and statistical procedures to use in analyzing these data and in arriving at conclusions.

3. *Collect the data* in accordance with the research design. Often it will be necessary to change the design to meet some unforeseen difficulty.

4. *Analyze the data.* Classify, tabulate, and compare the data, making whatever tests and computations are necessary to help find the results.

5. *Draw conclusions.* Was the original hypothesis confirmed or rejected? Or were the results inconclusive? What has this research added to our knowledge? What implications has it for sociological theory? What new questions and suggestions for further research have arisen from this investigation?

SOCIOLOGY AS A SCIENCE

Science may be defined in at least two ways: (1) A science is a body of organized, verified knowledge which has been secured through scientific investigation; (2) a science is a method of study whereby a body of organized verified knowledge is discovered. These are, of course, two ways of saying much the same thing.

If the first definition is accepted, then sociology is a science *to the extent that it develops a body of organized verified knowledge* which is based on scientific investigation. To the extent that sociology forsakes myth, folklore, and wishful thinking and bases its conclusions on scientific evidence, it is a science. If science is defined as a method of study, then sociology is a science *to the extent that it uses scientific methods of study.* All natural phenomena can be studied scientifically, if one is willing to use scientific methods. Any kind of behavior—whether of atoms, animals, or adolescents—is a proper field for scientific study.

During most of man's history, few of his actions were based on verified knowledge, for man through the ages has been guided mainly by folklore, habit, and guesswork. Until a few centuries ago, very few people accepted the idea that man should find out about the natural world by systematic observation of the natural world itself, rather than by consulting his oracles, his ancestors, or his intuition. This new idea created the modern world. A few decades ago, man began acting on the assumption that this same approach might also give useful knowledge about man's social life. Just how far he has replaced folklore with knowledge in this area will be explored in the chapters which follow.

THE DEVELOPMENT OF SOCIOLOGY

Sociology is the youngest of the social sciences. Auguste Comte in France coined the word "sociology" in his *Positive Philosophy,* published in 1842. He believed that a science of sociology should be based on systematic observation and classification, not on authority and speculation. This was a relatively new idea at that time. Herbert Spencer in England published his *Principles of Sociology* in 1876. He applied the theory of evolution to human society and evolved a grand theory of "social evolution" which is no longer accepted, but helped to launch sociology as a field of study. America's Lester F. Ward published his *Dynamic Sociology* in 1883, calling for social progress through intelligent social action, which sociologists should guide. All these "founders" of sociology were basically social philosophers. They developed grand systems of thought, but did little research, verification, or measurement. They did not collect and classify facts and then develop the grand theory from these facts; they thought out the grand theory and sought for facts to support the theory. They called for scientific investigation, but did little. Yet they took the necessary first steps, for the *idea* of a science of sociology had to precede the building of one. Courses in sociology appeared in many universities in the 1890s. The *American Journal of Sociology* began publication in 1895, and the American Sociological Society (now the American Sociological Association) was organized in 1905.

Most of the sociologists at the turn of the century were social reformers. Many were either former ministers or ministers' sons, and nearly all were of rural background. Urbanization and industrialization were creating grave social problems, and these sociologists groped for "scientific" solutions. They saw sociology as a scientific guide to social progress. The early volumes of the *Journal* contained many recommended solutions, but very few research studies testing whether these solutions would work out. A second generation of pioneers—Durkheim, Simmel, Cooley, Weber, Park, Thomas, and others—built on these foundations. They proceeded with the theoretical formulations and empirical studies necessary for a scientific development of sociology [Barnes, 1948; Vine, 1959]. By the 1930s, the several sociological journals were well filled with research articles. Sociology was becoming a body of scientific knowledge with its theories based on scientific observation rather than on armchair speculation.

SUMMARY

In his search for truth, man has relied upon: (1) *intuition,* ranging from brilliant imagination to naïve guesswork; (2) *authority,* which tells him what is true; (3) *tradition,* which finds truth in whatever has been long accepted as true; (4) *common sense,* a convenient catchall which includes casual observation plus any or all of the above sources; and (5) *science,* the newest method of seeking truth. Science differs from other sources of truth in that (1) since scientific truth is based on verifiable evidence, science studies only those questions on which verifiable evidence can be secured, making no attempt to answer many important questions of value, purpose, or ultimate meaning; furthermore science realizes that all scientific truth is tentative, subject to revision in the light of new evidence; and (2) science is ethically neutral, seeking to discover knowledge no matter what values or institutions it may undermine or reinforce.

The basic technique of scientific investigation is *observation.* Scientific observation differs from just looking at things in that scientific observation is: (1) *accurate,* seeking to describe what really exists; (2) as *precise* and exact as is necessary; (3) *systematic,* in an effort to find all the relevant data; (4) *recorded* in complete detail as quickly as possible; (5) *objective,* in being as free from distortion by vested interest, bias, or wishful thinking as is humanly possible; (6) *conducted by trained observers,* who know what to look for and how to recognize it; (7) *conducted under controlled conditions* which reduce the danger of fraud, self-deception, or mistaken interpretation. The several steps in a scientific research project are: (1) Formulate the problem; (2) plan the research design; (3) collect the data; (4) analyze the data; and (5) draw the conclusions.

Whether the study of man's social relationships is a science is often debated. Sociology is a very new science, recently emerged from the speculations of nineteenth-century social philosophers and social reformers. To the extent that man's social life is studied through scientific methods so that a body of verified knowledge is developed—to that extent these studies become social sciences.

QUESTIONS AND PROJECTS

1. Does the rigorously trained scientist make use of any sources of truth other than scientific observation in his daily life? Which ones? How often?

2. Distinguish between the critical and uncritical uses of authority.

3. Will a scientist ever make use of sacred authority?

4. Discuss the proposition: "Modern man should discard all ideas which are not scientifically verified." Should he? Can he?

5. Can scientists prove that ghosts and spirits do not exist, or that fortune telling and mind reading do not work? Why are scientists so skeptical?

6. Suppose a foreman says, "I've supervised all kinds of workers, and the Negro workers just don't measure up to white standards." What will be necessary for this statement to be a scientifically justified conclusion?

7. What difficulties in being objective would confront a scholar writing a biography of Martin Luther if the scholar were a devout Catholic? A devout Protestant? A convinced atheist?

8. Suppose you wished to get an accurate description of a riot which happened five years ago in a city of 100,000 people. Make an outline showing where you would look for data, and suggest the limitations or inadequacies of each type or source of data.

9. Read Sinclair Lewis's novel, *Arrowsmith*. What are some of the difficulties Martin had to meet in becoming rigorously scientific?

10. Suppose you, a college student, were to take a summer job working as a laborer in a factory. Make a list of the biases which might distort your impressions of factory workers as you size them up. Subject these lists to class comparison and criticism.

11. Prepare three statements of some issue or event, one written as a neutral scientist, the second as a supporter, and the third as an opponent.

SUGGESTED READINGS

*BECK, WILLIAM S.: *Modern Science and the Nature of Life*, Harcourt, Brace & World, Inc., New York, 1957, chap. 3, "The Nature of Science." A brief essay on the history and nature of the scientific method. (N8-NHL)

*CHASE, STUART, WITH EDMUND DE S. BRUNNER: *The Proper Study of Mankind*, Harper & Row, Publishers, Incorporated, New York, 1956. A highly readable treatise on the contribution of social science to the solution of human problems. (CN/10-CN)

*DUNHAM, BARROWS: *Man against Myth*, Little, Brown and Company, Boston, 1947. A critical examination of some of the major myths of the Western world. (AC56-AM CEN)

*EVANS, BERGEN: *The Natural History of Nonsense*, Alfred A. Knopf, Inc., New York, 1946. An entertaining examination of many popular myths and superstitions, which are demolished with a rare blend of wit and learning. (V64-Vin)

*GARDNER, MARTIN: *Fads and Fallacies in the Name of Science*, Dover Publications, Inc., New York, 1957. Earlier edition under the title, *In the Name of Science*, G. P. Putnam's Sons, New York, 1952. An interesting account of many unscientific and pseudoscientific theories and the cults which promote them. (Dov)

*INKLES, ALEX: *What Is Sociology*, Prentice-Hall, Inc., Englewood Cliffs, N.J., 1965. A brief description of what sociology is and what sociologists do. (P-H)

KAUFMANN, FELIX: *Methodology of the Social Sciences*, Oxford University Press, Fair Lawn, N.J., 1944, especially chaps. 10, 14, and 15. A penetrating discussion of major questions of scientific method in the social sciences; for the more advanced student.

*MACDOUGALL, CURTIS D.: *Hoaxes*, Dover Publications, Inc., New York, 1958. An entertaining survey of frauds in art, history, science, literature, politics, and journalism. (K-136-Ace)

VINE, MARGARET WILSON: *An Introduction to Sociological Theory*, David McKay Company, Inc., New York, 1959. Outlines the contributions of each of the pioneers of sociology.

2

FIELDS AND
METHODS OF
SOCIOLOGY

What are the social scientists up to today?

A television camera could show a number of professors lecturing to more or less eager students in more or less stuffy classrooms; experiments being performed in psychological laboratories; two-way communication systems between men and management being installed in large corporations; teams of investigators taking notes in communities like Middletown; social workers making case reports on their rounds; a battery of electronic computers clicking away while they sort cards for opinion polls; interviewers taking a sample of the unemployment situation in Illinois; sunburned persons in pith helmets asking questions of puzzled natives in New Guinea. Finally, the camera would focus on shelf after shelf of books. . . .

Here in America, 165 million people, scattered over 3 million square miles of plain, valley, and hillside, form and re-form into numberless groups and organizations, with loyalties and sentiments woven around each. . . . The camera might go on to indicate the many curious methods by which Americans earn their living, or try to offset the boredom of earning a living under machine-age conditions. . . .

This is the field of the social scientists: watching these people behave, and searching out the laws which govern their behavior. (Stuart Chase, with Edmund de S. Brunner, *The Proper Study of Mankind*, Harper & Row, Publishers, Incorporated, New York, 1956, pp. 19–20.)

W HAT WILL you say when you go home next weekend and your younger sister asks, "Sociology? Well, what *is* sociology?" If you reply, "Sociology is the scientific study of human social relationships with special emphasis upon groups and institutions," she may say, "Oh," and you will guess that she is as confused as you are. If you tell her, "Sociology is the scientific study of social problems, like race, crime, divorce, etc.," your definition will give her *some idea* of what sociology is about, and may be a pretty good description to give to someone who is unfamiliar with sociology. But your answer will not be entirely correct, for sociology is much more than the study of social problems. As a student of sociology, you need a better definition.

THE FIELD OF SOCIOLOGY

First of all, *forget whatever you have read about sociology in popular magazines and newspapers,* for most of it is absurd. When a magazine writer wishes to make some of his offhand guesswork sound more impressive, he may preface it with the phrase, "Sociologists fear that . . . ," "Sociologists are alarmed by . . . ," or "Sociologists are wringing their hands over. . . ." This journalistic device helps a writer to speak authoritatively without knowing very much about the subject. Often a writer sets up his "straw man" by attributing to sociologists the viewpoints which he is about to demolish. For example, one magazine writer [Bliven, 1960] lists nine developments over which he states that "the sociologists, of course, are wringing their hands. . . ." Of these nine propositions, six would be flatly rejected by most sociologists, two are marginal, and only one bears much resemblance to what most sociologists believe. Such writing makes for colorful journalism, but it caricatures the sociologist as a frustrated do-gooder in a perpetual state of shock over the mess we are in.

Careless use of the term *sociologist* is also confusing. Magazine and newspaper writers, social workers, labor leaders, government officials, or anyone else who is interested in social relations may be described as sociologists. This is incorrect. A sociologist is one who has earned advanced degrees or pursued other advanced studies in sociology (not in psychology, theology, social work, or some other field) and is engaged in teaching, research, or other professional work as a sociologist.

No formal definition of sociology is very satisfactory. Short definitions do not really define; long, explicit definitions are usually cumbersome. Yet a definition of some sort is needed, and sociology is often defined as *the scientific study of man's social life.* Man behaves differently from other animals. Man has unique forms of group life, pursues customs, develops institutions, creates values. Sociology applies scientific methods to the study of these phenomena in the search for scientific knowledge. It may be helpful to give some definitions in reverse—to state what sociology is *not.*

Sociology is science, not social philosophy. A science is a body of knowledge; a philosophy is a system of ideas and values. A social philosophy is a set of ideas about how men *ought to* behave and treat one another; a social science studies how they actually *do* behave, and the consequences of this behavior.

Sociology is social science, not socialism. Socialism is a social philosophy with a political program, whereas sociology is a search for scientific knowledge.

Sociology is interested in the way groups interact with one another.

Socialists sometimes find in sociological research some material they can use in their propaganda; so do Republicans and Democrats. A few sociologists have been socialists; many more have been Republicans or Democrats.

Sociology concentrates its study upon man's group life and the products of his group living. The sociologist is especially interested in the customs, traditions, and values which emerge from group living, and in the way group living is, in turn, affected by these customs, traditions, and values. Sociology is interested in the way groups interact with one another and in the processes and institutions which they develop. Sociology is subdivided into many specialized fields, of which a partial list includes:

Communication and public opinion
Criminology
Demography (population)
The family
Industrial sociology
Medical sociology
Methodology of social research
Occupational sociology
Political sociology
Race and ethnic relations
Rural sociology

Social disorganization
Social psychology
Social stratification
Sociological theory
Sociology of the arts
Sociology of complex organizations
Sociology of education
Sociology of law
Sociology of religion
Sociology of small groups

These topics are not the exclusive property of sociology, for other fields share our interest in them. For example, our interest in communication and public opinion is shared by psychology and political science; criminology is shared with psychology, political science, law, and police science, and so on. No science can fence itself off from other sciences, least of all sociology. Our field is especially close to those of psychology and anthropology, and overlaps theirs so constantly that any firm boundaries would be arbitrary and unrealistic. The more we learn about man's behavior, the more we realize that no one field of knowledge can fully explain him.

THE METHODS OF SOCIOLOGICAL RESEARCH

The methods of sociological research are basically those outlined in the preceding chapter and used by all scientists. As Karl Pearson has remarked, "The unity of all science consists alone in its method, not in its material. The man who classifies facts of any kind whatever, who sees their mutual relation and describes their sequences, is applying the scientific method and is a man of science'' [1900, p. 12].

While scientific methods are basically alike for all sciences, scientific *techniques* differ, for techniques are the particular ways in which scientific methods are applied to a particular problem. Each science must, therefore, develop a series of techniques which fits the body of material it studies. What are some of the techniques of sociological research?

Cross-sectional, longitudinal, and ex post facto studies

Every study has some sort of time setting. A study which limits its observations to a single point in time is called a *cross-sectional* study. For example, Freedman, Whelpton, and Campbell [1959] interviewed a national sample of 2,713 young married women to discover their childbearing frequency and expectations. If the study extends over time, describing a trend or making a before-and-after set of observations, it is called a *longitudinal* study. Thus Campbell and McCormack [1957] sought to find out whether military training develops authoritarian attitudes. They gave an authoritarianism scale (a questionnaire designed to measure authoritarian attitudes) to Air Force cadets at the beginning of Air Force training, and repeated the test a year later. Contrary to expectation, the retest showed authoritarian attitudes lower than the original test. While a single study, on a rather small sample, is not conclusive, this study points up the danger of simply making assumptions about the personality effects of any kind of experience.

An *ex post facto* study seeks to trace a present situation back to some earlier factors which may have been involved. For example, Glick [1957, p. 112] compared divorcées with married persons as to their age at marriage, and found divorce among those married before the age of eighteen to be almost three times as common as among those marrying between the ages of twenty-two and twenty-four. A great deal of sociological research is of the *ex post facto* sort.

Planned experiments

All sciences use planned experiments. The concept of the experiment is simple: Hold all variables constant except one; cause it to vary and see what happens. Do we want to know whether vitamin X will prevent colds? We need two groups, a test group and a control group, who are alike in all other significant respects —income, education, occupation, diet, health habits, general health level, or anything else suspected of being related to colds. The test group takes vitamin X while the control group takes placebos (dummy pills), without knowing which they are getting; then any differences in cold incidence must be due to vitamin X.

There are two common ways of setting up test and control groups. One is the matched-pair technique. For each person in the test group, another person like him in all important variables (such as age, religion, education, occupation, or anything important to this research) is found and placed in the control group. Another technique is to make statistically random assignments of persons to test and control groups—such as assigning the first person to the test group, the next to the control group, and so on. Suppose we wish to measure the effectiveness of an experimental treatment program for delinquents in a reformatory. Using one technique, we should match each delinquent who received the experimental treatment (test group) with another delinquent, matched for all other variables thought important, who received only the usual treatment (control group). Using the other technique, every second (or third, or tenth) delinquent would be assigned to the experimental group upon arrival at the reformatory, with the others becoming the control group. Wherever the researcher is permitted to make assignments in this way, the random-assignment technique is far easier and at least as accurate; but often, when the research situation precludes this technique, the matched-pair technique may be used.

Sometimes the research situation provides ready-made test and control groups. For example, during World War II there was some debate over whether it was more efficient to use Negro troops in segregated or in mixed units. A few experimental units were organized with Negro platoons within white infantry companies. Some time later a sample of servicemen were asked how they would feel about serving in such a mixed outfit. As shown in Figure 1, it was found that the servicemen who actually served in mixed companies offered the least objection, while those in divisions with no mixed companies were the most unfavorable. In other words, those who were nearest to the mixed com-

FIGURE 1 *Attitudes toward Serving in a Company Containing Negro and White Platoons among Men Who Have Done So and Men Who Have Not (Europe, June, 1945).*
SOURCE: Reproduced from Samuel A. Stouffer et al., *Studies in Social Psychology in World War II,* vol. 1, *The American Soldier: Adjustment during Army Life,* Princeton University Press, Princeton, N.J., 1949, p. 594.

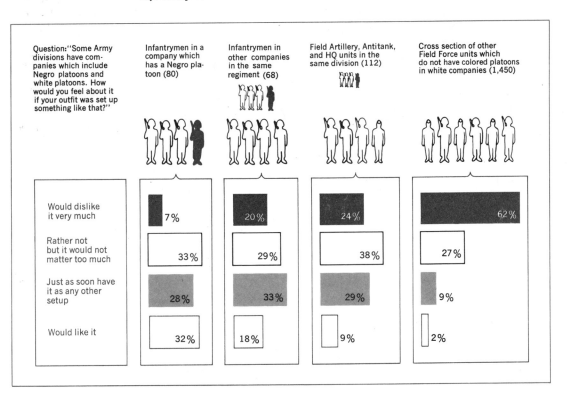

panies liked them best. And, while most of those in mixed companies had objected strongly *before* their organization, they offered the least objection after having actual experience in a mixed company. This experiment clearly showed that a great change in attitude took place as a result of enforced contacts.

These research findings formed the basis for the decision to end segregation in the armed services. As a result, the armed services now have much less racial "trouble," and are making far more efficient use of Negro troops [Nichols, 1954]. We see, from this example, how a planned experiment in the social sciences can provide knowledge which is useful in the making of practical social policy.

Planned experiments in sociology face certain difficulties. An experiment involving thousands of people may be prohibitively expensive. It may take many years to complete an experiment. Our values forbid us to use people for any experiments which may injure them. When people are unwilling to cooperate in an experiment, we cannot force them to do so (although we may occasionally trick them into unconscious cooperation). Furthermore, when people realize that they are experimental subjects, they begin to act differently, and the experiment may be spoiled. Almost any kind of experiment upon people *who know they are being studied* will give some interesting findings which may vanish soon after the experiment is ended. This is known as the Hawthorne effect, named after some experiments with temperature, humidity, rest periods, and other working conditions at the Hawthorne plant of Western Electric Company [Roethlisberger, 1949]. It was found that *any* change in the working conditions—more humidity, less humidity, longer rest periods, shorter rest periods—was followed by a temporary gain in work output. This illustrates how the findings of many experiments may be due to the attention the subjects are getting, not to the factor which is being tested.

Planned experiments upon human subjects are most reliable when these subjects do not know the true object of the experiment. They may be given a rationale, a reasonable explanation of what the experimenter is doing, but this rationale may be a harmless but necessary deception which conceals the true purpose of the experiment. For example, an experiment to determine the effect of background music upon work output in a factory might be explained as a trial to see whether workers *liked* the music. But as Kelman points out [1966] the use of deception in social research poses the ethical question of distinguishing between harmless deception and intellectual dishonesty, and may even produce errors in the outcome (subjects may detect the deception and begin second-guessing the researcher!).

Because of all these limitations, social sciences (excepting psychology) make limited use of planned experiments. We use them wherever practical, but depend more heavily on other techniques.

Observational studies   Observational studies are like planned experiments in all respects except one: In the planned experiments the scientist arranges for something to happen so that he can observe what follows, whereas in the observational study the scientist observes something which happens, or has already happened, by itself. Both rely upon systematic observation under controlled conditions in a search for verifiable sequences and relationships. Both are used in all the sciences, but the procedures for using them vary according to the material being studied. The types of studies which follow are not mutually exclusive, for a study may use several different techniques.

Impressionistic studies   These are informal descriptive and analytic accounts, based on observations which are less fully controlled than in more formal studies. Suppose a sociologist with a special interest in the family makes a tour of Russia. He is alert for information on the Russian family, asks questions about Russian family life of most of the people he meets, scans the papers and magazines for their pictures of family life. He returns home with some very definite impressions of Russian family life, but they are not based on a systematic, scientifically controlled investigation—on an orderly search of the published literature, on scientifically constructed sample of informants, and so on. If he is a responsible scholar, he will state his judgments as *impressions,* not as scientifically established conclusions.

No matter how elaborate, carefully planned, and systematically conducted a study may be, if the recorded data consist of the impressions of the observer, it is classed as an impressionistic study. Thus the Lynds [1929, 1937] spent many months in "Middletown" (Muncie, Indiana); they systematically searched the newspaper files, interviewed virtually everyone who held a position of authority or was locally said to be important, and participated in community life. They ended up with a large mass of impressions which were highly perceptive and probably accurate, but largely unverifiable except through long and costly research.

Impressionistic studies are highly useful in social science. They provide many hypotheses and research leads, and suggest many insights which might be overlooked by other methods. The best of the impressionistic studies hold an honored place in sociological literature.

Statistical comparative studies   If everything which could be found through an experiment is already written down somewhere, it is sensible to look up the record. Much sociological research consists of looking up recorded statistical facts and comparing and interpreting them. For a simple example, consider the question, "Now that women have greater freedom to lead an interesting and independent life without marriage, are more women remaining single?" The answer is easily derived from census data, which show the proportion of single women dropping from 24.3 per cent in 1890 to 18.2 per cent in 1965. (These figures give the percentage of all American women fourteen years old or older, who had never been married, with correction for changes in the age distribution of the population.) Many such questions can be answered quickly by checking data in the annual *Statistical Abstract of the United States,* which summarizes statistics collected by many government and other agencies and is available in nearly any library. Other questions may require study of more specialized statistical sources, such as the many *Special Reports* issued by the Bureau of the Census.

Many research questions involve a comparison of several kinds of statistical data from several sources. For example, Lander [1954] wondered about the relation between juvenile delinquency and overcrowded, substandard housing. From court records he compiled delinquency rates for 155 census districts in

Baltimore, and from census data he found the average number of persons per room and the percentage of officially substandard housing units for each census district. He found that delinquency rates closely followed rates of overcrowding and substandard housing, but that this association disappeared when he controlled the other variables, such as race, income, education, and occupation. However, he found one variable—home ownership—which remained highly associated even when all others were controlled. He concluded that home ownership was an index of family stability, and that this connection helped to explain the lower delinquency rates in areas where home ownership prevailed.

Sometimes the research scholar must go out and collect the raw statistical data to clarify a problem. For example, consider the question, "Why are some marriages happier than others?" Many research studies of several kinds have tried to help answer this question. In each of two especially interesting studies, a sample of several hundred married couples was divided into several groups of differing degrees of marital happiness or unhappiness; then these groups were compared with one another on dozens of points. One of these studies centered upon the circumstances preceding the marriage of the couple—age at marriage, length of courtship and engagement, education completed, approval or disapproval of marriage by parents, employment history, and dozens more. This study [Burgess and Cottrell, 1939] found that the happily and unhappily married groups differed strikingly in many of these background circumstances. The other study [Terman, 1938] compared the personality characteristics of happily and unhappily married informants and found marked personality differences between the two groups.

Many people "have no use for statistics." Often they don't like statistics because they don't understand them. Statistics, like shotguns, are dangerous when handled by the ignorant, as is shown in Huff's entertaining little book, *How to Lie with Statistics* [1954]. Those who know the uses and abuses of statistics realize that statistics are nothing more or less than *organized, measured facts*. They are as trustworthy or untrustworthy as is the scientific method of the person who compiles them. To reject statistics is but a way of rejecting facts.

Sociologists make a great many comparative statistical studies. As almost any kind of research is likely to involve statistical organization and comparison of facts at some point or other, the sociologist must be something of a statistician, and the citizen who hopes to be intelligently aware of the world he lives in must have some understanding of statistical interpretation.

Questionnaire and interview studies   Sometimes the facts we need are not recorded anywhere, and we can find them only by asking people. For example, what is the "ideal-size family" in the eyes of American young people? This question has some importance for population prediction, business planning, educational planning, and many other purposes. We can find the answer only by asking people what they think is the ideal size for a family. Questionnaire and interview studies are systematic ways of asking questions under scientific controls. A questionnaire is filled out by the informant himself; an interview schedule is filled out by a trained interviewer who asks the questions of the informant. Both methods have their pitfalls, which the trained sociologist should be able to avoid. While it is fairly easy to get purely factual information quite accurately (e.g., "Do you own or rent your home?" "Are you married?"), surveys of attitudes and opinions have greater margins of error. The informants may not understand the question; they may pick an answer even though they do not have any firm opinion on the matter; they may give an "acceptable" answer rather than the real one; or they may be swayed by the way the question is worded. A survey may also give false conclusions because the sample of persons surveyed is not a representative cross-section of the population. Questionnaire and interview studies, like other research methods, must be used by trained scholars who are aware of their pitfalls.

Even though questionnaire and interview studies have a margin of error, they may still be useful, for they are more reliable than guesswork. For example, after victory over Germany in 1944, the Army had more men in uniform than were needed. *Which* men should be demobilized? This was an explosive question, with grave consequences for morale. The Army made a questionnaire study [Stouffer, 1949, chap. 11] in which several thousand servicemen were asked:

After the war when the Army starts releasing soldiers back to civilian life, which of these two groups of men do you think should be released first? (Check only one.)
——— *Men with dependents*
   or
——— *Men over 30 years of age*

This question was repeated several times with various pairings of overseas service, combat experience, length of time in service, age, and number of dependents. Responses showed that the largest number of servicemen would give first priority to men who have seen combat, next priority to married men with children, and so on. Using these responses, the Army developed a point system for determining eligibility for discharge. That this approach was highly practical was shown by the fact that the Army discharge policy proceeded with very little criticism or resentment, either from servicemen or from civilians.

Participant-observer studies   No man will fully know what it feels like to be a mother, nor will any civilian completely understand army life. Some things can be fully understood only by experiencing them. The *participant observer* seeks insight by taking part himself in whatever he is studying. If he wishes to understand labor unions, he will join one, work in the shop, attend the union meetings, possibly become a minor union official or a union organizer. If he wishes to study a religious sect, he will join it and try to share in its worship. Through his own participation, together with the opportunity for very intimate observation, he may gain insights which no amount of *external* observation would provide.

At the height of the flying-saucer craze, an interesting cult arose in a Midwestern American city. A small group

The participant observer seeks insight by himself taking part.

of believers received certain "revelations" that the earth would soon be destroyed, and that only a faithful few would be rescued by flying saucers and carried to a friendly planet. Several participant observers joined the group, concealing their scientific identities, and taking part in the group's activities until it dissolved some months later [Festinger, 1956]. In another instance, a white novelist [Griffin, 1961] was commissioned by a Negro magazine to make a participant-observer study of Negro life. With his hair trimmed short and his skin darkened by a drug, he traveled about the South where everyone identified him as a Negro. Although he was a native Southerner, he found that his view of Negro life from the inside brought many surprising revelations.

There are pitfalls in this technique. The participant observer may become so emotionally involved that he loses his objectivity. Or he may overgeneralize; that is, he may assume that what he finds in the group he studies is also true of all other groups. Since his data are largely impressionistic, his conclusions are not easily verified. Yet the participant observer is not just "looking at things," but is applying a sophisticated scientific methodology [Bruyn, 1966] which has given us many insights and suggested many hypotheses for further study.

Is it ethical to pretend to be a loyal member of a group in order to study it? Is such a deception justifiable? It is not easy to say when a deception ceases to be harmless. Perhaps the best answer is that a reputable scientist will be careful not to injure the people he is studying.

The *eyewitness account* is an amateur, small-scale participant-observer study. How do people act after a disaster, such as a tornado or an explosion? What happens at a religious revival, a riot, a picket-line disturbance? Rarely is there a visiting sociologist, pencil in hand, ready to record the event. Social scientists often seek eyewitness accounts from persons who were there. A detailed eyewitness account, collected as soon as possible after the event, is a useful source of information. Such accounts must be used with care, for the eyewitness is usually an untrained observer, and his own excitement or involvement may have impaired his accuracy and objectivity. Yet the eyewitness account is a priceless source of data for the social scientist.

Case studies The case study is a complete, detailed account of some phenomenon. It may be a life history of a person, or a complete account of a brief event. The case history of a group—a family, a clique, a union, a religious movement—may suggest some insights into group behavior. An accurate, detailed account of a riot, a panic, an orgy, a disaster, or any social event may have scientific value. An unhappy family, a happy family, a community, an organization—almost any phenomenon can be studied by the case-study technique.

Perhaps the greatest value of the case study is in the suggestion of hypotheses, which can then be tested by other methods. Most of our reliable knowledge about juvenile deliquency, for instance, has developed through the testing of hypotheses which were suggested by early case studies of delinquents [Thomas, 1923; Shaw, 1931]. Much of our present knowledge of personality disorganization stems from hypotheses suggested by a classic collection of case studies in Thomas and Znaniecki's *The Polish Peasant in Europe and America* [1923]. These hypotheses are not often *tested* by the case-study method, but by other methods.

A generalization cannot be based upon a single case, for a case can be found to "prove" almost anything. Generalizations must be based upon a large mass of carefully processed data, and the collection of a great many case studies is expensive. Also it is difficult to "add up" a number of case studies or compute averages or other statistical computations. Therefore we seldom use case studies when seeking to test a hypothesis. But after the hypothesis has been tested and we have arrived at some sound generalizations, a good case study may give a beautiful illustration of these generalizations. For example, there is conclusive evidence that juvenile delinquency is closely associated with unsatisfactory family life [Glueck and Glueck, 1959]. A case study, showing how unsatisfactory family life has apparently encouraged delinquency in a particular family, makes a vivid illustration of this generalization [Shaw, 1938].

SOME DIFFICULTIES IN SOCIOLOGICAL RESEARCH

Complexity of phenomena Social phenomena are so complex, subtle, and elusive that the sociologist sometimes wonders where to begin. Yet a science is defined, not by the simplicity of its raw materials, but by the rigor of its methods. To some extent, the subtlety and elusiveness of phenomena are in proportion to our ignorance about them. The causes of a patient's fever, which may elude the layman, may be easily perceptible to the pathologist. As any science gains in maturity and knowledge, its confusing complex phenomena become somewhat more orderly and systematic, and its data somewhat less puzzling and elusive.

It is unlikely, however, that any amount of knowledge will ever make our phenomena appear as orderly as those of the natural sciences. Boyle's law deals with only three variables—volume, temperature, and pressure of enclosed gases, all of which are easily controlled; criminal behavior deals with two or three dozen variables, none of which is very easily controlled. The truly great complexity of social phenomena poses a lasting challenge to the methodology of sociological research.

Constant change Social phenomena are constantly changing. How can scientific truth be based upon data which are so slippery that today's truth is untrue tomorrow? This real difficulty is not peculiar to the social sciences, for many sciences must make allowance for changing phenomena. The geographer's landscape is constantly changing, although very slowly. The meteorologist must allow for shifting wind systems. The immunologist and the entomologist must concern themselves with changes in the tolerance or resistance of bacteria, viruses, and insects. The social sciences, however, study phenomena which are vastly more changeable than the phenomena of most other sciences.

But, as already stated, it is not the materials but the methods of study which identify a science. Since many of the phenomena of sociology are constantly changing, each sociological generalization must have a time-and-place qualification. Therefore, when we speak of "the family," we must show whether we are speaking of the family in all its forms and variations of whether we are speaking of, say, the contemporary, urban, American, middle-class family.

All sciences must qualify their generalizations by stating the conditions under which they hold true. The physicist must say, "Water boils at 100 degrees centigrade—providing it is chemically pure and at an atmospheric pressure of 14.7 pounds per square inch." And the sociologist may say, "Contact and association between members of prejudiced groups will reduce prejudices, *provided* these contacts are cooperative and equalitarian in nature."

The very great changeability and variability of the phenomena of sociology compel the sociologist to qualify his generalizations with especial care. The student will find many carefully qualified statements such as, "In the contemporary American middle-class family, education and the drive to 'get ahead' are major goals," or "Among the small, nontypical samples studied to date, young American married couples living with in-laws are as happily married as those living by themselves." This incessant hedging may become tiresome to the student, who may be tempted to agree with the definition of sociology as "the science that is never sure of anything." Yet careful qualification is the price of accuracy, and the scientist never intentionally generalizes beyond the limitations of his data.

Unpredictability of behavior Some critics maintain that, since all people are different, human behavior is unpredictable. People may even deliberately change their behavior in order to upset our predictions. A true science can predict and sometimes control. Can sociology?

It is true that all persons are different in some respects. It is also true that all persons are alike in some respects. Sociology seeks to learn more about the ways in which people are different and the ways in which they are alike and act alike, so that their behavior can be understood and predicted.

In considering scientific prediction, the student must grasp two principles. First, *predictions hold true only under certain stated conditions.* The physicist can predict with great exactness the behavior of a specially manufactured ball rolling down a perfectly smooth plane in a vacuum chamber. If asked to predict the behavior of a driverless truck rolling downhill, his prediction must be less exact, since the conditions are not fully controlled.

Accurate and exact prediction, in any science, is possible only when all variables can be controlled or mathematically calculated. The agronomist may predict, "About 20 per cent of these seeds will fail to grow, if placed in good Indiana soil about May 15 and if temperature and rainfall conditions are similar to those of last year." Likewise, the sociologist may predict, "About 20 per cent of the male teen-agers in this particular slum area will be officially recorded as delinquent this year, if social influences and law-enforcement practices in the area remain like those of last year." But if several of the variables cannot be controlled, then accurate prediction is impossible. For example, will we have a "white Christmas" next winter? The meteorologist cannot predict, unless he knows what the wind systems and pressure areas are going to be next December. Or, what will the population of the United States be by the end of the century? The demographer cannot predict this without knowing what the birth rates, death rates, and rates of migration are going to be during the rest of the century; and these, in turn, hinge upon such variables as age at marriage, the popularity of large families, the level of prosperity, the progress of medical science, and several other variables.

The problem of prediction, then, is similar in all sciences. Our success in prediction is in proportion to our accurate knowledge of the variables involved. As the following chapters will show, there are some topics upon which sociologists are able to make reasonably dependable predictions.

A second principle of scientific prediction derives from the fact that *most scientific prediction deals with collectivities, not individuals.* The agronomist predicts what proportion of seeds will grow, without telling which little seed will die. The chemist predicts the behavior of several billion hydrogen and oxygen atoms, without predicting the behavior of any single atom of hydrogen or oxygen. The sociologist can rarely predict what any one person will do, although he may be able to predict what most of the members of a group will do. In other words, the sociologist may predict the *probability* of an action, just as the life insurance actuary predicts the probability that an insured will die. Predictions may be useful even when we cannot predict the behavior of any particular individual. It is not necessary to know *which* persons will die of typhoid fever to know that polluted water is deadly. Nor need we stop predicting population movements just because we cannot name the persons who are going to move. Sociological prediction can be a useful basis for social policy if it can foretell what certain *groups* or *proportions* of people are going to do; it is quite unnecessary to predict the behavior of each individual.

In the making of *socially significant* predictions, the social sciences already compare favorably with the natural sciences. The natural scientist can predict to the minute the next eclipse of the sun, but cannot predict the next flood or drought as accurately as the social scientist can predict the next recession. Natural science prediction is most accurate in artificial laboratory situations, and least accurate when directed to those matters upon which important social decisions hinge. On questions like, "How soon can we expect a major breakthrough in cancer research?" or "Which raw materials will be indispensable and which will have become unnecessary by the twenty-first century?" natural science is not very helpful. In the making of socially significant predictions, neither natural nor social scientists have attained any great accuracy, but the social scientists appear to be at least as successful as their critics.

PURE AND APPLIED SOCIOLOGY

A distinction between pure and applied science is drawn in every scientific field. *Pure science* is a search for knowledge, without primary concern for its practical use. *Applied science* is the search for ways of using scientific knowledge to solve practical problems. A biochemist who seeks to learn how a cell absorbs food or how a cell ages and grows old is working as a pure scientist. If he then tries to find some substance or procedure which will control the aging process, he is working as an applied scientist. A sociologist making a study of "the social structure of a slum neighborhood" is working as a pure scientist; if he then follows with a study of "how to prevent delinquency in a slum neighborhood," he is working as an applied scientist. Many people view sociology entirely as an applied science—trying to solve social problems. Properly viewed, it is both a pure and an applied science. For unless a science is constantly searching for more basic knowledge, its "practical applications of knowledge" are not likely to be very practical.

Practical applications of sociological knowledge are not widely appreciated. Some sociologists are employed by corporations, government bureaus, and social agencies, usually as research scholars, and sociologists are sometimes consulted by legislative committees who are planning new legislation. But the private citizen rarely bases his social decisions upon sociological knowledge. If a man wants to know how to fertilize artichokes, he generally collects some scientific data before deciding. But how are social-policy decisions made? Each year dozens of communities vote on whether to allow liquor to be sold by the glass in taverns and restaurants. Arguments about automobile accidents, crime, drunkenness, and other evils are hurled around with abandon. But has any *comprehensive, carefully controlled* comparison of communities with and without liquor sale by the glass ever been conducted? Your authors know of none. Local groups in hundreds of communities are promoting a crusade against pornography. Yet there is virtually *no scientific evidence,* one way or the other, on the question of whether pornography is a dangerous stimulant or a harmless outlet for salacious impulses. This decision, like many others, is being made by people who are happily indifferent to the fact that their decision is based upon ignorance and emotion, not upon knowledge.

On many other social questions, such as the causes and treatment of crime and delinquency, drug and alcohol addiction, sex offenses, the causes and consequences of racial discrimination, or the adjustment of the family to a changing society, there *is* considerable scientific knowledge, but this knowledge is rejected by many persons who prefer their prejudices. As a nation, we have only begun to apply scientific methods to our thinking about social issues.

Popular sociology A great deal of sociological material gets into print through the agency of people who are not sociologists. The popular magazines are studded with articles on crime, family life, sex, education, suburbia, social class—practically every sociological topic imaginable. This is popular sociology—treatment of sociological topics, often by writers without much formal sociological training, and aimed at a popular audience. Popular sociology at its worst is seen in articles like the "sex-and-sin" exposés upon which certain men's magazines dwell so fondly. Such articles are generally descriptively inaccurate, with a total lack of the interpretative analysis which would fit the facts into a relevant social context. At the opposite pole are many writers for magazines which do a fairly creditable job of popularizing sociological findings. Perhaps the best-known popular "sociologist" is Vance Packard, whose books on social class [The Status Seekers, 1959; The Pyramid Climbers, 1962] and other topics have been read by millions—and severely criticized by sociologists [Petersen, 1960; Goldner, 1963]. The writings of the sociological popularizers often contain inaccuracies and instances of misplaced emphasis, doubtful interpretation, oversimplification, and too sweeping generalization. Yet it is likely that popular understanding of sociological topics has been greatly increased by such writers.

Why isn't popular sociology written by professional sociologists? For the same reason that popular medicine and popular science are usually written by journalists, rather than by physicians and scientists. Popular writing is a special skill which few scientists or professors have mastered. The scientist's passion for accuracy and for a careful qualification of his statements is a positive handicap in popular writing. His unwillingness to oversimplify, to overdramatize, or to indulge in the grandly sweeping generalization all make his writing more accurate but less exciting. Sociologists write for the scholarly audience, while journalists popularize sociology, more or less accurately, for the public.

THE ROLES OF THE SOCIOLOGIST

What is the proper task of the sociologist? Should he merely observe human action with the calm, detached curiosity of the ecologist who counts the lemmings as they dive into the sea? Or should he plunge into social action to avert the dangers he foresees? Should the professor of sociology encourage students to develop a detached understanding of social phenomena, or should he inspire them to man the barricades for social reform? What is the proper role for the sociologist in a changing society?

The sociologist as a scientific scholar and teacher

Like all scientists, sociologists are concerned with both collecting and using knowledge. They share in these tasks in various ways.

Conducting scientific research   The sociologist's foremost task is to discover and organize knowledge about social life. Most research today, in any science, is too demanding to be done as a spare-time hobby. Many sociologists are employed as full-time research scientists, usually by universities, government agencies, foundations, or corporations. These same agencies make many research grants to sociologists who submit a proposal for research on a specific topic. Obviously, those who control the granting of research funds (often nonsociologists) have great power to control the direction of sociological research —a situation with which sociologists are not entirely comfortable. Former Senator Goldwater introduced amendments to the National Defense Education Act in 1961 and 1963 providing that no Federal funds be used ". . . for the conduct of any test . . . dealing with the personality, environment, home life, parental or family life, economic status or sociological or psychological problems of the student involved." This proposal, although defeated, illustrates how the funding of research carries a threat to freedom of scientific inquiry.

Correcting popular nonsense   Another task of the sociologist as a scientist is to clear away the intellectual rubbish of misinformation and superstition which clutters so much of our social thinking. Sociologists have helped to bury a great deal of nonsense about heredity, race, class, sex differences, deviation, and nearly every other aspect of behavior. It is due partly to the findings of sociology that today we rarely hear an educated person argue that the white race is innately superior, that women are intellectually inferior to men, that behavior traits are inherited, that punishment reforms criminals, or that rural people are less "immoral" than urbanites,—ideas which nearly every educated person accepted a half century ago. By helping replace superstition and misinformation with accurate knowledge about human behavior, sociologists are perhaps performing their most important function.

Making sociological predictions   Sociological prediction should be of interest to legislators and all others who are concerned with social policy, for every major policy decision makes certain assumptions about the present and future structure of society. When a legislator says, "Schools must operate within their present income," he is assuming that present school funds are adequate to prepare children for the society in which they will be living for another seventy-five years, while the legislator who says, "We must raise more funds for schools," makes an opposite assumption. Unavoidably, every policy pronouncement makes an assumption about the kind of society we shall have in the future. What sort of predictions do sociologists offer? Here are a few samples, offered without explanation or documentation at this point, as examples of the kind of predictions sociologists can make:

Urban sprawl will spread rapidly along the superhighways and will result in the creation of regional planning and administrative authorities.

The income gap between the poor and the rest of us will grow larger during the next decade or two.

The trend toward the employment of mothers will continue until most women are working for a substantial portion of their married lives.

The present racial disorders will continue until all forms of institutionalized segregation or discrimination are destroyed.

Birth rates will, sooner or later, fall to approach death rates, or death rates must rise to approach birth rates.

Farm organizations and perhaps labor unions have passed the peak of their power; both will suffer a relative decline in membership and in power.

There is no certainty that any one of these predictions will be fulfilled, only a strong likelihood that most of them will come true. Such predictions help to clarify the kind of social setting in which we must function for the next generation or two.

The sociologist as policy consultant   Sociological prediction can also help to estimate the probable effects of a social policy. Every social policy decision *is* a prediction. A policy (e.g., Federal grants for urban renewal) is begun in the hope that it will produce a desired effect (e.g., halt the spread of urban blight). Policies have often failed because they embodied unsound assumptions and predictions. Sociologists can help to predict the effects of a policy, and thus contribute to the selection of policies which achieve the intended purposes. For example:

What effect would the removal or the addition of the death penalty have upon the murder rate? (Practically none.)

What effects do brotherhood propaganda and "education for brotherhood" efforts have on race prejudices? (Practically none.)

What effects do attempts at enforced desegregation have upon race prejudices? (Momentary tension, followed by substantial reduction.)

If welfare payments were withheld from illegitimate mothers, what effect would this have on illegitimacy rates? (Little or none.)

Would publishing the names of juvenile delinquents help to reduce delinquency? (No; it would more likely increase it.)

Would the suppression of obscene literature help to reduce sex crimes and sex immorality? (Nobody knows, for there is no dependable scientific evidence on this question.)

These are a few of the many social-policy questions which sociologists could help to settle. So far our society has not generally accorded the sociologist a status as technical expert on social-policy matters. The image of the sociologist as a professional bleeding heart, so often reflected in the popular press, does not help the public to visualize the sociologist as a technical expert. Congressional committees, however, often consult sociologists and other social scientists when holding hearings on proposed legislation. In some areas, especially in criminology and race relations, the conclusions of sociologists (and other social scientists) have had considerable influence. It was, in considerable part, the findings of sociologists and psychologists which led the United States Supreme Court to rule that "segregated schools are inherently unequal."

One of the greatest services any scholarly group can offer is to show the society what policies are most likely to work in achieving its objectives. This is a service which sociologists are qualified to perform.

The sociologist Today sociologists are increasingly finding employment with government
as a technician departments, corporations, hospitals, large welfare agencies, and other large organizations. Aside from research, they are engaged in planning and conducting community action programs; advising on public relations, employee relations, problems of morale or of "intergroup relations" within the organization; working on human relations problems of many sorts. The "staff sociologist" is becoming more familiar in all kinds of large organizations [*Business Week*, 1959]. Often he has specialized in social psychology, industrial sociology, urban or rural sociology, or the sociology of complex organizations.

In such positions the sociologist is working as an applied scientist. His employer has engaged him to use his scientific knowledge in pursuing certain values—a harmonious and efficient working force, an attractive public image of the industry, or an effective community action program. This role raises a question of ethics. When a sociologist accepts employment as a technician, pursuing values chosen by his employer, has he compromised his scientific integrity? To take an extreme example, there is evidence [Monroe, 1962] that gambling operators engaged social scientists to find out why people do or do not gamble, so that the operators will know how to attract more customers. (We do not know whether any sociologists were included.) Would this be a form of scientific prostitution?

One answer to this question is that neither the profession nor the public expects the same neutrality from a General Motors economist or sociologist that they expect from a university professor. The university professor is expected to search for and teach the truth; the technician is expected to serve the interests of his employer, *within certain limits*. He must not betray the values of accuracy to which science is dedicated or the values of decency and propriety which his fellow sociologists, as persons, feel to be acceptable. Thus a corporation's sociologist might seek to locate and remove some unnecessary sources of friction within the organization, or a hospital staff sociologist might advise on internal organization, fund raising, community relatons, or out-patient operations. All of these would be viewed by his fellows as legitimate professional activities. Your authors know of no sociologists who have accepted positions which involve them in union busting or strike breaking, in serving antidemocratic causes or movements, or in campaigns to deceive or misinform the American people. If any were so to commit themselves, they would become sociological outcasts for serving values which most sociologists privately despise, and which in some cases are a betrayal of truth.

The sociologist and social action Scientists seek to discover knowledge. Should scientists also tell the society how this knowledge *should* be used? For example, the geneticists already know something about human heredity, and before very long it may be possible to "order" babies according to a specifications list. Who should decide what sort of baby should go to whom? The scientists? The parents? The government?

The basic question is whether science—specifically sociology—should be value-free. For example, sociologists know some things about population growth, race relations, urban development, and many other matters involving questions of public policy. Should sociologists become public advocates of birth-control programs, racial integration, urban renewal, and many other pro-grams which they may consider socially desirable?

Early sociologists gave an emphatic "yes" to this question. Without an ade-quate foundation of scientific knowledge, they rushed into support of all sorts of public policies they believed wise. Between 1920 and 1940, many sociolo-gists shifted to the view that sociology should be a more nearly "pure" science, discovering knowledge, but not attempting to decree how it should be used. They sought to build sociology on the model of physics or chemistry, as a value-free science. As such, it should be committed to no values except those of free scientific inquiry. Sociologists generally avoided involvement in contro-versial issues and sought the status of "pure" social scientists.

More recently, this view has been challenged in both physical and social science. *The Bulletin of the Atomic Scientists* carries many articles by scien-tists urging their fellows to claim a larger role in making the decisions about the uses of nuclear science discoveries. Many sociologists today believe that sociologists should claim a major role in making decisions about public policy and should involve themselves in the major issues of our society [Lindesmith, 1960; Horowitz, 1964; Stein and Vidich, 1964; Lee, 1966; Becker, 1967]. They charge that sociologists have buried themselves in "safe" research topics, leaving the really important questions to be explored by nonsociologists —questions such as, "How can poverty be reduced?" "How can schools be integrated?" "How can communities be organized for more civilized social living?" "Should the goals and values of American society be altered to pro-mote human welfare?" They feel that sociologists not only should say what society *might* do about problems of race conflict, population growth, birth control, drug addiction, divorce, sex deviation, medical care, etc.; they feel that sociologists have a duty to say what our society *should* do about such problems. Books like Shostak's *Sociology in Action* [1966] provide some con-crete examples of how sociologists are involving themselves in social issues and constructive social action and show what they have learned from these experiences.

As a citizen, he is perfectly justified in supporting causes.

Whether sociology should be value-free is an unsettled question. But sociologists *are* agreed upon the following propositions:

(1) Sociologists should show the relationships between values. In short, sociologists may say, "If *this* is what you want, *here* is what you must do to get it." If stable, enduring marriages are more important than marriage happiness, then divorce should be made more difficult; if *happy* marriages represent the more important value, then fairly easy divorce should permit the unhappily married to separate and try again. If we wish to arrest urban blight and suburban sprawl, some private property rights will have to be sacrificed. If we wish to clean up polluted rivers, we must be prepared to spend a lot of tax moneys in doing so. Sociologists may clarify what value sacrifices must be made if we wish to attain certain other values.

(2) A sociologist *as an individual* may properly make value judgments, support causes, and join reform movements, like any other citizen. As a scientist, he may not be able to prove whether television violence is harmful to children, and therefore will make no public recommendations; but as a parent he makes a decision according to his beliefs and values. As a scientist, he may not be able to say whether gambling should be forbidden or whether contraceptives should be distributed to unmarried coeds; but as a citizen he is free to express his opinions and support his own value judgments.

Beyond this, there is no complete agreement among sociologists concerning what role they should assume. Most sociologists have some firm opinions on what policies society should follow and are in considerable agreement with one another upon many of these policies. Possibly the time will come when the social policies which seem best to sociologists will also seem best to the rest of the society. As persons who cannot and would not divorce themselves from the society in which they live, most sociologists hope so.

THE STUDY OF SOCIOLOGY

Some students will learn little in a sociology course because they feel that they already know everything worth knowing about social life. Having prowled the same haunts in a dozen towns and made the same encounters in a dozen or a hundred bars, they know all about *life*. Those who feel this way will learn very little, here or anywhere.

A lifetime of eating food does not make one a dietitian, nor does surviving a number of traffic jams make one a traffic engineer. Each student, true enough, has been having social experiences all his life, and from these he has learned many things, some true and some false. To separate truth from falsehood is one of the objectives of sociology. Only those students who are willing to learn —who are willing and able to subject their beliefs, assumptions, and practices to objective scientific scrutiny—will gain much from the study of any of the social sciences.

The use of concepts in sociology

Every field of study makes the student memorize many words to which that field attaches special meanings. This is not an idle ritual; it is done because precise concepts are necessary. First, *we need carefully expressed concepts to carry on a scientific discussion*. How would you explain machinery to a person who had no concept of "wheel"? How useful to a specialist would a patient's medical history be if his physician had recorded it in the language of the layman? The several dozen sociological concepts which will harass the student in this book are necessary for a clear discussion of social phenomena. Secondly, *the formulation of concepts leads to increased knowledge*. Some accurate descriptive knowledge must be organized before a concept can be framed. Then the analysis and criticism of this new concept point up the gaps and errors in present knowledge. The *use* of the concept often calls attention to facts and relationships which may have been overlooked. Years ago, while studying the mulatto, Stonequist [1937] framed the concept of the *marginal man* who is on the fringes of two groups or two ways of life while fully belonging to neither. The use of this concept quickly led to the recognition that there were many kinds of marginal persons—the foreman, who is not clearly either "management" or "labor"; the immigrant, partly adapted to two ways of life while fully adapted to neither; the ambitious climber, no longer in the working class yet not securely a middle-class person; and many others. Sound concepts like that of the marginal man lead to increased knowledge.

Most of the concepts of sociology are expressed in words which also have a popular meaning, just as the term *order* has one meaning in zoology and another at the restaurant table. Every science appropriates some common words and makes them into scientific concepts by giving them a specific definition. Sociology is no exception.

Careers in sociology

If a subject interests a student, he may wonder what possibilities it holds for a career. A combination of courses which constitutes an undergraduate major or minor in sociology is not, in itself, preparation for a professional career as a sociologist. Undergraduate majors and minors are useful mainly as background preparation for other careers. (1) In *social work,* the better jobs demand a graduate degree in social work, and usually recommend a strong undergraduate major in sociology. (2) *The professions*—medicine, law, engineering—are increasingly urging more undergraduate social science upon their students, since some understanding of people and society is necessary for success in these professions [Turner, 1958; Boodish, 1957]. (3) *Secondary schools* present a growing demand for sociology teachers, with about one-fourth of the schools offering sociology as a separate course and another one-fourth including sociology in a composite course [S. Anderson et al., 1964; Wright, 1965]. (4) *Civil service positions* often include undergraduate sociology among the acceptable educational qualifications for a wide variety of positions in lower and middle brackets. (5) *Newly emerging careers* are to be found in many sorts of action programs—local human relations councils, fair employment practices commissions, economic opportunity and Job Corps programs, Peace Corps and foreign aid programs, and many others. Such careers are too new and too rapidly expanding to have developed any rigidly standardized courses of professional preparation, but sociology majors are often sought for these positions.

An M.A. degree is usually sufficient to obtain a position at a junior college or community college, but promotions and university appointments usually require a Ph.D., which is even more necessary for a distinguished career in sociology than it is in the other sciences. Among those scientists with enough "professional standing in the scientific community" to be listed in the 1964 National Register of Scientific and Technical Personnel, a doctor's degree was held by 81 per cent of the sociologists, 65 per cent of the biologists, 61 per cent of the psychologists, 42 per cent of the physicists, 35 per cent of the chemists, and so on down to 9 per cent of the meteorologists [Hopper, 1966]. Of these sociologists, 75 per cent were employed by colleges and universities, with the remainder scattered among many employers, including government agencies and private foundations. Teaching was the primary work activity of 57 per cent of the sociologists, with 22 per cent engaged primarily in research, and 16 per cent in management and administration, most often management and administration of research. Employment opportunities are steadily growing, and any well-qualified sociologist can take his pick of several kinds of work.

For most students, sociology will not be a career but merely a part of their general liberal arts education. Whatever career they enter, including that of housewife, they will be members of a society, residents in a community, participants in many groups, and carriers of the culture to the next generation. The study of sociology may aid them to fill with greater insight these varied roles which are their inescapable destiny.

SUMMARY

Sociology attempts to study society scientifically. Sociology is science, not social philosophy; it is knowledge, not social reform; it is social science, not socialism. Each social science has its own focus, and sociology's is upon man's group life and the social products of this group life.

The methods of sociological research include studies which are cross-sectional, longitudinal, or *ex post facto*. They may be planned experiments, or they may be observational studies of several kinds—impressionistic studies, statistical comparative studies, questionnaire and interview studies, participant-observer studies, and case studies. Some difficulties in sociological research pose a challenge to our methodology—the complexity of social phenomena and the limitations of possible prediction when one is working with many variables. Sociology, like all sciences, may be either pure or applied. Pure sociology searches for new knowledge, while applied sociology tries to apply sociological knowledge to practical problems. A good deal of more or less accurate sociology is popularized by professional journalists, who are sometimes incorrectly called sociologists.

The sociologist in his professional role as a social scientist tends to be a pure scientist who devotes himself to discovering and teaching truth; occasionally he makes sociological predictions. He may function as an applied scientist when employed as a technician or consultant, or when he fills his private role as a citizen. Whether sociologists as scientists should select and recommend the policies society *should* follow is an unsettled question among sociologists. The study of sociology will be successful only if the student is willing to learn about matters which he may think he is already familiar with. He must learn some concepts which are needed for a precise scientific discussion. Granted a willingness to engage in serious preparation, he may even find a prospective career in sociology.

QUESTIONS AND PROJECTS

1. How would you define sociology to an uneducated person with no understanding of the fields of knowledge? How would you define it to a well-educated person whose education had included no sociology?

2. What is a sociologist? How is the term often misused?

3. What is the difference between social science and social philosophy? Which do you think is more important?

4. Are sociologists interested in social reform?

5. Why are sociologists sometimes confused with socialists? What is the difference?

6. How do you "control" a variable? If studying the possible effects of student marriage on college achievement, what other variables would need to be controlled? How could they be controlled?

7. Why are planned experiments rather rare in sociology?

8. What precautions are needed in using eyewitness accounts as sources of scientific data?

9. How does the participant-observer technique differ from merely looking at things? Isn't everyone a participant observer?

10. What are some things that a sociologist may do as a private citizen which he may not do as a scientist? Are there any other professions in which one may do, as a citizen, things which he may not do in his professional capacity?

11. When you are in an informal student "bull session," listen to each statement with these questions in mind: "How scientifically sound is this statement? Is it based upon scientific fact or upon guesswork, folklore, and wishful thinking? Could it be documented with adequate scientific support?" At the conclusion, try to estimate what proportion of the statements could be scientifically substantiated.

12. Write a brief, impressionistic account of some group or some community you have observed. Then list several of your generalizations about the group, and outline a research project for collecting the empirical data which would enable you to test the accuracy of these statements.

SUGGESTED READINGS

ADAMS, SAMUEL HOPKINS: "The Juke Myth," *Saturday Review*, Apr. 2, 1955, pp. 13ff.; reprinted in EDGAR A. SCHULER ET AL. (EDS.): *Readings in Sociology*, 2d ed., Thomas Y. Crowell Company, New York, 1960, pp. 40–46. An amusing account of the method whereby the author of a famous study arrived at some highly dubious conclusions about heredity and crime.

ALLPORT, GORDON W., J. S. BRUNER, AND E. M. JANDORF: "Personality under Social Catastrophe: Ninety Life-histories of the Nazi Revolution," *Character and Personality*, 10:1–22, 1941; reprinted in CLYDE

KLUCKHOHN AND HENRY A. MURRAY (EDS.): *Personality in Nature, Society, and Culture*, Alfred A. Knopf, Inc., New York, 1949, pp. 347–366. Shows how a collection of life histories can be used in arriving at scientific generalizations.

*BATES, ALAN P.: *The Sociological Enterprise*, Houghton Mifflin Company, Boston, 1967. A brief paperback telling what sociologists do and how they become sociologists. Ch. 5, "Training for Careers in Sociology," and ch. 6, "Careers in Sociology" are especially recommended. (HM)

FORM, WILLIAM, AND SIGMUND NOSOW, WITH GREGORY P.

STONE AND CHARLES WESTIE: *Community in Disaster,* Harper & Row, Publishers, Incorporated, New York, 1958. A case study of community reaction to a severe tornado, showing how eye-witness accounts and other observational data can be used in sociological research.

LANTZ, HERMAN R.: *People of Coal Town,* Columbia University Press, New York, 1958. A largely impressionistic case study of a community. Gives few statistics and no sweeping generalizations, but presents some hypotheses and interesting sociological description.

LAZARSFELD, PAUL F., WILLIAM H. SEWELL, AND HAROLD L. WILENSKY: *The Uses of Sociology,* Basic Books, New York, 1967. A comprehensive review of the practical applications of sociology to a wide range of problems.

MCCORMICK, THOMAS C., AND ROY G. FRANCES: *Methods of Research in the Behavioral Sciences,* Harper & Row, Publishers, Incorporated, New York, 1958. A brief handbook on planning and conducting a social research project.

*PETERSEN, WILLIAM (ED.): *American Social Patterns,* Doubleday & Company, Inc., Garden City, N.Y., 1956. An Anchor paperback containing a good collection of sociological research examples. (A86-Anch)

PHILLIPS, BERNARD S.: *Social Research,* The Macmillan Company, New York, 1966. A standard text in social research methods.

SELLTIZ, CLAIRE, MARIE JAHODA, MORTON DEUTSCH, AND STUART COOK: *Methods in Social Relations,* Holt, Rinehart and Winston, Inc., New York, 1959. A standard textbook in sociological research methods.

*SHOSTAK, ARTHUR B. (ED.): *Sociology in Action: Case Studies in Social Problems and Directed Social Change,* Dorsey Press, Homewood, Ill., 1966. Tells how sociologists may become involved in social action. (Dor)

Statistical Abstract of the United States, published annually by the Bureau of the Census, and *The World Almanac and Book of Facts,* published annually by the *New York World-Telegram and Sun.* Two useful sources of statistical and factual information on practically any subject, available in any library. Every student should be familiar with them.

Two

CULTURE AND PERSONALITY

Part Two shows how man develops a remarkable thing called culture, and how his culture in turn shapes man's behavior. Chapter 3, "The Nature of Culture," tells what culture is and how it develops. Chapter 4, "The Meaning of Culture," shows in greater detail how the thoughts and actions of a person are a reflection of his culture.

Chapter 5, "Personality and Socialization," shows how individual personality is developed through the interaction of heredity, environment, culture, and both group and unique experience. In Chapter 6, "Role and Status," we see how most behavior is organized into a series of roles which men can fill easily only if they are properly prepared. Chapter 7, "Social Control and Social Deviation," shows how most people are led to act as they are expected to act, and attempts to explain the deviations of the minority.

The cars of the migrant people crawled out of the side roads onto the great cross-country highway, and they took the migrant way to the West. In the daylight they scuttled like bugs to the westward; and as the dark caught them, they clustered like bugs near to shelter and to water. And because they were lonely and perplexed, because they had all come from a place of sadness and worry and defeat, and because they were all going to a new mysterious place, they huddled together; they talked together; they shared their lives, their food, and the things they hoped for in the new country. Thus it might be that one family camped near a spring, and another camped for the spring and for company, and a third because two families had pioneered the place and found it good. And when the sun went down, perhaps twenty families and twenty cars were there. . . .

Every night a world created, complete with furniture—friends made and enemies established; a world complete with braggarts and with cowards, with quiet men, with humble men, with kindly men. Every night relationships that make a world, established; and every morning the world torn down like a circus.

At first the families were timid in the building and tumbling worlds, but gradually the technique of building worlds became their technique. Then leaders emerged, then laws were made, then codes came into being. And as the worlds moved westward they were more complete and better furnished, for their builders were more experienced in building them.

The families learned what rights must be observed—the right of privacy in the tent; the right to keep the past black hidden in the heart; the right to talk and to listen; the right to refuse help or to accept, to offer help or to decline it; the right of son to court and daughter to be courted; the right of the hungry to be fed; the rights of the pregnant and the sick to transcend all other rights.

And the families learned, although no one told them, what rights are monstrous and must be destroyed: the right to intrude upon privacy, the right to be noisy while the camp slept, the right of seduction or rape, the right of adultery and theft and murder. These rights were crushed, because the little worlds could not exist for even a night with such rights alive.

And as the worlds moved westward, rules became laws, although no one told the families. It is unlawful to foul near the camp; it is unlawful to eat good rich food near one who is hungry, unless he is asked to share.

And with the laws, the punishments—and there were only two—a quick and murderous fight or ostracism; and ostracism was the worst. For if one broke the laws his name and face went with him, and he had no place in any world, no matter where created.

In the worlds, social conduct became fixed and rigid, so that a man must say "Good morning" when asked for it, so that a man might have a willing girl if he stayed with her, if he fathered her children and protected them. But a man might not have one girl one night and another the next, for this would endanger the worlds.

The families moved westward, and the technique of building the worlds improved so that the people could be safe in their worlds; and the form was so fixed that a family acting in the rules knew it was safe in the rules. (John Steinbeck, *The Grapes of Wrath*, The Viking Press, Inc., New York, 1939, pp. 264–266.)

3

THE NATURE OF CULTURE

From their life experiences, a group develops a set of rules and procedures for meeting their needs. The set of rules and procedures, together with a supporting set of ideas and values, is called a *culture*. This chapter and the one which follows are devoted to the explanation of this very important concept.

We commonly say that a person is cultured if he can identify operatic arias, read a French menu, and select the right fork. But people who are bored by the classics, eat peas with their knives, and speak in four-letter words also have a culture. Like most sociological concepts, *culture* is a word with both a popular and a sociological meaning.

The classic definition of culture, framed by Sir Edward Tylor [1871, vol. 1, p. 1], reads, "Culture . . . is that complex whole which includes knowledge, belief, art, morals, law, custom and any other capabilities and habits acquired by man as a member of society." Stated more simply, *culture is everything which is socially learned and shared by the members of a society.* The individual receives culture as part of his social heritage, and, in turn, he may reshape the culture and introduce changes which then become a part of the heritage of succeeding generations.

This social heritage may be divided into *material* and *nonmaterial culture.* Nonmaterial culture consists of the words people use, the ideas, customs, and beliefs they hold, and the habits they follow. Material culture consists of man-made objects such as tools, furniture, automobiles, buildings, irrigation ditches, cultivated farms, roads, bridges, and in fact, any physical substance which has been changed and used by man. In the game of baseball, for instance, the gloves, bats, uniforms, and grandstands are a few elements of material culture. The nonmaterial culture would include the rules of the game, the skills of the players, the concepts of strategy, and the traditional behavior of players and spectators. The material culture is always the outgrowth of the nonmaterial culture and is meaningless without it. If the *game* of baseball is forgotten, a bat becomes just a stick of wood.

The destruction of World War II, while the most extensive in history, has left little lasting physical impression because men retained the knowledge and skills (nonmaterial culture) needed to rebuild their ruined cities. The Pyramids of Egypt, on the other hand, would not be rebuilt, for they are entirely divorced from the nonmaterial culture that led to their construction—a culture that would include both the methods of construction and the values that inspired the Pharaohs to want to build such monuments. Today the value system that motivated their behavior has disappeared, and the Pyramids are merely monuments to a dead culture, of interest only as a tourist attraction. People are likely to place a great value on impressive parts of the material culture, even though these may easily be replaced if the relevant nonmaterial culture is active, or may be completely useless if the nonmaterial culture which produced them has disappeared. Since *the heritage of ideas is the most important part of man's culture,* the major emphasis of this book will be on this nonmaterial culture.

We also make a distinction between culture and society. A culture is a *system of behavior* shared by the members of a society; a society is a *group of people* who share a common culture. A society is made up of people who are interacting on the basis of shared beliefs, customs, values, and activities. The common patterns which govern their interaction make up the culture of the society. There cannot be a culture apart from society, and no society exists without a culture. As Gillin and Gillin [1948, p. 188] state, "Culture is the cement binding together into a society its component individuals . . . human society is *people* interacting; culture is the *patterning* of their behavior." The two terms may be used almost interchangeably in places; yet we must remember that society refers to people, and culture to patterns of behavior.

CULTURE AS A SYSTEM OF NORMS

Since culture tells us the way in which things should be done, we say that it is *normative,* which is another way of saying that it provides standards of proper conduct. For shaking hands, we extend the right hand; our culture defines this as proper. For scratching our heads we may use either hand; our culture has no norm for head scratching. The term *norm* has two possible meanings. A *statistical norm* is a measure of what actually exists; a *cultural norm* is a concept of what is expected to exist. The famous Kinsey studies sought to find some statistical norms of sexual behavior in the United States. The effort infuriated many people who confused statistical with cultural norms. A cultural norm is a set of behavior *expectations,* a cultural image of how people are supposed to act. A culture is an elaborate system of such norms—of standardized, expected ways of feeling and acting—which the members of a society follow more or less perfectly. Except where otherwise indicated, it is the cultural norms to which the sociologist refers. These norms are of several kinds and several degrees of compulsion.

Folkways Social life everywhere is full of problems—how to wrest a living from nature, how to divide up the fruits of toil or good fortune, how to relate ourselves agreeably to one another, and many others. Man seems to have tried every possible way of dealing with such problems. Different societies have found a wide variety of workable patterns. A group may eat once, twice, or several times each day; they may eat while standing, seated in chairs, or squatting on the ground; they may eat together, or each may eat in privacy; they may eat with their fingers or use some kind of utensils; they may start with wine and end with fish, start with fish and end with wine, or they may reject both fish and wine as inedible. And so it goes for thousands of items of behavior. Each trait is a selection from a number of possibilities, all of which are more or less workable. Through trial and error, sheer accident, or some unknown influence a group arrives at one of

Folkways are simply the customary ways a group does things.

these possibilities, repeats it, and accepts it as the normal way of meeting a particular need. It is passed on to succeeding generations and becomes one of the ways of the folk—hence, a folkway. *Folkways are simply the customary, normal, habitual ways a group does things.* Shaking hands, eating with knives and forks, wearing neckties on some occasions and sport shirts on others, driving on the right-hand side of the street, and eating toast for breakfast are a few of our many American folkways.

New generations absorb the folkways, partly by deliberate teaching, but mainly by observing and taking part in the life about them. The child is surrounded by folkways. Since he constantly sees these ways of doing things, they become to him the only real ways. If he chances to hear of the customs of other groups, they appear as quaint oddities and not as practical, realistic ways of getting things done. Even the most primitive society will have a few thousand folkways; in modern, industrialized societies they become even more numerous and involved. Sorting out the proper folkway becomes so difficult that Emily Post was able to earn a sizeable fortune as an interpreter of our folkways, even though her fat volume does not catalog those followed by all Americans, but lists only some of the nonoccupational folkways of the urban upper class.

Mores   Some of the folkways are more important than others. If one uses the wrong fork for one's salad, there is momentary embarrassment but no great injury. But if, in our society, a woman chooses anyone but her husband to sire her child, many aspects of financial obligation, property inheritance rights, family relationships, and sentimental linkage become disrupted. We therefore recognize two classes of folkways: (1) those which should be followed as a matter of good manners and polite behavior and (2) those which *must* be followed because they are believed essential to group welfare. These ideas of right and wrong which attach to certain of the folkways are then called *mores*. By the mores (a Latin plural, long a part of our language) we mean those strong ideas of right and wrong which require certain acts and forbid others.

The members of a group normally share a sublime faith that violation of their mores will bring disaster upon the group. Outsiders, however, often see that at least some of the group's mores are irrational. They may include food taboos which make cattle, hogs, or horses unfit to eat, modesty taboos which forbid exposure of the face, the ankle, the wrist, the breast, or whatever is considered "immodest"; language taboos which forbid misuse of certain sacred or obscene words; and many others. Such taboos seem very important to their believers but may be entirely unknown in other cultures and seem to have no necessary connection with group welfare. It is not necessary that the act forbidden by the mores should actually be injurious. If a society believes that the act is injurious, it is condemned by the mores. Mores are *beliefs* in the rightness or wrongness of acts.

Mores are not deliberately invented or thought up or worked out because someone decides they would be a good idea. They emerge gradually out of the customary practices of the people, largely without conscious choice or intention. Mores arise from a group decision that a particular act seems to be harmful and must be forbidden (or, conversely, that a particular act is so necessary that it must be required). Originally, then, mores are a practical group judgment about group welfare. For example, suppose that through some coincidence several members of a tribe have nasty accidents after swimming in a certain pool. The tribe draws the logical conclusion that there is something dangerous about the pool. As soon as they firmly agree that people should stay away from the pool, the mores have defined this act as wrong. Persons who swim in the pool thereafter are likely to expect misfortune, and others who know of their act will wait to see how they are punished. Thus any misfortune will be interpreted as a punishment and will reinforce these mores. Before long, their origin is forgotten and people think of a dip in this pool as being wrong *in and of itself,* not just because it seems to have been followed by misfortune. In this way, mores, which originate as practical group judgments of the effects of actions, become transformed into absolutes—into things which are right because they are right, and wrong because they are wrong. In other words, *mores become self-validating and self-perpetuating.* They become sacred. To question them is indecent, and to violate them is intolerable. Every society punishes those who violate its mores.

Mores are taught to the young, not as a set of practical expedients but as a set of sacred absolutes. Wherever the mores are firmly established, obedience is automatic. When fully internalized by the individual, the mores control behavior by making it psychologically very difficult for him to commit the forbidden act. For example, we do not refrain from eating our children or our enemies because of an intellectual decision that cannibalism is impractical or wasteful, but because the idea of cannibalism is so repellent to us that the thought of eating human flesh never seriously occurs to us. Most of us would be unable to eat human flesh even if we tried to do so. Mores function by making their violation emotionally impossible. In a society with a clearly defined, firmly implanted set of mores, there is very little personal misconduct.

Some people claim that mores are just group opinions and are not the same as "real" right and wrong. They argue for absolute standards of morality, claiming that the nature of the universe makes certain actions definitely wrong and others definitely right, regardless of time, place, or circumstances. This is an important ethical issue but one which has had meaning for only philosophers and theologians. As far as the behavior of most people is concerned, "mores" is simply another word for "real" right and wrong. For, as Sumner [1906] has observed, the mores can make anything right and prevent condemnation of anything. Our mores define the killer as either a villain or a hero, according to the circumstances. Medieval mores made it right for the church to tolerate prostitution and even share in its income. Most of the Reformation churchmen, both Catholic and Protestant, who ordered the torture and burning of heretics were not cruel or evil, but were decent and often kindly men who did what the mores of the time and place required them to do. Mores of our recent past have approved child labor, slavery, and persecution of minorities, and have condemned pacifism, woman suffrage, and sex education. And at all times and places, good people feel pure and righteous when following the mores, whatever they may be.

Institutions Some folkways and mores are more important than others; for example, those concerned with forming families and raising children are more important than those concerned with playing football. *An organized cluster of folkways and mores centered upon a major human activity is called a social institution.*

In most complex societies there are five "basic" institutions which provide for family life, religion, government, education, and the organization of economic activities. Beyond these the concept tapers off into less significant clusters of behavior patterns like those surrounding baseball, hunting, or beekeeping, which are sometimes loosely called institutions, but probably should not be included because they are so much less important.

Institutions are among the most formal and compelling of the norms of a society. As already outlined, folkways emerge from the trial-and-error experience of the group; some of the folkways come to be viewed as essential to group welfare, and are therefore supported by the mores; when the folkways and mores surrounding an important activity become organized into a quite formal, binding system of belief and behavior, an institution has developed. An institution thus includes a set of behavior patterns which have become highly standardized, a set of supporting mores, attitudes, and values, and generally a body of traditions, rituals and ceremonies, symbols and vestments, and other paraphernalia. Social institutions will be treated in detail in later chapters, but are introduced here because the concept must be used throughout our discussion.

Laws   While some of the mores function simply as mores, there is a strong tendency for them to become incorporated into the laws of a society. Many people will obey the mores automatically or because they want to do the "right" thing. A few people, however, are tempted to violate the mores. These people may be forced to conform by the threat of legal punishment. Thus the law serves to reinforce the mores. Those who still will not conform are imprisoned or executed.

Some observers believe that law can be effective only when it seeks to support mores which are already firmly accepted by most members of the society. National prohibition is offered as an example. The Eighteenth Amendment was ratified in 1918 to end all sale of intoxicating beverages in the United States. It clearly expressed the mores of many persons and groups. But for many others, the prohibition amendment was not a legal sanction of *their* moral beliefs, but an effort by the state to impose an unreasonable restriction. To these people the use of alcoholic beverages was a part of family social life and sometimes of religious celebration. The members of these groups reinforced one another's belief that prohibition was absurd and obedience unnecessary. The bootlegger who sold liquor illegally became, not a criminal to be reported to the police, but a folk hero somewhat in the Robin Hood tradition. Under these circumstances, law enforcement was ineffective. The illegal consumption of alcohol was widespread, corruption was rampant in police departments, and the public in general became disgusted with the prohibition law. The Eighteenth Amendment was repealed in 1933, only fifteen years after it had been introduced. Other examples of laws unsupported by the mores include the Fugitive Slave Act, widely violated by persons who believed that escaped slaves should be helped to escape their owners, and World War II price and rationing controls, widely violated by Americans trained to believe that they had a right to buy anything they could pay for. Such examples show how difficult it is to enforce a law that is not backed by a nation's mores.

On the other hand, seldom is any legislation in agreement with the mores of all groups in a society. Nor can one measure the precise degree of agreement needed between laws and the mores for the law to be effective. Perhaps a better way to state the relationship between law and mores is to say the law *is most effective when it is in harmony with changes which are affecting the mores*. Some examples of conflict between law and the mores will illustrate this idea. National Prohibition was passed at a time when social changes tended to make the mores permissive rather than restrictive. The Fugitive Slave Act faced a mounting opposition to slavery which undercut any effort to support slavery by legislation. Increasingly strict divorce laws in the twentieth century (reduced number of grounds, waiting periods, interlocutory decrees) failed to stem a rising divorce rate. In other words, all three examples are of cases in which the trend of the mores was in the opposite direction from that indicated by the law.

This does not mean that law is always ineffective when it is in opposition to the mores of a part of the population. A case in point is the civil rights legislation since 1960 which has certainly increased the opportunity for minority groups to vote, to find a job appropriate for their capabilities, and to enjoy full access to public accommodations. The opposition to the law is bitter and formidable, but it comes at a time when the trend toward equal treatment of colored peoples is undermining the mores supporting segregation. Under these circumstances the law and the trend of the mores are working in harmony and tend to support each other. Incidentally, similar civil rights legislation passed just after the Civil War in a different type of racial climate was completely ineffective.

In complex societies, law also becomes a means of regulating many kinds of behavior which are not clearly covered by the mores. Our culture changes rapidly, while mores change more slowly, and new situations must be handled in an orderly way. A vast array of laws and regulations—building codes, zoning ordinances, business law, traffic codes, and many others—has developed to regulate matters which are too detailed, specialized, technical, or changeable to be controlled successfully by mores. Some sociologists [Odum, 1947, pp. 227–229] have used the term *stateways* to include all this regulatory machinery of the state, and this is a useful label since the term *law* is used in many other contexts. Scientific laws, for instance, are statements of an "orderly and dependable sequence presumably of a causative character" [Fairchild, 1957, p. 171]. Scientific laws are not passed by anyone but refer to man's observation of persistent regularities in interaction. They have no necessary relationship with the stateways which concern the legislation and administrative rules determined by government.

THE STRUCTURE OF CULTURE

A culture is not simply an accumulation of folkways and mores; it is an *organized system* of behavior. Let us see some of the ways in which it is organized.

Cultural traits and complexes   The smallest unit of culture is called a *trait*. This is a somewhat arbitrary definition since what is a single unit to one individual may appear as a combination of units to another. Hoebel's definition [1949, p. 499] is apt at this point: "A reputedly irreducible unit of learned behavior pattern or material product thereof." Traits of the material culture would include such things as the nail, the screwdriver, the pencil, and the handkerchief. Nonmaterial culture traits would include such actions as shaking hands, tipping hats, the practice of driving on the right-hand side of the road, the kiss as a gesture of affection between the sexes, or the salute to the flag. Each culture includes thousands of traits.

Is the dance a trait? No; it is a collection of traits, including the dance steps, some formula for selecting the performers, and a musical or rhythmic accompaniment. Most important of all, the dance has a meaning—as a religious ceremonial, a magical rite, a courtship activity, a festive orgy, or something else. All these elements combine to form a *culture complex*, a cluster of related traits. Another cluster of objects, skills, and attitudes forms the football complex.[1] The saying of grace, the reading of the Bible, and evening prayers may form a family religious complex. Similarly, there is a dating complex which includes many activities and attitudes with which students may have some familiarity.

The complex is intermediate between the trait and the institution. An institution is a series of complexes centering upon an important activity. Thus the family includes the dating complex, the engagement-and-wedding complex, the honeymoon complex, the child-care complex, and several others. Some complexes are parts of institutions; others, revolving around less important activities—such as stamp collecting—are simply independent complexes.

Universals, alternatives, and specialties   Linton [1936, chap. 16] has pointed out that some culture traits are necessary to all members of the society, while other traits are shared by only some members. A trait required of all members of the society he calls a *universal*. Certain values, gestures, and meanings must be shared by all members if there is to be an orderly social life. When a person approaches us with the right hand extended, we must know whether this indicates a friendly greeting or a physical attack. Without a set of understanding shared by all normal members in the society, such confusion would prevail that the ordinary business of social life would never get done. In our culture one must be monogamous if he marries, must clothe certain parts of the body, and drive on the right side of the street; he must condemn free love and infanticide; he must praise free enterprise and motherhood. Punishment—legal or social, or both—awaits the man who does not conform.

In every society there are some areas of life in which the individual must choose among several possibilities. These Linton calls *alternatives*. Americans may choose among a number of religious faiths, or even—at the price of some disapproval—adopt none. We may travel by automobile, railroad, or airplane, eat at home or in restaurants, purchase or make our own clothing. Our family patterns allow a man or woman to marry or remain single; intermediate or simultaneous arrangements are disapproved. The couple may be married in a religious or a secular ceremony. They may live with the groom's parents, with the bride's parents, or by themselves. The bride may be either a full-time housewife or a "working" wife. Either party, if widowed, is free either to remarry or remain widowed.

All these are matters in which many societies allow no individual choice. In

---

[1] The term should not be confused with the term in psychology (e.g., inferiority complex) where the meaning is quite different.

other words, alternatives in our society may be universals elsewhere. Some societies allow parents either to keep or to destroy their babies and allow a husband either to forgive or to execute a wife who has been unfaithful. So some matters which are universals in our society are alternatives in others.

Specialties are elements of the culture which are shared by some, but not all, groups within a society. Baby nursing is obviously a female specialty not shared by men. Occupational skills are specialties, shared by the occupational group along with the technical knowledge, private vocabulary, and special folklore of the occupation. Nearly every group in society—each age group, sex group, occupational group, religious group—has certain traits not shared by other groups.

One should remember that the universals, alternatives, and specialties apply only within a given society. Although there are a few needs which all societies try to meet, there is no collection of traits present in all cultures.

Subcultures and contracultures   Sometimes the special culture traits of a particular group are too numerous and too interwoven with one another to be called simply specialties. Immigrant groups, for example, develop a blend of the culture of their host nation and of the mother country. Economic groups, whether of high, low, or middle status, usually develop ways of behavior that mark the group off from the rest of society. The adolescent has special styles of behavior, thought, and dress, and a private vocabulary which adults can scarcely translate, so that one may speak of "teen-age culture." Institutions tend to produce behavior patterns not required outside of the institutional setting, and the expressions "culture of the school" or "culture of the factory" suggest special sets of behavior patterns. Such terms as "army life," "preacher's kid," and "ivory tower" evoke pictures of a cultural setting different from the conventional.

Clusters of patterns such as these, which are both *related to the general culture of the society and yet distinguishable from it, are called subcultures.* The subcultures in our society include occupational, religious, national, regional, social-class, age, and sex subcultures, and many others. Literature abounds in descriptions of subcultures, ranging from serious studies like Coleman's *The Adolescent Society* [1961] to Clausen's lighthearted description of carnival life in *I Love You Honey, but the Season's Over* [1961].

Subcultures are important because all complex societies have, not a single, uniform culture, but a core of universals plus an assortment of subcultures. The individual lives and functions mainly within certain of these subcultures. The immigrant may live within the immigrant subculture, and the army wife on a military post may

The individual lives and functions mainly within certain of these subcultures.

have very little contact with civilian people or civilian values. The child passes through several age subcultures and behaves according to their values, often distressing his mother, who applies the values of a different age subculture.

Several sociologists feel that the term *contraculture* should be applied to designate those groups which not only differ from the prevailing patterns but sharply challenge them. The delinquent gang, for instance, is not a group with no standards or moral values; it has very definite standards and a very compelling set of moral values, but these are quite the opposite of conventional middle-class precepts. Youth, trained in this culture, are influenced *against* the dominant cultural norms; hence the term *contracultural*. Similarly, the "hippie" conforms to a culture depicting work as undesirable, sexual monogamy as "square," patriotism as *passé*, and the accumulation of material possessions as irrelevant.

Most subcultures serve to reinforce the dominant cultural patterns by offering a variety of ways in which the individual may respond to the basic values of the larger society while still retaining allegiance to his particular subculture. The contraculture, on the other hand, serves to reinforce the individual's rejection of the patterned ways of the society. The delinquent may be accused of being disloyal to the conventional mores, but he comforts himself by resolute adherence to the mores of the gang. The gang mores sustain him in deviant behavior by proclaiming that everyone steals, that "squealing" is the worst possible sin, and that only dopes go to school, save money, or try to hold steady jobs.

Contracultures arise out of the needs of individuals to find group support for their failure to follow the dominant patterns [Yinger, 1965, p. 233]. The growth of such contracultures may be expected to reflect the quality of frustration within a society.

Age, sex, class, and occupational subcultures are probably inevitable in a complex culture, and economic specialization tends to increase them. Whether national, religious, and regional subcultures are desirable has been a subject of debate. Some Americans feel that such subcultures add a variety and richness to their national life, others argue that true Americanization requires total cultural conformity. The existence of such subcultures is strengthened by the diversity of national backgrounds but is weakened by the standardizing effects of television and other mass-communication media.

Cultural integration   The culture of the Plains Indians centered upon the buffalo. From its carcass they drew most of their material culture, as they used its flesh, hides, tendons, bones, sacs, membranes, and many other parts for one purpose or another. Their religion was mainly directed at ensuring the success of the buffalo hunt. Their status system measured success largely according to a man's hunting skill. Their nomadic way of life was attuned to the buffalo migrations. In other words, the different parts of the culture all fitted together in an interrelated system of practices and values. When the white man killed off the buffalo, he did so in a deliberate and successful effort to demoralize the Indian by destroying the focal point of his culture.

Just as a pile of bricks is not a home, a list of traits is not a culture. A culture is an *integrated system* in which each trait fits into the rest of the culture. It is no accident that hunting peoples worship hunting gods, fishing peoples worship sea gods, and agricultural peoples worship sun and rain gods. The different parts of a culture must fit together if the culture is to function efficiently. Over a period of time, a people tends to reject or discard inharmonious elements, gaining from their elimination a reasonably integrated culture.

Linton [1936, pp. 189–195, 348–354] illustrates the concept of integration with a description of the Tanala of Madagascar. Their main crop was rice, grown on dry land by slash-and-burn agriculture. An extended family group of several adult males with their wives and children formed the basic social unit. This extended family formed a cooperative work force of the right size for clearing the land and growing rice. As land became exhausted, the village would move on to fresh lands. The family heads formed a tribal council, whose main task was to reassign land annually to different families according to their size and needs. This system of land tenure prevented any great differences in wealth or income, and the society was quite democratic and equalitarian. The authority of the family head was limited and rested upon his abilities in personal leadership more than upon inheritance. Religion was centered upon ancestor worship, the founders of a family receiving special veneration. Whenever a family became much larger than necessary for working efficiency, it was likely to divide, some members remaining at home, some members leaving under the leadership of a new founder, who was thus assured of great honor. When attacked by unfriendly neighboring tribes, the people simply fled into the jungle, for their flimsy, temporary villages could be easily rebuilt. Thus their family life, religion, tribal structure, defense measures, and economic procedures all fitted together into an efficient, mutually harmonious system. Stated somewhat differently, the culture of the Tanala was highly integrated around the dry-rice complex.

All this changed when wet rice growing spread to the Tanala from neighboring peoples. It was adopted first as an individual hobby rather than as a family activity. It took a lot of work to prepare the necessary dikes and ditches along the river. Furthermore, the season was continuous and unending, so that such land never reverted to tribal ownership for the annual reassignment. Thus, private ownership of land appeared, and differences in wealth developed. Disputes within each family arose over the division of work time between family work and private hobby, and over the sharing of the wet-rice crop. When the dry-rice land was exhausted and it was time to move the village, the wet-rice growers declined to abandon their laboriously prepared wet-rice plots. When white men arrived, they found a landed nobility of wet-rice aristocrats, living in permanent homes in well-fortified villages, and a landless proletariat of dry-rice growers, living in simple shelters and moving farther and farther away from the river, while the tie between the two branches of each family gradually weakened. In a few more generations, they would have become two entirely separate societies. The addition of an important new culture trait had disrupted the existing integration and had brought about a new integration of the culture.

Failure to appreciate the integration of culture leads to many failures in dealing with other cultures. When the American Indians were herded onto reservations and supplied with cattle by the government, the Indians hunted the cattle instead of tending and milking them as expected. The idea of tending and milking cows did not tie in with anything in their culture; to introduce a completely foreign complex was a far more complicated task than had been first imagined. Today, the industrialization of the undeveloped areas of the world is delayed because "backward" patterns are tightly interwoven into the native culture. For example, the Bantu of South Africa are overgrazing their lands with oversized herds of scrawny, infected cattle. Reduction of herds and selective breeding are clearly indicated; but in the Bantu culture a man's wealth and status and his ability to purchase wives are measured by the number, not the quality, of his cattle. To introduce scientific livestock practices will require changes in customs and values which weave through the entire culture. Since a culture is integrated, we cannot change one part of it without producing some change in the whole.

Cultural integration and the spread of Western culture   The Western nations, especially the United States, are now engaged in a major effort to transplant democracy and industrial technology into the world's undeveloped areas. These undeveloped peoples yearn for popular self-government and industrial development, but they also cherish a traditional culture which is incompatible with these developments. Democratic government flourishes best in a nation whose citizens are both literate and accustomed to making decisions through deliberative group action. Its export to areas which have lacked these cultural patterns has meant that, although the forms of democracy may exist, the actual power usually gravitates to some type of dictator. Similarly, an industrialized society not only needs engineers and machinery but also businessmen who are willing to risk capital in new enterprises, workers who are willing to submit to the routine discipline of regular factory labor, and a government which provides needed services, maintains order, and is reasonably honest and efficient. Industrialism is favored by a family system which allows individuals to strike out on their own and by religious institutions which encourage thrift, hard work, and responsibility. Some of the difficulties met in trying to graft democracy and industrialism upon an incompatible culture are seen in the following statement written some years ago but still applicable today:

India, it seems, wants to improve her standard of living and desires technical assistance and foreign capital, but is in no mood to accept uncritically the whole pattern of Western culture. Rather than wholesale adaptation of Western customs, the Indians desire to pick and choose the cultural elements they will accept. Industrial techniques and public health practices may be valid, but Western patterns of family life, political institutions, religious movements, and business enterprise may be disregarded as either harmful or irrelevant to the aims of a modern oriental state. Even the Philippines, an area more subject to American influence than any other spot in Asia, shows some of the same symptoms.

India and the Philippines are by no means unique in this respect. This effort to achieve improved economic standards while rejecting the cultural changes associated with industrial development is prevalent throughout the world. . . .

In most of the world today, the individual is still submerged in a strong family group which chooses his mate, absorbs his money and makes the major decisions of life on a basis of family rather than individual needs. Such a family usually includes three generations and several households, with decisions made on an authoritarian basis by the oldest active family members. It may be no coincidence that countries with this family system complain of lack of individual initiative and pioneering spirit and of nepotism in both business and government. . . .

The peoples who wish to avail themselves of the advantages of a higher output of goods while avoiding drastic changes in their life patterns may protest that they are trying to gain the benefits of industrialism while avoiding its evils. A more sophisticated observation would be that the underdeveloped countries wish to acquire the end results of economic development while resisting the attitudes which make such development possible.

This discussion implies that democracy and industrialism must be integrated into a total culture which is consistent with the type of economic structure the society seeks to develop. This does not mean that American institutions must be exact blueprints for the rest of the world, but it does imply that if an agricultural nation is to be industrialized, the entire culture will be forced to change in a direction in harmony with the new economic ethos. It demands the development of both social and personal attitudes able to cope with the opportunities and problems of mass production. This, in turn, implies that government, education, religion and family structure will encourage a social milieu favorable to industrial development.

Adapted from Chester L. Hunt, "Cultural Barriers to Point Four," *Antioch Review*, 14:159–167, Summer, 1954.

Without an appreciation of the concept of cultural integration, one cannot either understand a culture or know how to make successful changes in it. These processes of change will be discussed in greater detail in a later chapter.

THE DEVELOPMENT OF CULTURE

Subhuman societies Many subhuman species have an orderly system of social life. Many bird species mate for a lifetime and (in contrast to humans) are absolutely loyal to their mates. Many species of insects, such as ants and bees, have an elaborate pattern of social life, complete with specialized occupations, lines of authority, and detailed distribution of duties and privileges. But the *subhuman social life is based upon instinct, not upon social learning.* Within a given species of ants, all anthills are very much alike, while human dwellings vary tremendously. For man's instincts, unlike those of the subhumans, do not give him any inborn patterns of behavior, but only a set of needs, urges, and hungers that he must satisfy in some way or other. In his trial-and-error efforts to satisfy his urges, man creates his culture, with its tremendous variations from society to society. Unable to rely upon instinct, man must build culture in order to survive.

As an animal, man is among the larger and more powerful of beasts. Fewer than a dozen other species will ordinarily attack an adult human unless wounded or provoked. Man's physical structure and processes are similar to those of other animals, and he shares many of their diseases. He has certain physical disadvantages. He is far from the strongest of animals; he lacks the physical agility of his cousins, the apes; his claws and teeth are puny weapons; and he has no hide, scales, or fur to protect him. He cannot hibernate or adjust organically to great temperature changes.

Man also has some advantages. He can digest a wider variety of foods than most other animals. His eyesight is fairly good at all distances from a few inches to many miles—a characteristic that many animals lack. Alone among the animals, he is well balanced on only two of his feet, freeing the other two for all sorts of mischief. He can oppose his thumb to each of his fingers and is capable of more delicate manipulations than any other animal. No chimpanzee, no matter how brilliant, could perform skillful surgery, for its hands lack dexterity.

Man's learning capacity   These advantages would mean little unless man had a greater learning capacity. This does not deny that other animals do think, reason, and learn, for their ability is shown by many tests. In some experiments a chimpanzee must figure out that he can get a banana, placed beyond reach, only by fitting together two sticks to make a longer one. In other experiments, where slugs must be put into a slot machine in order to get food, the chimpanzees quickly learn which size or color slugs are valuable, and sort out, hoard, hide, and steal them from one another in a quite human manner. Many such experiments with many species have clearly established that animals *do* learn, and apparently they learn *in the same way* that humans learn; they just don't learn as fast or as much. A famous experiment [Kellogg and Kellogg, 1933] in which a human infant and a chimpanzee infant were raised together and treated alike, showed that they behaved alike in many ways, but that before long the human greatly outdistanced the chimpanzee in learning.

Communication   Animals can learn; they can form interacting groups and have a social life; they can even communicate with one another at a very simple level. These facts lead a few scholars to conclude that some animals have a culture. Several experiments have shown that animal learning is affected by their social setting. For example, Kuo [1931] found that when kittens could watch the mother cat catching rats, 85 per cent of them were catching rats themselves by the time they were four months old. Other kittens were raised with rats as companions; none of them killed the type of rats they grew up with and only 16 per cent killed any kind of rats. This suggests that animals can learn through example, and that it may be a form of social learning. But if cats have a "rat-killing culture," it is far removed from the hunting complex of the Plains Indians or the English gentry.

The idea of animal culture becomes rather farfetched if we try to imagine Leo the Lion acting in a manner governed by custom, tradition, or sacred ideal. As Myerson observes,

We cannot imagine him, for example, stopping in palpitating pursuit of a tawny female because some Leo the Saint, a hundred lion generations ago, reached the conclusion that burning desire might be satisfied only under very special circumstances. Nor can we visualize this same Leo aching for food yet withholding his mighty paw from a delicacy because that delicacy has been staked off for another lion or because old lions in a congress a hundred years before decreed private ownership in delicacies and forbade even ravenous hunger to satisfy itself except under strict rule and regulation.

We cannot imagine the young lion contemplating the life of some past Leo the Great and planning his entire career in emulation of the dead hero. . . . We cannot imagine him in agonies of self-condemnation because he has fallen short of an

ideal which has been incorporated within him by the teaching and preaching of a thousand years and of countless lions. . . .

He does not foresee his own death, and knows nothing of his own birth. Sex means to him only the satisfaction that an individual of the opposite sex can bring him. It does not mean parenthood, domesticity, respectability, the fulfilling of an ideal, a responsibility, and the becoming part of a great racial sweep.

Abraham Myerson, *Social Psychology*, Prentice-Hall, Inc., Englewood Cliffs, N.J., 1934, pp. 3–6. Adapted by permission.

It is fashionable to believe a great deal of nonsense about animal behavior. A faithful dog, gazing intently at his master, inspires all sorts of fanciful notions as to what he is thinking! Dogs are often credited with remarkable homing instincts; yet, for every dog who finds his way home across a continent, the lost-and-found ads list a hundred dogs who can't find their way home from the next block. Mama Bear is pictured as patiently "teaching" her cubs how to fish, yet we have no evidence that she is consciously trying to teach them anything. Perhaps she is just hungry! Only for man is there conclusive evidence of deliberate teaching and intentional communication of ideas.

This may be mankind's greatest advantage—*his ability to communicate his learnings to others.* The chimpanzee may learn how to get the banana, but he has no effective way of communicating his insight to others; each of his brothers must get the idea for himself, either through imitation or through his own imagination. Each chimpanzee stands, or rather crouches, on his own feet and must face the world without the advantage of simian learning. Man stands on the shoulders of his ancestors and brings to his problems a great heritage of accumulated wisdom.

Language and symbolic communications   Many animals can exchange feelings through growls, purrs, mating calls, and other sounds. Some animals give off odors or make bodily movements which convey meanings to one another. These sounds and motions are not *language,* for each is largely or entirely an inborn, instinctive response rather than an acquired, symbolic response. There is no evidence that a dog growls or barks because he wants to tell another dog something; perhaps he barks just because he feels like barking. As far as we know, no dog has yet developed a barking code (e.g., one short bark for "let's eat," two yips for "after you," etc.). A language is just such a code— *a set of sounds with a particular meaning attached to each sound.* A largely emotional or instinctive set of yips and yells is not a language, even though these sounds do serve to carry some accurate meanings to others of the species. A mother soon learns from her baby's cry whether he is hungry, sick, or angry; but the baby is simply expressing his emotions, not using language. Only when an *artificial* meaning is attached to each sound, so that the sound becomes a symbol—only then do we have language. The idea of "chair" might be represented by any one of thousands of vocal sounds; when the members of a society agree in dependably recognizing one particular vocal sound as meaning "chair," then a *word* has been added to the language. We limit the term *language* to symbolic communication and exclude the exchange of meanings through instinctive cries and sounds as not being true language.

Only man uses symbols; therefore, only man's communication reaches

Only man uses symbols.

beyond the level of exchanging very simple feelings and intentions. With symbolic communication men can exchange detailed directions, share discoveries, organize elaborate activities. Without it, they would quickly revert to the caves and treetops.

Somewhat as speech separates man from the animals, the written language is a dividing line between primitive and civilized cultures. The man in the preliterate culture must memorize traditional lore, and the man with a fine memory is valued as a walking library. Old people are useful in a society which must rely on human memory to preserve its culture. But the human memory is not limitless. A culture dependent upon human memory and oral tradition must remain fairly simple. The use of writing allows an almost limitless expansion of the culture, since endless bits of lore can be stored away until needed. Techniques and processes of infinite complexity can be recorded in precise detail and endless variety. Even the illiterate person is affected by living in a literate culture since his entire life is colored by the fact that others can draw upon the storehouse of the written word. The dictum of Pharaoh's court, "Thus it is written; thus it shall be done," is the basis of every civilized society.

Language is so intimately tied up with culture that every new addition to the group's cultural heritage involves additions to the language. In order to know a group one must learn to speak its language. Even special groups within a society, such as hoboes, soldiers, railroad men, or teen-agers have their own vocabularies. College students are painfully aware that each new field of study forces them to learn many new words and to learn new meanings for many of the old ones.

Language is related to the rest of culture in other ways. Not only does culture produce language, but language helps or hinders the spread of culture. It is difficult to think without language, for one's thought are likely to be vague until put into words. One can, perhaps, visualize objects or actions without using words, but ideas require language. Try visualizing ideas such as "goodness," "never," or "necessary" without using words! Sometimes an idea or concept is hard to translate because the language has no words with which to express it. The translation of Papal encyclicals into classical Latin is complicated by the lack of Latin terms for modern words like "automation" and "atomic reactor." India's effort to limit the use of English and to employ the traditional Hindustani as the national language is facing similar difficulties. Since Hindustani developed before the dawn of modern science and industry, either a whole new set of expressions must be hastily coined, or Hindustani must absorb words borrowed at a tremendous rate from other languages. Hence the zealous Indian attempt to support Hindustani is being followed by a reluctant admission that English might have to be the language of university instruction for the indefinite future [Rao, 1956, pp. 1–12]. An adequate language is the indispensable means of communication through which culture is shared, transmitted and accumulated.

Language is so closely bound to culture that translators must have an understanding of the culture of both societies if they are to translate from one language to the other. The following incident is a case in point:

A story is making the rounds these days about some scientists who designed an English-to-Russian translating machine. To test the device they fed in the sentence, "The spirit is willing but the flesh is weak." Back came the translation: "The liquor is good but the food is lousy."

John G. Fuller, "Trade Winds," *Saturday Review,* 45:12 Feb. 17, 1962.

The accumulation of culture   A look at prehistory shows that man once lived very much like his animal cousins. Our early human ancestors lived in the open, wore no clothes, raised no crops, domesticated no animals, and used no fire. Archeological reports indicate that hundreds of thousands of years passed before man learned to cook his food, plant crops, or build shelters. We who have come to expect a "new model" every year find it hard to visualize an era when man made no great change in his habits for perhaps a thousand generations and, like the animals, lived at the mercy of an unfriendly nature.

Man spent ages in making his early discoveries and inventions, but these became the *cultural base* for more rapid discovery and invention in the future. It took him several hundred thousand years to invent the wheel; once invented, the wheel might then be used in thousands of other inventions. For this and other reasons, man's culture has accumulated exceedingly slowly in prehistoric times, more rapidly in historic times, and with breakneck speed in modern times. Man's greatest problem today is how to adjust himself and his social arrangements to the speed with which his culture is changing. The accumulation of culture is treated in greater detail in Chapter 19.

SUMMARY

Culture consists of the socially learned behavior norms and patterns accumulated and shared by a group, and transmitted from generation to generation. A *society* is a group of people who share a common culture. Man's greatest difference from other animals is his ability to absorb and transmit culture, mainly through the use of language.

Folkways are types of habitual behavior which have the force of custom but do not have a moral connotation, while *mores* carry the idea of right and wrong. Both folkways and mores develop gradually through social living, without conscious plan or design. Important clusters of folkways and mores centering upon major activities are called *institutions*. Mores may become sanctified by religion and strengthened by incorporation into the law as part of the stateways.

A *trait* is the smallest unit of culture, and related traits are grouped into *complexes.* The *universals* of a culture are certain behavior patterns which are

Table 1 *If a million years* of human history were compressed into the lifetime of one seventy-year-old man*

1,000,000 years of history	Compressed into one 70-year lifetime
1,000,000 years ago	*Pithecanthropus erectus is born.*
500,000 years ago	*He spends half his lifetime learning to make and use crude stone axes and knives.*
50,000 years ago	*And most of the next half in improving them.*
40,000 years ago	*Three years ago he began to use bone and horn tools.*
10,000 years ago	*Nine months ago the last ice age ended, and he left his cave dwellings.*
7,000 years ago	*Six or eight months ago he began to make pottery, weave cloth, grow crops, and domesticate animals.*
5,000 years ago	*About three months ago, he began to cast and use metals and built the Pyramids.*
3,000 years ago	*Ten weeks ago he invented the spoked wheel and began making glass.*
2,000 years ago	*Seven weeks ago, Christ was born.*
700 years ago	*Two weeks ago man finished the Crusades.*
185 years ago	*Five days ago he crossed the Delaware with Washington.*
60 years ago	*Yesterday he invented the airplane.*
25–30 years ago	*This morning he fought World War II.*
In the year 2,000 A.D.	*Tonight he will celebrate the arrival of the twenty-first century!*

* Or several million years, according to some anthropologists.

shared by all normal members of a society. *Alternatives* are traits or complexes between which one may choose, while *specialties* are traits or complexes which are expected only of particular groups in the society. A *subculture* is the behavior system of a group which is really part of a larger society, but which has certain unique cultural patterns that mark it off as a distinctive unit. *Contraculture* refers to a type of subculture which is opposed to the dominant cultural values of the larger society.

A culture is an *integrated* system of behavior, with its supporting ideas and values. In a highly integrated culture, all elements fit harmoniously together. The adoption of Western technology by non-Western societies will inevitably bring many other changes in their traditional culture.

QUESTIONS AND PROJECTS

1. Which would give the greater understanding of the culture of the Romans—studying the ruins, sculpture, and public works that have been excavated or studying the records of the nonmaterial culture preserved in literature, letters, and legal documents? Why?

2. How do you differentiate between society and culture?

3. Distinguish between the symbolic communication among humans and the instinctive communication among animals.

4. What is meant by the statement that, when firmly established, the mores operate automatically?

5. Of the following acts, which would violate American folkways and which would violate American mores?
a. Attending church in a bathing suit
b. Nude bathing at a public beach
c. Nonsupport of one's children
d. "Standing up" a date

6. Classify the following in terms of alternatives, specialties, and cultural universals:

a. Spending a vacation at a ski resort
b. Selecting the premedical curriculum in college
c. The American practice of restricting marriage to one mate
d. Physical bravery on the part of policemen

7. Why, when the government first gave cattle to the American Indians, did the Indians hunt and kill the cattle instead of herding and milking them?

8. Apply your knowledge of the integration of culture in evaluating the proposal that our society should return to the "simple life."

9. Make a list of ten folkways on the college campus that are different from those in the rest of the community. Make a list of the folkways and mores of fraternity life.

10. Select an occupational group, and describe the *special* behavior typical of that occupation.

11. Describe the traits, complexes, attitudes, and values making up a subculture with which you are familiar.

SUGGESTED READINGS

BERNSTEIN, WALTER: "The Cherubs Are Rumbling," *New Yorker*, Sept. 21, 1957, pp. 129–159. An account of juvenile gang mores.

COLEMAN, JAMES S.: "The Adolescent Subculture and Academic Achievement," *American Journal of Sociology*, 65:337–347, 1960. Relation of teen-age values to academic achievement.

CRESSEY, PAUL FREDERICK: "Chinese Traits in European Civilization: A Study in Diffusion," *American Sociological Review*, 10:595–604, October, 1945. A study of the extent to which European culture is built on traits borrowed from the Orient.

HALL, EDWARD T.: "Our Silent Language," *Americas*, 14:5–8, February, 1962; reprinted in *Science Digest*, 52:19–23, August, 1962. Description of non-verbal cues which indicate differences between North and South American cultural norms.

*LINTON, RALPH: *The Study of Man*, Appleton-Century-Crofts, Inc., New York, 1936. A classic analysis of the role of culture in human affairs. Chapters 5, 6, 20, and 25 are especially recommended. (Appl)

LIPSET, SEYMOUR MARTIN: "The Value Patterns of a Democracy: A Case Study in Comparative Analysis," *American Sociological Review*, 28:515–531, August, 1963. Comparison of value systems in Australia, Canada, Great Britain and the United States.

LEZNOFF, MAURICE, AND WILLIAM WESTLEY: "The Homosexual Community," *Social Problems*, 3:257–264, April, 1956. A treatment of the folkways and mores found within this particular subculture.

SALE, J. KIRK, AND BEN APPELBAUM: "Report from Teeney-Boppersville," *New York Times Magazine*, May 28, 1967, pp. 25ff.; or, "The Hippies: Philosophy of a Subculture," *Time*, July 7, 1967, pp. 18–22. Popularized descriptions of a contemporary, rapidly changing subculture.

SANDERS, IRWIN T.: *Societies around the World*, Holt, Rinehart and Winston, Inc., New York, 1956. Detailed description of six contrasting societies—Eskimo, Navajo, Baganda, Chinese peasant, the Cotton South, and the English Midlands.

SCOTCH, N. A.: "Magic, Sorcery, and Football Among the Urban Sulu: A Case of Reinterpretation Under Acculturation," *Journal of Conflict Resolution*,

5:70–74, March, 1961. An example of cultural integration involving a mixture of traditional and modern elements.

*SUMMER, WILLIAM GRAHAM: *Folkways,* Ginn and Company, Boston, 1906. A source book on folkways and mores. (Dov)

WHITE, LESLIE A.: "Culturological vs. Psychological Interpretations of Human Behavior," *American Sociological Review,* 12:686–698, December, 1947; Bobbs-Merrill reprint S-309. An exposition of the far-reaching influence of culture by one of the most extreme advocates of the importance of culturological influence.

*WHYTE, WILLIAM F.: *Street Corner Society,* The University of Chicago Press, Chicago, 1955. Describes the subculture of street-corner gangs in a large Eastern city. (Chic)

YINGER, J. MILTON: "Contraculture and Subculture," *American Sociological Review,* 25:625–635, October, 1960. Distinguishes between subcultures which are variants on the general ethos and those which are definitely hostile to the dominant culture.

THE MEANING
OF CULTURE

"You said the fellow you killed provoked you?"

"So it was."

"He insulted Asiak?" [an Eskimo wife]

"Terribly."

"Presumably he was killed as you tried to defend her from his advances?"

Ernenek [her husband] and Asiak looked at each other and burst out laughing.

"It wasn't so at all," Asiak said at last.

"Here's how it was," said Ernenek. "He kept snubbing all our offers although he was our guest. He scorned even the oldest meat we had."

"You see, Ernenek, many of us white men are not fond of old meat."

"But the worms were fresh!" said Asiak.

"It happens, Asiak, that we are used to foods of a quite different kind."

"So we noticed," Ernenek went on, "and that's why, hoping to offer him at last a thing he might relish, somebody proposed him Asiak to laugh [have sexual intercourse] with."

"Let a woman explain," Asiak broke in. "A woman washed her hair to make it smooth, rubbed tallow into it, greased her face with blubber, and scraped herself clean with a knife, to be polite."

"Yes," cried Ernenek, rising. "She had purposely groomed herself! And what did the white man do? He turned his back to her! That was too much! Should a man let his wife be so insulted? So somebody grabbed the scoundrel by his miserable little shoulders and beat him a few times against the wall—not in order to kill him, just wanting to crack his head a little. It was unfortunate it cracked a lot!"

"Ernenek has done the same to other men," Asiak put in helpfully, "But it was always the wall that went to pieces first."

The white man winced. "Our judges would show no understanding for such an explanation. Offering your wife to other men!"

"Why not? The men like it and Asiak says it's good for her. It makes her eyes sparkle and her cheeks glow."

"Don't you people borrow other men's wives?" Asiak inquired.

"Never mind that! It isn't fitting, that's all."

"Refusing isn't fitting for a man!" Ernenek said indignantly. "Anybody would much rather lend out his wife than something else. Lend out your sled and you'll get it back cracked, lend out your saw and some teeth will be missing, lend out your dogs and they'll come home crawling, tired—but no matter how often you lend out your wife she'll always stay like new." (Hans Ruesch, *Top of the World*, Harper & Row, Publishers, Incorporated, New York, 1950; Pocket Books, 1951, pp. 87–88.)

As THIS INCIDENT shows, a particular social situation gets its meaning from the culture in which it appears. A situation has very different meanings in two different societies. The members of each society are so completely immersed in their own body of belief and custom that they generally fail to sense that they are obeying *belief* and *custom*, and fail to wonder *why* they believe and act as they do. Only by imaginatively stepping outside his own body of belief and custom can a man become aware of their actual nature. The purpose of this chapter is to help us to see our own behavior as a system of beliefs and values, of customs and traditions, of gadgets and properties, and of social contacts and relationships which we call our culture.

Let us consider the morning of an American college student. He awakens on a large, rather soft pad held above the floor on a wooden framework and covered with several layers of soft woven material between which he sleeps. He is roused at a carefully predetermined moment by a tinkling sound from a tiny box on a platform near his sleeping pad. He reaches out and silences it and after various scratchings and gruntings arises and enters a small adjoining room and gazes intently at a large shiny surface that reflects his image. He strokes his face and meditatively fingers a small object with a sharp cutting edge, then lays it down and shakes his head. He turns some knobs, and water gushes from small stems and fills a bowl into which he dips and splashes. He squeezes some white stuff onto a small tufted stick and stirs it about in his mouth while he foams and sputters. He dries himself on a large soft cloth, returns, and makes several selections from a large number of variously colored fabrics that are shaped to fit different parts of his body. He then leaves his room and walks to a much larger room where he and many other students form a single line. Each is served some food, which he loudly criticizes and greedily consumes. After eating, he leaves the building and approaches a wide pathway filled with passenger wagons that move very fast and pass very close to one another without striking, since each stays on a certain side of this pathway. He stares at a colored light above the pathway until it changes color, whereupon the wagons stop and he crosses the pathway. Ahead of him he observes a young female and considers asking her for an appointment to face each other and jump up and down whenever loud noises are made by a team of professional noise makers. Deciding against this, he hurries into a large building, seeks out a particular room, slumps into a chair and whispers to another student, "What's that 'culture' stuff this prof's always talking about?"

A Purari youth in New Guinea awakens at sunrise from his sleep on a woven reed mat on the floor of the men's house. With other unmarried young men, he sleeps here because it would be shockingly indecent for him to sleep in the same house with his female relatives. He yawns, stretches, and rises to perform his first assigned task of the day—he checks the row of human skulls on the display racks to see that they are in neat and orderly array. He gazes at them and remembers the mighty enemies they represent. He wishes he were old enough to share in the next cannibal feast. Then the enemy's powers would surge through his own muscles, and his enemy's craft would lodge in his own brain! Truly, it will be wonderful to be a Purari warrior!

But meanwhile there is work to do. He takes a quick plunge into a muddy stream, then goes to his father's house for a breakfast of sago sticks. He finds his mother and sisters in the house, so he returns to the men's house to eat his breakfast, as any well-mannered young man should do. Since today's work is to be a pig hunt, he collects bow and arrows and joins several other young men, mostly relatives on his father's side of the family. While they are waiting, a Purari maiden strolls casually by with her grass skirt swinging gaily, and he chats with her for a moment. He suspects that she may like him, but their fingers do not even touch, for both are above any vulgar public display. As the party leaves for the jungle, her younger brother appears and unobtrusively falls into step with him. Quietly and wordlessly this boy slips a small gift—which happens to be a roll of tobacco leaves—into his hand and then drifts away. Now his step becomes more elastic and the set of his shoulders more assured. Now he knows that she likes him and that the costly love-magic he placed under his sleeping mat last night has worked well. Truly it would be good to be a Purari warrior, but meanwhile, it is good to be a Purari young man!

For descriptions of the Purari, see F. E. Williams, *The Natives of the Purari Delta, Anthropological Report no. 5*, Port Moresby, Territory of Papua, 1924; J. H. Holmes, *In Primitive New Guinea*, G. P. Putnam's Sons, New York, 1924; Robert F. Maher, *The New Men of Papua*, The University of Wisconsin Press, Madison, Wis., 1961.

These two sketches show that a culture is a system of behavior norms which people follow habitually and unthinkingly. They seldom realize how closely their behavior is guided by system. In the culture of his own society a man lives and dreams, shapes his ideals, formulates his questions, stages his rebellions, trains his body, and disciplines his mind. He dreams the dreams his culture suggests, wishes the wishes his culture develops, and fears the fears his culture inspires. He takes pride in the achievements his culture applauds and feels shame at the impulse his culture condemns. Each person is, far more than he will ever know, *the product of his culture*. If we would understand people, we must study culture.

People are often misled by the fact that certain primitive groups may permit behavior which advanced cultures prohibit; thus we may picture the "free" savage happily clothed in fig leaves, living with no sense of responsibility. Actually, his culture defines his daily life at least as closely as ours. The traditional Polynesian girl, for instance, does not debate the question of marriage versus career. Her culture rigidly decrees what she may and may not do until married, whom she will marry, when she will marry, and exactly the kind of work she will do. A similar cultural patterning applies to other activities. The dance forms of a primitive society may seem to the outsider to be simply wild random movements, but careful observation shows that they are more rigidly stylized than the dancing in an American ballroom. Since the culture of a primitive group often permits only *one* type of behavior for a particular occasion, there is not even as much choice between culturally sanctioned alternatives as exists in more complex societies. The "noble savage" whom Rousseau imagined free of restraint is actually, even more than a modern man, the slave of custom.

SOME FUNCTIONS OF CULTURE

As we have already stated, a culture is no more an assortment of curious ways of doing things than a heap of spare parts is an automobile. A culture is an *organized system of behavior*, together with its supporting ideas and values.

How does the culture of a society—of any society—function to control and direct the life of the individual?

Culture defines situations An early sociologist, W. I. Thomas, coined the phrase, "the definition of the situation." Suppose someone approaches you with right hand outstretched at waist level. What does this mean? That he wishes to shake hands in friendly greeting is perfectly obvious—obvious, that is, to anyone familiar with our culture. But in another place or time the outstretched hand might mean hostility or warning. One does not know what to do in a situation until he has defined the situation. Each culture has many subtle cues which define each situation, revealing whether one should prepare to fight, run, laugh, or make love. The stranger who misinterprets the cues and wants to run when he should make love, or vice versa, is a stock comic figure in the literature of many cultures. Each society has its insults and fighting words. In many primitive societies a man would be unperturbed at the suggestion that his mother's husband was not his father, but it is unwise to call an American a "bastard" unless one is ready for a brawl.

The cues which define situations appear in infinite variety and subtlety. When a Dobuan man cuts or delouses a woman's hair in public, this means that they have committed adultery and he is challenging her husband to make something of it. Owen Wister's "Virginian" says, "When you call me that, smile!" A word spoken in one manner is an insult that demands manly vengeance; but delivered with a different inflection, it becomes a bit of harmless banter. A person who moves from one society into another will spend many years misreading the cues, laughing at the wrong places, and committing *faux pas*. In fact, it is debatable whether a person who enters another society as an adult ever fully absorbs the endless nuances of meaning within that culture.

Culture defines attitudes, values, and goals Each person learns from his culture what is good, true, and beautiful. It matters not whether female charm is represented by a flat-chested, straight-hipped flapper of the American 1920s, a chubby butterball of the French Regency, or a mountainous heap of Dahomean blubber—to each, man has reacted with predictable longing, for each had been defined by his culture as desirable. When a Rhodesian chieftain once told Lillian Russell, a famous beauty of the last century, "Miss Russell, had Heaven only made you black and fat, you would be irresistible," he revealed how his feelings were channeled by his society's concept of beauty.

Attitudes, values, and goals are defined by the culture, while the individual normally learns them as unconsciously as he learns the language. Sociology has no special definitions for these terms; they are used in their popular meaning by sociologists. Attitudes are tendencies to feel and act in certain ways. Values are measures of goodness or desirability; e.g., we value private property, representative government, romantic love, and many other things and experiences. Goals are those attainments which our values define as worthy, e.g., winning the race, gaining the affections of a particular girl, or becoming president of the firm. An interrelated and interdependent system of attitudes, values, and goals is an important part—probably the *most* important part—of any culture. Why will twenty-two healthy young Americans, after hours of grueling practice, pound one another into sweaty exhaustion in a mighty effort to boost the air-filled skin of a dead pig over a pair of posts? Why is it a moral obligation of every Marindese husband to hunt heads? Each culture defines the desirable goals and the praiseworthy values. One society admires lusty brawlers; another prefers gentle souls. One society expects its heroes to be sybaritic libertines; another demands that they be ascetics.

By approving certain goals and denigrating or ridiculing others, the culture channels individual ambitions. The American high school male graduate may wonder whether to become a carpenter, a salesman, or a physician, but he "decides" against being a dressmaker or a eunuch without ever considering the matter. Young American women today wonder what career to enter—a question which did not arise a century earlier, when our culture approved no role for a woman except that of housewife. Since domesticity was the only goal for women which the culture respected, this was the only role most women wanted.

In these ways culture determines the goals of life. Although the young person looking for a career may feel that he has a free choice, he will choose one of the relatively few lines of work his culture has taught him to value. Whether it is praiseworthy to become a mighty warrior, a powerful capitalist, a great land-owner, or a wandering, penniless holy man—the choice is defined by the culture and sanctified by its religion. An extreme example of this channeling can be seen in Tibet where, prior to Chinese annexation, it was estimated that about one-third of the males became Buddist monks. This occupational distribution, which would seem absurd to most other societies, is understandable in view of Tibetan cultural values. In the United States we have long known the "white-collar" complex which highly values occupations not involving manual labor. The preference has been criticized, but it would seem to be consistent with other aspects of a society that is steadily replacing human labor by machines and IBM cards.

Even one's play is culturally defined. Hunting, which was work for primitives, is play for moderns. Golf is acceptable in the United States, but cricket or lacrosse, although far more vigorous, are not "masculine." Few American men will brag about their skill in the kitchen; but at a charcoal grill—that's different!

The cultural definition of goals helps to explain the achievements and failures of different societies. Why did Germany lead the world in music, Italy in art, and England in commerce during the eighteenth century? Laymen often attribute such achievements to some racial or national aptitude, but a more careful look shows that each society excels in those activities which the culture rewards and encourages.

The individual may develop, modify, or oppose the trends of his culture, but he always lives within its framework. What would Bach have done in a culture with no musical instruments or Einstein in a culture without a number system? The "great man" is one whose talents can find an outlet in the culture; without appropriate cultural channels his genius will either take a different form or remain dormant. In more ways than there is space to tell, we are the reflections of our culture. It provides channels for our individual talents and shapes our general attitudes and view of life.

Attitudes, values, and goals are related to norms but are not identical with them. Norms are standards of behavior in the society which state how things ought to be done. Attitudes, values, and goals are individual preferences within the range of culturally approved alternatives. The norms indicate the approved ways in which we may realize our goals, follow our values, and express our attitudes; but they do not directly determine them. For example, people have various attitudes about automotive speed, but the norms require all of us to stop at red traffic lights. The norms of the culture demand that the adult male should earn an income, while his values determine the decision he will make if he is offered a promotion carrying higher income but less leisure. In brief, norms define the behavior acceptable to society, while attitudes, values, and goals determine the selection we will make within the range of socially acceptable choices.

Culture defines myths, legends, and the supernatural

Myths and legends are an important part of every culture. They may inspire, reinforce effort and sacrifice, and bring comfort in bereavement. Whether they are true is sociologically unimportant. Ghosts are real to people who believe in them and who act upon this belief. We cannot understand the behavior of any group without knowing something of the myths, legends, and supernatural beliefs they hold. Could the Jews have survived centuries of persecution without the chosen-people myth to sustain them? Try to explain the rise of Hitler without exploring the heritage of Teutonic mythological heroes with which he identified the Nazi movement! In an effort to promote loyalty and sacrifice, Communist China is today reviving the ancient myths of Han superiority, an image of a favored people surrounded by barbarian hordes. The legend that one sturdy freeborn American can lick any number of decadent foreigners has helped to keep us unprepared for every war we have entered. Myths and legends are powerful forces in a group's behavior.

Culture provides myths.

Culture also provides the individual with a ready-made view of the universe. Questions as to the origin of the world, the nature of divine power, and the important moral issues are defined by the culture. The individual does not have to grope or select, but is trained in a Christian, Buddhist, Hindu, Moslem, or some other religious tradition. This tradition gives answers for the major imponderables of life, and fortifies the individual to meet life's crises.

Culture provides behavior patterns

The individual need not improvise; he need not go through painful trial-and-error learning to know what foods can be eaten without poisoning himself, or how to live among people without fear of mayhem. He finds a ready-made set of patterns awaiting him which he needs only to learn and follow. This is a tremendously important fact. Without it we should still be living in caves and hollow trees—those of us who have survived long enough.

For example, if a society is to function without unbearable chaos, it must provide some standardized way of forming new families. In the United States our culture has encouraged a set of romantic attitudes and developed a dating system that leads to marriage. Other societies are shocked that marriage partners should be selected through youthful impulse and romantic illusion, and they have made different provisions. In some Arab groups the young man knows that he is predestined to mate either with the oldest available female daughter of his father's brother or with the nearest kinswoman equivalent in relationship. Until quite recently, parents in the Tinguian tribe of the Philippines selected mates for their children and often arranged the betrothal in infancy so that the matter would be settled at an early age. Different as these methods are, they have one feature in common: The culture maps out the path to matrimony. The individual does not have to wonder how one secures a mate; he *knows* the procedure defined by his culture. He accepts without question this path to matrimony because he has been trained to view it as the only proper way to get a mate, and considers himself fortunate to have been provided for in this manner.

From before he is born until after he is dead, man is a prisoner of his culture. His culture directs and confines his behavior, limits his goals, and measures his rewards. His culture gets into his mind and shutters his vision so that he sees what he is supposed to see, dreams what he is expected to dream, and hungers for what he is trained to hunger. He may imagine that *he* is making choices, or that *he* rules his destiny, but the choices of the normal person always fall within a series of possibilities which the culture tolerates. The individual is thus prepared to fill his role among his fellows while the smooth, orderly operation of the society is assured. The occasional individual who deviates from these expected patterns is scorned and punished by his fellows, for he upsets the smooth operation of society, and if people are to be comfortable, society must carry on in an orderly and predictable manner.

Culture molds national character The system of norms and values which give a characteristic feeling or tone to the culture is called its *ethos*. A culture's ethos is difficult to define precisely; yet there is difference in the cultures of various societies which goes beyond the mere listing of traits and complexes. The concept of national character, which implies that members of a society share so many common cultural norms that they have certain tendencies in common, is similar to that of ethos. The individual differences between members of a society are striking; but they should not obscure the similarities they share. Even the casual traveler senses a difference in the cultural atmosphere when he moves from Paris to Berlin or from Tokyo to New York. The many jokes about the Frenchman, the Englishman, the Irishman, the Scotsman, and others are popular oversimplifications of the ideas of ethos and national character. Some research efforts have been made to test the idea of national character. Germans, for instance, are often considered to have a greater tendency to accept regimentation and to subordinate the individual to the state than Americans have. Obviously not all Germans are regimented and not all Americans are individualistically inclined. The question is whether there is a significant difference in the proportions who have each tendency in the two countries. Acting on the assumption that people like to sing about sentiments dear to them, Seabold [1962] analyzed a sample of popular songs in each country. Some 36 per cent of the German songs sang of devotion to some supraindividual entity such as nation or society, as compared with only 1 per cent of the American lyrics. While over 8 per cent

Table 2   *Cultural attitudes differ from society to society*

What should a newspaper publish?
Answers in percentages to the question, "In your opinion should a newspaper publish:
(a) What they wish, or (b) only what is good for the country?"

Societal groups	(a)	(b)	No answer
American sample (200)	*65*	*33*	*2*
German sample (191)	*51*	*43*	*6*

Which boys are worse?
Answers in percentages to the question, "Which of these boys in your opinion is the worse?
(a) The boy who tyrannizes and beats up smaller children, or (b) the boy who disobeys his
superiors, such as his elder brother, parents, teachers, leaders, employer, etc."

Societal groups	(a)	(b)	No answer
American sample (200)	*68*	*29*	*3*
German sample (191)	*41*	*30*	*29*

Donald V. McGranahan, "A Comparison of Social Attitudes Among American and German Youth,"
Journal of Abnormal and Social Psychology, 41:245–257, July, 1946.

of the German songs dealt with heroic death, this theme was entirely absent from the American songs. Another effort to establish a German-American difference was carried on through an attitude survey of a sample of youth from both countries. The results seen in Table 2 indicate a considerable emphasis on submission to authority in the German sample.

Perhaps an even more striking comparison concerns Menominee Indians who were divided into four groups according to their degree of participation in general American society. The most isolated group held a large number of attitudes considered related to the traditional Menominee culture, while the group with the most participation in the general society showed little variation from white Americans. These examples do not prove that all individuals in a given society will act in the same manner; but they do indicate that different cultural influences have enough effect on the behavior of large numbers of citizens so that national character is a useful concept [Spindler, 1957].

ETHNOCENTRISM

Oliver Wendell Holmes once observed that "the axis of the earth sticks out visibly through the center of each and every town and city." Sumner called this outlook *ethnocentrism,* formally defined as "that view of things in which one's own group is the center of everything and all others are scaled and rated with reference to it" [Summer 1906, p. 13]. Stated less formally, ethnocentrism is the tendency for each group to take for granted the superiority of its culture. We assume, without thought or argument, that monogamy is better than polygamy, that young people should choose their own mates, and that it is best for the young married couple to live by themselves. Our society is "progressive," while the non-Western world is "backward"; our art is noble and beautiful, whereas that of other societies is grotesque and degraded; our religion is true; others are pagan superstitions. Ethnocentrism makes our culture into a yardstick with which to measure all other cultures, which are good or bad, high or low, right or queer in proportion as they resemble ours. It is expressed positively in such phrases as "chosen people," "progressive," "superior race," "true believers," and negatively by epithets like "foreign devils," "infidels," "heathen," "backward peoples," "barbarians," and "savages." Like the Bostonian who "didn't need to travel because he was already here," we are usually quick to recognize ethnocentrism in others and slow to see it in ourselves. Thus it was often remarked that Americans could not possibly believe Hitler's claim that the Germans were a nation of supermen, because they knew this could be true only of Americans!

All known societies are ethnocentric. The "backward" native peoples, to whom we feel so superior, have a similar feeling of superiority to us. Even while they are adopting our technology, they generally consider most of the rest of our culture quaint and absurd. Worsley describes the New Guinean's evaluation of white men:

The Europeans were not regarded as all-powerful, but as rather pathetic, ignorant people who could be easily cheated or stolen from. Their ignorance of sorcery was lamentable. "These are not men; they are merely gods," said the natives, judging the whites to be beings whose lives were inferior to those of living men. Again, they spoke the indigenous tongues very badly; why should one bother trying to make out their uncouth speech?

Peter Worsley, *The Trumpet Shall Sound,* MacGibbon & Kee, London, 1957, pp. 208–209.

Most, if not all, groups within a society are also ethnocentric. Caplow [1958, p. 105] studied 55 sets of six organizations each, including fraternities, churches, insurance companies, colleges, and many others. He found that members overestimated the prestige of their own organizations eight times as often as they underestimated it. Ethnocentrism is a universal human reaction, found in all known societies, in all groups, and in practically all individuals.

A few persons reject their group or some part of its culture. There are anti-Semitic Jews, anti-Negro Negroes, aristocrats who lead revolutions, intensively trained believers who abandon their faith, and so on. This rejection of one's group or culture is a form of deviant behavior and will be discussed in Chapter 7.

Although ethnocentrism is partly a matter of habit, this is not the whole story. We are also ethnocentric because we are encouraged to be ethnocentric. Our culture complex of nationalistic patriotism is perhaps the greatest source of deliberately cultivated ethnocentrism. From early childhood we learn about national heroes and the national mythology. Self-appointed patriotic organizations comb our textbooks and pounce upon any statements lacking in ethnocentric coloration. Anybody who is of doubtful commitment to nationalistic loyalties may be denounced as an undesirable citizen. Thus, both the United States and the Philippines have had "un-American" and "un-Philippine" activities committees which investigated people who were suspected of deviating from true ethnocentric devotion to national principles.

College students should find ethnocentrism easy to understand, since they experience so much of it. They are subjected to a barrage of ethnocentric cultivation from before they arrive until the moment of graduation—when the alumni office takes over. College newspapers and annuals, pep rallies, trophy cases, and countless "bull sessions" all combine to convince the neophyte that Siwash U. has unique virtues denied to all lesser institutions. Rush week reaches a high point in ethnocentric indoctrination. An elaborate drama is staged to allow the pledge to perceive how only this particular fraternity has the social values, the illustrious membership, the burnished traditions, and the shimmering prestige which make joining it a privilege. Other fraternities are counterfeits, to whose members one condescends; the unaffiliated student one simply ignores. Without the successful cultivation of ethnocentrism, few fraternities could meet the payments on the mortgage, and every college "homecoming" would be a flop!

There are many other sources of ethnocentrism. Almost every race, social class, regional or sectional group, occupational group, recreational group, or group of any kind encourages the ethnocentrism of its members.

Personality and ethnocentrism All groups stimulate the growth of ethnocentrism, but not all members of the group are equally ethnocentric. There is some evidence that many people in American society develop a personality which is basically more ethnocentric than that of other people. How can we explain this? One answer is that some of us are strongly ethnocentric as a defense against our own inadequacies.

Many research studies have explored this hypothesis. One group of studies [O'Connor, 1952; Brown, 1953] finds that the ethnocentric person is apt to have difficulty in following abstract reasoning and tends to be intolerant of ambiguity in a threatening situation. By the first criticism we mean that he has difficulty in placing specific events in the framework of a complicated chain of reasoning and therefore easily accepts simplified explanations that fit ethnocentric prejudices. "Intolerance of ambiguity" means that the ethnocentric person sees the experiences of life as polar opposites with no indeterminate shadings; that is, everything must be either "good" or "bad," with no confusing mixtures. This polarity is especially necessary when he feels that his status or his group's welfare is involved; his need for security demands that his enemies and friends must be clearly identified. He cannot attribute adversity either to his own limitations or to a complex chain of events, but must fix the blame on some specific personal or ideological devil. In this way he can simplify a baffling world and escape the need to deal realistically with his own short-comings.

Two large-scale research projects and a number of smaller projects stimulated by their findings have given us information on the kinds of people most apt to hold strong ethnocentric views. One of them, *The Authoritarian Personality* [Adorno, 1950], sought to discover the personality types most apt to accept a fascist philosophy. Most of the data were gathered through interviews with people on the West Coast of the United States during and after World War II. The authors developed a scale designed to measure ethnocentrism. They found that the ethnocentric personality is not just prejudiced against one group but against many. The people they questioned who denigrated Negroes also expressed suspicion of other minorities in the society, and were distrustful of many "foreign" groups and influences.

Another major study, *Communism, Conformity, and Civil Liberties* [Stouffer, 1955], gives some characteristics of people who are apt to be ethnocentric. This study developed a "tolerance" scale to measure attitudes toward nonconformists. The scale would seem to include the same attitudes that were measured on the ethnocentrism scale, and when both tests were given to the same group, the correlation was in the expected direction. The result suggests that people classified as ethnocentric are also apt to be intolerant of nonconformists. From these and other studies of ethnocentrism, Altus and Tabejian [1953] arrive at some general characteristics of the kinds of Americans who are most likely to be highly ethnocentric. Five social categories among whom ethnocentrism has been found to be high are women, older people, the less educated, those who are less active in community affairs, and the religiously orthodox. The categories may be more ethnocentric because these groups are somewhat restricted in their interaction with other groups in our society. Seclusion of one kind or another is obviously characteristic of the aged, the less educated, and those who are inactive in community affairs. It is also true that many women are still confined to contacts with their families and those in the immediate neighborhood, although this situation is rapidly changing. The religiously orthodox develop an intense and unquestioning loyalty to a religious creed while living in a society which permits religious variation. Religious orthodoxy, with its sharp distinction between truth and error, would seem to appeal to the desire of the ethnocentric person for definite, unambiguous answers and a positive identification of good and bad people.

These studies have also found ethnocentrism to be higher among people with certain personality characteristics: the sexually inhibited, those with obsessive compulsions, those with paranoid feelings (of persecution), those with stunted egos (lack of self-confidence), and the poorly socialized (ruthlessly self-centered). While this is not the place for a detailed psychoanalytic interpretation of ethnocentrism, it is clear that individual differences in ethnocentrism are related both to the group affiliations and to the personality structure of the individual.

We should remember that not everyone in each of these categories is highly ethnocentric; these are group averages. Also we often find that a particular form of ethnocentrism is a local tradition which one absorbs along with the rest of the culture, without necessarily becoming ethnocentric about other topics. Thus, Southern whites learn a set of ethnocentric reactions to Negroes; but Prothro [1952] finds no evidence that Southerners are more ethnocentric about other groups than comparable persons from other parts of the country. The intense ethnocentrism which some localities, such as Boston, cultivate in matters of local pride and history may not extend to other topics. In other words, it takes more than one ethnocentric reaction to identify a highly ethnocentric person.

Effects of ethnocentrism   Is ethnocentrism good or bad for people? First, we should have to decide how to define "good" and "bad," and even then we might find the question very unsettled. Ethnocentrism gets us into many of our muddles; yet it is doubtful whether groups can survive without it.

Promotion of group unity, loyalty, and morale   Ethnocentric groups seem to survive better than tolerant groups. Although most of the tolerant religions have disappeared, the ruthlessly ethnocentric ones have, in the main, survived and maintained missionary zeal. Ethnocentrism justifies sacrifice and sanctifies martyrdom. The attitude, "I prefer my customs, although I recognize that, basically, they may be no better than yours," is not the sort of faith for which dedicated believers will march singing to their death.

Ethnocentrism reinforces nationalism and patriotism. Without ethnocentrism, a vigorous national consciousness is probably impossible. Nationalism is but another level of group loyalty. Periods of national tension and conflict are always accompanied by intensified ethnocentric propaganda. Perhaps such a campaign is a necessary emotional preparation for the expected sacrifices.

Protection against change   If our culture is already the world's most perfect, then why tinker with alien innovations? From the Biblical Hebrews to nineteenth-century Japan, ethnocentrism has been used to discourage the acceptance of alien elements into the culture. Such efforts to prevent culture change are never entirely successful; change came to both the Hebrews and to the Japanese. Yet if people share a serene, unquestioning faith in the goodness of their culture—a conviction so completely accepted that no proof is necessary—then change is delayed.

Ethnocentrism also acts to discourage change in the internal arrangements of a culture. Privileged and wealthy groups are apt to feel that their society is "the best of all possible worlds," since a society which treats them so well must be good. Those who can buy the symbols of success but have not yet been fully accepted socially—the "new rich"—are apt to hold an even stronger belief in the virtues of the aristocratic group they hope to join. In either case a defense of the group distracts attention from the weakness of the individual while preserving the class system against change.

While ethnocentrism provides rationalization for the privileged, it also brings compensation to those of low status. An example is seen in the attitude of Southern "poor whites" toward Negroes. Myrdal [1944, pp. 597–599] found that the poor whites, low in income and social status, were the strongest exponents of the doctrine of white supremacy. As Sinclair Lewis writes, "Every man is king so long as he has someone to look down upon." Belief in the moral and mental inferiority of Negroes and perhaps "damyankees" compensates for their own wretched position. These attitudes are powerful barriers to change in the American South.

In discouraging culture change, ethnocentrism is undiscriminating. It discourages both the changes which would disrupt the culture and the changes which would help it attain its goals. Ethnocentrism led the Biblical Hebrews to reject both the pagan gods who would have disrupted their culture and the superior farming techniques of their neighbors which would have advanced their culture. Since no culture is completely static, every culture must make some changes if it is to survive. Ethnocentrism in India today helps to keep her from turning

Ethnocentrism also acts to discourage change.

Communist, but India may not remain non-Communist unless she rapidly modernizes her technology and controls her population growth, and these changes are delayed by ethnocentrism. In an age of atom bombs and push-button warfare, when the nations must probably either get together or die together, ethnocentrism helps to keep them tied to concepts of national sovereignty. Under some circumstances, then, ethnocentrism promotes cultural stability and group survival; under other circumstances, ethnocentrism dooms the culture to collapse and the group to extinction.

An evaluation of We can see that there is no simple answer to the question whether ethnocen-
ethnocentrism trism is good or bad. It is inevitable. It has a number of effects, some of which most of us would consider good and some bad. Our interest is neither to justify nor to condemn it, but to understand it. We must understand that no one can help being ethnocentric. As Ruth Benedict has observed,

The life history of the individual is first and foremost an accommodation to the patterns and standards traditionally handed down in his community. From the moment of his birth the customs into which he is born shape his experience and behavior. By the time he can talk, he is the little creature of his culture, and by the time he is grown and able to take part in its activities, its habits are his habits, its beliefs his beliefs, its impossibilities his impossibilities.

Ruth Benedict, *Patterns of Culture,* Houghton Mifflin Company, Boston, 1934, pp. 2–3.

Rarely are we able to question the basic values of our culture until we come into direct contact with people from another background. Even at the point of this contact our tendency is not to question the values of our culture, but rather to defend them vigorously against the assaults of members of the other group, whom we tend to classify as "backward" or "immoral" and therefore unworthy of serious consideration. To understand our own ethnocentrism will help us to avoid being so gravely misled by it. We cannot avoid *feeling* ethnocentric, but with understanding, we need not *act* upon these irrational feelings. We may learn to base our actions upon rationally perceived facts, rather than upon thoughtless ethnocentric evaluations.

To achieve an efficient balance between a useful pride in our own culture and subcultures and a realization of the real qualities of other groups is a difficult task. It requires both an emotional maturity which enables the individual to face his world without the armor of exaggerated self-esteem and an intellectual realization of the complexity of cultural processes. There is no guaranteed way to achieve this maturity. Wealth may be accompanied by psychological insecurity; travel may simply give us more vivid examples

No one can help being ethnocentric.

of the backwardness of other peoples; religion may cast even the deity in the image of our own group values; and education may only provide a more sophisticated justification for an ethnocentric bias. But unless we can understand and control our ethnocentric impulses, we shall simply go on repeating the blunders of our predecessors.

CULTURAL RELATIVISM

We cannot possibly understand the actions of other groups if we analyze them in terms of *our* motives and values; we must interpret their behavior in the light of *their* motives, habits, and values if we are to understand them. Consider, for example, the administration of justice in the far North. The Canadian Mounties are occasionally called to go into the arctic region to apprehend Eskimos who have committed a murder. This action in terms of our culture is a crime, and the individual has violated the mores. In the culture of many Eskimo tribes, however, the killing may have been justified, since their mores demand that a man avenge an injury committed upon a kinsman. This type of revenge is not considered unruly or deviant but is the only kind of action which an honorable man could take. We would condemn the man who takes the law into his own hands and seeks revenge, while they would condemn the man who has so little courage and group loyalty as to allow his kinsman to go unavenged.

Few culture traits are so disturbing to most Americans as the primitive practice of head hunting—an apparently useless and bloodthirsty pastime. However, this trait nearly everywhere has a fairly complex meaning. The Marindese of New Guinea, a quite gentle and affectionate people, hunted heads in order to provide names for their children [Van der Kroef, 1952]. Since they firmly believed that the only way a child could get a name and a separate identity was to take it from a living person, they hunted heads from neighboring tribes. A Marindese husband had a moral obligation to have one or two head names on hand, in case he was presented with a child. Thus head hunting, like any other important trait, was deeply integrated into a total cultural system within which it was moral and necessary.

These illustrations show what we mean by cultural relativism—that *the function and meaning of a trait are relative to its cultural setting.* A trait is neither good nor bad in itself. It is good or bad only with reference to the culture in which it is to function. Fur clothing is good in the arctic, but not in the tropics. Premarital pregnancy is bad in our society, where the mores condemn it and where there are no comfortable arrangements for the care of illegitimate children; premarital pregnancy is good in a society such as that of the Bontocs of the Philippines, who consider a woman more marriageable when her fertility has been established, and who have a set of customs and values which make a secure place for the children. Adolescent girls in the United States are advised that they will improve their marital bargaining power by remaining chaste until marriage. Adolescent girls in New Guinea are given the opposite advice, and in each setting the advice is probably correct. The rugged individualism and peasant thrift of early America would produce great unemployment if they were widely practiced in our present mass-production economy. From such examples we see that *any cultural trait is socially "good" if it operates harmoniously within its cultural setting to attain the goals which the people are seeking.* This is a workable, nonethnocentric test of the goodness or badness of a culture trait.

The concept of cultural relativism does not mean that all customs are equally valuable nor does it imply that no customs are harmful. Some patterns of behavior may be injurious in any milieu, but even such patterns serve some purpose in the culture, and the society will suffer unless a substitute is provided.

Sociologists are sometimes accused of undermining morality with their concept of cultural relativism, and their claim that almost "everything's right somewhere." If right and wrong are merely social conventions, say our critics, one might as well do whatever he wishes. This is a total misunderstanding. It is approximately true that "everything's right somewhere"—but not everywhere. The central point in cultural relativism is that in a particular cultural setting, certain traits are right because they work well in that setting, while other traits are wrong because they would clash painfully with parts of that culture. This is but another way of saying that a culture is integrated, and that its various elements must harmonize passably if the culture is to function efficiently in serving human purposes. The person who invokes cultural relativism to excuse his own unconventional behavior is showing that he does not understand the concept, and perhaps that he has no concern for the welfare of his society.

REAL AND IDEAL CULTURE

In most societies some behavior patterns are generally condemned yet widely practiced. In some places these illicit behavior patterns have existed for centuries side by side with the norms which are supposed to outlaw them. Malinowski cites as an example of this type of behavior, the Trobriand islanders, a group whose incest tabus extend to third and fourth cousins.

> *If you were to inquire into the matter among the Trobrianders you would find that . . . the natives show horror at the idea of violating the rules of exogamy and that they believe that sores, disease and even death might follow clan incest. . . .*
>
> *[But] from the point of view of the native libertine, suvasova (the breach of exogamy) is indeed a specially interesting and spicy form of erotic experience. Most of my informants would not only admit but actually did boast of having committed this offense or that of adultery (kaylasi); and I have many concrete, well-attested cases on record.*

Bronislaw Malinowski, *Crime and Custom in Savage Society,* Routledge & Kegan Paul, Ltd., London, 1926, pp. 79, 84.

Like all societies, the Trobrianders have some standardized ways of evading punishment, Malinowski [p. 81] observes, "Magic to undo the consequences of clan incest is perhaps the most definite instance of methodical evasion of law."

This case illustrates the difference between the real and ideal culture. The ideal culture includes the formally approved folkways and mores which people are supposed to follow (the cultural norms); the real culture consists of those which they actually practice (the statistical norms). For example, Warriner [1958] found that many residents of a town in Kansas, a legally "dry" state at the time of his research, drank in private while supporting the "temperance" morality in public. He concluded that the official morality served to prevent a disruptive public controversy, without interfering with their drinking behavior. There are many such divergences between the real and ideal culture in our society. As a sample, Williams lists ten examples of "patterned evasion" of our formally approved norms:

1. *Prohibition vs. the bootlegging and speakeasy industry, prior to repeal of prohibition*
2. *Impersonal, disinterested governmental services vs. political graft, "fixing," "status justice"*
3. *Family mores vs. prostitution*
4. *Classroom honesty vs. accepted patterns of "cribbing"*
5. *Promotion by technical competence vs. nepotism, racial discrimination, etc.*
   a. *Systematic evasion of civil service laws*
6. *Universalistic legal justice vs. white-collar crime, the public defender system, bias in jury selection*
7. *Prescribed patterns of sexual behavior vs. the patterns revealed in the Kinsey reports*
8. *Legal rules regarding divorce vs. actual court practice ("void" divorces, the "alimony racket")*
9. *Professional codes of conduct vs. such practices as fee splitting among doctors, ambulance chasing among lawyers*
10. *Ethical concepts of truth vs. some advertising, financial transactions, etc. ("business is business")*

Robin M. Williams, Jr., *American Society*, Alfred A. Knopf, Inc., New York, 1960, p. 382.

A clash between the real and ideal culture patterns is generally avoided by some kind of rationalization which allows people to "eat their cake and have it." For example, Lowie [1940, p. 379] describes some Burmese villages which are Buddhist, and whose inhabitants are therefore forbidden to kill any living thing, yet are dependent upon the murderous occupation of fishermen. They evade this contradiction by not literally killing the fish, which ". . . are merely put out on the bank to dry after their long soaking in the river, and if they are foolish and ill-judged enough to die while undergoing the process, it is their own fault."

No society is free of such inconsistencies, and complex societies like ours have many patterns which are formally condemned, enthusiastically practiced, and skillfully rationalized. We cherish monogamous marriage but tolerate quasilegalized prostitution. The practices seem to be incompatible, but there is little conflict between them since our culture trains us both to applaud the virtuous woman and to tolerate the prostitute. Tax evasion is legally and morally wrong, but apparently it is practiced by most people who have a good opportunity. Business life demands rigid honesty, but alongside this upright-ness may be found a pattern of bribery and special favors which is said to facilitate the making of business agreements. All are equal before the law in

America—except Negroes, immigrants, poor people, radicals, women, children, and the unemployed. Such contradictions could be extended into an impressive list for any modern society.

In the long-run viewpoint, the clash between real and ideal culture patterns may simply illustrate the fact that we have gone only part way in developing social control, and that eventually there may be a greater consistency between the actual behavior and the moral precepts of the culture. The extension of the voting privilege regardless of race or sex narrows the gap between precept and practice in our democratic mores. The abolition of child labor and the social security provisions for the aged and the handicapped are fulfilling the implications of the humanitarian mores in areas which have often been neglected. These and many other developments exemplify what Sumner [1906, p. 66] called a "strain toward consistency in the mores." In spite of frequent discrepancies, there is still a strong tendency for a society, sooner or later, to bring its various ideas and practices into harmony with one another.

On the other hand, in some circumstances it may be possible that the illicit patterns of behavior allow society to engage in conduct which seems essential to the welfare of the group but for which it has not been able to find a moral sanction. Thurman Arnold expressed this viewpoint in a book called *The Folklore of Capitalism* [1937]. He argued that the large-scale consolidation of industry was an essential part of modern technological development. This trend, however, is inconsistent with the American mores which sanction the value of small-scale competitive business. To meet the situation, he claims that the United States evolved unenforceable antitrust laws which expressed our moral condemnation of bigness in business, and at the same time permitted business to gain the advantages of continued consolidation. This procedure reminds us of the practice in some primitive societies in which courtship and marriage regulations are so complicated that most marriages occur through a type of elopement which is vigorously condemned by the mores. If the couple are unusually awkward, they may be caught and severely beaten, but ordinarily they are able to make good their escape. After a period of penance, they are welcomed back into the social group. Thus society is able to maintain the expression of sentiments sacred to the mores along with the existence of a useful practice in violation of the mores, thereby promoting a type of adjustment which seems necessary to the smooth functioning of the society.

Real and ideal patterns are both definitely a part of the culture. The real patterns are not mentioned in formal statements or deliberately taught as part of the program of church and school, but they are transmitted by an informal communication network of gossip and advice which may be even more effective than the formal channels. For this reason it is sometimes suggested [Yinger, 1966, p. 75] that the terms *overt* and *covert* might indicate their nature. Ideal patterns are overt, that is, openly announced, while the real patterns are often covert, transmitted in an unofficial and perhaps clandestine fashion.

CULTURE AND HUMAN ADJUSTMENT

Is culture a help or a burden to mankind? Some of each. It helps him to solve some problems, gets in his way as he grapples with others, and itself creates still others.

Culture and biological adjustment

Man's culture contains many gadgets which help him in his unremitting battle with nature. Since man freezes and sunburns easily, he wears clothes and builds houses. Nature offers wild fruits, seeds, and berries; man domesticates them and increases their yield. His hands are poor shovels, but his bulldozers remake the surface of the earth. He cannot run fast, swim well, or fly at all; yet no living thing travels so fast as he. Man was created a fragile, delicate being, quickly prey to death through heat or cold, thirst or hunger. Through his culture, man can moisten the desert and dry the swampland, can survive arctic cold and tropic heat, and can even survive a trip through outer space.

While culture helps man to adjust to his environment, it also interferes with his biological adjustment in many ways. Every culture offers many examples of patterns harmful to man's physical well-being. The Hindu belief that man should not kill anything has filled India with stray dogs, scrawny cattle, and all manner of parasites, wasting food and spreading diseases. Man has improved his weapons until he can destroy the entire human race. He follows methods of agriculture and land use which destroy the soil and flood the land. He pollutes the air, fouls the streams, and poisons his foods. If he is rich enough he generally eats, smokes, and drinks more than is good for him. He eats polished rice or white bread which are stripped of vital food elements, while he may pass up beef, pork, horse meat, snake meat, snails, milk, or whatever valuable source of nourishment is under taboo in his society. If he were descended from cats instead of anthropoids, he would be better equipped for the night hours he likes to keep.

In nearly every culture men (and women) have twisted, stretched, squeezed, gouged, painted, trimmed, and scarred the human body in an effort to be beautiful. The clumsy platters inserted in the slit lips of the Ubangi, the foot binding as practiced upon upper-class female children in classical China, and the precarious high heels of our women are all efforts to improve upon nature by deforming and distorting the natural body contours—along with those interesting Western devices intended to squeeze, shift, uplift, and supplement various parts of the female anatomy. Our culture causes men to wrap themselves in useless garments in the summer while in winter women expose their legs to the icy blasts. Our culture encourages men to dangerous overexertion in sports, yet encourages them to miss healthful exercise by taking a car for a trip to the corner, and by hauling their children to school even when they

Efforts to improve upon nature.

would be better off walking. Automobile buyers are far more interested in a stylish appearance than in passenger safety—so much so that "safety" has been a nasty word in Detroit. Our culture includes traits that lead communities to build new hospitals and other traits that cause them to oppose fluoridation programs to reduce tooth decay. American culture includes both the scientific milieu that developed an effective polio vaccine and the folkways and vested interests that made it difficult to pursue an effective mass-immunization program for making efficient use of this vaccine. When the values of the culture are not in harmony with the needs of biological adjustment, the culture may cause man to work against his own physical welfare.

Even the principle of self-preservation, which is said to be the first law of nature, sometimes gives way to cultural considerations. The Japanese culture provides obvious examples of this tendency in institutionalized suicide, hara-kiri, and in the wartime kamikaze pilots who dove to their death in airplanes used as guided missiles. This sacrifice of human life for other values is not a monopoly of any culture, and the Japanese might regard the American mania for speed on the highways as a similar value which retains its appeal in spite of the cost to human life. The appearance of impressive statistics on the relation of cigarette smoking to cancer of lungs and throat has not caused any bankruptcies in the tobacco industry, nor have predictions of perhaps 50 million deaths in an atomic war produced any panic among us. We are apparently less concerned with how long we live than we are with preserving the practices and values which our culture has taught us to consider important.

Is culture, then, good or bad for man? It may be either. Culturally sanctioned behavior may prolong life, or it may prevent man from using nature for his own physical welfare.

Culture and social adjustment Just as culture may either promote or impair man's physical health, so it may either encourage or impede the harmonious operation of the society and the development of well-adjusted personalities. American culture, for instance, has so highly valued the "practical" pursuits that it has been hard to interest enough young people in theoretical science or higher learning. The term "egghead" is a cultural stereotype which reflects a disdain of intellectuality that slows our scientific development and threatens national survival. In the Ottoman Empire the military and agricultural activities were highly valued, while commerce was disdained to such an extent that the Turks could not maintain their leadership in a world increasingly dominated by industrialism. In the Philippines the culture encourages an extremely high status for the legal profession with the result that other occupations are neglected while the country has thousands of lawyers without a practice.

The cultural guides to religious belief and family formation may also have mixed effects. The religious emphasis on the next world may cause the individual to ignore the need for making practical day-to-day adjustments in this world. Similarly a family-determined choice of marriage partners may lead to a rule of the elders which retards social change, while the belief in romantic choice of mates by individuals may lead them on a fruitless round of divorce and remarriage in search of ecstatic happiness probably unattainable by the human family. The culture may ascribe roles without providing adequate preparation for them, or may require a succession of roles which impose painful transitions upon individuals. It may build conflicting pressures into a role so that few individuals can possibly avoid mental conflict, or it may require difficult role choices of individuals or encourage role ambitions which doom most persons to failure.

The culture provides patterns of behavior, organized into a series of ascribed and achieved roles, and thus provides for getting the routine work of society accomplished. It may overelaborate these to a point of impracticality. It is said that Marie Antoinette was unable to get a glass of cold water; court etiquette required it to pass through so many hands that it was always tepid by the time it reached her. Rivers [1912] tells how on Torres Island in Melanesia, canoe building was surrounded with such an elaborate set of magical rites and taboos that only a small group of hereditary canoe builders dared to try to build one. Others were familiar with the manual skills for canoe building, but since they lacked the secret magic, it was unthinkable that they should build the craft. Therefore when the hereditary canoe-builder families died out, the Torres islanders went without canoes despite their desperate need for them. If this deliberate frustration seems stupid to the reader, let him try to explain why in our society, any people should be hungry, ill-housed, or ragged while food rots in warehouses and men rot in unemployment! In our society our building codes, union rules, and other monopolistic practices in the construction industry make building unnecessarily complicated and costly. In every society the culture organizes the work of the society in ways that are sometimes cumbersome and impractical; yet, without a culturally organized system for getting things done, most of them wouldn't get done at all.

If a culture is to survive, it must cultivate the values and practices necessary for its survival. A culture is weakened if it encourages the individual in lines of endeavor which will lead to personal frustration and rob his society of needed types of activity. The culture may lead the individual into successful activity, or it may cause him to follow a blind alley. The culture may produce either a society with qualities which make for world leadership or a society which lacks the elements needed for survival in competition with other world societies.

SUMMARY

From before one is born until after he is dead, his life is circumscribed by his culture. His culture (1) defines the meaning of situations and thereby indicates the behavior expected; (2) defines the attitudes he should hold, the values he should cherish, and the goals which are worthwhile; (3) provides the myths, legends, and supernatural beliefs he will live by; and (4) gives him ready-made behavior patterns to carry out all of these.

All societies and all groups assume the superiority of their own culture; this reaction is called *ethnocentrism*. We are ethnocentric because (1) we are so habituated to our culture's patterns that other patterns fail to please us; (2) we do not understand what an unfamiliar trait means to its user and therefore impute our reactions to him; (3) we are trained to be ethnocentric; (4) we find ethnocentrism a comforting defense against our own inadequacies. Ethnocentrism (1) promotes group unity, loyalty, and morale, and thereby reinforces nationalism and patriotism; (2) protects a culture from changes, including those needed to preserve the culture. Sociology does not either applaud or condemn ethnocentrism, but seeks to understand it and its effects upon society.

Cultural relativism describes the fact that the function and meaning of a culture trait depends upon the culture in which in operates. Traits are judged "good" or "bad" according to whether they work efficiently within their own culture.

Every society has an ideal culture, including the patterns which are supposed to be practiced, and a real culture, including illicit behavior which is formally condemned but widely practiced. Clashes between the two are evaded by rationalization. In some cases, illicit patterns are ways of getting necessary tasks done and thus, even though the mores do not approve the illicit actions, may actually contribute to cultural stability.

Culture both aids and hinders human adjustment. It enables man to survive in an inhospitable physical environment, although in many respects it sustains habits which are physically injurious. We couldn't live without culture; sometimes it isn't easy to live with it.

QUESTIONS AND PROJECTS

1. Why must we "define a situation" before we can do anything?

2. What goals do you think are most widely approved in our society? How is your present behavior related to these goals?

3. Are there any myths or legends in the history of your church? Of your college or university? What is their function?

4. Is ethnocentrism the opposite of cultural relativism? Explain.

5. Is there any difference between ethnocentrism and patriotism? Are the most ethnocentric groups also the most patriotic?

6. In what ways does ethnocentrism aid in national survival in the modern world? In what ways does it jeopardize national survival?

7. What effects do you think an extended trip around the world is likely to have upon one's ethnocentrism?

8. Cheating in college is sometimes defended on the ground that it is necessary if a student is to reach the goal of graduation. Is this position defensible in terms of cultural relativism? Why or why not?

9. In terms of cultural relativism, how would you appraise the old Chinese custom of binding upper-class women's feet? How about the extravagances of the American standard of living?

10. Are there any respects in which the real campus subculture differs from the ideal campus subculture?

11. In a perfectly integrated culture, would there be any divergence between the real and ideal culture patterns?

12. Apparently, culture can be both a help and a hindrance to man. How can this be?

13. How would you rank the following organizations and activities in terms of their tendency to encourage ethnocentrism, and how would you justify your ranking?
   College alumni association
   College fraternity or sorority
   College student council
   Daughters of the American Revolution
   International Geophysical Year
   Olympic Games
   Peace Corps
   United Nations
   United States Army

SUGGESTED READINGS

"The American Way of Life," *Fortune*, February, 1950, p. 63. A comment on the goals, values, and regional subcultures of American life.

BAIN, READ: "Our Schizoid Culture," *Sociology and Social Research*, 19:266–276, January, 1935. A classic discussion of our cultural contradictions.

CARNEIRO, ROBERT L.: "The Culture Process," in Gertrude E. Dale and Robert L. Carneiro (eds.), *The Science of Culture*, Thomas Y. Crowell Company, New York, 1960, pp. 145–161. Uses a brief description of the Protestant Reformation to distinguish between the historical treatment of unique events and the anthropological analysis of repetitive cultural processes.

CHASE, STUART: "On Being Culture Bound," *Antioch Review*, 9:293–306, September, 1949. Shows how the habit of thinking in terms of one's own culture makes it difficult for persons from different cultures to understand one another.

GILLIN, JOHN P.: "The Old Order Amish of Pennsylvania," in *The Ways of Men*, Appleton-Century-Crofts, New York, 1948, pp. 209–220. A summary of John W. Kollmorgen's research on the Old Order Amish, who are seeking to preserve a distinct subculture.

LABARRE, WESTON: "Professor Widjojo Goes to a Koktel Parti," *New York Times Magazine*, Dec. 9, 1956, pp. 17ff. A brief, highly entertaining picture of our folkways as seen through the eyes of an imaginary African anthropologist doing field work in "darkest America."

MERYMAN, RICHARD S., JR.: "South Dakota's Christian Martyrs," *Harper's Magazine*, December, 1958, pp. 72–79. A description of a group of Americans who were persecuted because of their subculture, which includes a form of New Testament communism.

*MICHENER, JAMES A.: *Return to Paradise*, Random House, Inc., New York, 1950; Bantam Books, 1952, section entitled, "Povenaaa's Daughter." A popular writer's hilarious tale of ethnocentric Americans' inability to comprehend the customs of Polynesian society, a fairly comfortable mixture of native and Western elements. (Ban)

MINER, HORACE: "Body Ritual among the Nacirema," *American Anthropologist*, 58:503–507, June, 1956; Bobbs-Merrill reprint S-185. An anthropologist describes the quaint customs and odd values of a well-known modern culture which the student may recognize.

VOGT, EVON Z. AND THOMAS F. O'DEA: "Cultural Differences in Two Ecologically Similar Communities," *American Sociological Review*, 18:645–654, December, 1953; reprinted in THOMAS E. LASSWELL ET AL., *Life in Society*, Scott, Foresman and Company, Chicago, 1965, pp. 34–41. Comparison of a Mormon and a non-Mormon community operating in comparable circumstances.

WILLIAMS, ROBIN M., JR.: *American Society*, Alfred A. Knopf, Inc., New York, 1960, chap. 10, "Institutional Variation and the Evasion of Normative Patterns." A perceptive discussion of the differences between our real and ideal cultures.

5

PERSONALITY

AND

SOCIALIZATION

Every man is in certain respects
  a. Like all other men
  b. Like some other men
  c. Like no other man

(Clyde Kluckhohn and Henry A. Murray (eds.), *Personality in Nature, Society and Culture*, Alfred A. Knopf, Inc., New York, 1949, p. 35.)

THERE ARE SOME ELEMENTS of a man's personality and socialization which he shares with all other men, some which he shares with some other men, and some which he shares with no other man. What these are and how they operate is the subject of this chapter.

MEANING OF PERSONALITY

Personality is one of those terms which is seldom defined in exactly the same way by any two authorities. All definitions of personality suggest that it represents a tendency for a person to act in a somewhat predictable manner. While some authorities are concerned with inborn predispositions which they credit to each person, others assume that behavior is largely a product of social experience. A quite satisfactory definition is offered by Yinger [1965, p. 141], who sees personality developing from the interaction of both elements: "Personality is the totality of behavior of an individual with a given tendency system interacting with a sequence of situations."

The phrase, "a given tendency system," suggests that the behavior of a person is fairly consistent. He acts much the same way day after day. When we remark, "Isn't that just like Ruth," we recognize that Ruth has a behavior "tendency system" that is quite characteristic of her. The phrase, "interacting with a sequence of situations," indicates that personality is never rigidly fixed but is constantly being remolded by experience. To understand personality we need to know how behavior tendency systems develop through the interaction of the biological organism with various kinds of social and cultural experience.

FACTORS IN THE DEVELOPMENT OF PERSONALITY

The factors in personality development include (1) heredity, (2) physical environment, (3) culture, (4) group experience, and (5) unique experience.

Biological inheritance A brick house cannot be built of stone or bamboo; but from a pile of bricks, a great variety of houses can be built. Heredity provides the raw materials of personality, and these raw materials can be shaped in a great many different ways.

Unlike many species, the human animal is sexually active throughout the entire year, and this characteristic guarantees the more or less constant association of the sexes. The human infant is born helpless and will survive only if given tender care for many years. Such biological facts provide a basis for man's group life. Some species are monogamous by instinct; that man is not is a biological fact which every society must deal with in some manner. Some of the similarities in man's personality and culture are due to his common heredity. As far as we know, every human group in the world inherits the same general set of biological needs and capacities. According to Montagu [1958, p. 85], these needs include oxygen, food, liquid, rest, activity, sleep, bowel and bladder elimination, escape from frightening situations, and the avoidance of pain. Our common heredity thus explains some of our similarities in personality, while individual differences in heredity explain some of the individual differences in personality. But *group* differences in personality cannot be attributed to heredity unless there is convincing evidence that the groups differ in average inheritance.

The American Negroes were taken from a number of tribes, mostly in West Africa. Promptly upon arrival, they began absorbing a culture and developing a personality quite different from that of their African kinsmen. Americans of many racial and national origins now share a common culture, and their differences in personality are not closely related to their different ethnic origins. We could cite dozens of examples of a rapid change in culture and personality without any change in heredity. All that we know of heredity suggests that the heredity of a group does not change rapidly enough to account for such changes in group behavior. What heredity does is to provide the set of needs, limitations, and capabilities with which other factors interact in shaping human personality.

Physical environment Some of our earliest manuscripts are attempts to explain man's behavior in terms of climate and geography. Sorokin [1928, chap. 3] summarizes the theories of hundreds of writers, from Confucius, Aristotle, and Hippocrates down to the modern geographer, Ellsworth Huntington, who have claimed that group differences in behavior are due mainly to differences in climate, topography, and resources. Such theories fit beautifully into an ethnocentric framework, for geography provides a respectable, apparently objective explanation of our national virtues and other peoples' vices.

The difficulty with geographic explanations is that they allow too many exceptions. If a hot climate favors dictatorship and a temperate climate encourages democracy, then how do we explain the Nazi and Communist dictatorships or the early Roman Republic? If the excitability of the Italians and the stolidity of the Scandinavians is climatically caused, then what explains the dignified Aztecs and the good-natured Eskimos?

The fact is that most kinds of personality and culture are found in every kind of climate. We find sharply differing cultures in similar physical environments, as witness the American Indians and the American colonists, or Tibet and the Peruvian highlands. We also find similar cultures in differing physical environments, as in the British settlements in England, India, Australia, and South Africa. Tradition is more important than physical environment in shaping most of our behavior. Social life in an area some-

Tradition is more important than physical environment.

times changes rapidly, without any change in physical environment. Obviously, the physical environment is only one of the factors in social life.

Physical environment sets the limits within which the culture can develop. A desert people will not use boats or live in log houses. A desert people usually live as small nomadic bands or in remote oases, and their shifting habitation profoundly affects much of their social life. Physical environment is, unquestionably, a highly important factor in social life, especially among the more primitive societies. It accounts for some similarities in the social life of all desert peoples, highlands peoples, seafaring peoples, or hunting peoples. Men can use only the materials present in their environment (at least, until they develop trade and transportation). Diet is limited to those foods which are available; but it is further limited by cultural preference, for almost all societies reject some of the edible foods available to them. Environment is a persuasive, but seldom a controlling factor in social life. A mountainous terrain isolates people in pockets and encourages separate units like the Greek city-states; yet the Incas in Peru built an empire upon an equally mountainous and unpromising terrain, while the Venetians and the Aztecs built city-states in shallow waters.

Today, culture minimizes the importance of physical environment upon social life. Trade and transportation move the more portable materials wherever they are needed. There are no longer many truly isolated groups. Drainage and irrigation are making many barren regions productive. Air conditioning reduces the enervation of a steaming climate for at least a few of the people. While mankind remains absolutely dependent upon his physical environment for the necessities of living, his ability to manipulate his environment is constantly growing, and the importance of regional variations in physical environment is steadily diminishing.

Heredity and environment set the limits within which personality can develop. Similarities in personality among all men are due partly to their common heredity. Then cultural experience shapes personality development, providing for both similarities and differences.

Cultural variation in personality Some cultural experience is common to all mankind. Everywhere infants are nursed or fed by older persons, live in family groups, learn to communicate through language, experience punishments and rewards of some kind, and have some other experiences common to the entire human species. It is also true that each society gives to virtually all its members certain experiences which many other societies do not offer. From the social experience common to virtually all members of a given society, emerges a characteristic personality configuration which is typical of

Some cultural experience is common to all mankind.

many members of that society. DuBois [1944, pp. 3–5] has called this the "modal personality" (taken from the statistical term, "mode," referring to that value which appears most frequently in a series). How the modal personality may vary between two different societies is seen in the following contrast.

The anxious Dobuan [Fortune, 1932; Benedict, 1934, chap. 5] The Dobuan child in Melanesia might think twice about coming into this world, if he had any choice in the matter. He enters a family where the only member who is likely to care much about him is his uncle, his mother's brother, to whom he is heir. His father, who is interested in his own sister's children, usually resents him, for his father must wait until he is weaned before resuming sexual relations with his mother. Often he is also unwanted by his mother, and abortion is common. Little warmth or affection awaits the child in Dobu.

The Dobuan child soon learns that he lives in a world ruled by magic. Nothing happens from natural causes; all phenomena are controlled by witchcraft and sorcery. Illness, accident, and death are evidence that witchcraft has been used against one and call for vengeance from one's kinsmen. Nightmares are interpreted as witchcraft episodes in which the spirit of the sleeper has narrow escapes from hostile spirits. All legendary heroes and villains are still alive as active supernaturals, capable of aid or injury. Crops grow only if one's long hours of magical chants are successful in enticing the yams away from another's garden. Even sexual desire does not arise except in response to another's love magic, which guides one's steps to his partner, while one's own love magic accounts for his successes.

Ill will and treachery are virtues in Dobu, and fear dominates Dobuan life. Every Dobuan lives in constant fear of being poisoned. Food is watchfully guarded while in preparation, and there are few persons indeed with whom a Dobuan will eat. The Dobuan couple spend alternate years in the villages of wife and husband, so that one of them is always a distrusted and humiliated outsider who lives in daily expectation of poisoning or other misadventure. Because of numerous divorces and remarriages, each village shelters men from many different villages, so that none of them can trust either their village hosts or one another. In fact, no one can be fully trusted; men are nervous over their wives' possible witchcraft and fear their mothers-in-law.

To the Dobuans, all success must be secured at the expense of someone else, just as all misfortune is caused by others' malevolent magic. Effective magic is the key to success, and a man's success is measured by his accomplishments in theft and seduction. Adultery is virtually universal, and the successful adulterer, like the successful thief, is much admired.

On the surface, social relations in Dobu are cordial and polite although dour and humorless. There is very little quarreling, for to give offense or to make an enemy is dangerous. But friends are also dangerous; a show of friendship may be a prelude to a poisoning or to the collection of materials (hair, fingernails) useful for sorcery.

What kind of personality develops in such a cultural setting? The Dobuan is hostile, suspicious, distrustful, jealous, secretive, and deceitful. These are rational reactions, for he lives in a world filled with evil, surrounded by enemies, witches, and sorcerers. Eventually they are certain to destroy him. Meanwhile he seeks to protect himself by his own magic, but never can he know any sense of comfortable security. A bad nightmare may keep him in bed for days. As measured by Western concepts of mental hygiene, all Dobuans are paranoid to a degree calling for psychotherapy. But simply to call them paranoid would be incorrect, for their fears are justified and not irrational; the dangers they face are genuine, not imaginary. A true paranoid personality *imagines* that other people are threatening him, but in Dobu, other people really *are* out to get him. Thus the culture shapes a personality pattern which is normal *and useful* for that culture.

The cooperative Zuñi [Benedict, 1934, chap. 4]   The Zuñi of New Mexico are a placid people in an emotionally undisturbed world. The child is warmly welcomed, treated with tender fondness, and receives a great deal of loving attention. He is never disciplined or punished, yet becomes a well-behaved member of a society in which crime is rare and quarreling almost unknown.

Cooperation, moderation, and lack of individualism are carried into all Zuñi behavior. Personal possessions are unimportant and readily lent to others. The members of the matrilineal household work together as a group, and the crops are stored in a common storehouse. One works for the good of the group, not for personal glory. (Zuñi children do poorly on competitive examinations in the government schools, for it is impolite to answer any question whose answer may be unknown to one's classmates.)

The magical forces in the Zuñi world are never malevolent and often helpful. Since the supernaturals have the same tastes as living men, they need not be feared. Supernatural and magical aid is sought through many long ceremonials, yet the ceremonial dances are never frenzied or orgiastic. Violence or immoderation is distasteful, and even disagreements are settled without open bickering. For example, one wife who became weary of her husband's many amours decided to settle the matter. "So," she said, "I didn't wash his clothes. Then he knew that I knew that everybody knew, and he stopped going with that girl." Without a word the issue was settled. [Benedict, 1934, p. 108.] Unlike most Indians, the Zuñi rejected alcohol because it tempts men to immoderate, undignified behavior. They do not use peyote or other drugs, or resort to self-torture or prolonged fasting in an effort to induce ecstasies, visions, or other unusual sensory phenomena. They desire only the normal sensory experience of moderate behavior. The individual Zuñi craves no power or leadership, and the necessary leadership roles must be thrust upon him. Responsibility and power are distributed; the group is the real functioning unit.

The Zuñi have no sense of sin. They have no picture of the universe as a conflict between good and evil, nor any concept of themselves as disgusting or unworthy. Sex is not a series of temptations but part of a happy life. Adultery is mildly disapproved, but is largely a private matter and a probable prelude to a change of husbands. Divorce is simple; the wife simply piles her husband's things outside the pueblo, where he finds them, cries a little, and goes home to his mother. Since the family is matrilineal and matrilocal (descent follows the mother's family line, and family residence is with the mother's family), a divorce and the disappearance of the father does not seriously disrupt the life of the children. Yet divorce is not very common, and serious misconduct is very rare.

The normal personality among the Zuñi stands in stark contrast to that of the Dobuans. Where the Dobuan is suspicious and distrustful, the Zuñi is confident and trusting; where the Dobuan is apprehensive and insecure, the Zuñi is secure and serene. The typical Zuñi has a yielding disposition and is generous, polite, and cooperative. He is unthinkingly and habitually conformist, for to be noticeably different from his fellows is something neither he nor they can tolerate. Apparently this serves to control his behavior without the sense of sin and the guilt complexes found in many societies, including our own.

The cultural patterning of personality As the two foregoing sketches illustrate, personality differs strikingly from society to society. *Each society develops a basic personality type which fits the culture.* The Dobuans do not consciously or intentionally train their children to be hostile and suspicious; yet the atmosphere of constant treachery and fear has this result. Each culture, simply by being what it is, shapes personality to fit the culture. Let us consider some aspects of the culture which affect the process of personality development.

Norms of the culture From the moment of birth, the child is treated in ways which shape the personality. Each culture provides a set of general influences, which vary endlessly from society to society. As Linton writes,

In some [societies] infants are given the breast whenever they cry for it. In others they are fed on a regular schedule. In some they will be nursed by any woman who happens to be at hand, in others only by their mothers. In some the process of nursing is a leisurely one, accompanied by many caresses and a maximum of sensuous enjoyment for both mother and child. In others it is hurried and perfunctory, the mother regarding it as an interruption of her regular activities and urging the child to finish as rapidly as possible. Some groups wean infants at an early age; others continue nursing for years.

In the techniques of caring for infants there is an even greater cultural range. One society may make the baby the center of attention for the entire family, various adults constantly carrying it about, playing with it, and giving it anything it wants. Another society may regard infants as a nuisance and pay little attention to them outside the satisfaction of their physical needs. In some societies the child is in almost constant bodily contact with its mother during the first two years. Madagascar mothers keep their infants in the backs of their dresses, leaving them there even when working in the fields. In other societies this constant bodily contact is lacking, but the child is handled frequently. In still others it is rarely touched except at feeding time. In some societies the child is allowed to tumble about without interference. In others it spends its first eighteen months bound to a board, even its arms sometimes being wrapped. . . .

Turning to the more direct effects of culture patterns upon the developing individual, we have an almost infinite range of variations in the degree to which he is consciously trained, discipline or the lack of it and responsibilities imposed upon him. Society may take the child in hand almost from infancy and deliberately train him for his adult status, or it may permit him to run wild until the age of puberty. He may receive corporal punishment for even the smallest offense or never be punished at all. As a child he may have a claim upon the time and attention of all adults with whom he comes in contact or, conversely, all adults may have a claim upon his services. He may be put to work and treated as a responsible contributing member of the family group almost from the moment that he is able to walk and have it constantly impressed upon him that life is real and earnest. Thus in some Madagascar tribes children not only begin to work at an incredibly early age but also enjoy full property rights. I frequently bargained with a child of six for some object which I needed for my collection; although its parents might advise, they would not interfere. On the other hand, the children in a Marquesan village do no work and accept no responsibility. They form a distinct and closely integrated social unit which has few dealings with adults. The boys and girls below the age of puberty are constantly together and often do not go home even to eat or sleep. They go off on all-day expeditions, for which no parental permission is required, catch fish and raid plantations for food, and spend the night in any house they happen to be near at sunset.

Examples of such cultural differences in the treatment of children could be multiplied indefinitely. The important point is that every culture exerts a series of general influences upon the individuals who grow up under it. These influences differ from one culture to another, but they provide a common denominator of experience for all persons belonging to a given society.

Ralph Linton, *The Study of Man*, Appleton-Century-Crofts, New York, 1936. Copyright, 1936, and reprinted by permission of Appleton-Century-Crofts.

Some of the American literature on psychoanalysis and child development, drawing heavily upon the theories of Freud, has attached great importance to specific child-training practices. Breast feeding, gradual weaning, demand-feeding schedules, and easy and late induction to bowel and bladder training have often been recommended, with the opposite practices being blamed for all sorts of personality difficulties. These recommendations are generally unsupported by any carefully controlled comparative studies, although dramatic case histories may be cited in illustration. One serious effort [Sewell, 1952] to test these recommendations made a comparison of American children who had received differing child training practices. This study found that no measureable adult personality differences were associated with any particular child-training practices. Studies of personality development in other cultures have likewise failed to substantiate Freudian theories of the results of specific child-training practices [Dai, 1957; Eggan, 1943]. Apparently, it is the total atmosphere, and not the specific practice, which is important in personality development. Whether a child is breast-fed or bottle-fed is unimportant; what *is* important is whether this feeding is a tender, affectionate moment in a warmly secure world, or a hurried, casual incident in an impersonal, unfeeling, unresponding environment.

Cultural personality types A society poses one or more personality types which children are urged to copy. Among most of the Plains Indians, the approved personality for the adult male was that of a vigorous, self-reliant, aggressive warrior. Under many circumstances, to take what he wanted from the weak was a virtue; any tendency to overlook insults or to compromise disagreements was a weakness. Since only these personality characteristics were admired and rewarded, they were the ones most youths developed.

The most widely approved personality in our culture is probably friendly and

Children are urged to copy.

sociable, somewhat cooperative yet quite competitive and aggressively individualistic, progressive, yet practical and efficient. Many features of our social life conspire to develop these characteristics within us. We live in a society where sociability has a cash value. Cordiality is taught and cultivated as a necessity in almost any career. The child is trained to make all requests with a "Please," and receive all favors with a smiling "Thank you." Television commercials, clerks, and salesmen mount an unending barrage of smiling, friendly-sounding appeals. While much of this outward show of friendliness is phony, it nonetheless surrounds one with an atmosphere of sociability which probably leaves some residue. Our society forces people to develop an acute time consciousness, since nearly everything is done on a time schedule. The Indian's serene unconcern with time is exasperating to whites who have dealings with him, just as the white man's endless fretting and clock watching perplexes and bores the Indian.

Most of the world's people could see little if any social change within their own lifetimes. They lived in an unchanging world, a world of customs supposedly unchanged over countless generations, of legends passed down from remote ancestors, and a world expected to extend endlessly into the future. We live in a culture permeated by change and expectations of change. Each child is surrounded by adults busily contrasting the present with their childhood reminiscences. Change is accepted, expected, and even discounted, as we base our future plans on the changes which we expect to have taken place by the time our plans mature. Cultural influences such as these help to develop the bustling, restless, energetic personality that is admired in our culture.

A close relationship between personality and culture should be expected, because in a sense, personality and culture are two aspects of the same thing. As Spiro [1951] has observed, "the development of personality and the acquisition of culture are not different processes, but are one and the same learning process. . . ." In a stable, well-integrated society, personality is an individual aspect of culture, while culture is a collective aspect of personality. This discussion could be prolonged indefinitely; but we have said enough to illustrate the point that every culture, including our own, surrounds the individual with experiences that develop a normal personality, more or less perfectly reflected by most members of that society.

Subcultures and personality. This picture of a single approved personality type (for each sex and age level) in a society holds fairly true for the simple society with a well-integrated culture. But in a complex society with a number of subcultures, the picture changes. Are there personality differences between the Yankee and the Deep Southerner? Does the sharecropper think and feel as does the urban professional? In a complex society, there may be as many "normal personality types" as there are subcultures.

The United States has many subcultures—racial, religious, ethnic, regional, social-class, perhaps even occupational. The boundary lines are indistinct, and some subcultures are more important than others. For example, the Catholic and Protestant subcultures probably affect less of a member's life than the Jewish subculture, and still less than the Amish subculture. Yet subcultures are real, and we have some justification for speaking of the "urban middle-class personality" or of the "typical salesman." Of course, we must not exaggerate; it is likely that personality similarities within our culture greatly outnumber personality differences between subcultures, and there are individual personality differences within each subculture. But the physician, the minister, the carnival worker, and the migrant fruit picker show some predictable personality differences from one another. Therefore we cannot describe *the* normal American personality without first naming the subculture we have in mind.

Individual deviation from modal personality.   In even the most conformist of societies, there is some individuality in personality. The modal personality merely represents a series of personality traits which are most common among the members of a group, even though comparatively few of them may have developed every one of the traits in the series. Wallace [1952 *a*] used Rorschach tests on a sample of Tuscarora Indians, and concluded that only 37 per cent of them showed all twenty-one of the modal personality traits. Other similar studies [Kaplan, 1954; Wallace, 1952 *b*] show that while a modal personality type characteristic of a society exists, it is not a uniform mold into which all members are perfectly cast. Likewise, in discussing the "typical" personality of nations, tribes, social classes, of occupational, regional, or other social groups, we must remember that the typical personality merely describes a series of personality traits, a *great many* of which are shared by *most* of the members of that group. Each society and each social group allows a certain amount of individual deviation from the modal personality. When this deviation extends beyond what the group or society considers "normal," then that person is considered to be a "deviant." Such deviation will be considered in some detail in Chapter 7.

SOCIALIZATION AND THE SELF

The infant enters this world as a biological organism preoccupied with his own physical comforts. He soon becomes a human being, with a set of attitudes and values, likes and dislikes, goals and purposes, patterns of response, and a deep, abiding concept of the sort of person he is. He gets these through a process we call *socialization*—the learning process which turns him from an animal into a person with a human personality. Put more formally, socialization is *the process whereby one internalizes the norms of his groups so that a distinct "self" emerges, unique to this individual.*

Group experience and socialization   As one's life begins there is no self, for the individual is simply an embryo sharing the life processes of the mother's body. Nor do birth and the severing of the umbilical cord produce any awareness of self. Even the distinction between the limits of the physical self and the rest of the world are a matter of gradual exploration as the infant discovers that toes are a part of his body, not like the rattle or the bars on his crib which belong to the external world.

The realization of a distinctive personality is an even more complicated process which continues throughout life. The child learns to differentiate between various other people by names—Daddy, Mummy, and Baby. At first, any man is a "daddy" and any woman a "mummy," but eventually he moves from names which distinguish a status to specific names which identify individuals, including himself. At about the age of two he begins to use "I," which is a sign of definite self consciousness—that he is becoming aware of himself as a distinct human being [Cooley, 1908; Bain, 1936]. As time passes and social experiences accumulate, he forms an image of the kind of person he is—an image of self. One ingenious way of trying to get some impression of a person's self image is the "Twenty Questions Test" [Kuhn and McPartland, 1954], in which the informant is asked to write twenty answers, exactly as they occur to him, to the question, "Who am I?" One's formation of his image of self is perhaps the most important single process in personality development.

Social isolates To some degree, personality is dependent upon physical-growth processes. But personality development is not simply an automatic unfolding of inborn potentials, as is shown by the social isolates whose physical growth has not been accompanied by corresponding personality development. Several times each year the newspapers report instances of neglected children who have been chained or locked away from the normal family group. They are always found to be retarded and generally antisocial or unsocial. Without group experience, human personality does not develop. The most dramatic reports are those of so-called "feral" children, separated from their families and supposedly raised by animals [Singh and Zingg, 1942; Krout, 1942, pp. 106–114]. Social scientists doubt that a child would live for long in the care of animals, and suspect that so-called feral children simply had been lost or abandoned by their parents and then discovered by others shortly thereafter [Ogburn, 1959].

An explanation of the reported "animal" behavior of feral children is offered by Professor Bettelheim, who states that severe cases of infantile autism being treated at the Orthogenic School of the University of Chicago show symptoms like those of the feral children, although there was no claim that the Chicago children had ever been in a nonhuman environment.

During one year a single staff member had to have medical help more than a dozen times for bites she suffered from Anna, and the children regularly bare their teeth when annoyed or angry. Different, and again reminiscent of animals is their prowling around at night, in marked contrast to their quiet withdrawal to a corner during the day. . . . Then there is their great preference for raw food, particularly for raw vegetables. . . . Some of these children on seeing animals, respond as though they had found a dear, long-lost friend. One girl for example, became extremely excited on seeing a dog; she showed a strong desire to run toward it and cried or howled like an animal. . . . She fell on all fours, jumped like a dog with her head down and made biting gestures. Now had we believed in the feral origin of this girl—whose total life-history incidentally, is well known to us—we would probably have been convinced that, on seeing that wolflike creature, she was filled with memories of her happy times among wolves and was reverting to what she had learned from them.

Bruno Bettelheim, "Feral Children and Autistic Children," *American Journal of Sociology,* 54: 458, March, 1959.

Bettelheim found that the autistic children in the Chicago clinic showed traits commonly attributed to "feral" children and concludes that the "feral" children were probably simply suffering from infantile autism—defined as "the inability to relate themselves in the ordinary way to people and situations from the beginning of life." He says that the autistic children known to the clinic had invariably been rejected by their parents and deprived of normal human love and concludes that this may be the real difficulty with the reported cases of feral children:

Study of the so-called feral children, and comparison of them with known and well-observed wild autistic children, suggests strongly that their behavior is due in large part, if not entirely, to extreme emotional isolation combined with experience which they interpreted as threatening them with utter destruction. It seems to be the result of some persons'—usually their parents'—inhumanity and not the result, as was assumed, of animals'—particularly wolves'—inhumanity. To put it differently, feral children seem to be produced not when wolves behave like mothers but when mothers behave like nonhumans. The conclusion tentatively forced on us is that, while there are no feral children, there are some very rare examples of feral mothers, of human beings who became feral to one of their children.

Bruno Bettelheim, op. cit., 467.

It is highly doubtful, then, that allegedly feral children are examples of animal nurture. It does seem evident, however, that children who are emotionally rejected and deprived of normal loving care fail to develop the type of personality we usually consider human. This conclusion is consistent with the findings of a number of experiments in which animals were raised in isolation from their normal groups. Harlow [1961] raised monkeys in isolation, with only a heated terry cloth-covered wire framework as a substitute "mother," from which they received their bottle and to which they clung when frightened. As infants, they seemed satisfied with this substituted "mother," but as adults, they were almost entirely asocial. Many were apathetic and withdrawn; others were hostile and aggressive. None showed the social group behavior of normal adult monkeys. Apparently the substitute mother met the infant's need for affection and security, but was unable to carry the monkey through any further stages of psychosocial development. Other animal experiments show similar failures of isolated animals to develop the behavior normal for their species [Krout, 1942, pp. 102–105]. Both animals and human beings need group experience if they are to develop normally.

Cooley and the looking-glass self　Just how does a person arrive at a notion of the kind of person he is? He develops this concept of self through a gradual and complicated process which continues throughout life. The concept is an image that one builds only with the help of others. Even the elementary knowledge that one tends to be fat or thin, tall or short is a comparative judgment that we cannot make until we have had the opportunity to compare ourselves with others. One of your authors, a modest 5 feet 7 inches in height, had internalized the notion that he was a relatively short man and looking with awe upon the 6-foot stalwarts around him. A short stay in an Asian area where most of the men appeared to be about 5 feet 5 completely changed his perspective. Now he was the tall person who towered, slightly but definitely, above his fellows. His actual height had not changed, but the perception of his own relative stature had definitely altered.

If one's definition of himself as tall or short is a response to the perception of those about him, his notion of qualities which are harder to define is even more dependent upon other people's ideas. Whether one is intelligent, average, or stupid; attractive, homely, downright ugly; righteous or sinful; these and many other ideas of the self are learned from the reactions of our associates. This process of discovering the nature of the self from the reactions of others has been labeled the "looking-glass self" by Cooley [1902, pp. 102–103], who carefully analyzed this aspect of self-discovery. He may, perhaps, have been inspired by the words in Thackeray's *Vanity Fair:* "The world is a looking glass and gives back to every man the reflection of his own face. Frown on it and it will in turn look sourly upon you; laugh at it and with it, and it is a jolly, kind companion."

There are three steps in the process of building the looking-glass self: (1) our perception of how we look to others; (2) our perception of their judgment of how we look; and (3) our feelings about these judgments. Suppose that whenever you enter a room and approach a small knot of people conversing together, the members promptly melt away with lame excuses. Would this experience, repeated many times, affect your feelings about yourself? Or if whenever you appear, a conversational group quickly forms around you, how does this attention affect your self-feelings? A wallflower is a person who learned early in life that she could not make conversation. How did she discover this?

Just as the picture in the mirror gives an image of the physical self, so the perception of the reactions of others gives an image of the social self. We "know," for instance, that we are talented in some respects and less talented in others. This knowledge came to us from the reactions of other persons. The little child whose first crude artistic efforts are sharply criticized learns that he lacks artistic talent, while the child whose first efforts win praise from a considerate parent may build up a belief in his own ability in this field. As he matures, others will also give a reaction which may differ from that of his parents, for the social looking glass is one which is constantly before us.

Still more important are the impressions that the individual receives as to whether he is an attractive person who inspires love or an inadequate person who is incapable of stimulating affection and respect. As with specific talents, this type of self-knowledge is first gained from parents and is modified by the reactions one receives from other individuals in later life. It is difficult to change completely an impression formed in early childhood. A child who learns from his family that he is inferior and unwanted may cling to a belief in his personal inadequacy in spite of spectacular success in adult life. Conversely, one who seems to be a failure in life may carry a feeling of security, developed through favorable early childhood experience, which survives adult disappointments. This does not mean that personality is frozen in a rigid mold at the time of early childhood, but it does suggest that the adult does not easily change his childhood conception of self. Sometimes he must reinterpret his childhood experience in great detail, with the aid of psychotherapy, before he can recon-struct a concept of self with which he can live more comfortably.

Another difference between the functioning of the "looking glass" in early childhood and in later life is that the child may be deeply affected by the response of anyone with whom he comes in intimate contact, whereas the older individual is more discriminating in appraising the importance of the response he receives from various individuals. The baby-sitter's responses affect the child more than they affect the parent. Thus we say that as one matures he develops *reference groups* to whom he gives special attention [Rosen, 1955 a]. A child may base his estimate of his musical talents on the opinions of parents regardless of their musical sophistication; an adult is more likely to give special attention to the opinions of musical experts and ignore the reactions of others. Not only do we become more selective in choosing the reference groups who comprise our social looking glass but we also are selective in the perception of the images which do influence us. We pay more attention to some reactions than to others; or we may misjudge the reactions of others. It may be that the ego-boosting remark which we take at face value is mere flattery; a scolding may have been caused by the boss's headache rather than by our own errors. Thus the looking-glass self which the individual perceives may easily differ from the image others have actually formed of his personality. Several research efforts have sought empirical evidence of the correlation between one's *perception* of responses of others and the *actual* judgments they have made of him. These studies find that there is often a significant variation between the individual's perception of how others picture him and the views they actually hold. Calvin and Holtzman [1953] found that individuals vary considerably in their ability to perceive accurately the judgments of others about them, and that the less well-adjusted person was less accurate in these perceptions. Another experiment by Miyamoto and Dornbusch [1956] found that a subject's self-conception is closer to his perception of a group's impression of him than to their actual reported impression of him, as is shown in Table 3.

In this study of ten groups totaling 195 subjects, the "perceived response" is each subject's estimate of how the other members of the group rate him according to the four characteristics above. The "actual response" is the rating

Table 3   *Self-conception as related to perceived and actual group response*

Characteristic	Groups in which subjects' self-conceptions were closer to their perceptions of group response	Groups in which subjects' self-conceptions were closer to actual group response
Intelligence	8	2
Self-confidence	9	0 (1 tie)
Physical attractiveness	10	0
Likeableness	7	3

SOURCE: S. Frank Miyamoto and Sanford M. Dornbusch, "A Test of Interactionist Hypothesis of Self-Conception," *American Journal of Sociology*, 61:399–403, March, 1956.

actually assigned to him by the others in the group. In most of these groups (of fraternity members and classmates who knew each other well) the subjects' self-conceptions were closer to their perceived response than to the actual response of the group to them. Clearly, it is our perception of the responses of others and not their actual responses which shapes our self-image, and these perceptions are often inaccurate.

Mead and the generalized other The process of internalizing the attitudes of others has been aptly described by George Herbert Mead [1934, part 3, pp. 140–141] who refers to "the generalized other." This "generalized other" is an individual's total impression of the judgments and expectations that other people have toward him. He then looks at himself as though he were another person and judges his actions and appearance according to these judgments of his "generalized other." This theory may be illustrated in terms of the development of play activities. At first the young child simply imitates the actions of his elders without much realization of why they act the way they do. Later, in games such as "hide and seek" he begins to make a partial response to what he assumes will be the actions of others since he tries to predict the places they would look, and seeks to find less accessible hiding places. Later, in the organized game he finds that others have definite roles assigned to them and must act in a given manner. In order to play the game successfully he must internalize the expected actions of others as well as their expectations of his actions, and conduct himself accordingly. When a girl plays with a doll, she acts out the part of the mother and gives the doll the part of the child; she can doll-play *only* as she puts herself into the role of another. Thus the individual is never truly alone, for always in his own mind he is responding to a pattern of behavior he attributes to other people. The self is thus inevitably social, since the individual incorporates the attitudes of other people in his own mind. His developing awareness of the social expectations of others is a vital part of self-development.

This development of the self involves two additional problems: finding an "identity" and gaining "self respect." Identity refers to the elements which distinguish the individual and enable him to be placed in an acceptable category of persons. The problem in establishing a satisfactory sense of identity is that the individual needs to be distinguished by characteristics which carry prestige in the eyes of his "generalized other." Often one is assigned an identity on the basis of characteristics of his race, nationality, religion, or occupation, and these characteristics of his may have low standing in the eyes of those who "count." Hence the individual engages in a vigorous (but sometimes futile) struggle to find a more prestigious identity which is more acceptable to others and consequently to himself [Merrill, 1957]. The feeling of "self respect" is also socially determined. One's ability to respect himself is dependent on his perception of how he is rated by others, especially the others whom he considers important. The man whose interpretation of the "generalized other" leads him to perceive a favorable reaction to his own personality will develop a sense of self respect. Otherwise he is likely to turn on himself, lack self respect, and regard himself as unworthy and deficient.

Freud and the antisocial self Our treatment thus far implies a basic harmony between the self and society. In the words of Cooley:

A separate individual is an abstraction unknown to experience. . . . In other words "society" and "individuals" do not denote separate phenomena but are simply collective and distributive aspects of the same thing. . . . And just as there is no society or group that is not a collective view of persons, so there is no individual who may not be regarded as a particular view of social groups. He has no separate existence; through both the hereditary and the social factors in his life a man is bound into the whole of which he is a member, and to consider him apart from it is quite as artificial as to consider society apart from individuals.

Charles Horton Cooley, *The Nature of Human Nature*, Charles Scribner's Sons, New York, 1902, pp. 1–3.

This concept of the socialized self was challenged by Freud, who saw no identity of self and society. Freud believed that the rational portion of human conduct was like the visible portion of an iceberg, with the larger part of human motivation resting in the unseen, unconscious forces which powerfully affect human conduct. He divided the self into three parts: the *superego*, the *ego*, and the *id*. The superego, or the conscience, represents the social ideals which one has internalized; the ego is the acting individual; the id represents instinctive desires which may be viewed as an unsocialized aspect of human nature. Since society restricts the expression of aggression, sexual desire, and other impulses, the id is continually at war with the superego. The id is usually repressed, but at times it breaks through in open defiance of the superego, creating a burden of guilt that is difficult for the self to carry. At other times the forces of the id find expression in disguised forms which enable the ego to be unaware of the basis of its actions, as when a parent relieves his aggressions by beating his child, believing that this is "for his own good." Thus Freud finds that the self and society are often opponents, and not merely different expressions of the same phenomena. He asserts,

If civilization imposes such great sacrifices not only on man's sexuality but upon his aggressivity we can understand better why it is hard for him to be happy in that civilization . . . .

We may expect gradually to carry through such alterations in our civilization as will better satisfy our needs and will escape our criticisms. But perhaps we may also familiarize ourselves with the idea that there are difficulties attaching to the nature of civilization which will not yield to any attempt at reform . . . .

In all that follows I adopt the standpoint, therefore, that the inclination to aggression is an original, self-subsisting instinctual disposition in man, and I return to my view that this constitutes the greatest impediment to civilization.

Sigmund Freud, *Civilization and Its Discontents, Standard Edition of the Complete Psychological Works of Sigmund Freud*, vol. 21, The Hogarth Press Ltd., London, 1961, pp. 115, 122. Quoted by permission.

Freud's theories have inspired bitter controversies, rival "schools," and numerous interpretations and revisions. His concepts represent ways of looking at personality rather than actual entitities which can be verified through specific experiments. There is no simple empirical test which can be used to determine whether the superego, ego, and id are the best possible concepts to use in describing the component parts of the human personality. As our understanding of human nature grows, we may expect to develop additional forms of analysis which will relegate Freud's concepts to the status of pioneering ventures rather than ultimate truths. The fact that theories are subject to revision and modification does not lessen the importance of their contribution. Social scientists today agree that Freud was probably right in his claim that human motives are largely unconscious and beyond rational control, and do not always harmonize with the needs of an orderly society.

Social and individual aspects of the self   On the other hand, Cooley, Mead, and many others have demonstrated that the very emergence of the self is a social process. From this social process, however, a self emerges which is not altogether harmonious with the society that created it. Man's readiness to respond to sexual stimuli is far greater than any society has felt could be safely permitted, and his tendency to meet any kind of frustration with aggressive violence must likewise be restrained in the interest of social order. Further, he may lack the type of physical stature, the muscular coordination, or the ability to engage in complex thinking which his society values. The ability of the individual to develop a self in harmony with the image his society prefers may depend, at least in part, on his possession of biological traits needed to match the social image. In a society rewarding tallness or thinness, the short and fat are likely to feel that they are social misfits, and neither girdles nor elevator shoes can completely conceal the discrepancy between the biological reality and social expectations.

Multiple groups and socialization   Another reason for lack of harmony between the self and society is that society itself is torn by conflict, and the individual is presented with models of behavior which are rewarded at one time and condemned at another, or approved by some groups and criticized by others. Thus the boy learns that he should be tough and able to "stand up for his rights" and at the same time that he should be orderly, considerate, and respectful. Some people caution the girl that society demands modesty and maidenly reserve, while others show how a bold, provocative approach is rewarded. In a society where the individual participates in a number of groups, often with conflicting standards and values, he must work out some way of dealing with these opposing pressures. Failure to do so is likely to bring personal maladjustment and even mental illness. He may deal with this problem by compartmentalizing his life, developing a different "self" for each group in which he moves. Or he may select a favorite reference group to conform to and have his real life within, rejecting other groups, as in the case below:

"Thirteen arrests." The judge shook his head over my file. "Gang fightings, shootings, burglary, stealing a car . . . I don't know what to make of you. Your parents are hardworking, religious people in pretty good circumstances. Your IQ is extraordinarily high. Why do you do these things?"

I shrugged. What a dumb question. Every boy I knew did these things. Maybe I just did more of them and better.

"A Gang Leader's Redemption," *Life,* Apr. 28, 1958, pp. 69ff.

This boy had adopted the standards of a delinquent peer group rather than those of his family. Research studies [Warner and Lunt, 1941, p. 351; Rosen, 1955 b] have usually emphasized the power of the peer group to cultivate behavior patterns contrary to those of the family. Not all youth, however, are as firmly wedded to peer-group standards, and not all peer groups are as much in conflict with family or the society. Most youths find their principal extra-family group allegiance in athletic teams, church youth groups, neighborhood clubs, or youth cliques which are in harmony with the standards of adult society. Such groups frequently operate to support the parental standards, as seen in this case:

Bill was a late adolescent who began to run around with a girl who not only lived on the other side of the railroad tracks, but who had most of the traits associated with that oft-used phrase. Bill's family was upper class, Bill was personally most attractive, and his mother knew the power of a peer group. Calling Bill to her, she explained with disarming friendliness that she had heard of his new girl and wanted to meet her. Wouldn't he bring her to the house, and to make it less formal, she would invite a few of his favorite friends. Upon securing Bill's wondering and semireluctant consent, the mother proceeded to promote, secretly, a gala event, to which she invited all of Bill's extended clique. Bill's relations with the new girl just barely survived until the end of the party.

James H. S. Bossard, *The Sociology of Child Development,* Harper & Row, Publishers, Incorporated, 1948, p. 507.

Why do some youths select peer groups which generally support the socially approved adult values while others choose peer groups which are at war with adult society? The choice seems to be related to self-image. The habitual delinquent is usually one who sees himself as unloved, unworthy, unable, unaccepted, unappreciated; he joins with other such deprived youth in a delinquent peer group which reinforces and sanctions his resentful, aggressive behavior. The law-abiding youth sees himself as loved, worthy, able, accepted, appreciated; he joins with other such youth in a conforming peer group which reinforces socially approved behavior. Truly, seeing is behaving. How we see ourselves is how we behave.

Unique experience and socialization   Why is it that children raised in the same family are so different from one another, even though they have had the same experiences? The point is that they have *not* had the same experiences; they have had social experiences which are similar in some respects and different in others. Each child enters a different family unit. One is the firstborn; he is the only child until the arrival of the second, who has an older brother or sister to fight with, and so on. Parents change, and do not treat all their children exactly alike. The children enter different peer groups, may have different teachers and survive different incidents. Identical twins, in addition to having identical heredity, come very close to having the same experience. They enter a family together, often have the same peer groups, and are treated more nearly alike by other people; yet even twins do not share *all* incidents and experiences. *Each person's experience is unique in that nobody else perfectly duplicates it.* A detailed inventory of the daily experiences of the several children in the same family will reveal an impressive number of differences. So each child (excepting identical twins) has a unique biological inheritance, exactly duplicated by no one, and a unique set of life experiences, exactly duplicated by no one.

Furthermore, *experiences do not simply add up; they integrate.* Personality is not built by piling one incident upon another, like a brick wall. The meaning and impact of an experience depends upon the other experiences which have preceded it. When a popular girl is "stood up" by her date, this is not the same experience for her as it is for the wallflower. Psychoanalysis claims that certain incidents in one's experience are crucial because they color one's reaction to all later experience. "Psychological" movies often imply that psychoanalysis consists of probing into one's unconscious and dredging up *the* traumatic experience which caused all the trouble. This is a gross oversimplification. No woman has had her personality blighted *because* papa stomped on her dollie when she was five. But it is possible that such a traumatic episode might become the beginning of a series of mutual rejection experiences and thus color the meaning of a great many later experiences. This means that each person's experience is an infinitely complicated network of millions of incidents, each gaining its meaning and impact from all those which have preceeded it. Small wonder that personality is complex!

Still another factor appears in the selection of roles to play within the family. Children imitate each other a great deal, but they also strive for separate identities. Younger children often reject those activities which their older siblings already do well and seek recognition through other activities. Parents may unwittingly aid this selection process. Mother may say, "Susie is mama's little helper, but I guess Annie is going to be a tomboy," whereupon Susie starts clearing the table while Annie turns a few handsprings. Sometimes a child in a well-behaved family selects the "badboy" role, and scowls impressively while his parents describe their problem to the visitors. In large families a child may be hard pressed to find a role which has not already been annexed by an older sibling. Thus, in these and many other respects, each person's life experience is unique— unique in that nobody else has had exactly this set of experiences, and unique in that nobody else has the same background of experience upon which each new incident will impinge and draw its meaning.

SUMMARY

Personality is one's total behavior tendency system. Our *heredity* gives us a set of needs and potentialities which other factors may channel and develop; our *physical environment* sets certain limits to our behavior; our *culture* provides certain fairly uniform experiences for all members of our society; our *group experience* develops personality similarities within groups and differences between groups; the *unique experience* of each person shapes his individuality.

The normal personality differs dramatically from society to society, as is shown by the suspicious, treacherous, insecure Dobuan and the amiable, secure, cooperative Zuñi. Each society develops a normal personality, produced by the total experience of a person raised in the society. Such cultural influences include the norms of the culture, the ideal personality types presented as models, and many other kinds of experience. All these influences tend to develop a modal personality type for the society.

The more complex societies may have a number of subcultures, each developing its characteristic personality, and reducing the overall uniformity of personality within the culture. Even in the simpler societies, there is no complete uniformity in personality; only a minority of the members share all the traits of the modal personality. In complex societies, the variation in personailty is still greater.

Socialization requires group experience, and *social isolates* fail to develop a normal human personality. Socialization is heavily centered upon the development of the concept of *self*. One's image of self is largely perceived in the looking glass of other people's reactions to him and his feelings about these perceptions. Through play and other group activities, one is also helped to perceive the feelings of others and their feelings toward him. Cooley viewed self and society as two aspects of the same thing, whereas Freud viewed self as basically antisocial, with most personality difficulties arising from the clash between the impulses of the self and the restraints of society.

In the complex culture with many kinds of groups, one may have difficulty in developing a satisfactory self image and an integrated system of behavior. One may resolve this problem by compartmentalizing his life and acting differently in each group, or by conforming to one group while, if possible, ignoring any others whose standards conflict. Failure to do either may bring confusion and maladjustment. While there are common elements in the experience of all men and even more in the experience of men within a particular society, each man is still unique. Thus each man is socialized in such a way that his personality is at the same time much like that of others in his society and yet unique.

QUESTIONS AND PROJECTS

1. How do we know that personality is not simply the maturing and unfolding of inherited tendencies?

2. What might be some possible differences in social life and human personality if human infants were normally born (and nursed) in litters instead of one at a time?

3. Is the influence of physical environment upon culture increasing or diminishing? Why?

4. It has been said that a person raised in one culture may learn to act like people in an adopted culture, but will never be able to think and feel like a person of his adopted culture. Do you agree?

5. Suppose the Dobuans were visited by a person who persistently acted in a straightforward, trusting, confident manner. Tell why you believe they would, or would not:
a. Admire him
b. Copy him
c. Fear him
d. Pity him

6. If culture develops similarities in personality within a society, how do we explain personality differences within a society? Are such personality differences greater within a simple or a complex society? Why?

7. How would you explain the fact that groups which have a major socializing influence upon one person may leave another person in the same vicinity unaffected?

8. Can you recall a specific "looking-glass" incident in your experience? Write it up, describing your actions, others' reactions, your perception of their reactions, and your feelings about that perception. How do you think this incident affected you?

9. How is the self a social product?

10. How do games contribute to the development of the self?

11. Do you feel that Freud and Cooley are in basic disagreement on the nature of the self? Explain.

12. How can children in the same family develop such strikingly different personality traits?

13. Write an account of a typical day in your life, listing all the standardizing cultural influences which you have experienced along with nearly every other American, and state how you suspect each has helped to shape your personality.

14. Prepare an analysis of the behavior of "Yank," the fireman in Eugene O'Neill's The Hairy Ape. Is his behavior consistent with what this chapter outlines about others and the concept of self?

SUGGESTED READINGS

*BENEDICT, RUTH: *Patterns of Culture,* Houghton Mifflin Company, Boston, 1934; Penguin Books, Inc., Baltimore, 1946. Shows how each culture develops a behavior and personality which is normal and useful for that society. (8-SEN ED)

BERREMAN, GERALD D.: "Aleut Group Alienation, Mobility and Acculturation," *American Anthropologist,* 66:231–250, April, 1964. A comparison of Aleuts who became alienated from Aleutian culture with those who remain loyal to the Aleut membership group, and the problem of retaining loyalty to an original ethnic group while becoming acculturated to a new one.

BRONFENBRENNER, URIE: "The Changing American Child—A Speculative Analysis," *Merrill-Palmer Quarterly of Behavior and Development,* 7:73–84, April, 1961; reprinted in THOMAS E. LASSWELL, ET AL., *Life in Society,* Scott, Foresman and Company, Chicago, 1965. Appraises the effect of cold war competition in stimulating a shift from socialization for conformity to socialization for achievement.

GARABEDIAN, PETER G.: "Socialization in the Prison Community," *Social Problems,* 2:139–152, Fall, 1963. How "square Johns" learn to become "right guys" according to the definition of prison inmates.

*GOFFMAN, ERVING: *Presentation of Self in Everyday Life,* Social Science Research Center, University of Edinburgh, 1956; Anchor paperback, Doubleday & Company, Inc., Garden City, N.Y., 1959. A detailed picture of how the self emerges through everyday experiences. (A174-ANCH)

HAVIGHURST, ROBERT J., AND ALLISON DAVIS: "A Comparison of the Chicage and Harvard Studies of Social Class Differences in Child Rearing," *American Sociological Review,* 20:438–442, August, 1955. Two separate studies show that cultural influences on personality development differ from one social-class subculture to another, and also differ by region, religion, and ethnic group within the same social class.

KUHN, MANFORD: "Self-attitudes by Age, Sex, and Professional Training," *Sociological Quarterly,* 1:39–55, January, 1960. Exploration of self-attitudes by members of different social categories through use of the Twenty Questions Test.

LEZNOFF, MAURICE, AND WILLIAM A. WESTLEY: "The Homosexual Community," *Social Problems,* 3:257–264, April, 1956. Describes efforts of homosexuals in a Canadian city to organize a "third-sex" community.

*MEAD, MARGARET, AND MARTHA WOLFENSTEIN (EDS.): *Childhood in Contemporary Cultures,* The University of Chicago Press, Chicago, 1955. A number of studies of patterns of child development in different cultures. (P124-PHOEN)

MERRILL, FRANCIS E.: "The Self and the Other: An Emerging Field of Social Problems," *Social Problems,* 4:200–207, January, 1957. An analysis of anxiety over others' image of the self in a society stressing achieved status.

RIESMAN, DAVID: "Some Questions about the Study of American National Character in the Twentieth Century," *The Annals of the American Academy of Political and Social Science,* 370:36–47, March, 1967. One of a series of articles in an issue devoted to national character; other articles consider Canada, Brazil, Mexico, England, France, Sweden, Russia, Israel, Japan, and China.

ROLE AND STATUS

On my third day at the hotel the chef du personnel, *who had generally spoken to me in quite a pleasant tone, called me up and said sharply:*

"Here, you, shave that moustache off at once! Nom de dieu, who ever heard of a plongeur with a moustache?"

I began to protest, but he cut me short. "A plongeur with a moustache—nonsense! Take care I don't see you with it tomorrow."

On the way home I asked Boris what this meant. He shrugged his shoulders. "You must do what he says, mon ami. *No one in the hotel wears a moustache, except the cooks. I should have thought you would have noticed it. Reason? There is no reason. It is the custom."* (George Orwell, *Down and Out in Paris and London,* Harcourt, Brace & World, Inc., New York, 1933.)

STATUS IS usually defined as the *rank or position of an individual in a group,* or of a group in relation to other groups. (In fact, some sociologists use the term *position* instead of *status.*) *Role* refers to the *behavior of one who occupies a certain status.* Children occupy a status usually subordinate to adults and are expected to show some degree of deference to adult authority. Soldiers occupy a status different from that of civilians, and their role calls for risks and duties which the general populace is not expected to bear. Women have a different status from men; their role calls for "feminine" behavior. Each person may occupy a number of statuses and be expected to perform the roles appropriate to them. In a sense, "status" and "role" are two words for the same phenomenon. A status is a set of privileges and duties; a role is the acting out of this set of duties and privileges.

SOCIALIZATION THROUGH ROLE AND STATUS

We become socialized largely through learning our roles. We must learn to fill roles as child, student, parent, employee, organization member or officer, member of a particular racial and social class, citizen, resident of a community, and many others. Role learning involves at least two aspects: (1) We must learn to perform the duties and claim the privileges of the role, and (2) we must acquire the attitudes, feelings, and expectations appropriate to the role. Of these two aspects the latter is often the more important. Almost any young woman who can read can learn the mechanical skills of housekeeping fairly quickly; what she cannot learn quickly are the attitudes and expectations which make housekeeping a satisfying and rewarding activity. One cannot fill a role successfully unless he has been socialized to accept that role as worthwhile, satisfying, and appropriate for him.

Imagine the mental state of a young German Jew, raised in a prosperous, cultivated home, who graduated from medical school just as the Nazi government closed the professions to Jews; at best, he could work only as a menial and live only as an outcast. Or consider the difficulties of a woman who has been socialized to view the role of housewife as the only really rewarding role for a woman, but who finds herself an unmarried career girl living alone and competing in a man's world.

Role training for most of the important roles begins early in childhood as one starts to form attitudes toward those roles and statuses. Most of the role training is painless and unconscious. Children "play house," play with the toys given them, watch and help mother and father, hear and read stories, listen to family talk and share in the countless incidents of family life. From all this experience, they gradually form a picture of how men and women act, and of how husbands and wives treat each other.

Social roles and personality The little child who assumes the role of his father while playing house is aware that he must think and act in a different manner than when he is simply playing his own role, that of child. At first he may have little understanding of the reasons which underlie his father's actions, but this understanding grows and his "pretend" roles will help prepare him for the time when he actually becomes a father. At a more mature level pretend role playing has been a helpful aid in assisting people to understand the reactions of others in a diagnostic and therapeutic technique known as the *psychodrama,* developed by Moreno [1940] and others. A husband, for example, may play the role of the wife while she assumes his role as they reenact in an unrehearsed dialogue some recent discussion or conflict. As each tries to play the part of the other, voicing the other's complaints and defenses, each may gain greater insight into the other's feelings and reactions.

The concept of role implies a set of expectations both of the one's own behavior and of the reciprocal behavior by other people in the situation. Whether a new role is taken on a pretend basis or as a genuine result of acquiring a new status, the person is forced to analyze the attitudes and behavior of himself and of those about him [Turner, 1956]. Obviously the self does not remain unchanged after this kind of experience. The married woman is in a different status from that of the single girl. Her role is different and in many ways she will seem a different personality. Occupational roles also produce personality changes, so that without knowing a person's occupation we may say that he "acts like" a teacher, a farmer, a businessman, or a minister. Personality and role have a reciprocal relationship in that certain personal characteristics favor or hinder the playing of social roles, while social roles in turn tend to develop the personal characteristics required. The extrovert, for instance, is a personality type who may find it easy to adjust to the role of salesman while, conversely, the daily routine of the salesman helps to develop an extroverted type of personality. Thus there is a constant interaction between role and personality.

ASCRIBED AND ACHIEVED STATUS

Linton [1936, chap. 8] has noted that statuses are of two sorts: those *ascribed* to us by our society, irrespective of individual qualities or efforts, and those we *achieve* through our own efforts.

Ascribed status and role If a society is to function efficiently, people must perform a vast number of daily chores willingly and competently. The simplest way to ensure the performance is to parcel most of the routine work of the society into a series of *ascribed* roles, and socialize people to accept and fill their ascribed roles. Since role training must therefore begin early in childhood, ascribed roles must be assigned according to some criterion which can be known in advance. Sex and age are universally used as a basis of role ascription; race, nationality, social class, and religion are also used in many societies.

Although role training may be largely unconscious, it is no less real. As a noted American educator has remarked, "Adults ask little boys what they want to be when they grow up. They ask little girls where they got that pretty dress." No wonder that by adolescence, boys are becoming concerned about careers while girls are preoccupied with baiting the man trap! This is no accident, since a major part of the socialization process consists of learning the separate activities of men and women. The little girl plays with dolls, helps mother in the housework, and is rewarded for being a "little lady," while learning that "tomboy" activities, though possibly tolerated, are not really "lady-like." The boy finds out that dolls are for girls and babies and that no worse fate can befall him than to be a "sissy." Many years of differential training, if successful, will bring boys and girls to maturity with great differences in their responses, feelings, and preferences.

In mature life, sex differentiation continues while the process of role definition becomes ever more complicated. The woman finds that she may have to become an economic provider as well as mother and housekeeper and that she must do this without robbing her husband of his masculine ego feelings. She must be an informed citizen, an intelligent conversationalist, and an active community worker, yet not neglect her primary duties in the kitchen and nursery. She must be a seductive siren, skillful, patient, and responsive, but she must also be a chaste creature, modest and demure, learning with wonderment the facts of life from the lips of her husband! She must be a skillful—but not *too* skillful—sportswoman, yet remain a feminine clinging vine. She must be a household purchasing agent, a business manager, and a financial consultant when necessary; at all other times she must be completely ignorant of money matters. Her total role as wife and mother thus includes many different roles, some of them inconsistent with one another. It is little wonder women often find it difficult to play this complex and paradoxical role.

We tend to attribute the complexity of sex roles in our society to the industrial revolution with its increase in women's occupational opportunities, but historical evidence suggests that *any* type of social change complicates the roles women perform. Before the United States became an industrial nation with women helping to man the offices and assembly lines, the pioneer women had already enlarged the feminine role:

Though careful to preserve the illusion of soft helplessness these Western dames were mostly as hard as nails. Wives of the Donner party survived that awful winter of snowbound death far better than the males. While passing through Montana in September, 1849, the men of the Riker family parked the wagon with Janette Riker in it and went hunting. They never returned. Janette kept herself alive alone in the wagon until Indians found her the following April. . . . A woman in Washington territory was planting precious seed corn, which was eaten by a rooster. When she caught on, the woman pounced on the bird, cut it open on the spot, removed the kernels and planted them again. An officer's wife carried her baby across the Arizona desert in a champagne basket. Sarah Royce rode horseback with her baby in her lap, canteen and diapers in one saddlebag, a pan in the other and necessities hanging from the pommel.

Marshal Sprague, "On the Western Trail There Was Nothing Like a Dame," *New York Times Book Review*, Apr. 20, 1958, p. 6, reviewing Dee Brown, *The Gentle Tamers: Women of the Wild West*, G. P. Putnam's Sons, New York, 1958.

Obviously, what it means to be "feminine" varies with the needs of time and place.

Nor is assuming the masculine role a simple task. The little boy must not be a sissy, but on the other hand he must become a gentleman and the line between often seems thin and tenuous. In mature life he may find himself sharing in household tasks while the little woman is on the night shift. If he wishes social approval in many groups today he finds that even the rugged male must profess an interest in the arts and take part in social life.

Every society handles many tasks by making them part of a sex role. Yet most of the sex-linked functions can be performed equally well by either men or women, provided they are socialized to accept the tasks as proper for them. Thus in Pakistan, men are the household servants; in the Philippines, pharmacists are usually women, while men are preferred as secretaries; in the Marquesas, baby tending, cooking, and housekeeping are proper male tasks, while women spend much of their time primping; in many parts of the world the heavy agricultural labor is performed by women. Occasionally there is a direct challenge to the mores which support the traditional sex roles, as in the case of the feminist movement in England and the United States during the past century; but normally the sexes accept their ascribed roles with little protest.

The definition of masculine and feminine roles is subject to infinite variation, yet every society has an approved pattern which the people are expected to follow. Individuals may be permitted to bypass some parts of the pattern at times, but they risk alienation from the society unless they can identify themselves with the role expected of their sex. A few individuals do fail to make this adjustment and become homosexuals or Lesbians, which means that they deviate from the roles expected of their own sex. While such individuals may attempt to develop a unique status for a "third sex," the task is difficult, and they usually become marginal to the culture. Only a few societies have developed an accepted status for homosexuals, for example, the Plains Indians, who consider the homosexual to be one who has been stricken by the gods and who thereby merits special consideration. In the majority of cases the homosexual is normal physically, and his condition is now viewed as a failure of socialization in relation to sex roles rather than as some type of biological deviation. Even in the case of hermaphrodites, who are biologically intermediate between the sexes, their biological "closeness" to one sex or the other is less important than the social definition of them as "boy" or "girl" by their family and others. In other words, ". . . sex orientation is much more dependent upon hair style and clothes than upon the morphologic criteria of sex." [Jones and Scott, 1958, p. 49.]

Each society also ascribes different roles according to age. The adjustment of age status is a perennial task; almost as soon as a person adjusts to one age level, he enters another with different status and role. Just at the time when the youth is beginning to master the bewildering complexities of adolescence, he finds himself facing the responsibilities of adult life. And although the adult period is the longest single time span, retirement and old age often seem to come just when one has begun to reach a position where he can fully exploit his mature power. Each age period brings different opportunities and responsibilities, which is to say that each period affords a new status and requires the learning of new roles. At any age one may have trouble in adjusting to new status and role demands. The child who is "old before his time" is one who has reached for adult status before fully realizing the potential of his childhood roles; on the other hand, the immature adult represents an attempt to combine adult status with attitudes and roles appropriate to childhood or adolescence.

In our society the socialization process is conspicuously inefficient in preparing for adolescence and for old age. In most primitive societies the adolescent period is not marked by any unusual stress. At any given age in most primitive societies, the individual has a clearly defined status and role; he, and everyone else, knows exactly what his duties and privileges are. Our society has no clearly defined age statuses, except for the relatively minor legal maturity at twenty-one. Recalling the concept of the "definition of the situation," we observe that age status in our society is an "undefined situation." The American youth and his parents have no standardized set of duties and privileges to guide them. Parents are uncertain about just how much "maturity" to concede to him, and they bicker with him endlessly about his choice of companions, the hours he keeps, his use of money, the use of the car, and whether he is old enough to marry. In most primitive societies the adolescent enters a period of training which ends in an elaborate ceremony, in which he may endure ordeals or submit to circumcision, tattooing, or scarification. Such ceremonies, called "rites of passage," establish his status and announce that the youth is now ready to assume adult responsibilities, and his successful role performance is almost guaranteed. Our closest equivalents are found in such events as confirmation or first Communion, getting a driver's license, holding a full-time job, graduating from high school or college, and getting married. Yet we lack any systematic preparation, or any general agreement upon the age, achievement, or type of ceremony which clearly establishes the transition into adult status.

The youth in primitive societies has few painful choices to make. He has little freedom, but little anxiety. There are no competing religious groups, political parties, or social clubs. Since occupations are limited, the youth escapes conflicting advice on the type of career he should choose. Religion, government, social activities, educational training, and occupation—all these are traditional and clearly defined. By contrast the American youth learns that there are 250 different churches and that he may select from, or even reject them all; his political views, if any, often conflict with those of his parents; he must choose between continuing school and the instant pleasures of a car and spending money; in earning a living a young man must choose among thousands of occupations. With so many alternatives, it is small wonder that many youths vacillate wildly before settling down or that others make decisions contrary to their parents' hopes and dreams.

The transition to middle age is not a happy one in our society, especially for women. Our accent on youth and glamour dooms every woman to feel her desirability slipping away from her. The menopause is a relentless announcement that youth, glamour, and romance are over; instead, she can become "matronly." Plastic surgeons, cosmeticians, and beauticians make fortunes by catering to women's futile efforts to stave off the ravages of time. We suspect that many of the physical and emotional difficulties that sometimes accompany the menopause are due to this painful role transition. And for men, the middle years are rightfully called the "dangerous age."

Old age in many primitive or traditional societies is highly honored, perhaps because in such a society the ancient are closest to the source of hallowed tradition. Thus in pre-Communist China the grandmother was the reigning female in a multiple-family home, and the grandfather was a patriarch whose whim was close to law. In contemporary industrialized society old age is a nuisance. A rapidly changing society looks for wisdom, not to the past but to the future, for people who were socialized two generations ago are likely to be behind the times. The compulsory retirement-at-age-sixty-five system is an expedient way of discarding the fossils. Multiple-family homes are scarce, and where they exist the aged are likely to be dutifully tolerated rather than revered as heads of the household. The role of the aged is a retirement in which their income is reduced, their responsibilities withdrawn, and their influence undermined; while their main function in life is to divert themselves while waiting to die. The unhappy position of our aged illustrates the fact that a role transition is difficult when the characteristics which one develops in one role may become useless or even troublesome as he moves into the next role.

Among the Plains Indians, the warriors were trained from childhood to become aggressive, hostile, and uncompromising; then upon retirement to "old man" status, they were expected to be placid peacemakers. This called for an abrupt reversal in personality, and few of them could make the transition gracefully. An equally painful transition is demanded in our society. To be successful in the active adult role, one must develop independence and self-reliance, must learn to find satisfaction in useful work, and in being adviser and protector of the young. As an aged person, he must become dependent and submissive, able to respect himself with no useful work to do, and must learn to keep his advice to himself while being ignored or patronized by the young. Is it little wonder that many of our old people sicken and die soon after retirement, while many others become bored and fretful? The rapidly developing field of *geriatrics* indicates a serious concern with this topic, and the picture may change in the future. One such change is emphasis on the development of hobbies and activities that may be expanded on retirement since they are not associated either with the family or the job. Another trend is the growth of specialized facilities which may provide pleasant living in a society segregated on an age basis. These include housing, either in rest homes or specially designed apartments; recreation centers, often given some name such as the Golden Years Club; or even the development of an entire village as a living place for retired people, such as Ryderwood, near Longview, Washington. These trends are already changing the status of elderly people, but at present their role involves difficult adjustments at a time of life when such adjustments are not easy to make.

Sex and age are only two of many examples of ascribed status. All such statuses involve roles which can be filled successfully only when one has been socialized to expect and appreciate the role.

Achieved status and role   A social position which is secured through individual choice and competition is known as *achieved status*. Just as each person occupies a number of ascribed statuses, assigned without regard to individual ability or preference, so he occupies a number of achieved statuses which are secured through his ability, performance, and possibly good or ill fortune. The difference is aptly stated by Young and Mack:

"Princess" is an ascribed status; where there is a hereditary royalty a girl does not work her way up to being princess. She is born a princess, and whether she is pretty or ugly, tall or short, intelligent or stupid, a princess she remains. Achieved statuses, on the other hand, are not assigned at birth, but are left open to be filled by the persons who compete most successfully for them. Being male is an ascribed status.

It is determined at birth; either you are male or you are not. Being a husband is an achieved status; it does not result automatically from one's being born a male but depends upon a male's own behavior in the future. Negro is an ascribed status. One cannot change his color to white. But policeman is an achieved status. One is not born a policeman; he becomes one through his own talent or choice or action.

Kimball Young and Raymond W. Mack, *Sociology and Social Life,* American Book Company, New York, 1959, pp. 160–161.

Being a husband is an achieved status.

In traditional societies most statuses are ascribed, with one's occupation and general social standing determined at birth. Industrialized societies have a greater range of occupations, require a greater mobility of labor, and allow greater scope for the individual to change his status through his own efforts. The society stressing achieved status will gain in flexibility and in its ability to place people in occupations best suited to their talents. The price it pays for these advantages is seen in the insecurity of those unable to "find themselves" and in the strain of constant adjustment to new roles. Achieved status requires the individual to make choices, not only of occupation but also of friends, organizations, schools, and place of residence. Further, it leads the individual into roles which were not foreseen or desired by his parents. In the traditional society, where statuses and roles are ascribed, the individual is trained from childhood and guided through life by rules of conduct, which he has carefully learned in preparation for the roles he is destined to play. In a changing society where he is free to experiment, the individual meets situations far removed from the parental way of life and may have to feel his way awkwardly into unfamiliar roles.

Ascribed and achieved statuses are basically different; yet they interact with each other and may overlap. Thus it is easier for one with the ascribed status of male to reach the achieved status of President of the United States than it is for the one with the ascribed status of female. The achieved status of physician is open to both Negro and white, but in the United States whites reach it more easily than Negroes. General social standing in the community (social-class status) is partly ascribed, reflecting the status of one's parents, and partly achieved through one's own accomplishments. At many points the boundaries between achieved and ascribed status are indistinct; yet the concepts are useful.

ROLE CONFLICT AND PERSONALITY

Many of man's personality difficulties and maladjustments can be analyzed and better understood in terms of role incompatibilities and conflicts. In saying this, we do not deny the existence of the genetic or biological factor in personality disorder which is discussed in Chapter 7. It is agreed that whether people develop personality disorders depends partly upon their biological inheritance and partly upon the emotional stress they experience. Role conflicts are a major source of emotional stress and thus contribute to personality disorders. Role conflicts and role inadequacies are of several kinds.

Inadequate role preparation The little girl singing lullabies to her doll, the small boy building a model airplane, the maiden filling her hope chest, the apprentice copying the work techniques of the mastercraftsmen—all these are experiencing a *continuity of socialization* by learning skills and attitudes at one period of life which they can use at another. A classic summation of this process is attributed to the Duke of Wellington: "The battle of Waterloo was won on the playing fields of Eton." By continuity in socialization we simply mean that the experiences at each life stage are an effective preparation for the next stage. An example of how continuity in the socialization process provides a smooth transition into the adult role is seen in the child-training practices of the Cheyenne Indians, as described by Benedict.

> *The essential point of such child training is that the child is from infancy continuously conditioned to responsble social participation while at the same time the tasks that are expected of it are adapted to its capacity. . . . At birth the little boy was presented with a toy bow and from the time he could run about serviceable bows suited to his stature were specially made for him by the man of the family. Animals and birds were taught him in a graded series beginning with those most easily taken, and as he brought in his first of each species his family duly made a feast of it, accepting his contribution as gravely as the buffalo his father brought. When he finally killed a buffalo, it was only the final step of his childhood conditioning, not a new adult role with which his childhood experience has been at variance.*

Ruth Benedict, "Continuities and Discontinuities in Cultural Conditioning," *Psychiatry,* 1:161–167, May, 1938.

Such an easy transition from one status to the next is by no means universal. Our culture is characterized by built-in *discontinuities,* which make the socialization experience in one age period of little use in the next. In frontier America, boys and girls learned their adult roles by simply observing and taking part in whatever was going on around them—clearing land, planting crops, caring for babies, and so on. Today there is less opportunity for such continuity. Most adult male work is performed away from home, where boys and youths cannot watch and share it. Many households offer only a poor opportunity for a girl to learn the skills, attitudes, and emotional rewards of the housewife. Children and youths have few important tasks in most households, and much of the child's play activity is not closely related

Our culture is characterized by built-in discontinuities.

to adult tasks and responsibilities. Our maidens find that when they have internalized the roles of glamour girl and career woman as presented in magazines and movies, they are suddenly enveloped in maternity and housekeeping duties for which their previous experience has done little to prepare them. Then when they have become adapted to the housewife role, their children leave home, their housekeeping responsibilities diminish, and they must either face a late middle age of limited activity or transfer to roles much different from those they have known. Boys associate athletics with team sports such as basketball and football which are difficult for them to play in later life; thus even the athletic youth may learn a form of recreation which will not provide the physical activity he needs as an adult. When men reach the age of sixty-five they are apt to find that a life dominated by work has not prepared them for the leisure which comes with retirement.

Another imperfection in our socialization process is that the moral training of boys and girls introduces them mainly to the *formal* rules of social behavior rather than to the informal modifications of these rules which operate in the adult world. In other words, they are taught the ideal, not the real culture. The result is that young people become cynical as they find that the copybook maxims do not work out. The politician does not appear to be a public servant who negotiates a livable situation between bitter opponents, but a man who compromises on sacred principles; the businessman seems a greedy manipulator rather than an individual struggling to find his place in the market; the clergyman is apparently not one who mediates the ways of God to man, but a huckster who fails to live up to the ideals of *Holy Writ*. Thus we run the gamut from youthful idealism to mature cynicism without ever reaching an understanding of culture which can enable us to appreciate the services of those who work out livable compromises with the unsolved problems of society.

Some gap between the formal expressions of the mores and the actual adjustments of social life is probably found in all societies. The gap is probably far greater in a world so complex that the young have to find a considerable part of their socialization in separate educational institutions. Laboratory work, field experience, and "life-adjustment" education may narrow this gap, but there will probably always be some opposition between the precepts learned in church and school and the practices which hold sway in our competitive economic and social system.

Such discontinuities are also favored by rapid social change, since parents cannot possibly anticipate the type of world their children will face. While the emergence of new inventions is often recognized as a disrupting factor, the changing social climate is equally unpredictable. Thus the parent in Ceylon, who in the 1920s looked on Christianity as the religion of the enlightened and powerful, raised children who sometimes find this religious affiliation a social handicap, now that Buddhism has become identified with resurgent nationalism in a newly independent country. Conversely, the African, trained as a child to respect the traditions of the tribe and the authority of the chief, may grow up to live as an urban laborer in a culture where chiefs are powerless and tribal traditions are irrelevant. The American farmer may carefully train his children in the attitudes and techniques appropriate to farming, although it is a predictable certainty that many of these children are headed for an urban life and work.

Such examples could be multiplied indefinitely. They add up to the premise that it is impossible to prepare young people for precisely the roles they will play as adults in a changing society. Margaret Mead [1941] observes that the family and the school are adjusting to this situation by emphasizing the development of a broad range of qualities rather than attempting to prepare students for specific roles. Instead of training Susie to be a wife and mother *or* training her to be a career girl, Susie's home and school try to prepare her to fill either or both of these roles, as the occasion may demand. Thus "adjustment" is preferred to rote learning and students are introduced to "methods of thinking" rather than being trained in specific vocational techniques which may soon be outmoded. The rapidity of change in our day may make even such generalized training of doubtful help in meeting major shifts in roles, and the presence of cultural discontinuities is a part of the price we pay for rapid social change.

Conflicting roles   Not only does one fill a succession of roles throughout life; he also fills a number of roles at the same time. In our society a man may be filling roles as male, husband, father, son (to his aged parents), churchman, manager of a business enterprise, officer in the chamber of commerce, member of the local school board, and several others. In a complex and changing society like ours, he will almost inevitably find some of these roles in conflict with one another.

Cultural conflicts become upsetting to the individual when they produce conflicting role pressures upon him. Cultural conflicts and inconsistencies are probably found in every culture. In well-integrated cultures, these inconsistencies are so well rationalized, compartmentalized, and fenced off from one another that the individual does not sense them at all. Thus many primitives who treated one another with great tenderness were ruthlessly cruel to outsiders; their humanitarian mores applied only to tribal fellows, while outsiders were considered and treated like any other animals of the forest. By contrast, our belief in a universal God of all mankind makes it harder for us to bomb our enemies with a clear conscience. Our belief in democracy and our denial of equality to women and Negroes caused us few qualms as long as we believed that women and Negroes were on an intellectual level with children. *Cultural contradictions are upsetting only when they subject the individual to conflicting pressures in a situation that demands a single action.* For example, should the maiden respond to her lover's tender persuasions, or remember what her mother told her? Should the professor grade students with ruthless equality, or shade the grade of the boy who is about to lose his draft deferment (and thus send some *other* boy off to the army)? Should a government or corporation official use his authority to find positions for his relatives? In our society, such an official is not expected to find jobs for unqualified relatives, and is criticized if he does so. In many non-Western societies, his family role demands that he find jobs for as many of his relatives as possible, without too much regard to their qualifications. But in some countries now in transition to Western technology, it is becoming unclear which role takes precedence, so that family role and professional role come into conflict.

Role conflicts in our society are unavoidable. Our moral and ethical training teaches us values which are inconsistent with some of the roles we must fill. The church teaches us to be gentle, forgiving, and sympathetic, while military

He develops a wardrobe of role personalities.

training prepares our youth to be tough, aggressive, and hostile. Jesus Christ said that we should love our enemies, but pacifists are seldom admired, usually persecuted, and sometimes jailed. Our democratic ethos, as reflected in orations, legends, slogans, and schoolbooks, teaches us to be individualistic and independent, to stand up for our rights, and not to allow ourselves to be "pushed around." But when members of racial minorities follow this course of action, they court severe reprisals. Family and church encourage us to be generous, self-sacrificing, and helpful to the weak; an indiscriminate application of these virtues in the business world would guarantee bankruptcy.

If one is successfully socialized, he develops a wardrobe of role personalities, and slips into one or another as the situation demands. At home he is tender and indulgent; while working at the office he is brisk and formal. This process of switching role personalities creates emotional strain whenever the attitudes called for in one role clash sharply with those needed in the other. Many a businessman, faced with the necessity of laying off employees, finds it painful to ignore their human needs and treat them impersonally as "cost factors in production." The dishonesties, deceptions, and exploitations that are a part of many occupational roles are inconsistent with the usual moral and religious training. If the individual is not fully successful in fencing his behavior off into compartments, these cultural contradictions become mental conflicts within the individual. Some psychiatrists [Horney, 1937] hold that such culture conflicts, and the mental conflicts they produce, are major causes of personality disorder.

Not only must the individual reconcile the conflicting pressures of his different roles; sometimes there are conflicting pressures and demands within a single role itself. For example, the clergy or priests in a well-integrated society have a definitely established role which places them in a relatively well-understood position in relation to the rest of society. Today, however, clergymen of all faiths in our society complain of being asked to be many things to many men. A priest may find it difficult to be at once a prophet, an executive, a hail-fellow-well-met, an ascetic saint, a social group worker, and a spiritual philosopher. The following statement suggests that even the ministers of churches like the Pentecostalists, who deliberately seek to separate themselves absolutely from "wordly" affairs are still beset by role conflicts.

In testimonies and even sermons frequent contrast is made between divine election and "futile" book-learning and schooling. . . . There is a strong distrust of Catholic and Anglican priests, and the role of the ministry in the movement must always be distinguished from that of a priesthood, and its status consequently diminished.

Pentecostalists, however, do necessarily if involuntarily, accept the status system of the society at large and consequently their status assumptions oscillate between this and that of the sect itself. The professional minister is very differently placed in these two systems—there are pronounced status contradictions. Undoubtedly, the minister is accorded status in the sect because of symbols such as ministerial dress, which, up to a point, evoke responses more typical of society at large than of the sect and set him above the status ordering within the group. Yet he must not presume too much, and it is interesting that he will not infrequently conduct meetings, particularly midweek meetings, in ordinary dress.

Pentecostalists, like most sectarians, though despising the world, often accept worldly estimates of themselves or their activities when these are favorable, if, for example, an Elim minister is shown respect in public or in the press. The enjoyment of privileges in common with other ministers has not, however, been without its problem; this is particularly true of the exemption from military service granted to Pentecostal ministers in the second World War. This lifted the ministry from its lay following by according it privileges for which other members had to fight as rights of conscience in the law courts. . . .

That the Pentecostal ministry has assumed conventional clerical garb indicates a search for status outside the movement and perhaps also inside. Yet the minister is aware that even though, as a minister, he enjoys relatively high status, as a Pentecostalist, his social status is low. And even high status is, for the sect, tainted: it were better to be despised among men. . . .

Bryan R. Wilson, "The Pentecostalist Minister: Role Conflicts and Status Contradictions," *American Journal of Sociology*, 54:503–504, March, 1959.

Other roles in our society are beset with similar internal uncertainties. Should a wife and mother stay home and take good care of her husband and children, or should she take a job so that the family can live better? Our culture presses her to do both, and this is impossible. According to Komarovsky [1946 a], neither role is, therefore, completely satisfying or free of guilt. From role uncertainties and conflicts such as these come much of the mental conflict and tension of our age.

Role failure In a stable, well-integrated society with a high proportion of ascribed roles, most people fill these roles successfully. Most of the roles in any society can be filled by almost any member, if he has been adequately prepared for them. But in a rapidly changing and less well-integrated society like ours, where we cannot predict all adult roles in advance and where discontinuities limit role preparation, a good deal of role failure is inevitable. Some persons even fail in their ascribed roles of male and female, as in the case of the homosexual, or of the woman with the complex of hostile, resentful, and aggressive attitudes toward men which is called the *masculine-protest* pattern, or of the man who never outgrows his dependence upon mother. Even more persons fail in some of their achieved roles. Some of them fail to achieve the role they court—the boy fails to become a physician or executive, or the girl fails to get a husband and become a wife and mother. Others achieve a role but fail to fill it successfully. Many husbands and wives fail as marital partners, and face either the often shattering experience of divorce or a lifetime of mutual frustration. Many parents fail to socialize their children successfully. Only a few in any occupation or profession can be spectacularly successful, because for each manager there must be many subordinates. Those who crave the highest levels of a particular role are usually frustrated. Role failures of many kinds and degrees keep providing recruits for the relief rolls and the mental hospitals.

Role personality versus true personality

Each role requires a certain series of personality traits if it is to be filled successfully. These traits may or may not be those most truly characteristic of the individual. For the ascribed roles and statuses, enough role preparation usually ensures that little clash will occur between role personality and true personality. Thus most adult males can fill the male role simply by "being themselves."

For the achieved roles and statuses, which often are not selected until after one's adult personality has already been formed, a divergence between role and true personalities is fairly common. For instance, in the role of salesman a man needs to be friendly, extroverted, and perceptive of the reactions of others. Suppose his true personality is shy, withdrawn, contemplative, and insensitive to the reactions of others. Such a person is unlikely to become a salesman or to succeed as one. If he does succeed, he does it by masking his true personality with an outward show of friendliness and a deliberately cultivated attentiveness to the clues to other's reactions. This role playing is not easy to accomplish successfully and may entail a good deal of emotional strain. If done successfully over a long period of time, however, the true personality may gradually be modified to come closer to the status personality. Mrs. Eleanor Roosevelt was a rather shy young woman and a hesitant and reluctant public speaker. In her role as wife to a politically ambitious but physically handicapped husband, she forced herself into vigorous political activity and became an eloquent speaker. Apparently she found the role a rewarding one, for long after her husband's death she accepted a diplomatic appointment, remained a tireless world traveler and public speaker, and became perhaps the most remarkable woman of her age. On the other hand, the wives of several men prominent in public life have rejected the role of politician's wife and divorced their husbands.

It is likely that a good deal of success and failure in achieved roles is explained by the degree to which the true personality coincides with the required role personality. Personnel management today is much concerned with this coincidence and uses job analyses, psychological tests, depth interviews, and other devices in an effort to fit people into jobs where there will be little clash between true and role personalities.

Psychic costs of achieved status

The ideal of the society which permits most statuses to be achieved is to place people according to their abilities. To some extent, this effort enables the highly talented to move upward, but it also destroys the alibi of the failures. In a society where most status is ascribed, the individual is not expected to improve his lot. He receives low rewards and little prestige, but he does not feel any guilt in occupying the lowly position in which society has placed him. He is taught that his role and status are right and proper. He can take pride in his accomplishments without any need to compare them with those of persons in other statuses. He is freed from the sense of insecurity, the nagging of ambition, or the sting of failure. Socialization is eased because he is not expected to change his status; he has only to learn and accept his social roles.

It is difficult to rationalize low status when hereditary barriers are removed and positions are open to all on the basis of ability. If positions are filled on competitive examinations and if schooling is free to everybody, then the reason for low status must be incompetence, and this is not a comfortable explanation. The low-caste person in India could blame his status on the inexorable laws of the universe; the American university student who fails to graduate is hard put to it to find a similar justification. In self-defense the mediocre generally support the attempt to limit achievement by the imposition of seniority rules, group quotas, veterans' preference, and similar techniques to assure that the "right" people get the proper rewards.

Achieved status makes maximum provision for the attainment of roles on the basis of individual ability. It provides a high degree of choice and flexibility at the cost of psychic insecurity for the individual who has limited talents or has unequal opportunity to develop and employ them. The roles which accompany achieved statuses may be difficult to learn and mutually conflicting. In essence the achieved status probably represents both the most efficient use of the human potential and the greatest threat to the individual's peace of mind.

SUMMARY

Socialization takes place largely through the learning of social roles. A *role* is a cluster of duties and privileges; a *status* is the social position which these duties and privileges create. Roles and statuses are of two sorts: those which are *ascribed* to individuals according to sex, age, race, or other characteristics, and those which are *achieved* through personal choice or effort. In well-integrated, traditional societies most statuses are ascribed, while in rapidly changing societies, many statuses are open to achievement.

Role conflicts may arise in several ways. Inadequate role preparation, especially in terms of attitudes and values, makes for difficult role adjustment. One's several roles may conflict with one another; or a single role may carry conflicting duties and pressures. One may fail in role performance, with consequent injury to the self. The role personality may call for traits which are not a part of one's true personality. In such cases one may reject the role; or he may counterfeit the required role personality; eventually he may somewhat modify his true personality in the direction of the role personality. Organizing society's work by ascribing statuses ensures that most roles will be filled adequately, with a maximum of emotional security but some waste of unusual abilities. Opening many statuses to achievement probably makes more efficient use of talent, at the price of many failures and greater emotional insecurity.

QUESTIONS AND PROJECTS

1. Are *role* and *status* two separate concepts or two aspects of the same phenomenon? Explain.

2. What is the function of children's play in socialization? How does play aid in role preparation?

3. Why is it a comparatively easy task to assume one's age roles in most primitive societies? Why do we not have a clearly defined set of age roles?

4. How does our culture make old age a difficult

period? Is it a difficult period in all cultures? Analyze our old-age problem in terms of discontinuities. In terms of conflicting roles.

5. Describe the shift from the status and role of a high school student to that of college student in terms of cultural continuities and discontinuities in socialization. From civilian to soldier.

6. In role preparation for most adult roles, which is more important: the attitudes and values which make that role acceptable, or the knowledge and skills necessary to fill the role? Illustrate for the homemaker, schoolteacher, army officer, research scientist, and old-age roles.

7. Is there any conflict between your roles as college student and as son or daughter? If you are a married student, a third (and possibly a fourth) role is added. What possible role conflicts are added?

8. What social costs accompany an emphasis upon achieved status? Ascribed status?

9. In what respects is your present role as college student preparing you for later roles? In what respects is your present role experience irrelevant or even dysfunctional?

10. Are there any respects in which you are already assuming role personalities which differ from your true personality? Are you aware of any stresses which this acting a part produces?

11. Describe in some detail a role and status with which you are familiar and which involves a good deal of conflicting pressure within the role. How do persons in that role usually resolve these conflicts?

12. Describe some situation you know about in which a person has been under pressure to fill two or more conflicting roles. How did he resolve the conflict? Would you say his resolution was successful or unsuccessful?

SUGGESTED READINGS

BURCHARD, WALDO W.: "Role Conflicts of Military Chaplains," *American Sociological Review,* 19:528–535, October, 1954. Conflict between chaplain's role as clergyman and as army officer, based upon interviews with chaplains and ex-chaplains in the San Francisco Bay area.

GOWMAN, ALAN G.: "Blindness and the Role of the Companion," *Social Problems,* 4:68–75, July, 1956. The process through which the companion develops a role relationship satisfactory to the blind person and the changes which occur in the definition of the situation.

GULLAHORN, JOHN T.: "Measuring Role Conflict," *American Journal of Sociology,* 61:299–303, January, 1956. An attempt to measure role conflicts of labor union leaders.

HOFFMAN, L. W., SIDNEY ROSEN, AND RONALD LIPPETT: "Parental Cohesiveness, Child Autonomy and the Child's Role at School," *Sociometry,* 23:15–22, March, 1960. A suggestive but inconclusive attempt to link family and school roles.

KOMAROVSKY, MIRRA: "Cultural Contradictions and Sex Roles," *American Journal of Sociology,* 52:184–189, November, 1946; Bobbs-Merrill reprint S-150. A brilliant discussion of the role conflicts of the college-educated woman.

MCCORD, JOAN, AND WILLIAM MCCORD: "Effects of Parental Role Models on Criminality," *Journal of Social Issues,* 15:66–75, 1958. A study of social worker reports upon the parents of delinquents; shows that some popular ideas are unsound.

STEINMANN, ANNE: "Lack of Communication between Men and Women," *Marriage and Family Living,* 20:350–352, November, 1958. A role-centered analysis of communication difficulties between the sexes.

TURNER, RALPH H.: "The Navy Disbursing Officer as a Bureaucrat," *American Sociological Review,* 12:342–348, June, 1947; Bobbs-Merrill reprint S-295. Shows some conflicting pressures within a formal role, and some informal ways of reconciling them.

WARDWELL, WILLIAM, AND ARTHUR L. WOOD: "Extra-professional Role of the Lawyer," *American Journal of Sociology,* 61:304–307, January, 1956. A discussion of the community service responsibilities involved in the role of lawyer.

7

SOCIAL CONTROL AND SOCIAL DEVIATION

The Hawaiians had long obeyed some of the Kanawai [laws]. They had always honored fathers and mothers, and their days had been long upon the land. They had utterly abolished idols before the Longnecks [whites] came.

Theft they had dealt with in a way that had served well enough, though it could scarcely have been pleasing to Jehovah. In the old days if a man took something from one below him in the social scale, it was not stealing; for that which was taken had in reality belonged by virtue of rank of the taker. And if a commoner made off with the calabash or the weapon of a superior, the injured man could go to the thief's house and take back his possession, along with anything else he saw that he wanted.

But when the hoales *[white traders] came with their bean pots and silver spoons, their monkey wrenches and linen towels, their sawed lumber and their keen-edged axes, this method no longer served. Complaints from foreigners rang unceasingly in the governor's ears. White men did not want to go poking into native huts to find their lost articles. They wanted Boki to haul up the thief and arrange for restitution and punishment.*

Gradually the enlightened chiefs saw what they must do. Some of them put their men in irons for proven theft or set them free only to work and pay for what they had stolen. The boy prince Kauikeaouli, when his beloved kahu was found accessory to a theft, consented quickly to the man's dismissal. "My kahu must go," he declared, "or by and by the foreigners will think that I myself am guilty."

The haoles *applauded such measures. Here was a Commandment they liked to see enforced.*

Then there was the Commandment forbidding murder in a few short words. Once, if a native killed in sudden anger, it was proper for the victim's relatives to avenge the deed, unless the murderer took shelter in a place of refuge. If the guilty man were of equal rank with the victim's avenger, there might be an appeal to the king or the governor or to the chief of the district. The aggrieved one and the accused would then sit cross-legged in the judge's yard and each would eloquently argue his case till the magistrate made his decision.

But these customs failed when Honolulu swarmed with hot-headed sailors, and brown and white alike drank rum and got huhu *[very angry]. Again, as with theft, the traders wanted stern laws, strictly enforced, so that the riffraff of all nations would think twice before bashing their fellows on the head. They told the chiefs to build a lofty engine of death which would string up a murderer by the neck and leave him hanging limp from a rope's end—a potent reminder to the living to restrain themselves.* (Reprinted by permission of Dodd, Mead & Company from *Grapes of Canaan* by Albertine Loomis, pp. 227–229. Copyright 1951 by Albertine Loomis.)

THE COLLAPSE of law and order when the European traders brought changes and new problems to Hawaii could be duplicated in many other lands. Changes in a society demand changes in its ways of maintaining social order. When the Hawaiian chiefs were shifting from their traditional customs to the jails and gallows suggested by the traders, they were seeking to adjust the techniques of social control to the needs of changing times—a problem which is a continuous concern of every modern society.

The study of *social control*—the means through which people are led to fill their roles as expected—begins with the study of the social order within which people interact. Consider, for example, the orderly arrangements which underlie the bustling confusion of a great city. Tens of thousands of people take their places and perform their tasks with no apparent direction. Thousands of vehicles butt their way through clogged canyons, missing by inches, but seldom actually colliding. Thousands of kinds of merchandise arrive at the proper places in the proper amounts at the proper times. Ten thousand people whom an individual never sees will labor on this day so that meals will be ready for him when needed, drinking fountains will flow, drains will carry off the wastes, bulbs will blink and glow, traffic will part to let him pass, and various conveniences will meet his other needs. A hundred people may serve him within an hour, perhaps without a word from him to any of them.

This is what is meant by *social order*—a system of people, relationships, and customs operating smoothly to accomplish the work of a society. Unless people know what they may expect from one another, not much will get done. No society, even the simplest, can function successfully unless the behavior of most people can be reliably predicted most of the time. Unless we can depend upon police officers to protect us, workers to go to work on schedule, and motorists to stay on the right side of the road most of the time, there can be no social order. The orderliness of a society rests upon a network of roles according to which each person accepts certain duties toward others and claims certain rights from others. An orderly society can operate only as long as most people reliably fulfill most of their duties toward others and are able successfully to claim most of their rights from others.

How is this network of reciprocal rights and duties kept in force? Sociologists use the term *social control* to describe *all the means and processes whereby a group or a society secures its members' conformity to its expectations.*

SOCIAL CONTROL AND SOCIAL ORDER

How does a group or a society cause its members to behave in the expected manner? In a number of ways, whose relative importance is difficult to measure.

Social control through socialization Fromm [1944] has remarked that if a culture is to function efficiently, "its members must acquire the kind of character which makes them *want* to act in the way they *have* to act as members of society. . . . They have to *desire* to do what objectively is necessary for them to do."

People are controlled mainly by being socialized so that they fill their roles in the expected way through habit and preference. How do we compel women to accept the endless drudgery of household and child care? Mainly by socializing them so that they *want* husbands and children, and feel cheated without them. How is man, unlike the male of most other species, persuaded to exchange his freedom for a sense of social responsibility toward the offspring he sires? Mainly by cultivating within him a set of cherished sentiments and yearnings which this troublesome little creature promises to fulfill. As we stated in an earlier chapter, the crucial part of one's role preparation is his development of the attitudes and wishes which make the role attractive. Most role failures come, not because one is unable to perform the role's tasks, but because he is trapped in a role he does not really want or enjoy.

Socialization shapes our customs, our wishes, and our habits. Habit and custom are great time savers. They relieve us of the need for countless decisions. If we had to decide whether and how to perform each act—when to arise, whether and how to wash, shave, dress, and so on—few students would get to class at all! The members of a society are schooled in the same customs and tend to develop much the same set of habits. Thus habit and custom are great standardizers of behavior within a group. If all members of a society share similar socialization experiences, they will voluntarily and unthinkingly act in very much the same ways. They will conform to social expectations without any conscious awareness that they are "conforming," or any serious thought of doing otherwise. The American college male's attempt to date a cute coed arises from motives less academic than a wish to "conform to the courtship pattern"; yet such conformity is the result.

Social control through group pressure In a novel by Sinclair Lewis, George F. Babbitt, a small-town realtor, somehow strays into "radical" notions about government and politics. Soon his business declines, his friends begin to avoid him, and he grows uncomfortably aware that he is becoming an outsider. Lewis describes with rare perception how Babbitt's associates apply a variety of subtle pressures until, with a sigh of relief, Babbitt scurries back into a comfortable conformity [Lewis, 1922, chaps. 32, 33].

Our need for acceptance within intimate groups.

LaPiere [1954] sees social control as primarily a process growing out of the individual's need for status within his primary groups. He claims that these groups are most influential when they are small and intimate, when the individual expects to remain in the group for a long time, and when he has frequent contacts with them. All authorities agree that our need for acceptance within intimate groups is a most powerful lever for the use of group pressure toward group norms.

The individual experiences this group pressure as a continuous and largely unconscious process. Its operation is illustrated by the life of one of the author's acquaintances. He spent most of his working life as a small farmer in central Michigan; like most of his neighbors, he thought conservatively, voted Republican, and scolded labor unions. During World War II he moved to Detroit and worked in a war plant, joined a union, became a union officer, and voted Democratic. After the war, he retired to a small central Michigan village where he again thinks conservatively, votes Republican, and scolds labor unions. He explains these about-faces by claiming that the parties and the unions have changed. He does not realize that it is *he* who has changed. Like most of us, he soon came to share the views of his group associates. This tendency to conform to group attitudes is so compelling that the Catholic church in France found it necessary to abandon its worker-priest program. This was an effort to stem the drift of French workers toward communism by sending out priests who would take ordinary jobs and work beside the workers, meanwhile leading them back to the church. After a ten-year trial, when it became evident that the workers were converting the priests to the Marxian view of the class struggle, the program was curtailed [Brady, 1954].

Social psychologists [Sherif, 1935; Bovard, 1951] have made a number of experiments which show how a person tends to bring his expressions in line with those of the group. The method in such experiments usually consists of asking the members for individual estimates, attitudes, or observations on a topic, then informing them of the group norm, and finally asking for a new expression from each member. Many of the informants modify their second expression in the direction of the group norm. In a series of ingenious experiments, Asch [1951]; Tuddenham [1961], and others have shown that many people will even alter an observation which they *know* to be correct rather than oppose the group. Each subject in these experiments was surrounded by a group which, by secret prearrangement, made factual observations that the subject *knew* to be wrong; yet one-third of these subjects accepted the wrong observation when opposed by a unanimous group opinion to the contrary. Schachter [1951] has also shown experimentally how the member who sharply deviates from group norms in opinion is rejected by the group.

We often notice that a new member of a group is more carefully conformist and more fiercely loyal than the old members. Religious converts and naturalized citizens often show a zeal which puts lifelong members to shame. An experiment by Dittes and Kelley [1956] helps to explain this. They found that among members who equally value their membership in a group, those who feel *least accepted* are the most rigidly conformist to the group's norms. Meticulous conformity is a tool for gaining acceptance and status within a group, while rejection is the price of nonconformity.

It is probable that no other structure even approaches the tremendous controlling power of the group over the individual. Any parent who has tried to counter a teen-ager's argument, "*All* the kids are wearing them!" is fully aware of the controlling power of the group.

Informal primary-group controls Groups are of two kinds, primary and secondary; these concepts will be analyzed in detail in a later chapter. For our present discussion, it is sufficient to note that primary groups are small, intimate, informal, face-to-face groups, like the family, clique, or play group, while secondary groups are larger, more impersonal, more formal, and more utilitarian, like a labor union, trade association, church congregation, or student body.

Within primary groups, control is informal, spontaneous, and unplanned. The members of the group react to the actions of each member. When a member irritates or annoys the others, they may show their disapproval through ridicule, laughter, criticism, or even ostracism. When a member's behavior is acceptable, a secure and comfortable "belonging" is his usual reward. Countless novelists have used the subplot in which a character violates the norms of his group in some way, is disciplined by group disapproval which he cannot endure, and must earn his way back into group acceptance through penitence and renewed conformity.

In most primitive societies where virtually all groups were primary groups, there was very little serious misconduct. Each person was born into certain kinship groups—for example, a family, a clan, and a tribe. He could not move on to another tribe or clan, for a man divorced from his kinship ties had no social existence—that is, no one was obligated to regard and treat him as a fellow human being. If a man were to survive, he *had* to get along with the groups in which he found himself. Since there was little privacy and no escape, the penalty of serious nonconformity was an intolerable existence. For example, the polar Eskimo institutionalized ridicule and laughter as a social control. The person who violated cultural norms was mercilessly ridiculed. Birket-Smith writes of the Chugach Eskimo:

Once a habitual thief entered a house, and an old woman sitting there began to sing:

> *Analurshe*
> *Analurshe*
> *Makes me ashamed*
> *He was looking at me*
> *While I was eating*
> *Analurshe*
> *Analurshe*

He immediately left the house, but the children used to sing the song whenever they saw him. Thus he acquired the nickname Analurshe, i.e., Old Excrements, and after that he stopped stealing.

Kaj Birket-Smith, *The Eskimos*, Methuen & Co., Ltd., London, 1959, p. 151.

Lowie describes the use of scorn and ridicule by a number of American Indian peoples:

When a Fox Indian boy in Illinois was taught not to steal and never to abuse his wife, his elder did not hold up to him any tangible punishment here or hereafter nor any abstract rule of morality. The clinching argument was, "The people will say many things about you, although you may not know it."

Gossiping sometimes took special forms of ridicule. An Alaskan youth thus reports his experience: "If you do not marry within your village, they joke about you— they joke so much that it makes it disagreeable." The Crow sang songs in mockery of a miser, a bully, or a man who should take back a divorced wife—the acme of disgrace. Certain kinsmen had the privilege of publicly criticizing a man for breaches of etiquette and ethics, and there was nothing he would fear more than to be thus pilloried. This system was developed by the Blackfoot along slightly differ-

*ent lines. "For mild persistent misconduct, a method of formal discipline is some-
times practiced. When the offender has failed to take hints and suggestions, the
head men may take formal notice and decide to resort to discipline. Some evening
when all are in their tipis, a head man will call out to a neighbor asking if he has
observed the conduct of Mr. A. This starts a general conversation between the many
tipis, in which all the grotesque and hideous features of Mr. A.'s acts are held up to
general ridicule, amid shrieks of laughter, the grilling continuing until far into the
night. The mortification of the victim is extreme and usually drives him into a
temporary exile or, as formerly, upon the warpath to do desperate deeds."*

*A primitive man sacrifices half his property lest he be dubbed a miser; he yields his
favorite wife if jealousy is against the code; he risks life itself, if that is the way to
gain the honor of a public eulogy. That is why savages of the same tribe are not
forever cutting one another's throats or ravishing available women, even if they
lack written constitutions, jails, a police force, and revealed religion.*

Robert H. Lowie, *Are We Civilized?* Harcourt, Brace & World, Inc., New York, 1929. Copyright 1929,
by Harcourt Brace & World, Inc., renewed © 1957, by Robert H. Lowie, and reprinted with the
publisher's permission.

In many authenticated instances where primitives have violated important
norms, they have committed suicide because they could not endure the penalty of group disapproval [Malinowski, 1926, pp. 94–99]. In such a group
setting, the penalty for serious nonconformity is so unendurable as to make
serious nonconformity quite rare. Likewise in complex cultures, wherever
persons are trapped in primary group settings which they cannot easily escape,
as in a prison cell or a military unit, this great controlling power of the primary
group comes into operation.

In many societies, the group is held responsible for the acts of any of its members. For example, if a Tlingit murders a member of another clan, his own clan
must provide for execution a person equal in social status to the murdered
victim, while the actual murderer is punished by living with the knowledge that
he has caused the execution of a clansman. In our military units, one dirty rifle
or messy locker may deprive an entire company of their week-end passes.
Such forms of collective punishment may seem unjust, *but they work!* A
soldier whose carelessness has once caused his company to lose their week-
end passes is unlikely to repeat his error—or to be permitted to forget it!

A great deal of "leadership" and "authority" rest upon the skillful manipulation of the group as a control device. The successful schoolteacher, for example, often uses the class to maintain discipline; she manipulates the situation so that the child who misbehaves will look ridiculous before the class. But
if she allows a situation to develop wherein the misbehaving child appears as a
hero or a martyr to the class, her control is lost.

Normal people everywhere need and seek the approval of others, especially
of the primary group associates upon whom they depend for intimate human
response. Thousands of novels, dramas, and operas have elaborated this
theme. Most people will give almost anything, even their lives if necessary, to
retain this approval and the comforting feeling of belonging to the group. It is
the overwhelming need for group approval and response that makes the
primary group the most powerful controlling agency known to man.

Secondary-group controls   As we shift from primary- to secondary-group situations, we also shift from informal to more formal social controls. Secondary

groups are generally larger, more impersonal, and specialized in purpose. We do not use them to meet our need for intimate human response, but to help us to get certain jobs done. If a secondary group does not meet our needs, we can generally withdraw with no great anguish, for our emotional lives are not deeply involved. To maintain our status in the secondary group is desirable but not a desperate emotional necessity as it is in the primary group. True, it is possible in our society for people to change their primary groups—leave their families, divorce their mates, find new friends—but the process is generally painful. The secondary group is a less compelling control agency than the primary group.

The secondary group is still an effective control. Some of the informal controls still operate in the secondary group. No normal person wants to appear ridiculous at the union meeting, the church worship service, or the chamber of commerce banquet. Such informal controls as ridicule, laughter, gossip, and ostracism operate in secondary-group settings, but generally with a reduced impact. Meanwhile, other more formal controls are characteristic of secondary groups—parliamentary rules of order, official regulations and standardized procedures, propaganda, public relations and "human engineering," promotions and titles, rewards and prizes, formal penalties and punishments, and still others.

The more formal controls of the secondary group are most effective when reinforced by a primary group. A prize or decoration is more sweet when an admiring family and an applauding clique of close friends can watch the presentation ceremony. Within the large impersonal secondary group may be many very closely integrated primary groups, such as squads within an army or work crews within a corporation. These primary groups can either reinforce or undermine the formal secondary-group controls and greatly affect the performance of the secondary group. Much of the human-engineering approach in industry is an effort to use these primary groups to reinforce the controls and the objectives of the corporation [Gross, 1953].

Special language as a social control   An argot, a special vocabulary restricted to a particular subculture, serves important functions of social control. An argot promotes communication within the group, since each unique expression is freighted with meaning which only the group members can comprehend. Conversely the argot shields the group from outside influence which might introduce discordant ideas. Learning the argot thus not only strengthens the tie between the individual and the group; it also cuts down communication with the world outside. No individuals are entirely cut off from contacts outside the subculture, but as Bernstein [1966] observes, the argot serves to maximize the social barriers between the group and the rest of society.

Running It Down on the Set

Some vocabulary of street life in the Negro ghetto.

COOL PEOPLE, DUDES, REGULARS—*members of street groups, mostly young unemployed males*

A LAME, SQUARE—*one who lacks knowledge of street life*

THE MAN—*the police, white men generally*

THE SET—*both the peer group and the places where the peer group hangs out*

RAP—*street repartee*

BREAD—*money*

PILLS—*barbiturates, benzedrine, or dexedrine*

POT, GRASS, WEED—*marihuana*

HEAT—*police pressure*

BUST—*an arrest*

A PROCESS—*having hair straightened and styled*

DUKING—*fighting or at least looking tough*

CONKED TO THE BONE—*having processed hair*

GIGGING—*having a party*

HUSTLING—*any way of making money except through legitimate work: conning, stealing, gambling, selling dope*

BURN, PUT THE BUMP ON A CAT—*get money or service from someone*

WOMAN GAME—*obtaining a woman's welfare check*

MOTHER'S DAY—*when the welfare child-support checks arrive*

TO BE LEGIT—*not working for the police*

LAYING DEAD, DOING DEAD TIME—*hanging around the street, doing nothing*

JIVING—*kidding around, putting someone on*

HOLD HIS MUD—*keep cool and out of trouble*

Adapted from John Horton, "Time and Cool People," *Trans-action*, 4:5–12, April, 1967. For an extended glossary of current youth argot (which changes so rapidly that it may be dated by the time students read this), see J. L. Simmons and Barry Winograd, *It's Happening*, Marc-Laird Publications, Santa Barbara, California, 1966, pp. 167–174.

Control through force Many primitive societies succeeded in controlling the behavior of individuals through the mores, reinforced by the informal controls of the primary group, so that no formal laws or punishments were necessary. But with larger populations and more complex cultures, formal governments, laws, and punishments are developed. Wherever it becomes possible for the individual to become lost in the crowd, informal controls are inadequate and formal controls are necessary. For example, in a clan of one or two dozen adult kinsfolk, informal food sharing is practical; each person can take what he needs and contribute whatever he can catch, while informal group pressures can be trusted to prevent laziness and control greed. But in a village of hundreds of persons, it would be impossible to keep tab on each person informally; individual laziness and greed would make a system of informal food sharing unworkable. Some *system* of assigning work and distributing rewards becomes necessary. Thus, with larger populations and cultural complexity comes a shift to impersonal secondary-group controls—laws, regulations, councils, and formalized procedures.

When the individual does not wish to follow these regulations, the group tries to compel him to do so. In such large groups he is too anonymous for informal group pressures to be brought to an effective focus upon him. Furthermore, in larger groups with complex cultures, some subcultures that conflict with the culture of the majority are likely to develop. The individual who rejects the conventional regulations of the society may find emotional support from other persons who think and act as he does. Although he is still subject to group pressure, it now comes from a nonconforming group which insulates him from the pressures of conventional society. So conventional society uses force upon him—force in the form of laws and formal punishments—to compel his con-

formity. This force is not always successful; yet no complex culture has survived without it.

Situational When a layman sees some behavior he does not like, he often attributes it to
determinants evil human nature, wicked impulse, weak character, or some other *individual*
of behavior cause. What separates the sociologist from the layman here is the sociologist's
habit of looking for *social* factors in the causation of behavior. True, when one
individual or a few people change in character or behavior, the explanations
may be purely individual. But when any *large number* of people change their
character or behavior in the same way, we look for the probable cause in some
change in the social and cultural influences upon behavior.

*Behavior in a particular situation is the result of the needs
of that situation.*

To a far greater degree than
most people recognize, one's
behavior in a particular situation is a result of the needs,
pressures, and temptations
of that situation. There is ample evidence that many people
who would not cheat a blind
newspaper man will cheat the
national supermarket if they
get a chance to do so; war
veterans who did not rob their
neighbors back home "liberated" many articles from the enemy population;
people do things as part of a mob which they would never do as individuals.
War atrocities are committed by all armies. Whether a surrendering enemy
is shot or taken prisoner depends more upon the circumstances at the moment
of surrender than upon the character of the capturing troops [Draper, 1945].
Kinsey's data show that most civilian husbands are faithful to their wives, at
least most of the time; but it appears that most overseas military personnel,
when long separated from their wives, seized almost any attractive opportunity
for infidelity. Labor union officials believe in labor unions—except for their
own employees! So when the staff employees of the large unions seek to
organize and bargain collectively with their bosses, these union official-bosses
seem to react just like any other employer.[1] Boys from satisfactory homes in
stable neighborhoods rarely become delinquent, but most boys from unsatisfactory homes in a slum neighborhood will become seriously delinquent
[Glueck and Glueck, 1959; Reckless et al., 1957]. Argyris [1967] reports,
"Not long ago, as a sociological experiment, two Detroit ministers went to
work on an assembly line and soon found themselves cheating on quality,
lying to their foremen and swearing at the machines." Their new work situation carried pressures and frustrations to which they responded like any other
workers. Illustrations of how the total behavior situation affects the behavior
outcome could be multiplied almost without end. Many more are found in
Chapter 16, "Collective Behavior."

True, the character one brings to a situation is a factor in his behavior; occasionally it is the determining factor. A few people are honest in *all* situations; a

[1] See "The Class War," *Reporter,* Jan. 9, 1958, p. 6.

few husbands will be faithful despite *any* temptation. But more often than our folklore admits, a situation develops a characteristic kind of behavior among most of the participants. This is why the upper floors of girls' dormitories are forbidden to male callers. A major part of social control consists of trying to manipulate the kinds of situations which people enter, for we know that most of them will respond with the kind of behavior which a particular situation encourages.

This is not a complete catalog of the means of social control. There are many others which are described by Lumley [1925] and Landis [1956]—symbols, traditions, myths, legends, threats, intimidations, tortures, and still others— but they would be only an elaboration of the above outline.

SOCIAL DEVIATION

No society succeeds in getting all its people to behave as expected all the time. The term, *social deviation* is given to *any failure to conform to the customary norms of the society.* Deviation takes many forms. The juvenile delinquent, the hermit, the ascetic, the hippie, the sinner and the saint, the artist starving in his garret and the miser gloating over his wealth—all have deviated from the conventional social norms.

In a simple society where all members accept a single set of norms, deviation is easy to define. In a complex society with many different competing norms, the problem grows more complicated. In a neighborhood where most of the boys are delinquent, and many of the adults are repeatedly violating the law, who is the deviant—the delinquent or the nondelinquent? Obviously, deviation needs more detailed definition.

Basic types of deviation   **Individual and group deviation**   A boy in a "good" neighborhood of stable families and conventional people may reject the norms which surround him and become a delinquent. In this case, the individual deviates from the norms of his subculture. He is thus an *individual deviant.* In a complex society, however, there may be a number of *deviant subcultures,* whose norms are condemned by the conventional morality of the society. Thus in the deteriorated areas of the city, Cohen [1955] and Miller [1958] find a delinquent subculture in which many of the youths participate. For many of them the life of the street gang is the only life that seems real and important. In such neighborhoods, delinquent behavior is as "normal" as law-abiding behavior. When boys from these neighborhoods become delinquent, they are not individually deviant from their subculture; it is their subculture (the group, not the boy) that is deviant from the conventional norms of the society. The delinquent episodes are not revolts against the area subculture but are "status-seeking mechanisms within the group [Short and Strodtbeck, 1965, p. viii].

These delinquent boys are not individually deviant in the beginning; they are conforming normally to the norms of a deviant subculture. This subculture directs them into patterns which eventually result in many of them becoming individually deviant. As they graduate from the adolescent gang into adult society, their gang experience has placed them at war with conventional society, so that they often become and remain individual deviants.

They tend to become subcultures.

We therefore have two ideal types of deviants: (1) individual deviants, who reject the norms which surround them and deviate from their subculture; and (2) group deviants, wherein the individual is a conforming member of a deviant group. In practice, deviant persons are not sharply divided into two such distinct groups. The "ideal type" always is a clearcut expression of an idea, while most real persons fall somewhere between the sharply contrasting images presented by the "ideal types." This is the reason for constructing the ideal types; they clearly express an idea. Meanwhile, we remember that very few people perfectly fit into an ideal type, but are intermediate; for example, few people are either "dominant" or "submissive"; most people show some of each characteristic.

In the case of deviant persons, many deviants are not perfect examples of either individual or group deviation, but show elements of both. Rarely is an individual deviant *completely* surrounded by conventional groups and influences. If he were, it is unlikely that he would ever deviate at all! But even the most carefully sheltered child hears about crimes and immorality, comes across literature his parents would censor, and observes other children violating the norms his parents revere. In other words, even a highly conventional subculture does not completely isolate the person from deviant patterns which he can observe and follow.

Furthermore, deviant persons tend to join with other similar persons into deviant groups. The "bad boys" in the schoolroom tend to form a clique, reinforcing one another's boisterous behavior. Individual hot-rodders, hippies, drug addicts, or homosexuals tend to drift together into groups of deviants. These groups reinforce and sanction the deviation, give the member emotional protection against conformist critics, and possibly help to cultivate new deviants. These groups of deviants tend to develop a private language and a set of rigidly stereotyped behavior norms of their own. In short, they tend to develop subcultures. Thus it becomes hard to say whether the beatnik of the 1950s was a deviant nonconformist or a rigidly conforming member of a deviant subculture. In practice, then, the distinction between the individual and the group deviant becomes blurred; yet the theoretical distinction is an important one, as our later discussion will elaborate.

Cultural and psychological deviation   One may deviate from the norm in his social behavior, in his personality organization, or sometimes in both of these. Sociology is primarily interested in the cultural deviant, who deviates in his behavior from the norms of his culture. Psychologists are primarily interested in the psychological deviant, who deviates from the norm in his personality organization—the psychotic, the neurotic, the paranoid personality, and others. These two categories often converge. Deviant behavior may spring from personality abnormality, and many studies of deviant behavior report evidence of such an association. Radical political behavior is often interpreted as an outlet for emotional hostilities [Ernst and Loth, 1952; Almond, 1954]. The prostitute is often explained as a product of an emotionally deprived childhood, in which she had little opportunity to integrate a secure personality [Greenwald, 1959]; and other sex deviations, along with alcoholism, drug addiction, and compulsive gambling, are often attributed to personality disorder of some sort.

Personality disorder, however, is far from the sole cause of deviant behavior. While some psychologically abnormal people have a compelling urge to be bad, other psychologically abnormal people have an equally compelling urge to be good. These disturbed people become overconformists. The insecure, complex-ridden neurotic who *must* do his work perfectly, cannot stand disagreements, obeys all the mores, and finds comfort in meticulously following all the rules and regulations is fulfilling a neurotic need to conform. This shows that cultural and psychological deviation are related, but not in any simple cause-and-effect relationship. The puzzling question of why personality abnormality sometimes leads to deviant behavior and sometimes to conforming behavior is a question which continues to interest both psychologists and sociologists.

Culturally approved deviation Deviant behavior is culturally evaluated. Some deviation is condemned; some is applauded. The wandering holy man of one society is the worthless bum of another; the rugged hero of the raw frontier is the uncouth boor of an urban community. In our society, the genius, the hero, the leader, and the celebrity are among our culturally approved deviants.

Causes of individual distinction   There has been much speculation about what contributes to individual greatness. A large number of studies have compared leaders with followers, both among children and in adult groups; and some studies [Gibb, 1954] have also surveyed the "great men" of history to see what distinguished them from ordinary people. Most of the studies find that leaders (but not necessarily scholars or creative artists) tend to be taller than average. Several studies find that attractive appearance and dress is associated with leadership. Several find that leaders are considerably, *but not too greatly*, above average in intelligence; those who are greatly above average apparently seek learning or creative work instead of political or institutional leadership. Several studies find associations between leadership and self-confidence, sociability, will, dominance, or other traits. But these many studies do not agree in finding any consistent pattern of traits for great men or leaders.

Efforts to find *the* causes of greatness are probably doomed by the fact that different roles call for different personal qualities. The saint, the war hero, the revolutionist, the artist, the scientist, and the tycoon are far from uniform in their attributes or their paths to greatness. A look at some possible "causes" of greatness will reveal the difficulty of assigning any general causes of individual achievement.

1. *Intelligence.*   Intelligence is more useful in some roles than in others. The intellectual mediocrity is unlikely to gain fame as a scientist or mathematician, but extraordinary intelligence is less necessary to the actor, the athlete, or the religious or political leader; in these roles, certain other qualities of talent, physique, character, or personality are especially important. Great

intelligence may even be a handicap in some roles, as it may isolate the gifted person from ordinary people, or bar him from the comfortable oversimplifications which allow lesser men to act with confidence. Fools rush in—and sometimes succeed—where wiser men fear to tread because the wise are able to foresee the hazards and possible consequences of such rash action. All in all, the factor of intelligence in personal greatness is probably exaggerated in popular thought—possibly because it seems so unkind to suggest that behind the great man's sterling character, magnetic personality, and benign smile, there sometimes lurks a mediocre brain.

2. *Special aptitudes.*   As implied above, the greatness of the athlete, the musician, the actor, the ballerina, the artist, and certain others rests more heavily upon special aptitudes than upon superior general intelligence. Some intelligence is necessary if one is to use his aptitudes effectively; yet many famous men have also been famous for their naïveté and poor judgment outside their field of special talent. The difference between the great artist and the rest of us seems to be found in a greater special aptitude, not in greater intelligence.

3. *Motivation.*   We speculate much upon the topic of motivation, but actually we know relatively little. Motivation is clearly a factor in success, but just why a person becomes highly motivated is not easy to determine. Group pressure is probably a factor. For example, the drive for success and upward mobility in the United States appears to be stronger among Jews than gentiles, and among middle-class than lower-class persons. Family tradition is probably a factor, but tradition is difficult to measure since it cannot be separated from the other aids and opportunities which a distinguished family gives to its children.

Social scientists suspect that intense motivation is often *compensatory.* This is to say, one may be highly motivated as an unconscious response to some frustration or deprivation. Hitler and Napoleon may have drawn their motivation from their lonely, rejected childhoods, Richard III from his deformity, and Theodore Roosevelt from his childhood delicacy. We suspect that such wishes as the desire to win the affectionate approval of an unresponsive or demanding parent, the wish to humble a resented relative, or to prove one's worth to a skeptical home town may form the core of many a successful person's motivation. Feelings of insecurity, inferiority, resentment, or hostility may thus find outlet through intense efforts at personal achievement. This possibility is difficult to prove, disprove, or measure, but holds an important place in our thinking about motivation.

4. *Personality traits.*   The effort to identify the personality traits which make for greatness has produced much speculation and a number of studies. But such studies are doomed to be contradictory and inconclusive because different roles require different personality traits. Physical courage is essential to a soldier but unnecessary to an artist; sociability and conviviality, useful to the businessman or politician, may be a positive interference in the career of the writer, artist, or scientist.

Popular thinking is confused by a number of popular stereotypes about individual distinction—the mad scientist, the temperamental musician, the Bohemian artist, and so on. Some of these stereotypes may not be entirely untrue, for the "self-fulfilling prophecy" may help them to become true. A "self-fulfilling prophecy" is one in which the prophecy starts a series of events which make it come true [Merton, 1957a, chap. 11]. (For example, if I point at a girl in the class and say, "You are going to blush! Watch her blush, everybody!" she nearly always blushes brightly.) If great musicians are expected to be highly temperamental, and their outbursts of rudeness and immaturity are excused as "artistic temperament," such outbursts may be encouraged. If the great actor or artist is expected to pursue his amours with a zest which others dare not imitate, we should not be surprised when he does so. However, very little empirical evidence either confirms or disproves these popular stereotypes, and the serious student will not rely upon them.

The stereotype of the mad genius, however, has been thoroughly exploded. The belief that extraordinarily gifted people are nearly always unstable, erratic, physically delicate, and precariously poised on a thin dividing line between genius and insanity is nonsense. We hear of child prodigies who mature into an ineffectual obscurity, and we may not realize that most child prodigies become distinguished adults—Mozart, Francis Bacon, John Stuart Mill, Albert Einstein, and Norbert Wiener, for example. The stereotype of the sexually irresponsible artist is fed by the Casanova types like Wagner and Liszt, although they were outnumbered by good family men like Bach and Mendelssohn. Several studies of great men of history have concluded that the majority of them were quite normal in their personal and family relationships. [Dempsey, 1958]. For many years, Terman [1959] has followed the careers of a sample of 1,000 exceptionally gifted children (as measured by intelligence quotient, an admittedly imperfect measure, but the only practical one available). He finds that, both as children and as adults, the gifted group is well above average in physical development, emotional stability, and nearly every other "desirable" attribute, and that their adult achievement is greatly above average. He furthermore finds that, up to IQs of about 170, the more highly gifted among his sample average higher in most of these other respects. The mad genius makes good melodrama but poor social science.

Personality characteristics are doubtless extremely important factors in achievements, often the most important factors. A man's childhood experiences, his parental relationships, and his relations with wife and relatives all have profound effects upon his work. But we dare not generalize. One man's achievement is encouraged by an adoring wife and an admiring clan of relatives; another's is a refuge from a shrewish wife and a revenge upon disbelieving relatives. Bach was immersed in music by a large affectionate family of musicians; Mozart's interest is music was applauded by an exploitative father; Handel fought his way into music over the bitter protest of a tyrannical father. Many different kinds of social situations and personality attributes may enter into great achievement, and it is hazardous to generalize about them.

5. *Cultural evaluation.* The values of the culture determine whether a particular deviant is praised or pilloried. This is another example of cultural relativism. Each culture encourages some deviations and discourages others. Some cultures, such as the Zuñi or Hopi, encourage very little deviation of any kind whatever; persons of remarkable individual achievement are rare in such a culture. Other cultures, such as the Haida or Kwakiutl, or the contemporary American culture, encourage individual distinction of certain approved sorts. In such cultures, persons of great achievement are fairly nu-

merous, highly honored, and widely emulated. A culture may thus encourage or discourage great personal achievement, direct it into one channel or another, or even block it completely. What would Einstein have accomplished in a society which had no need to count beyond ten? Beethoven among the American Indians might have added a new drum beat, but he would never have written the Ninth Symphony.

Some people will insist that a genius in any society would still find some way to express his talents through great achievements. Since we cannot reincarnate Einstein for a second try among the Hottentots, such statements cannot be either proved or disproved. But we suspect that when a primitive genius came up with a new idea, it was accepted and used only if it fitted in with the needs and values of his society; otherwise it was generally suppressed, ignored, or ridiculed, and thereby lost and forgotten. Thus the genius in any society is able to contribute only the kinds of contributions which are welcomed by at least some groups in his society.

6. Luck.   Good fortune cannot make a genius of a dullard, but fortune can give or withhold a favorable opportunity to display one's abilities. Would Eisenhower have become President if there had been no World War II? Would he have been picked as Allied Commander if he had been a few years younger or a few years older? Great achievement requires not only that one have certain talents, but that he have them at just the right place at the right time. History is filled with gifted generals and statesmen, like Smuts, Masaryk, and Sequoia, who are buried in the footnotes because they led one of the minor nations. The factor of luck can easily be exaggerated by the cynic, but the serious student of individual achievement does not overlook it.

To summarize.   A number of factors in extraordinary personal achievement are difficult to isolate and measure. Since different kinds of achievement differ so greatly in their requirements, there probably are no general "qualities of greatness." Popular thinking about greatness is confused by many romantic stereotypes, and fails to give proper weight to the social and cultural factors in individual achievement.

Culturally disapproved deviation   Most societies permit and reward deviation in the form of extraordinary achievements in activities already approved by the values of the culture. But most societies are unhappy about individual failure to attain the norms in approved activities, while deviation from the mores is even more severely disapproved.

Deviation through inability to conform   Those with physical or mental defect may be incapable of normal achievements or normal social behavior. The term *mental defect* refers to limited learning capacity, either through inheritance or brain damage. The diagnosis and treatment of physical or mental defect lie largely outside the field of sociology. Popular beliefs about mental defect, however, and social policies concerning defectives do interest sociologists. The popular belief that all mental defectives multiply like hamsters is incorrect. Birth rates are high only among the "high-grade morons" or borderline defectives; among the more seriously defective, the greater the defect, the lower tends to be the birth rate and the survival rate. Most of the inherited severe mental defect appears among children of normal parents who carry recessive gene defects, so that only a small fraction of severe mental defect could be prevented by sterilizing all mental defectives. Since all true mental defect and most physical defect is incurable at present, social policy is mainly concerned with preparing defectives to be as socially useful as their abilities permit.

Mental illness is a disorganization of behavior rather than a lack of learning capacity. In mental illness, a person within the normal range of learning capacity is unable to perceive and respond to realities in an orderly and rational manner. His reality perceptions may be so distorted that he imagines that people are persecuting him or that he hears strange voices and commands, or he becomes disoriented and forgets where he is and what he is doing. His self-perceptions may become distorted, so that he becomes obsessed with his own worthlessness, sinfulness, or incompetence, or perhaps develops delusions of grandeur and power. His reactions to reality may become confused and erratic, or he may withdraw from reality into an inner world of fantasy.

The classification, diagnosis, and treatment of mental illness lie in the fields of psychology, psychiatry, and medicine. Sociologists are mainly interested in the social and cultural factors involved in producing mental illness, and in our social attitudes and policies toward it.

The causes of mental illness appear to be both physical and social, but in unknown proportions. All students of mental illness agree that heredity is a factor, but the exact degree and operation of the hereditary factor has not been established [Jost and Sontag, 1944; Kallman, 1946; Coleman, 1964, pp. 117–129]. The fact that mental illness often runs in a family is not very helpful, since the members of a family generally share both a similar heredity and a similar social experience. Yet each individual is biologically and biochemically unique. Williams [1956] has shown that individuals vary considerably, even in the size and location of internal organs, the chemical composition of body fluids, the number of branch arteries, the branching of trunk nerves, and many other respects. It is known that severe malnutrition can induce personality disorders [Keys, 1952; Wilder, 1952]. Kretschmer [1925] and Sheldon and Stevens [1942] have shown how at least some types of mental illness seem to show some association with constitutional body type, but constitutional factors and their exact roles remain to be established. The entire question of the hereditary, constitutional, or organic causation of mental illness is not yet settled.

There is widespread agreement among scientists that most mental illness is precipitated, or "triggered," by mental conflicts, especially the conflicts provoked by guilts, frustrations, and anxieties. Yet some people survive terrific stress without becoming disorganized, while others succumb quickly. Obviously, people differ in their ability to endure mental conflicts. It is not known whether this difference is partly physical; some people may be biologically better able to endure mental conflict without becoming disorganized. Certain physical changes or disorders may make a healthy person become susceptible to mental illness. There is widespread agreement among scientists, however, that the socialization process is extremely important. It may develop a secure and confident personality, well able to meet the stresses and conflicts of social life, or it may develop an insecure and complex-ridden personality, unable to survive even mild stress without disorganization.

Sociologists are especially interested in the ways a culture may create mental conflicts for individuals. The culture may impose difficult role transitions, such as our transition from youth into adulthood or from active adulthood into retirement. It may require difficult choices, so arranged that neither alternative is fully comfortable; an example is the American wife who is under pressure to get a job so that the family can live better, and also under pressure to stay home and take care of the family. Our massive advertising campaigns guarantee that people's wants will constantly outrun their means; this fostering of desires may be economically useful but it is emotionally costly. Our culture teaches many contradictory values: Be generous, but hang on to your money; be modest and unassuming, but be sure to get ahead; don't take advantage of others' hardship, but remember that business is business; be thrifty and saving, but keep spending lest you touch off a recession; be virtuous, but don't be inhibited; love your enemies, but extend no sympathies lest you be disloyal. Any complex, changing culture includes many such culture conflicts, and these become mental conflicts for individuals. To some students of mental illness, such conflicts within the culture are largely responsible for the mental conflicts which precipitate much of our mental illness [Horney, 1937].

The simple well-integrated societies, then, should provoke fewer mental conflicts and have less mental illness than we have. There is some evidence that this is true [Carothers, 1947], but it is difficult to be certain. Many difficulties arise when an observer from our society tries to diagnose and measure mental illness in a different cultural setting. Sometimes later studies of a group have concluded that the earlier studies underestimated the amount of mental illness in that group [Kaplan and Plaut, 1956]. Furthermore, if increasing cultural complexity produces mental illness, then our rates should have increased during the past century. Whether they have is uncertain; one recent study [Goldhamer and Marshall, 1953] concludes that there has been no noticeable increase between 1840 and 1940. Yet it is significant that "no field worker has reported a high rate of schizophrenia [our most common form of mental illness] in a stable primitive society which is isolated from white influences. Wherever schizophrenia is recorded, the society is in the process of change." [Miller and Swanson, 1960, p. 42; also Demerath, 1942.] Until more is definitely known, we may only conclude that it *seems likely* that the mental conflicts produced by the culture are a major factor in mental illness.

Social attitudes toward mental illness show a fascinating variety. Some primitive societies assumed that the mentally ill were supernaturally favored and gave them special privileges and recognition. Medieval Europeans blamed mental illness upon demon possession and therefore tortured and abused the victim to chase the demons from his miserable body. (There are no reliable data measuring the success of this heroic treatment!) Even today, many people cannot accept mental illness as an *illness* without connotations of humiliation or disgrace. This attitude is revealed in their preference for the euphemism, "nervous breakdown," and by their unwillingness to admit that an illness is mental or to visit patients at a mental hospital, or to accept members back into the family when they are ready for release [Weinberg, 1952, pp. 466–473; Freeman, 1961]. Such attitudes have the effect of prolonging mental illness, since they lead people to delay treatment, and make recovery more difficult even after treatment is sought. As long as such prescientific attitudes persist, they will remain among the "causes" of mental illness.

Deviation through failure to conform　Some persons fail to behave in the usual ways even though they are physically and mentally capable of learning conventional behavior. Criminals, bums, sex deviants, alcoholics, drug addicts, political extremists, hermits, and "cranks" of many varieties are examples. What causes such deviation?

Causes of failure to conform　**Some debatable theories**　Several theories have become quite popular, although evidence for them is either contradictory or incomplete.

1. Physical-type theories attempt to associate deviant behavior with body type. A number of students, including Lombroso [1912], Kretschmer [1925], Hooton [1939], Von Hentig [1947], and Sheldon [1949] have made studies claiming to find that certain body types are more prone to deviant behavior than others. The most recent and elaborate theory is that of Sheldon, who identifies three basic body types: endomorph (round, soft, fat); mesomorph (muscular, athletic); and ectomorph (thin, bony). For each type, Sheldon describes an elaborate series of personality traits and behavior tendencies. For example, he finds that delinquents and alcoholics are generally mesomorphs. He attributes neurosis largely to one's effort to be different from what his body type predisposes him to be.

Physical-type theories appear occasionally as "scientific" articles in popular magazines and Sunday papers. They have become quite popular, possibly because they seem to offer a simple, scientific way of classifying people and predicting or explaining their behavior. Social scientists, however, are quite skeptical of the body-type theories [Clinard, 1963, pp. 119–125]. Although these theories are supported by impressive empirical evidence, critics have noted serious errors in method which cast doubts upon their findings. For example, the process of classifying subjects into the several body types included no adequate methodological safeguards against unconscious bias; consequently, a borderline subject may have been placed in whatever body-type class he "belonged" in order to support the theory. The subject groups used in most of these studies were composed of institutionalized delinquents, who are not properly representative of all types of delinquents. Furthermore, none of the studies used adequate control groups of "normal" people. For example, over half of Hooton's control group were firemen and militiamen, persons who are especially selected for physical fitness. Because of such errors in method, most social scientists doubt that a reliable association between physical type and deviant behavior has been established.

2. Psychoanalytic theories of deviant behavior are also popular and have provided many plot themes for TV and the "adult westerns." Psychoanalysis is firmly rooted in Freud's concepts of the id, ego, and superego, as described in the preceding chapter. Deviant behavior is attributed to conflicts between the id and the ego, or between the id and the superego. Crime, for example, takes place when the superego, the civilized self-control of the individual, is unable to restrain the savage, primitive, destructive impulses of the id [Zilboorg, 1943; Abrahamsen, 1944].

Do the id, ego, and superego represent major aspects of the human personality, or are they merely words that psychoanalysts quote to one another? Do death wishes, castration complexes, and Oedipal stages actually exist in the normal personality, or does the psychoanalyst unconsciously plant the expected symptoms in the patient's mind and dig them up in subsequent interviews? We do not definitely know. Psychoanalytic theory is almost totally unsubstantiated by empirical research, while a number of such efforts have been inconclusive or nonconfirmatory. In Chapter 5 we cited Sewell's findings [1952] which cast doubt on psychoanalytic theory about specific child-training practices. Barnes [1952] sought to test the Freudian theory of the successive oral, anal, and phallic levels of psychosexual development and concluded that "the Freudian theory of levels of psychosexual development has not been supported as a whole." In all, comparatively few empirical attempts to test psycholanalytic theory have been made. It would, in fact, be quite difficult to design research that would either establish or disprove the usefulness of such concepts as the id or the ego. But until such research is attempted, psychoanalytic theory remains debatable, even though it is widely used in the treatment of behavior disorders. Its clinical success is sometimes cited as proof of psychoanalytic theory; i.e., since some of the patients improve under psychoanalytic treatment, the theory must be sound. But such claims for successful treatment are not accompanied by a comparison of these patients with a control group of untreated patients, who often improve without treatment. Consequently, we cannot know whether the patients improved because of the treatment or because of other factors.

If, without using psychoanalytic terminology, we merely state that culture often frustrates biological drives, little argument is possible. While the id may be debatable, there is no doubt about the existence of biological drives such as hunger and sex, or of the organic reactions associated with fear and anger. Clearly, too, culture often frustrates these drives and impulses. Our culture, for example, makes no socially approved provision for the sexual drives of those who are unmarried, widowed, or separated. If one gratifies such impulses in defiance of cultural taboos, he is engaging in deviant behavior. If, however, he disposes of the impulse by *repressing* it into his unconscious (to return to psychoanalytic theory), it does not go away, but remains as part of his unconscious motivation and may still give rise to deviant behavior of some kind. Thus the sex-starved spinster may repress her sex drives into her unconscious, where they remain active, perhaps impelling her to extreme prissiness, to religious fanticism, to health anxieties, or to some other emotional "cover-ups." Stated in this less tortuous manner, psychoanalytic theory, while still unproved, becomes a highly plausible explanation for much deviant behavior.

Failures in socialization   Every member of a society is frustrated by the clash of his biological drives with the taboos of his culture. But not everyone becomes a deviant. Why, when most persons conform to the norms of the culture, do some become deviant? There is no convincing evidence that most of these deviants differ significantly from the conformists in their inherited or constitutional behavior impulses. Therefore, *social scientists assume that they are deviant because the socialization process has failed in some way to integrate the cultural norms into the individual's personality.* Where the socialization process is successful, the individual adopts the norms which surround him, and the approved goals and values of the culture become his own emotional needs, while the taboos of his culture become a part of his conscience. He *internalizes* the norms of his culture so that he automatically and mechanically acts in the expected manner most of the time. His lapses are rare, and both he and others recognize that they are lapses from his normal behavior.

Behavioral scientists are agreed that moral values and behavior norms are learned mainly in the family. Where the child is socialized in a happy, affectionate, conventional family, he usually develops a secure, well-adjusted personality, behaves conventionally in most respects, marries successfully, and provides a happy, affectionate, conventional home for his children, who then repeat the cycle. Where family life is unsatisfactory, the children often develop personality difficulties and behavior deviations. The Gluecks [1959], after many years of carefully controlled comparisons of delinquent and nondelinquent youth, predict that juvenile delinquency is at least a 90 per cent probability when the "five highly decisive" factors in family life are unfavorable: father's discipline (harsh, erratic, unsympathetic); mother's supervision (indifferent, unconcerned); father's affection (lacking); mother's affection (cold, indifferent, hostile); cohesiveness of the family (unintegrated, empty of companionship). Where all five of these factors are favorable, they find virtually no serious delinquency.

The exact manner in which one's family life molds personality into conforming or deviant channels shows an endless variety. Some families make no real effort to transmit the cultural norms to their children, while others try but fail, as is shown in this personal history taken from the authors' files.

As far back as I can remember anything, I can recall those scenes which always ended with my mother's tearful lament, "Why can't you be more like your brother?" While I kept to myself the thought, "Be like that big sissy? Not on your life." He was older and was expected to look after me, which I resented. So anything he counseled against, I promptly did. I think it was emotionally necessary for me not to be or do anything he was or did. He was studious; I avoided school books like they were disease germs. He was neat, orderly, punctual, and methodical; I shunned these weaknesses. He did exactly what our parents and teachers asked; I did nothing they asked. He was a "good boy," and they showed their pride in him on every occasion; they were never proud of me. He and my father were close confidants and companions; my only companions were other "bad boys" from whom my parents made strenuous—and unsuccessful—efforts to separate me. When I finally stood, dry-eyed, beside my father's casket while my brother sniffled, my only thought was, "Why don't you die too, you stupid square!"

We cannot be certain just why this boy rejected parent values and standards while his brother was accepting them. One might guess that his parents showed some favoritism and perhaps a lack of sympathetic interest, and made a clumsy use of the older brother as model. Yet a similar family atmosphere had an opposite effect upon another child, as is shown in this case, also taken from the authors' files.

All my life I have been competing with my older brother. From the first I felt that he was better, smarter, and more handsome than I. He was the one whom my parents loved the more, criticized more gently, praised more highly, and proudly showed off before the relatives and guests. I recall that at such moments, I harbored no feelings of resentment, but only feelings of wistful longing that I might also deserve such appreciation. I became very dutiful and obedient, and my intense efforts to do what they wished were sometimes rewarded.

Today, as a middle-aged adult, I feel a good deal of resentment toward them. I suppose that my dedicated efforts to earn their affection are responsible both for my success, which greatly surpasses my brother's, and for my anxieties and tensions, which are considerable. Although both parents have been dead for years, my persistent emotional need to seek approval through perfect performance is both my virtue and my curse. I often wonder what I would be today, had I received the warm acceptance my brother always enjoyed.

These two cases illustrate the fact that *there is no social situation which has uniformly predictable effects upon all persons in that situation.* All attempts to link predictably a particular behavior outcome with a particular type of family experience are doomed to failure. The most we can say is that certain kinds of family experience *usually* produce well-adjusted, conforming people, while family life which is deficient in certain characteristics is more likely to produce poorly adjusted personalities and behavior deviation. The specific deficiencies may be of many sorts—parental neglect or abuse, lack of sympathy and affection, harsh or erratic discipline, lack of family cohesiveness, excessive parental demands and unrealistic standards, or any of a number of other defects which keep the home from being a pleasant, comfortable place.

Inadequate parents may fail in at least two general ways: (1) They may fail to provide a satisfactory model of normal behavior for their children to copy. If the parents are themselves deviant persons, their children have little opportunity to learn the conventional behavior norms. There is a good deal of speculation upon the possibility that much alcoholism, drug addiction, sex deviation, marital inadequacy, and other behavior difficulty may stem from a boy's inability to identify with his weak, ineffectual father, so that the son was never able to form a satisfactory masculine self-image. Feminine difficulties are often attributed in like manner to a girl's unsatisfactory mother-model. This theory is plausible and widely accepted, although as yet largely unsubstantiated.

(2) Parents may strive to instill the cultural norms in their children, but may succeed only in arousing their children's resistance. Perhaps they are too demanding, too critical, too strict, too erratic, or too unloving. At any rate, a child sometimes develops a strong emotional need to resist parent goals and standards and to shock parents and others by unconventional behavior. A study of American ex-Communists by Ernst and Loth [1952] found that most of them were resentful, somewhat unhappy children of conventional, domineering parents, and had joined the Communist party briefly during young adulthood as a means of emancipation from and revenge upon their parents. Psychiatrists are convinced that some alcoholics are resentful persons who, probably unconsciously, are revenging themselves upon their families by destroying themselves [Podalsky, 1960; Fox, 1956]. L. Young [1954] studied 1,350 unmarried mothers, and concluded that most of them *wanted* an illegitimate child as a form of revenge, usually upon their mothers. An endless variety of behavior difficulties are often traced to some disturbance in the parent-child relationship. Such conclusions are difficult to prove or disprove, but are widely held by behavioral scientists.

Cultural conflicts   In a well-integrated culture with a single set of behavior codes and moral values, socialization is smooth and untroubled. Parents express the cultural norms in their words and actions, and these are reinforced by the rest of the society. But in a heterogeneous, changing society there is no single set of norms; instead many sets of norms and values compete with one another. Many parents find that their efforts to train their children are undermined by other groups and influences. Parents who wish their teen-age children to remain chaste and sober must struggle, not only against the rash, exploratory self-confidence of youth, but also against a variety of commercial panderings and group encouragements which tempt youth to seek "sophistication" and indulgence. Our formal mores demand chastity until marriage, but young people are subjected to a ceaseless barrage of commercial sex stimulation, are exposed to a pseudoscientific literature which encourages and justifies indulgence, and are largely removed from any effective adult chaperonage. Is it surprising that most unmarried young people dally on the borders of unchastity while at least half of them step across it [Reiss, 1960]?

The extreme heterogeneity of American society produces many conflicting norms and values. A variety of immigrant groups have brought differing cultural traditions which are difficult to fuse into a common set of norms. Even the different branches of the Christian faith cannot agree on several questions of morality. Some Protestant groups condemn all alcoholic beverages, dancing, and all kinds of gambling as sinful, while certain other Protestant groups, together with the Catholics, claim that under certain conditions these activities are harmless. The Catholic Church condemns divorce and contraception, while most Protestant bodies will permit them. All American churches teach that one should be generous, sympathetic, and self-sacrificing, but our economic system rewards those who are ruthless, selfish, and grasping. This list of culture conflicts could be extended indefinitely. They are not unique to our society, for culture conflicts are probably found in virtually all societies, and especially in all heterogeneous, changing societies. But wherever they exist, culture conflicts encourage deviant behavior by undermining and weakening the common set of norms and values upon which social order depends. A fairly high rate of deviation is part of the price we pay for a complex, rapidly changing society.

Anomie and deviation From such a variety of conflicting norms arises a condition which Durkheim [1897] called *anomie,* a condition of "normlessness." He did not mean that modern societies have no norms; instead they have many sets of norms, with none of them clearly binding upon everybody. Later sociologists extended the term to include the state of mind in which the person has no firm sense of belonging to anything dependable or stabilizing. As Parsons writes, anomie is

. . . the state where large numbers of individuals are in a serious degree lacking in the kind of integration with stable institutions which is essential to their own personal stability and the smooth functioning of the social system. . . . The typical reaction of the individual is . . . insecurity.

Talcott Parsons, *Essays in Sociological Theory,* The Free Press of Glencoe, New York, 1954, pp. 125, 126.

This approach implies that anomie arises from the confusion and conflict of modern society. People move about too rapidly to be bound to the norms of any particular group and, as a result, have no stable perspective from which to make decisions. In this sense anomie is the result of freedom of choice without the balance assumed to come from stable relationships to church, state, family, or community.

Merton [1938] suggests that anomie comes not from freedom of choice but from the inability of many individuals to follow norms which they are perfectly willing to accept. He sees the major cause of this difficulty as a disharmony between cultural goals and the institutionalized means for reaching them. He notes that while our society encourages *all* its members to aspire to wealth and social position, our approved modes of attaining these goals are so restrictive that only a few have any realistic prospect of reaching them. True, an exceptional poor boy reaches wealth and fame, and these rare exceptions help to preserve the myth of equal opportunity. But a poor boy with a family background of ignorance and apathy and without valuable "connections" has to struggle for success even if he is highly talented. If he has only average abilities, he has still less chance of ever reaching the goals which our culture holds before him unless he violates the rules for seeking them. So Merton concludes:

It is only when a system of cultural values extols, virtually above all else, certain common success-goals for the population at large while the social structure rigorously restricts or completely closes access to approved modes of reaching these goals for a considerable part of the same population, that deviant behavior ensues on a large scale. . . .

The moral mandate to achieve success thus exerts pressure to succeed, by fair means if possible and by foul means if necessary.

Robert K. Merton, "Social Structure and Anomie," in his *Social Theory and Social Structure*, The Free Press of Glencoe, New York, 1957, chap. 3, pp. 146, 169.

The approved path to success in our society lies in education and occupational advancement. To many people, however, education is a frustrating, boring experience which they escape as soon as possible; occupational advancement eludes them, and the idea of saving and investing is not even seriously considered. Since these people still feel entitled to affluence, they proceed to look for other means than those society approves. These deviant routes to legitimate ends may include gambling, swindling, participation in the rackets, or resort to violent crime. When the condition of anomie becomes so widespread that deviancy becomes the rule rather than the exception, then social control may be considered to have completely broken down.

This substitution of illegitimate for legitimate means is only one of several possible reactions to the disparity between universalized goals and restricted methods of obtaining them. Other reactions noted by Merton include (1) *apathy*, a rejection of both goals and means without any alternative focus, (2) *rebellion*, an effort to alter the social system so that both goals and means will be changed, (3) *ritualism*, a slavish devotion to the means while ignoring the end result, (4) *retreatism*, which involves escape through daydreaming, drugs, alcohol, etc. Retreatism is often the route for those whose ability or prepartion is inadequate, but it also involves a number of seemingly competent individuals who have become alienated from conventional norms. All of these are forms of deviation.

Whereas Merton sees deviation growing from one's inability to achieve culturally inspired goals, Riesman [1950] sees it growing from the shift to *other-direction* in modern society. In traditional societies, people are *tradition-directed;* that is, they are guided by a coherent set of traditions which they follow with little deviation. Later the society becomes *inner-directed,* with people guided by a conscience which has internalized the rather authoritarian indoctrination of family and other groups in a stable community. Today man is increasingly *other-directed,* for lack of a coherent tradition or a stable community is leaving him with no clear guide to conduct except the judgments of other people. But since modern societies have many groupings, with differing norms, other-direction provides no dependable guide to conduct. Consequently the behavior of the individual often lacks consistency and conforms to no dependable norm. Since it is impossible, in our complex and changing society, to reestablish stable communities, Riesman looks to the development of "autonomous" persons who can order their lives responsibly without being rooted in stable communities or being puppets of their peer groups. Whether this autonomy is possible remains an unanswered question.

McClosky and Schaar [1965] suggest that anomic normlessness may be simply one aspect of a negative and distrustful outlook on life and society. They present evidence that anomie appears, not only among Merton's frustrated failures, but also among the highly successful. They find that persons who score high on anomic scales also show high scores for hostility, anxiety, pessimism, authoritarianism, political cynicism, and other symptoms of alienation.

All authorities agree that anomie is not the only explanation for deviant behavior, but that anomie is an important factor. Just *how* important it is and exactly *how* anomie produces deviant behavior are still unsettled questions.

Significance of deviant behavior **Deviation is relative, not absolute** People are not completely conformist or completely deviant. A completely deviant person would have a hard time staying alive. Even the more spectacular deviants, such as criminals or sex deviants, are generally fairly conventional in dress, food habits, recreation, and many other activities. And nearly all "normal" people are occasionally deviant. Kinsey [1948, p. 392, 576] has shown how over half our adults could be imprisoned for sex deviations with which they have experimented. A number of studies have shown that most people have committed a number of major crimes for which they could be imprisoned [Porterfield, 1946; Wallerstein and Wyle, 1947]. It is clear that nearly everyone in our society is deviant to some degree; but some are more frequently and broadly deviant than others, and some conceal their deviant actions more fully than others. To some extent, the recognized deviant is one who does openly what others do secretly.

Deviation from real or ideal culture? Since the real and ideal cultures often diverge, as mentioned in Chapter 4, conformity to one may be deviation from the other. For example, the ideal culture includes the cultural norm of obedience to all laws, yet practically no one does so.

Where important values are involved in the divergence between what people say (ideal culture) and what they do (real culture), this becomes an important distinction. In each discussion of deviation where this distinction is important, the normative base—real or ideal culture—should be either implied or expressly stated. For example, in any discussion of premarital chastity or of certain sex "crimes" which are widely practiced by married couples, the normative base should be specified.

Popular labeling of deviants   Whether one is labeled by others as a deviant depends upon the definitions of these other people. A single known homosexual act or a single armed robbery is usually enough to label one a homosexual or criminal; yet many acts of discreet adultery or many tax-chiseling frauds are unlikely to label one a deviant, especially if he is not legally prosecuted. Popular labeling as a deviant apparently depends upon whether the particular act is one which greatly disturbs others, or is defined by others as being outside the tolerance range of the real culture as they perceive it [Becker, 1963, chap. 1].

Norms of evasion   Whenever the mores forbid something that many people strongly wish to do, *norms of evasion* are likely to appear. These are the patterns through which people indulge their wishes without openly challenging the mores. For example, Roebuck and Spray [1967] show how the cocktail lounge functions to facilitate discreet sexual affairs between high-status married men and unattached young women.

   The fact that a particular norm is often violated does not necessarily create a norm of evasion. It is only when there is a *pattern* of violation which is *recognized and sanctioned by one's group* that we have a norm of evasion. Patronizing a bootlegger became a norm of evasion when it became a standard, group-approved way of getting the forbidden alcoholic beverages. In becoming group-sanctioned, the evasion loses its moral censure. Among many groups, success in "fixing" traffic tickets or in seducing women will earn one the admiration of his fellows. Norms of evasion thus are a semi-institutionalized form of deviant behavior.

Deviation and social stability   Deviation is both a threat and a protection to social stability. On the one hand, a culture can function efficiently only if there is order and predictability in social life. We must *know*, within reasonable limits, what behavior to expect from others, what they expect of us, and what kind of society our children should be prepared to live in. Deviant behavior threatens this order and predictability. If too many people fail to behave as expected, the culture becomes disorganized and social order collapses. Economic activity may be disrupted, and actual shortages may appear. The mores lose their compelling power, and the society's core of common values shrinks. Individuals feel insecure and confused in a society whose norms have become undependable. Only when most of the people conform to well-established norms most of the time can a society function efficiently.

   On the other hand, *deviant behavior is one way of adapting a culture to social change*. No society today can possibly remain static for long. Even the most isolated of the world's societies faces sweeping social changes within the next generation. The population explosion, technological change, and the passing of tribal or folk cultures will require new behavior norms of the more primitive peoples, while changing technology continues to demand adaptations from the more advanced peoples. But new norms are not produced by deliberative assemblies of people who solemnly pronounce the old norms outworn and call for new ones. New norms emerge from the daily behavior of individuals, responding in similar ways to the impact of new social circumstances. The deviant behavior of a few individuals may be the beginnings of a new norm. As more and more people join in the deviant form of behavior, a new norm will eventually be established, and the behavior will cease to be "deviant."

The emergence of new norms is neatly illustrated in the decline of the patriarchal family. In an agrarian society where all the family worked together under the father's watchful eye, it was easy to maintain male dominance. But changing technology moved the father's job to the shop or office, where he could no longer keep his eye on things; changing technology also began drawing the wife into jobs where she worked apart from her husband and earned her own paycheck. The husband was no longer in a strategic position to assert his male authority, and, bit by bit, it slipped from him. In the nineteenth century, the relatively independent, equalitarian woman with a mind of her own and a habit of firmly voicing it was a deviant; today she is commonplace. The deviant behavior of one generation may become the norm of the next.

Deviant behavior thus often represents tomorrow's adaptations in their beginnings. Without any deviant behavior, it would be difficult to adapt a culture to changing needs and circumstances. A changing society therefore needs deviant behavior as the incubator of the new norms it must develop if it is to operate efficiently. The question of *how much* deviation and *what kinds* of deviation a society should tolerate is a perpetual puzzle. It is easy now to agree that the eighteenth-century republicans and the nineteenth-century suffragists were socially useful deviants, while the utopians were harmless and the anarchists were socially destructive. But which of today's deviants will prove to be tomorrow's trail blazers—the Communists, nudists, hippies, pacifists, free-lovers, one-worlders, or who? It is difficult to say.

Not all forms of deviation will fit the above analysis. The behavior of the criminal, the sex deviant, or the alcoholic rarely contributes to the forging of a useful new social norm. At any particular moment, deviant behavior takes many forms, only a very few of which are destined to become tomorrow's norms. Much deviation is entirely destructive in its personal and social consequences. But *some* deviation is socially useful, as is indicated above. To separate the socially harmful from the socially useful deviations requires an ability to predict the social norms that tomorrow's society will require. Although sociologists cannot forecast future norms with any certainty of accuracy, they may, however, forecast them somewhat more accurately than others who are not professionals in the study of culture and social change.

SUMMARY

A society must have *social order* if it is to function smoothly. A society maintains *social control* over its members in three principal ways. First, it socializes them so that they will want to behave as they should. Second, society imposes *group pressure* upon the individual so that he must conform or be punished by his group. This group pressure may be expressed through the informal controls of the primary group—approval and disapproval, praise, scorn, ostracism, etc.; or it may operate through the more normal controls of secondary groups—rules and regulations, standardized procedures, propaganda, rewards, titles, and penalties. Finally, control through *force* is used where other controls fail. But in many social situations, behavior is more greatly controlled by the needs and pressures of the situation—the *situational determinants of behavior*—than by the character one brings to the situation.

Social deviation arises whenever a person fails to conform to the usual norms of the society. Deviation may be individual, in that a person deviates from the normal behavior of his group; or it may be group deviation, in which the entire group deviates from social norms, so that the individual is a conforming member of a deviant group or subculture. In practice these two types tend to merge, since deviants tend to seek out other deviants and form deviant groups. Deviants are also divided into *cultural deviants* and *psychological deviants*. Cultural deviants simply deviate from the expected behavior norms. Psychological deviants are deviant from the norm in their personality integration; in their social behavior they may be either deviant or conformist.

Some forms of deviation are approved—the leader, hero, genius, and saint are often (although not always) honored and revered. Efforts to determine which factors account for outstanding individual achievement are not very conclusive, but it appears that social circumstances and personality factors other than pure intelligence play a larger role in "greatness" than is generally known.

Many forms of deviation are disapproved by the culture. Deviation through *inability* to conform—often caused by physical or mental defect or illness—is usually viewed with sympathy. The role of social and cultural influences in producing mental illness cannot be exactly measured, but there is widespread agreement that our culture provokes mental conflicts which contribute to mental illness.

Other deviation arises through *failure* to conform, and the causes are debatable. Physical-type theories are popular but unproved. Psychoanalytic theories are popular and plausible, but also unproved. Most of the disapproved individual deviation probably stems, at least partly if not entirely, from failures in socialization, so that the norms and values of the culture are imperfectly integrated into the personality of the individual. The family plays the key role in socialization and is the main channel through which the child absorbs the society's norms and values. Unsatisfactory family life is, therefore, the principal factor in disapproved individual deviation. The family, however, is a part of the culture, and unsatisfactory family life is often a reflection of conflicts within the culture. Such conflicts surround cultural norms with uncertainty, and by thus imposing pressures upon individuals, help to produce a state of normlessness called *anomie*. The disharmony between our cultural goals and our means for attaining them encourage anomie and deviation.

Deviation is relative, not absolute, in that most people are deviant to some degree. Wherever a particular pattern of deviation becomes widely followed and excused, it is called a *norm of evasion*. Whenever a culture becomes unbearably confining, norms of evasion are likely to appear. In time, these may become the new norms. Thus deviation, while an enemy of social stability, is also a means of introducing the changed norms which become necessary if a changing society is to remain reasonably integrated and efficient.

QUESTIONS AND PROJECTS

1. How does social order depend upon predictability of behavior?

2. Some ancient societies required many human sacrifices. Why did the victims consent to die quietly instead of revolting?

3. Evaluate this statement: "Only weaklings follow the herd. A person with true strength of character will do what he knows is right without being swayed by the group."

4. In the factory a "rate buster" is a worker on piece-work who produces and earns so much that management may revise the piece rate downward. How do the other workers treat him? Is he anything like a "course spoiler" in college, who works so hard in a course that the professor begins to expect more from the other students?

5. What do you think of the Tlingit practice of holding the entire group morally responsible for the acts of each member? Does the practice make for effective social control? How widely could we follow it? Is it consistent with our ethos? Does our society have the kind of group structure in which such a practice is workable?

6. Under what circumstances will practically all students cheat? When will very few students cheat? How does this contrast in attitude illustrate "situational determinants of behavior"?

7. Distinguish between individual and group deviants. How do these two ideal types tend to merge in practice?

8. Is overconformity a mark of successful or unsuccessful socialization?

9. Why do "backward" or primitive societies have less crime and fewer violations of the mores than "progressive" societies like ours?

10. How would you interpret our high Negro crime rate in terms of Merton's theory of cultural goals and institutionalized means?

11. Discuss these propositions: (1) "Norms of evasion are a threat to the stability of a society." (2) "Norms of evasion are a protection to the stability of a society."

12. Read one of the disaster studies such as William Form et al., *Community in Disaster,* Harper & Row, Publishers, Incorporated, New York, 1958, or Harry E. Moore, *Tornados over Texas,* University of Texas Press, Austin, Tex., 1958. Show how social order breaks down and then is restored, following a physical disaster.

13. Compare and explain the differing success of two families in their effort to insulate their children from the influences of a slum neighborhood, as described in Betty Smith, *A Tree Grows in Brooklyn,* Harper & Row, Publishers, Incorporated, New York, 1943, and James T. Farrell, *A World I Never Made,* Vanguard Press, Inc., New York, 1936.

14. Do you think the Presidents of the United States have had greater abilities than the men they defeated? Read Irving Stone, *They Also Ran: The Story of the Men Who Were Defeated for the Presidency,* Doubleday & Company, Inc., Garden City, N.Y., 1943, 1945.

SUGGESTED READINGS

BAVELAS, ALEX: "Communications Patterns in the Task-oriented Groups," in DORWIN CARTWRIGHT and ALVIN ZANDER (EDS.), *Group Dynamics,* Harper and Row, Publishers, Incorporated, New York, 1953, pp. 493–494; Bobbs-Merrill reprint P-25.

*BECKER, HOWARD S.: *Outsiders: Studies in the Sociology of Deviance,* The Free Press of Glencoe, New York, 1963, 1966. A concise description of how people become deviant, applied particularly to marihuana users and dance musicians. (Free P)

BERNSTEIN, BASIL: "Elaborated and Restricted Codes: An Outline," *Sociological Inquiry,* 36:254–261, Spring, 1966. Analysis of the role of language in facilitating communication within the group and simultaneously isolating it from outside contacts.

BINGER, CARL: "The Pressures on College Girls Today," *Atlantic Monthly,* 207:40–44, February, 1961. A popular account of contemporary emotional stress.

BROWN, PAULA: "Changes in Ojibwa Social Control," *American Anthropologist,* 54:57–70, January, 1954. Tells how loss of traditional controls and lack of effective replacements leaves the Ojibwa with an unsolved problem of social control.

CLINARD, MARSHALL: *Sociology of Deviant Behavior,* Holt, Rinehart and Winston, Inc., New York, 1963. A comprehensive textbook on deviation.

GREEN, ARNOLD: "Why Americans Feel Insecure," *Commentary*, 6:18–28, July, 1948; reprinted in EDGAR A. SCHULER ET AL. (EDS.), *Readings in Sociology*, 2d ed., Thomas Y. Crowell Company, New York, 1960, pp. 812–821; 3rd ed., 1967, pp. 793–801.

HORNEY, KAREN: *The Neurotic Personality of Our Time*, W. W. Norton & Company, Inc., New York, 1937. A classic description of how a competitive, stressful society encourages mental disorders.

KLAPP, ORRIN E.: "The Folk Hero," *Journal of American Folklore*, 62:17–25, January, 1949; and "Hero Worship in America," *American Sociological Review*, 14:53–62, February, 1949. A study of those who deviate through superfulfillment of cultural norms, and a study also of their admirers. Also, **Heroes, Villains, and Fools: The Changing American Character*, Prentice-Hall, Inc., Englewood Cliffs, N.J., 1962. A study of deviant social types and of the society which poses them as models. (S-31-Spec)

LANDIS, PAUL H.: *Social Control*, J. B. Lippincott Company, Philadelphia, 1956. An interestingly written textbook on social control.

LEMERT, EDWIN H.: *Social Pathology*, McGraw-Hill Book Company, New York, 1951, chaps. 1–3. A perceptive outline of social deviation.

MERTON, ROBERT K.: *Social Theory and Social Structure*, rev. ed., The Free Press of Glencoe, New York, 1957, chaps. 3 and 4, "Social Structure and Anomie," and "Continuities in the Theory of Social Structure and Anomie." A classic statement upon anomie and deviation in modern society; chap. 11, "The Self-fulfilling Prophecy," is a description of the self-fulfilling prophecy as a basic process in society.

SIMMONS, JERRY L.: "On Maintaining Deviant Belief Systems: A Case Study," *Social Problems*, 11:250–256, Winter, 1964. Description of the way in which acceptance of a bizarre ideological viewpoint is secured.

Three # SOCIAL ORGANIZATION

This section describes how society is organized. People are not independent units, like grains of sand on the beach. The members of a society are organized into many kinds of groups, associations, and relationships. Chapter 8, "Groups and Associations," describes the kinds of groups and associations which appear in any society—ours in particular. Chapter 9, "Social Institutions," describes how the norms of the society and the relationships of its members are organized into working systems in order to meet people's needs. Chapter 10, "The Family," is a detailed description of one of these social institutions—probably the most important. Chapter 11, "Social Class," describes an extremely important set of status relationships among individuals, and shows how these relationships affect their entire lives. Chapter 12, "Social Mobility," shows how people change their class status.

8

GROUPS AND ASSOCIATIONS

Take each of us alone, a man apart from the Cheyenne people who remember the same things and wish for the same things. Take each one of us that way, and you have nothing but a man who cannot respect himself because he is a failure in the white man's way. A man who does not respect himself cannot make a good future. There is no strength in his spirit. Now take all of us together as Cheyenne people. Then our names are not the names of failures. They are the names of great and generous hunters who fed the people, fighters who died for freedom just as white men's heroes died, holy men who filled us with the power of God. Take us together that way and there is a drink for every man in the cup of self-respect, and we will have the strength of spirit to decide what to do and to do it. We will do good things as a tribe that is growing and changing that we cannot do as individual men cut off from their forefathers. (From a statement by the Northern Cheyenne, quoted by Oliver la Farge in *Indian Affairs*, News Letter of the Association for American Indian Affairs, Inc., no. 37, New York, June, 1960.)

HE CHEYENNE are not the only people who find that individual strength and character come from association with the group. All men, regardless of race or culture, find personality fulfillment through group life. The infant becomes "human" as he takes his place in the family; the autistic children mentioned in Chapter 5 are extreme examples of the personality distortion associated with a lack of normal family interaction. As the child moves beyond the family circle he enters into still other group relationships which will continuously remold his personality until death ends the process.

To define a "group" presents certain problems, because it is often difficult to distinguish between categories, aggregates, and groups. A *category* is any number of items (or people) which have some characteristic in common. For example, males, one-eyed people, and high school graduates may be considered categories. An *aggregate*, or *aggregation*, is any number of individuals who are clustered together in space. The population of the Tenth Federal Reserve District may be considered an aggregate. The passengers on a train may also be considered an aggregate. All groups are categories, and most are aggregates; but not all categories or aggregates constitute groups.

One sociologist [Bogardus, 1949, p. 4] suggests this definition of *group*: "A number of persons who have common interests, who are stimulating to each other, who have common loyalty and participate in common activities." This definition covers the groups in which the members come to know each other personally but does not fit groups such as the national fraternal order, the political party, or the national state. Yet all these and many other similar aggregations are important groups in society. For a more inclusive definition, let us say that *groups are aggregates or categories of people who have a consciousness of membership and of interaction*. This definition includes both the large groups in which one never sees most of the members and also the smaller groups such as the family.

This definition excludes certain types of aggregations. A busload of passengers would not ordinarily be a group because they have no consciousness of interaction with each other but simply happen to be in the same place at the same time. It is possible that interaction may develop in the course of the trip and groups may form. When children begin to play together, or boy meets girl, or businessmen discover a common interest in the stock market or the baseball game, groups begin to develop—transient and amorphous though they be. On occasion the entire aggregate may become a group, as in this instance related by Bierstedt.

Subway passengers in New York, for example, are notoriously indifferent to one another. But only the slightest stimulus is needed to transform [them] . . . into a social group. The writer was in a fairly crowded car one evening in the spring when a very young, very tipsy Scandinavian sailor happened to stroll in from the adjoining car. He began to sing aloud in his native language, a gay, pleasant song, and the passengers, aroused from their reveries and their newspapers, responded warmly to his effort and began to exchange smiles with one another. With unexpected and indeed, unusual solicitude for subway passengers, several of the men in the car asked the sailor where he wanted to go and made sure that he did not ride past his destination. After he left, the remaining passengers, augmented now by others who were strangers to the episode, returned to their reveries and their newspapers. The spell was broken. What for a few transitory moments had been a social group became once again . . . people with no more in common than their accidental togetherness at the same time and place, enough to give them a consciousness of kind but not enough, without this extra stimulus, to induce them to enter into social relations with one another.

Robert Bierstedt, *The Social Order*, McGraw-Hill Book Company, New York, 1957, p. 257.

The essence of the social group is not physical closeness but a consciousness of joint interaction. The passengers in the subway car were close together, but until the entry of the sailor gave them a common interest, they were not engaged in joint interaction. Other kinds of stimulus incidents may change an aggregation into a group. For example, a rate increase for passenger fares or a threat to discontinue commuter service may change an unstructured aggregation of passengers into an effective, self-conscious group, developing the usual group patterns as they seek to safeguard a privilege which they might lose. This consciousness of interaction depends on many factors and may be present even when there is no personal interaction between individuals. Thus we are members of a national group and think of ourselves as nationals even though we are acquainted with only a tiny fraction of those who make up our nation. Nevertheless, we interact through political campaigns, the payment of taxes, the use of government services, the response to symbols such as the flag and the national anthem, and perhaps most of all through our consciousness that as citizens of one nation we are bound together in a way that distinguishes us from the citizens of other nations. The definition of group includes the family, the peer group, the neighborhood gang, the work crew, the church, the nation, and many others. Groups vary tremendously in size, purpose, and degree of intimacy among their members, and the individual is involved with them in many different ways.

THE GROUP AND THE INDIVIDUAL

Our individualistic ethos tempts us to assume that the individual is in full command of his behavior and blinds us to the degree to which individual behavior is controlled by group experience. This assumption is revealed by the popular reaction to the announcement that some American soldiers held prisoner by the Chinese in the Korean War had collaborated with the enemy. There was a popular disposition to blame individual weaknesses and character defects, but a more scientific inquiry found that the captured soldiers had been demoralized by a systematic attack upon their group loyalties.

To explain this process we must describe the types of conduct in question. First, all evidence shows that the American soldiers were patriotic men who fought bravely and surrendered only in hopeless situations. There were no wholesale conversions to communism, for when prisoners were given their choice at the end of hostilities, only 21 Americans chose to remain with the Chinese forces as against over 20,000 Chinese prisoners who chose to go to Formosa rather than return to mainland China.

Critics of the conduct of the captive Americans point out that there were no organized escape attempts from prison camps and charge that approximately one in three of the Americans collaborated to some extent with the enemy. A death rate of 38 per cent in the prison camps is also attributed, in part, to the American prisoners' lack of concern for the welfare of their comrades [*U.S. News and World Report,* 1955]. On the other hand, it is also true that conditions of physical terrain and distance from friendly territory made prison camp escape more difficult than in previous wars, that many Americans did resist the demands of their captors, that never before had American prisoners been placed under such intensive pressure to collaborate, and that the prisoner death rate in previous wars was comparable to that in the Korean conflict [Biderman, 1963]. In summary, it appears that the captured Americans stood up about as well as could be expected, but the Chinese and North Koreans were still able to utilize some of them in ways embarrassing to the United States.

Physical hardship, poor food, limited medical attention, and inadequate shelter played a part in weakening the resistance of the American prisoners, but these conditions were not considered sufficiently severe to account for their behavior. Torture and, more frequently, the threat of torture did take place on occasion but affected only a minority of the prisoners. The major means of demoralization used by the Chinese was something more powerful than physical force—*the systematic attack upon group ties,* described by Biderman [1960] and Schein [1960]. Just as "dying is easy for anyone left alone in a concentration camp,"[1] death came easily to prisoners of war who were isolated from their fellows.

The Chinese used such techniques as solitary confinement, isolation of small groups of prisoners, and frequent shifting of personnel to hamper the formation or survival of cohesive groups. More important, they also sought to divide the prisoners in their attitude to each other and to cut off the prisoners from any feeling of effective links with the homeland. Casual information gathered in interviews was used to convince them that all other Americans were informers and that they might as well give in too. If a prisoner resisted what he thought were improper demands from the Chinese, the whole unit was denied food or a chance to sleep until the objector had been forced to come round by his own buddies. The following description of mail censorship gives an idea of some of the procedures used:

Another method of isolating these people from each other was through their selection of mail. . . . This effectively separates people one from another by shearing away what ordinarily serves as a common basis for unified effort and unified activity. When two soldiers get together and compare their letters from home about their kids and about their family and about their house, this has a unifying effect. This binds men closer together. But when your letters are restricted to letters very often which announce some major or minor domestic crisis, when your letter turns out to be a notice from a collection company, or what a soldier calls a "Dear John" letter, this isn't the kind of thing you get together with your buddy and talk about. Consequently, men were deprived of this common emotional basis for sticking together.

[1] An anonymous concentration-camp survivor, quoted in *Life,* Aug. 18, 1958, p. 90.

They also used this control of the mail to make men feel that what the Communist says about capitalism and what it does to its members was demonstrably true, in this respect: It said that our system of free enterprise leads to selfishness, grasping, caring only for what is in it for you, little regard for another individual, especially if he is not there. They said, "Your people at home have forgotten about you. They don't really care about you." What little mail you got was likely to bear this out. Of course this helped make men feel that they were alone and abandoned and isolated.

It was interesting that they routinely did not allow a photograph to come through. A man might get an intact letter in which it said "Here is a picture of me and the kids." No picture. This was almost invariably true, because they didn't want this kind of reminder. They didn't want to give him supports of an emotional kind. It is a diabolical kind of censorship and it is bound over a period of time to be extremely effective.

They cut these people apart, making them isolated and thus obviously much more helpless.

Testimony before the permanent Subcommittee on Investigations; testimony of Major William E. Mayer, Medical Corps, United States Army, before the Committee on Government operations, U.S. Senate, 84th Cong., 2d Sess. Cited in Eugene L. Hartley and Gerhart D. Wiebe, *Casebook in Social Processes*, Thomas Y. Crowell Company, New York, 1960, pp. 76–77. Our general treatment of this topic is based on testimony by Major Mayer and Major Marion R. Panell.

Normally the GI is a gregarious soul, looking for amusement in the company of his buddies and anxious to maintain his home ties. Observers reported that over half of the first group of liberated American prisoners passed up an offer for a free long-distance phone call to the States and that, when given leave in Tokyo, they went to town alone. These are clues to the success with which they had been isolated—from their buddies, from their families, from everyone! How this separateness contrasts with the kind of group experience that makes a soldier effective may be seen in a dispatch by the late Ernie Pyle, a World War II correspondent:

The ties that grow up between men who live savagely and die relentlessly together are of great strength. There is a sense of fidelity to each other among little corps of men who have endured so long and whose hope in the end can be but so small.

One afternoon while I was with the company, S. Sgt. Buck Eversole's turn came to go back to rest camp for five days. The company was due to attack that night.

Buck went to his company commander and said, "Lieutenant, I don't think I better go. I'll stay if you need me."

The lieutenant said, "Of course I need you, Buck, I always need you. But it's your turn and I want you to go. In fact, you're ordered to go." . . .

I walked with him toward the truck in the dusk. He kept his eyes on the ground, and I think he would have cried if he knew how, and he said to me very quietly:

"This is the first battle I've missed that this battalion has been in, and I sure do hope that they have good luck."

And then he said:

"I feel like a deserter."

He climbed in and the truck dissolved into the blackness. I went back and lay down on the ground among my other friends, waiting for the night orders to march. I lay there in the darkness thinking—terribly touched by the great simple devotion of this soldier who was a cowboy—and thinking of the millions far away at home who must remain forever unaware of the powerful fraternalism in the ghastly brotherhood of war.

Ernie Pyle, *Brave Men*, Holt, Rinehart and Winston, Inc., New York, 1944, pp. 197, 198.

The remarkable tenacity with which the German army survived years of unbroken defeats in World War II is testimony to the importance of group unity to fighting effectiveness. During the war the Allies nursed the hope that "psychological warfare" could undermine the German soldier's faith in his cause and his loyalty to his government and thus impair his fighting morale. Postwar studies [Shils and Janowitz, 1948] have shown that this approach was not very effective. It was rooted in the unsound theory that the soldier is sustained mainly by loyalty to his country and faith in the rightness of its cause, whereas postwar investigations found that he is sustained mainly by his unity with, and loyalty to, the small military units to which he is attached. As long as the soldier's immediate group—the primary group which we shall analyze within a few pages—remained integrated, he continued to resist. Even those who were critical of their "cause" remained effective soldiers because of their group loyalties. Among the comparatively few German deserters, their failure to have become fully absorbed into the primary-group life of the army was far more important than any political or ideological doubts. Long after their cause was clearly lost, most German units of all sizes continued to resist until their supplies were exhausted or they were physically overwhelmed.

Such is the sustaining power of a unified group. When bound to his fellow soldiers by shared experience and group loyalties, the soldier was able to face death itself in heroic fashion, but when he was cut off from the support of his group his fighting effectiveness quickly ebbed. Individual qualities certainly played a part, but beyond them was the vital question of whether the soldier was an isolated individual or a member of a group drawing strength from the consciousness of his relationship to others. Pasley [1955] has shown how, of the twenty-one American soldiers who defected to the enemy after being taken prisoner in Korea, eighteen had no close family ties and had never taken part in school activities or sports during their school life. This shows that these were men who had never really "belonged" and were therefore easily open to treason.

The concept of group, then, is not just a sociological plaything. It is a vital social reality, with profound effect upon the behavior of individuals in all social situations. Cut a man off from all group ties, and in many cases he will soon sicken and die; unite him in group loyalty and his endurance and sacrifice are almost beyond belief.

SOME MAJOR GROUP CLASSIFICATIONS

In-groups and out-groups There are some groups to which I belong—my family, my church, my clique, my profession, my race, my sex, my nation—any group which I precede with the pronoun, "my." These are *in-groups,* because I feel I belong to them. There are other groups to which I do not belong—other families, cliques, occupations, races, nationalities, religions, the other sex—these are *out-groups,* for I am outside of them.

In-groups and out-groups.

The least advanced primitive societies live in small, isolated bands which are usually clans of kinsmen. It was kinship which determined the nature of the in-group and the out-group, and when two strangers met, the first thing they had to do was establish relationship. If kinship could be established, then they were friends—both members of the in-group. If no relationship could be established, then in many societies they were enemies and acted accordingly.

Modern society is based upon many ties besides those of kinship, but the establishment and definition of in-groups is equally important to us. People placed in a new social situation will usually make cautious conversational feints to find out whether or not they "belong." When we establish that people have a common economic level with ourselves, a common religious background, a common political viewpoint, are interested in the same types of sports or music, then we may have some assurance that we are in an in-group. Members of the in-group are likely to share certain sentiments, laugh at the same jokes, and define with some unanimity the activities and goals of life. Members of the out-group may share many of the same cultural traits, but they lack certain essentials which are considered necessary to break into this particular social group.

In modern society, we find that individuals belong to so many groups that a number of their in-group and out-group relationships may overlap. A member of a senior class will consider that a freshman belongs to an out-group; yet the same senior and freshman may both be members of an athletic team in which they have an in-group relationship to each other. Similarly, men who have an in-group relationship based on membership in the same church may discover that this association does not extend to economic relationships; and women who work together in the PTA may find that they are no longer in the same in-group when making plans for a party at the country club.

The fact that in-group and out-group classifications cut across many lines does not minimize their intensity; the subtlety of some distinctions makes exclusion even more painful. One may crave membership in a group which excludes him. Thus the "new rich" who have all the surface qualifications for admittance to "society" may still find themselves excluded from the social register. The teen-ager who hopes desperately for acceptance may find that no clique welcomes him; the housewife may be left out of the coffee klatsch; and the man on a work gang may find himself the butt of ridicule rather than one of a group of comfortable companions. Exclusion from the in-group can be a brutal process. Most primitive societies treated outsiders as part of the animal kingdom; many had no separate words for "enemy" and "stranger," showing that they made no distinction. Not too different was the attitude of the Nazis, who excluded the Jews from the human race. Rudolf Hoess, who commanded the Auschwitz concentration camp in which 2 million Jews were put to death, characterized this slaughter as "the removal of racial-biological foreign bodies."[2]

It is impossible to understand the repeated brutalities of history without understanding in-groups and out-groups. This distinction makes it psychologically possible for even decent and humane men to commit cruel acts. Trevor-Roper writes:

Seventeenth-century Englishmen were generally tolerant and humane. Even in their civil war and revolution, they constantly remembered that their enemies were like themselves; they fought them with mildness and courtesy. Oliver Cromwell himself was ahead of his age in tolerance. But when Cromwell invaded Ireland, he assumed a new character. To him and his followers, the Irish were quite different. A generation of ideological propaganda against creatures safely invisible in another island made it possible for Englishmen to regard the Irish as "sub-human," and for Cromwell (who was surprisingly tolerant of Roman Catholics in England) to write from Drogheda that his "knocking on the head" of obstinate Irishmen was "a righteous judgment of God" on "these barbarous wretches."
H. R. Trevor-Roper, *New York Times Magazine*, Sept. 17, 1961, p. 108.

In-groups and out-groups are important, then, because they affect behavior. From fellow members of an in-group, we expect recognition, loyalty, and helpfulness. From out-groups, our expectation varies with the kind of out-group. From some out-groups we expect hostility; from others, a more or less friendly competition; from still others, indifference. From the sex out-group we may expect neither hostility nor indifference; yet in our behavior a difference undeniably remains. The twelve-year-old boy who shuns girls grows up to become a romantic lover and spends most of his life in matrimony. Yet when men and women meet on social occasions they tend to split into one-sex groups, for each sex is bored by many of the conversational interests of the other.

Social distance   We are not equally involved in all our in-groups. One might, for example, be a passionate Democrat and a rather indifferent Rotarian. Nor do we feel equally distant from all our out-groups. A loyal Democrat will feel far closer to the Republicans than to the Communists. Bogardus [1958, 1959] and others [Westie, 1959] have developed the concept, *social distance*, to measure the *degree of closeness or acceptance we feel* toward other groups. While most often used with reference to racial groups, social distance refers to closeness among groups of all kinds.

Social distance is measured either by direct observation of the relationships which people have with other groups, or more often by questionnaires in which people are asked the relationships in which they would accept or reject members of certain other groups. In these questionnaires, a number of groups may be listed and the informants asked to check whether they would accept a member of each group as a neighbor, as a fellow worker, as a marriage partner, and so on through a series of relationships. Table 4 shows a study of social-distance reactions of a sample of college students to eleven different groups.

[2] See Rudolf Hoess, *Commandant of Auschwitz*, tr. by Constantine Fitzgibbon, The World Publishing Company, Cleveland, 1960, in which Hoess tells with nostalgic pride how efficiently he organized this operation; reviewed in *Time*, Mar. 28, 1960, p. 110.

Table 4   *Social distance on the campus: Percentage of students in 40 American colleges who would accept or reject personal contacts with other group members*

Other groups	Work beside on job	Live on same block	Have as intimate friend	Date or allow child to date	Marry	Bar from social club	Bar from block
Italians	92%	84%	84%	76%	65%	4%	4%
Negroes	89%	58%	63%	24%	29%	24%	26%
Jews	93%	84%	85%	60%	37%	12%	6%
Japanese	90%	74%	72%	46%	24%	11%	8%
Catholics	95%	83%	92%	73%	56%	3%	1%
Filipinos	89%	73%	69%	42%	24%	12%	11%
Protestants	95%	96%	92%	83%	74%	1%	1%
Mexicans	88%	66%	68%	45%	31%	15%	14%
Greeks	93%	82%	80%	64%	50%	6%	4%
Irish	95%	88%	87%	77%	64%	3%	2%
Polish	93%	83%	83%	72%	61%	4%	3%

SOURCE: Albert I. Gordon, *Intermarriage*, Beacon Press, Boston, 1964, pp. 389–399.

The social-distance questionnaires may not accurately measure what people actually would do if a member of another group sought to become a friend or neighbor. The social-distance scale is only an attempt to measure one's feeling of unwillingness to associate equally with a group. What a person will actually do in a situation also depends upon the circumstances of the situation, a point which will be discussed at some length in the chapter on race and ethnic relations.

Reference groups   There are groups which are important to us as models even though we ourselves may not be a part of the group. The opinions of "high society" may be important to the social climber who has not yet made the social register. At times the in-group and the reference group may be the same, as when the teen-ager gives more weight to the opinions of the gang than to those of his teachers. Sometimes an out-group is a reference group: American Indians wore war paint to impress their enemies, and little boys (of all ages!) show off to impress girls. A reference group is any group to which we *refer* when making judgments—any group whose value judgments become our value judgments. You will recall that we mentioned the concept of reference group when speaking of the "looking-glass" self, indicating that the young child is interested in the reactions of everyone with whom he is in contact, while the more mature person selects particular groups whose approval—or whose disapproval—he especially desires.

Primary and secondary groups   Primary groups are those in which we come to know other people intimately as individual personalities. We do this through social contacts that are *intimate, personal,* and *total* in that they involve many parts of the person's life experience. In the primary group, such as family, clique, or set of close friends, the social relationships tend to be informal and relaxed. The members are interested in one another as persons. They confide hopes and fears, share experiences, gossip agreeably, and fill the need for intimate human companionship. In the *secondary group* the social contacts are *impersonal, segmental,* and *utilitarian.* One is not concerned with the other person as a person, but as a functionary who is filling a role. His personal qualities are not important; his performance—only that part, or segment, of his total personality involved in playing a role—is important. The secondary group might be a labor union or a trade association, a country club, or a PTA, or it might be two persons bargaining briefly over a store counter. In any case the group exists to serve a specific, limited purpose involving only a segment of the personalities of the members.

The terms *primary* and *secondary* thus describe a type of relationship rather than the relative importance of the group. The primary group may serve objective functions such as the provision of food and clothing, but it is judged by the quality of its human relationships rather than by its efficiency in meeting material needs. The secondary group may function in pleasant surroundings, but its principal purpose is to fulfill a specific function. One does not consider a family successful because the house is clean, nor does one judge the New York Stock Exchange mainly by the pleasant manner in which the broker's clerk answers the phone; indeed telegraphic communication is apt to eliminate even this vestige of a human touch. Primary groups are not judged so much by their "efficiency" in performing some task as by the emotional satisfactions they bring to their members. Thus the quartet of ladies who meet for bridge Tuesday afternoons may play a pretty indifferent bridge game but share a lot of pleasant, gossipy conversation. Tournament and duplicate bridge are another matter. Here, virtual or total strangers meet and play to win. A "good partner" is a skillful player who wastes no time on distracting small talk. The major goal is a winning score (and master points chalked up), not sociability. A good lunch-table clique is one that has fun; a good union is one that succeeds in protecting its members' interests. Primary groups are judged by the satisfying human response they supply; secondary groups are judged by their ability to perform a task or achieve a goal. Although secondary groups sometimes also provide pleasant human relationships, sociability is ordinarily not their goal. In brief, *primary groups are relationship-directed, and secondary groups are goal-oriented.*

Primary and secondary groups are important because feelings and behavior are different. It is in the primary group that personality is formed. In the primary group one finds intimacy, sympathy, and a comfortable sharing of many interests and activities. In the secondary group one finds an effective mechanism for achieving certain purposes, but often at the price of suppressing one's true feelings. For example, the saleslady must be cheerful and polite, even when she has a splitting headache and the customer is a boor. The concepts are useful because they describe important differences in behavior.

Gemeinschaft and Gesellschaft

Somewat similar to the concepts of primary and secondary groups are the concepts of *Gemeinschaft* and *Gesellschaft,* developed by the German sociologist Ferdinand Tönnies [1957]. The gemeinschaft is a society in which most relationships are personal or traditional, and often both. A good example is the feudal manor, a small community held together by a combination of personal relationships and status obligations. Although great inequality existed, the lord of the manor was personally known to his subjects while their duties to him were balanced by his obligation for their welfare. When money was used, economic transactions were governed by the concepts of a just price; more often the people involved simply carried out a network of customary obligations to one another. Written documents were scarce, formal contracts unknown, bargaining rare, and behavior of all types operated in traditional patterns that were known and accepted by all the community. Men had little hope of surpassing their fathers and equally little fear of falling behind the parental status. Except for occasional feast days, life was monotonous; but loneliness was rare in a community of lifelong neighbors.

The gesellschaft has replaced the society of tradition with the society of contract. In this society neither personal attachment nor traditional rights and duties are important. The relationships between men are determined by bargaining and defined in written agreements. Relatives are separated as people move about and live among strangers. Commonly accepted codes of behavior have less force than rational—or "cold-blooded"—calculation of profit and loss. The gesellschaft flourishes in the modern metropolitan city. Some of the contrasting characteristics of gesellschaft and gemeinschaft relationships are summarized in this table:

Gemeinschaft relationships	Gesellschaft relationships
Personal	Impersonal
Informal	Formal, contractual
Traditional	Utilitarian
Sentimental	Realistic, "hard-boiled"
General	Specialized

MODERN TREND TOWARD SECONDARY-GROUP ASSOCIATION

Our sentiments and emotional ties are centered in primary groups, but an accelerating trend toward a gesellschaft society based on secondary groups has been irresistible in the modern era. The small principalities of feudal Europe have given way to national states, and the intimate association of master and workmen in the guild workshop has yielded to the giant corporation employing thousands of men. Population has moved from the country to the city, and lifetime residence in familiar surroundings has become a rarity as approximately one American family in five moves each year.

An industrialized urban society attacks the primary group in at least two ways. First, it increases the relative proportion of secondary-group contacts, as one activity after another is withdrawn from the primary group and assumed as a secondary-group function. Second, the primary-group associations which remain are at the mercy of secondary-group developments. Changes in industry may move the wage earner about, disrupting his local associations. Industrial changes also influence the roles played in the family. A prolonged depression, the result of a maladjustment of secondary relationships, may deprive the father of his earning power and substitute the wife and the relief administrator as symbols of authority. Changes in office and factory work lead to the employment of women, so that the mother has the same kind of career as the father, and both share in the domestic tasks of the home. Changes in the international political scene may take the husband or son out of the family locale and move him to the other side of the world. The worker's family must adjust itself to whatever working hours the corporation finds most profitable. Negotiations between the international union and the corporation may result in work changes which break up informal primary groups formed on the job. The "little red schoolhouse" where a small group of children and a teacher formed an intimate primary group lasting for years is succeeded by the consolidated school, drawing hundreds of children from a large area and shifting them about from class to class and teacher to teacher. Scores of similar examples show how primary groupings have become transient and changing units, swept along by the heedlessly changing trends of a gesellschaft society.

Such a trend is not universally welcomed. Critics maintain that it produces shallow and rootless personalities which lack the calm certainty and deep friendship which supposedly characterized personal relationships in the gemeinschaft setting. A visiting Filipino educator expressed this view in his reaction to America's largest city:

In New York, people seem so busy and so deeply concerned with their own affairs that they no longer know how to smile. Some of them wear masks like "guys and dolls" who conceal their inner world from the busy chatter outside. They walk hurriedly—tack! tack! tack!—on the sidewalks, like robots, unfeeling and unconcerned.

Vidal A. Tan, "Visit to America," *Sunday Times Magazine*, Manila, Dec. 28, 1952.

Durkheim [1897] in his study of suicide came to the conclusion that not only high rates of suicide but many other behavior difficulties are explained by the lack of traditional and personal ties in a secondary society, where the individual is engulfed by anomie. Many students of society have followed his lead in regarding the secondary trends of the modern world as an evil force destructive of the relationships that assured man of membership in a warm and secure society where his tendencies toward crime or despair were curbed by his obligations to a stable and intimate social community.

Contributions of the gesellschaft   While the gesellschaft has brought problems to man, it has also brought benefits. The most obvious is the efficiency of large-scale impersonal organizations in which sentiment is subordinated to the need to get the job done in the most practical way. The tremendous advances in material comfort and in life expectancy in the modern world would be impossible without the rise of goal-directed secondary organizations, in which the paternal squire has been replaced by the efficiency expert and the production manager.

Nor has the rise of the gesellschaft and the accompanying division of labor had only materialistic advantages. These changes have opened channels of opportunity and specializations of function which, while they fragment society, also open a greater chance to develop individual talents. The contrast between the thousands of occupations in the metropolis and the handful of pursuits in the rural village shows how a society dominated by secondary groups opens the way for specialized careers. This process has gone so far today that not only is the talented individual able to rise from an obscure background but society actively seeks out those whose abilities may be developed along professional, artistic, scientific, or managerial lines.

The secondary group also has a tendency toward the imposition of patterns of conformity on its members. In this way it offers a counter-balance to the prejudices or vested interests of the immediate locality. Since its boundaries extend beyond the primary group, it forces a consideration of events from a larger perspective. This difference in attitudes may be seen in the tendency of religious organizations, operating on a national or international scale, to espouse viewpoints which may be unpopular in local congregations. The reaction of the Southern Baptist Churches to the school-integration issue is a case in point. With a membership of white Southerners, most congregations have been strongly segregationist in their beliefs and practices. Prominent members, including some pastors, have been active in the efforts to keep racial separation in the schools. Nevertheless, when meeting as a national body somewhat removed from the pressures of local groups, the convention of the Southern Baptist Churches voted in 1954 to *endorse* the Supreme Court decision [Fey, 1954]. A similar type of reaction to the segregation issue occurred among Roman Catholics in Louisiana. Here the violently prosegregationist stand of local Catholics contrasts sharply with the prointegration stand of the church as a whole as voiced by the Archbishop [*America*, 1957].

Lest these be viewed as isolated incidents peculiar to an especially violent racial controversy, we should add that this disparity between national and local views is common in many church groups on many questions. For example, a study [Glock and Ringer, 1956] of the Protestant Episcopal Church showed a wide divergence between statements of the national body and views of members of local congregations on eight out of nine issues. Such a divergence between national and local sentiment is sometimes attributed either to hypocrisy at the local level or to a misrepresentation of the "real" views of the organization at the national level. A more penetrating analysis would emphasize the fact that while the local group and the national organization interact, the national body has concerns which may override local feelings.

This tendency for the secondary organization to be more universal in its judgments and the primary units to be more particularistic—that is, influenced by local concerns and personal attitudes—is not confined to churches and may be observed in the deliberations of business, labor, and political organizations. The emphasis on goals rather than on personal relationships and the need to accommodate a large number of individuals and localities tend toward an outlook which reaches beyond the primary group. Such an outlook is, however, not necessarily more liberal or humanitarian. Communist Russia and Nazi Germany are extreme examples of situations in which the goals of secondary organizations demanded action which violated the local code of human decency. The expulsion of the more well-to-do peasants in Russia from their farms and the large-scale use of concentration camps in Germany were motivated by goals beyond the usual concern of a local community, but they diminished rather than increased the area of human fellowship. Secondary groups may restrain local greed and shatter the bonds of provincialism, or they may let loose a ruthless force which transgresses the traditional mores in pursuit of institutional goals.

Persistence of The secondary group has overshadowed but not destroyed the primary group.
primary groups In fact, the two major primary groups, the clique and the family, appear to be
stronger than ever. The clique is a small group of intimates with intense in-
group feelings based on common sentiments and interests. It may develop in
almost any situation, and nearly every secondary group shelters a large number of cliques which add a highly personal note to an otherwise impersonal
environment. As for the family, more people get married today, and get married
earlier, than in any other period on which we have reliable data. Furthermore,
today's family is steadily becoming less directed toward mundane goals and
more concerned with human relationships. Yesterday's family was primarily
a work crew, sometimes a brutally repressive one; today's family is primarily
a companionship group, and a perfect example of primary-group persistence.

Primary groups persist in a secondary-group-dominated world because the
human need for intimate, sympathetic association is a continuous need. Man
cannot function well unless he belongs to a small group of people who really
care what happens to him. Wherever people are ripped from family and friends
and thrust into large, impersonal, anonymous groups, as in a college dormitory
or an army camp, they feel such great need for primary groups that they
promptly re-form them.

Primary groups If we classified groups according to the extent to which they show primary- or
in a secondary secondary-group traits, the result would be a listing of secondary groups such
setting as the army, the corporation, and the national state, and a list of primary
groups such as the family, the clique, and the gang. Proceeding in this fashion,
we should then contrast the impersonal goal-directed nature of the large organization with the personal, relationship-oriented focus of smaller intimate
groups. Such a separation is often assumed when we attempt to analyze the
efficiency of large organizations. If we are interested in the productivity of
industrial labor, we might study the goals, techniques, and rewards of the
factory and then look at the character and training of the individuals who make
up the labor force.

The fallacy of this approach is that it overlooks the extent to which every
large organization is a network of small primary groups. A person is not simply
a unit in an organization chart designed by top management; he is also a member of a smaller informal group with its own structure and its own system of
statuses and roles defining the behavior of its members. In the factory the
workman finds his place in a group of his fellows with its own leadership, from
which the foreman is usually excluded since his very position bars him from
this in-group relationship. Since the workman needs the approval and support
of his clique more than he needs the approval of his supervisors, he responds
to the demands of management only as these demands are consistent with his
primary-group relationships.

The influence of the primary group is one reason why incentive pay plans
giving the worker a bonus for greater output have frequently been ineffective.
The logic of such plans is that many workers who fail to exert their maximum
efforts will work harder if paid in proportion to the work they do. The major
defect in such plans is that their effective operation destroys the unity of
primary groups. Rather than a number of equals cooperating together, the
work gang would become a number of competing individuals each striving to

Primary groups persist in a secondary-group dominated world.

outdo his fellows. Aside from the strain of continuous competition, this situation threatens the workers' social relationships. As a defense, factory cliques develop a norm of a "fair day's work." The man who attempts to ignore this norm is the butt of ridicule, ostracism, and possible violence. Management may employ time and motion study experts to decide a "reasonable" output, but new norms cannot be effective unless they are also accepted by the group [Roethlisberger and Dickson, 1939, chaps. 22, 23; Moore, 1947, chap. 15].

While the primary group in the secondary setting can be an obstacle, it can also be a positive aid in the accomplishment of organizational objectives. Gross [1953] has examined the way in which informal cliques that cut across formal work assignments may lead to cooperation and smoother functioning of the organization. He finds that the clique may even reinforce the idea of organization loyalty, as one private secretary reveals:

A private secretary is the top of the heap. You need something else beside the ability to type and take shorthand. You've got to feel that you are working for the company and not just for yourself. Now Mildred and Emma [other private secretaries], we see eye to eye on that. Louise—she's a good little stenographer, but she'll never be a secretary. She doesn't fit into our crowd. When we go out for coffee she usually tags along. Then she'll complain about her boss. She can't accept the idea that you don't work for a boss, you work for the company.

Edward Gross, "Some Functional Consequences of Primary Controls in Formal Work Organizations," *American Sociological Review*, 18:372, August, 1953.

At times the primary groups may even violate the rules of the larger secondary organization in order to get things done. If the formal rules are not always workable in all situations, primary worker groups simply trim some corners—that is, break a few rules—in order to get the work out [Roy, 1955].

Perhaps the most dramatic of all illustrations of the influence of the group is found in studies of the extent to which American combat soldiers actually fired their guns in combat. Since the soldiers have been trained to shoot and may die if they fail to shoot, one would take their reaction for granted. Actually many men found that at the crucial moment they were unable to fire. In fact, studies in World War II [Marshall, 1947; Davidson, 1952] indicated that only 12 to 25 per cent of combat soldiers in a position to fire were able to pull the trigger. Apparently the soldiers had been so strongly conditioned against taking human life that even when self-defense and the call of duty demanded that they kill the enemy, they were unable to overcome the effect of the mores of the civilian culture. Research on combat behavior found that patriotism, hatred of the enemy, military training, and fear of punishment are not very effective in making a man perform well in combat. The main variable that determines how well a man will fight is his degree of integration with his unit. Men who will not shoot to save themselves will shoot to save their comrades. Highly integrated units fought bravely. Poorly integrated units, although identical in individual abilities and training, fought poorly, with a high proportion of non-shooters, deserters, and mental breakdowns. The authors of the research study, *The American Soldier*, conclude that the primary group "served two principal functions in combat motivation: it set and emphasized group standards of behavior and it supported and sustained the individual in stresses he would otherwise not have been able to withstand" [Shils, 1950].

Training methods and combat techniques now are designed to create the closest possible unity of member and group. For example, two men are assigned to a foxhole instead of the men being scattered as much as possible. Instead of keeping silence in combat, men are now encouraged to yell and scream while attacking, as this binds them into a group. Officers are told to spend their time crawling from foxhole to foxhole to keep the mob psychology going. In such ways, the primary group may be used to achieve secondary-group objectives.

Integration of primary and secondary groups   Just as we cannot realistically consider the individual apart from society, so we cannot understand secondary and primary groups completely except in relation to each other. In modern society the functions and influence of primary groups have been weakened by a growth of impersonal, goal-directed secondary groups which are assuming an increasingly dominant role. Each of these secondary groups, however, creates a new network of primary groups that provide intimacy and personal response in an otherwise impersonal situation. While these and other primary groups are often destroyed or modified by the impact of secondary groups, the primary groups in turn exert a major influence on the secondary groups. Primary groups may resist the goal-directed efforts of secondary organizations, or they may help to integrate disparate parts of the organization and provide an emotional security which reinforces the individual's ability to play the roles demanded by his status in the secondary group.

VOLUNTARY ASSOCIATIONS

It has been said that if three Americans were shipwrecked on a remote island, they would spend the first day forming an organization, electing officers, and appointing a committee! All of us are compelled to become members of some organizations. We are born into membership in the nation; parental influence largely determines our membership in churches; the need to make a living causes us to be employees of business concerns; the need to protect our economic interests and, sometimes, the direct compulsion of a "closed shop" compel some of us to be members of a labor union. On the other hand, there are many groups in which membership is much more voluntary. We are not forced to become members of the Rotary Club, the Americans for Democratic Action, the John Birch Society, the Boy Scouts, the athletic association, the "little theater," or the country club. One authority [Morris, 1965] defines voluntary associations in these terms: "Voluntary associations are groups in which membership is in no sense obligatory, which have a formal constitution but which usually do not have paid officials at the local level." Sometimes, however, while membership may not be obligatory, it is highly expedient, as when the businessman finds it very wise to join some church and attend Rotary Club.

Voluntary associations are an important part of the life of many people, especially in the urban middle class. For example, consider how voluntary associations affect the life of many a businessman. After luncheon at the chamber of commerce he rushes back to the office to get in a little work before spending the rest of the afternoon soliciting for the community chest. When he returns home after a weary round of pledging, he finds that his children have gone on an overnight hike with the scout troop and that dinner is delayed because his wife spent the afternoon at a board meeting of the Children's Aid Society. In the evening his wife will be attending a League of Women Voters' session while he joins an initiation ceremony at his lodge. During the week his leisure and working hours are sprinkled with club luncheons, committee sessions, and organization meetings. On weekends he and his family spend much of their time at the country club, and on Sundays the children are apt to find themselves involved in a church youth group. These are only the beginning. He or his family are sought by the symphony society, the art center, and the little-theater group; the taxpayers' association, the good-government league, and a dozen reform organizations beckon to him; the PTA, several church groups, and a dozen welfare organizations crave his support. Obviously, he cannot support them all!

Voluntary associations attract many types of people. The young businessman finds that he is expected to take a major part in civic organizations, and labor leaders view invitations to serve in such groups as a sign that they have begun to be recognized by the rest of the community. Smaller towns supposedly offer a sense of community which might make formal organizations less necessary, but a survey [Scott, 1957] of a New England town of about 7,500 found a higher level of participation in organized groups than in most large cities. Surveys of participation usually show less activity among Negroes than among whites, but the existence of 4,000 associations among Chicago Negroes indicates that any Negro-white gap in this respect will probably be of short duration [Myrdal, 1944, pp. 952–955]. Roman Catholicism has usually not encouraged voluntary associations, and Catholic membership in such groups is ordinarily low in Catholic countries and among Catholic minorities in other countries. In the United States, however, the Catholic Church met the attraction of secular associations by promoting a large number of Catholic organizations in an effort to keep the voluntary-association tendency within the Catholic framework. In short, voluntary associations in great variety and number are a conspicuous feature of American life.

A voluntary association differs from a social institution by having a rather narrowly limited purpose (e.g., to enjoy bowling, to protect neighborhood property values, or to secure a particular social reform), while the institution pursues a series of rather broad, general purposes. Also, an institution is basically a set of *norms* and *ideas*, together with the necessary people and procedures, while an association is basically a *group of people* who have organized to pursue a particular activity or objective. Some associations are attached to an institution, helping it to pursue one, or a few, of its purposes. Thus the PTA and the alumni association serve the school, while a church has its youth groups, men's clubs, and ladies' guilds. Other associations, like the photography club or the neighborhood-improvement association, may be independent of any institutional connection. Rose [1954, p. 52] makes a distinction between *expressive* associations such as sport groups and hobby clubs, and *social-influence* groups such as taxpayers associations, chambers of commerce, and the National Association for the Advancement of Colored People. The expressive groups provide activities for their members; the social-influence groups are directed toward achieving some sort of social power.

Functions of voluntary associations

An outlet for individual interests   The major appeal of the voluntary association lies in its ability to provide a means of satisfying the proclivities of a number of citizens even though their interest is not shared by the total society. A few men who like to play golf can band together and provide a country club even though the city council may be cool to the use of tax money for adult playgrounds. A few individuals may band together to found a planned-parenthood association to take action in a controversial field where it is politically unwise for the government to act. Rose [1954, p. 58] maintains that a variety of voluntary associations provide a type of "cultural pluralism," in which varied interests may be supported within the same society. Whatever the purpose, the voluntary association has the supreme merit of enabling a minority of the people to take some action toward realizing their aims without being held back by a hostile or indifferent majority.

A testing ground for social programs   The voluntary association can develop a program and so demonstrate its value that it is ultimately taken over by the church or the state. The Sunday school began as an individual project by Robert Raikes, then was promoted through the London Sunday School Society, and is now an organic part of most Protestant churches. Most of the welfare functions of the modern state were born in voluntary associations which saw a social need, pioneered a program, and educated the public to the point where government was expected to assume the responsibility.

A channel of purposive social action   The voluntary association enables the private citizen to share in the making of major social decisions. Many observers feel that this is a vital part of the democratic process. One sociologist observes:

More specifically, the hypothesis is that the voluntary associations have three important functions in supporting political democracy in the United States: (1) They distribute power over social life among a very large proportion of the citizenry, instead of allowing it to be concentrated in the elected representatives alone, so that the United States has a little of the character of the ancient Greek democratic city-state, as well as of the modern European centralized republic. (2) The voluntary associations provide a sense of satisfaction with modern democratic processes because they help the ordinary citizen to see how the processes function in limited circumstances, of direct interest to himself, rather than as they grind away in a distant, impersonal, and incomprehensible fashion. (3) The voluntary associations provide a social mechanism for continually instituting social changes, so that the United States is a society in flux, constantly seeking (not always successfully, but seeking nevertheless) to solve long-standing problems and to satisfy new needs of groups of citizens as these needs arise.

Arnold Rose, *Theory and Method in the Social Sciences,* The University of Minnesota Press, Minneapolis, 1954, p. 52.

Voluntary associations are almost the only means whereby the average citizen can share actively in democratic policy formation. It is indeed doubtful whether American democracy could survive without them.

Participation in voluntary associations Activity in voluntary associations is so conspicuous in the American community that observers tend to view it as a universal interest. Thus the historians Charles and Mary Beard [1930, pp. 730–731] report that "It was a rare American who was not a member of four or five societies. . . . Any citizen who refused to affiliate with one or more associations became an object of curiosity if not suspicion." Statements of this kind reflect the impressions that men of social prominence have when they observe their peers. It is true that the better-educated and higher-income groups participate actively in association work. Careful surveys reaching a cross section of the population, including those whose economic and educational handicaps make them less conspicuous, present a different picture.

A look at the characteristics of people who participate actively will tell us a good deal not only about voluntary associations but also about the general topic of social participation in American society [Scott, 1957; Wright and Hyman, 1958; Komarovsky, 1946b; Bell and Force, 1956; Foskett, 1955; Axelrod, 1956]. High rates of participation characterize the upper-income groups, the more highly educated, and those living in high-status urban communities. Men have a higher rate of participation than women, and Jews and Protestant a higher rate than Catholics. Studies of high school youth [Stone, 1960] show higher organizational participation among youth whose families come from higher income and educational levels. They also show a higher rate among girls than boys, and a higher rate among youth who classify their family relationship as satisfactory than among those who have family problems.

Participation in voluntary associations in the United States

High participation	Low participation
Protestants	*Roman Catholics*
Jews	*No religious affiliation*
Men	*Women*
College-educated	*Elementary school only*
Children of native-born parents	*Children of foreign-born parents*
Business and professional occupation	*Manual occupation*

Colleges, like urban communities, have a proliferation of organizations in which some students participate to a great extent, others moderately, many students not at all. Organization work might be thought to conflict with studies, but surveys show that the better students are most apt to be members and officers of numerous organizations [Burma, 1947; Chapin, 1931].

From our study of voluntary associations we find that they have provided a means of social interaction through which the citizen can understand and, to some extent, control his society. But voluntary associations are largely an activity of the middle and upper classes. Possibly the lower classes, less mobile geographically and with more opportunity to rely on family relations (the ex-

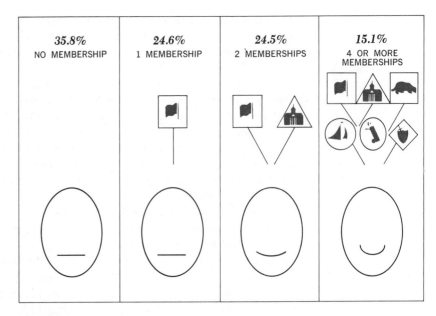

| 35.8%
NO MEMBERSHIP | 24.6%
1 MEMBERSHIP | 24.5%
2 MEMBERSHIPS | 15.1%
4 OR MORE
MEMBERSHIPS |

FIGURE 2 *A Nation of Joiners?*

Organizational participation reported by residents of a New England small city.

SOURCE: Based on a survey in Bennington, Vermont, reported by John C. Scott, Jr., "Memberships and Participation in Voluntary Associations," *American Sociological Review,* 22:315–326, June, 1957. Surveys in other communities arrived at quite similar conclusions.

tended family) for social relationships, feel less need for activity in voluntary associations. Apparently the better-educated and more prosperous persons find organization activity a useful means of adjusting to a complex modern society; and their children acquire the same pattern at an early age. The manual workers, the less educated, and the residents of substandard neighborhoods are indifferent to appeals to join in such activity. Neighborhood improvement associations flourish in prosperous areas where they might seem superfluous and founder in deteriorating neighborhood which seem to need some concerted attempt to improve community life. Bewildered and lonely individuals seldom find their way into associations, while the well informed and gregarious are overwhelmed with organization activity. Those who might gain the most from voluntary associations are least equipped to participate in them and least inclined to seek them.

Voluntary associations are important in all industrialized countries, and to a lesser extent are found in other areas as well, but in no other major country are they as numerous and influential as in the United States.[3] European coun-

[3] Kenneth Little ("The Role of Voluntary Associations in West African Urbanization," *American Anthropologist,* 59:579–596, August, 1957) states that the West African cities may be an exception, with many associations, often based on tribal or kinship lines, involving many people and functioning to provide sociability and mutual aid as well as social control. More typical of the developing areas is the situation reported by Floyd Dotson ("A Note on Participation in Voluntary Associations in a Mexican City," *American Sociological Review,* 18:380–386, August, 1953) in a study of Guadalajara, the second largest city of Mexico, where he found voluntary organization was rudimentary and participation far less widespread than in American cities of comparable size.

tries in the past have been suspicious of voluntary associations, feeling that they might represent a conspiracy against the state or the church. Even today the increase in voluntary associations in Europe has been mostly along the lines of cooperatives, church-sponsored societies, political parties, and labor unions. The notion that active participation in strictly voluntary single-purpose groups is both an obligation and an opportunity of the citizen is still primarily an American idea, not widely shared by the rest of the world.

GROUP DYNAMICS

For a long time sociologists were busy trying to convince a skeptical world that the group was real and not simply a collection of individuals. Only recently have sociologists turned their attention to the specific factors which affect the functioning of groups. Obviously many possible patterns may occur. A group may be dominated by one or two individuals, or it may involve the participation of all its members; leadership may be democratic or authoritarian, transitory or enduring; the group may stimulate productivity or hold it down; its atmosphere may be relaxed and friendly or tense and charged with hostility; it may forge new approaches to problems or stick to old routines. These and many other patterns have often been observed. The question arises, "What factors produce one or another type of group life and how can these factors be controlled?"

The academic interest of sociologists in expanding the frontiers of knowledge in this area has been stimulated by demands from organizations who want help in solving their problems. Social agencies such as the Scouts and the YMCA and YWCA wish to use leaders more effectively and secure more intensive participation from their members. Governmental bodies hope to make their employees more efficient and more responsive to the needs of the people. The armed forces are constantly revising their policies in the search for the type of organization which will lead to the most effective use of military manpower. Industrial corporations seek knowledge which will help them plan their work groups in a way to minimize friction and to secure the maximum efficiency in their operations.

These practical needs of organizations, joined by the intellectual curiosity of scholars, have led to a field of research usually labeled either "group dynamics" or "small-group research." Such research painstakingly records the interaction which actually occurs in group activities, oftentimes using such devices as a conference room in which one-way visibility enables observers to see the interaction and record conversations without being noticed by the participants. The problems to be solved are difficult because groups are affected both by the specific way in which they are organized and also by the general cultural background of their members. In spite of the complexities of the task, however, this type of research is gradually enlarging our understanding of the nature of group operations. Since it would be hopeless to try to summarize many volumes of research [Strodtbeck and Hare, 1954; Cartwright and Zander, 1960; Bales, 1959] in a few pages, we shall limit our discussion to a short exposition of two topics in the hope that students will gain some idea of the questions usually raised and the type of research that has developed.

Formal and informal structures In the armed forces a table-of-organization chart shows the exact rank and duties of every category of personnel. The recruit soon learns that he must "go through channels," that is, take up his business with the appropriate officer, without going over his head to any of this officer's superiors. In a short time, however, the perceptive soldier will learn that the organization chart does not really tell how the army operates. He will find that sometimes, but not always, a sergeant or secretary has more to do with decision making than the commanding officer. As he continues in an army career he will, if successful, learn that there is a "shadow" table of organization, different for every unit and not printed in any headquarters, which he must learn in order to get things done. This shadow table is a list of the men who have "influence." Sometimes they are the men named in the official organization chart, sometimes not; but the individual who can discern the real pattern of power will find adjustment easy in the armed forces, whereas the man who relies on the official table of organization will experience bewildering delays and frustrations.

The individual who can discern the real pattern of power will find adjustment easy.

All groups have a *structure,* that is, *a network of relationships among the members.* Primary groups usually have no formal structure, no list of officers, ranks, or formal duties. But within the group certain members have influence over others, some assume leadership while others follow, and definite roles within the group are filled. The group has a real structure, based on a network of personal relationships instead of an organizational chart.

Secondary groups have both a formal and an informal structure. The formal structure is that which can be shown on an organizational chart—positions or ranks, duties and privileges of each, lines of authority, and the like. The informal structure is the network of personal relationships found in every formal organization. It arises from the fact that the formal pattern is developed on a relatively impersonal basis, giving weight to such factors as hereditary social position, seniority, education, and proficiency in passing examinations. This formal pattern becomes limited in its effectiveness as people develop relationships based on the primary-group traits which cause them to be accepted or rejected as individuals. Even under the best of personnel systems the two patterns will not completely coincide. There will be natural leaders who acquire power greater than their position in the organization chart would warrant. These persons get enthusiastic support from their subordinates and favorable attention from their superiors. They can often gain through persuasion the decisions which they lack the authority to command. Other officials have formal authority but no personal influence. They get little real support from subordinates and no special consideration from superiors. They can accomplish nothing beyond the measures which they have the authority to order, and these orders may be frustrated by delay and concealed resistance.

If the disparity between the formal and informal systems becomes too great, it may be readjusted to give formal power to the informal leader. An extreme example of this shift was seen in Tunis in 1957 when Premier Habib Bourguiba arranged to have his National Assembly depose his nominal chief, the Bey of Tunis, and establish a republic with himself as president. The Bey had top place in the formal system, but Bourguiba had secured the support of the people and was able to topple the Bey from his throne without difficulty. Such a solution to tension between formal and informal systems of power is not uncommon, but it is probably the exception rather than the rule.

Organizations have devised ways to protect themselves from the strain of deviation between their formal and informal structures. Thus members of a religious group are advised to honor the clergyman regardless of his personal traits, and soldiers are told that they "salute the office not the man." It still remains true however that the group is more efficient if the formal and informal systems support each other. The priest is more effective in his work if he is pious and devout than if he is lecherous and dissolute. The army officer can better command his troops if he inspires personal confidence as well as respect for his office.

The relative importance of formal and informal organization will vary in different associations. Frequently, in the beginning stages of an association, people will be drawn together by ties of congeniality and common interest. The association, be it a good-government league, stamp-collectors' club, or society to aid unmarried mothers, has few formal rules and operates with the volunteer labor of its members. Decisions are made through the personal influence of the individuals involved rather than according to rules as to the authority or responsibility of different functionaries. Eventually the members of the association feel a need for professional employees with definite responsibilities, to be supervised by a set of association officers with definite authority. Often this need for a more formal bureaucratic structure comes when enthusiasm has waned and it is more difficult to secure member participation on an informal basis. In a study of the formalization trend in a voluntary association, Chapin and Tsouderos [1955, 1956] found that informal contacts between members declined as expenditures for hired personnel increased and a more formal organization was adopted. In other words the formal organization devices used to strengthen the informal organization had the reverse effect. The paid executive may draw up a more coherent program, keep better accounts, and put out more attractive publicity material, but the members now feel that the formal organization can handle matters and that the association no longer requires their personal efforts. This result does not mean that the total effectiveness of the association has decreased but simply that the gain from the greater efficiency of the association must be balanced against the loss from a decline in the informal participation of its members.

Bierstedt has catalogued a list of contrasting traits associated with formal and informal organization:

Formal organization	Informal organization
Associational norms	*Communal norms*
Statuses	*Roles*
Prestige	*Esteem*
Authority	*Leadership*
Superordination	*Dominance*
Subordination	*Submission*
Extrinsic evaluation of persons	*Intrinsic evaluation of persons*
Status relations	*Personal relations*
Positions	*Personalities*

SOURCE: Robert Bierstedt, *The Social Order*, McGraw-Hill Book Company, New York, 1963, p. 337.

It will be noted that the list under "formal organization" applies to traits which can be defined with some precision regardless of the personalities or the situation. Traits listed under "informal organization" are less definite and depend a great deal on the personalities and the specific situation in which they are involved. Prestige for instance, may be designated by a badge of rank easily recognizable, while esteem is a personal judgment of individuals and can only be appraised indirectly. Associational norms refer to the formal standards of the organization, while communal norms refer to the mores and folkways of the general community. This comparison shows how formal organization is mechanical and impersonal, and how informal organization rests upon the personal qualities of the individuals involved.

Communication patterns   One of the important problems in any group is communication among its members. Communication is not merely a matter of the language spoken and the types of printed or audio-visual material used to get across messages, even though these are important. Communication is also a matter of the structure of the group and the physical and social proximity of its members. Any group must devise some way for its members to share their information. There are many possible ways of arranging the flow of communication, and possibly not all these patterns have the same effect on the work of the group and the relationship among its members.

The influence of different patterns of communication in a problem-solving group has been listed by Bavelas [1953]. He arranged groups of five men in different communication patterns which may be described as the circle, the chain, the Y, and the wheel. In the circle everyone had an equal chance to communicate with everyone else; in the other patterns the man at the center had maximum communication and the others were restricted. Morale and leadership turned out to be closely related to centrality of position. Member satisfaction with the situation was greatest in the circle, where no one man emerged as a leader. In the wheel, where the man in the center became the leader, production was greater but group satisfaction less. As an offset to its lower production, the circle was found to adapt more quickly to new tasks than the other patterns.

Effective communication promotes satisfaction of the individual with the group and enables him to express himself freely and to receive the impressions of others. A centralizing of communication focuses the attention of group members on specific topics and promotes a concentration of effort. The implications for the organization of school classrooms and industrial work plans depend on whether the major emphasis is on routine productivity or on developing flexibility and achieving satisfaction in the group situation. Research on the lecture versus the discussion method of college instruction, for instance, reports that students memorize as much even in very large groups with the lecture method (analogous to the wheel pattern) but that they have greater stimulus to do their own thinking in the discussion method (analogous to the circle pattern) [Bloom, 1954, pp. 37–38]. These are a few examples of how small-group research can help in solving practical problems.

SUMMARY

Both strength and weakness are largely the result of the manner in which a person is integrated into a network of groups. A fundamental distinction is that between *out-groups* and *in-groups*—a distinction which has been measured by the use of the concept of *social distance*. *Reference groups* are those which we accept as models and as guides for our judgments and actions. Emotional conditioning is largely the result of *primary-group* contacts, but our society is increasingly affected by the growth of *secondary-group* relationships. While many groups may be easily characterized as either primary or secondary, the two types of influence interact, each influencing the other.

Since the industrial revolution, the trend has been from the traditional *gemeinschaft* toward the *gesellschaft*. This has meant a loss of intimacy and security, which has been countered to some extent by the growth of new primary groups and adjustment through the rise of voluntary associations.

Voluntary associations represent a type of organization in which small groups of citizens may work for goals not yet accepted by a more lethargic majority, or pursue special interests not shared by everyone. Voluntary associations are most prominent in the highly industrialized areas, chiefly the United States, and even here involve mainly the middle- and upper-class citizens.

Formal patterns of group interaction based upon the standards of secondary relationships are accompanied by informal patterns arising out of primary-group relationships. Group members usually have unequal access to communication, and it has been found that this inequality affects both morale and participation. Small-group research is now providing much knowledge useful to administrators and others responsible for group management.

QUESTIONS AND PROJECTS

1. Which of the following social aggregates or categories are groups: citizens of a country; commuters waiting for a train; husband and wife; members of an international labor union; residents of cities of between 50,000 and 100,000 population?

2. Comment on this statement: "A group is made up of individuals; and the characteristics of a group are the sum of the characteristics of its members."

3. Is courage an individual character trait or a response to group patterns?

4. What differences are found in the in-group–out-group distinction in primitive and modern societies?

5. Why are primary and secondary groups important? In-groups and out-groups?

6. To what extent would you expect social distance to coincide with geographical distance?

7. College is often an introduction to the complexities of secondary-group relationships. Is this experience worthwhile for a young woman whose major interests are centered in the primary-group relationships of family life? Defend your answer.

8. Suppose that production engineers design a new layout in a factory which spaces the work force differently and thereby achieves a smoother flow of goods from the raw material to the finished product. Is this a case of secondary- or primary-group behavior? What types of resistance would the engineers be apt to encounter in putting their plan into effect?

9. A new employee has thoroughly studied the organization chart of a company where he is going to work. Will this enable him to understand the distribution of power and influence among the employees?

10. Does the conduct of American prisoners of war in Korea indicate that a greater knowledge of communism is essential for our soldiers? What other needs are indicated by this experience?

11. The early Christians were sometimes crowded into large prison cells and later marched into the Colosseum to be crucified or fed to the lions before thousands of spectators. They could have saved themselves by denying their faith, but few did so. Why?

12. Make a simple questionnaire study of associational memberships on the campus. List all campus organizations, together with blanks for sex, class rank, religion, rural-urban background, occupation and education of father, and possibly other factors. Control for class rank, and then see whether this chapter's data on associational memberships apply to your sample.

SUGGESTED READINGS

BABCHUCK, NICHOLAS, AND CHARLES K. WARRINER (eds.): "Signposts in the Study of Voluntary Groups," *Sociological Inquiry*, vol. 35, Spring, 1965. Ten different articles on voluntary associations including an analysis of the leadership of sociological societies.

BALES, ROBERT F.: "How People Interact in Conferences," *Scientific American*, 192:31–35, March, 1955. A popular description of social interaction in the conference.

BARBER, BERNARD: "Participation and Mass Apathy in Associations," in Alvin W. Gouldner, *Studies in Leadership*, Harper & Row, Publishers, Incorporated, New York, 1950, pp. 477–504. Describes some organizational obstacles to mass participation.

BOGARDUS, EMORY S.: "Racial Distance Changes in the United States during the Past Thirty Years," *Sociology and Social Research*. 43:127–135, November, 1958. Shows how the acceptance and rejection of different racial or national groups has changed during this period.

BURMA, JOHN H.: "Student Attitudes toward and Participation in Voluntary Organizations," *Sociology and Social Research*, 32:625–629, November, 1947. A study of the relation between social participation and academic performance of college students.

GROSS, EDWARD: "Some Functional Consequences of Primary Groups in Formal Work Organizations," *American Journal of Sociology*, 18:368–373, August, 1953; Bobbs-Merrill reprint S-106. A description of some ways in which primary groups may support the aims of secondary groups.

JANOWITZ, MORRIS: *Sociology and The Military Establishment*. Russel Sage Foundation, New York, 1962, 1965, ch. 4, "Primary Groups and Military Effectiveness;" reprinted in ALVIN W. GOULDNER AND HELEN P. GOULDNER, *Modern Sociology*, Harcourt, Brace & World, New York, 1962, pp. 70–82. An analysis of the role of primary group relationships in various types of military situations.

*OLMSTEAD, MICHAEL S.: *The Small Group*, Random House, Inc., New York, 1959. A brief and highly readable description of small-group research. (SS16-RH)

ROSE, ARNOLD: *Theory and Method in the Social Sciences*, The University of Minnesota Press, Minneapolis, 1954. Chapters 3 and 4 contain a description of voluntary associations in the United States and France.

SCHEIN, EDWARD H.: "Interpersonal Communication, Group Solidarity and Social Influence," *Sociometry*, 23:148–161, June, 1960. Describes how group disintegration was used as a technique of psychological warfare against American prisoners in Chinese camps.

SHILS, EDWARD A., AND MORRIS JANOWITZ: "Cohesion and Disintegration in the Wehrmacht in World War II," *Public Opinion Quarterly*, 12:280–315, Summer, 1948; Bobbs-Merrill reprint S-263. Tells how morale and resistance continued in the German army as long as primary-group structures remained intact.

WARRINER, CHARLES K.: "Groups are Real: A Reaffirmation," *American Sociological Review*, 21:549–554, October, 1956; reprinted in MILTON BARRON, *Contemporary Sociology*, Dodd, Mead & Company, Inc., New York, 1964, pp. 120–127. Shows how the nature of the group is not completely represented by the individuals who compose its membership.

9

SOCIAL INSTITUTIONS

Work expands so as to fill the time available for its completion. General recognition of this fact is shown in the proverbial phrase, "It is the busiest man who has time to spare." Thus, an elderly woman of leisure can spend the entire day in writing and dispatching a postcard to her niece in Bognor Regis. An hour will be spent in finding the postcard, another in hunting for spectacles, half an hour in a search for the address, an hour and a quarter in composition, and twenty minutes in deciding whether or not to take an umbrella when going to the mailbox in the next street. The total effort that would occupy a busy man for three minutes all told may in this fashion leave another person prostrate after a day of doubt, anxiety, and toil.

Granted that work (and especially paperwork) is thus elastic in its demands on time, it is manifest that there need be little or no relationship between the work to be done and the size of the staff to which it may be assigned. . . . The thing to be done swells in importance and complexity in a direct ratio with the time to be spent. . . . The fact is that the number of the officials and the quantity of the work are not related to each other at all. The rise in the total of those employed is governed by Parkinson's Law and would be much the same whether the volume of work were to increase, diminish, or even disappear. The importance of Parkinson's Law lies in the fact that it is a law of growth based upon an analysis of the factors by which that growth is controlled. (C. Northcote Parkinson, *Parkinson's Law and Other Studies in Administration*, Houghton Mifflin Company, Boston, 1957, pp. 2–4.)

IN THIS FAMOUS essay, Parkinson has written with tongue in cheek of the tendency for all bureaucracies to expand. Bureaucratic behavior, however, is only one of the many forms of institutional behavior which interest sociologists. What are social institutions, and what is their importance?

Sociologists have not been entirely consistent in their use of the term *institution*. Some have applied the term to any large-scale organization, like the American Legion or the YMCA, using the term *association* for smaller organized groups like the local photography club. This makes the distinction between institution and association purely one of size and obscures the basic difference in nature between institution and association. The more common practice is to call any organized group of any size an association and to define an institution as "an organized way of doing something" [Bierstedt, 1963, p. 341]. Kingsley Davis [1949, p. 71] defines the institution as "a set of interwoven folkways, mores, and laws built around one or more functions." Hertzler [1961, p. 77] calls them "great clusters of established, accepted, and implemented ways of behaving socially." Clearly, the association is an organized *group of people* while an institution is an organized *system of behavior*.

An institution embodies certain common values and procedures.

All these definitions of institutions imply both a set of behavior norms and a system of social relationships through which these norms are practiced. Let us suggest a formal definition which clearly includes both ideas: *An institution is an organized system of social relationships which embodies certain common values and procedures and meets certain basic needs of the society.* In this definition, "common values" refers to shared ideas and goals; the "common procedures" are the standardized behavior patterns the group follows; the "system of relationships" is the network of roles and statuses through which this behavior is carried out. Thus the family includes a set of common values (about love, children, family life), a set of common procedures (dating, child care, family routines), and a network of roles and statuses (husband, wife, baby, teen-aged child, fiancé), which form the system of social relationships through which family life is carried out. Five important basic institutions in complex societies are the familial, religious, governmental, economic, and educational institutions. Today, the values and procedures of science are so important and so highly standardized that some would add the "scientific institutions" to the list. The activities involved in social work or medical care have become so definitely patterned that we might speak of either of these systems of behavior as institutions. In referring to the Middle Ages one could speak of chivalry and knighthood as aspects of the institution of feudalism.

While they are separate concepts, institutions and associations are not entirely separate from each other. An institution is a set of relationships and a system of behavior, and these require *people*. Although the institution itself consists of relationships and norms, it is people who fill these relationships and practice these norms. And people organize themselves into groups, forming associations. Thus each institution has many satellite associations which carry out institutional behavior. By *institutional behavior* we mean the carrying of institutional norms and values into practice. Institutional behavior is carried out, in large part, through these satellite associations. The church has its organized local congregations, Sunday schools, clubs, and groups of many kinds, carrying out the work of the church; the school has its PTA, alumni association, athletic association; the state has its political organizations, voters' leagues, taxpayers' associations, and organized pressure groups. Institutions and associations are very much interrelated; yet the concepts are distinct and should not be confused. *The* church is a social institution; the First Methodist Church on Main Street is an association. *The* corporation is a social institution; the First National Bank and the Ford Motor Company are associations.

THE DEVELOPMENT OF INSTITUTIONS

The process of institutionalization

Institutions emerge as the largely unplanned products of social living. People grope for practical ways of meeting their needs; they find some workable patterns which harden through repetition into standardized customs. As time passes, these patterns acquire a body of supporting folklore which justifies and sanctions them. The custom of "dating" developed as a means of mate selection. Banks gradually developed as the need for storing, transferring, borrowing, and lending money gave rise to a series of practices for accomplishing these purposes. From time to time, men might gather to codify and give legal endorsement to these practices as they continued to develop and change. In such manner, institutions arise.

Institutionalization consists of the establishment of definite norms which assign status positions and role functions in connection with such behavior. A norm is a group expectation of behavior. Institutionalization involves the replacement of spontaneous or experimental behavior with behavior which is expected, patterned, regular, and predictable. Thus the preinstitutional period of a religous movement brings forth spontaneous ecstatic and often confused behavior as the followers of the new leader respond to his dynamic appeal. Every day is an adventure, and every religious meeting is an unpredictable sequence of emotional events in which no man is able to predict what he will do. As the institutionalized church emerges, the participants acquire definite roles, and their activities begin to follow a routine pattern. Some people are simply worshipers; others assume specialized roles such as choir member, clergyman, teacher, usher, secretary, janitor, and so on. Novelty and excitement fade as procedures come to be governed by definite norms, and the behavior of each participant becomes standardized and predictable.

A tavern brawl is noninstitutionalized behavior; a professional boxing match is institutionalized. A set of social relationships has become institutionalized when (1) a regular system of statuses and roles has been developed, and (2) this system of status and role expectations has been generally accepted in the society. Dating in American society meets both of these qualifications. A rather clearly defined set of courtship roles has emerged, in which the duties and privileges of each party are defined (he asks, she accepts, he pays, etc.), and safeguarded with some limitations or restraints (e.g., no all-night dates) intended to prevent complications; thus dating became part of our marriage and family institutions.

When we say that dating has become institutionalized, we mean that it is generally accepted by the society as a necessary and proper activity whereby young people mature emotionally and eventually find agreeable partners. Many societies have also institutionalized premarital sexual intercourse, making it a normal and expected part of the activities leading to marriage. Although premarital intercourse is fairly common in American society, it has not been institutionalized; that is, it is not a part of a standardized, approved, and culturally safeguarded pattern of behavior.

Even carefully organized patterns of behavior differ in the extent to which they receive social acceptance. In American society the corporation has full institutional status. The labor union, on the other hand, would be classified as an *emergent* institution, not yet completely accepted as a proper and necessary part of society. The first six grades of the elementary school are accepted as necessary in all American localities, whereas the provision of kindergarten facilities is still a matter of controversy. Although the need for some basic social institutions is recognized in all societies, their subsidiary units vary. Time will see some subsidiary forms becoming accepted institutions and others passing from the scene. As an example, Smith [1955] gives an interesting account of psychiatry as an emergent institution.

Individual roles in Not all roles are institutionalized. The "bad boy" and "mother's little helper"
institutional roles in the family are noninstitutionalized roles, while son and daughter are
behavior institutionalized roles. An institutionalized role is a set of behavior expectations that leaves little room for personal eccentricity. All judges act a good deal alike when on the bench, however much they differ at other times. Every Methodist minister and every Catholic priest finds that his duties and privileges are quite precisely defined by his institutional role; to deviate from his expected role in any way is hazardous. Even presidents and kings, apparently so powerful, are in fact most highly circumscribed in their freedom of action. If they fail to operate within the role expectations of the institution they generally lose their influence.

An interesting example of the persistence of institutional roles is seen in the transition of the English coal mines from private to public ownership [Koening, 1948]. Under private ownership the miners were supervised by the "boss," an agent of the private capitalists who owned the mines. Acting in this role, the boss sought to get the greatest production at the least possible cost. When the government took over the mines, some of the miners thought the new ownership meant the end of annoying rules and regulations. The boss, however, was still with them. Although now an agent of the state, he still had the job of making the nationalized mines produce the greatest possible amount of coal at the lowest possible cost. Ownership and sometimes personnel had changed, but the system of roles which had grown up in response to institutional needs remained pretty much the same.

This lack of change in the role of the supervisor in the coal mines under nationalization is not an isolated example; similar experiences occur in other institutional settings. Occasionally a man contrasts the smooth and efficient way in which his secretary anticipates his needs in the office situation with the rather demanding attitude of his wife at home. Sometimes a discontented husband divorces the wife and marries the secretary, only to find that when the secretary assumes the role of wife, she begins to act like a wife! Many an employee who is promoted to a supervisory role tries to retain his old rapport with his former crew; this rarely succeeds, for the new role inevitably alters his relationship to the old buddies whom he now bosses.

It is true that individual personality differences do affect institutional behavior to some degree. One foreman is grouchy and another is cheerful; one professor is stimulating and another is dull. But the range of individual variation is limited and is greatly overshadowed by role requirements. The conflicts that arise within an institution are sometimes due to clashes of personality but more often to the clash of institutional roles. The foreman and the inspector clash because the foreman must keep production going while the inspector keeps finding defects that must be corrected. The salesman is frustrated when the credit manager refuses to extend more credit to a slow-paying customer. The university professor's wish to stimulate intellectual controversy on the campus may clash with the dean's or president's wish to avoid off-campus criticism. Many such clashes are inherent in the interrelation of roles within an institution. With some modification, Gertrude Stein's famous statement, "A rose is a rose is a rose," may be applied to institutional roles. A wife is always a wife; a husband is always a husband; and a supervisor is always a supervisor. The difference made by individual personalities in institutional roles is comparable to the difference between a mediocre and a highly talented actor in a dramatic production. The highly talented actor realizes more fully the potentialities of the part he is playing, but at the same time his expression must be channeled within the limitations of the role. Organizations function most smoothly when they can attract competent personnel, and sometimes they are handicapped by personnel unequal to the roles assigned them. Regardless of differences in personnel, however, the persistence of role requirements will require some degree of uniformity in the conduct of those who carry out a particular institutional role.

INSTITUTIONAL TRAITS

While each institution has its peculiarities, each institution is also like all others in some respects. All institutions must maintain the loyalty of their participants, assign authority to different functionaries, formulate standards of behavior, and develop methods of dealing with other institutions. Since these are common problems, it is not surprising that institutions with very different goals may use quite similar techniques.

Cultural symbols All institutions develop symbols which serve as a shorthand reminder of the institution. The citizen is reminded of his allegiance to the state by the flag, to the church by a crucifix, crescent, or star of David, to the family by a wedding ring, to the alma mater by the school colors or animal totem (mascot), and to the business concern by brand names and trademarks. Music also has symbolic meanings. National anthems, school songs, religious hymns, and the singing "commercials" all use the art of melody to strengthen institutional ties. Buildings may become institutional symbols, so that it is hard to think of home without a house, religion without a church edifice, education without a school building, or government without the government house or king's palace.

Codes of behavior Along with inculcating a general sense of loyalty, institutions must prepare their members to carry out the roles the institution has assigned them. These roles are often expressed in formal codes, such as the oath of allegiance to the country, the marriage vows, the medical profession's oath of Hippocrates, and the codes of ethics of several other groups. As we saw in Chapter 7, these institutionally defined roles are an important part of social control.

A formal code of behavior, however impressive, is no guarantee of proper role performance. Husbands and wives may prove unfaithful to marital vows; citizens who fervently repeat the oath of allegiance may commit treason; and church members who have sworn fidelity to their religion may lapse into indifference. If the affirmation of a verbal or written code is the climax to a long process of attitude formation and role preparation, it may be observed; if not, and if there are no swift and sure punishments for violation, the code may be quietly ignored.

A formal code is only a part of the total behavior that makes up an institutional role. Much of the behavior in any role—parent, soldier, priest, professor, politician—consists of an elaborate body of informal traditions, expectations, and routines which one absorbs only through long observation and experience with the role. Children who have never lived in a harmonious family setting are likely to have greater difficulty in ever filling the roles of parent and husband or wife [Terman, 1938]. They have had no good chance to observe these roles in successful operation or to absorb the attitudes needed for successful role performance. Like roles of all kinds, institutional roles can be filled most successfully by those who have fully learned the proper role attitudes and behavior.

Ideologies An ideology may be loosely defined as a *system of ideas which sanction a set of norms.* The norms define how people are expected to act; the ideology explains *why* they should act that way, and why they sometimes fail to act as they should. The ideology of an institution includes both the central beliefs of the institution and an elaboration of these beliefs which will explain the rest of the world in terms acceptable to the participants in the institution. Whereas the repetition of an oath formally binds the individual to follow institutional norms, the ideology gives him a rational justification for the application of institutional norms to the problems of life.

For instance, juvenile delinquency is a problem in all complex societies. All institutions tend to develop an explanation for this problem consistent with their basic norms. Juvenile delinquency may be interpreted by the Communist as the result of capitalist exploitation, by the conservative businessman as the result of coddling by a paternalistic government, by the churchman as caused by the neglect of religious teaching and practice, by the educator as the result of an inadequate school system, and by the family-oriented persons as a symptom of the breakdown of the home.

Ideological explanations persist in spite of changing circumstances. In Russia, after more than fifty years of Communist rule, juvenile delinquency is still viewed as either the result of organic ailments which might resist even a perfect social order, or is attributed to the fact that the Soviet Union is still in the process of transition to the ideal Communist state [Alt and Alt, 1959, pp. 201–202, 216–217]. Similarly, in African or Asian countries under Western rule, nationalist leaders have long attributed social problems to the evil effects of foreign rule. After independence is achieved, social problems are still attributed to a "colonialism" which is now said to be all the more potent because it is disguised [Lava, 1958]. The Communist Party in the United States was viewed as a major menace by many Americans who called for stern measures of repression. But even after the party had practically disappeared, J. Edgar Hoover [1958, p. 78] warned us that it was more dangerous than ever.

Such examples might be extended indefinitely. The point they illustrate is simply that an ideologically satisfying explanation of a social problem is not easily abandoned even when changing circumstances make it outmoded.

The usefulness of an ideology is measured, not by its literal correctness, but by its ability to inspire the loyalty and cooperation of an institution's personnel. Any shortcoming in society is blamed upon competing institutions or upon the inadequate devotion of the institution's own followers. Institutional leaders claim credit for practically all favorable developments and define all problems as simply a challenge to greater efforts along present lines. Criticisms of institutional ideology are defined as heretical or subversive attacks which must be repelled. False doctrine (any belief that attacks the ideology) breaks down the attitudes supporting institutional role performance and so strikes at the heart of institutional functioning.

INSTITUTIONAL STRUCTURES

Institutions have *structure*. The *normative* structure is the cluster of norms—of expectations, rules, and procedures—written or unwritten, formal or informal. The *personnel* structure is the network of persons, roles, and statuses through which the activities of the institution are carried on. Both the normative and the personnel structures can be closely or loosely structured.

Closely structured and loosely structured institutional units   Some institutional units are termed *closely structured* because authority is highly centralized and procedures are highly standardized with little autonomy for either local groups or individuals. Other *loosely structured* institutional units have less centralization and allow more freedom of action. In the closely structured institutional unit, roles are rigidly defined, even to the prescription of specific rules for most situations; in the loosely structured institutional unit, the roles are less rigidly defined and may be adjusted by the individual or local group as circumstances may warrant. The state and the military institution are normally closely structured institutions, with a precisely defined role

Table 5 *Traits of major American social institutions*

Family	Religion	Government	Business	Education
Attitudes and behavior patterns				
Affection	*Reverence*	*Loyalty*	*Efficiency*	*Love of*
Loyalty	*Loyalty*	*Obedience*	*Thrift*	*knowledge*
Responsibility	*Worship*	*Subordination*	*Shrewdness*	*Class attendance*
Respect	*Generosity*	*Cooperation*	*Profit making*	*Studying*
				"Cramming"
Symbolic culture traits				
Marriage	*Cross*	*Flag*	*Trademark*	*School colors*
ring	*Ikon*	*Seal*	*Patent sign*	*Mascot*
Wedding veil	*Shrine*	*Mascot*	*Slogan*	*School song*
Coat of arms	*Hymn*	*Anthem*	*Singing*	*Seal*
"Our Song"			*commercial*	
Utilitarian culture traits				
House	*Church building*	*Public buildings*	*Shop, factory*	*Classrooms*
Apartment	*Church*	*Public works*	*Store, office*	*Library*
Furnishings	*equipment*	*Office*	*Office*	*Stadium*
Car	*Literature*	*equipment*	*equipment*	*Books*
	Liturgical	*Blanks and*	*Blanks and*	
	supplies	*forms*	*forms*	
Code of oral or written specifications				
Marriage	*Creed*	*Charter*	*Contracts*	*Accreditation*
license	*Church law*	*Constitution*	*Licenses*	*Rules*
Will	*Sacred books*	*Treaties*	*Franchises*	*Curricula*
Geneology	*Taboos*	*Laws*	*Articles of*	*Graduation*
Marriage law			*incorporation*	*requirements*
Ideologies				
Romantic love	*Thomism*	*Nationalism*	*Laissez faire*	*Academic*
"Togetherness"	*Liberalism*	*States rights*	*Managerial*	*freedom*
Familism	*Fundamentalism*	*Democracy*	*responsibility*	*Progressive*
Individualism	*Neo-orthodoxy*	*Republicanism*	*Free enterprise*	*education*
			Rights of labor	*Three "r"s*
				Classicism

SOURCE: Adapted from F. Stuart Chapin, *Contemporary American Institutions,* Harper & Row, Publishers, Incorporated, New York, 1935, p. 16.

and status for each rank, rigid obedience to orders, and detailed organization patterns. The family in our society is a loosely structured institution, in which roles and statuses are so uncertain that they are sometimes confusing.

Associations which carry out institutional behavior may also be either closely or loosely structured. Business corporations may be classified in either category according to their pattern of organization. The corporation which controls all activities by detailed direction from a central office would be in the closely structured category. The loosely structured approach is manifested by an increasing number of concerns which give their branch managers freedom to set their own policies as long as they show a profit.

Associations with a similar ideology may differ in structure. The Catholic Church is closely structured, with a strong central authority, elaborate organization, and detailed rules and procedures. The Baptist Church is very loosely structured. Congregations are highly autonomous; they select and dismiss their own ministers, run their own affairs, and are very loosely tied together into a denominational organization. Likewise the Communists and Socialists both base their ideology on the writings of Karl Marx. Yet the Communist party is one of the most closely structured organizations developed, whereas the Socialist parties operate in a loosely structured system which somewhat resembles the congregationally organized Protestant churches.

Which is more effective—the closely structured or the loosely structured institutional pattern? Neither, apparently. A large army must be fairly closely structured; a smaller military unit can be quite loosely structured. Under some circumstances, loosely structured guerilla units are the more effective, as in the defeat of the carefully organized troops of General Braddock by a less orderly collection of French and Indians. Churches and political parties apparently can be effective with varying degrees of close or loose structuring. Any intrinsic superiority of one over the other is difficult to prove. The loosely structured organization is apt to pride itself on freedom, tolerance, and individual responsibility while being criticized for inconsistency, laxness, and ideological deviations. The closely structured unit prides itself on the purity and consistency of its ideology and the close integration of its component parts, while it is criticized as dogmatic, intolerant, and heedless of local problems far removed from the central office.

Formal and informal structure of institutions Institutional units have a formal and informal structure similar to the formal and informal structuring of groups as discussed in Chapter 8. An organizational diagram of an army would show the ranks from general to private, with the powers and duties of each. It would show the formal structure of the army, with every task and duty accounted for. But an institution is more than a system of roles. These are filled by a network of people who relate themselves to one another in ways not covered by the organizational diagrams. A constantly changing complex of personal friendships, antagonisms, obligations, and admirations is operating behind the facade of institutional titles and formal roles. It is this network of personal relationships which either fulfills or frustrates the purposes of the institution.

A crucial distinction must obviously be made between *authority* and *influence*. Authority is an official right to make and enforce decisions; influence is the ability to affect the actions of others apart from any authority to do so.

It is often easiest to go outside regular channels.

Authority stems from rank; influence rests largely upon personal attributes. Authority is based upon the status one holds; influence is based upon the esteem one receives. A professor has authority to make assignments and assign grades; he may have much or little influence upon his students, depending upon how they feel about him. An admired institutional officer will have both authority and influence; an unpopular officer has authority but little influence; a competent, popular subordinate may have much influence even though he has little authority.

This informal structure grows partly from the personality differences among individuals and partly from the fact that no system of roles is completely successful in meeting all the needs of the institution. In order to get things done, one may prefer to go outside regular channels and use the informal structure of the institution. This procedure is sometimes risky and must be handled skillfully if it is not to backfire; yet it is very common. The Navy even has an institutionalized name—"cumshaw"—for the use of this informal structure. Without informal structures and procedures, many things would not get done quickly or efficiently.

The real operation of an institution cannot be understood without understanding its informal structure. In an institutional unit we may find the "operator" who can pull strings and get things done outside the usual channels; there is the old-timer whose support is valuable because he knows all the routines and because he knows "where all the bodies are buried"—that is, he knows of past errors and incidents which can be used as gentle blackmail; there are the friends and relatives of the higher officials who presumedly have influence upon them; there is the "fair-haired boy" who appears to have been selected for promotion; there is the subordinate who is so widely admired and respected that the officials find it wise to consult him; there is even the pariah who is so disliked that his support is to be avoided. The interplay of such personalities has great effect upon the decisions made by those in authority and upon the way these decisions are interpreted and carried out in practice. The interactions of authority and influence in the upper levels of government is perceptively described in the popular novel, *Advise and Consent* [Drury, 1959] and in the several novels of C. P. Snow.

INSTITUTIONAL FUNCTIONS

Society is so complex and its forces so interrelated that it is impossible to foresee all consequences of a particular action. Institutions have *manifest* functions which are easy to recognize as part of the professed objectives of the institution, and *latent* functions which are unintended and may be unrecognized, or, if recognized, regarded as by-products [Merton, 1957b, pp.

19–84]. The manifest function of our economic institutions is to produce and distribute goods, services, and profits, their latent functions may be to promote urbanization, alter family life, promote the growth of labor unions, redirect education, and produce many other changes. Men with important institutional roles often fail to realize the latent effects of the activities they promote. Henry Ford, the founder of the company that bears his name, is a case in point. He cordially detested labor unions, big cities, mass credit, and installment buying; yet through his promotion of the assembly line and mass production he probably did more than any one man to stimulate these very developments. The latent functions of an institution may support the professed objectives, or be irrelevant, or even lead to consequences quite damaging to the norms of the institution. A brief look at some of the latent functions of educational and religious institutions will illustrate some of the types of unintended consequences.

Latent functions of educational institutions   The manifest function of mass public education is to enable all to share the knowledge and skills once confined to a privileged few. Some of the latent functions of this activity would include keeping youth off the labor market, weakening the control of parents, promoting the Americanization of immigrants, and altering the class system.

To a great extent, the complaints about the schools are a reaction to these latent functions. Keeping youth off the labor market may be attractive to labor unions, but it appears in a different light to farmers who need seasonal workers or to those remaining industrialists who rely on cheap and unskilled labor. Parents want their children to achieve higher status through education but are distressed when their children learn about ideas that conflict with parental norms; immigrant parents who wish children to cling to the practices and customs of a foreign culture have mixed feelings about the Americanization of the school. Altering the class system by enabling youth from low-income families to get the education needed for higher-status positions likewise meets with a mixed response. Some laud this as a step toward a better society; others fear the increase of competition or fear a shortage of workers who will be content with low status jobs. The American school system is now engaged in probably the most bitter controversy in its history—over whether its latent functions should include the promotion of racial integration.

Latent functions of religious institutions   Few Americans will object to the manifest functions of religious institutions— the worship of God and instruction in religious ideology. Some of the latent functions of the churches, however, bring consequences which often surprise even the faithful, while they may stimulate either approval or opposition from those who do not consider themselves very religious.

Christian missions in colonial areas have often served to stimulate nationalistic feeling. This was not the intention of the missionaries who, though not mainly concerned with government, usually considered Western rule essential to the progress of an underdeveloped area. Rather than a direct goal, the stimulus of nationalistic feeling was a latent result of the training received in mission schools and the need to treat potential converts with some measure of equality. The manifest function was simply to produce Christians, but the latent function has often been to train nationalist leaders who became bitter enemies of colonial rule.

The Christian emphasis on monogamous marriage has some latent consequences quite the opposite of the desires of churchmen. Protestant countries tend to emphasize the sexual exclusiveness of marriage and, partly in consequence, have a high divorce rate. Catholic countries generally prohibit or restrict divorce and, partly in consequence, see the rise of a number of more or less permanent extramarital relationships. Many among the lower classes react to the prohibition of divorce by setting up households without legal marriage and shifting mates when they wish. Most of the middle- and upper-class people are properly married, but a discontented husband may establish a relationship with a mistress which the wife is powerless to prevent, since divorce is either completely outlawed or religiously taboo. Thus both the Protestant and the Catholic approach to ideal family life have latent consequences which modify the monogamous character of the family.

One of the most often cited latent effects of religion is the relation between the "Protestant ethic" and the "spirit of capitalism." Protestant leaders of the Reformation had no desire to erect the spiritual foundations for a capitalistic society and often denounced capitalistic trends in their day. Yet the industrial revolution and the growth of large-scale business concerns was much more rapid in predominantly Protestant than in largely Catholic areas, and in mixed areas Protestants were much the more active in business development. This circumstance helps explain the economic depression in France which followed the revocation of religious tolerance and the expulsion of the Huguenots. The phrase "as rich as a Huguenot" became a popular stereotype, and the expulsion of the Protestants slowed down French industry while accelerating business development in the countries where they settled as refugees.

The Protestant ethic made religious virtues of individualism, frugal living, thrift, and the glorification of work—practices which obviously favored the accumulation of wealth. These practices are usually attributed to the Protestant emphasis on individual responsibility rather than churchly sacraments, to the interpretation of worldly success as a sign that one was predestined for salvation, and to the reaction against the symbols of wealth which had been accumulated by the traditional church. None of these Protestant practices originated in a deliberate desire to encourage commerce, and perhaps for that reason, their effect was all the more potent. The classic presentation of this theory is found in Max Weber, *The Protestant Ethic and the Spirit of Capitalism*. While most social scientists accept Weber's theory as probably correct, some disagree [Fanfani, 1955].

Catholics today are increasingly accepting the values of a business society, whereas the power of the Protestant ethic has been weakened by the installment buying and the general emphasis on leisure, recreation, and luxury in an affluent society. A few decades ago it was fashionable among Protestant leaders to glorify business activity, but in more recent years capitalism has come under heavy criticism, and modern Protestants are uncertain whether their identification with business development is a virtue to be proclaimed or a mistaken emphasis to be corrected [Boulding, 1950]. A Detroit study, however, claims that the Protestant ethic still lives [Lenski, 1961]. This study found more commitment to work, thrift, and individualism among Protestants than among Catholics, and also a more rapid social mobility.

Manifest functions of institutions Every institution has two types of manifest functions: (1) the pursuit of its objectives in a world which is often indifferent or hostile to these objectives and (2) the preservation of its own internal cohesion so that it may survive. The family, for instance, is concerned both with raising its children and with maintaining harmony and loyalty among its members so that it does not dissolve in the divorce courts. The national state must serve its citizens and protect its boundaries and, at the same time, escape the peril of revolution or conquest. The church which seeks to convert outsiders and increase its influence must also hold the loyalty of its members and enhance their feeling of satisfaction with the institution. When an institution fails in either of these manifest functions, it either suffers disorganization and change, or its necessary functions are absorbed into some other institution.

INTELLECTUALS AND BUREAUCRATS

In all complex societies, social institutions are the objects of constant comment by the intellectuals, while the bureaucrats supervise institutional behavior.

Role of the intellectual An intellectual is one who, regardless of education or occupation, devotes himself seriously to the analysis of ideas. The importance of ideology in sustaining loyalty to institutional norms leads all institutions to develop mixed attitudes of appreciation and fear toward those men who are able to manipulate ideas. Intellectuals are needed to perform the vital service of explaining social developments in terms harmonious with institutional norms. Communist intellectuals, for instance, have the task of showing how all recent history really fulfills the predictions of Marx and Lenin, although this task requires a spectacular distortion of the facts. China's 1966 campaign to destroy the influence of the intellectuals reflected Mao Tse-tung's fear that the intellectuals were wavering in their support of the revolutionary regime [Bloodworth, 1966]. The intellectual cannot be fully trusted, because the training that equips the intellectual to defend the ideology may also enable him to analyze its deficiencies. He may even develop a rival ideology more satisfying to the demands of the time. It is the intellectuals who promote revolutions and lead the attack upon entrenched institutions. Conversely, it is the intellectuals who are called upon to defend institutions under attack.

No institution can avoid the constant need to justify its basic beliefs and practices. Any institution needs intellectuals who are able to interpret the social situation in terms harmonious with the institutional ideology. The difficulties of the intellectual come from the fact that his devotion to the institution may be subordinated to his concern for the truth. Conflict is minimized when the two types of interest converge, as was illustrated by Adam Smith's argument that the pursuit of private gain by businessmen served the public good. More recently, however, economists have come under criticism when their research led them to the conclusion that, under modern conditions, the public good may require some limits upon the quest for private gain [Galbraith, 1958].

Sometimes the intellectual is alternately praised and condemned during his lifetime, as were Plato, Galileo, Luther, Trotsky, and many others. In his youth, Milovan Djilas interpreted communism as the main hope for achieving social justice. His writings were widely quoted, and he became Vice-president of Yugoslavia. On more mature reflection he wrote a book describing communism as a new form of human exploitation [1957]; its publication resulted in his being imprisoned by the same authorities who had praised his previous works.

The intellectual best able to serve as an institutional spokesman is a man acknowledged to be devoted to the truth as he sees it regardless of institutional commitments. Such a man is both helpful and dangerous to the welfare of his institution—helpful because his support gains respect for the institution; dangerous because his search for truth may lead him to conclusions which provide ammunition for institutional critics while weakening the convictions of its supporters. This dual role creates a problem of discipline for the institution and a problem of conflicting loyalties for the intellectual.

Role of the When man first tackled projects which demanded an organizing of human
bureaucrat activity beyond what family and clan organization could provide, bureaucrats first appeared. Some feel that perhaps the ancient irrigation and flood-control projects first gave rise to the need for a disciplined and organized division of labor [Wittfogel, 1957]. Bureaucrats are never very popular. Most men regard themselves, rightly or wrongly, as productive workers and look with suspicion upon the bureaucrat who "does no real work" but just organizes and records the work of others.

Bureaucracy is defined [Coser and Rosenberg, 1957, p. 433] as "that type of hierarchical organization which is designed rationally to coordinate the work of many individuals in pursuit of large scale administrative tasks." A bureaucracy, therefore, is a pyramid of officials who conduct rationally the work of a large organization. Except for the family, which requires no large associational organizations for its tasks, all basic institutions carry out their functions through the associational structures forming the bureaucracy of the institution. Thompson [1961, pp. 13–17], drawing mainly on the work of Max Weber, gives the main characteristics of bureaucracy as: (1) *specialization*, to assign each task to an expert; (2) *merit appointment and job tenure*, to ensure competent personnel; (3) *formalistic impersonality*, to see that a set of formal procedures is carried out impartially; and (4) a *chain of command*, to define each person's authority and responsibility.

Bureaucracy inevitably develops in all large organizations—government departments, churches, universities, voluntary associations, and private business concerns. Suppose, for example, a business concern has an office force of three persons. They can divide the work casually and informally, and each can get from the supply closet whatever office supplies he needs. Suppose the office force grows to three thousand. Now an orderly division of work and authority is necessary to get the work done; a set of formal policies is needed to keep the supplies in order, along with a system of inventory control and requisitions to keep supplies in stock and to prevent pilferage. Bureaucracy thus has at least three roots: the needs for efficiency, for uniformity, and for prevention of corruption.

Civil service as a bureaucratic model The origin of the civil service type of governmental employee is due both to the expansion of government functions and to a new concept of the nature of the state. The state is no longer the property of either an hereditary ruler or a successful politician but is the servant of the people. As such it performs many functions which it did not assume in an earlier era. If governmental employees are not just loyal henchmen claiming their just rewards then a system must be devised to obtain people who will assume their responsibilities in an impartial and capable manner. To gain this type of employee, civil service rules carefully define qualifications, duties, authority, and compensation. The civil service employee ordinarily makes decisions, not to please the political ruler or to gratify his own prejudices, but according to definite rules. His income is not based on either his ability to gather taxes or the generosity of the ruler; he receives a salary according to his rank in the governmental organization. His tenure is usually for life, and he may be promoted on the basis of seniority or proved competence; he can be dismissed only for wrongdoing or lack of efficiency.

The civil service system is designed to secure uniformity of administration by employees who have a special competence for the particular task to which they are assigned. The fact that it is still subject to criticism, even though it has largely succeeded in reaching the objectives for which it was established, reveals some of the problems of bureaucratic operation [Merton et al. (eds.), 1952, pp. 397–424]. The criticisms of civil service may be summarized as: (1) creation of an invidious status, (2) rigidity of performance, (3) division of responsibility and excessive clerical routine, (4) bifurcation of focus [Selznick, 1943; Merton, 1949, pp. 151–160]. To some extent these tendencies may be alleviated by changes in the structure, but they appear in all bureaucracies and are probably impossible to eliminate.

An *invidious status* in one which automatically tends to create ill will, resentment, or animosity. It arises from the fact that although the bureaucratic employee is supposed to be the servant of the public, he is often in a position where he makes decisions that vitally affect the welfare of the citizen. The clerk who informs a jobless man that he is ineligible for unemployment benefits or tells a homeowner that his tax assessment has been raised is probably acting according to regulations, but he is in the position of handing down a distasteful decision to the citizen who is nominally one of his employers. It is easy for the bureaucrat to defend himself by citing the regulations and his duties as a public official, but this Olympian detachment may simply infuriate the citizen who already believes himself the victim of an unfair decision. Such resentment is increased by the security of the official's way of life in contrast to the insecurity of those who do not have a salaried civil service position.

Rigidity of performance is an attribute of men who have learned a great respect for written rules. When conditions unforeseen by the rules come up, they may be unable to act, both from a real lack of authority and from an acquired disposition to do nothing not sanctioned by precedent. A striking example of the difficulty of the bureaucratic person in situations without a clear precedent is afforded by the case of Bernt Balchen, Admiral Byrd's pilot in his South Pole flight:

According to a ruling of the department of labor, Bernt Balchen . . . cannot receive his citizenship papers. Balchen, a native of Norway, declared his intention in 1927. It is held that he has failed to meet the condition of five years' continuous residence in the United States. The Byrd Antarctic voyage took him out of the country, although he was on a ship carrying the American flag, was an invaluable member of the Antarctic expedition, and in a region to which there is an American claim because of the exploration and occupation of it by Americans, this region being Little America.

The bureau of naturalization explains that it cannot proceed on the assumption Little America is American soil. That would be trespassing on international questions where it has no sanction. So far as the bureau is concerned, Balchen was out of the country and technically has not complied with the law of naturalization.

Chicago Tribune, June 24, 1931.

A more amusing example of the bureaucrat's habit of blindly following the rules occurred when the cold wave of 1962 brought freezing temperatures to many Southern cities which had not had a freeze in decades. In at least one city the street department proceeded with its regular street-sprinkling schedule. The water promptly froze, bringing traffic to a standstill. After all, nobody *told* them not to water the streets that day.

The disadvantages of rigidity are recognized by governmental administrators, and they have made efforts to counter it by giving more discretion to subordinate officials as well as by leaving some positions free to be filled by appointees selected without regard to the usual civil service regulations. But the granting of a great deal of discretionary authority to officials will increase favoritism and corruption, and this in turn will lead to a new set of regulations. Rigidity remains a problem, and the civil service official usually has difficulty in coping with a situation not clearly defined by regulations.

Division of responsibility is another irritating aspect of bureaucracy. In order to be sure that a uniform policy is followed and all individuals are treated equally, it may be necessary to build up an elaborate file and to consult several officials at different levels of the hierarchy. The citizen often feels that he is getting the "runaround" as he tries to find some official whom he can pin down to a decision. If this difficulty is minimized by decentralization to give subordinate officials more power, then the bureau faces the danger of criticism because of favoritism and inconsistent decisions.

Bifurcation of allegiance is perhaps the most deep-rooted of the objections to any bureaucracy, civil service or otherwise. Bifurcation means a splitting off in two divergent paths. In the bureaucracy, this may take the form of a split between service to the clientele and adherence to the norms and procedures characteristic of the bureaucratic structure. Supposedly the bureaucracy exists to serve its clientele, and procedures are developed with service in mind. Actually the procedures sometimes become an end in themselves. For example, the prison and the mental hospital have the goal of rehabilitating inmates or patients. But in each institution an employee culture develops, oriented toward controlling the inmates or patients in the easiest way, which sabotages the formal goals of the prison or hospital [Dunham and Weinberg, 1960]. Every bureaucracy offers similar examples of means becoming ends. An office may go through the motions without ever actually solving a problem. A bureaucrat may handle a citizen's complaint by filing a report, or by referring him to Mr. X. The official who follows this path may feel that he has done all that could be expected according to the rules; but the public is dissatisfied because its needs have not been met. Efforts to punish an official are usually fruitless when he can prove that he has followed the letter of the regulations. Again, a greater amount of freedom for the official, though it would enable him to meet problems more realistically, would destroy uniformity in treatment and invite corruption.

A number of these dysfunctional tendencies in bureaucracy are summed up in the concept of *bureaupathology,* a word apparently coined by Thompson [1961, chap. 8]. All large impersonal organizations produce a great many tensions among their personnel. Anxieties and frustrations over promotions, criticisms, failures, lack of recognition, unwelcome demands of others, and conflicting pressures of many sorts all combine to produce great stress in the individual. He often responds in ways which reduce his tension but sabotage the goals of the organization. The insecure employee plays it safe by concentrating on report filing and record keeping. Buck passing and responsibility ducking are ways of keeping one's record "clean." Bureaupathic behavior is oriented to personal needs rather than to institutional goals. Since it arises from the anxiety and insecurity created by all large organizations, it is a problem in organizational theory, not in psychopathology.

Reactions to bureaucracy   The tendency for bureaucracies to accumulate rules and procedures is well known. In fact, many bureaucracies become so entangled in red tape that their daily work can be accomplished only by violating or evading some of the rules. Employees find it possible to go "on strike" by simply abandoning their shortcuts and following the rule book. In this way the employees of the British Post Office slowed the mails to a crawl during a dispute in 1962 [*Time,* Jan. 19, 1962, p. 35].

The difficulties of bureaucratic organization lead both to attempts to improve it and to revolt against it. The formal study of administration with a careful analysis of bureaucratic forms and functions is an attempt to make the bureaucracy an efficient instrument for meeting institutional needs. Training programs for businessmen, educators, public officials, and clergymen, all stress courses in "administration" (a more popular term for bureaucratic procedures). The basic premise of this attempt at improvement is that bureaucracy is a necessary aspect of modern culture and that its evils can be reduced through the study of institutional organization and the careful training of personnel.

Revolts against bureaucratic rigidities take many forms. In government they may be seen in the persistence of "machine politics." The political machine is sometimes regarded as an effort to outflank the bureaucracy, since the citizen who is frustrated by the bureaucracy may have his needs cared for by a political boss who gives preferential treatment in return for votes. The boss is usually less honest than the bureaucrat but more skillful in primary-group relations. While he ignores red tapes and violates rules, he gets things done.

Other institutions also show discontent with bureaucratic rule. The elaborate ecclesiastical structure of the major denominations is often threatened by irregular clergy or by less formal churches which provide religious solace to those who distrust the formalized institution. The elaborately organized business may be undercut by a smaller competitor which can more swiftly pursue profitable opportunities. Schools find themselves confronted with taxpayers' revolts which are due in part to a feeling of helplessness of the average citizen in dealing with educational administration. Labor-union leaders often find their control is jeopardized by wildcat strikes in which the rank and file take action that the official union leaders would rather suppress.

Both the need for bureaucratic structures and the resentment which they arouse seem inherent in the nature of modern large-scale organizations. A growing understanding of the techniques of administration may enable institutions to function in ways that may lessen public resentment against bureaucratic red tape, but some degree of dissatisfaction will probably always remain. If future trends follow those of the past, we may expect to see rank-and-file revolts against bureaucratic rule followed by the rise of new bureaucracies differing in personnel but following essentially the same procedures as the old ones.

THE INTERRELATIONS OF INSTITUTIONS

No institution operates in a vacuum. The preceding sections of this chapter show that one cannot understand a social institution unless one studies its relationships with the rest of the culture. Religion, government, business, education, and the family all exist in a constant state of mutual interaction. Business conditions determine the number of people who feel able to marry; the marriage and birth rates affect the demand for goods. Education creates attitudes which influence the acceptance or rejection of religious dogma; religion, in turn, may either exalt scholarship because it reveals the truths of God or denounce scientific inquiry because it threatens the faith. Businessmen, educators, clergymen, and the functionaries of all other institutions seek to influence the acts of government, since governmental action may make the difference between success and failure in their institutional enterprises.

The interrelationship of institutions explains why institutions are seldom able to control their members' behavior in a manner fully consistent with institutional ideals. Schools may offer a standard curriculum to all children, but the reaction of students depends on many factors outside the control of the educational institution. Children from a home which offers stimulating conversation and challenging reading materials are more apt to acquire intellectual interests than are children in homes where comic books and confession magazines are the reading fare and where television replaces conversation. Churches profess high ethical ideals, but their members often feel obliged to compromise these ideals in their adjustment to business, politics, or the process of securing a mate. Patriotism glorifies self-sacrifice and a devotion to the welfare of the state that conflict with the citizen's desire to accumulate a substantial nest egg for his family.

The need to harmonize the roles which different institutions seek to impose on the same individuals has often led to a deliberate effort to arrange institutional alliances. Our nineteenth-century alliance between business and government made it possible for business to pursue maximum profits with government assistance instead of governmental restraint. A state church ensures that church and state will support, rather than oppose or undermine, each other. Education has such a profound influence on the rest of the society that other institutions attempt to capture it by controlling the schools. Business and labor associations attempt to influence the schools by propaganda in the guise of free "educational" materials; politicians investigate them to be sure they conform to the current standards of nationalism; and some churches operate schools of their own in an effort to guarantee that education will support religious indoctrination.

The family affects participation in other institutions and in turn is the object of concern by other parts of the social order. The state regulates the process of marriage and divorce and at the same time sets minimum standards for the care of children. The schools provide "family-life" courses and seek family cooperation through the formation of parent-teacher associations. Churches set ideals for family life and strive to keep the observance of family ceremonies in the religious setting. Business advertises its products as essential to proper family life.

All organizations face a conflict between career loyalty and family loyalty on the part of their functionaries. Business concerns try to secure "corporation wives" [Whyte, 1951] who will cheerfully adjust their family concerns to harmonize with the demands the corporation makes on its executives. The army discourages marriages for privates and tries, by providing living quarters for the upper-officer ranks, to enable them to adjust their family life to the needs of military service. The most thorough effort to control family influence is seen in the Roman Catholic Church which strives to free its priesthood entirely from family entanglements through the requirement of celibacy.

All institutions face the necessity of continuously adapting themselves to a changing society. Changes in one institution compel changes in other institutions. Since family patterns change, the state sets up a system of social security. Since workers drift from farm to factory, the church must revise its language, its procedures, and possibly its doctrines. No institution can avoid affecting other institutions or avoid being affected by other institutions.

Institutional autonomy The fact that institutions are interdependent does not mean that any institution willingly surrenders ideological or structural control. Each institution tries to preserve its own autonomy while at the same time seeking to influence, if not to dominate, the others. Two of the basic institutions, education and religion, have developed patterns of behavior that are intended to prevent domination by other institutions and to maintain some degree of independence for schools and churches.

Educators are a relatively conservative group, somewhat more apt than average men to be loyal citizens, to accept the prevailing economic institutions, and to be faithful churchmen and conventional family members. Nevertheless, educators have a rationale of their own and are restive when other institutions attempt to exert control over the schools. The rationale of the educator is that schools exist to disseminate the truth as it is discovered by each academic discipline. Usually this search for truth does not have revolutionary implications, but it frequently issues forth in a form somewhat different from that preferred by the representatives of other institutions. Further, the very process of intellectual inquiry is upsetting to those who have made an absolute commitment to institutional goals and accompanying ideologies. Hence the schools are often under suspicion of undermining the faith of the citizens and are closely watched by representatives of other institutions.

The ideology used to safeguard the autonomy of educational institutions is *academic freedom*. This means that schools are to be run by their own authorities rather than being directly subservient to other institutions and that professors are free to conduct research, publish, and teach their findings without fear of reprisal if the results of research should prove unpopular. From the point of view of educators, academic freedom is the passport to their search for truth wherever it may lead. From the viewpoint of society, this means of assuring educational autonomy may at times prove embarrassing to other institutions whose leaders feel they have not received the proper support from the school. Its merit lies in the assurance that both students and the general public will receive what is actually the truth as the professor understands it, rather than some position to which the professor is forced to subscribe because of pressure.

Religious organizations face a similar pressure to support other institutions. The national state often wishes to equate the idea of the good churchman with the good citizen. The forces of the existing order wish the churches to bless the *status quo* in the name of peace and responsibility. The forces of revolution wish the churches to endorse drastic change in line with religiously expressed ideas of equality and social justice. The functionaries of every institutional system crave the blessings but not the ethical judgments of the church; that is, they wish the church to endorse, but not to criticize or evaluate, their institutional practices.

Religious organizations have developed various means of coping with these threats to their independence and freedom of action. One method is that of the state church, sometimes designated the *ecclesia*. This may be found in a society where the great majority of the people are also members of the same church. Under these circumstances a type of *modus vivendi* is worked out under which the church accepts the main features of the institutional life of the country and in turn is protected and oftentimes financially supported by the state. Somewhat attenuated versions of the state church are found in the Lutheran Church in Scandinavian countries and the Church of England in Great Britain. Tibet, before the Communist invasion, was a country in which state and church were so thoroughly intermingled that it was hard to tell them apart. Currently, Islam in Saudi Arabia and Roman Catholicism in Spain are vigorous examples of the state church practice. The state church not only accepts the main features of the society, but oftentimes accepts some measure of government control. The Spanish government, for instance, was given the right to approve or reject bishops nominated by the Vatican.

The *sect* and the *cult* are at the opposite pole from the ecclesia. The cult is a comparatively small religious organization which stresses the ecstatic experience of its members, is usually uninterested in most types of personal morality, and is relatively unconcerned about the ethics of governmental or economic activities. It is thus seldom directly concerned with interests affecting other institutions and asks only to be let alone. Cults have a special appeal for older rural migrants to urban centers. California is considered to be the most flourishing ground for such groups in the United States.

The sect is also comparatively small, but unlike the cult, its religious interest takes in a wide range of personal and social morality. Of all the religious groups, the sect is the most insistent that its members actually live according to its doctrines. Its mores may be greatly different from those of the general society. It may be pacifist in a warlike nation, collectivist in an individual economy, agrarian in an urban culture, and austere in an affluent society. The sect is so small that deviations are easily detected, and deviants may be expelled. The sect's variation from the ideals and practices of the general culture is tolerated only because it comprises so small a minority that it is not thought to be a threat. A nation would not tolerate pacifist attitudes if they were widespread, but it can ignore a few Quakers or Mennonites without seriously affecting its military power. The sect usually gives up any serious attempt to sway the total society and asks only that the society tolerate its peculiar practices and beliefs.

Another type of religious organization is the *denomination,* a group which has a large membership but less than a majority of the nation's inhabitants. Since membership does not cover a majority of the country's citizens the denomination does not feel the same pressure for support of state objectives that is found in the ecclesia, and it may hold viewpoints not generally accepted in the country. Thus in the United States, the Methodists have espoused a policy toward liquor and gambling which did not meet majority approval, and the Catholics have been in a similar position in regard to birth control. On the other hand, a large and widely dispersed membership is difficult to discipline, and the members of a denomination find themselves in agreement with the majority position on most questions considered vital by the national state. Occasionally a nation will subsidize different religious denominations on the ground that their activities work for the general good, but usually they are supported by the voluntary contributions of their members.

In summary, the ecclesia seeks to dominate secular life through an alliance with the state but finds that it must surrender some of its own autonomy in the process. The denomination may be at odds with secular society on some issues but is unable either to secure control of the state or to enforce a rigid pattern of conduct on its members. It seeks to secure both acceptance of its internal autonomy and a greater degree of influence in the total society. The sect withdraws from the rest of society in an effort to keep the faith pure and remove its members from pressures to conform to the larger society. The cult finds its major role in emotionally expressive activities, and its ethical demands are largely irrelevant to other social institutions.

Classification of a religious group as cult, sect, denomination, or ecclesia does not imply any value judgment concerning its validity or prestige. Rather the classification is an indication of a difference in type of emphasis and in pattern of relationship to the general society. There are, however, no churches which are "pure" types, and the classification is a continuum with degrees of difference rather than a dichotomy with absolute contrasts. Since no single church claims a majority of Americans, it is probably correct to say that the

United States does not have an ecclesia and that all the larger groups are denominations. The Amish and the Hutterites could be cited as two groups which most nearly match the definition of sect. Numerous small groups would probably be listed as cults. Marty [1960] mentions the following as a partial list: Peace Mission Movement of Father Divine; "I Am" movement; in some respects, Oxford Group Movement; Unity School of Christianity; Theosophy; New Thought. Sociologists of religion disagree somewhat about the exact definition of the various categories and the number of subtypes which might be added to their classification. They are, however, in fairly general agreement that such a typology indicates the main ways in which religious organizations have responded to pressure from other institutions.

American society has not encouraged the complete domination of any institution by another. It has fostered the separation of church and state, a rejection of widespread government ownership of industry, the preservation of private business enterprise, a somewhat uncertain tradition of academic freedom for educational institutions, and a considerable degree of freedom for individuals in making their own family arrangements. These methods of assuring institutional autonomy are not completely accepted, and each institution makes a continued effort to increase its influence upon other social institutions. While institutions do develop distinctive attitudes and goals, their members carry into one institutional arrangement the attitudes formed in another, and the social order is the stage for a continual interplay, adjustment, and competition among different institutionalized groups.

CYCLES OF INSTITUTIONAL CHANGE

The birth or death of an institution is a rare event. New institutional norms may replace old norms, but the institution generally goes on. For example, the modern family has replaced a set of strongly patriarchal norms with a set of more equalitarian norms, while *the family* continues. When feudalism "died," government did not end; one pattern of institutional structure with its attendant associations was replaced by a different one; governmental and economic functions continued to be fulfilled, although according to changed norms. All the basic institutions are thousands of years old; the present institutional norms and the forms of association which carry out institutional functions are much newer. Sometimes this institutional change takes place gradually and informally. Old practices fall into disuse and are replaced by new ones which gradually appear, become customary, and eventually become fully supported by the mores (that is, become institutionalized). For example, strict parental control over the courtship choices of their children has faded away in most western societies, while "dating" and "going steady" have appeared and become institutionalized. From time to time, changes in the law provide legal sanction for changes in institutional norms that have already taken place. American colonial law provided for legal punishment of youths who persisted in courting a girl without her father's consent; American law today protects the right of young people (above certain ages) to court and marry in opposition to their parents' wishes. In such informal ways, much institutional change takes place.

Many other institutional changes are accomplished through the formal organization of new associations; for example, the organization of the parent-teacher associations has promoted a number of changes in our educational institutions. This establishment of new institutional norms and supporting associations often follows a familiar sequence of stages, as is suggested by Dawson and Gettys [1948, pp. 705–709] and Hertzler [1961, pp. 155–157].

The initial phase   Winning recognition for a new institutional norm is often the outgrowth of a struggle—the culmination of a successful social movement. The successful establishment of a new association also involves a struggle for acceptance from a society which is often skeptical or hostile. The battle for acceptance

is likely to develop a heroic loyalty which the founders never forget. Countless novels and epic poems have immortalized the burning faith of the founder of a new religion or a new religious order, the patriotism of revolutionary armies, and the zealous conviction of the founders of a new political party. Individual interests have

The battle for acceptance often develops a heroic loyalty.

been largely submerged in dedication to the establishment of the new norm or association, and its progress gives its members new roles providing them with a sense of fulfillment. If personal rivalries develop, they are handled in an improvised and perhaps violent manner. Stern and even harsh actions are justified by the belief that they are necessary to protect the institution. The leader during this period is often a person of magnetic personality, who receives a fanatical devotion from his followers. In his person people see a "charisma" which personalizes their image of the crusade and sustains their loyalty.

The consolidation phase   An association cannot survive on spontaneous enthusiasm; it must be organized. In this period the thrill of novelty is largely gone, and the new roles and statuses become routinized. People no longer are fighting for a cause; instead they accept the remodeled association as a natural part of the social order and seek to find in it a desirable personal status. The virtues of dignity and responsibility replace spontaneous enthusiasm among participants. Capable administrators replace leaders of magnetic personality. In rare cases is the early popular leader able to develop administrative talents and retain associational leadership; in others he is shoved aside by coldly efficient "organization men." The religious saint or martyr is succeeded by the ecclesiastical diplomat; the daring business promoter gives way to the efficiency expert; and the revolutionary hero yields to the shrewd political administrator.

During the initial phase, institutional change is supported by an ideology which is a flaming faith that inspires a challenge to the social order. Now it becomes a comfortable system of beliefs which serve to reinforce the *status quo*. The consolidation process generally demands some compromises in the original beliefs. When the early Christian faith—communal, frugal, and pacifistic—gained recognition as the official faith of the wealthy and powerful

Roman Empire, some compromises were necessary. Those who cannot make such compromises may become a nuisance, and like Trotsky in Russia, may have to be silenced. Thus "the revolution devours its children," as ardent devotees of the early ideals give way to practical men who can adjust their ideological beliefs to the needs of institutional power.

The major activity in this period is the development of institutional procedures. It is a time when the statuses become formalized so that titles and established privilege mark off one status from another. Decisions become the precedents for future action. Many personal rivalries appear, and in dealing with them the institution develops a rigid pattern of procedures. Changes do occur, but these must be pictured as though they were logical and proper developments from the past, latent always in the life of the institution.

The disorganization phase   The routinization of the institution during the period of consolidation does not mean that it has lost its attractiveness. Indeed, the very fact that it can be sustained without fanatical enthusiasm may indicate that people generally find it a satisfying way of meeting their needs, and it may continue to gain fairly complete and uncritical acceptance for a long period of time. Eventually, however, social changes are apt to bring about situations which the institution fails to meet successfully. Gunpowder and trade destroyed feudalism; nationalism destroyed the Holy Roman Empire; today the atom bomb has (we most fervently hope) made total war obsolete. Social change will shake the firmest institution. The first symptom is often a widespread cynicism about the motives of the leaders of the institution, followed by demands for reforms and then by the threat of replacement of present norms and associational structures by alternative ones.

In this period of change the associational structures attached to the institution may fail to attract either the idealist or the practical citizen. The practical man seeking a career may look elsewhere for personal opportunities; the idealist may be dismayed by the traditional inertia apparently making the institution unresponsive to human needs. The institutional officers are apt to be either aristocrats who inherited their position, opportunists callously exploiting the institution for personal advantage, or passionate antiquarians living in a bygone world. As acceptance dwindles and criticism mounts, frantic attempts may be made to restore prestige through the sporadic persecution of critics and the expansion of symbols of wealth and power. Often the most impressive monuments are completed just as an institution or state enters a period of disorganization and perhaps decline—the Hanging Gardens of Babylon, the Acropolis at Athens, St. Peter's Cathedral at Rome, or the Palace at Versailles. Such displays of institutional splendor seldom regain the loyalty of an apathetic public.

If an association fails to adjust to changing conditions, it dies. A corporation whose products no longer appeal to its customers will become bankrupt. If the corporation as an institutional system of business organization fails to adapt itself to meet changing social needs, it is either compelled by outside pressure to change or is discarded in favor of some other (possibly socialist) form of business organization.

The church whose doctrines and activities are out of touch with current needs will lose it followers to other churches. An ineffectual political system will be replaced by a competing institutional form as monarchies yield to republics or democracies to dictatorships. History is strewn with the wreckage of once powerful institutions which relied on prestige, wealth, or force instead of making adaptations to a changing scene.

The reorganization phase It is not easy to reformulate institutional norms and structures, for they are highly resistant to change. The institution tends to become tradition-encrusted, and its procedures and symbols become sacred, so that a proposal for change appears to be subversive and wicked. It was traitorous and sinful to question the absolute authority of seventeenth-century kings or nineteenth-century husbands.

An institution may be so involved in procedures that members lose sight of its objectives. The church may become preoccupied with its rituals, the government with its paper work, the army with its parades, equipment, and traditional training procedures, and the school with its established courses of study. The *means* of the institution may have become the *ends* of the institution. Proposed changes in procedures are bitterly denounced as attacks upon the institution itself.

To reorganize an institution demands leadership capable of adapting the institution to meet changing needs. Such leadership rarely arises within an institution, for it generally promotes men who venerate its traditions and respect its present operation. To get leaders who will make drastic changes new blood must be brought in. The reorganization may involve new associational structures, new procedures, new objectives, or perhaps a reinterpretation of neglected earlier ideals of the institution.

Religious institutions offer many examples of institutional reorganization. To Western eyes. Buddhism and Islam appear to be outmoded faiths, irrelevant to the needs of the modern world. But a skillful alliance with the newer nationalism has made Buddhism in Burma, Ceylon, and Thailand a symbol of national unity with which every ambitious man must be identified [Cady, 1953]. In Africa and the Middle East, a similar identification with nationalism has brought a fresh dynamism to Islam [Northcott, 1959]. An enlargement of objectives has strengthened both these faiths. Meanwhile the struggle of the Christian faith to gain institutional status in Asia and Africa has been severely, and perhaps fatally, handicapped by its identification with Western colonialism [Jacob, 1957].

Sometimes an institutional reorganization consists of a change of methods as in the counterreformation led by Ignatius Loyola, which helped the Catholic church to regain some of the ground lost in the Protestant Reformation. Sometimes an emphasis on latent ideals, long neglected in practice, may gain new power for the church. A case in point here is the emphasis of American Negro pastors on the ideals of brotherhood and nonviolent resistance, a strategy that has enabled their churches to assume a prominent position in the fight against segregation. Similar examples could be cited from the fields of politics, education, and business. Problems and methods of coping with them may vary, but all institutions face the necessity of periodic changes of norms, objectives, procedures, and leadership if they are to survive in a changing society. In modern societies, change is so rapid that most institutions are in a continuous state of disorganization and reorganization.

SUMMARY

As roles are defined by mores, folkways, and laws, role behavior becomes predictable or institutionalized. Such role behavior is carried on in a regular pattern which is relatively independent of the personalities involved. Institutions tend to interpret both their own behavior and that of the rest of society in ideological terms. This mode of interpretation strengthens the institution by enabling people to explain events in terms consistent with the ideology of the institution.

Institutions may be so loosely structured that no central authority has the power to make binding decisions, or their system of defining role behavior may be so closely structured that rigid specifications for all participants in the institution are centrally determined. Institutional functions may be categorized as manifest or latent depending on the degree to which they are deliberately planned. Latent functions may be completely at variance with the professed aims of the institution, and devoted members of the institution may be unaware of their existence. Manifest functions include activities sustaining the internal functioning of the institution and also measures designed to extend its influence in the total society. Functions, morale, ideology, and type of personnel vary at different periods in the life cycle of the institution, and behavior common in one period may be unusual in another. Intellectuals are valued for their ability to defend the ideology and at the same time are feared because of their ability to develop opposing ideologies.

Bureaucratic structures in institutions are not necessarily confined to political organizations but develop wherever it is necessary to coordinate the activities of many people. Bureaucracy offers both an efficient mechanism for reaching institutional goals and the danger of allowing the mechanism to seem more important than the service it is supposed to perform. Civil service systems offer vivid illustrations of both the functions and problems of bureaucratic development.

Regardless of the unique qualities of each institution, its functioning is affected by its relationship to the rest of society. This relationship is seen both in behavior patterns which spread unconsciously from one institution to another and in the conscious efforts to establish the supremacy of church, state, business, or family. Adjustments to the struggle for power are seen in the development of the concept of academic freedom among educational institutions and various church-state arrangements espoused by the sect, the denomination, and the ecclesia. Institutions are interrelated, so that changes in one institution affect the others in a continuous mutual cause-and-effect relationship.

QUESTIONS AND PROJECTS

1. Emerson made the statement, "An institution is the lengthened shadow of one man." To what extent is this definition consistent with that used in this chapter?

2. What changes occur as a procedure becomes institutionalized?

3. "Turn the rascals out," is a frequent battle cry in politics. Comment on the effectiveness of this procedure as a means of changing role behavior.

4. Is it correct to say that modern labor unions are a latent effect of changes in business enterprise brought about by the industrial revolution?

5. Religious institutions are often charged with having abandoned the faith as originally conceived. How does this charge, if true, relate to the theory of the life cycle of institutions?

6. Why does dissatisfaction arise with bureaucratic developments? What is the major obstacle in eliminating bureaucratic features which cause resentment?

7. Can you cite any examples of bureaupathic behavior in any bureaucracy with which you are familiar? By college students? By professors?

8. The Socialist Workers' party in the United States, a small group with no hope of winning an election, is bitterly critical of other parties who have missed the true path of Marxian socialism and is very proud of its own steadfast devotion to basic principles. What type of religious group does it resemble? What kind of motivation keeps parties of this type alive?

9. What is meant by the interrelationship of institutions? How does the shift from rural to urban living affect the church? Can the development of the social security system be related to any other changes in economic institutions? In the family?

10. Make a comparison of the Communist party and the Christian church(es) as institutional structures. (William Ebenstein, *Today's Isms,* Prentice-Hall, Inc., Englewood Cliffs, N.J., 1964, chap. 1, is a good source on the Communist party.) For each, identify its sacred writings, saints and martyrs, absolute truths, symbols, codes of behavior, manifest and latent functions, and recent examples of disorganization and reorganization.

11. Read the fictional or biographical presentation of institutional roles in James Gould Cozzens, *Guard of Honor* (army officer); A. J. Cronin, *The Keys to the Kingdom* (Catholic priest); Pearl S. Buck, *Fighting Angel: Portrait of a Soul* (missionary); Sara Lucille Jenkins, *Lost Lamp* (Protestant minister); Theodore Morrison, *Stones of the House* (college president); James Hilton, *Good-bye, Mr. Chips* (old schoolmaster); Cameron Hawley, *Executive Suite* (business executive); Fortune (editors of), *The Executive Life* (business executive).

SUGGESTED READINGS

BLAU, PETER M.: *The Dynamics of Bureaucracy,* The University of Chicago Press, Chicago, 1955. A study of interpersonal relations in two government agencies. *Bureaucracy in Modern Society,* Random House, Inc., New York, 1956. A brief handbook on bureaucracy. (SS12-RH)

DAVIS, A. K.: "Bureaucratic Patterns in the Navy Officer Corps," *Social Forces,* 27:143–153, December, 1948. A description of the relation of bureaucratic patterns to institutional needs in the Navy setting.

DOUGLASS, H. PAUL, AND EDMUND DE S. BRUNNER: *The Protestant Church as a Social Institution,* Harper & Row, Publishers, Incorporated, New York, 1935. Pages 3–19 present a vivid picture of both the advantages and the difficulties of research on this topic. This material is reprinted in LOUIS SCHNEIDER,

Religion, Culture and Society, John Wiley & Sons, Inc., New York, 1964, pp. 9–21.

*ETZIONI, AMITAI (ED.): *Complex Organizations,* Holt, Rinehart and Winston, Inc., New York, 1961. A collection of essays and research on the structure and functions of large organizations. (P-H)

HERTZLER, J. O.: *American Social Institutions,* Allyn and Bacon, Inc., Englewood Cliffs, N.J., 1961. A textbook on social institutions.

HOULT, THOMAS FORD: *The Sociology of Religion,* Holt, Rinehart and Winston, Inc., New York, 1958, especially chap. 4, "The Institutionalization and Differentiation of Religion." Discusses principally the relationship of religion to other social institutions.

HUNT, CHESTER L.: "Moslem and Christian in the Philippines," *Pacific Affairs,* 28:331–350, December,

1955. Interaction among religious, economic, and political institutions in the southern Philippines.

MERTON, ROBERT K.: "Manifest and Latent Functions: Toward the Codification of Functional Analysis in Sociology," *Social Theory and Social Structure,* The Free Press of Glencoe, New York, 1957, pp. 19–84. A discussion of latent and manifest functions.

SMITH, HARVEY L.: "Psychiatry: A Social Institution in Process," *Social Forces,* 33:310–317, May, 1955. A description of the factors affecting the success of psychiatry in gaining institutional status.

THOMPSON, VICTOR A.: *Modern Organization,* Alfred A. Knopf, Inc., New York, 1961, chap. 8, "Bureau-pathology." An original analysis of some dysfunctional aspects of bureaucracy.

*GOSLIN, DAVID A: *The School in Contemporary Society,* Scott, Foresman and Company, Chicago, 1965, (5535-Scott); *SMELSER, NEIL J., *The Sociology of Economic Life,* Prentice-Hall, Inc., Englewood Cliffs, New Jersey, 1963 (P-H); *YINGER, J. MILTON, *Sociology Looks at Religion,* Macmillan, New York, 1961. (09029-Macm) Several small, inexpensive paperback books which present an excellent treatment of the sociological aspects of the institutions with which they are concerned.

THE

FAMILY

It happened one morning when Johnny [an American ex-GI] came to work and found Maggi, Kim Sing, Povenaaa, and three other men rolling dice. Teuru [Johnny's native girl] stood nearby, watching the game with interest, advising Maggi, "You better try harder! You need three more sixes!"

"What's the game?" Johnny asked.

"Dice," Teuru said.

"I can see that. What's it about?"

Teuru blushed and looked away, so Johnny asked Povenaaa. "Don't bother me now," the excited man cried. Suddenly there were shouts of triumph and Maggi swore the Chinaman·had cheated, but Kim Sing grinned happily and picked up the dice.

"The damned Chinaman gets the baby," Povenaaa spat.

"Gets what?" Johnny asked.

"The baby."

"Whose baby?"

"Teuru's."

"I didn't know Teuru had a baby."

"She doesn't . . . yet."

"You mean . . . my baby?" Johnny fell back with his mouth gaping. Then he yelled, "Hey! What's this about my baby?"

"He won it," Maggi said disconsolately.

Grabbing Teuru the American cried, "What are they talking about?"

"When it's born," Teuru said. "All the people in Raiatea would like to have it. So we rolled dice."

"But it's your own baby!" he stormed.

"Sure," she said. "But I can't keep it. I'm not married."

"Your own flesh and blood!"

"What's he mean?" Teuru asked Maggi.

Johnny Roe looked beseechingly at the fat woman and asked, "Would you give away your own baby? Would you give away Major?"

The crowd in the vanilla shed burst into laughter and Johnny demanded to know the joke. "It's Major!" Povenaaa roared, punching Johnny in the ribs. "Major's not her baby. She's Hedy's."

"You mean that Hedy. . . ."

"Of course," Maggi explained. "Hedy had to go to Tahiti for a good time before settling down. So she gave me Major."

Johnny Roe had heard enough. He stormed off and bought two bottles of gin, and when Teuru found him he had returned to his Montparnasse days except that now he blubbered, "Our baby! You raffled off our baby with a pair of dice!"

He kept this up for a whole day and Teuru became afraid that it was the start of another epic binge, so she broke the gin bottles and said, "All girls give away their first babies. How else could they get married?"

Johnny sat upright, suddenly sobered. "What do you mean, married?"

"What man in Raiatea would want a girl who couldn't have babies?"

"You mean . . . the men don't care?"

"Very much! Since people find I'm to have a baby, several men who never noticed me before have asked when you were going away."

"What happens then?" Johnny asked suspiciously.

"Then I get married."

Johnny fell back on his pillow and moaned, "It's indecent. By God, it's indecent."
(James A. Michener, *Return to Paradise*, Random House, Inc., New York, 1951, pp. 115–117.)

FAMILY PATTERNS show a fascinating variation from society to society, and persons from one society who become involved in the family patterns of a different society generally react in a predictably ethnocentric manner. Why, if the family is so important, has mankind been unable to find and agree upon some ideal pattern of family life which best serves human needs?

In the most primitive societies, the family is the only institution. Among the polar Eskimos, there are no other institutions—no chiefs or formal laws, no priests or medicine men, no specialized occupations. Within the family all the business of living is fulfilled. In other words, they have no physical or social needs that call for an institutional structure other than that provided by their family.

As a culture grows more complex, its institutional structures become more elaborate. The family is an adequate structure for handling the economic production and consumption of primitive hunters and farmers. But what happens when they develop trade with neighboring or distant tribes? Before long the group includes traders, shippers, and other specialists whose work is no longer a part of the family life of the society. Later, specialized craftsmen begin to produce trade goods, giving rise to further occupational differentiation. Economic institutions exist whenever economic functions are performed in routine ways by specialists, operating outside their family roles and functions.

In the most primitive societies, order is maintained with no formal laws, police, or courts. The only authority known in many simple societies is family authority; that is, certain family members have certain authority over others. With increasing tribal size and growing cultural complexity, more formal political organization is needed. Family heads are joined into tribal councils, tribes combine into confederations, and bureaucracies begin to develop. Warfare, in both primitive and modern societies, is a powerful stimulus to political organization, for only through political organization can an aroused rabble be mobilized for an effective military effort. In like manner, religious and educational institutions develop as professional functionaries, following standardized procedures, and withdraw from the family certain activities too complicated for the family to handle well.

The family, then, is the basic social institution, from which the others have grown as increasing cultural complexity made them necessary. A study of the family will tell us something about the family and about institutions in general.

STRUCTURE OF THE FAMILY

Like all institutions, the family is a system of accepted norms and procedures for getting some important jobs done. The family is defined as a *kinship grouping which provides for the rearing of children and for certain other human needs.* If a society is to survive, people must find some workable and dependable ways of pairing off, conceiving and raising children, and fulfilling the other functions of the family. These family functions vary less than the family forms through which people seek to meet them. In fact, if one were to list every possible way of organizing family life, a search of anthropological literature would probably reveal that each form of organization was the accepted pattern in at least one society. With only a few exceptions, where family patterns are concerned, everything's right some place.

Composition of the family group

When we speak of the family, we think of a husband and wife, their children, and occasionally an extra relative. This is called the *conjugal family*, since its core is the married couple; or it is sometimes called the "nuclear family." The *consanguine family* is founded, not upon the conjugal relationship of two people, but upon the blood relationship of a large number of kinspersons. The consanguine family is an extended clan of blood relatives together with their mates and children. Sometimes it is called the "joint" or "extended" family. There are certain technical differences between the joint and the extended family [see Queen et al., 1961, p. 69], but they need not concern us here. While we use the consanguine family pattern for family reunions and other ceremonial purposes, our important family functions proceed on a conjugal-family basis. Our folklore warns against in-laws and urges the couple to set up a household of their own. Our laws require a husband to maintain his wife in a home apart from other relatives if she insists, and she sometimes does. Our laws require parents to support their own children, but impose only slight obligation to care for their parents, and no obligation to care for brothers and sisters, cousins, uncles and aunts, nephews and nieces, or other relatives.

The consanguine family has a very different atmosphere. Whereas the conjugal family has a married couple at its core, surrounded by a fringe of blood relatives, the consanguine family has a group of brothers and sisters at its core, surrounded by a fringe of husbands and wives. In most instances of the consanguine family, a married man (or woman) remains primarily attached to his parental family, and remains a semioutsider in his wife's (or husband's) family. This has important consequences. One's principal responsibilities are toward the family into which one was born, not the family into which one has married. Thus a woman may depend not upon her husband but upon her brothers for protection and help in raising her children. Her husband does not escape, however, for he is saddled with his sister's children. [For descriptions of the consanguine family, see Linton, 1936, chap. 10; Murdock, 1949, chap. 3.]

In such a family, affection and responsibility are widely diffused among a fairly large group of people. Children are the joint responsibility of the entire family, and a child develops a relationship with his aunts very like that with his mother. He is surrounded by many adults, any of whom may momentarily act as parents toward him. The family tends to turn out personalities with less individuality than ours, since each child has more nearly the same socialization experience. Such a family protects the individual against misfortune. If a child's mother dies or is neglectful, good substitutes are at hand. The consanguine family offers little opportunity for individuality and little danger of loneliness or neglect.

Where family patterns are concerned, almost everything is right some place.

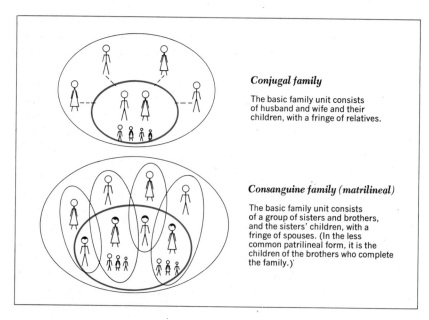

Conjugal family

The basic family unit consists of husband and wife and their children, with a fringe of relatives.

Consanguine family (matrilineal)

The basic family unit consists of a group of sisters and brothers, and the sisters' children, with a fringe of spouses. (In the less common patrilineal form, it is the children of the brothers who complete the family.)

FIGURE 3 *Conjugal and Consanguine Family Types.*

Obviously the consanguine family is not practical everywhere. Where both the family of birth and the family of marriage are in the same village, it is easy to be with one's mate while fulfilling one's family obligations. If they are in different villages, a strain is imposed. In a highly mobile, individualized, specialized society like ours, the consanguine family would be unworkable. But for the Tanala of Madagascar, whose farm work required a cooperative team of a half dozen or more adult males, the consanguine family was ideal [Linton, 1936, chap. 12].

Forms of marriage The path to marriage is lined with a variety of impediments, requirements, preliminaries, and ceremonials which would be downright discouraging—were not the objective so compelling. Rare is the society which simply allows a couple quietly to pair off and start playing house. Marriage is too important for such casual arrangements. Marriage is *the approved social pattern whereby two or more persons establish a family*. It involves not only the conceiving and rearing of children (who are sometimes conceived as an institutionalized preliminary to marriage), but also a host of other obligations and privileges affecting a good many people. Every society has, therefore, developed a pattern for guiding these marriages.

In this matter of guidance our ethnocentrism is likely to be evident. To us it is monstrous that parents should arrange and compel the marriage of two persons who may never even have met! How do they know whether they will love each other? Why are not their wishes consulted? Our reaction illustrates the usual error of ethnocentrism—assuming that people of another culture will think and feel as we should think and feel if transplanted into their situation. It overlooks the fact that most people wish and feel only what their culture trains them to wish and feel. We think of marriage as a romantic adventure with a person we have come to love. The girl in classical China, about to enter an arranged marriage with a stranger, eagerly anticipated her marriage as a desirable status and a comfortable companionship with a man she would come to love, because he had been wisely chosen by her parents. Each society viewed the other with an ethnocentric pity; we pitied their young people for their lack of freedom; they pitied our young people for their lack of parental assistance. In neither case did the young people themselves feel any need for pity. Today, of course, the Chinese family is changing rapidly and painfully under the new Peoples' Republic [Levy, 1949; Chandrasekhar, 1959; Yang, 1959; Huang, 1961].

Endogamy and exogamy Every society limits choice in marriage by requiring that one choose a mate outside his own group. This is called *exogamy*. In our society the prohibition applies only to close blood relatives; one may not marry his sister, first cousin, and certain other close relatives. Many societies extend the circle of prohibited kin to forbid marriage within the clan, the village, or sometimes even the tribe.

Most societies also require that mates be chosen within some specified group. This is called *endogamy*. Clan, village, and tribal endogamy are quite common among primitive societies. In our society, racial endogamy was required by law in many states until the U.S. Supreme Court held all such laws unconstitutional in 1967, while custom and social pressure strongly discourage racial intermarriage throughout our society. With varying degrees of pressure, we also encourage religious endogamy and class endogamy in our country.

Every society practices both exogamy and endogamy, as it specifies the limits of group closeness (exogamy) and the limits of group distance (endogamy) within which mates must be found. Sometimes between these two limits there is little room for hunting! The Aranda of Central Australia have a complicated marital pattern known to anthropologists as an "eight-class system with exogamy and indirect patrilineal descent." To skip the detailed explanations, this means that a man can marry only a woman from a particular group within the proper subsection of the opposite half of his tribe [Murdock, 1936, pp. 27–30]. In a number of societies, a formula such as this makes an actual choice unnecessary, for only one girl may be in the permissible category for a boy to marry. If there is none at all, then the couple who are supposed to become his parents-in-law normally adopt a marriageable girl from another family with a surplus. After all, an institution is a structure for meeting human needs, and it usually does so in one fashion or another.

Marital choice The process of arranging a marriage shows a fascinating range of possibilities. As shown above, some societies follow a formula whereby the children of certain socially designated kinsmen marry each other, so that the individual choices may be unnecessary. Where actual choices are necessary, they may be made in many ways. The couples can do their own choosing, sometimes with parental guidance or parental veto. The parents can arrange the marriage, with or without considering the couple's wishes. A wife may be purchased, or perhaps a complicated series of gifts are exchanged between families. Wife capture is not unknown. All these patterns exist as the standard way of arranging marriages in some of the world's societies. All of them work—within the society in which they exist—and are supported by the surrounding values and practices of the culture. Wife capture worked very well for the Tasmanians, who practiced village exogamy and were not greatly concerned over the differences between one woman and all the others. For our society, it would be less practical.

Monogamy and polygamy To us, the only decent and civilized form of marriage is *monogamy*—one man to one woman (at a time). Yet a majority of the world's societies have practiced *polygamy*, allowing a plurality of mates. There are three theoretical forms of polygamy. One is *group marriage*, in which several men and several women are all in a marriage relationship with one another. While this is an intriguing theoretical possibility, there is no authentic instance of it among human beings, with the possible exception, at one time, of the Marquesans. A very rare form is *polyandry*, where several husbands share a single wife. The Todas of Southern India provide one of our few examples. Here, as in most other cases, polyandry was fraternal, meaning that when a woman married a man, she automatically became wife to all of his brothers, and they all lived together with little jealousy or discord. Toda polyandry becomes understandable when one learns that it accompanied female infanticide and a shortage of women [Murdock, 1936, pp. 120–121; Queen et al., 1961, chap. 2]. Only where some situation has created a shortage of women is polyandry likely to be found [Unni, 1958]. But the scattered handful of societies which practice polyandry serve to show how a practice which seems to us to be contrary to human nature can still be the accepted and preferred pattern for people who are socialized to expect it. The usual form of polygamy is *polygyny*—a plurality of wives, not necessarily sisters and generally acquired at different times during one's life.

Mention of polygyny will arouse a predictably ethnocentric response from almost any American. He conjures up images of female degradation and helpless enslavement and rises to impressive heights of moral indignation at such heathen brutishness (or possibly of harem delights as pictured in Hollywood's mass-produced daydreams!). The facts are otherwise. It would be difficult to show that women have generally had a more satisfactory status in monogamous than in polygamous societies. Even in polygynous societies, most of the marriages are monogamous. It is generally only the more successful and powerful men who can afford or attract more than one wife. In many polygynous societies, the second wife fills the status function of the second Cadillac in our society. Far from feeling resentful, the first wife often urges her husband to take more wives, over whom she generally reigns as queen bee. Polygyny in operation takes many forms in different societies, all of them far removed from the imagination of the normal ethnocentric American.

Divorce What is to be done when a married couple can't stand each other? Although most societies make some provision for divorce, some make it very difficult or perhaps give the privilege of divorce only to the men. Some make divorce very simple. Among the Hopi, divorce is rather rare but very uncomplicated. The husband merely packs up and leaves, or in his absence his wife tells him to get lost by piling his things outside the door.

The social and family structure of many societies makes divorce a fairly pain-less and harmless operation. Where there is no great emphasis upon romantic love and no intense individual love attachments, divorce entails no great heart-break. Where the consanguine family surrounds the child with a protective clan of kin, and designates the mother's brother as the responsible male in a child's life, the loss of a child's father is hardly noticed. The meaning of divorce depends upon how it relates to other aspects of the institution of the family. In our society, with its strong accent upon individual love attachments within an independent conjugal family unit, a divorce is likely to mean the collapse of the emotional world for both child and adult.

Other variations in family structure   We could extend the list of "odd" family patterns indefinitely. Some societies, like ours, encourage an informal camara-derie between brother and sister; among others, such as the Nama Hottentots, brother and sister are expected to treat each other with great formality and respect, may not address each other directly, or even be alone together. Such *avoidances* are found in many societies. Mother-in-law avoidance is very com-mon; the Crow husband may not look at or speak to his mother-in-law, or even use a word which appears in her name. In many societies, avoidance taboos demand extreme decorum toward other relatives. Thus the Crow, who must act with great decorum toward his sister, mother-in-law, son-in-law, and his wife's brother's wife, is socially expected to show great familiarity toward his sister-in-law, joke with her, and engage in various immodesties. Among the Nama Hottentots, brother-sister incest is the worst of all offenses, but cross-cousins[1] enjoy a "joking relationship" which includes loose talk, horseplay, and sexual intimacy. All this is merely to say that the family includes a varying number of people whose relationship to one another is defined differently in different societies.

Is there any sense in all this, or is the family an irrational jumble of odd no-tions and historical accidents? Two things we should remember. First, many different patterns will "work," as long as all members of the society accept them. Wife purchase, wife capture, or wives-for-the-asking—any one of these patterns works out acceptably, provided the people view it as the proper way to stake out a mate. Thousands of societies have been in existence at some time or other. It is not surprising that most of the possible ways of organizing human relationships have been tried out sometime, somewhere. Many of them have survived, showing that man is a highly adaptable animal, capable of being trained to find his satisfactions in a remarkable variety of ways.

Second, we invoke the concept of cultural relativity and repeat that how a custom works depends upon how it relates to the rest of its cultural setting. Where wife purchase exists, the transaction is not merely a way of arranging marriages but a central feature of the entire economic and social system. The consanguine family exists in certain societies because it is an efficient eco-*nomic* unit in such societies, and not just because it is nice to have the family together [Sahlins, 1957; Nimkoff and Middleton, 1960]. As we stated in the preceding chapter, institutions are interrelated.

---

[1] *Cross-cousins* are the children of a brother and a sister; where the related parents are of the same sex, the cousins are called parallel cousins.

FUNCTIONS OF THE FAMILY

The family in any society is an institutional structure which develops through a society's efforts to get certain tasks done. What are the tasks commonly performed through the family?

The sexual regulation function The family is the principal institution through which societies organize and regulate the satisfaction of sexual desires. Most societies provide some alternative sexual outlets. With varying degrees of indulgence, each society also tolerates some sex behavior in violation of its norms. But all societies expect that most sexual intercourse will occur between persons whom their institutional norms define as legitimately accessible to each other. These norms sometimes allow for considerable sexual variety; yet no society is entirely promiscuous. In every society there are mores which forbid certain persons access to one another. What may look to us like promiscuity is more likely to be a complicated system of sexual permissions and taboos which we do not fully understand.

A clear majority of the world's societies allow young persons to experiment with sexual intercourse before marrying [Murdock, 1949; 1950]. Many societies think the idea of virgin marriage is absurd. Yet in such societies, this premarital sex experience is viewed as a preparation for marriage, not as a recreational pastime. Its principal purpose is generally to determine fertility; a girl who conceives shows her readiness for marriage. Most of these societies have not merely *allowed* premarital sexual behavior; they have *institutionalized* it. They have defined it as a proper and useful activity and have developed a supporting set of institutional arrangements which make it safe and harmless. Since there is full social approval, there is no fear, shame, or disgrace. The family structure and living arrangements in such societies are generally of a sort where one more baby is no special inconvenience or burden. Premarital sex experience can be a useful and harmless preparation for marriage in a society which has institutionalized it. Ours has not, as many young people learn to their dismay.

Some societies provide for the sexual needs of virtually all adults; others do not. Many primitive societies provide for the unmarried through some form of sexual hospitality or occasional license. An unmarried or widowed brother may be permitted occasional access to his brother's wife. A widow may automatically become wife to her deceased husband's brother (the *levirate*); and, less commonly, the widowed husband becomes husband to his deceased wife's sister (the *sororate*). Celibacy is exceedingly rare in primitive societies. Contemporary Western societies are less solicitous. No approved sexual outlet is provided for the widowed or the unmarried adult. Just how easily Western societies *could* make such provision, without severe disruption of other institutions and values, is a matter of debate. Yet the war-decimated populations of countries like Germany and the Soviet Union have several millions of women who are condemned to a life without husband, legitimate children, or a legitimate sex and love experience. In this respect, contemporary Western society is, perhaps, less well organized than many primitive societies.

The reproductive function   Every society depends primarily upon the family for the business of producing children. Other arrangements are theoretically possible, and many societies arrange to accept children produced outside a marriage relationship. But no society has established a set of norms for providing children except as part of a family.

The socialization function   All societies depend primarily upon the family for the socialization of children into adults who can function successfully in that society. Thinkers from Plato to Huxley [1932; 1958] have speculated about other arrangements, and dozens of experiments in communal child rearing have been attempted and abandoned. After the Russian Revolution, the Soviet Union experimented with raising children in institutions, hoping to free their mothers for labor and to rear the children more "scientifically." But Russia never practiced this idea very widely, soon gave it up, and then did everything possible to strengthen the family [Alt and Alt, 1959]. In modern Israel, children in the kibbutz (co-operative farm) are raised in communal cottages and cared for by nursery workers while the other women work elsewhere in the kibbutz. Parents are normally with their children for a couple hours a day and all day on Sundays. This communal rearing seems to work very successfully in the kibbutz [Bettelheim, 1964], although some critics disagree [Spiro, 1958]. Yet only a few of the Israeli live in the kibbutzim, and in Israel as elsewhere, the family survives as the standard institution for looking after children. The family is the child's first primary group, and this is where his personality development begins. By the time he is old enough to enter primary groupings outside the family, the basic foundations of his personality are already firmly laid.

One of the many ways in which the family socializes the child is through providing models for the child to copy. He learns to be a man, a husband, and a father mainly through having lived in a family headed by a man, a husband, and a father. Some socialization difficulties are encountered where such a model is missing and the child must rely upon the second-hand models he sees in other families or upon other relatives. There is no fully satisfactory substitute for a mother and a father, although they need not be the biological parents.

Sometimes, although both parents are present, they are not satisfactory models. If the father is an ineffectual, timid, hesitant incompetent in a society which expects men to be bold, confident, and successful, the son is torn between his need to identify with a father as a model and his growing awareness that he should not grow up to be like his father. A girl's mother may be agressive and masculine, with a resentful hostility toward men; she may be exploitatively feminine, selfishly using femininity to manipulate men; she may be timid, overdependent, and insecure, lacking any confidence in her ability to function as a wife and mother. A girl with such a mother has no opportunity to imitate the attitudes and skills needed for a successful adult role in our society. Many psychiatrists trace many personality difficulties to one's childhood lack of suitable parental models [Parsons, 1947; La Piere and Farnsworth, 1949, chap. 8].

The function of models in socialization can be seen in the role-taking play of children. Children often "play house," passing out roles among one another

("You be the mama, and you be the papa, and I'll be the little girl, and you be the baby!"). They proceed to act out these roles as they perceive them, and they perceive them largely as they have seen them being played in their own families. Many a parent, overhearing such play, has been chagrined to learn how his child perceives his behavior! All this, however, is more than just "play." Through such role taking, the child's perception of adult roles is refined and corrected ("You stop doing that and act like a papa is supposed to act, or we won't play!"). Such play probably contributes insights into the feelings of others. When in play a child "misbehaves" and is "punished" by the "papa," each of them probably gains some insight into the feelings of the real father who punishes a child. Both are also recognizing the boundaries of conduct when they define an act as misbehavior. Role-taking play is thus a way of socializing children to accept and fill both their present and their future family roles.

The affectional function   Whatever else he needs, man needs intimate human response. Psychiatric opinion holds that probably the greatest single cause of emotional difficulties, behavior problems, and even of physical illness, is *lack of love*, that is, lack of a warm, affectionate relationship with a small circle of intimate associates [Fromm, 1956; Schindler, 1954, chap. 10]. A mountain of data shows that the serious delinquent is typically a child whom nobody cares very much about. Infants who get good physical care but are not cuddled, fondled, and loved are likely to develop a condition medically known as *marasmus* (from a Greek word meaning "wasting away"). They lose weight, fret and whimper listlessly, and sometimes even die [Ribble, 1943, chap. 1]. Several studies have shown how children in the sterilized but impersonal atmosphere of hospital or foundling home will suffer in emotional development and often show startlingly high rates of illness and death [Spitz, 1945]. Lack of affection actually damages an infant's ability to survive.

The evidence is overwhelming that our need for companionship and intimate, affectionate human response is vitally important to us. Indeed, this is probably our strongest social need—far more necessary than, for example, sex. Many celibates are leading happy, healthy, and useful lives, but a person who has never been loved is seldom happy or healthy.

Most societies rely almost entirely upon the family for affectionate response. The companionship need is filled partly by the family and partly by other groupings. Many primitive societies had organizations and clubs somewhat like modern lodges and fraternities, filling much the same functions. Yet even these were often organized on a kinship basis and were, therefore, another aspect of the family.

The status function   In entering a family one inherits a string of statuses. One is ascribed several statuses within the family—age, sex, birth order, and others. The family also serves as a basis for ascribing several social statuses—as, for example, a white, urban, middle-class Catholic. Class ascription is especially important, for the class status of a child's family largely determines the opportunities and rewards open to him, and the expectations through which others may inspire or discourage him. Class status can be changed through some combination of luck and personal efforts, as is described in chapter 12, "Social Mobility."

But each child *starts out* with the class status of his family, and this initial placement probably has greater effect upon achievement and reward than any other single factor. The assignment to a class may seem unfair; yet it is inevitable. The family cannot avoid preparing the child for a class status similar to its own, for the very process of living and growing up in such a family is preparation for its class status. The child normally absorbs from his family a set of interests, values, and life habits which make it easy for him to continue in the class status of his family and difficult for him to achieve a different class status.

The protective function
In all societies the family offers some degree of physical, economic, and psychological protection to its members. In many societies any attack upon a person is an attack upon his entire family, with all members bound to defend him or to revenge the injury. In many societies guilt and shame are equally shared by all family members. In most primitive societies the family is an extended food-sharing unit which starves or fattens together; as long as a man's relatives have food, he has no fear of hunger. And in many primitive societies, as in ours, very few persons outside one's family really care what happens to him.

The economic function
As stated earlier, the family is the basic economic unit in many societies. Its members work together as a team and share jointly in their produce. In some societies the clan is the basic unit for working and sharing, but more often the family performs the function. This situation, however, is now changing, as will be seen in the following section.

THE CHANGING AMERICAN FAMILY

The family is a prime example of the interrelatedness of institutions, for the changes in the family mirror the changes in the other institutions with which it dovetails. For example, in most hunting societies the men are clearly dominant over women, who make inferior hunters because of their limited strength and incessant child bearing. But as the economic base shifts from the hunt to the garden, women's role in the family grows somewhat more influential, for women can and do perform most of the hoe agriculture. As the plow replaces the hoe, male dominance again tends to grow, for plowing generally calls for the greater strength of the male. Thus there is some relation between one's power within the family and the importance of his (or her) economic contribution. Other examples of interrelatedness will follow.

Changing family structure
The size of the American family has decreasd   It is no secret that the twelve-child families of the last century are rare today. The birth rate in the Western world began falling about a century ago. It reached a low during the great Depression of the 1930s, when in the United States it fell to 16.6 births per thousand in 1933, rose to 26.6 in 1947, and is expected to fall to 18.7 by 1977. Today's "smaller family," however, does not mean that all families are proportionally smaller. As Figure 4 shows, small and medium-sized families are about as common as they were a half century ago, but very large families are in-

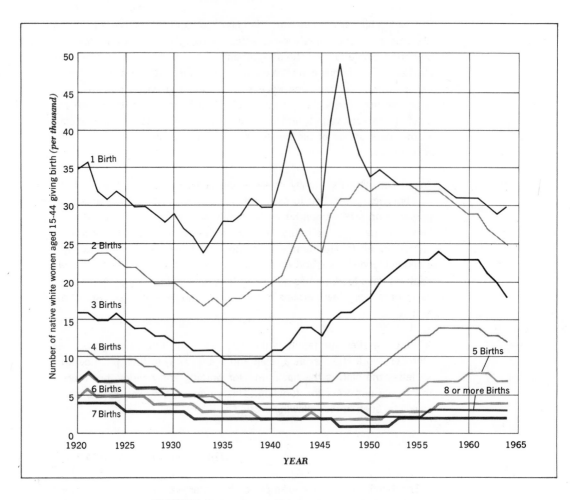

FIGURE 4 *Family Size in the United States since 1920.*

SOURCE: *Vital Statistics of the United States*, 1964, vol. 1, *Natality*, U.S. Department of Health, Education, and Welfare, pp. 1–11.

creasingly rare. As birth control becomes increasingly available to the poor and uneducated, this trend away from the very large family will probably continue.

Why has overall family size declined in the Western world? Contraceptive devices have provided the means but not the motive. Contraceptives are not the cause of smaller families any more than ropes are the cause of suicides. The motives for desiring smaller families carry us into many other aspects of the culture. The shift from an illiterate agricultural society to a literate, specialized, industrialized society has changed children from an economic asset into an expensive burden. Shifts in patterns of recreation, in aspirations for education and social mobility, and changing concepts of individual rights have all united to curb indiscriminate child bearing. Thus changing technology, changing economics, and changing values are all involved in the change in family size.

The status of divorce has changed   Divorce is the object of much agonized dismay by Americans who cannot accept divorce as an integral part of the modern American family system. A society can secure a very low divorce rate in at least four ways. First, it can deemphasize love. In many societies marriage is a working partnership, but not a romantic adventure as well. If less is expected of marriage, more will be "successful." Second, it can separate love from marriage. Romantic love appeared in Western societies several centuries ago, but only recently has it become the standard basis for marriage. A number of societies have a series of men's clubs for companionship, and allow men a wide freedom to prowl in search of sex adventure. Here again, less is demanded of the marriage. Or the society can socialize its members to be so much alike in personality and expectation that practically all marriage will work out successfully. The stable, well-integrated society generally succeeds in accomplishing this leveling; our society does not. Finally, divorce can be made so difficult that most unhappily married couples are unable or unwilling to seek divorce as a solution. Our society has actually done none of these things. It socializes people so that they differ more and more greatly in personality and expectation, gives them values which lead them to expect a great deal of marriage and to demand a high level of love satisfaction in marriage, and provides no approved outlet for their frustrated marital needs when they fail. All this makes a fairly high rate of marital failure and divorce an inescapable part of our modern family structure. The American divorce rate increased gradually to a peak of about one divorce for every four new marriages in 1946 and has remained at about that ratio ever since. From being a rare example of moral disgrace, divorce has become a fairly common, more-or-less respectable way of dealing with an intolerable marriage.

Where children are involved, a divorce creates a broken home. But while divorce has been creating more broken homes, falling death rates have reduced the number of homes broken by the death of parents. When both causes of broken homes are combined, we find that we now have proportionately fewer broken homes than formerly [Landis, 1965, pp. 3–4]. The proportion of children who reach adulthood under the care of their own parents is higher today than in the "good old days" when families were supposed to be stable. This suggests that the popular practice of blaming rising delinquency and other problems on broken homes is not supported by the facts.

The division of labor and authority has changed   The traditional American family was highly patriarchal. A century ago, a married woman's property, earnings, and even her body were legally beyond her control and at her husband's disposal. Today both law and custom have changed. Even among groups whose family is often said to be patriarchal, such as Catholics, immigrants, or farmers, recent investigation shows that ". . . the patriarchal family is dead" [Blood and Wolfe,

They differ more and more greatly in personality and expectation.

1960, p. 29]. In their investigation of 909 Detroit-area marriages, Blood and Wolfe found that power or domination of decision making was about equally divided between white husbands and wives [p. 35]. Among Negro couples, the wife was normally the more dominant, perhaps because our economy offers more steady jobs to Negro women than to Negro men [Kephart, 1961, pp. 217–225].

Blood and Wolfe's research clearly shows the relationship between economic role and family role. Husbands exercised less dominance over working wives than over nonworking wives; unemployed husbands of working wives ranked far down the dominance scale. The more highly educated, prosperous, and successful the husband, the greater his degree of dominance over the wife [Blood and Wolfe, 1960, pp. 37, 40–41, 60–61; Wolfe, 1959]. Thus the upper-class family more nearly approaches the patriarchal tradition than the lower-class family.

The "quiet revolution" in women's employment. Perhaps the greatest change of all has been the increase in "working wives." Women today make up one-third (32 per cent) of our labor force. Slightly over one-half (52 per cent) of all women are in our labor force at any single moment, and three-fourths (76 per cent) of these are married. Nine out of ten married women work at some time during their marriage. Of the married workers, almost half (7.5 million) have children under eighteen, and one-sixth (2.9 million) have children under six years old. Almost one-third of all mothers with children under eighteen are employed, and about 4 million preschool children have working mothers [Herzog, 1960, p. 3; Leaflet no. 37, Women's Bureau, 1961, p. 196]. Educated women are still more likely to be employed. Of 1957 women college graduates, those employed in 1964 included 41 per cent of those who were married and 94 per cent of those who were single, widowed, or divorced; 28 per cent of those with children under 6 years old; and 91 per cent with all their children

FIGURE 5 *Women in the Labor Force (United States, 1920–1975).*
SOURCE: Department of Commerce, Bureau of Labor Statistics.

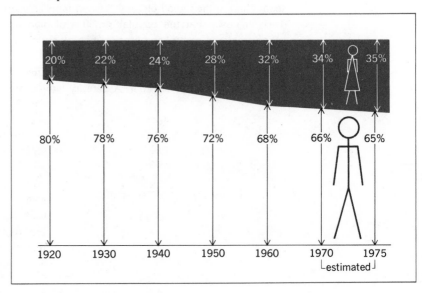

over 6 years old [*Business Week,* Nov. 26, 1966, p. 170]. From these figures, the "normal" pattern of the American woman emerges. Typically, she begins working before marriage, works until her children arrive, takes off a few years, then returns sometime after her children get into school [Smutz, 1959, p. 60]. Obviously, it has become normal for the American wife to work for a major part of her lifetime.

Historically, a woman who worked was living evidence that she had no husband able and willing to support her. A survey of 140 married women workers in 1908 found only six husbands held jobs above the grade of unskilled laborer [Bureau of Labor Statistics, 1916, pp. 163–164]. The working wife, once a lower-class phenomenon, is increasingly common among the prosperous middle classes. There is no reason to believe that this trend will be reversed. The "American standard of living" now assumes two incomes. A survey of incomes received in 1961 [Barlow et al., 1966] finds a working wife in 40 per cent of all American families in the $10,000 to $30,000 family-income bracket. As the "normal" standard of living increasingly becomes insupportable on a single income, the pressure grows upon the nonworking wives to get a job. A large majority of the readers of this textbook will be either working wives or the husbands of working wives for a major portion of their married lives.

This quiet revolution has transformed the household division of labor as well. A French study finds that married women workers actually work, at job plus housework, only six to eight hours a week more than nonworking wives with several children [Stoetzel, 1956]. Blood and Wolfe's study shows that husbands of working wives must expect to help out more at home. Many of the male readers of this text will (if they have not already done so) eventually learn whether their masculinity will dissolve in dishwater!

Changing family functions

Structure and function are two aspects of the same thing. Changes in one are both cause and effect of changes in the other. What changes in function accompany the changes in family structure?

The sexual-regulation function probably shows no great change   Illicit sexual behavior is fairly common, but, according to Kinsey, at least 90 per cent of all American sexual intercourse is marital [1948, p. 588]. There is evidence of a good deal of premarital sexual intercourse, most often with one's intended marital partner, and with considerable evidence that such behavior has been increasing. But is premarital sexual intercourse evidence of the *failure* of family regulation of sex? Or are we developing premarital relations with an intended mate as a form of family regulation of sex? In other words, are we actually beginning to institutionalize premarital sex relations? Some scholars suspect so [Ehrmann, 1959; Reiss, 1960]. They point to the increasing acceptance of the "permissiveness with affection" pattern, in which serious emotional attachment rather than marriage is the primary test of propriety in sexual intimacy. The "situation ethics" concept is part of the "new morality" which would judge behavior, not according to moral absolutes, but according to whether the behavior is harmful or fulfilling for the particular persons in their particular situation [Kirkendall, 1961; Fletcher, 1966]. Meanwhile, improved antibiotics and contraceptives are weakening some of the supports of the traditional moral code. Whether the "new morality" is an enlightened adaptation to new conditions or a dangerous rationalization for self-indulgence and exploitation is an important question [Schur, 1964, pp. 63–118]. The cultural norm (virgin marriage) and the statistical norm (increasing premarital experience) are in growing divergence. Young people, parents, relatives, and friends all conspire to maintain the illusion of virgin marriage, complete with pure white gown and veil, whereas at least half our brides today should be wearing polka dots [Burgess and Wallin, 1953; Kinsey, 1953; Kanin and Howard, 1958]. It is uncertain whether the cultural and statistical norms will eventually be brought into closer harmony, or whether this will continue as one of our norms of evasion.

The reproduction function is little changed   True, birth rates are much lower than a century ago, but if one considers only the size of the *surviving* family, then the family reproductive function is not so greatly changed. A century ago, half the children died in infancy or childhood; today over 96 per cent reach adulthood. Today's average American family of three or four surviving children (3.2, to be exact) is not far from what it has been through most of recent Western history.

The socialization function claims increased attention   The family remains the principal socializing agency, although the school now plays an important role. Other social agencies are occasionally called in for guidance. The major change has been in our *attention* to the socialization function. An earlier generation knew little about "personality development"; today nearly every literate parent knows about Dr. Spock [1945, 1957]. We know something today of the role of emotional development in school progress, career success, physical well-being, and practically all other aspects of the good life. Our great-grandparents worried about smallpox and cholera; we worry about sibling jealousies and peer-group adjustment.

How has the quiet revolution affected the socialization function? Does the child suffer when mother takes a job? There have been several dozen studies of this question [reviewed by Stolz, 1960; Herzog, 1960; Nye and Hoffman, 1963]. The earlier studies failed to control for such variables as social class or family composition. As a result, the working-mother sample had a higher proportion of poor, uneducated slum dwellers, widows, and divorcées than the nonworking-mother sample. Such poorly controlled studies seemed to show that children suffered when mother worked. Later studies compared children of working mothers with children of *otherwise comparable* nonworking mothers. Although not entirely conclusive, these studies do not show any general tendency for children to suffer when the mother is employed. The Gluecks [1959] compared 500 delinquents with 500 nondelinquents, carefully matched for social class, age, ethnic-racial derivation, and intelligence. They found no difference between the delinquency rates of the children of nonworking and those of regularly employed mothers, while children of irregularly employed mothers had a higher delinquency rate. They attributed this higher delinquency rate to the fact that the irregularly employed mother more often had an unstable husband with poor work habits; they suspected that the mother herself was more often unstable and, consequently, was a poor mother whether working or not.

Whereas the Gluecks studied working-class mothers, Nye [1958] studied middle-class mothers and found greater delinquency among the children of working mothers. On the other hand, several studies [Nye, 1952; 1959; Douvan, 1963] find that part-time employment of the mother seems to be beneficial to the adolescent child. Although the evidence is somewhat mixed, it is clear that *whether* the mother works is not very important, while the *kind* of mother she is and the kind of home she and the father provide are the important variables [Hoffman, 1963].

The affectionate and companionship functions have gained Among Blood and Wolfe's 909 families, "Companionship has emerged as the most valued aspect of marriage today" [p. 172]. Here we have two apparently contradictory developments. We have become *more* dependent upon the conjugal family for affection and companionship while we have become *less* dependent upon the extended family, the clan of relatives. We are so mobile and so individualized in our interests that we sometimes find that we have nothing in common with our cousins, uncles, and aunts except our ancestors. The extended family is less effective in offering companionship, and this lack increases our dependence upon the immediate family. Furthermore, the primary community, the small group of neighbors who knew one another well and had much in common, has disappeared from the lives of most Americans. Urbanization and specialization have destroyed it. In an increasingly heedless, impersonal, and ruthless world, the immediate family becomes the bulwark of emotional support. A man may be insulted by his boss, patronized by his colleagues, and ignored by his neighbors, but at home he can be King Solomon to his wife and Hercules to his children! Herein lies one of the greatest functions and strengths of the family.

Herein also lies one of the greatest weaknesses of the modern American family. When the family fails to provide affection and companionship—the key functions of the modern American family—little is left to hold it together. Most of the other functions can be performed for the individual outside the family relationship. We can even question whether the married man is better off, economically or sexually, than the bachelor. Yet most people marry, perhaps because sex without enduring affection is not enough. Nonetheless, when we place so much responsibility upon the conjugal family group for providing the basic emotional support for the individual, many families will fail.

The status-definition function continues Many families continue to prepare children to retain the class status of the family; a growing fraction seek to prepare their children for social mobility. They do this mainly by trying to give children the kind of ambitions, attitudes, and habits which prompt them to struggle for a higher status. At best, the effort is only partly successful. No family can fully succeed in socializing children in a way of life not practiced by the family.

The protective functions have declined The traditional family in Western society performed most of the functions of organized social work today—nursed the sick, gave haven to the handicapped and shelter to the aged. Today, we have a medical technology which only specialists and hospitals can handle. Today's urban household is an impractical place in which to care for many kinds of handicapped people. Family care of the aged was a practical arrangement when the aging couple stayed on the farm, joined by a married child and

Table 6   Subsistence production in city and farm families

Families producing "most" or "all" of each item	City, per cent	Farm, per cent
Baked goods	55	79
Summer vegetables	9	87
Canned, frozen foods	7	74
Dresses	7	15

SOURCE: Robert O. Blood and Donald M. Wolfe, *Husbands and Wives,* The Free Press of Glencoe, New York, 1960, p. 82.

mate. The parents could retire gradually, shifting to less strenuous tasks, but remaining useful and appreciated. This pattern is available today to only a tiny minority, and many elderly couples feel—and are—useless and unappreciated in the homes of their children. Our rapid rate of social change and social mobility also mean that many tensions may develop when three generations live under one roof. So for a variety of reasons—most of which have nothing to do with selfishness or personal irresponsibility—many of the protective functions of the traditional family have been shifted to other institutions.

The economic functions have changed most greatly   A century ago the American family was a unit of economic production, united by shared work on the farm. Today only one-fourteenth of our families are farmers, and even the farm family is not the self-sufficient unit of the past. Except on the farm, the family is no longer the basic unit of economic production; this has shifted to the shop, the factory, the office. The family is no longer united by shared work, for its members work separately. Instead, the family is a unit of economic *consumption,* united by companionship, affection, and recreation together.

THE FUTURE OF THE FAMILY

The family is unquestionably here to stay, but its forms and functions will constantly change along with the rest of the society. Our family has largely completed the transition "from institution to companionship"—from a family wherein the role of each person was rigidly fixed by tradition and enforced by law, custom, and social pressure to a family wherein the roles and tasks are arranged according to the wishes of the members [Burgess and Locke, 1953]. It is united not by work and external pressures but by shared interests and affections. It shows a far greater variety, since no uniform set of marriage roles and duties are impressed upon all without regard for individual preferences and aptitudes.

Such a family has a far greater potential.

Such a family has a far greater potential for personality development and individual fulfillment than the traditional pattern. This potential, though not always realized, influences the form our family is taking.

A look at our other institutions tells us why this is so. Our economic system demands specialization and mobility. The American standard of living, supported by advertising and salesmanship, guarantees the continuing march of women from the kitchen to the time clock. No amount of lecturing about "women's place" will change the trend. In time we shall adjust our family life to this fact. Our value system prizes individuality and personal happiness at the expense, if necessary, of family stability. In a society of mass production, automation, and the forty-hour week, family play takes the place of family work as the great unifying agent. Under our political system the welfare state has assumed many of the protective functions which the mobile, urban, individualized family is poorly adapted to fulfill. Our religious institutions have tempered their former preoccupation with sin and eternity with a concern for individual fulfillment in the present world.

The modern American family is thus moving in harmony with the rest of our institutions. There is little reason to believe that present trends will be reversed. Our family will for some time continue to be medium in size, to accept and appreciate mothers who work, to have a fairly high divorce rate, and to be integrated around companionship and common interests. Only major changes in our other institutions would be likely to change these tendencies.

Elsewhere in the world, the family is changing even more rapidly. All over the world, women are shedding their veils and other symbols of sexual subordination. Not everyone is copying American family patterns, but nearly everywhere traditional family patterns are rapidly eroding. In most of the underdeveloped countries, the traditional family patterns are incompatible with the economic development which they covet. It is difficult to proceed with the rational industrialization of a country where the family is still the dominant social institution. Such a society may have separate governmental and economic institutions, but they tend to operate along family lines rather than to act independently. Thus jobs are given, supplies purchased, and money loaned on a basis of kinship instead of rational economic advantage. Government office is viewed as a chance to extend family opportunity, and political power is often based upon a network of kinship alliances. Such family dominance tends to inhibit and delay industrial development, but finally, industrial development is inevitable. This makes the eventual disorganization of the traditional family norms equally inevitable. Some partly industrialized nations have limited kinship control of economic affairs by prohibiting nepotism (employment of relatives) and by using the corporation for large-scale enterprises beyond the resources and control of a single family [Fox, 1959]. Nothing is more certain than that the economic development of underdeveloped countries will be purchased at the price of vast family change.

SUMMARY

The family is the basic social institution. It varies greatly in form. The Western family is normally *conjugal*, composed of man, wife, and children. But in many societies the family unit is *consanguine*, a much larger group of blood relatives with a fringe of spouses. All societies practice *endogamy*, requiring selection of mates within some specified groups, as well as *exogamy*, requiring that one go outside certain of his groups for selection. Although most marriages are *monogamous*, many societies permit *polygamy*, generally *polygyny*, wherein it is the husband who has more than one mate at a time. Most societies provide for divorce, with wide variance in grounds and procedures. The fascinating variety of family forms shows how man's basic needs can be satisfactorily met under a great variety of institutional arrangements. In all societies the family performs certain functions—regulates sex relations, provides for reproduction, socializes children, offers affection and companionship, defines status, protects its members, and serves as a working and sharing team.

The present American family is in the midst of sweeping changes. It is somewhat larger than a generation ago, perhaps a little smaller than a century ago. Divorce has become common and almost respectable. Male authority has declined, and the division of labor has changed since it has now become normal for the wife to hold a job during a considerable part of her married life. This development has aroused many alarms over the welfare of children, but the evidence suggests that these alarms are largely unjustified.

The sex-regulatory, reproductive, and status-definition functions of the family have probably been the least affected by recent social changes. In economic function, the production activities of the family have been largely absorbed by separate economic institutions, leaving the family mainly a unit of economic consumption. The protective functions have been largely shifted to other institutions. The socialization and affectionate functions of the family have gained greatly in relative importance, both because of changes in other institutions and because of our increased knowledge about man's personal and social needs. Probably these trends will continue, and tomorrow's family in America will be equalitarian, oriented toward companionship and family recreation. It is not certain what kinds of family patterns will develop in other parts of the world, but the incompatibility of traditional family forms with economic development makes sweeping family changes inevitable.

QUESTIONS AND PROJECTS

1. Why is the family found in all societies? Would it be possible, with modern technology, to dispense with the family?

2. Why do American parents today play only a limited role in guiding the courtship choices of their children? Would it be desirable for them to play a larger role in determining marriage choices?

3. In societies where a girl normally produces a child before she is considered marriageable, is this child "legitimate"? Would it belong to a family, or would it have been produced outside the family?

4. In a society such as the Trobriand, where a man has no special duties or particular affection for his own children, how can he possibly take a truly "fatherly" concern for his sister's children?

5. What could be said for allowing polygynous marriages in American society? What could be said against such permission?

6. We use the term "uncle" for the brothers of our father or mother. Among the Todas the term "father" includes not only one's father but all his uncles. What is the importance of such variations in terminology? Some societies have no word for "illegitimate." What does the omission mean?

7. How do recent and current family changes illustrate the interrelationship of institutions?

8. Defend each of these positions: (1) "Divorce is a necessary and useful institution for a society like ours." (2) "Divorce is cause and evidence of family breakdown, and should be avoided at all costs."

9. Discuss these two propositions: (1) "The proper socialization of the child requires the intimate, continuous, affectionate supervision that only a full-time mother can give." (2) "An uninterrupted mother-child contact encourages an excessive dependence; the child develops most healthfully when cared for by several warmly responsive adults."

10. Discuss these two propositions: (1) "The American family is badly disorganized by the sweeping social changes of the past century." (2) "The American family is reorganizing itself to meet changing human needs in a changing society."

11. Prepare a statement of the reasons why you believe you will, or will not: (1) be a working wife, if you are female, or (2) have a working wife, if you are male. Then identify each reason as to whether it is a value judgment—a statement of what you like or dislike—or whether it is a statement of social forces and trends which may affect your decision.

12. Read John P. Marquand's *H. M. Pulham, Esq.,* Little, Brown and Company, Boston, 1941. How does the Pulham family prepare Harry for his sex role and class status, and generally socialize him to act in the expected manner?

13. Read Hans Ruesch, *Top of the World,* Harper & Row, Publishers, Incorporated, New York, 1950; Pocket Books, 1951, a novel about Eskimo life. Evaluate the Eskimo family as an institutional structure for meeting the needs of people in a particular environment.

SUGGESTED READINGS

*BLOOD, ROBERT O., JR., AND DONALD M. WOLFE: *Husbands and Wives,* The Free Press of Glencoe, New York, 1960. A research study of 909 marriages in the Detroit area, which presents evidence contradicting many widely held notions about the American family. (90407-Free P)

DOTEN, DANA: *The Art of Bundling,* Holt, Rinehart and Winston, Inc., New York, 1938. An entertaining account of the rise and fall of a quaint American custom, showing how it related to the other institutions of the period.

FOLSOM, JOSEPH K.: *The Family,* John Wiley & Sons, Inc., New York, 1934, 1943, chap. 1, "The Family Pattern." An interesting parallel-column comparison of the American and Trobriand family patterns.

HESS, ROBERT W., AND GERALD HANDEL: *Family Worlds,* The University of Chicago Press, Chicago, 1959. A study of five differing but "typical" American families, showing how each has worked out an acceptable adaptation to the gratifications and stresses of family life.

KOMAROVSKY, MIRRA: *Blue Collar Marriage,* Random House, Inc., New York, 1962, 1964. An interesting research study of working-class marriage, showing many contrasts with middle-class marriage.

*LINTON, RALPH: *The Study of Man,* Appleton-Century-Crofts, New York, 1936, chap. 10, "The Family," chap. 11, "Marriage," and chap. 12, "Social Units Determined by Blood." An anthropologist's description of various forms of marriage and family life. (Appl)

*MURDOCK, GEORGE P.: *Social Structure,* The Macmillan Company, New York, 1949. An anthropological study of the family and kinship systems of 250 societies. (92229 Free P)

QUEEN, STUART A., ROBERT W. HABENSTEIN, AND JOHN B. ADAMS: *The Family in Various Cultures,* J. B. Lippincott Company, Philadelphia, 1952, 1961, 1967. Readable descriptions of the family in a dozen cultures, primitive and civilized, ancient and modern.

*REISS, IRA L.: *Pre-marital Sexual Standards in America,* The Free Press of Glencoe, New York, 1960. An analysis of contemporary sex standards in America. (92620 Free P)

SCHUR, EDWIN M. (ED.): *The Family and the Sexual Revolution,* Indiana University Press, Bloomington, Ind., 1964. Selected readings on our changing sex and family patterns.

WHYTE, WILLIAM H., JR.: "The Wives of Management," *Fortune,* October, 1951, pp. 86ff.; "Corporation and the Wife," *Fortune,* November, 1951, p. 109ff. Describes the role of the executive wife and the efforts of the corporation to control the family life of its executives.

YOUNG, KIMBALL: *Isn't One Wife Enough? The Story of Mormon Polygamy,* Holt, Rinehart and Winston, Inc., New York, 1954. A readable analysis, by a Mormon and distinguished sociologist, of the only serious attempt to establish polygamy in America.

11

SOCIAL CLASS

CAPTAIN: (. . . walks upstage, then turns to ROBERTS) *I think you're a pretty smart boy. I may not talk very good, Mister, but I know how to take care of smart boys. Let me tell you something. Let me tell you a little secret. I hate your guts, you college son-of-a-bitch! You think you're better than I am! You think you're better because you've had everything handed to you. Let me tell you something, Mister— I've worked since I was ten years old, and all my life I've known you superior bastards. I knew you people when I was a kid in Boston and I worked in eating- places and you ordered me around. . . "Oh, bus-boy! My friend here seems to have thrown up on the table. Clean it up, please!" I started going to sea as a steward and I worked for you then. . . "Steward, take my magazine out to the deck chair!" . . . "Steward, I don't like your looks. Please keep out of my way as much as pos- sible!" Well, I took that crap! I took that for years from pimple-faced bastards who weren't good enough to wipe my nose! And now I don't have to take it any more! There's a war on, by God, and I'm the Captain and you can wipe my nose! The worst thing I can do to you is to keep you on this ship! And that's where you're going to stay! Now get out of here.* (Thomas Heggen and Joshua Logan, Mister Roberts, Random House, Inc., New York, 1948, pp. 87–88.)

I N THESE LINES from the play, *Mister Roberts,* the Captain explodes with resentment against those whose class origin is higher than his. Popular literature abounds with dramatic illustrations of class attitudes, class prejudices, and class-typed behavior. What is social class, and how does it affect behavior?

Aristotle observed two millenia ago that populations tended to be divided into three groups: the very rich, the very poor, and those in between. For Karl Marx the principal social classes were the wage workers (the proletariat) and the capitalists (the bourgeoisie), with a middle group (the petty bourgeoisie) which was on the way out. Adam Smith divided society into those who lived on the rent of land, the wages of labor, and the profits of trade. Thorstein Veblen divided society into the workers who struggle for subsistence and a leisure class which has become so wealthy that its main concern is a "conspicuous consumption" which proves how far this group has risen above the common herd. Franklin D. Roosevelt in 1937 gave a vivid description of lower-class life when he said in his inaugural address, January 20, 1937, "I see one third of the nation ill-housed, ill-clad, and ill-nourished." All these descriptions of social class imply that money separates people into different groupings.

ARE THERE SOCIAL CLASSES?

Although the concept of social class has long been used by sociologists, some sociologists today feel that it is not a useful concept [Faris, 1954; Nisbet, 1959; Lasswell, 1965]. They state that there are no definite boundaries or dividing lines for social classes, that persons placed in one class according to one measure belong in another class according to another, and that, consequently, the members of a "class" differ from one another too greatly for the concept of class to be valid.

The following pages will show why, despite the above objections, your authors believe that social class *is* a valid and useful concept.

WHAT IS SOCIAL CLASS?

Is social class purely a matter of money? If so, the rich gambler would outrank the minister, nurse, or professor. While money is a factor, social class is not directly measured by one's bank account. A social class is defined as *a stratum of people of similar position in the social status continuum.* The social position of the janitor is not the same as that of the college president; a student will not greet them in exactly the same manner. We are deferential toward those whose social position we believe to be above ours; we are condescending to those whom we consider socially below us. These processes of snubbing and kowtowing, of trying to claw one's way in or of shouldering out the person who doesn't "belong"—these provide the inexhaustible material for hundreds of novels, plays, and scripts every year.

The members of a social class view one another as social equals, while holding themselves to be socially superior to some other groups and socially inferior to still others. In placing a person in the proper social class, one asks such questions as: "To whose dinner party will he be asked as a social equal?" or "For whose daughter will his son be an 'acceptable' escort?" The members of a particular social class often have about the same amount of money; but what is much more important is that they have much the same attitudes, values, and way of life.

How many classes are there? This question is hard to answer. Classes are not sharply defined status groupings like the different ranks in an army. Social status varies along a continuum, a gradual slope from top to bottom, rather than a series of steps. As "youth," "middle age," and "old age" are points along an age continuum, the several social classes may be viewed as points along a status continuum. Consequently, the number of social classes is not fixed, nor do any definite boundaries and sharp status intervals separate them. Instead, persons are found at all status levels from top to bottom, just as persons are found at all weights and heights, with no abrupt gaps in the series.

Such a series can be broken up into any convenient number of "classes." Clothing makers have found it practical to divide people into a dozen or more size classifications. Earlier students of social class broke up the status continuum into three classes—upper, middle, and lower. Later students found this division unsatisfactory for many communities, because it placed persons in the same class even when they were much too far apart to treat one another as equals. Later students have often used a six-fold classification by breaking each of these three classes into an upper and lower section. The top, or *upper-upper* class, is composed of the wealthy old families, who have long been socially prominent, and who have had money long enough for people to have forgotten when and how they got it. The *lower-uppers* may have as much money but have not had it as long, and their family has not long been socially prominent. The *upper-middle* class includes most of the successful business and professional men, generally of "good" family background and comfortable income. The *lower-middle* class takes in the clerks, other white-collar workers and semiprofessionals, and possibly some of the foremen and top craftsmen. The *upper-lower* class consists mainly of the steadily employed workers, and is often described as the "working class" by those who feel uncomfortable about applying the term, "lower," to honest workmen [Miller and Riessman, 1961]. The *lower-lower* class includes the irregularly unemployed, the unemployable, migrant laborers, and those living more or less permanently on public assistance.

This six-fold classification, used by Warner and associates [1941, 1942] in studying an old New England town, is probably fairly typical of the large and medium-size cities in the more settled parts of the country. In the rapidly growing Western regions, "old family" may be less important. In smaller towns, the class system is less complex. In studying a small city in the Midwest, Hollingshead [1949] used a five-fold classification in which the two upper classes were combined into one. In a small rural community, West [1945] found no agreement among the residents upon the number of classes, although the status range probably would correspond to the bottom half of the six-class system of an urban society. Lynch [1959], studying the class system of an impoverished agricultural community in the Philippines, found only two classes —the self-sustaining and the destitute.

The number of social classes, therefore, varies from place to place; possibly

People do classify others into equals, superiors and inferiors.

it also varies with the observer's appraisal of the number of social strata whose members have the same general status. When we speak of, for example, the middle class, we do not refer to a group of people who are clearly set off from others by a definite status interval; we refer to a group of people who cluster around a midpoint in a status scale and who view and treat one another as social equals. The fact that the terms have no distinct boundaries does not keep the terms from being useful concepts and research tools. Social class is a significant social reality, not just a theoretical construct, for people *do* classify others into equals, superiors, and inferiors. Whenever people define certain other people as social equals and treat them differently from those who are not so defined, their behavior creates social classes.

GENESIS OF SOCIAL CLASSES

All complex societies have some system of stratification which unequally ranks people. The extent and kind of inequality varies tremendously, but there are always some accepted standards by which men distinguish their peers from their inferiors. This is true in Communist countries which deplore class divisions and in capitalist countries which may justify them; it is true in both democracies and autocracies and in agricultural as well as industrial societies. The only possible exception is in the most primitive food-gathering societies where people live by collecting roots and berries. Here there is little possibility of any division of labor and hence little possibility of rank which may lead to group differentiation.

As soon as the society develops enough complexity to require coordination, the basis is formed for the development of social classes. Some men will be in charge of the work of other men, and their authority will inevitably be reflected in privileges which they try to pass on to their descendants. Warner describes the process in the following terms:

For example, among primitive peoples simple fishing expeditions may be organized so that the men who fish and handle each boat are under the direction of one leader. The efforts of each boat are directed by the leader and, in turn, each boat is integrated into the total enterprise by the leader's taking orders from his superior. The same situation prevails in a modern factory. Small plants with a small working force and simple problems possess a limited hierarchy, perhaps no more than an owner who bosses all the workers. But a large industrial enterprise with complex activities and problems, like General Motors, needs an elaborate hierarchy of supervision. . . . The same holds true for political, religious, educational, and other social institutions; the more complex the group and the more diverse the functions and activities, the more elaborate the status system is likely to be.

W. Lloyd Warner, with Marchia Meeker and Kenneth Eells, *Social Class in America*, Harper & Row, Publishers, Incorporated, New York, 1960, pp. 8–9.

Although social class includes many features besides occupation, it is fundamentally based on the division of labor. A complex society requires many workers with varying degrees of skills and many coordinators with varying realms of authority. Prestige and power attach to the higher-ranked occupations and in turn enable the men in these occupations to confer advantages on their descendants. Thus a group of people arise whose hereditary privileges are greater than are those of people who have descended from less highly regarded ranks.

An agricultural society with only two or three categories of responsibility may have a completely rigid system of stratification in which the gulf between nobles and commoners is never bridged. An industrial society is apt to have a far greater variety of occupations with greater ease of movement from one level to another, but distinct levels still remain. Social class, then, grows out of the system of division of labor, and the ease of movement from one level to another depends upon the complexity and flexibility of the occupational structure of the society. Class mobility within a society is a highly complicated topic and is considered in some detail in the following chapter.

Social classes as subcultures   *It is, after all, this division into working class and business class that constitutes the outstanding cleavage in Middletown. The mere fact of being born upon one or the other side of the watershed roughly formed by these two groups is the most significant single cultural factor tending to influence what one does all day long throughout one's life; whom one marries; when one gets up in the morning; whether one belongs to the Holy Roller or Presbyterian church; or drives a Ford or a Buick; whether or not one's daughter makes the desirable high school Violet Club; or one's wife meets with the Sew We Do Club or with the Art Student's League; whether one belongs to the Odd Fellows or to the Masonic Shrine; whether one sits about evenings with one's necktie off; and so on indefinitely throughout the daily comings and goings of a Middletown man, woman, or child.*

Robert S. Lynd and Helen H. Lynd, *Middletown*, Harcourt, Brace & World, Inc., 1929. Copyright 1929, by Harcourt, Brace & World, Inc., renewed © 1957 by Robert S. Lynd and Helen H. Lynd, and reprinted with the publisher's permission.

Each social class is a system of behavior, a set of values, and a way of life. While some overlapping and some exceptions occur, it remains true that the average middle-class child has a socialization vastly different from that of the average lower-class child. Let us take just one aspect of socialization—those experiences which shape ambition, education, and work habits—and see how they differ between two social-class worlds.

The typical upper-middle-class child lives in a class subculture where he is surrounded by educated, cultivated persons who speak the English language correctly most of the time, enjoy classical music, buy and read books, travel, and entertain graciously. He is surrounded by people who are ambitious, who go to work even when they don't feel like it, and who struggle to make their mark in the world. He is acquainted with the successes of ancestors, relatives, and friends, and it is normal for him simply to assume that, like them, he is going to amount to something in the world.

When he goes to school, scrubbed and expectant, he finds a teacher whose dress, speech, manner, and conduct norms are much like those he already knows. He is met by a series of familiar objects—picture books, chalkboard, and others—and introduced into a series of activities which are already familiar. The teacher finds him an appealing and responsive child, while he finds school a comfortable and exciting place. When the teacher says, "Study hard so you can do well and become a success some day," her exhortation makes sense to him. His parents echo these words; meanwhile he sees people like him— older brothers, relatives, family acquaintances—who actually *are* completing educations and moving on into promising careers. For him, to grow up means to complete an advanced education and get himself launched into a career.

The lower-lower-class child lives in a class subculture where scarcely anybody has a steady job for very long. To be laid off and go on relief is a normal experience, carrying no sense of shame or failure. He lives in a world where one can spend his weekends in drinking, gambling, and sexual exploration and miss work on Monday without sacrificing the respect of his friends or neighbors. In his world, meals are haphazard and irregular; many people sleep three or four to a bed; and a well-modulated speaking voice would be lost amid the neighborhood clatter.

He goes to school, usually unwashed and often unfed, and meets a woman unlike anyone in his social world. Her speech and manner are unfamiliar, and when he acts in ways that are acceptable and useful in his social world, she punishes him. The classroom materials and activities are unfamiliar. The teacher, who usually comes from a sheltered middle-class world, is likely to decide that he is a sullen, unresponsive child, while he soon concludes that school is an unhappy prison. He learns little. The school soon abandons any serious effort to teach him, defines him as a "discipline problem," and concentrates upon keeping him quiet so that the other children can learn. When the teacher says, "Study hard so you can do well and become a success some day," her words make no sense to him. They receive no reinforcement from his parents, who are apt to be hostile and uncooperative toward the school. More important, he sees almost nobody *like him,* nobody in his world, who actually *is* using school as a steppingstone to a career. In his world, the big cars and slender blondes are possessed by those who picked a lucky number, or got into the rackets, or found an "angle." Thus the school fails to motivate him. For him, "growing up" means to drop out of school, get a car, and escape from the supervision of teachers and parents [Davis, 1952]. The child's horizon of ambition seldom extends beyond the next weekend. His work habits are casual and irregular. Soon he marries and provides for his children a life which duplicates the experiences of his own socialization. Thus the class system operates to prepare most children for a class status similar to that of their parents.

Such differences in class behavior are found in virtually every activity of life— food habits, personal care, discipline and child care, reading tastes, conversational interests, vocabulary and diction, religious behavior, sleeping arrangements, sex life. Even the procedures followed in making love, according to

Kinsey [1948, pp. 355–357], show important class differences. This is what we mean in speaking of class subcultures—that a great many of the normal life experiences of people in one class differ from those of people in another class. It is true that there are no sharply defined boundaries. From top to bottom, one kind of behavior shades gradually off into another; for example, vocabulary gradually becomes less genteel and diction less precise as we descend the class continuum. But if we pick several points along this continuum for comparison, then the class differences are easy to see.

Determinants of social class   What places one in a particular social class? Is it birth, money, occupation, or what? The answer to each question is "Yes," for all these attributes are involved.

Wealth and income   Money is necessary for upper-class position; yet one's class position is not directly proportional to his income. An airline pilot has less status than a college professor at half the income; a clergyman may outrank a prizefighter at fifty times his income.

To understand the place of money in class determination, we must remember

Table 7   *Distributions of prestige ratings, United States, 1963*

Occupation	Rank	Occupation	Rank
U.S. Supreme Court justice	1	Biologist	24.5
Physician	2	Sociologist	26
Nuclear physicist	3.5	Instructor in public schools	27.5
Scientist	3.5	Captain in the regular army	27.5
Government scientist	5.5	Accountant for a large business	29.5
State governor	5.5	Public school teacher	29.5
Cabinet member in the Federal government	8	Owner of a factory that employs about 100 people	31.5
College professor	8	Building contractor	31.5
U.S. representative in Congress	8	Artist who paints pictures that are exhibited in galleries.	34.5
Chemist	11	Musician in a symphony orchestra	34.5
Lawyer	11	Author of novels	34.5
Diplomat in the U.S. foreign service	11	Economist	34.5
Dentist	14	Official of an international labor union	37
Architect	14	Railroad engineer	39
County judge	14	Electrician	39
Psychologist	17.5	County agricultural agent	39
Minister	17.5	Owner-operator of a printing shop	41.5
Member of the board of directors of a large corporation	17.5	Trained machinist	41.5
Mayor of a large city	17.5	Farm owner and operator	44
Priest	21.5	Undertaker	44
Head of a department in a state government	21.5	Welfare worker for a city government	44
Civil engineer	21.5	Newspaper columnist	46
Airline pilot	21.5	Policeman	47
Banker	24.5	Reporter on a daily newspaper	48

that a *social class is basically a way of life*. It takes a good deal of money to live as upper-class people live. Yet no amount of money will gain *immediate* upper-class status. The "new rich" have the money, but they lack the way of life of the upper-class person. They can buy the house, cars, and clothes, and hire a decorator to select the proper furnishings, books, and paintings. It takes a little longer to learn the formal manners of the upper class, but some careful observation, plus intensive study of Emily Post or Amy Vanderbilt, will probably suffice. But to acquire the attitudes and feelings and habitual responses of the upper-class person takes far longer. Unless one is born and socialized in an upper-class subculture, he is almost certain to make occasional slips which betray his plebeian origin. Novels and plays abound with social climbers who never quite "make it" because they occasionally use the wrong word or reflect the wrong attitude and thereby betray their humble origin. Most of the "new rich" are no more than marginal members of the upper classes during their lifetimes.

Their children, however, have a better chance, and for their grandchildren, a secure upper-class status is practically assured. Money, *over a period of time*, usually gains upper-class status. People who get money begin to live like

Occupation	Rank	Occupation	Rank
Radio announcer	49.5	*Milk route man*	70
Bookkeeper	49.5	*Streetcar motorman*	70
Tenant farmer—one who owns livestock and		*Lumberjack*	72.5
machinery and manages the farm	51.5	*Restaurant cook*	72.5
Insurance agent	51.5	*Singer in a nightclub*	74
Carpenter	53	*Filling-station attendant*	75
Manager of a small store in a city	54.5	*Dockworker*	77.5
A local official of a labor union	54.5	*Railroad section hand*	77.5
Mail carrier	57	*Night watchman*	77.5
Railroad conductor	57	*Coal miner*	77.5
Traveling salesman for a wholesale concern	57	*Restaurant waiter*	80.5
Plumber	59	*Taxi driver*	80.5
Automobile repairman	60	*Farmhand*	83
Playground director	62.5	*Janitor*	83
Barber	62.5	*Bartender*	83
Machine operator in a factory	62.5	*Clothes presser in a laundry*	85
Owner-operator of a lunch stand	62.5	*Soda-fountain clerk*	86
Corporal in the regular army	65.5	*Sharecropper—one who owns no livestock or*	
Garage mechanic	65.5	*equipment and does not manage farm*	87
Truck driver	67	*Garbage collector*	88
Fisherman who owns his own boat	68	*Street sweeper*	89
Clerk in a store	68	*Shoe shiner*	90

SOURCE: Robert W. Hodge et al., "Occupational Prestige in the United States, 1925–63," *American Journal of Sociology*, 70:290–292, November, 1964.

upper-class people. By the time their grandchildren mature, they are becoming "old family," while the grandchildren have fully absorbed upper-class behavior. Thus the two requisites of upper-class status are fulfilled.

Money has other subtle overtones. Inherited money is better than earned money, for inherited wealth shows family background. Income from investments also suggests family background. Income from genteel professions is better than wages; money from speculating on stocks is better than money from gambling on horses. The nature and source of one's income carry suggestions as to one's family background and probable way of life.

Money one used to have is almost as good as money one has now. The "real" aristocracy of the South, for example, no longer has great wealth, partly because its class values prevented it from engaging in the grubby scrabbling which eventually created the oil millionaires and the industrial magnates. Yet the impoverished aristocrat can still retain upper-class status as long as he has enough money to eke out an upper-class pattern of living, even though it is somewhat frayed around the edges.

Money, then, is an important determinant of social class, partly because of the way of life it permits or enforces, and partly because of what it suggests about one's family background and way of life.

Occupation   Occupation is another determinant of class status. As soon as man developed specialized kinds of work, he also got the idea that some kinds of work were more honorable than others. In a primitive society, the spear maker, the canoe builder, and the medicine man each holds a definite social status because of his work. Classical China honored the scholar and despised the warrior; Nazi Germany reversed the formula. Table 7 gives a prestige ranking of some occupations in the United States, according to one national-opinion survey.

Just why one occupation should carry greater prestige than another is a question which has long fascinated social theorists. The high-prestige occupations generally receive the higher incomes; yet there are many exceptions. A popular night-club singer may earn as much in a week as a Supreme Court justice earns in a year. The relatively low-paid clergymen, diplomats, and college professors rank far above the higher-paid airline pilots and building contractors, and have about equal ranking with the far wealthier physicians and lawyers. The high-ranking occupations generally require advanced education, but again the correlation is far from perfect. The importance of the work is an unsatisfactory test, for how can we say that the work of the farm hand or policeman is less valuable to society than the work of the lawyer or corporation director? In fact, it has been suggested that the low-ranking garbage collector may be the most essential of all workers in an urban civilization!

Obviously, the prestige ranking of occupations cannot be easily explained on a purely rational basis; yet it can hardly be an accident that all complex cultures have developed much the same hierarchy of occupational status. A survey of data from many countries by Inkeles [1960] finds that a particular occupation has about the same status rating in all urbanized, industrialized societies. Apparently the industrial system fosters certain attitudes, perceptions, and status relationships wherever it develops. And in all societies, industrial or preindustrial, we see that persons tend to be assigned a class status according to their occupation, and that people will find those occupations open to them which are appropriate to their present class status.

Occupation is an exceedingly important aspect of social class because so many other facets of life are connected with occupation. If we know a man's occupation, we can make some fairly accurate guesses about the amount and kind of education he has had, the standard of living he can afford, the kind of people he associates with, the hours he keeps, and the daily routines of his family life. We can even make some guesses about his reading tastes and recreational interests, his standards of moral conduct, and his religious affiliations. In other words, each occupation is part of a way of life that differs considerably from that which accompanies certain other occupations. It is one's total way of life that ultimately determines which class one belongs to, and occupation is one of the best clues to one's way of life, and therefore to one's social-class membership.

The underdeveloped countries have a class structure which reflects a society which has limited use for professional, white collar, or highly skilled workers and hence has a small middle class and a very large lower class. This pattern is changing as these countries become industrialized. Mexico, for instance, is a nation which is making rapid strides in this direction, and Table 8 shows the changes in social-class distribution. The *popular* category (Mexican term

FIGURE 6 *The Public Classifies Occupations in the United States.*

Non-response accounts for per cent totals of less than 100.

SOURCE: Joseph A. Kahl, *The American Class Structure*, Holt, Rinehart and Winston, Inc., New York, 1957, p. 81. Based on data in Richard Center's "Social Class, Occupation, and Imputed Belief," *American Journal of Sociology*, 58:543–555, May, 1953.

PER CENT OF PUBLIC

Occupation	Upper class	Middle class	Working class	Lower class
Big businessmen	82%	11%	3%	
Doctors and Lawyers	57%	33%	7%	
Schoolteachers	13%	53%	31%	1%
Small businessmen	4%	65%	26%	3%
Foremen	3%	41%	51%	2%
Office workers	2%	40%	54%	2%
Salesclerks	1%	29%	63%	5%
Carpenters	2%	20%	74%	2%
Factory workers	1%	15%	69%	12%
Janitors		5%	59%	34%

for lower class) now comprises only 40 per cent of the population as compared with 90 per cent in 1890.

Education   Social class and education interact in at least two ways. First, to get a higher education one needs money plus motivation. Lack of money is less of a barrier than it used to be, now that scholarships and student loans are so widely available; yet relatively few students complete college without some financial aid from their families. Even if it is no more than free room, board, and laundry for all or part of the year, this is a considerable help. Upper-class youths already have money for the finest schools; they also have family tradition and social encouragement. For the upper-class or upper-middle-class high-school youth, the question is, "What college are you going to?"; lower-middle-class and perhaps upper-lower-class youths ask one another, "What will you do after graduation?"; lower-lower class youths are more likely to ask, "How soon can I quit school?" Second, one's amount and kind of education affects the class rank he will secure. Education is one of the main levers of the ambitious. Higher education brings not only occupational skills; it also brings changes in tastes, interests, goals, etiquette, speech—in one's total way of life. Level of education is probably the most important single clue to a man's social class.

Although a distinguished family background is a necessity for secure upper-class status, education may substitute for family background at the intermediate class levels. The middle classes are so large and move around so much that it is impossible to know the family background of each individual. Newcomers to a locality are likely to be accepted into whichever of the middle or lower classes their behavior fits them. Education, occupation, and expended income are three fairly visible clues, and with these are associated most of the other behavior characteristics which make one "belong."

Social scientists make great use of these three criteria—education, occupa-

Table 8   *Changing class structure in Mexico, 1895–1960 (percentages, varying bases)*

Classes and subclasses	1895	1940	1950	1956	1960
Upper					
Leisure	*0.4*	*0.4*	*0.5*	*1.0*	*1.5*
Semileisure	*1.1*	*2.5*	*1.5*	*4.0*	*5.0*
Subtotal	*1.5*	*2.9*	*2.0*	*5.0*	*6.5*
Middle					
Stable	*6.1*	*6.1*	*8.0*	*15.0*	*17.0*
Marginal	*1.7*	*6.5*	*17.0*	*15.0*	*16.5*
Subtotal	*7.8*	*12.6*	*25.0*	*30.0*	*33.5*
Transitional	*00.0*	*6.5*	*20.0*	*20.0*	*20.0*
Popular (lower class)	*90.7*	*78.0*	*53.0*	*45.0*	*40.0*

SOURCE: Adapted from Howard F. Cline, *Mexico*, Oxford University Press, Fair Lawn, N.J., 1963, Table 30, p. 124.

TABULAR PRESENTATION: per cent of total employed in each group.

	Elementary: Nongraduate	High school: Nongraduate	High school: Graduate	College: Nongraduate	College: Graduate
Professional	1	2	7	23	65
Managerial	6	9	12	19	15
Clerical and Sales	4	14	35	33	13
Skilled and Semiskilled	37	44	29	15	4
Laborers, Farm, Service	52	31	17	10	3
	100	100	100	100	100

GRAPHIC PRESENTATION: per cent of total employed in each group.

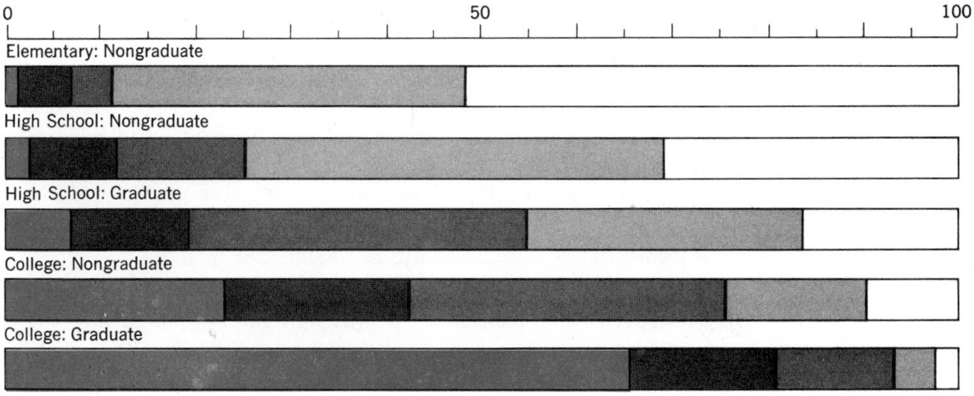

FIGURE 7 *Education and Occupation in the United States, 1959.*
SOURCE: The National Industrial Conference Board.

tion, and income—in dividing people into social-class levels for research purposes. As we have already explained, these are fairly reliable clues to the total way of life distinguishing social classes. Furthermore, these criteria are fairly easy to objectify. It would, for example, be difficult to use "crude or cultivated speech" as a test of class rank in a research study, because speech, though easy to notice, is hard to measure.[1] Finally, the data on education, occupation, and income are available from the census reports, broken down by "census

[1] For a discussion of speech as an indication of social class, see William Labov, "The Effect of Social Mobility on Linguistic Behavior," *Sociological Inquiry,* 36:186–203, Spring, 1966.

tracts," or areas of a few blocks each. Suppose a sociologist wishes to compare death rates, or polio rates, or average family size, or practically anything, as it varies among social classes. Using census data on occupation, education, and average income of the different census tracts within the community, he could easily locate an upper-class tract, a middle-class tract, and a lower-class tract for comparison. While social class involves more than these three criteria, they are adequate to identify social classes for most research purposes.[2]

Self-identification and class consciousness   Most sociologists consider social class a reality even if people are not fully aware of it. American democratic beliefs emphasize equality and tend to inhibit a frank recognition of class lines. People will deny that there are social classes in their community, yet state this denial in terms which reveal that classes really do exist. Lantz cites one of many such statements by the residents of a small town:

You see, this no-class idea makes it a good place to live. The Company houses are called "Silk Stocking Row" but I would feel as good with the mining superinten-dent's wife as I would with anybody else. You see, this is a melting pot. Our people, you see, all came from foreign countries. Why, my grandparents came from Eng-land. You see, I belong to the DAR. I can trace my family tree all the way back through the Revolutionary War into England. I take a great deal of pride in this. Why, I can trace my ancestry back to a captain who was a friend of Washington's in the Revolutionary War.

Herman R. Lantz, *People of Coal Town*, Columbia University Press, New York, 1958, p. 216.

The belief that the American people lack "class consciousness" was sup-ported by early surveys [Cantril, 1943; Gallup and Rae, 1940; *Fortune*, Feb-ruary, 1940], which found from 79 to 88 per cent of the people claiming to be "middle-class"; yet Warner's [1941, p. 88] careful analysis of the actual class distribution of the population of "Yankee City" (Newburyport, Massachusetts) placed only 38 per cent in the two middle classes, and other studies agree in finding that only a minority of people belong in the middle class. More recent surveys suggest that people may be resisting the word more than the reality. When informants are permitted to select the term "working class" rather than "lower class," they classify themselves in a way which more closely resembles the class division made by the social scientists [Centers, 1949; Manis and Meltzer, 1954, 1963].

Is one's class membership, then, determined by his feeling that he belongs in a particular class, or by the facts of his occupation, education, and income? Largely by the latter, for they determine his overall way of life. Yet his *feeling* of class identification is of some importance, for he tends to copy the behavior norms of the class with which he identifies himself. Eulan [1956] found that those informants who placed themselves in a class in which they did not ob-jectively belong, shared the political attitudes of the class they claimed rather than those of the class in which they belonged. Self-identification with a social

[2] See Joseph A. Kahl and James A. Davis, "A Comparison of Indexes of Socioeconomic Status," *American Sociological Review*, 20:317–325, June, 1955, for a defense of the view that occupation is the best overall measure of class behavior. For a claim that a composite "index of status characteristics" is a better measure of class behavior, see John L. Haer, "Predictive Utility of Five Indices of Social Stratification," *American Sociological Review*, 22:541–546, October, 1957.

class apparently has some effect upon behavior, whether one actually is a member of that class or not.

Size of each social class A number of studies show considerable agreement in placing something over half the population in the two lower classes, using Warner's six-class typology. Warner's 1941 study, and two national self-identification surveys in 1945 and 1946 [Centers, 1949] agree in placing about 57 per cent of the population in the two lower classes (lower-lower and upper-lower). Davis [1952, pp. 22–23] concluded that each of the two lower classes provided about one-third of the elementary school children. Table 9 presents some more data on several groups, most of whom are probably lower-lower class. To summarize, somewhat over half the people seem to fall in the two lower classes, with slightly less than half divided, in decreasing numbers, in the middle and upper four classes.

Measurement of classes is complicated by the fact that there are several criteria of membership in a given class and many families do not show *all* the characteristics of any one class level. For example, the "ideal type" lower-lower-class family would live in an urban slum or rural shack; one or more adult members would drink quite heavily, and the male family head would not be consistently in the household; the family would have little education or interest in education; and its low income would be derived partly from intermittent unskilled labor and partly from welfare sources. Probably comparatively few lower-lower-class families meet all of these conditions. While class differences are real, the boundaries and membership of each class cannot be clearly fixed.

Table 9 How large is our lower class? Proportion of United States population in selected educational, occupational, and income categories (arranged in order of descending magnitude)

Type of individual or group	Approximate percentage of population	Year or period
Adults (18 or over) in labor force who did not complete high school	*42.5*	*1965*
Adults in civilian labor force in "semiskilled" and "unskilled" positions	*33.0*	*1965*
Adults with 8 grades of education or less	*22.9*	*1965*
Family units with income under $3,000	*18.0*	*1964*
Household units reporting female head	*10.0*	*1965*
Family units with incomes under $2,000	*9.5*	*1964*
Unemployed and seeking work	*4.7*	*1965*
Adult illiterates	*2.4*	*1960*

sources: *Statistical Abstract of United States 1966;* Denis F. Johnston and Harvey R. Hamel, "Educational Attainments of Workers in March 1965," *Monthly Labor Review,* 89:251–255, March, 1966; Vera C. Perrela and Elizabeth Waldman, "Marital and Family Characteristics of Workers in March 1965," *Monthly Labor Review,* 89:260, March, 1966; *Manpower Report to the President,* U.S. Department of Labor, March, 1966, p. 189.

Class distribution appears to be changing in the United States. The middle class and possibly the upper classes are growing; the lower classes are shrinking. Changing technology is destroying lower-class jobs and creating middle-class jobs. In 1900, "unskilled laborers" comprised 13 per cent of the labor force; by 1950 they had fallen to 8 per cent, and are expected to fall to 4 per cent by 1975; meanwhile, the "professionals" in the labor force have risen from 4 per cent in 1900 to 8 per cent in 1950 and are expected to reach 14 per cent by 1975 [National Education Association, 1959]. Almost every kind of middle-class job is expanding as the changes in economic life continually demand more technical and professional personnel. Furthermore, as technology changes the content of jobs, their status also changes. Historically, most factory jobs were dirty, filled by men who were comparatively unskilled and low paid. Today a growing fraction of factory jobs are clean, calling for highly trained and well-paid workers. Such workers seem likely to move into the middle class. We have not yet become a "middle-class" society in the sense that the middle class is becoming the largest class, but we seem to be moving in that direction.

THE SIGNIFICANCE OF SOCIAL CLASSES

Determining life opportunities From before one is born until after he is dead, his opportunities and rewards are affected by his class position. A study of Chicago death rates in 1940 found a life expectancy at birth of 61 years for the lower-class female and 70.3 years for the upper-class female, while for males the expectancies were 58.7 and 67.8 years, a difference of over 9 years for each sex. A comparison of the death rates for the highest economic group and the rest of the city indicated that 21 per cent of all Chicago deaths in 1940 would have been avoided if the style of life, attitudes, and use of medical care for the rest of the city had been equal to that of its most prosperous segment [Mayer and Hauser, 1950].

In mental health, the disparity is even greater [Hollingshead and Redlich, 1958]. The lower the class, the higher is the rate of mental illness; the increases, however, are small at all levels except the lowest class, whose rate is much higher than the others [Miller and Mishler, 1959]. The "treatment" received by the lower-class mentally ill is sometimes only custodial, which simply removes the patient from society, rather than the complete medical and psychotherapeutic treatment which might effect a cure. In no other major form of health care is the disparity between the classes as great as in the treatment of mental illness [Hollingshead and Redlich, 1953; Robinson et al., 1954].

The school attended by the lower-class child has usually been one of the drab and dingy schools of the community built a half century or more ago; although in recent years some of these have been replaced by gleaming modern structures. His teachers may be either dedicated mentors hopefully utilizing the latest educational methods or weary drudges who have long since given up in what seems a hopeless battle against ignorance and apathy. In any case, the effectiveness of the school is largely determined by the attitudes of the students which, in turn, reflect the spirit of the neighborhood. The neighborhood is likely to be an area of drab, crowded housing, of irregular family life, of per-

Table 10   Korean war-casualty rate per 10,000 occupied dwelling units; by median income of census tract, Detroit, Michigan

Median income, dollars	Casualty rate per 10,000 occupied DU's
Under 2,500	*14.6*
2,500–2,999	*10.8*
3,000–3,499	*9.1*
3,500–3,999	*8.6*
4,000–4,499	*7.5*
4,500–4,999	*6.6*
5,000–5,499	*5.8*
5,500 and over	*4.6*

SOURCE: Albert J. Mayer and Thomas Ford Hoult, "Social Stratification and Combat Survival," *Social Forces*, 34:155–159, December, 1955. Copyright © 1955, The University of North Carolina Press, Chapel Hill, N.C.

sons whose goals are short-term just as their grasp on jobs, health, and housing is short-term.

When the lower-class youth comes to seek a job, he lacks the education, the work habits, and the poise or bearing to command a job with a promising future. The lower-class occupations, such as farm laborer, unskilled laborer, or dock worker, carry low wages, irregular employment, and few welfare or "fringe" benefits. Often they involve high accident danger or health hazard; yet this class can afford only the poorest living conditions and the least medical care. In wartime the lower-class youth is less likely to be deferred as a college student or an essential worker; when drafted he is less likely to become a commissioned officer or earn a specialist's rating. There is one place where his chances are better; he has a better chance of being killed, as is seen in Table 10.

Coloring personality development   Since social classes are subcultures, the personality development of the child is affected in many ways [Davis and Havighurst, 1946; Sears et al., 1957; Havighurst and Davis, 1955]. As has been already suggested, his goals, interests, and habits are affected by the kind of social world he lives in. His moral standards are equally class-typed. The lower-class family is less stable, more often broken by death or separation. It is larger in size, yet occupies smaller living quarters. At almost every point of contact between child and parent, there are class differences in socialization experience. Middle-class child training encourages individual achievement and the urge to "succeed," encorges competition and rivalry while discouraging direct aggression, uses parental love systematically as a control device, avoids severe physical punishment, imposes numerous restrictions, and produces a good many anxieties and guilt feelings. Lower-class child training more rapidly pushes the child into adult roles, places less stress on individual achievement, accepts the idea that the child will probably retain the social status of its father, seldom uses parental love as a systematic reward, uses physical punishments readily, imposes fewer

Two patterns of child rearing: Those conducive to educational achievement and those characteristic of low-income families

Conducive to achievement	Low-income
1. *Child given freedom within consistent limits to explore and experiment.*	1. *Limited freedom for exploration (partly imposed by crowded and dangerous aspects of environment).*
2. *Wide range of parent-guided experiences, offering visual, auditory, kinesthetic, and tactile stimulation.*	2. *Constricted lives led by parents: fear and distrust of the unknown.*
3. *Goal commitment and belief in long-range success potential.*	3. *Fatalistic, apathetic attitudes.*
4. *Gradual training for and value placed on independence.*	4. *Tendency for abrupt transition to independence: parents tend to "lose control" of children at early age.*
5. *Educational-occupational success of parents; models as continuing "learners" themselves.*	5. *Tendency to educational-occupational failure; reliance on personal versus skill attributes of vocational success.*
6. *Reliance on objective evidence.*	6. *Magical, rigid thinking.*
7. *Much verbal communication.*	7. *Little verbal communication.*

SOURCE: Adapted from Catherine S. Chilman, "Child Rearing and Family Relationship Patterns of the Very Poor," *Welfare in Review*, 3:10, January, 1965.

restrictions upon organic functions and pleasures, accepts direct aggression and encourages aggressive self-defense, places little stress on language facility, literacy, or school advancement, and probably produces fewer guilts and anxieties. Middle-class socialization is strongly oriented toward upward social mobility through risk taking; lower-class socialization in a risk-filled world is strongly oriented towards reducing risks by attaining economic security and stability [Miller and Riessman, 1961].

As compared with lower-class personality, adult middle-class personality tends to be more ambitious, more competitive but less aggressive physically, more rigidly conformist to conventional mores, outwardly more poised and self-assured, but possibly beset by greater inner guilts and self-doubts. Such differences are not predictably true for all members of either class, for there are many exceptions and much overlapping. But such differences are frequent enough to be socially significant [Barber, 1957, chap. 12].

Assigning social responsibilities and privileges   A lot of unpleasant work must be done in any society, and someone must be persuaded to do it. Occasionally special rewards may be used—honor for the warrior, or wealth and fame for the prizefighter, for example. But each complex society relies mainly upon the class system to compel someone to do the drudgery. A combination of cultural background, educational limitation, and job discrimination all work together to make the lower-class person unable to compete for the better jobs; as a result, only the poorer jobs are left. The result, though it may be entirely unintentional, is no less real. Social class gets the grubby work of the world done by excluding part of the people from the nicer jobs.

There is a lot of unpleasant work.

The lower class also functions as a storehouse for surplus unskilled labor. Our economy requires a good deal of seasonal or irregular labor, especially in farm labor and construction projects. Those who are not continuously needed are "stored" in the lower class, where the class subculture makes it possible to survive periods of unemployment and go on relief without guilt or sense of failure. The lethargy, lack of ambition, and willingness to accept squalor which middle-class people criticize so self-righteously are, in fact, the *necessary and useful* life adjustments of the lower class. Such attributes are necessary to the mental health and sanity of our "stand-by" unskilled labor supply.

The lower-class culture makes a positive contribution to the society. Men who seem to lack ambition and responsibility have shouldered jobs which were rough, monotonous, temporary in duration, often far from settled communities, yet essential to the economic life of the nation. The lower-class women, often frowned upon by higher-status women because of their irregular family life, have learned to adjust to the unreliable habits of fathers and husbands whose lives have been shaped by irregular and uncertain employment. These women have reared children in manless households and, at the same time, cleaned the homes and offices used by other classes. Lower-class life produces people able and willing to work and live under conditions which those raised in other class levels would find intolerable.

Other social classes also provide their members with distinctive subcultures that prepare them for specialized functions in society. Looking at the upper class, one sees a group which is removed from the fear of being unable to make a fairly adequate income. Their position in society does not have to be earned by unusual achievement, although they may have to validate their status through some form of public service. At its best this class produces men like Franklin D. Roosevelt, Nelson Rockefeller, and the Kennedys, who have been able to devote a major portion of their lives to public service without having to worry about personal fortune. The fact that all these men accept government programs commonly identified with lower-class interests indicates both an emancipation from economic concern and an acceptance by the masses of the leadership of an elite whose wealth and background are strikingly different from those of the common man.

A most vulnerable aspect of upper-class claims to social usefulness is the existence of a group who become playboy types and devote their time and money to expensive dissipation in an endless search for novelty to stimulate jaded senses dulled by little responsibility and much indulgence. Persons of this type may be a minority of the upper class, but they are very conspicuous in an era of mass communication, and the envy and resentment they arouse is a major obstacle to the acceptance of the legitimacy of an upper class by the rest of society.

Vigorous controversy has developed in sociological circles over the question of whether social-class stratification is useful as an efficient means of role allocation. Some claim that society requires a variety of occupational roles, and one's social class background gives one the attitudes desirable for his occupational function. The following is a typical statement of this viewpoint:

Social inequality is an unconsciously evolved device by which societies insure that the most important positions are filled by the most qualified persons. Hence every society, no matter how simple or complex, must differentiate persons in terms of both prestige and esteem, and must therefore possess a certain amount of institutionalized inequality.

Kingsley Davis and Wilbert Moore, "Some Principles of Stratification," *American Sociological Review,* 10:242–249, April, 1945.

This position has been sharply criticised on the grounds that social-class conditioning and role ascription may make it difficult for the individual to make the best use of his potential abilities. The brilliant man from a lower-class background may have neither the objective opportunities to prepare himself for an important career nor the value system which will encourage him to pursue long years of education apprenticeship. Conversely the upper-class moron may be kept from useful service by family privilege and may lack completely the attitudes which enable unskilled laborers to adjust to their occupational roles. These and other criticisms have been made by Tumin [1953] who suggests that social class may be disfunctional, i.e., it hinders social adjustment, whereas a better system of allocating occupational roles could be devised.

This is another form of the argument over ascribed versus achieved roles. A plausible summation is suggested by Gordon [1958, pp. 166–173] who points out that, while an equalitarian society might be ideal, such a society has never existed. Some system of differential reward always develops, and men do seek to transmit their advantages to their children. The resulting class system has a major influence in the allocation of occupational roles. It is not a perfect system, but is only seriously wasteful of talent when a "closed" system develops which does not allow people to cross class lines. This is a topic we will take up in more detail in the following chapter, "Social Mobility."

Cultivating class ethnocentrism

There is an anecdote of a private tutor in a wealthy family who sought to teach her pupil about the life of the poor. Then the little rich girl wrote a story about the poor, beginning:

"Once upon a time there was a very poor family. Everybody was poor. The Papa was poor, the Mama was poor, the children were poor, the cook was poor, the maid was poor, the butler was poor, the gardener was poor—Everybody was poor."

Members of one class cannot help judging members of other classes in terms of their own class expectations and values. The middle class scorns upper-class snobbishness, but strives desperately to raise its own children in a "good" neighborhood. People at every class level tend to see those above themselves as effete, snobbish, and pretentious, and those beneath as either disgusting or pathetic, as either good-for-nothing or "awfully pushy." At all intermediate status levels one tends to attribute one's own status to personal achievement, the status of those above to luck, and that of those beneath to inability and laziness. Miller suggests that, of all forms of ethnocentrism, class ethnocentrism is one of the most difficult to restrain:

It is considerably easier to manifest "tolerance" for the ways of the Zulu, Navaho, or Burmese than to achieve emotional acceptance of features of lower-class culture in our own society; in the former case it is relatively easy to recognize that disapproved or exotic behavior is a direct product of the group's culture and to accept such behavior on the grounds that it is "their way" of doing things, a way which is different from ours. In the case of lower-class culture, however, there is an almost automatic tendency to view certain customary behaviors in terms of right and wrong and to explain them as blameworthy deviations from accepted moral standards rather than as products of a deep-rooted cultural tradition. It is not too difficult to view the device of polygamous marriage and the mother-centered household among the Zulus as one alternative arrangement for meeting the problem of marriage and child-rearing; it is much harder to see the practice of serial mating and the female-based household in our own society as social forms which may constitute a practical or effective adaptation to the milieu in which they are found. . . .

The basic values and emphases of lower-class culture produced a vast army of woodsmen, construction workers, cattlemen, Indian fighters, frontier women, and many others without whose labors our country would never have achieved its present strength. . . . It is precisely these qualities and abilities which constitute the major emphases of lower-class male culture and which, in fact, comprise the basic set of qualities and skills learned and practiced in the "gang."

Walter B. Miller, "Implications of Urban Lower Class Culture for Social Work," *Social Service Review*, 33:232–234, September, 1959. Copyright, 1959, by The University of Chicago.

Defining the conventional morality The classes do not merely differ in etiquette; they also differ in moral judgments. The term "loyal worker" has one meaning in the union hall, another at the chamber of commerce. Kinsey [1948, pp. 375–379] has shown how sex mores differ between the classes. The lower-class emphasis is upon naturalness, not upon chastity; thus premarital sex experience is viewed rather tolerantly, since it is "natural"; but the lower classes strongly condemn as degenerate and "unnatural" the adolescent masturbation which the middle classes view more tolerantly, or the elaborate love play which the middle-class marriage manuals recommend. On almost every point of moral conduct, class-typed mores differ.

Middle-class mores, however, tend to become the conventional mores. The church, the school, and the welfare and "uplift" agencies are middle-class institutions, staffed and run by middle-class persons, and dedicated to the cultivation of middle-class values. Political candidates must be models of middle-class virtue; stupidity is forgivable, but not immorality. The laws are written by middle-class legislators and enforce middle-class values. The mass magazines righteously reflect middle-class mores, while the "confessions," aimed at the lower-class market, are even more undeviating in their unctuous approval of middle-class conventionality [Gerbner, 1958]. The upper classes may own or control these agencies, but it is not to their advantage to veto a middle-class morality which helps to protect upper-class interests. Thus the middle-class mores tend to become the official or conventional morality of the society.

The lower classes feel that they are constantly being prodded, scolded and "pushed around."

This tendency creates certain strains for the lower-class person. He often finds that behavior which is normal and acceptable in his class subculture is condemned and punished when he steps outside this subculture, as he must do at school and in nearly all his dealings with persons in positions of authority. A good deal of resentment and class antagonism accumulates among the lower classes, who feel that they are constantly being prodded, scolded, and "pushed around" by middle- and upper-class people.

Explaining many other group differences   Many other kinds of group differences—racial, religious, regional—are really class differences. For example, almost any Negro-white comparison will prove to be very flattering to whites. Negroes have proportionately more crimes, more venereal disease, more illegitimate births, more drunkenness, more desertions, more broken families, and proportionately more people on relief. Their record of dereliction is due largely to the fact that discrimination and lack of opportunity have kept most Negroes in the lower class. When Negroes and whites are compared as racial groups, therefore, we are comparing an overwhelmingly lower-class group with another group having vastly larger middle- and upper-class segments.

Variations in the class composition of religious groups affect comparisons between them. One would expect Baptists and Catholics to have a higher rate of juvenile delinquency than Episcopalians and Congregationalists simply because juvenile delinquency usually is more frequent in lower-social-class groups. For the same reasons exclusive residential suburbs of Long Island will have lower death rates than slum districts in New York City. Therefore, whenever data for two groups are compared, the critical observer will always wonder, "Are these groups comparable in class composition?" If not, some very misleading conclusions may be drawn.

Shaping life-adjustment patterns   The way people handle life situations varies with social class, as is illustrated in the following incident, reported to one of the authors by a perceptive student.

> *I was in a small two-man garage on a Saturday morning, making small talk with the proprietor as he worked on my car. He pointed to another car parked nearby.*
> *"How much do you think that car is worth?" he asked.*
> *I studied it a moment, and ventured, "Oh, perhaps $300."*
> *"I bought it a few minutes ago for $150," he remarked.*
> *"Now, I wonder why a fellow would sell his car so cheaply," I mused.*
> *He paused a moment, and said, "Oh, . . . you wouldn't understand."*
> *Suddenly I did understand. The proprietor was thinking "You, in your sheltered middle-class world of careful plans, long-term goals, and wisely rationed puritan pleasures, are unable to understand how a fellow would turn his car into quick cash to gratify a pressing impulse. Perhaps his eye is on something he can't wait to buy,*

or he needs money to finance a big weekend or to gain a new girl friend's gratitude. In his world, these may be more important than protecting his capital investment."

Social class affects the way people deal with virtually every aspect of reality. As space forbids examining them all, let us describe just two areas of life in which class background appears to produce contradictory tendencies: political attitudes, in which the lower classes appear to be more liberal (some would say "radical"), and social attitudes, in which the lower classes appear to be more conservative. (The terms, "liberal" and "conservative" are here used to describe differing degrees of receptivity to social change.)

Social class and political attitudes   If social class influences the basic outlook of people, we should expect people to support the party and candidates closest to their class interests. Several surveys [Centers, 1949, chap. 5] seem to confirm this expectation in showing that the lower classes are more favorable toward government welfare benefits and services and government regulation of business than are the other classes. Since 1936 the electorate has divided quite sharply along class lines, and in recent decades "every cross-section political survey ever conducted shows the inevitable pattern of low-income people being dominantly Democratic and upper-income people being Republican" [Harris, 1957]. In the 1956 campaign, the list of those who contributed over $5,000 to either political party numbered 269 Republican and 56 Democratic contributors [*New York Times*, Feb. 3, 1957, p. 52]. In 1952 and 1956, the immense personal appeal of Eisenhower made deep inroads into the normally Democratic labor vote; yet these voters did not change their *party* preference and continued voting Democratic for other offices. In 1964, Johnson captured many middle-class and upper-class voters, but they returned to their usual voting habits in 1966.

Party alignment by social class is not perfect; some lower-class people vote Republican, and a few upper-class people vote Democratic. Class interest is not the only factor in voter behavior, although it does appear to be the greatest factor. Whenever the political candidates are clearly identified with issues that appear to threaten or favor the welfare of a particular segment of the population, most members of that segment will vote accordingly. But other considerations may overrule class interest for some people, or they may fail to understand the issues and unwittingly vote against their own class interests. For example, many lower-class people favor a sales tax over an income tax, perhaps because of its more "painless" collection, or perhaps because they do not realize that a sales tax places a larger share of the tax burden upon the lower incomes. Often there is no clear-cut issue of class interest involved in a particular election. Kornhauser summarizes several studies of social class and political attitudes:

The opinion surveys and political and social studies as a whole indicate that class differences are greatest in regard to issues that obviously and directly affect the interests of people at upper, middle, and lower levels differently. Rather consistently the lower income groups are more in favor of government control of business and extending government welfare activities, sacrificing certain institutional property rights and unlimited opportunities for individual achievement in the interests of increasing security, overcoming the concentration of influence in the hands of the

*wealthy. There is also evidence that the poorer groups have more extreme national-
istic attitudes, greater religious traditionalism, and generally a more restricted outlook on the world, associated presumably with limited education.*

*It is tempting to catch up the main differences in a simple generalization that
upper classes are more conservative, lower classes more radical; that the former
rest content with things as they have been, while the have-nots desire reform. . . .
If one accepts a definition of radical and conservative opinion that is limited to
question responses pertaining to distribution of income, regulation of economic
effects in the interests of the common man, and similar economic-political reforms,
there can be little doubt that pronounced differences are found in relation to socio-
economic status. Questions on other issues, however (religious doctrine, international questions, race relations, for example), fail to support the conception of a
neat general pattern of radicalism-conservatism in which social classes manifest
consistent contrasts.*

Arthur Kornhauser, "Public Opinion and Social Class," *American Journal of Sociology,* 55:333–345,
January, 1950. Copyright 1950, by The University of Chicago.

In political attitudes and behavior, then, social class appears to be the most
important determinant. The loyal Republican or Democrat will defend his
allegiance with a string of arguments without realizing that these particular
arguments make sense to him largely because of his set of class interests,
traditions, habits, and associations. Thus, on economic issues, the lower class
tends to be politically liberal and the upper class politically conservative. Is this
division true in other fields of interest besides economics?

Social class and social attitudes   The lower class tends to be liberal on economic questions but conservative in many other social attitudes. The lower
class appears reluctant to accept new ideas and practices and is suspicious of
the innovators. Changes in health practices, food usage, religious doctrines,
family life, or educational procedures are likely to find their strongest opposition among lower-class groups. Their limited education, reading habits, and
associations isolate the lower class from a knowledge of the reasons for these
changes, and this ignorance, together with their class position, makes them
suspicious of the middle- and upper-class "experts" and "do-gooders" who
promote the changes.

A case in point is an experiment in the use of the Salk vaccine for the prevention of poliomyelitis [Deasy, 1956]. The experiment occurred in a suburban
area near Washington, D.C., where a large-scale trial program of the vaccine
was attempted before it was released for use in general. Parents were notified
of the opportunity in a letter from the school asking permission to give a free
vaccination to the child. A follow-up survey disclosed that proportinately twice
as many parents of upper and middle socioeconomic status gave permission,
as is shown in Table 11. The reasons for lower-class refusal were explored.
Fewer of the lower-class mothers had read about the program in the newspapers or discussed it with friends, and more of them expressed worries over
its possible dangers. Lower-class participation was inhibited by lack of knowledge, lack of communication, lack of confidence in scientific experts, a greater
fear of the new and untried, and a tendency to be unconcerned about actions
whose results would not materialize until a future date.

*Table 11   Per cent of respondents who gave consent for their child to partici-
pate in poliomyelitis vaccine trial*

| | Socio-economic status | | |
	Highest (N-42) per cent	Middle (N-44) per cent	Lowest (N-44) per cent
Gave consent	*86*	*84*	*43*
Did not give consent	*14*	*16*	*57*
Total	*100*	*100*	*100*

SOURCE: Leila Calhoun Deasy, "Socio-economic Status and Participation in the Poliomyelitis Vaccine Trial,"
American Sociological Review, 21:185–191, April, 1956.

Many other examples of lower-class conservatism could be cited. "Contemporary" design in art and home furnishings is first found in the shops catering to the wealthy and later is vulgarized for the lower-class tastes. The lower class is last to feel the trend toward the democratic family, permissive child-training practices, and birth control procedures [Bossard, 1954, chap. 15]. It does not follow that *all* social changes filter downward from the top, but a pattern of lower-class conservatism does seem to apply to many activities and interests.

Social class and social participation   Social class largely determines which parts of the culture one will experience—opera, country club, and cotillion, or jukebox, tavern, and brawl. This is illustrated by class differences in degree of social participation. In general, the lower the social class, the fewer are the associations and social relations of the individual. In Chapter 8 we saw that lower-class people belong to fewer organizations of any kind—clubs, civic groups, or even churches—than do middle and upper-class people. We might assume that this lack of organized sociability is compensated by more numerous informal contacts, but we find that these also diminish as we go down the class continuum. Lower-class people have fewer acquaintances, fewer friends, gossip with and about fewer other people, and do less informal visiting [Shuval, 1956].

The age of mass communications cuts across class lines, and while the lower classes read and travel less than other classes, they spend more time with radio, television, and movies [Bogart, 1958, p. 91]. This greater audio-visual exposure is still a selective process, since lower-class listeners shun "serious" programs and stick as far as possible to entertainment, which in turn is shaped along stereotypes already accepted in lower-class culture. Mass communication undoubtedly speeds the acceptance of new gadgets, but other than this, its influence on lower-class listeners would appear to be mainly to intensify their social conservatism. In substance then, the lower-class person has only limited participation in any kind of social interaction which might lead to the rapid acceptance of new ideas.

Some of the patterns of behavior related to social class are indicated in the following digest of class attitudes toward governmental, religious, and educational institutions. All these propositions are supported by research findings, although the evidence for some is far more conclusive than for others. Some are documented elsewhere in this chapter; documentation for the rest is omitted because of space limitations.

A SUMMARY OF SOME CLASS ATTITUDES TOWARD SOCIAL INSTITUTIONS

Attitudes toward governmental institutions

Upper class Appreciate effect of government on own affairs; know leading officials and are interested in politics. Majority will regard governmental regime as basic to their own security and will resist any type of drastic change. A minority will take their own security for granted and work energetically for an "efficient" or "humanitarian" regime.

Middle class Conscious of duty to be "good citizens." Responsive to appeals for "clean" or "honest" government, but for the most part will resist major change.

Lower class Many are completely indifferent to government since it seems remote and evidently has little effect on them. Some view it as the dispenser of petty favors such as minor jobs and possible payments for votes. A few may be consciously discontented with status and work for a revolutionary change that promises them greater benefits.

Attitudes toward religious institutions

Upper class Often take positions of leadership in lay movements and like to be considered "patrons" of the church. Some are critical of church dogma, but interested in the aesthetic aspects of religion. Some feel above the need for religion and show little interest except when custom demands their attendance on special occasions.

Middle class Apt to be responsive to appeals on a moral or intellectual basis. Somewhat uncertain about attitude toward traditional church dogmas. Highly critical of religious practices that seem to be excessively emotional.

Lower class Responsive to emotional services with (among Protestants) little ritual. Protestant groups often accept highly puritanical dogma which is often evaded in practice. Readily accepts reports of modern miracles. Some feel that the church is an upper-class institution and are either indifferent or openly hostile. Many join "store-front" churches that stress emotional expression and informal association.

Attitudes toward economic institutions

Upper class Take superior position and high standard of living for granted. Normally believe the traditional economic system is the best possible arrangement. Sometimes morally uneasy because of special privileges and seek to compensate by charity or civic service. Small minority may worry about "social injustice" and promote social reforms.

Middle class Laud virtues of thrift, ambition, and "decent" living. Torn between desire to improve status by saving money and need to prove their importance by expensive living. Tend to accept prevailing system, but hope to rise within it.

Lower class   Usually take inferior position for granted. Have little real hope of improvement. Little chance for thrift, and occasional windfalls are used for immediate consumption. Some have acquired middle-class aspirations and seek rise in status through thrift and increased educational attainments. A few resent inferior position and hope for change through revolution and different type of economic structure.

Attitudes toward educational institutions   **Upper class**   Many assume that their children will attend fashionable private schools and will make acceptable but not necessarily outstanding records. Education is regarded as a means of securing social acceptance and enriching cultural values rather than of preparation for earning a living. They support private schools generously, but some oppose raising taxes for public education. Others send their children to public schools in fashionable neighborhoods and to the major state universities. These parents are "patrons" of the schools and use their influence to increase community support of public education.

Middle class   Life adjustment, vocational preparation, and opportunity for meeting suitable marriage partners are major aspects sought in higher education. Parents are concerned about standards of public education, join parent-teacher associations, and generally support higher school taxes. Children are expected to have a good school record. Some view the degree or certificate as more important than the content of education. Such parents refuse to be involved in maintaining educational standards and may resist increases in taxes. These parents are anxious that students graduate but not greatly concerned about high marks.

Lower class   Many consider the school not very important, perhaps even a nuisance. Their children are not encouraged either to excel in studies or to remain in school. Increases in school taxes often receive the most opposition from this group. Some, especially among the upper-lowers, become "middle-class" converts who view the school as a channel of occupational mobility, and make great sacrifices to see that children have a chance for education.

THE FUTURE OF AMERICAN CLASSES: FROM "PROLETARIAT" TO "STATUS SEEKERS"

Karl Marx, in the volumes entitled *Das Kapital* and in the *Communist Manifesto*, probably did more to emphasize the importance of social class than any other thinker in history. In the Marxian view, conflict between social classes has been continuous since the dawn of history, and the rise and fall of various social classes offer the key to the understanding of history. Prior to the industrial revolution the top social class was a landed aristocracy which owned great estates by virtue of inheritance and noble rank. This class was forced to share top status with the manufacturers, traders, and financiers whose wealth and prestige were greatly increased by the expansion of business since the time of the industrial revolution. Marx prophesied that the ultimate struggle would take place between the proletariat (wage workers) and the bourgeoisie (capitalists) and would end in the inevitable triumph of the proletariat, who would in turn establish a classless society under the banner of communism. This interpretation of history gave to communists a sort of "messianic hope" which enabled them to believe that, in spite of present obstacles, history was on their side and their final triumph was certain. For many years discussion of social class centered on the validity of the Marxian analysis.

The current opinion among social scientists is that Marx was only partly correct and that the class struggle is not proceeding on the lines he predicted. Marx predicted, for example, that classes would grow farther apart as industrialization advanced. Hence the lower class would become more conscious of its distinct interests and more hostile to the upper class, while the middle classes would gradually be pushed down into the proletariat. Actually the exact opposite seems to have taken place; classes are coming closer together both in possessions and in attitudes. The middle class is stronger than ever in Western societies, and the lower class is gaining a stake in the society which Marx wanted them to overthrow. Marx had predicted that communism would follow industrialization and that the most advanced countries would be ripe for communism under the influence of revolutionary urban wage earners. Since the writing of Marx, communism has spread in many places, but not in the manner that Marx predicted. The industrial countries have not developed Communist parties strong enough to take over the government (both Russia and China were primarily agricultural at the time of their Communist revolutions in 1917 and 1949), and expansion has come either through Chinese or Russian military conquest or by movements in agricultural areas led by the urban intellectuals with the support of a landlord-hating peasant population.

Skepticism about the Marxian prediction of an eventual classless society has also been strengthened by the difficulties of eliminating social class in Communist-controlled countries. Considerable evidence has filtered through the Iron Curtain to the effect that the Communist party officers, factory managers, government officials, professional men, scientists, and artists in the Soviet Union tend to form a distinct self-perpetuating social class with special privileges and a distinct style of life with appropriate attitudes [Inkeles, 1950; Feldmesser, 1953]. A strong statement on the development of social-class lines in Communist society comes from the pen of Milovan Djilas, formerly vice-president of Tito's government in Yugoslavia, who was later thrown into prison for making statements such as this:

The establishment of the ownership of the new class was evidenced in the changes in the psychology, the way of life, and the material position of its members, depending on the position they held in the hierarchical ladder. Country homes, the best housing, furniture, and similar things were acquired; special quarters and exclusive rest homes were established for the highest bureaucracy, for the elite of the new class. The party secretary and the chief of the secret police in some places not only became the highest authorities but obtained the best housing, automobiles, and similar evidences of privilege. Those beneath them were eligible for comparable privileges depending upon their position in the hierarchy. . . . More than anything else, the essential aspect of contemporary Communism is the new class of owners and exploiters.

Milovan Djilas, *The New Class*, Frederick A. Praeger, Inc., New York, 1957, pp. 57–58.

Far from achieving a classless society, the Communists have set in power a new class, based on the possession of nearly absolute power, which is even more rigid in its composition and more differentiated from the masses in its privileges than the upper class of capitalist societies. The dreams of the new freedom have given way to a regimentation more rigid than the old slavery. Judged by its creed, Communist society is the enemy of class privilege; judged by its results, it is class privilege's newest and strongest bastion.

In non-Communist societies the possibilities of a Marxian-style class struggle for the control of society seem to be diminishing, but we are becoming increasingly aware of class struggle of a different type—the pursuit of status. This struggle is the main theme of Vance Packard's *The Status Seekers* [1959], a best-selling piece of "popular sociology." Packard is not a professional sociologist, and his book has been criticized, among other reasons, for depicting class lines as a recent development .when, in reality, they have long been present on the American scene [Lipset, 1959]. There is no doubt, however, that he has correctly identified the desire for social mobility as the major class concern in the United States today. Instead of seeing life as a struggle between classes with a fixed membership, the average American today sees it as a contest in which the reward is individual advancement from a lower- to a higher-class status. Although class barriers may produce frustration, most Americans do not respond by trying to overthrow the system; either they accept a low status or they try to advance themselves within the system through getting a better job so that they too can move into a better neighborhood, buy wall-to-wall carpeting, and fight crab grass.

Changes in relative class status One reason for the lack of revolutionary fervor among workers is that many of the changes that Marx, Debs, and others worked for have now taken place without revolution. Such commonplace arrangements as legalized collective bargaining through labor unions, minimum wage laws, old-age pensions, and vacations with pay, which would have been considered fantastic dreams in the 1920s, are now taken for granted by most industrial workers. The result is that those who have usually been placed in the lower class now have many of the privileges of the middle class.

The essence of the Marxian appeal for class warfare was the belief that with the passing of time the rich would become increasingly wealthy and the poor increasingly miserable. This is not exactly what has been happening. All income levels have shared in the increasing productivity of our society and have gained in *absolute* standard of living; yet not all have shared equally in our growing prosperity. As shown in Figure 8, the share of our national income received by the top fifth has diminished very slightly, the middle-income receivers' share has grown somewhat, and the poorest fifth are *relatively* poorer than ever.

There is a widespread impression that taxes and welfare expenditures go a long way to redistribute income more equally. This is doubtful, possibly entirely false. Contrary to popular opinion, lower-income families pay a *higher* fraction of their income in taxes than more prosperous families.[3] Most of the very rich avoid the maximum income tax rates by taking advantage of the many tax loopholes thoughtfully provided for them. Although some government welfare

[3] According to the Tax Foundation, the percentage of income collected in Federal, state, and local taxes of all kinds rises steadily as income falls below $10,000, from 23.9 per cent at $10,000 to 28.3 per cent at $1.450. See *Allocation of the Tax Burden by Income Class*, The Tax Foundation, New York, 1960, p. 12.

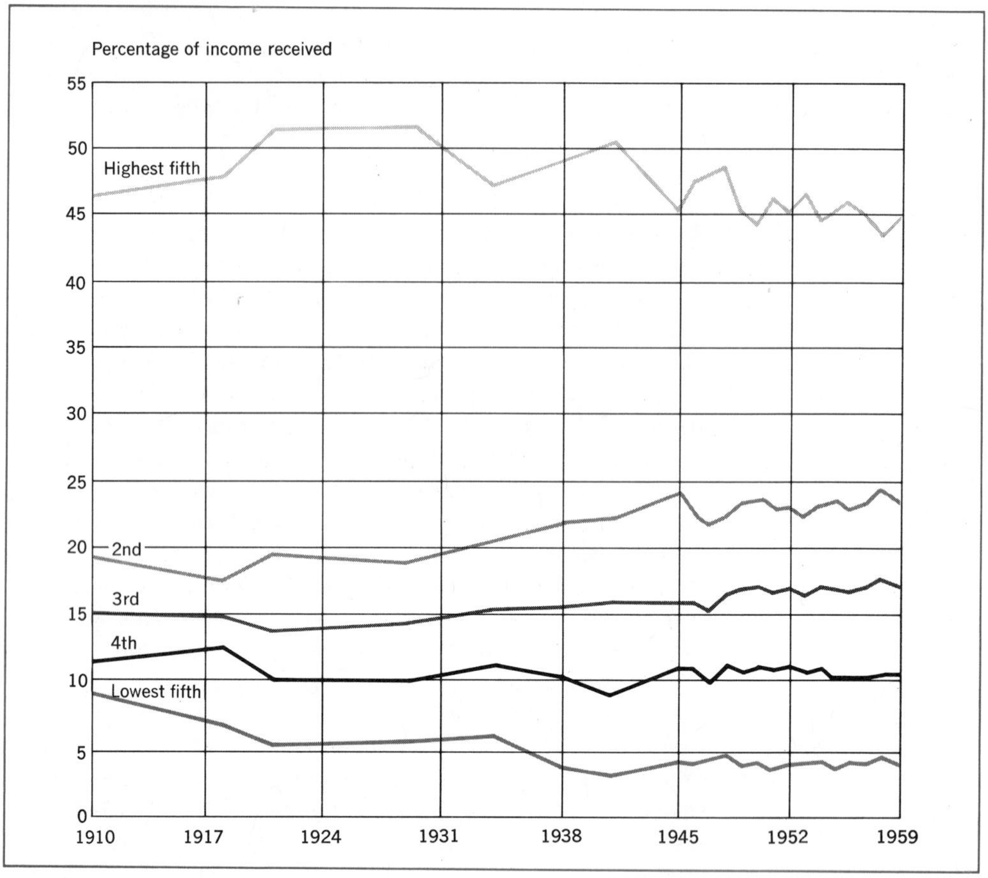

Percentage of income received

FIGURE 8 *Who Gets Richer in the United States?*
Percentage of national personal income, before taxes, received by each income fifth, 1910–1959.
SOURCE: Adapted from data presented in Gabriel Kolko, *Wealth and Power in America*, Frederick A. Praeger, Inc., New York, 1962, p. 14.

programs benefit mainly the poor, others benefit mainly the prosperous and the rich—government expenditures for airports and air terminals, yachting facilities, interstate highways, irrigation projects which turn owners of desert wasteland into millionaires, and business subsidies of many kinds, to give a few examples. Whether the subsidies of the rich to the poor are greater or lesser than the subsidies of the poor to the rich has not been exactly determined. The following anecdote, related by a friend of one of the authors, is a case in point.

As my host guided his 55-foot yacht toward its slip, he applauded the decision of [a Florida] city commission to cancel an urban renewal project, largely federally financed, which would benefit mainly the city's Negro slum area. As he expanded on the "taint" of Federal funds to solve "local" problems, he tuned in on a weather report from a federally operated weather station, waved at the captain of a federally operated coast guard vessel which stood ready to rescue him if he got into trouble, carefully noted the position of the federally placed bouys and channel markers, nosed down a channel dredged with Federal funds, and entered a marina financed partly from Federal funds and tied up to a federally subsidized dock, concluding his lecture on the evils of government welfare programs with the sage observation, "We coddle people too much. People should stand on their own feet and pay their own way."

Although class privileges and obligations differ, all classes make useful contributions to society, and all types of class environments produce individuals who are problems to themselves and to society. Whether a class system is the best means of assigning different social functions is probably a question of only academic interest, since all modern societies follow the system. Ethical interest focuses on two questions: First, should the privileges and responsibilities of different classes be modified in the direction of minimizing differences between them? And second, can, or should, we promote the opportunities for individuals to change their class levels? Most societies are now more or less seriously committed to a program of curtailing upper-class privileges and improving levels of living for the lower class. The possibilities of individual movement between classes will be explored in a later chapter on social mobility.

SUMMARY

A social class is made up of people of similar social status who regard one another as social equals. Each class is a subculture, with a set of attitudes, beliefs, values, and behavior norms which differ from those of other classes. Social class is based on total social and economic position in the community, including wealth and income, occupation, education, self-identification, hereditary prestige, group participation, and recognition by others. Class lines are not clearly drawn but represent points along a continuum of social status. The exact size and membership of a given class is difficult to establish.

Social class is an important social reality. Social class largely determines one's life opportunities and colors one's personality development. Social class assigns privileges and responsibilities to individuals and thereby helps to get necessary work accomplished. Social-class subcultures breed a highly subtle and tenacious class ethnocentrism, which prevents classes from fully understanding one another. It is mainly the standards of the middle class that are written into law and sanctioned by the conventional morality. Many differences ordinarily assigned to race, religion, ethnic group, or to some other kind of group difference, are actually class differences; confusion arises from the fact that racial, religious, and other groups may be unevenly distributed along the class continuum.

Social class molds the life-adjustment patterns of the individuals; the lower class tends to be liberal in political action connected with economic benefits and conservative in accepting other social changes, while the opposite tends to be true of the upper class. This is partly explained by the fact that the lower the class level, the more limited tends to be the participation of the individual in social and community life.

Current scientific interest in class has shifted from the Marxian theory of class warfare to the struggle for individual social mobility. Current technological, economic, and governmental changes are increasing the relative size of the middle classes and bringing us closer to a middle-class society.

QUESTIONS AND PROJECTS

1. Distinguish among *evaluated participation, status characteristics, and self-identification* as methods of determining social-class status. Which method do you think is best? Why?

2. Are Americans class-conscious? Can class lines exist when people deny their existence?

3. How can social classes really be subcultures when children of all class levels attend school together?

4. Given unlimited money, to what degree could a government or a community provide children with complete "equality of opportunity"?

5. Is there a relation between the problems of health and education and the attitudes engendered by lower-class life? Explain.

6. How does class affect political attitudes? When a college student switches from his father's political party, does he do so because of increased knowledge, parental rebellion, or social mobility? Outline each possibility.

7. When a college student from a wealthy family takes a summer job working in a factory, how much does he learn about the "working class"?

8. What is meant by the "messianic hope" of Marxism? Have recent developments supported the Marxian theory of social class?

9. Do you feel that social-class stratification is harmful or beneficial to society as a whole? Why?

10. Is the United States primarily a middle-class country? Defend your answer.

11. Make a chart of officers in your senior high school class (or some other organization you know well). From which social-class level does each come? Are the officers proportionately representative of the social class present in the organization? Do members from different social classes view the group in the same way? Wherein, and why, do they differ?

12. Read and analyze the treatment of social class in one of the following novels: *Kitty Foyle* by Christopher Morley, *Marjorie Morningstar* by Herman Wouk, *Studs Lonigan* by James T. Farrell, *The Forge* by Thomas S. Stribling, *Mansfield Park* by Jane Austen, *The Age of Innocence* by Edith S. Wharton, *Fraternity* by John Galsworthy, *Tobacco Road* by Erskine Caldwell, *Hunky* by Thomas R. Williamson, *Babbitt* by Sinclair Lewis, *So Little Time* or *B. F.'s Daughter* by John P. Marquand.

SUGGESTED READINGS

*BALTZELL, E. DIGBY: *Philadelphia Gentlemen: The Making of a National Upper Class*, The Free Press of Glencoe, New York, 1958, chaps. 2 and 4. Brief descriptions of the American upper class. (90743 Free P)

BENDIX, REINHARD, AND SEYMOUR LIPSET (EDS.): *Class, Status, and Power*, The Free Press of Glencoe, New York, 1966. A collection of essays and research studies on social class.

HODGE, ROBERT W., ET AL.: "Occupational Prestige in the United States, 1925–63," *American Journal of Sociology*, 70:286–302, November, 1964. Analyzes

data relating to occupational prestige and finds that this has been remarkably stable.

KOLKO, GALRIEL: *Wealth and Power in America: An Analysis of Social Class and Income Distribution*, Frederick A. Praeger, New York, 1962. The economic basis of social-class distribution.

LENSKI, GERHARD E.: *Power and Privilege: A Theory of Social Stratification*, McGraw-Hill Book Company, New York, 1966. Bases social stratification on the functioning of distribution processes and concentrates more on the causes of social stratification than on the consequences.

LIPSET, SEYMOUR MARTIN, AND NATALIE ROGOFF: "Class and Opportunity in Europe and the United States: Some Myths and What the Statistics Show," *Commentary*, 18:562–568, December, 1954. Reprinted in ROBERT W. O'BRIEN, ET AL., *Readings in General Sociology*, Houghton Mifflin Company, Boston, 1963, pp. 395–401. Finds that social mobility in some European countries is as high as in the United States.

MANIS, JEROME, AND BERNARD MELTZER: "Some Correlates of Class Consciousness among Textile Workers," *American Journal of Sociology*, 69:177–184, September, 1963. A study of class consciousness among textile workers in an Eastern American city.

MARTINEAU, PIERRE: "Social Classes and Spending Behavior," *Journal of Marketing*, 23:121–130, October, 1958; also, "Social Class and Its Very Close Relationship to the Individual's Buying Behavior," in JOHN S. WRIGHT AND DANIEL S. WARNER, (eds.), *Speaking of Advertising*, McGraw-Hill Book Company, 1963, pp. 147–153. Show class influences on buying habits.

MILLER, WALTER B.: "Implications of Urban Lower-class Cultures for Social Work," *Social Service Review*, 33:219–237, September, 1959. A description of the problems faced by social workers in serving lower-class clients.

MITCHELL, ROBERT EDWARD: "Class-linked Conflict in Liberalism-Conservatism," *Social Problems*, 13:418–427, Spring, 1966. Contrasts in social-class attitudes on the national and local levels as seen in Berkeley, California.

*SHOSTAK, ARTHUR B., AND WILLIAM GOMBERG: *New Perspectives on Poverty*, Prentice-Hall, Englewood Cliffs, N.J., 1965. A series of articles devoted to the culture of poverty and to methods by which the lower class might absorb some elements of middle-class standards. (P-H)

WARNER, W. LLOYD, AND PAUL S. LUNT: *The Social Life of a Modern Community*, Yale University Press, New Haven, Conn., 1941, chap. 7, "Profiles of Yankee City." A long chapter, reading like a novel, in which the attitudes and behavior of the different classes are dramatized.

12

SOCIAL
MOBILITY

When Paul Stanley (upper-lower to lower-middle and still moving) was in high school he played football well enough to gain a reputation which brought him several offers of scholarships. He chose Eastern College because there he would have less competition and would be sure of being subsidized for his four college years. After finishing he sought to enter Harvard Law School, but his college record was not sufficiently good to be passed by the board of admissions. He chose a less difficult, professional law school in Boston and in time received his law degree. Meanwhile, he had supported himself by working in the law office of John Bates (upper-middle).

Mr. Bates was a loyal alumnus of the local high school. He once said to Mr. John Breckenridge (upper-upper) that "Paul Stanley's a good sound boy. Hard worker and knows people. He's a fellow to watch."

Paul's father and mother (upper-lower) had come over from Poland with their respective parents when they were still children. After they had met and married they settled in the downtown region of Yankee City where Paul, their first child, grew up. They both had worked in the shoe factory and gone to an "Americanization school" to improve their English.

The Stanleys were proud of their home. They owned it outright, and the husband and wife had planted the flower garden. Mr. Stanley had painted the house and the fences with two coats of white paint. He had placed cast-off tires in appropriate places in the front yard and had given them a coating of white paint. After Mr. Stanley had spaded the ground inside the tires, his wife had planted petunias. Rows of hollyhocks grew beside the white fences. . . .

On his son, Paul, he lavished the greatest affection. When Mr. Stanley wanted to expand and demonstrate how he had gone up in the world since coming from Poland, he first talked of his son's college education and then spoke of "my beautiful white house." He then made comments about "all these Yankees who have lived here forever and never got any place." . . .

When younger, Paul had been proud of the home of his parents. It was the nicest house in their neighborhood. But now he saw it not as the nicest house in the neighborhood but in the larger context of the whole town, and this made it appear just a little ridiculous. . . . The house he bought was over in Newtown. He wanted to raise his family away from everything which would make them think of what he had gone through. He wanted a nice new house—"one of those cute little bunga-

lows with a big lawn in front and a concrete sidewalk on the street with new curves and a high-class name."

He had been flattered after graduating from law school when some members of the Caribous (upper-middle to lower-lower) had invited him to join their organization. There were only a few Poles in the Caribous and most of the members were Yankees. They were all good fellows.

Before he had left the bank after negotiating with some of the officials for his money, he had been congratulated by several of the bank employees on acquiring the new house. They had kidded him about his coming marriage. A few evenings later one of the bank clerks told a clique mate of his, the manager of a hardware store, that Mr. Breckenridge thought very highly of Paul Stanley. At the moment he was talking, they were enjoying a glass of prohibition beer at the hall of the American Order of Antlers (upper-upper to lower-middle). The Antlers, they felt, had "everyone who counted in Yankee City" as members.

"Paul Stanley's come a long way," he said, "and he's come the hard way. And what's more, he's going a lot further. Nobody who's got what it takes and who's got the backing of Mr. Breckenridge can help but succeed. You know, I think Paul would make a swell member of the Antlers."

"That's a swell idea," his companion replied.

Within the year, Paul was a member in good standing of the Antlers, and he played bridge there several nights a week. He still belonged to the Caribous, but some of the members of the latter organization were beginning to complain that he didn't come around any more.

The Stanleys were now in a clique with Mr. and Mrs. Tim Pinkham, Mr. and Mrs. Dick Jones, and Mr. and Mrs. Jerry Thomas (lower-middle), but people like the Camps, the Frenches, and the Flahertys (upper-middle), whom Paul knew at the Antlers, never invited them to dinner, nor did any of the "nice ladies of Hill Street" ever call on Annie. It is possible that this occasionally worried them, but there is more evidence that their past success was still a pleasant reward and that the present filled them with hope for the future.

"And anyway," they said, "we're going to see to it that our children have every advantage." (Quoted with very slight adaptation from W. Lloyd Warner and Paul S. Lunt, *The Social Life of a Modern Community*, Yale University Press, New Haven, Conn., 1941, pp. 188–193.)

THREE THINGS stand out in the above sketch of Paul Stanley. He had ability. He had a family from whom he learned ambition and good work habits. He gained the endorsement of some influential persons. Ability, ambition, sponsorship—without these, few men rise much above their social origins.

THE NATURE OF SOCIAL MOBILITY

No doubt talented persons are born into all class levels. If there were no barriers to social advancement, we could expect a great deal of mobility as some persons climbed while others slipped. But obviously barriers of many sorts block men's progress upward. The grandson of Henry Ford and the grandson of an Alabama sharecropper did not have an equal opportunity to become a corporation executive. It is true, however, that considerable movement goes on up and down the social ladder. This mobility is aided by all the influences that give people a more nearly equal chance to develop and use their talents. Mobility is discouraged by all the influences that tend to hold one in the same class as his parents. *Inherited wealth* makes it easy for upper-class children to remain upper-class; its lack makes it likely that lower-class children will remain lower-class. *Discrimination* of many sorts limits mobility. Many exclusive schools admit students only after a look at the applicant's family background. The high school student is often funneled into curricula according to social class more than ability, with upper-class students taking the college preparatory courses while the lower classes are shunted into the vocational curriculum [Hollingshead, 1949, chap. 8]. In vocational guidance, the class background of the child, rather than the abilities of the child, sometimes guides the counselor's recommendations. For members of racial minorities, discrimination is an even greater barrier to class mobility.

Class discrimination is not always conscious or intentional. When a successful attorney seeks out the bank president at the country club and casually remarks that he has a nephew, graduating next year, who aspires to a career in banking, he is not intentionally trying to discriminate against some ambitious youth who has no uncle at the country club. He is merely trying to help his nephew to find a good opening. Yet the effect of such favors is to discriminate heavily against those who have no influential family friends or relatives.

The greatest barrier to class mobility, however, springs from the fact that *social classes are subcultures which fit the child for participation in the class subculture to which he has been socialized.* The average lower-class child does not have the ambition and study habits needed for upward mobility because he has had little chance to learn them in his subculture. The middle-class child has this chance; meanwhile, he is denied the chance to learn the habits and values that would be appropriate for a lower-class world. The process of growing up in a class thus sets forces in motion which tend to hold one in the same class position.

Mobility runs both ways—up and down. Some people fail to maintain the social-class rank into which they were born. Loss of wealth or income, acceptance of a lower-status occupation, and settling into a lower-status pattern of life are both the symptoms and the processes of downward mobility. Contrast this case, supplied by a student of one of the authors, with the example of upward mobility at the start of the chapter.

Peter Wilson's father was a successful small-town lawyer who lived modestly but comfortably and was a pillar of small-town respectability. Peter was always a "different" child, obstinate and selfish; his parents indulged his whims and excused his shortcomings. Peter flunked out of two colleges in prompt succession and evaded two shotgun marriages as quietly as his father's legal skill could arrange. At this point his father gave up hope and moved to another locale.

For several years Peter clung to the edges of the lower-middle class. He held a succession of lower-middle-class jobs—cashier in a garage, inspector in a furniture factory, timekeeper on a construction project—but never held them for long. Nor did he ever get a very good job, for he lacked both education and dependability. Also, he never looked clean-shaven, and every suit he wore promptly assumed a slept-in look.

He finally drifted into a semiskilled factory job which he has now held for over a dozen years. He earns average wages, buys the food for the family, and spends the rest of his wages and most of his time with his cronies who work at the same factory. His father is still paying the rent, and his wife does housework to pay for other family needs.

The older sons have finished high school and hold semiskilled jobs. Both have married daughters of unskilled or semiskilled workers. The third generation now appears firmly fixed in the upper-lower or "working" class.

Such a spectacular drop from upper-middle to upper-lower or lower-lower class is unusual but not impossible. Lack of ability, lack of emotional stability, or possibly misfortune may prevent one from holding a suitable occupation and living the life appropriate to one's parental status. Sometimes an entire group may suffer downward mobility, as in the case of victims of the "dust bowl" during the 1930s, or members of a skilled trade whose jobs are destroyed by technological advance. Downward mobility is not proudly announced and may go unnoticed, but it is constantly in process all around us.

CLASS, CASTE, AND ESTATE

Some societies have developed structures which greatly hamper any kind of social mobility; in others, people are relatively free to rise or fall. An *open-class* society is one in which people move up or down in the social structure strictly on the basis of personal effort and ability; a *closed-class* society is one in which position is fixed at birth and cannot be changed by individual achievement. Perfect examples are hard to find, but the frontier society of early America is often regarded (not entirely correctly) as a society in which inherited prestige was of little importance, while the classic representation of the closed society is the caste system of ancient India.

In this caste system, social position was entirely determined by parentage. Since intermarriage between castes was strictly prohibited, the individual was practically helpless to change either his status or that of his children. The barriers between castes were rigid, and exceptions were practically unknown. Caste specified type of occupation, place of worship, use of separate roads

for travel, and separation to the greatest possible degree in all social relationships. The Brahmin in the upper-caste was likely to be a person of wealth and
education, but even if he were bankrupt and illiterate he still retained his caste
status. The "untouchable," whose position was so low that he was outside the
framework of the caste system, could not raise his status by individual accomplishments. Even if he was able to overcome his handicaps and acquire wealth
and fame, he still retained his lowly social status in the eyes of the members
of the regular castes [Hocart, 1950; Ryan, 1953; Marriott, 1955].

Recent legislation has attacked caste discrimination in India, but it is deeply
rooted in the mores and difficult to change. The system is sanctioned by Hindu
religious beliefs and regarded as the will of the gods by members of both the
higher and the lower castes. The only escape mechanisms are a very limited
possibility of changing caste through adoption and the hope that one may have
a higher status in his next incarnation. The Hindu believes in a prolonged
round of rebirths; if he is unfortunate in his present life, he may be more
favored in the next. This religious sanction of caste is not unchallenged, however, for some of the most prominent Hindus, including the late Mahatma
Gandhi, have attacked caste barriers as a perversion of the essence of true
Hinduism.

The position of the American Negro is sometimes regarded as an example
of the caste system, since his position is determined by his racial classification. Even the Negro who is well educated and is successful in a profession
or business will still be regarded as an inferior by many less distinguished
whites. There is some debate over whether Negroes and whites form true
castes in the United States. Critics of the concept point out, for example, that
while most whites may feel superior to all Negroes, they do not treat all Negroes alike. Even the most bigoted white is unlikely to treat the Negro university president as he treats the Negro sharecropper. Exceptions to the caste
barriers are constantly being made for particularly distinguished Negroes.
Does this disprove the existence of caste, or merely show that we recognize
class differences within the two castes? The latter idea is expressed in the
caste-class hypothesis diagramed in Figure 9. The figure describes two castes
with a virtually impassable barrier; on each side of the caste barrier is a comparable set of class levels. No Negro will be treated in all respects as though
he were white, and vice versa; in some respects, Negroes and whites may be
treated alike; in others a caste difference is noticeable. Thus, Negroes and
whites are treated approximately alike when they are buying cars, but differently when they are buying houses. The heart of a caste system, moreover,
is the preservation of hereditary distinctions through the prohibition of legal
intermarriage. State laws prohibiting racial intermarriage in the United States
were held unconstitutional in 1967, but strong social pressures remain. Wherever racial intermarriage is prohibited or severely restricted, the central feature of a caste system is present.

The caste-class concept is, in your authors' opinion, a valid and useful concept. It describes the fact that certain privileges and duties are assigned to
whites and Negroes according to race, while certain other privileges and duties
are received by both whites and Negroes according to their social class.

Estate is the term designating rank in a society where drastically unequal
ownership of land makes for what is practically a closed society without a for-

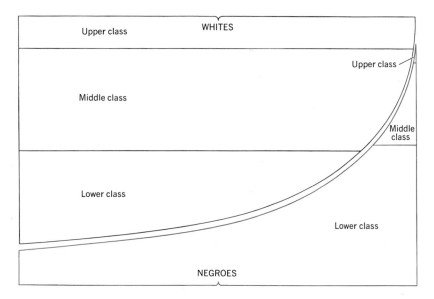

FIGURE 9   *The Caste-Class System in the United States*
This figure probably exaggerates the size of the white upper and middle classes, but it aptly illustrates the fact that there are classes within each caste, although the proportion of people in each class differs greatly between castes.
SOURCE: Reproduced from Allison R. Davis, Burleigh B. Gardner, and Mary R. Gardner, *Deep South*, The University of Chicago Press, Chicago, 1941, p. 10.

mal caste system. The extreme example of the estate system is represented by the feudal period when the top estates were the land-owning nobility and the clergy, with the peasants and workers occupying lesser rank. During the French Revolution the newspapers had become so powerful that journalists were referred to as the "fourth estate." Powerful landlords owning thousands of acres are still a feature of many countries today so that "estate" is a continuing form of social stratification. Hence the move for land reform (breaking up large holdings and giving land to peasants) can be seen as an effort to shift from an estate system to a class system.

Open and closed classes   No society has an absolutely open or a completely closed class system. Even in societies such as the United States, which lays great stress on individual initiative, family position plays a great role, since it prevents men from having the type of equal start in life that would be necessary for a completely open society. In every society, no matter how democratic or equalitarian its ethos may be, the successful parents will find ways to help their children hang on to the status and privileges the parents have enjoyed. This makes complete equality of opportunity impossible. The children of the most successful will inherit not only some of their parents' prestige, but also a better chance to acquire a good education, a driving ambition, and a chance to begin their working life with a fair supply of capital. In every society unsuccessful parents will, helplessly and unwittingly, handicap their children in their competition for status. The children of the poor have to live down their parents' lowly status, have more trouble in acquiring a good education, and will have great difficulty in obtaining the capital needed for business success. Unlike the untouchables of India, however, if they can overcome these obstacles, they will then be able to rise in status.

The concept of open and closed classes is more useful than the concept of caste, because it can be used as a measuring stick to determine the freedom of movement in different societies. If a society has many individuals who came from lowly homes and rose to high positions, along with others who fell from the high status of their parents, then we say there is a high degree of social mobility and an approximation of the open-class society. A society in which only a few rise or fall from their parental status is closer to the caste system. The variations in rates of mobility are due both to the general rate of occupational improvement—the number of higher-status jobs appearing in the society —and the barriers against mobility within the society. Regardless of the attitude of the society toward social mobility, not many people will find an opportunity to improve their lot unless the society is making rapid economic advance. France, for instance, is a country that has emphasized freedom, equality, and social welfare; but until recently it has lagged in technological advance. The result is that many Frenchmen remained on small farms, and relatively few had the opportunity to move into urban industrial and white-collar occupations [Rogoff, 1953, b]. Spain has, until very recently, lagged in industrial advance even more than France, and in Spain lower-class people have found great difficulty in reaching a higher occupational status [Matthews, 1957, pp. 108–111]. India is usually classified as "underdeveloped" (a country which has made little advance in the use of mechanical techniques or rationalized agriculture), and caste barriers are still strong enough so that the top castes secure most of the better opportunities which are created by the industrialization now taking place [Gist, 1954].

Social mobility in underdeveloped countries is not simply a matter of reaching a higher level within an established status system. It also generally involves a shift from being a part of a traditional farming culture to becoming a participant in a modern plantation or industrial economy. The individual leaves the water buffalo, the rice paddy, and a system of farming ruled by tradition and family authority, and enters the world of the tractor, time sheet, and rational agricultural techniques decreed by a remote and strange authority. It is not too difficult to recruit enough unskilled laborers, but competent skilled workers, technicians, and supervisors are scarce. In underdeveloped countries, the low status of manual labor tends to extend, to some degree, to the engineers and technicians, since they are also engaged in getting manual labor accomplished. The high-status occupations are those completely removed from manual labor—law, government, teaching, writing, and the like. The campaign for national independence in colonial areas has also focused the attention of ambitious young people on law and government. The results are that the underdeveloped society quickly accumulates many lawyers and civil service clerks, while independent businessmen, mechanics, and engineers will be in short supply for some time. Even though government employment may expand tremendously, it is still unable to take care of all who seek a career while agricultural and industrial development languishes, partly because of a lack of competent personnel [Van der Kroef, 1956; Hunt, 1956].

ETHNIC AND RELIGIOUS FACTORS IN MOBILITY

In most societies there is a tendency for national, racial, and religious groups to be distributed differently among the various social-class levels. Usually the social status of an ethnoeconomic group is determined by a combination of the following factors: (1) the length of time the group has been in the country; (2) the circumstances under which it entered the country; (3) the success of members of the group in improving their economic status; (4) stereotypes about the status of the group which may be widely believed, either by outsiders or by members of the group themselves; and (5) "visibility," or the ease with which outsiders can identify members of the group.

Table 12 illustrates the relationship between ethnic background and occupation in Canada. This table indicates the differential participation in various occupations by ethnic group. The English have twice the expected number of professional and financial posts in proportion to the size of the English population, while the French have about half the expected number of such posts. Scandinavians, who are mostly immigrants attracted to Canada by the prospect of cheap land, have ten times the expected number of farmers, while largely urbanized Jews have less than one-eleventh of their expected number of farmers.

A similar study made in a New England village by Warner in 1941 found that the upper class was entirely composed of Protestants of Anglo-Saxon background, although more recent immigrants of Catholic or Jewish faith were making a rapid rise [Warner 1941]. While occupation was only one of the traits considered by Warner in ranking social class, his findings were similar to those that would be expected on the basis of the Canadian data, thus indicating that the social mobility tendencies of a specific ethnic group may be similar in two different nations.

Table 12   Ethnic origin and occupational classes, male labor force, Canada, 1961, proportion of over-representation in occupation by ethnic group

	British	French	Ger-man	Italian	Jew-ish	Dutch	Scandi-navian	East Euro-pean	Other Euro-pean	Asian	Indian and Eskimo	Total male labor force
Professional and financial	+2.0	−1.9	−1.8	− 5.2	+ 7.4	− .9	− 1.9	−1.2	−1.1	+ 1.7	− 7.5	8.6
Clerical	+1.3	− .2	−1.8	− 3.2	− .1	− 1.7	− 2.4	−1.7	−2.0	− 1.5	− 5.9	6.9
Personal service	− .9	− .2	− .7	+ 2.9	− 2.4	− .5	− 1.1	+ .9	+5.1	+19.1	+ 1.3	4.3
Primary and unskilled	−2.3	+2.8	−2.1	+11.5	− 8.9	− 2.0	− .2	0.0	+1.8	− 3.6	+34.7	10.0
Agriculture	−1.5	−1.4	+8.8	− 9.5	−11.7	+10.3	+10.6	+6.9	+ .6	− 6.5	+ 6.9	12.2
All others	+1.4	+ .9	−2.4	+ 3.5	+15.7	− 5.2	− 5.0	−4.9	−4.4	− 9.1	−29.5	58.0
Total	0.0	0.0	0.0	0.0	0.0	0.0	0.0	0.0	0.0	0.0	0.0	100.0

A +2.0 sign would indicate that the ethnic group has twice as much as its proportionate share of a given occupation, whereas a −2.0 sign would indicate that the ethnic group has only one-half as much as its expected occupational quota, considering the ethnic group's size in proportion to the total population.

SOURCE: Adapted from presentation in John Porter, *The Vertical Mosaic*, University of Toronto Press, Toronto, Canada, 1965, p. 87.

Table 13 Composition of selected religious bodies, by social-class level, United States, 1945–1946

Denomination	Class levels		
	Upper class, per cent	Middle class, per cent	Lower class per cent
Congregational	24	43	33
Episcopalian	24	34	42
Presbyterian	22	40	38
Methodist	13	35	52
Lutheran	11	36	53
Roman Catholic	9	25	66
Baptist	8	24	68

SOURCE: Derived from a breakdown of four polls taken by the American Institute of Public Opinion in 1945–1946 covering 12,000 cases. Reported in Liston Pope, "Religion and the Class Structure," *Annals of the American Academy of Political and Social Sciences*, 256:84–91, March, 1948.

Most religious groups are highly conscious of how they differ from other groups in religious doctrines and practices, but are less aware that they also differ in social class, nationality, and racial and regional background. As is shown in Table 13, Protestant denominations not only differ from Catholics and Jews but differ greatly from one another in class composition. Data of this type are seldom available. A sampling study by the Survey Research Bureau of The University of Michigan in 1957 [Lazerwitz, 1964] found that the relative position of denominations in terms of education and occupation was comparable to those indicated for social class in the 1945–1946 study shown in Table 13. There are, however, many indications of accelerated social mobility by Roman Catholics, and it is possible that this church currently has a higher proportion of upper- and middle-class members than is indicated in these studies of a few years ago.

Differences in class background greatly influence a group's adjustment to economic life, and it is not surprising that ethnoreligious groups differ in their rate of social mobility. Jewish immigrants to the United States came from urban European backgrounds; they adapted easily to our urbanized, industrialized society and rapidly developed traits of upward mobility, although discrimination has made it difficult for them to reach the topmost rungs of the ladder. On the other hand, distinctive racial groups such as the Negroes and American Indians, along with distinctive cultural groups such as the French Canadians and the economically impoverished Southern whites, are retarded in social mobility. These groups are handicapped both by discrimination and by a background in a subsistence type of agriculture which has not developed the traits required for success in urban economic competition.

Both the successful climber and the derelict member of the "best" family are exceptions to the general association between group affiliation and class status. Top-status groups often feel that such persons are a threat to their group status, and react to this threat by a concerted effort to keep their members on top and to resist the advance of those from lower levels. For example, in exclusive Grosse Pointe, Michigan, the Grosse Pointe Property Owners'

Association and the local real estate brokers had in operation for many years an elaborate screening program for new residents. Such items as occupational status, way of living, American-sounding name, swarthy complexion, flashy dress, and many others were measured on a 100-point scale. Prospective purchasers needed a minimum score of 50 to pass. Southern Europeans had to score 65, and Jews, 85, with no passing scores at all for Negroes and Orientals [*Time,* Apr. 25, 1960; *New York Times,* Apr. 24, 1960]. Ironically, several of Detroit's leading gangsters had "passed," although it is unlikely that Jesus Christ would have been acceptable. Probably Grosse Pointe was only doing systematically what most other exclusive residential areas do informally. When the high-status group is comparatively small in numbers, it may make a vigorous effort to see that all its members either pláy upper-class roles or else are removed from public view. Thus, during the American control of the Philippines, American citizenship conferred high social status since Americans had political, economic, and educational prestige. Some Americans, however, were either unable or unwilling to play the role expected of an upper-class group; they became itinerant laborers who were often involved in petty crime and alcoholism and, most disturbing of all, often associated with lower-class Filipinos on an equal-status basis. Such Americans were encouraged to accept free transportation back to the United States, where they would not disturb the status image of Americans abroad.

All upper-class groups find their popular image threatened by members whose downward social mobility has made them *déclassé.* At times an upper-class group may be able to conceal their black sheep from public view. In parts of South and Central America or the Pacific Island areas where living is inexpensive and pleasant, the "remittance man" is a familiar figure. He is usually an European who has failed to fill the upper-class role acceptably and who is sent a monthly income by his family on condition that he get lost. Often an upper-class family will maintain its unsuccessful members in an upper-status role by the support of trust funds along with family advice and supervision. If the unsuccessful group is too large, these measures are impractical, and the amount of downward mobility may be too great to be concealed. One interesting example of this situation is found in the Union of South Africa, where the advocates of white superiority have been embarrassed by the presence of several thousand "poor whites." In spite of their alleged biological superiority, these people live on a plane little better than that of the "black" industrial laborers and considerably below that of the most mobile part of the black population. Recent industrial expansion has given the poor whites new opportunity, but a considerable number still remain as a visible contradiction of the notion that there is a natural link between a white skin and high social status [Robertson, 1957, pp. 45–48].

Just as the status of a group is diluted by the downward mobility of its members, so it is weakened by the upward mobility of outsiders. If the Brahmin must share high occupational status with those of lower caste, then the importance of being a Brahmin is no longer so great as when his group had a monopoly of high-status occupations. In a static society the caste rules made it exceedingly difficult for the low-caste members to enter prestige occupations. High-prestige occupations were reserved for the upper castes, just as American society has had Negro jobs and white jobs. It is good for the lower-status person to be hard-working; but when he gets "out of his place," he threatens the status of those who regard the top levels as their private preserve.

When an ethnoreligious group is forced to share high economic status with a different group, it may still resist the entry of the newcomers into other upper-class relationships. Thus Jews often find that entry into exclusive clubs is denied them because, although they have enough money, they belong to the wrong ethnic group. Or the New England Yankees may be forced to share economic and political leadership with Irish and Italians but still maintain social events from which these out-groups are excluded. The out-group member finds that certain economic advantages usually go to members of the in-group; and if he is successful in circumventing these barriers to economic advance, he still finds a lack of complete social acceptance in the upper strata. If the differences between the group affiliations of the new rich and those already established are slight, they eventually become assimilated in upper-class society. When the differences are based on sharply variant cultural practices or on recognizable physical features, then a long-established ethnoreligious group may be able to block the complete acceptance of the new recruits for a long time.

THE PROCESS OF SOCIAL MOBILITY

The American dream tells each young person to hope for a higher status and a better life than his parents. The emphasis seems to be on higher status more than upon money, for many a skilled workman takes pride in a son who enters schoolteaching at a salary less than he would earn as a skilled workman. This accent on status is revealed in a study of workers in automobile factories, which described them as prosperous but dissatisfied [Chinoy, 1952]. In terms of income and possessions they had done far better than their parents would have thought possible. The parents of many of them had lived either in slum tenements or in rural shacks, while these men lived in neat suburban cottages with all the usual modern conveniences. The pay was good and supplemented by fringe benefits such as pensions, insurance, and medical-care plans. Their dissatisfaction was not directed at their compensation, but grew from a feeling that they had no chance to escape the category of semiskilled workers.

In other words, the lower class had been upgraded; but the American dream also implies that one has a chance to rise to higher-class status, and for these men that possibility seemed remote. Some protected their egos by exaggerating the significance of minor promotions within the plant, while others daydreamed about someday leaving the factory and starting their own businesses. In neither case, however, was there any real chance of a significant rise in occupational status. In another era an intelligent workman who had mastered mechanical skills might be steadily promoted through supervisory levels until he reached a position in top management; or if these roads were blocked, he might use his mechanical skills to start a shop of his own. Today's workers find that supervisory positions above the level of foreman are usually filled by college-trained specialists, and that routine assembly-line work does not even give them mechanical skills which may be used elsewhere; in fact, it usually provides no mechanical skill at all. This situation represents a "break in the skill hierarchy," meaning that one may move from unskilled to skilled labor and eventually become a foreman, but that beyond that point lie barriers which are difficult to pass without the proper educational qualifications. Thus we have not one occupational ladder, but two: One stops with foreman; the other begins with a college diploma and a job in the "executive-development program" and ends with the presidency. To leap from the top rung of the first to the bottom rung of the second is rarely possible.

While the break in the skill hierarchy has largely destroyed the stock-boy-to-president route, there are other roads to upward mobility. Education is more necessary to occupational mobility than before, but education is also more readily available than ever before in the United States. Scholarships and other institutionalized aids to the talented youth are available in considerable number. While large-scale manufacturing may offer the poor boy few chances for promotion from within, the multiplication of the service industries—sales and service, retail trade, recreation, resort industry, and many others—do offer opportunities to persons with talent and ambition, even though they may lack college degrees.

In some occupations, the status of the occupation itself has changed. Farming has historically included a very few upper-class planters or plantation owners, a moderate number of fairly prosperous middle-status farm owners, and a large number of marginal farmers and tenant farmers of low income and low status. Today we have fewer farmers, but the average farm is larger and more prosperous, its owner is better educated, and his status and living standards compare more favorably with those of urban residents. Between 1940 and 1959 the number of tenant-operated farms declined from 39 to 20 per cent of all farms. These tenant farmers have moved to town or city. Those who remain farmers today are likely to have higher status and income than farmers a generation ago, while many of those who have left the farm have found a job of higher status than the one they left. Other occupations have shown a similar change in the nature or grade of work involved and the status of the occupation.

Prospects for social mobility Are class lines growing more rigid and upward mobility more difficult? Sometimes we note the impressive present barriers to upward mobility, contrast them with a fictitious reconstruction of the past as an era of individualistic opportunity, and draw the conclusion that class lines have grown more rigid. The facts justify no such conclusion. Studies of corporate structure made two or three decades ago pointed toward an increasing concentration of wealth and a narrowing of opportunity [Berle and Means, 1932], but more recent studies find no greater concentration of big business wealth than fifty years ago [Litner, 1959]. Warner and Abegglen's [1955] study of corporation executives finds that the proportion of owners' or top executives' sons who are promoted to top executive positions has actually declined in the past generation. A *Wall Street Journal* study of new millionaires finds that many of them were poorly educated, foreign-born, and from humble families [*Wall Street Journal*, 1961]. Natalie Rogoff [1953, *a*] studied the occupational status of workers and their fathers in the years 1910 and 1940. She found that a high proportion of farmers' sons had become urban factory workers. Her conclusion was that it was about as easy to move from a low-status to a higher-status occupation in 1940 as in 1910. Goldstein [1955] studied occupational mobility in a Pennsylvania town between 1910 and 1950, finding that both upward and downward mobility increased steadily during that period. Several other studies have reached the same conclusion that social mobility in American society is not declining and probably is increasing [Sjoberg, 1951; Kolko, 1957; Lenski, 1958].

The prospects for social mobility depend upon the total number of openings in higher-status occupations and upon the barriers to their attainment by the lowly born. The need for an increasing number of individuals in higher-status occupations depends on changes in society which create more upper-class jobs and on the extent to which the upper-class parents produce enough children to fill these places. The need for personnel in high-status occupations in the United States has been growing, as shown in Figure 10. Meanwhile the high-income groups have had until recently a birth rate too low to replace themselves. This makes room for a good deal of upward occupational mobility.

Table 14 estimates the amount of occupational mobility which took place between 1920 and 1950, considering both the effect of differential birth rates and the change in the demand for personnel. It will be noted that professional persons failed to replace themselves and that farmers had a surplus of births beyond what was needed to maintain their number. At the same time the demand for professionals was growing, along with the demand for all other urban workers except unskilled laborers, while the number of people engaged in agriculture was declining. Thus the farm "baby crop" moves to the city, while many of both the ex-rural residents and those born in the city have a chance to move into higher-status occupations.

Table 14   Male occupational distributions in the United States, actual and expected, 1920 and 1950

Social-economic group	(1) Actual, 1920	(2) Reproduction rate	(3) Expected, 1950	(4) Actual, 1950	(5) Mobility
Professional persons	1,062,000	0.87	924,000	3,025,000	+ 2,101,000
Proprietors, managers, and officials					
Farmers	6,122,000	1.52	9,306,000	4,205,000	− 5,101,000
Others	2,635,000	0.98	2,582,000	4,391,000	+ 1,809,000
Clerks, salespeople, and kindred	3,491,000	0.98	3,421,000	5,345,000	+ 1,924,000
Skilled workers and foremen	5,469,000	1.22	6,672,000	7,917,000	+ 1,245,000
Semiskilled workers	4,371,000	1.18	5,158,000	9,153,000	+ 3,995,000
Unskilled workers					
Farm laborers	3,162,000	1.52	4,806,000	2,048,000	− 2,758,000
Others	6,494,000	1.35	8,767,000	5,582,000	− 3,185,000
Total	32,806,000	1.27	41,636,000	41,666,000	+11,074,000

SOURCE: Joseph A. Kahl, *The American Class Structure*, Holt, Rinehart and Winston, Inc., New York, 1953, p. 257.

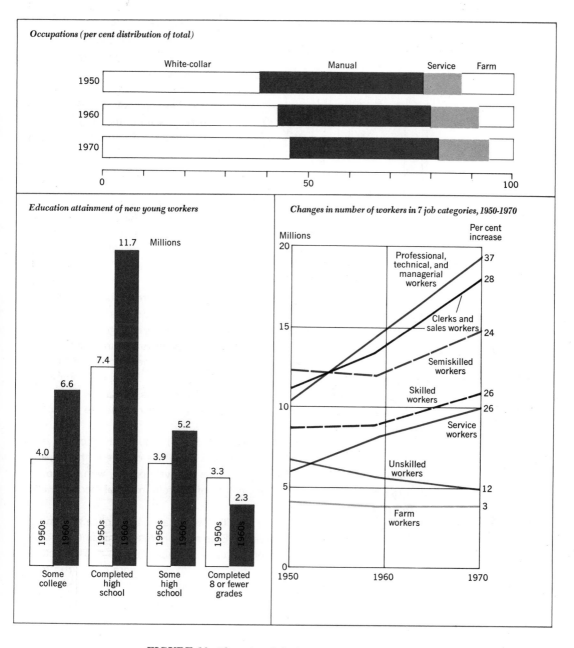

FIGURE 10 *Changing Job Opportunities Affect Prospects for Social Mobility.*
SOURCE: *Economic Growth in the 1960s*, The National Industrial Conference Board, New York, 1960, p. 11.

Social mobility includes all movement between social classes, either up or down. Kahl has compiled a table shown as Table 15, based on data from a nationwide survey of the National Opinion Research Council to show the percentage of people who moved up or down from the occupational status of their parents. Kahl [p. 263] concludes, "The upper levels have many new recruits from below, the semi-skilled level has recruits from above and below; . . . the

Social mobility probably is increasing.

unskilled group is recruited primarily from farm owners and laborers and secondarily from unskilled and semiskilled workers. Thus the bottom level has recruited from itself."

The development of automation is decreasing the demand for unskilled and semiskilled workers and for fine craftsmen, and is at the same time calling for a greater number of technicians capable of maintaining and coordinating complicated automatic machinery. This development is opening up a still larger number of higher-status positions, while still further decreasing the openings for the man who has little education or training. There will be a rapidly growing number of openings for graduate engineers and specialists of many sorts and for technicians with at least a high school or junior college education plus specialized technical training. Meanwhile the openings for unskilled laborers will continue their long-term decline. The youth who does poorly at school can no longer drop out and easily get a job. Conant [1961, p. 34] has commented on the social dynamite in slum neighborhoods where as high as 70 per cent of the boys and girls between the ages of sixteen and twenty-one are both out of school and out of work.

Although the absolute level of incomes of most groups has shown a rapid increase in the twentieth century, there has been little change in their *relative* position, except that the poor have become relatively poorer, with the bottom fifth receiving only about one-twenty-fifth of the total national income [Kolko, 1962, p. 14].

It is also possible that the route to skilled work via the apprentice system may yield a shrinking number of openings. Even now, apprenticeship in many crafts is closed to all but the sons or protegés of union members. The fact has prompted Conant [1961, p. 47] to remark: "It is far more difficult in many communities to obtain admission to an apprenticeship program which involves union approval than to get into the most selective medical school in the nation."

Formal education is, therefore, becoming more necessary for occupational advancement than ever before. This may be a barrier to some capable individuals who lack formal education, but the evidence indicates that higher education is open to a far larger proportion of the population than ever before. The situation is summarized by Dael Wolfle as follows:

In 1900 one youth out of every 60 graduated from college; now one in 8 does. . . . In 1900 nearly half of our college graduates trained for law, medicine, dentistry, or the ministry; now only 8% of the new graduates have prepared for traditional professions. In 1900 professional schools of education and of business were practically unknown; now more students graduate with specialized training in these fields than in any others.

Dael Wolfle, for the Commission on Human Resources and Advanced Training, *America's Resources of Specialized Talent,* Harper & Row, Publishers, Incorporated, New York, 1954, p. 24.

For many people the prospects for mobility are considerably brighter than they may appear to the frustrated automobile assembly-line workers cited a few pages earlier. Direct promotion from laborer to management may be blocked by educational requirements for managerial jobs, but a larger percentage of Americans than ever before is receiving advanced education and anticipating the possibilities for occupational advancement that may follow. While the frontier is gone and the number of farmers is diminishing, the expansion of business and the increase of technical and professional services are giving a chance for upward mobility to millions of Americans. Blind alleys have appeared in some lines and new hurdles to advancement have developed, but new opportunities have opened up along with opportunities for training. The net result of these changes would seem to be some increase in mobility, with the United States probably a more nearly open-class society today than it has been for several decades.

Channels of social mobility The availability of routes for social mobility depends both on the individual and on the structure of the society in which he lives. Individual ability is of little consequence when society allocates its rewards on the basis of ascribed status. On the other hand, an open society is of little help to the individual who is not equipped for a competitive struggle. Jews in the United States found barriers against many types of economic activity, but small business and the professions proved relatively open and have allowed this group to attain quickly an above-average prosperity. Irish immigrants found that their growing political power gave them opportunities for government jobs and that experience in construction work provided the knowledge essential for success in the contracting business. At an earlier date, immigrants found that the free land in the West offered opportunities more open than those they could discover in the

Table 15   *Upward and downward mobility in the United States°*

Social-economic group, 1950	Per cent who have			
	Moved up	Moved down	Remained	Total
Professional persons	77	—	23	*100*
Proprietors, managers, and officials, nonfarm	65	4	31	*100*
Clerks, salespeople, and kindred	53	32	15	*100*
Skilled workers and foremen	56	14	30	*100*
Semiskilled workers	43	38	19	*100*
Farmers and farm laborers	3	13	84	*100*
Unskilled workers, nonfarm	—	73	27	*100*

° National survey showing proportion of persons in each occupational group who have moved up, moved down, or stayed at the same occupational level as their fathers.
SOURCE: Joseph A. Kahl, *The American Class Structure,* Holt, Rinehart and Winston, Inc., New York, 1953, p. 263.

relatively closed urban communities. Negroes have found that opportunities were more open in government employment and in business and professional roles serving a largely Negro clientele. In traditional European and Latin American society, the hierarchy of the Roman Catholic Church and sometimes the army provided upward mobility for the poor but ambitious youth. Some competitive sports (professional boxing, football, baseball, basketball, but *not* polo, tennis, or golf) have usually been open to talented youth regardless of ethnic or social-class status and have usually been neglected by men from the more favored social strata.

In some societies the ambitious youth may find only one or two possible channels of mobility open to him; in others there may literally be hundreds of possible routes to higher social status. Some channels may be closed to the individual because of ethnic or social-class discrimination; others he may fail to perceive because of the limitations of his background or may be unable to utilize because his abilities have not been properly developed. This problem leads us to a consideration of the next topic: what techniques help one to make use of available mobility channels?

Techniques of social climbing

For the boy who wishes to elevate his social-class status, the prime essential is an education and an occupation which fit his class ambitions. For the girl, the problem is to snare the right husband, for her class status will ordinarily follow his. As already indicated, education, occupation, and income are the main factors which, operating over a period of time, will lift one's class status. There are, however, many ways for a skillful climber to speed up the mobility process.

Change in standard of living It is not enough merely to get and spend more money, for what one buys is more important than the amount one spends. To gain acceptance at a new status level, one must assume a material standard of living appropriate to that level. This means moving to an appropriate neighborhood, decorating one's house in an appropriate manner, driving a car which is neither too humble nor too ostentatious, and so on. The outward appearances must fit. After one is solidly established, he may ignore some of the appearances, especially at the upper-class level. The person whose secure upper-class status is beyond question can afford to drive a nondescript car and dress with a casual unconcern for fashion. But those who are on the way up must be careful about conformity to the pattern.

Cultivation of class-typed behavior The mobility-oriented person will not be fully accepted into a higher class until he has absorbed the behavior patterns of that class well enough to follow them without glaring errors over a considerable period of time. The time can be shortened by deliberate effort. The aspirant can study books on etiquette, read the magazines on home decoration, and consciously watch and copy the manners of those whose acceptance he craves. Patterns of dress, vocabulary and diction, recreational activities, reading interests—these can be overhauled and polished. The children can be given music and dancing lessons, and be sent to carefully chosen private schools and summer camps. It is true that not all aspects of a class subculture can be acquired through deliberate study and conscious imitation, but such efforts can speed up the process of acceptance.

Manipulation of associations If opportunities for social climbing were removed, many church organizations, civic associations, welfare societies, and other local associations would suffer a calamitous loss of membership. For how is the mobile person to meet and cultivate those who are a notch above him in social status? The very rich can engage a social secretary, part of whose task is to help them in the intricate art of social gamesmanship [Zorbaugh, 1929, pp. 55–56]. The new rich can even engage a professional service which is in the business of training the new rich in old rich behavior [Wakefield, 1961]. But the most useful device for social climbing is the association whose membership overlaps two or more class levels. The mobile person cultivates the highest-status members of an organization. Then he uses these friendships as levers to get himself into other higher-status organizations in which these friends are also members. Thus they climb, dropping out of the lower-status organizations as they gain admission to those of higher status [Chambers, 1954, pp. 384–406; Meeker, 1949; pp. 130–148]. The mobile Catholic can move to a better part of town, and thus transfer from a parish of lower-class members to a more aristocratic parish. The mobile Protestant may do likewise, or he may even switch to another denomination in which middle- or upper-class members are more numerous—from Church to God to Methodist, or from Methodist to Presbyterian. Church and welfare organizations are always in need of voluntary workers. A determined climber can easily find some whose members are worth cultivating. The informal clique, though perhaps harder to get into, is extremely useful because of its intimacy.

This, then, is the standard technique of the successful climber—to cultivate the upper-status members of one's cliques and associations, and use them to

FIGURE 11 *The Community is a Network of Overlapping Associations.*

The community is a network of associations or organizations whose membership may include persons at different class levels. Thus the organization helps persons to make social contacts across class lines. For the skillful manipulator, these associations are ladders of upward mobility, but few will climb more than one rung during a single lifetime.

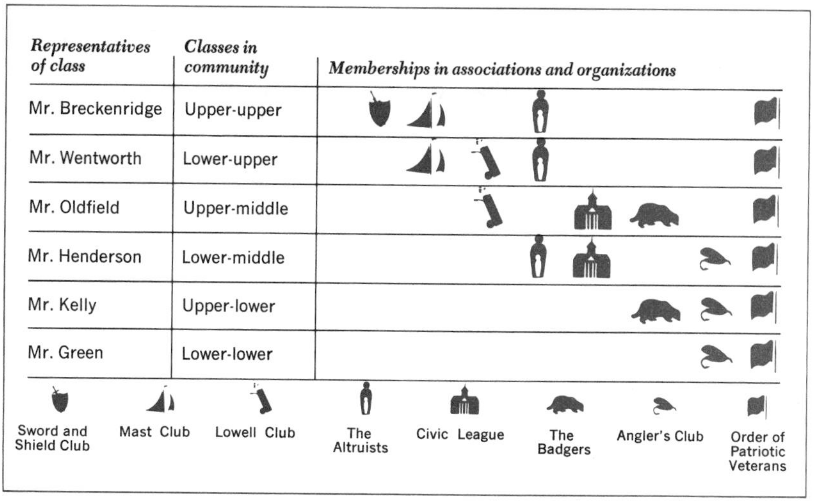

Representatives of class	Classes in community	Memberships in associations and organizations							
Mr. Breckenridge	Upper-upper	Sword and Shield Club	Mast Club		The Altruists				Order of Patriotic Veterans
Mr. Wentworth	Lower-upper		Mast Club	Lowell Club	The Altruists				Order of Patriotic Veterans
Mr. Oldfield	Upper-middle			Lowell Club		Civic League	The Badgers		Order of Patriotic Veterans
Mr. Henderson	Lower-middle				The Altruists	Civic League		Angler's Club	Order of Patriotic Veterans
Mr. Kelly	Upper-lower						The Badgers	Angler's Club	Order of Patriotic Veterans
Mr. Green	Lower-lower							Angler's Club	Order of Patriotic Veterans

Sword and Shield Club — Mast Club — Lowell Club — The Altruists — Civic League — The Badgers — Angler's Club — Order of Patriotic Veterans gain entrée into status groups in which one is not yet accepted. It takes a good deal of finesse to play this game. One must be socially perceptive, must learn quickly, and probably must have a certain amount of charm. Those who can play the game successfully achieve rapid mobility.

Marriage   People on the way up must be careful whom they marry. At the very least, they must choose a mate whose social finesse and learning abilities will not be a drag. At best, a "good" marriage is a priceless asset. By marrying into a family a notch or two above his, an ambitious youth gets a better opportunity to use his talents. He may get financial backing to complete an education or launch a business; he gets good connections and valuable introductions; he gets a wife who already fully understands the class culture he must absorb; he gets a powerful motive to "succeed" and prove himself worthy of his wife's confidence in him. A girl who "marries up" is not automatically accepted into her husband's social class, especially if the jump up has been a long one. Such marriages, however, are very rare. The upper-class college boy may romance the tavern maid, but he rarely marries her. Interclass marriages are generally between persons at adjacent class levels. Where the wife has the social finesse and learning ability to absorb the class culture quickly, she is likely to be accepted into her husband's social class with little difficulty.

When a woman "marries down," does she lose her class status? That depends upon him. If he soon gains the education, occupation, and income, and absorbs the class culture of her class level, he generally becomes accepted at her class level. But if he retains lower-status education, occupation, income, and behavior, she is likely to find that her old associates are forgetting her.

The celebrity: a special status   How about the famous baseball star or prizefighter who gets more newspaper space than all the nation's scientists combined? How about the singer or actor who zooms to wealth and fame, complete with swimming pool, press agent, and hordes of worshipful teeney-boppers? What is his social class status?

Celebrity status is a special kind of status, based on spectacular achievement, not upon one's total activities and behavior. The celebrity has a national public who follow his actions without ever knowing or interacting with him as a person. His social-class status would be measured by the status of those who would accept him, as a person, as their social equal, apart from his fame as a celebrity. President Roosevelt was clearly upper-class and President Truman just as clearly middle-class. Raymond Massey and Sir Cedric Hardwicke were members of the upper class before they became famous actors, and would remain so if they retired; many other famous actors and actresses came from lower-class backgrounds, and have never been accepted as upper-class, however much they have been feted as celebrities.

Since there are many wealthy celebrity chasers, the celebrity meets many upper-class persons at charity balls, house parties, and other occasions. But when he ceases to be a celebrity and becomes a "has-been," which people will accept and entertain him as a social equal? This selective treatment tells his true social-class status. Ex-Presidents and war-hero generals may always remain celebrities, but many other kinds of celebrities lose their claim to fame and descend to a humble status.

SOCIAL MOBILITY AND DEFERRED GRATIFICATION

So many aspects of life are determined by one's attitude toward social mobility that certain attitudes of the middle class, the most mobility-oriented group, have been grouped under the term *deferred gratification pattern* (abbreviated, DGP). This is simply the pattern of postponing immediate satisfactions in order to gain some later goal. You readers who are now studying this textbook, instead of playing poker or "goofing off," are practicing the DGP. The DGP may be described as a series of behavior tendencies of one who realizes that social mobility, either upward or downward, is a real probability in his life.

A deferment of present satisfactions.

Consequently, his attitudes and actions are guided by their supposed effect on his chances for upward social mobility. If the question is raised as to why this should be primarily a middle-class pattern, the answer may be that this is the group which can visualize the most gain from a deferment of present satisfactions for the sake of future gratification. The middle class has both the hope of reaching upper-class status and the fear of slipping into the abyss of lower-class torment. As for the other classes, their view of the life situation does not produce this type of anxiety. The upper class has arrived and feels secure. The lower class has already come close to hitting bottom, and unless converted to middle-class norms, sees little realistic basis for hope of status improvement. Thus both the top and bottom groups can enjoy whatever satisfactions are available in the present, while the middle class must always be planning with an eye to the future.

In this type of planning, any activity today is viewed from the question of its consequences for tomorrow. Marriage may be postponed until one has finished school and secured a job. Education is considered neither a luxury nor a bore but an investment in future prospects. Thrift will lay the basis for eventual economic power, and emotional control will permit eventual emotional satisfaction. Time is used for self-improvement instead of aimless relaxation. A good description of this pattern has been given by Schneider and Lysgaard.

Deferred gratification evidently refers to postponement of gratifications or satisfactions. . . . It may be contended that it does indeed fall into a pattern, characteristic of the so-called "middle class," members of which tend to delay achievement of economic independence through a relatively elaborate process of education, tend to defer sexual gratification through intercourse, show a relatively marked tendency to save money, and the like. . . . [An] important point is the normative character of the deferred gratification pattern. Middle-class persons feel that they should save, postpone, and renounce a variety of gratifications. There are very probably also normative elements in the "lower-class" pattern of non-deferment. Thus, Whyte notes that one of the important divergences between the social mobility pattern and the corner-boy activity pattern in Cornerville appears in matters involving expenditure of money. The college boys save money for educational purposes or to launch business or professional careers. But the corner boys must share their money with others and avoid middle-class thrift. Should a corner boy have money and his friend not have it, he is expected to spend for both. The corner boy may be thrifty, but, if so, he cannot hope to hold a high position in the corner gang.

Louis Schneider and Sverre Lysgaard, "The Deferred Gratification Pattern: A Preliminary Study," *American Sociological Review*, 18:142–149, April, 1953.

Evidence that the DGP really exists is found in several research reports [Rosen, 1956; McArthur, 1955; Kluckhohn, 1950; Kahl, 1953; Straus, 1962; Phillips, 1966]. Thus in a study of 2,500 high school students who classified themselves as "middle class" or "working class," the middle-class students showed many traits of the DGP. For the working-class youth, physical violence both among themselves and in adult associations was more common, occupational goals were lower, more youth expected to leave school before completing high school, and both the youth and their parents gave less emphasis to saving money [Schneider and Lysgaard, 1953]. Other studies have shown a relationship between the postponement of sexual gratification and middle-class status. Kinsey, in his study of the sex life of the American male, came to the conclusion that early sexual intercourse was a routine part of growing up for the lower-class male but a breach of the mores for the males of higher social status. In fact, he concluded that the lower-class boy who had not had sex relations by the age of sixteen was either a physical or mental defective or a middle-class convert "earmarked for moving out of his community and going to college." [1948, p. 381]. Lower-class youth also marry at earlier ages than middle- or upper-class youth [Glick and Landau, 1950]. In all areas of life the lower-class emphasis is on immediate satisfaction rather than waiting for the rewards of a doubtful future.

Why does the lower class so seldom defer gratification? Possibly because the insecurity of the lower-class world places so much pressure for immediate survival that deferring gratification now for the sake of rewards in the future seems both futile and difficult. Allison Davis describes the pressures of lower-class life:

The actual daily pressure of 5 to 10 hungry stomachs to fill, backs to clothe, and feet to cover forces the working-class parent to reduce his ambitions to the level of subsistence; to lower his sights as far as long-term planning and studying for better jobs and for finer skills are concerned; to narrow, limit, and shorten his goals with regard to the care, nutrition, education and careers of his childen.

This terrible pressure for physical survival means that the child in the average working-class family does not learn the "ambition," the drive for high skills, and for educational achievement that the middle-class child learns in his family. The working-class individual usually does not learn to respond to these strong incentives and to seek these difficult goals, because they have been submerged in his family life by the daily battle for food, shelter, and for the preservation of the family. In this sense, ambition and the drive to attain the higher skills are a kind of luxury. They require a minimum physical security; only when one knows where his next week's or next month's food and shelter will come from, can he and his children afford to go in for the long-term education and training, the endless search for opportunities, and the tedious apple polishing that the attainment of higher skills and occupational status require.

Allison Davis, "The Motivation of the Underprivileged Worker," in William F. Whyte (ed.), *Industry and Society*, McGraw-Hill Book Company, New York, 1946, p. 89. See also S. M. Miller and Frank Riessman, "The Working Class Subculture: A New View," *Social Problems*, 9:86–97, Summer, 1961.

The conditions of lower-class life inspire, not an acceptance of the DGP with redoubled efforts for advancement, but apathy or revolt. Older people are apt to surrender to a fatalistic view that nothing can be done and that they can only accept their status while taking advantage of any opportunities for momentary enjoyment that come their way. Cooperation cushions the shock of insecurity; as long as one's friends or relatives have money, one can eat. Younger people are more apt to revolt. This revolt often takes the form of juvenile delinquency; through fighting, sexual adventure, and theft, it provides the excitement and prestige among their peers that they cannot easily get in any other manner.

These attitudes are hard for middle-class people to understand. They reject fatalism, insisting that the individual can, at least to some extent, control his own destiny; they reject the notion that one should take care of improvident friends; and they prize the reputation associated with good conduct. For these reasons lower-class conduct seems either immoral or inexplicable. The lower-class convert to middle-class standards who accepts the DGP is considered good, while those who retain a lower-class outlook are thought to be lacking in character and undeserving of sympathy or assistance.

INDIVIDUAL COSTS OF SOCIAL MOBILITY

The idea that social mobility is good is part of our democratic ethos. We argue that a closed-class society thwarts the fulfillment of individual personality and deprives society of the contributions of many talented people.

Whether a society suffers because of limited mobility may depend upon its level of complexity. In a somewhat more simple society, such as existed in eighteeth-century Europe or America, very few roles could not be adequately filled by anyone of average ability, providing he were identified and prepared for his role from early childhood. Likewise, in a stable, unchanging society, the leadership roles, which consist mainly in carrying out the traditional rites and procedures, call for careful training rather than outstanding ability. A closed-class system is probably an asset to the simpler, more stable societies. It guarantees that most roles will be filled adequately, without wasting any talent really needed by the society.

A rapidly changing society, however, requires more of its leaders than an ability to preside over the traditional rituals. And a technologically advanced society requires vast numbers of highly intelligent, highly educated professionals, technicians, and experts. Such a society is less able to afford the waste of any of its brains. A fairly open class system may, therefore, be a necessity for "modern" society. Necessary though it may be, the open-class system has its penalties. In several ways, it exacts its price from those who compete within it.

Status insecurity   The medieval cobbler had little chance of rising but little danger of falling. He could be comfortable as a cobbler, free from the prod of ambition or the sting of failure. He could find fulfillment in his work without indignity or shame, and could enjoy his humble possessions and simple comforts without coveting the luxuries he was not encouraged to long for.

An open-class system grants man a chance to rise but charges him with the fear of failure. He cannot blame society for his lowly status but must shoulder this responsibility himself. There is no guarantee that he will not drop below his ancestral status, but even if he retains it, the retention does not mean that he has fulfilled his social obligations. His obligation is not merely to maintain his status but to improve it. Other men of lowly origin have reached high status. Why doesn't he?

This status anxiety is greatest in the middle class. The upper class has no need to struggle for higher status, and no great fear of losing it. At the lowest class level, few see much more hope of status gain, and few struggle to climb. But those at some intermediate status level feel a stronger desire for further status gain, and a greater fear of status loss.

Some men in an open-class society respond to the challenge and make rapid advancement; some are so demoralized that they seek escape in drink, narcotics, sex, or other distraction. Many try to protect themselves by supporting institutional arrangements to limit free social mobility. Perhaps the best example of this is seen in trade union, civil service, and business policies which place a premium on seniority as a basis for promotion. As long as one conforms to minimum standards and "keeps his nose clean," he is in line for a gradual advancement which depends less upon his own ability than upon the health of the man ahead of him and the number of new openings created by the growth of the enterprise. Funeral by funeral, he works his way up the seniority ladder. Some men chafe under the restrictions of the seniority system, but many prefer a slower rate of promotion if it will blunt the rigors of open competition.

Strain of new role adjustments   Upward mobility not only carries new privileges; it also carries new responsibilities and restrictions. Occasionally a man declines an offered promotion because he shrinks from the added responsibilities it carries. "Nervous breakdowns" among recently promoted executives are not uncommon.

Since social classes are subcultures, upward mobility requires the unlearning and relearning of a great many minor role adjustments. An interminable list of patterns of speech, dress, food preference, table manners, etiquette, recreation, and so on must be revised to fit one's new class status. One study [Hacker, 1962] reports a 50 per cent higher rate of heart symptoms among a group of young executives of working-class origin, as compared with a control group

Occasionally a man declines an offered promotion.

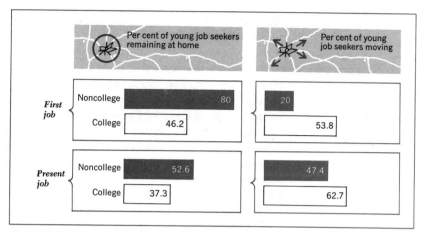

FIGURE 12 *Social Mobility Often Requires Geographical Mobility.*

SOURCE: Paul H. Landis, "The Territorial and Occupational Mobility of Washington Youth," *Agricultural Experiment Station Bulletin, 499*, Pullman, Washington, July, 1944.

of young executives of middle-class origin. The strain of such adjustments is seldom appreciated by one who has not needed to make them.

Disruption of primary-group relationships Among the student readers of this book will be many mobility-oriented students who are already becoming estranged from their parents. If their parents are working-class people of limited formal education, these students find that they are moving into a different social and intellectual world. On their successive visits home, they are finding fewer and fewer topics on which they can talk comfortably with their parents. Many parents sacrifice to help their children rise above their own position, only to watch sadly as their children become strangers to them. For both, the experience is painful.

Another point of strain comes from the tendency of social mobility to be correlated with geographic mobility, as is suggested in Figure 12. Contrary to the adage that "a rolling stone gathers no moss," the person who remains in his home town is less apt to reach the top of any occupational pinnacle. The life story of ambitious persons usually includes migration to another location for education or apprenticeship, a move to an outlying area to obtain experience, and then a move to the metropolis when he is considered ready to assume major responsibilities. At another level, the man on a run-down farm in New England, the laborer in a Puerto Rican village, or an Arkansas hill dweller must move to more industrialized areas if he wishes to improve his opportunities.

This frequent movement means that it is difficult to develop roots in the neighborhood and that one is constantly changing the circle of family friends and making new arangements with schools, churches, and local business establishments. The old family home, the familiar neighborhood, the friends of one's childhood—all these give way to a moving equilibrium of adjustment to new roles, new friends, and new places. The gain is excitement, novelty, and stimulation. The loss is reflected in brittle and temporary relationships which often lead to an ultimate loneliness and isolation. Indeed, one study [Hollingshead et al., 1954] suggests that mental illness may sometimes be the price for either upward or downward social mobility, and another [Ellis, 1952] finds an abnormally high rate of psychosomatic disorders among a group of upwardly mobile career women.

Even the marriage of the mobile couple is sometimes threatened. Often the two mates are not equally interested in mobility, or they may differ in their ability to learn the new role adjustments. One mate resents the implied insult of being constantly prodded, polished, and improved; the other resents his mate's lack of cooperation. The successful man who sheds the wife of his youth for a more cultivated partner is a familiar figure among the status seekers.

Other primary-group associates may also be sacrificed. One's easy camaraderie with his friends and fellow workers is threatened when he gains greater authority and income with the prospect of still further promotions. The wife of a major general recently remarked to the author, "I don't know who my friends are any more." Her friendships were now polite and correct, rather than relaxed and genuine. Many enlisted men in the army made no effort to gain officer status for fear it would alienate them from their "buddies" in the ranks; factory workmen sometimes hesitate to become foremen for similar reasons. Friendship under such circumstances may become "status-adulterated," in that those beneath him bootlick him while he bootlicks his superiors. In such a setting all motives become suspect, and genuine friendship may be a dim memory of the happier days before one had begun to climb the ladder of occupational success.

The other side of the picture is that upward mobility not only disrupts established social relationships but it may select those most willing to see such relationships disrupted. The person who leaves his home town, his friends, and his family in pursuit of fortune is often one who is dissatisfied with his primary-group associations and feels a need to escape from the surroundings of his childhood [Warner and Abegglen, 1955, pp. 80–81]. In this sense the boy who makes good is a social deviant who has left behind the attitudes and the associations he might normally have been expected to form in the process of growing up. Such a revolt against the standards of the social class of one's family may even be stimulated by parents who pass on to their children the standards they value but have been unable to attain. The father who left school in the middle of the eighth grade may urge his son to prepare himself for a professional career, and the mother who married early may encourage her daughter to complete college before marrying. Apparently there are two types of mobility-oriented children: those who identify with mobility-oriented parents and those who reject their static or downwardly mobile parents [Reusch, 1953]. In any case, the "middle-class convert" will experience a shift of attitudes and associations which will probably be even more drastic than that involved in the process of religious conversion or of changed citizenship. The fact that many social-class differences are subtle rather than pronounced makes the process all the more difficult, since the individual must be sensitive to nuances which are not easily recognizable. The shift from one class to another is a socially disruptive process which is easier for those who are already disenchanted with their pattern of life and anxious to make a complete break with the past.

Is a high rate of social mobility worth the cost? If a complex, changing society does not permit upward mobility to the talented and ambitious, it runs the risk of turning them into rebels and revolutionaries. The weakness of radical and revolutionary movements in the United States is generally attributed to our open-class system; if one has good prospects of self-advancement within the existing social order, why overthrow it? Thus a high rate of social mobility may tend to stabilize a social order by providing an encouraging outlet to talented persons who are dissatisfied with their social status. At the same time, a high rate of social mobility may tend to undermine traditions and develop in the old a cranky conservatism. It may lead to a contempt for "honest toil" and a drive for the "fast buck," and lead to anomie for persons who move rapidly through a succession of statuses and roles [Tumin, 1957]. But the question of whether mobility is good or bad is irrelevant, for a relatively open class system appears to be necessary and inevitable in a rapidly changing, technologically advanced society.

SUMMARY

Social mobility refers to movement up or down in social status. This usually involves a change in occupation. Differential reproduction rates and expanding industry offer a continuous chance for occupational advancement and social mobility; they are probably at least as great in the United States now as in earlier years. Some European countries also have considerable social mobility; in others the rate has been held down by the fact that a slower trend toward industrialization leaves a larger part of the population in rural areas. The under-developed countries are entering a period of industrialization which increases social mobility, but the amount of mobility in these countries is still less than in more industrialized areas. Mobility in the United States has been hampered by a trend toward rigid educational requirements in the proportion of youth gradu-ating from high school and college. Both societies and ethnic groups vary in the number of channels of mobility open to their members. Channels may be re-stricted by the limited technological development of the society, discrimination against an ethnic or social-class group, failure of perception, and lack of de-velopment of the necessary personal qualities.

A society in which people are ranked strictly according to individual ability and performance is known as an *open-class* society; one in which status is theoretically based strictly on heredity is known as a *closed-class* or *caste* society. No class system is entirely open or closed. Modern industrial societies tend toward the open-class system; traditional agricultural societies often develop caste or estate systems which restrict social mobiilty. Ethnic and reli-gious membership to a certain extent still affects class position. Negro-white relationships in the United States are often cited as a caste situation, although the class differences within each caste make the caste-class concept and designation more useful.

While a change in occupation is the crucial step in social mobility, the process may be speeded by: (1) revising one's standard of living, (2) cultivating class-typed modes of behavior, (3) manipulating associational memberships, or (4) a strategic marriage. The celebrity enjoys a special kind of status which gains him admittance to upper-class groups as long as he remains a celebrity.

Upward mobility is aided by a time perspective, most often found in the middle class, known as the *deferred gratification pattern*. The lower class tends to reject this pattern in favor of immediate gratification, whereas the upper class has a continuing status security that makes the deferment of gratification seem unnecessary. Lower-class norms are often regarded as immoral or pathological by middle-class critics, but have value in helping individuals adjust to the insecurities of life in the lower-class environment. Mobility brings new opportunities and greater outlets for potential ability, but it also brings emotional strains and threatens patterns of friendship, residence, and family ties. Those who are not firmly integrated into the social-class setting of their parental home appear to be most adaptable to the changes which make mobility possible. While bringing strain into the life of individuals, a high rate of social mobility may stabilize the social order, since discontented individuals may turn their energies to seeking personal advancement rather than to social revolution. High mobility may have certain other unapplauded consequences.

QUESTIONS AND PROJECTS

1. Why is it that persons at the very top of the status ladder often spend less freely and put up less "front" than many persons who are a level or two beneath them?

2. Distinguish between caste, class, and estate. Is there any caste aspect to stratification in the United States? How does the caste-class concept explain status variations in the United States?

3. What advantages and disadvantages does a closed-class system hold for a society? For the individual? Do you know of any deliberate attempts to decrease competition for status in the United States?

4. What advantages and disadvantages does an open-class system hold for a society? For the individual? What makes absolute equality of opportunity impossible?

5. Do you consider yourself to be highly mobility-oriented? What factors do you think explain your own mobility orientation?

6. Assume that a lower-class and a middle-class person each wins an unexpected $10,000 prize. How would you expect each to use this money? Relate your answer to the concept of the deferred gratification pattern.

7. Assume that higher education should become completely free of all costs and that all jobs were filled strictly on merit without regard to family connections. Would you expect the same proportion of lower- and middle-class youth to reach high-status positions? Why or why not?

8. Why do upward-mobile persons usually drift away from their relatives and old friends? Is the tendency due to snobbishness?

9. Is marriage while in college an aid or a threat to the student's prospects for social mobility? Will his social mobility become a threat to his marriage?

10. Read *A Tree Grows in Brooklyn*, by Betty Smith. What factors account for Francie's rejection of the slum subculture and her desire to escape it? Did she escape through luck or through her own efforts?

11. Analyze a pledge list in a fraternity or sorority in terms of those you would label socially mobile as contrasted to those who are simply maintaining the family status. Describe any contrasts between the personality traits of the socially mobile and the stationary pledges.

12. Describe the groups in your community characterized by the most rapid and least rapid rate of upward mobility. On the basis of present trends in both of these groups, attempt to predict their relative position fifty years hence.

SUGGESTED READINGS

BENDIX, REINHARD, AND SEYMOUR MARTIN LIPSET: *Social Mobility in Industrial Society*, University of California Press, Berkeley, Calif., 1959. Pulls together and analyzes material from a large number of empirical studies.

CHILMAN, CATHERINE S: "Child-rearing and Family Relationship Patterns of the Very Poor," *Welfare in Review,* 3:9–17, January, 1965. A consideration of the "cycle of poverty" indicating the mobility handicaps of the lowest income group.

ELLIS, EVELYN: "Upward Social Mobility among Unmarried Career Women," *American Sociological Review,* 17:558–563, October, 1952. A discussion of some of the effects of social mobility on personality.

HOLLINGSHEAD, A. B., R. ELLIS, AND E. KIRBY: "Social Mobility and Mental Illness," *American Sociological Review,* 19:577–584, October, 1954. Analysis of the strains of social mobility and their effect on mental health.

KANE, JOHN: *Catholic-Protestant Conflicts in America,* Henry Regnery Company, Chicago, 1955, chap. 5, "The Social Structure of American Catholics." An analysis of social status and mobility among American Catholics.

PHILLIPS, DEREK L.: "Deferred Gratification in a College Setting: Some Gains and Costs," *Social Problems,* 13:333–343, Winter, 1966. A study of deferred gratification in the college setting the results of which may be distorted by the fact that most college students probably practice some degree of deferred gratification.

SCHNEIDER, LOUIS, AND SVERRE LYSGAARD: "The Deferred Gratification Pattern: A Preliminary Study,"

American Sociological Review, 18:142–149, April, 1953; Bobbs-Merrill reprint S-250. A comprehensive periodical treatment of this topic.

*SOROKIN, PITIRIM: *Social and Cultural Mobility,* Harper & Row, Publishers, Incorporated, New York, 1927. A monumental study of social mobility in a variety of social systems and time periods. (93028 FreeP)

STRAUS, MURRAY A.: "Deferred Gratification, Social Class and the Achievement Syndrome," *American Sociological Review,* 27:326–335, June, 1962. A study of the relationship between social class and acceptance of the deferred gratification pattern.

TUMIN, MELVIN J.: "Some Unapplauded Consequences of Social Mobility in a Mass Society," *Social Forces,* 36:21–37, October, 1957; Bobbs-Merrill reprint S-294. Argues that social mobility imposes many personal and social costs upon a society.

WARNER, W. LLOYD, AND PAUL S. LUNT: *The Social Life of a Modern Community,* Yale University Press, New Haven, Conn., 1941. Description of social class and social mobility in a New England factory town. Chap. 7, "Profiles of Yankee City," is again especially recommended.

WILENSKY, HAROLD, AND HUGH EDWARDS: "The Skidder," *American Sociological Review,* 24:215–231, April, 1959. Analysis of the social attitudes of the downwardly mobile.

Four # SOCIAL INTERACTION

Part Four decribes some of the characteristic ways in which people treat one another. Chapter 13, "Social Processes," describes some fairly standardized types of interaction which appear in some form in most societies. Chapter 14, "Social Power," delineates the types of power and its use by different social groups. Chapter 15, "Race and Ethnic Relations," shows how facts and feelings about race enter into people's treatment of one another. Chapter 16, "Collective Behavior," analyzes a variety of forms of behavior in which the element of group encouragement and protection is especially important.

13

SOCIAL PROCESSES

The background of partition [of India and Pakistan] is long and involved. It was the culmination of more than a century of dual struggle—the struggle for national independence against England, and the struggle for power inside India between Hindu and Moslem. . . .

And in those early days of uncertainty and confusion people became panicky. Whatever the animosity had been between Hindu and Moslem before Independence, the people had managed to live side by side. With partition, however, millions of people suddenly became jittery and insecure. A Hindu who lived in a city near the border like Lahore wondered what was to happen to him now that Lahore was to become a part of Pakistan. A Moslem who lived on the outskirts of Calcutta wondered what was to happen now that there would be a separate Moslem government in Pakistan that did not include him. The insecurity and confusion became multiplied as millions of people decided to move in order to be governed by their own group.

Then came violence. At first there were only sporadic incidents. A Moslem in Dacca, for example, would smash the shopwindows of a clothing store owned by a Hindu, claiming he had heard that Hindus were looting Moslem shops in Calcutta or Delhi. A Hindu in Calcutta would set fire to a Moslem home, in open view of a crowd, yelling that he had heard that Moslems were burning homes of Hindus who remained behind in Dacca or Karachi. Some Hindus or Moslems would try to take advantage of the national turmoil by seizing business properties or homes.

Each incident, of course, fed on rumors and begat even greater rumors. Outrages were carried out in the name of retaliation. Soon a civil war without battle-lines or armies raged throughout the sub-continent. People rushed through the streets with sticks or torches or whatever could be used to kill a man. (Norman Cousins, ''Where Violence Begins,'' Saturday Review, Jan. 18, 1954, pp. 22ff.)

ERE WE HAVE an example of conflict—one of the social processes. What are social processes, and what is their importance?

THE NATURE OF SOCIAL PROCESSES

The term, *social processes*, refers to *repetitive forms of behavior which are commonly found in social life*. One of the most extensive treatments of social process is found in Park and Burgess, *Introduction to the Science of Sociology* [1921]. This highly influential textbook of an earlier period is primarily devoted to the classification and analysis of social processes. In recent decades sociologists have become less interested in social processes themselves and more intereted in the intensive analysis of behavior in specific institutional and cultural settings. Yet it still remains important for the student to be aware of the major social processes to be found in all groups and all societies. The most frequent classification of the major social processes is in terms of *cooperation, competition, conflict, accommodation,* and *assimilation*. These social processes apply to both individuals and groups. This chapter also includes two other social processes which apply only to groups—*boundary maintenance and systemic linkage*.

Social processes and value judgments

In the first part of the twentieth century, scholars engaged in heated arguments as to the relative importance of cooperation and competition in the natural world. Those who said that competition was the law of the universe often quoted Darwin's statement that evolution had been determined by a struggle for existence in which the strongest survived while the weaker were eliminated. Taking the name of "Social Darwinists," they argued that human life was also perfected by struggle and that philanthropy worked against the perfection of the race by allowing the unfit to survive [Simpson, 1959]. This theory was in turn attacked by Prince Kropotkin [1925] in his book *Mutual Aid*. Kropotkin used the works of Professor Kessler as his rationale for arguing that even the animal world was not one of unlimited conflict and that if humans were looking for biological analogies, they could find significant examples of cooperation in the realm of nature.

I obviously do not deny the struggle for existence, but I maintain that the progressive development of the animal kingdom, and especially of mankind, is favored much more by mutual support than by mutual struggle.... All organic beings have two essential needs: that of nutrition and of propagating the species. The former brings them to a struggle and mutual extermination, while the needs of maintaining the species bring them to approach one another and to support one another. But I am inclined to think that in the evolution of the organic world—in the progessive modification of organic beings—mutual support among individuals plays a much more important part than mutual struggle.

Statement of Kessler in *Memoirs of the St. Petersburg Society of Naturalists*, cited in Peter Kropotkin, *Mutual Aid*, Alfred A. Knopf, Inc., New York, 1925, p. 16.

Kropotkin added that while struggle exists between species, within species the dominant social process is cooperation, as is seen in flocks of birds, herds of buffalo, colonies of ants, and other group formations in the animal world.

Hence he argued that those species which have survived are precisely those which have developed the process of mutual aid to the highest degree.

Today the philosophical argument about the relative merits of cooperation and conflict has somewhat subsided. Few people are interested in abstract arguments about the superiority of the cooperative or the competitive way of life. But today all face the difficulties of cooperation in a society dominated by secondary groups and the perils of conflict in an age threatened by atomic destruction. The new problems may have renewed men's interest in the sociological analysis of these topics. In fact, one recently founded magazine bears the title, *Journal of Conflict Resolution.*

COOPERATION

Cooperation is derived from two Latin words, *co* meaning *together* and *operari* meaning *to work.* It may be formally defined as *joint activity in pursuit of common goals or shared rewards.* Cooperation may be found in groups as small as the dyad (group of two persons) and as large as the United Nations. Forms of cooperative endeavor in primitive societies are usually traditional and are acted out without any conscious design. Trobriand islanders do not "decide" to fish cooperatively; they just go fishing as their fathers always did. The more technologically advanced cultures often carry out elaborate plans for deliberate cooperative activities. Cooperation implies a regard for the wishes of other people and is often regarded as unselfish, but men may also find that their selfish goals are best served by working together with their fellows [Bogardus, 1946].

Deliberate primary-group cooperation Cooperation by members of small groups is so common in our society that the life history of most individuals may be written largely in terms of their attempts to become a part of such groups and to adjust to the demands of cooperative group life. Even the most ardent individualist will find that much of his life satisfaction arises from the give and take in the family, recreation groups, and work associates. The need for cooperation in these activities is so much taken for granted that we sometimes forget that the enjoyment of a stable group experience depends largely upon one's ability to enter comfortably into cooperative relationships. The person who cannot cooperate easily and successfully is likely to be isolated and perhaps maladjusted.

Deliberate primary group cooperation.

Not only is primary-group cooperation important in itself, but it is closely related to secondary-group cooperation. Most large organizations are networks of smaller primary groups in which cooperation functions on a face-to-face basis involving many highly personal relationships.

Deliberate secondary-group cooperation   When we think of cooperation, we often have in mind the kind engaged in deliberately by secondary groups. Consumer and producer cooperatives are an example. Consumer cooperatives are organizations of consumers which operate wholesale and retail stores and divide the profits (usually called "patronage dividends") among their members in proportion to their purchases. One form of consumers' cooperative, the credit union, pools the savings of members to form a loan fund handled on a similar basis. Members are paid the going rate of interest for their savings and are able to borrow funds at a set rate of interest, with rebates being divided among borrowers when a margin is available. Producers' cooperatives are most frequently used in the marketing of agricultural produce. Groups of farmers hope to eliminate the profits made by commercial middlemen through establishing their own warehouses and selling channels. Neither consumer nor producer cooperatives try to "undersell" other business concerns; they do business at competitive prices, then distribute profits among members in proportion to their purchases from, or sales to, the cooperative.

In the Scandinavian countries and in England, such cooperatives do a major proportion of the total business in the country. In the United States they handle only a small fraction of the total business but are highly important in dairy and fruit farming, and consumer co-ops are strong in some areas. Scandinavian immigrants have carried this pattern with them to the United States, and cooperatives seem to be strongest where a cohesive ethnic group regards them as a traditional part of the culture [Kercher et al., 1941].

As is true of all types of social interaction, the success of cooperatives seems to depend to a great degree on the culture of the area. Oddly enough, the most fertile ground for cooperatives seems to be a society in which there has already been a strong development of private business. In these areas cooperatives have often survived both capitalist competition and governmental discouragement. In underdeveloped areas cooperatives have had great difficulty in spite of the fact that they have often received governmental help [Hart, 1955]. In these areas the conduct of business is totally outside the experience of most of the people, and the middleman is usually an alien who is barred from participation in cooperative activity. As a result, even when the cooperative has had a government subsidy, it often has failed through corruption, mismanagement, or inability to repay loans. Cooperatives can succeed without governmental encouragement, but they rarely succeed unless the culture has familiarized the people with the practices essential to carrying on economic life in a market economy.

These "cooperatives" are but one of many forms of large-scale cooperative activity. The desire of people to work together for common goals is expressed through governments, fraternal bodies, religious organizations, and a host of special-interest groups. Such cooperation not only involves many people in the local community but also extends to a network of organized cooperative activity involving state, regional, national, and international relationships. Problems in such cooperation include decisions as to the geographical extent of cooperation, obtaining a consensus on the ends to be pursued and the means of reaching them, conflicts with other cooperative groups, and the inevitable difficulty of reconciling the conflicting claims of individuals and the subgroups with which they are associated.

Government may be taken as an example of such deliberate organized cooperation. When North America was first settled, it consisted of colonial regimes ruled by rival European nations. After a period of conflicts, the English achieved dominance, but soon the colonists revolted in order to gain the freedom to make their own cooperative arrangements. With independence, Americans organized state and national governments. The difficulty of reconciling the claims of state and national governments led to a civil war that, to some extent, established a pattern which has been followed since that time. Another type of cooperative adjustment has been the development of regional units such as the Federal Reserve Banks, now organized in twelve regions cutting across state lines. Our need for organized cooperation across national lines has led to the organization of the United Nations and determining the proper roles to be followed by the constituent members of that body is a major problem of our time.

Impersonal and *symbiotic* *cooperation* The world of nature is sometimes pictured as a world of conflict. Yet the concept of universal strife is contradicted by animals who hunt in packs, by insects who work together to maintain colonies, and even by the cooperation of dissimilar organisms. This cooperative interdependence of different species or orders upon one another is known in biology as *symbiosis.*

Darwin, in his description of the nexus between cats and next year's clover crop, provided the now classic illustration of the network of vital linkages which bind different organisms together. Humble-bees alone, his observations disclosed, visit the red clover; other bees and insects cannot reach the nectar. But the number of humble-bees in an area depends in a great measure on the number of field mice, since these latter invade the nests of humble-bees and rob them of their food stores. Cats, in turn, are the natural enemies of mice and hence control their numbers. In areas adjacent to villages the nests of humble-bees were found to be more numerous than elsewhere owing no doubt to the number of cats there. An increase in the cat population, it may be inferred, is followed by a decrease in the number of mice thus permitting an increase of humble-bees and, consequently, a more widespread fertilization of red clover. Creatures that, to all outward appearances, are "remote in the scale of nature" are found to be linked together in a chain of relations. Much has been accomplished since Darwin stirred the intellectual world by the publication of his observations and theories and much new light has been shed on the correlations of organisms and their collective adjustment to the varying physical environment. Darwin and his colleagues sketched the principal outlines in nature's pattern and subsequent students have been rapidly filling in the details of the pattern with many valuable discoveries. The deeper the analysis of the "web of life" is pushed the more meaningless becomes such a word as "independent."

Amos H. Hawley, *Human Ecology, A Theory of Community Structure,* The Ronald Press Company, New York, 1950, pp. 33–34. The reference to Darwin is from *Origin of the Species.*

Symbiotic relationships are not planned or deliberately established; they grow, as though by accident, from the groping efforts of organisms to survive. A great part of human cooperation may be said to be on the symbiotic level since it unites people in a mutual interdependence although they may have made no deliberate choice to cooperate. The marketplace draws men into a network of cooperation even though each wishes only to buy or sell for his own needs. The farmer, for instance, produces for the market which will give him the greatest net profit, but in this process he cooperates with many people about whom he neither knows nor cares. Most of our economic life is organized on the principle of pursuing self-interest by selling one's labor or goods at the highest price he can get. Although the goal is self-interest, the effect is to maintain a network of cooperative relationships in which men work to furnish goods and services needed by other men.

Even the dislocations of economic life may be viewed as furthering coopera-tion. If no one will buy a person's labor or his products, their refusal encour-ages him to shift into some type of labor or product that people will buy. The process is so painful that such market interferences as price supports, sub-sidies, and unemployment insurance have become common. Nevertheless, Western society may be said to rely to a great extent on mutual aid, which is no less effective because it is motivated by individualistic concerns. The main ideological controversies are not between those who reject cooperation and those who exalt it, but between the proponents of differing types of coopera-tion. The classical economists believed that the most effective integration of efforts would be ensured by a *laissez-faire* policy allowing men to be governed entirely by their pursuit of self-interest in the marketplace. Other men advocate various forms of deliberate cooperation, ranging from the consumers' coopera-tive to the enforced overall planning of the Soviet Union. Americans have generally followed the laissez-faire principle but have modified it by many types of cooperation undertaken deliberately either through government or through private associations.

COMPETITION

Competition is the struggle for possession of rewards which are in limited supply—money, goods, status, power, love—anything. It may be formally de-fined as *the process of seeking to obtain a reward by surpassing all rivals.* It is based on the inexorable fact that all people can never satisfy all their de-sires. It flourishes even in circumstances of abundance; in a time of full em-ployment rivalry is still keen for the top jobs. Regardless of the sex ratio, we find in many societies a bitter contest within each sex for the attentions of certain partners. Competition may be personal, as when two rivals contest for election to office; or it may be impersonal, as in a civil service examination in which the contestants are not even aware of one another's identity. Whether personal or impersonal, competition is conducted according to standards which focus attention on the surpassing rather than on the elimination of rivals.

American business sometimes seems to be in a flight from competition even as it praises its virtues. The antitrust laws represent an effort to keep competi-tion effective when many businessmen would rather modify or eliminate it. Monopoly, division of markets, price fixing, and "fair trade" laws are tech-niques for reducing business competition. In some instances these practices are fought by government, in others they are supported. In transportation and in such public utilities as light and telephone service, government regulation restricts competition by setting rates and assigning territories.

Competition a culturally patterned process

While competition is present to some degree in all societies, it differs greatly in degree from society to society. The fiercely competitive Kwakiutl and the relatively noncompetitive Zuñi offer a striking contrast. The Kwakiutl work very hard to accumulate wealth which is used primarily to establish status rather than to provide material comfort. The competition for status reaches its height at the famous "potlatch," in which the chiefs and leading families vie with each other to see how much they can give away or destroy [Murdock, 1936, pp. 242–248]. A family may spend a lifetime accumulating wealth, then bankrupt themselves in a single potlatch, thereby establishing the social status of their children. Members of a family who persisted in keeping their wealth would be criticized for their unwillingness to "do anything" for their children. The Zuñi, on the other hand, disdain any emphasis on the accumulation of wealth or the demonstration of individual skill. Most wealth is owned by the entire community, and it is bad form to demonstrate individual superiority of any kind. Thus the Zuñi child does not grow up believing that he should make the most money, get the highest grades, or run the fastest race.

Even such strong encouragement of competition as is found among the Kwakiutl does not mean that cooperation is completely absent. As the anthropologist Margaret Mead points out:

Nevertheless, no society is exclusively competitive or exclusively cooperative. The very existence of highly competitive groups implies cooperation within the groups. Both competitive and cooperative habits must exist within the society. There is furious competition among the Kwakiutl at the one stratum of society—among the ranking chiefs—but within the household of each chief cooperation is mandatory for the amassing of the wealth that is distributed or destroyed.

Margaret Mead, *Cooperation and Conflict among Primitive Peoples*, McGraw-Hill Book Company, New York, 1937, p. 360.

Sometimes, too, it is hard to distinguish competition from cooperation, for a variation in form may disguise a similarity in process. Jessie Bernard [1960] comments on the Hopi, another "noncompetitive" society: "The Hopi girls who attempt to outdo one another in lack of skill are just as competitive as the Kwakiutl chiefs who attempt to outdo one another in the potlatch. The difference lies in the thing being tested, not in the process itself." Far from being two mutually distinct processes, competition and cooperation overlap in various ways, while both may go on simultaneously, as is true of the group whose members cooperate with one another while the group competes with another group.

Competition in American society

In its competitive emphasis, the United States is probably closer to the Kwakiutl than to the Zuñi; yet this competition is sharply limited by many factors. Enactment of minimum wage laws works toward a situation in which men are not competing for a bare existence, and a growing emphasis on seniority as a basis of promotion means that many occupational goals cannot be reached by direct competitive efforts. In fact, the following description of the control of the competitive impulse in an American factory setting comes close to the Zuñi practice:

Worker: "*There's another thing; you know the fellows give the fast workers the raspberry all the time. Work hard, try to do your best, and they don't appeciate it at all. They don't seem to figure that they are gaining anything by it. It's not only the wiremen, the soldermen don't like it either. . . . The fellows who loaf along are liked better than anybody else. Some of them take pride in turning out as little work as they can and making the boss think they're turning out a whole lot. They think it's smart. I think a lot of them have the idea that if you work fast the rate will be cut. That would mean that they would have to work faster for the same money. I've never seen our rate cut yet, so I don't know whether it would happen or not. I have heard that it has happened in some cases though. . . .*"

F. J. Roethlisberger and William J. Dickson, *Management and the Worker,* Harvard University Press, Cambridge, Mass., 1939, p. 418.

Such practices modify but still do not eliminate the generally competitive pattern of American life. Athletics, politics, and business offer many competitive spectacles such as the World Series, the national presidential campaigns, and the struggle of the "independents" against the giants of the automobile industry. American men are encouraged to "make good," and neither the advantage of wealthy parents nor the drawback of being reared on the wrong side of the tracks completely absolves them from the pressure to get into the race for success. Women cannot rely on matchmaking parents to find a husband, and the sexual competition does not entirely cease when they are married since other women are still potential rivals. Even religion, often held to be the integrating force in society, functions on a competitive basis as numerous denominations compete for converts. In spite of efforts to moderate or limit the struggle, the average American is enmeshed in competitive activities from the time his mother purchases his first layette until he is buried in an expensive casket under an impressive headstone.

Effects of competition   Competition functions as one method of allocating scarce rewards. Other methods are possible. We might ration goods on some basis such as need, age, or social status. We might distribute scarce goods by lottery, or even divide them equally among all people. But each of these methods creates difficulties. Needs are highly debatable; any system of priorities will be disputed, for no group is likely to feel that another group is more deserving. Equal rewards to people who are unequal in needs, effort, or ability are hard to justify. Competition may be an imperfect rationing device, but it works and it eliminates a lot of arguments.

Another effect of competition is to shape the attitudes of competitors. When persons or groups compete, they normally develop unfriendly and unfavorable attitudes toward one another. Experiments have shown that when the situation is devised so that persons or groups cooperate in pursuit of a common goal, friendly attitudes are encouraged. When they meet under conditions which they consider competitive and frustrating, unfavorable attitudes and unflattering stereotypes appear [Sherif, 1958]. It has often been observed that when racial or religious groups compete, racial and religious prejudices appear and flourish [Berry, 1958, pp. 378–380]. Competition and cooperation differ sharply in the social attitudes they foster in the individual.

Competition is widely praised as a means of ensuring that each person will be stimulated to his greatest achievement. This belief is confirmed by many studies which show that wherever competition is culturally encouraged, it usually increases productivity although it sometimes lowers the quality [Murphy et al., 1937, pp. 476–495]. This generalization seems to apply to institutions as well as to individuals. It is often noted that while the competition of many different religious denominations in the United States may have produced many sects and congregations too small to support their programs efficiently, this competition has also promoted a greater alertness and aggressiveness in American religious institutions. Visitors to Europe often comment on Europe's impressive but empty churches, and evidence shows that Americans attend church and participate in church activities in far higher proportion than do Europeans [Vella, 1954; Frakes, 1958; McMahon, 1950]. In universities, too, competition seems beneficial. A recent study of medical education concludes that competition has stimulated scientific productivity [Ben-David, 1960]. This study compares the universities of France and England, where university education was highly centralized, with those of Germany, where the development of independent regional universities led to an intense competition for scientific prestige, favoring the rapid development of new discoveries. This finding is consistent with the experience of the Russians, who claim that competition between factories has increased production even though all the factories are part of the total Communist system. The Soviet Union has recently resurrected the profit system as a stimulus to productive efficiency, although the profits are not distributed to stockholders as they are in a capitalist system.

The stimulus of competition is, however, limited in at least three respects. First, people may decline to compete. Since competition requires that some must lose while all remain somewhat anxious and insecure, people try to protect themselves from its rigors. Businessmen develop monopolistic practices, set prices, and engage in collusive bidding; unions set work quotas, enforce promotion through seniority, and limit union membership; farmers want price protection; teachers want seniority salary schedules; practically every group promotes many competition-limiting arrangements.

Furthermore, many persons simply withdraw from competition whenever they lose too regularly. In singing the praises of competition, many people overlook the important fact that although competition stimulates those who win fairly often, it discourages those who nearly always lose. The slow learner in the classroom, the athletic "dub" on the playground, the adolescent who fails to draw the interest of the opposite sex—such persons usually quit trying, for the pain of repeated failure becomes unendurable. They withdraw from competition in these areas, having decided that the activity isn't worthwhile. There is even experimental evidence that repeated failures not only dampen one's willingness to compete, but may even impair one's actual ability to compete [Hurlock, 1927; Vaughn, 1936; Winslow, 1944]. It appears that repeated failures will so fill a man with a sense of his incompetence and an overwhelming expectation of failure that he is unable to use his abilities to good advantage. His failure becomes self-perpetuating. It may be that for every genius whom competition has stimulated to great achievement, there are a hundred or a thousand shiftless failures whom competition has demoralized.

A second limitation is that competition seems to be stimulating in only some kinds of activity. Where the task is simple and routine, competition is followed by the greatest gains in output; as the task becomes more intricate and the quality of work more important, competition is less helpful. In intellectual tasks, not only is the production of the cooperative group greater, but their work is of higher quality than the group whose members are competing with one another. [Deutsch, 1949]. The nature of work in today's world is steadily shifting away from the kinds of work where competition between individuals is most beneficial. Competition between groups in technical or intellectual tasks seems to be stimulating, but within the group, cooperation appears to be more stimulating than competition.

A third limitation upon competition is its tendency to turn into conflict. To accede peacefully while a coveted reward is claimed by a more skillful competitor is not easy, and the rules of competition are often breached by a resort to conflict.

CONFLICT

The conflict process is little praised but widely practiced. It develops whenever a person or group seeks to gain a reward not by surpassing other competitors, but by preventing them from effectively competing. It is formally defined as the process of *seeking to obtain rewards by eliminating or weakening the competitors.* A murder or beating, a threat, a law passed to injure a competing group, a "gentleman's agreement" to exclude Jewish or Negro home buyers—these are a few of many conflict devices. In its most extreme form, conflict leads to the total annihilation of opponents as when the Romans destroyed Carthage and exterminated its inhabitants, or as when American settlers exterminated many tribes of American Indians. In less violent forms, conflict may be directed toward displacing an opponent from effective competition by getting him fired, getting the building inspector to condemn his place of business, smearing his reputation, or any one of many devices men use to get their competitors out of the way.

Conflict between individuals may involve intense personal animosities, while group conflict, the type of greatest interest to sociologists, is highly impersonal. By this we mean that group loyalties and needs take precedence over individual feelings. Failure to understand this distinction often leads to the mistaken assumption that peace between nations is simply the result of good feeling between the individuals who compose the nations. Many Norwegians were shocked to see that many German children whom they cared for as refugees during World War I repaid their generosity by returning as German conquerors in World War II. Actually the apparent ingratitude should not have been a surprise since the German invasion of Norway was the result of conflict between nations in which individual

Eliminating or weakening the competitors.

Group interest and not personal relationships determine conflict alignments.

feelings were irrelevant. This observation is borne out by the frequent shifts in power alignments in international conflict. Germans and Italians were enemies in World War I and allies in World War II, not because personal feelings had changed but because the national interest was differently defined. Group interests rather than personal relationships determine conflict alignments, as is shown by the speed with which our German and Japanese enemies in World War II became our allies when the "cold war" with the Soviet Union began. Friendships across boundary lines may help to promote joint activities, but it is a mistake to regard personal relationships as the solution to problems of world peace. Individuals usually find their role in group conflict by reference to the groups to which they belong. When conflict breaks out—a war, a strike, a boycott, a legislative battle—the individual either fights for his group or is branded as a traitor. In such a situation his feelings about friends on the other side have less weight than his obligations to his group.

The cumulative nature of conflict   Once begun, the conflict process is hard to stop. Since each aggressive act inspires a still more hostile retaliation, the conflict process tends to grow more bitter as it proceeds. Grievances are told and retold within each group and hostile attitudes are intensified. Each group develops a set of moral sanctions which justify a chain of even more savage retaliations.

The atrocities in conflict are often mistakenly attributed to the sadism or brutality of the individuals who commit them. Yet most of the atrocities in group conflict are committed by ordinary people in an extraordinary situation. The conflict process often places people in roles where they *must* be brutal. Steinbeck's *The Moon is Down* [1942] pictures an intelligent, humane German commander of forces occupying a Norwegian town, who is forced to brutal acts of reprisal to keep the town under control. Under some battle conditions prisoners who can't be cared for must be slaughtered. During a strike union members may be forced to punish a strikebreaker, and management may be forced to punish strikers. Each, in fulfilling his role, is forced into acts of brutality and violence.

But the extremes of conflict cannot be understood unless we recognize that the individual, committing the most indescribable acts of brutality, is supported by his group. He sees his act, not as wanton inhumanity, but as a moral necessity. During the range wars of the American West, the cattlemen who harassed, threatened, burned out, and in some cases murdered the settlers did not see themselves as greedy tyrants, withholding land from its legal claimants; they saw themselves as embattled patriots who had fought Indians, drought, and plague to build up a country and a way of life which a horde of greedy scum and conniving politicians wished to steal from them [Dale, 1930, chap. 9; Wellman, 1939, chaps. 35 and 36]. To understand why normal people can commit gruesome atrocities in conflict, we must understand how the group provides the sense of righteousness which sanctions such actions.

Conflict defines issues Until the Supreme Court outlawed racial segregation in the public schools, there was much talk about brotherhood but no real decision as to whether Negroes were to have equal rights in American society. Since the Supreme Court decision, conflict has developed in many formerly peaceful areas and has increased the social distance between whites and Negroes. The issue can no longer be buried under platitudinous talk; conflict forces us to face issues and make decisions. The immediate effect of the conflict unleashed by the court decision may have been to shatter many peaceful relationships. The long-run effect, sociologists suspect, will be to reduce both discrimination and prejudice and eventually increase cooperative relationships between whites and Negroes in our society.

In this respect group conflict may be compared to the effect of fever in the human body—costly and dangerous, but calling attention to deep-seated tensions which must be relieved if health is to be maintained. Just as the treatment of fever goes beyond symptoms to the cause of the difficulty, so the effective handling of conflict goes beyond merely maintaining order and seeks to treat the basic disturbance. Any tendency to ignore controversial issues or to seek a moderate position might be compared to the tendency to ignore such symptoms of ill health.

Conflict forces a facing of social issues and polarizes our attitudes toward them. The moderates are pushed, distrusted, and attacked by both sides and eventually forced to make a choice. The end result of the conflict is that the issues are resolved, at least for a time, in a fairly definite fashion. The fact that the moderate is forced to take a more definite position means that he has to assume responsibility instead of simply standing aside and deploring violence. At the end of the Middle Ages, when men were being slaughtered because of religious differences, the moderates who were simply inclined to deplore fanaticism were driven to a definite program—the separation of church and state—so that religious differences might be tolerated. In present American racial controversies the moderate is pushed into support of integration as a result of his commitment to the maintenance of law and order:

In spite of the bad publicity and the damage to our prestige abroad, I should also like to comment on Little Rock. A distinguished religious leader from that community said to me this summer, "You know, while it was bad, maybe it was not a total loss." There is much more intelligent understanding of the responsibility of citizenship now. People of the moderate or middle group have come to realize that they do not have the privilege of sitting on the sidelines and letting the radicals at the two ends determine the outcomes. They had to learn that ultimately they had to get in there and get their hands dirty with the problem. They had to see that they were being made the testing place for the whole South, and that

when the chips were down they had to choose between law and chaos. "Maybe,"
he said, "we had to learn that, and it took the crisis to teach it to us."

Dan W. Dodson, "The Creative Role of Conflict Re-examined," *Journal of Intergroup Relations*,
1:5–12, Winter, 1959–1960.

The disintegrative **Conflict disrupts social unity**   Conflict is a highly disturbing way of settling
effects of conflict issues. Strikes may idle thousands of men and acres of costly machinery;
marital conflicts may wreck countless families; racial and religious conflicts
may prevent communities from facing their problems in a united spirit; and
atomic wars now threaten the total destruction of humanity. Even when conflict achieves a new equilibrium, the price may be very great. The Thirty Years'
War, 1618 to 1648, established the principle of religious toleration among
German states, but it also reduced the German population by at least one-
third, and much of the cultivated land became a wilderness.

Internal conflict disrupts group unity   Conflict within a group makes it hard
for members to agree on group goals or to cooperate in pursuit of them. At
any moment, in several of our states, one of the major political parties is split
into warring factions, giving the other party a fine chance to win the next election. It was often claimed that France fell to Germany so easily in 1940 because the French people were so divided into conflicting factions that they
were unable to unite against the enemy. Hitler confidently expected that the
United States, with its heterogeneous population, would also be so riven with
internal conflicts as to be unable to wage a united battle. This was one of his
more costly misjudgments!

The integrative **Internal conflicts are sometimes ultimately integrative**   A limited amount of
effects of conflict internal conflict may indirectly contribute to group interaction. Interests and
viewpoints within a group shift from time to time; new policies and new leadership may be needed. An occasional contest within a group may keep its
leadership alert and its policies up to date, whereas a suppression of internal
conflicts may allow disastrous lags and explosive discontents to accumulate.
Coser analyzes the role of conflict in promoting unity as follows:

> *In loosely structured groups and open societies, conflict, which aims at a resolution*
> *of tension between antagonists, is likely to have stabilizing and integrative func-*
> *tions for the relationship. By permitting immediate and direct expression or rival*
> *claims, such social systems are able to readjust their structures by eliminating the*
> *sources of dissatisfaction. The multiple conflicts which they experience may serve*
> *to eliminate the causes for dissociation and to reestablish unity. These systems*
> *avail themselves, through the toleration and institutionalization of conflict, of an*
> *important stabilizing mechanism.*

Lewis A. Coser, *The Functions of Social Conflict*, The Free Press of Glencoe, New York, 1956, p. 153.

External conflict tends to integrate the group   Conflict with another group
provides the members with an external outlet for their hostilities and resentments, and thus siphons off a lot of internal tensions. External conflict com-
pels each member either to cooperate loyally or to get out. Simmel, a very
perceptive early analyst of social conflict, defines the alternatives in these
words:

If a political party which unifies many different directions of interest is pushed into a decisive and one-sided position of conflict, an occasion for secession results. In such situations, there are only two alternatives—either to forget internal counter currents or to bring them to unadulterated expression by expelling certain members. . . . The group in a state of peace can permit antagonistic members within it to live with one another in an undecided situation because each of them can go his own way and avoid collisions. A state of conflict, however, pulls the members so tightly together and subjects them to such a uniform impulse that they must completely get along with or completely repel one another. This is the reason why war with the outside is sometimes the last chance for a state ridden with inner antagonisms to overcome these antagonisms, or else to break up definitely.

Georg Simmel, *Conflict*, tr. by Reinhard Bendix, The Free Press of Glencoe, New York, 1955, pp. 92–93.

External conflict also unifies the group through the imposition and acceptance of tighter controls than are normally accepted. The nation at war allows its business life to be completely directed toward national objectives in a way that would be unendurable in time of peace. The labor union gives "no-strike" pledges and accepts work rules which it would resist in peacetime. All groups tend to build bureaucratic structures and to centralize authority when faced by the need to organize resistance to an enemy.

While external conflict separates a group from its enemies, it also promotes federations or alliances with other groups. The phrase, "politics makes strange bedfellows," expresses the tendency to seek out allies in times of conflict even though they might be unacceptable in time of peace.

Effects of Conflict

Integrative Effects	Disintegrative Effects
Defines issues	Increases bitterness
Leads to a resolution of issues	Leads to destruction and bloodshed
Increases group cohesion	Leads to intergroup tension
Leads to alliances with other groups	Disrupts normal channels of cooperation
Keeps groups alert to members' interests	Diverts members' attention from group objectives.

Our disdain for communism did not keep us from being effective allies with Russia in World War II; when the cold war developed, our rapid *rapprochement* with Germany and Japan showed that alliance is based on mutual interest, not mutual affection. Wars and threats of war have unquestionably encouraged the growth of political states and governmental institutions from the earliest tribal alliance to the United Nations. War forces a nation into coordinated activity, stimulates inventions, and inspires heroic sacrifices. Wars have settled issues: The Mexican War ended controversy over American colonization of the Southwest; World War II appears to have ended efforts for territorial expansion of Japan and Germany; through war the Italian peninsula became a unified nation. By settling issues, wars often clear the way for cooperative action. Conflict thus performs an associative as well as a divisive function and may be considered in some ways an integrative factor in social life.

ALTERNATIVES TO CONFLICT

The conflict process may fulfill useful functions, but at so great a cost that man often seeks to avoid it. Conflict is often avoided through some form of two other processes, *accommodation* and *assimilation*.

Accommodation   *It really threw me when my folks got a divorce right after I was graduated. I never thought much about my parents' love life; I guess I just took them for granted. Our home always seemed to me about like most others. At graduation, they came and beamed, gave me graduation gifts, met my friends, and all that. Then Dad took me aside and said that he and Mom were calling it quits. He said that they had bugged each other for years but had stuck it out to give me a proper home. Now that I would be on my own, they were going to separate.*

Looking back on it now, I can remember little things that they let slip, but at the time I never noticed anything. They kept it pretty well covered up.

The above story, adapted from a student's life history in the authors' files, is an example of accommodation, a *process of developing temporary working agreements between conflicting individuals or groups*. It develops when persons or groups find it necessary to work together despite their hostilities and differences. Accommodation may be short-lived, or it may persist for centuries. No real settlement of issues is reached; each group retains its own goals and viewpoints, but arrives at an "agreement to disagree" without fighting and perhaps to resume peaceful interaction. It is what Sumner [1907] called "antagonistic cooperation."

Accommodation replaces conflict with peaceful interaction without fully settling basic issues, but it allows hostilities to subside while more friendly attitudes may grow from this peaceful interaction. This is illustrated in a Gallup poll showing that, whereas in 1942, the adjectives which Americans most frequently picked to describe Germans were "warlike," "hard-working," "cruel," "treacherous," and "intelligent," by 1961 the list had changed to "hard-working," "intelligent," "progressive," "practical," and "brave"—a much more favorable list [Associated Press, Apr. 26, 1961]. The accommodation process obviously affects people's attitudes and behavior. Accommodation takes a number of forms. Some are deliberately planned and formally negotiated; others arise as unplanned products of group interaction.

Displacement   Displacement is the process of ending one conflict by replacing it with another. A classic example is the use of war or the threat of war to end internal conflicts and bring national unity. It is a standard stratagem of dictators and not unknown among democracies.

Finding a scapegoat is a favorite displacement technique. The term refers to an ancient Hebrew ceremony in which the sins of the people were symbolically heaped upon a goat which was driven into the wilderness. Unpopular minorities often become scapegoats. Anti-Semitism has long been used to deflect criticism and to unite conflicting groups in blaming Jews for all the ills of the society. In the newly independent countries, all the nation's problems may be blamed upon the remaining "colonial influences." The true social influence of the scapegoat is of little consequence; what matters is that a ruling group may be able to avert a possible attack upon itself by diverting popular hostility to the scapegoat.

Institutionalized release of hostility   In many societies there are some institutionalized provisions for release of hostilities and tensions. Some primitive tribes regulated combat in a manner designed to express aggression, maintain "honor," and yet avoid destructive warfare. Warner [1931] describes an elaborate pattern of ritualistic warfare wherein Murngin tribes in Australia went through involved ceremonial combat in which, though nobody actually got hurt, a lot of hostility could be worked off. Then these rituals closed with a joint ceremonial dance expressing the renewed union and solidarity of the tribes. The Royal Copenhagen Porcelain Works, instead of junking the imperfect pieces, takes them to the Tivoli amusement park, where it collects a fee from people who are willing to pay for the privilege of smashing the rejects. It seems that "busting things up" serves to release hostility and tension.

Perhaps our spectator sports, especially the contact sports like football, hockey, boxing, and wrestling would be examples of opportunities for the institutionalized release of hostility in our society. Ceremonials and feast days, orgies and religious experiences of various kinds may also serve to release tensions or provide catharsis for hostilities and thus ease the pressures toward conflict. Karl Marx was quite correct in holding that believers in a biblical devil, heaven, and Christian forgiveness would be slow to join in class warfare.

Superordination   In some families one member totally and ruthlessly dominates the others. Some group conflicts end in the total defeat and submission of one group to the other. A war may "end" with the defeated people continuing resistance through guerilla warfare, assassination, sabotage, and noncooperation, thus continuing the conflict. Or they may accept defeat, submit, and make the best of it, as did Germany and Japan after World War II.

Superordination is likely to be accepted only when the parties are so unequal in power that resistance seems useless or impossible. When the subordinate group gains more power, the superordinate group must either relax its rule or risk a revolt. As Germany and Japan recovered from wartime devastation, the United States relaxed its rule rather than face growing resistance, while Russia's stern rule over conquered peoples provoked revolts in East Berlin, Hungary, and Poland, and seething resentment throughout her "colonies."

Conflict between two parties may sometimes be ended by their forced submission to a third party. History is crowded with instances. After Athens and Sparta had exhausted themselves, Macedonia conquered both. Only English rule brought peace between the Scottish clans. Most empires grew by picking off neighbors who were fighting among themselves.

Today the collapse of empires and the end of colonial rule in many areas is followed by the reappearance of local conflicts. The Near East peoples resumed ancient conflicts after the disintegration of the Ottoman (Turkish) Empire. As this is written, several African areas are precariously poised on the brink of tribal warfare. Whether stable national governments are possible for such areas is not yet certain.

Compromise   When all the parties are powerful enough so that none of them relish the prospect of conflict, they may compromise their differences. Compromise is a form of accommodation in which each party accepts less than its full goal in order to avoid or end the conflict. Each normally makes concessions according to its relative power, with the more powerful party making the fewer concessions.

Since a compromise leaves all parties somewhat dissatisfied, the compromise agreements are likely to be honored only so long as the respective power balance remains unchanged. As soon as either group gains in respective power, it is likely to press for a revision of the compromise, threatening renewed conflict if its demands are refused. During prosperous times, when the employer can scarcely fill his orders, the union will press for a more favorable contract; during a recession, when orders are fewer and stockrooms are full, the employer seizes the strategic moment to seek the revisions he desires. Politics may be seen as a continual round of shifting power positions and changing compromises. Politicians are often accused of dishonesty because of their compromising; yet without such compromises between the conflicting demands of many voting groups, democracy would become chaos.

Frequently the conflict has been so bitter and feelings so hostile that the parties are unable to reach a compromise. Several third-party techniques are often helpful in breaking such deadlocks.

Third-party roles in compromise   The techniques of conciliation, mediation, and arbitration use the services of a third party to help reach a settlement. In *conciliation* the third party functions by encouraging the disputants to keep talking; in *mediation* he suggests solutions and uses his personal influence and his powers of persuasion; in *arbitration* he hears their arguments and makes a decision, knowing that the contestants have already agreed to accept it. The third party may offer suggestions which the disputants could not offer without losing face, and he may be able to find new approaches to end a deadlock. Even if he is given the power of arbitration, his success depends mainly on his ability to gauge the relative power positions and suggest settlements fairly close to what might be obtained through all-out conflict.

Toleration   In some conflicts victory is either impossible or unbearably costly, and compromise is unendurable; some values may be too deeply cherished to compromise. In these circumstances the participants sometimes discover that agreement may not be absolutely necessary. In toleration, people accept each other's right to differ without demanding a settlement. Religious conflict is a classic example of this situation. In Europe at the time of the Reformation, both Protestants and Catholics were positive that they had the "true" version of the Christian faith which should be accepted by all men. Neither group was willing to compromise, and in spite of severe conflict, neither group could destroy the other. Adjustment has been made on the basis of toleration; each church ceases to persecute other churches while continuing to hold that these other churches are in error.

Why was religious toleration so long in developing? Partly because toleration requires a frame of mind in which people are willing to grant others the right to be different; ethnocentrism is the enemy of toleration. Furthermore, toleration is possible only for those matters on which agreement is not absolutely necessary. As long as church and state were combined, rejection of the established church automatically became treason to the state; not until their separation could one worship as he pleased and still be a loyal citizen. Catholic and Protestant neighbors may disagree on many religious questions without the disagreement impairing their interaction as neighbors, friends, or fellow workers. If they intermarry, some religious differences may still be open to toleration, but their interaction as husband and wife will absolutely require agreement upon a number of issues. Our rather wide use of toleration today rests not only upon a considerable readiness to tolerate differences but also upon a social structure in which many areas of peaceful interaction are open to groups who differ bitterly upon other matters.

Assimilation   Whenever groups meet, some mutual interchange or diffusion of culture takes place. Even groups who strenuously seek to prevent such diffusion, such as the modern Amish or the ancient Hebrews, do not fully succeed in protecting their culture from all cultural interchange. The Old Testament is filled with exhortations to avoid contact with the "heathen" peoples, and of their failure to heed this warning. The story of Samson was an object lesson on the folly of involvement with foreign women.

This process of *mutual cultural diffusion through which persons and groups come to share a common culture* is called *assimilation*. It is always a two-way process with each group contributing varying proportions of the eventual blend, depending upon respective group size, prestige, and other factors.

The assimilation process is nicely illustrated in the Americanization of our European immigrants. Arriving in great numbers between 1850 and 1913, many of them settled in immigrant colonies in the Northern cities. Within these "ethnic colonies"—Little Italy, Little Poland, and so on—they practiced much of their native European culture while absorbing some of the American culture. The immigrant parents often sought to transmit their European culture to their children, while the children generally sought to become American as rapidly as possible. This conflict often caused parental anguish, family disorganization, and loss of parental control, so that many second-generation immigrants became confused, rebellious, and delinquent. As the third generation matured, the assimilation difficulties generally subsided; Americanization became fairly complete, and the ethnic colony disappeared as the descendants scattered over city and suburb [Thomas and Znaniecki, 1927].

Assimilation reduces group conflicts by blending differing groups into larger, culturally homogeneous groups. The bitter riots against the Irish and the discriminations against the Scandinavians in the United States [Higham, 1955] have disappeared as assimilation has erased the group differences and blurred the sense of separate group identity. Anything which binds people into a larger group will tend to reduce rivalry and conflict between them. This is strikingly illustrated by an experiment which involved the experimental formation of different groupings at a summer camp [Sherif and Sherif, 1953]. The boys were all from the same community and were similar in religion, social-class status, age, and national background. For the first experimental period ("integrative") they were treated as a single group, and they showed no signs of

Table 16 *Choices of friends at end of integrative period and at end of segregative period*

Choices made by		Choices received by	
		in-group, per cent	out-group, per cent
End of integrative period	Eventual Red Devils	35.1	64.9
	Eventual Bull Dogs	35.0	65.0
End of segregative period	Red Devils	95.0	5.0
	Bull dogs	87.7	12.3

SOURCE: Adapted from Muzafer Sherif and Carolyn Sherif, *Groups in Harmony and Tension*, Harper & Row, Publishers, Incorporated, New York, 1953, p. 268.

incipient social conflict. In the second experimental ("segregative") period they were divided into two groups who were housed separately and encouraged to develop separate programs of activities. The groups took the names of "Red Devils" and "Bull Dogs." Group antagonisms quickly developed, and physical violence between the groups reached the point where it had to be suppressed by the adult leaders. Personal relationships followed the patterns of group division, as is shown in Table 16.

This experiment shows how, even when there are no real differences or issues to fight over, conflict still tends to develop wherever separate group identity is recognized. We can understand, then, why the assimilation of American Negroes or Japanese-Americans has not ended conflict. The Irish, Swedes, and Germans disappeared as separate groups as soon as they were assimilated. The Negroes and Japanese-Americans, although quite fully assimilated, remain identifiable as separate groups. For a variety of reasons, including historical tradition, the wish for scapegoats, and the desire to look down upon someone, these groups have not gained full social acceptability. Assimilation removes some but not all possible pressures toward conflict.

Boundary maintenance The importance of assimilation rests primarily in its elimination of boundary lines as two groups, formerly distinct, assume a common identity. Such boundary lines are a major aspect of social life, and we devote a great deal of energy to their establishment, maintenance, and modification. Questions such as the following are concerned with boundaries: Can a true believer attend services in another church? Do good girls have premarital sexual relations? Can a college athlete play semiprofessional baseball during the summer? Should foreign students be allowed to pursue an occupation in the United States? Can laymen conduct church services? Is racial integration really desirable?

Any answer to these and similar questions will either enlarge or restrict the membership of specific social groups and hence is a "boundary line" type of issue. National states indicate their territorial boundaries by markers, fences, and other evidence of the extent of their claims. Social groups without territorial limits face the necessity of establishing some type of social boundary lines which will separate their members from the rest of the society. For many groups a language, dialect, or specialized argot serves as a boundary which separates the members from outsiders: "If he doesn't speak our language, he certainly can't be one of us." Uniforms are also a device for separating members of one group from the rest of society, a practice found among clergy, policemen, nurses, and soldiers among others. Sometimes formal identifying insignia such as the Indian caste marks are utilized. Frequently there is no overt indication of group membership, and only a subtle sense of "belonging," related to group standards of conduct, is all that separates the in-group from the outsiders.

Groups need not only to establish definite boundaries but also to convince their members that the boundaries are important. Ethnocentrism usually develops and assists in this task by reassuring us about the virtue of our group and the shortcomings of others. Intense nationalistic indoctrination may build a patriotism which says that any weakening of national sovereignty through international agreements would be fatal. Similarly a religious body may seek to convince its members that it is the only true church. On a less formal basis, small suburbs may support a myth about the vices and high taxes of the big city as compared with the virtue and low cost of the suburb—a myth which has increasingly little basis in fact.

Loyalty on the basis of group pride is supported by sanctions which reward those loyal to the group, punish those deficient in group obligations, and keep out those the group wishes to exclude. Rewards may include access to employment through belonging to a union, social prestige which comes from being a club member, and the increased congeniality resulting from acceptance in the right circles. Punishment, or negative sanctions, consist largely in the lack of rewards which group membership offers. The alien is not allowed to vote, the lower-caste person is not allowed to worship in the higher-caste temples, the family not listed in the social register is left out of the glamorous parties. People seek the rewards offered by inclusion within the boundaries of powerful groups and try to avoid the penalties which follow inclusion in the boundary lines which define low-status groups or ineffectual units.

Not only are we concerned about boundaries which affect our own placement, but we also seek to set boundaries in ways which will keep undesirables out of the groups we value. In fact, the power of exclusion is often one of the rewards of group membership. By keeping others out, we assert our own superior status as social arbiters and emphasize the gulf which separates us from those of less esteem. Whatever the basis used for acceptance or rejection, it quickly becomes a trait which distinguishes one group from another. Those rejected by the dominant group establish their own sense of identity and utilize their own epithets to stigmatize those who have excluded them. Thus to the gentile the Jew is a "kike" or a "yid," but the Jew may retaliate by referring to gentiles as "goy" or "schottzim" or may use uncomplimentary phrases like "shicker as a goy" (drunk as a gentile). Such epithets set boundaries, since they convey a notion of relative status as well as of difference.

Social boundary lines are constantly shifting and often complex. Is a factory worker with a home in the suburbs lower class or middle class? If a man leaves Judaism for Presbyterianism, is he still regarded as Jewish? Is the Filipino a Westerner or an Asiatic? Is the Negro army officer defined in terms of military rank or racial status? These and countless similar boundary definitions are constantly being reformulated as groups strive to increase their rewards, avoid penalties, and place themselves in a favorable position. Sometimes boundary

determination is accomplished through formal means, as in the case of naturalization requirements or initiation ceremonies. In other cases there is a more
informal process of acceptance and rejection which indicates group boundary
lines in terms which are definite even though not defined in written documents.
In either case boundary establishment and modification is a continuous social
process. [Mack, 1965].

SYSTEMIC LINKAGE

Just as nations need both territorial limits and international trade, so other
groups which require boundaries also need some type of linkage with the rest
of society. The absence of boundaries means that the group is swamped by the
larger society, but the absence of relationship with other groups leads to isolation, stultification, lack of growth, and the attempt to perform functions for
which the group itself is not fitted. Even bitterly hostile primitive tribes have
recognized this fact by instituting a system of "blind barter" with their enemies. Since personal relationships were too bitter, no face-to-face contact
took place, but each group would leave trade articles at a mutually understood
spot and pick up the articles left by the other tribe.

Systemic linkage is defined by Loomis [1961, p. 16] as "the process whereby
the elements of at least two social systems come to be articulated so that in
some ways and on some occasions they may be viewed as a single system."

Even the Amish, a relatively isolated group, are linked to the rest of society
by education, agricultural marketing, and the payment of taxes. For other units
the linkages are usually far more numerous. The rural village is linked to the
urban metropolis by the market economy, by an educational system which
sends teachers into the community and takes advanced students out, by
churches and lodges which maintain contact with parent organizations, and
by many other links. Like the Amish, some groups try to reduce systemic linkage to the minimum because they see in it a threat to boundary maintenance.
Other groups promote such linkage deliberately, such as the church which belongs to an ecumenical organization, the labor union which sends a lobbyist
to the capitol, and the chamber of commerce which looks for new markets for
local industries. The methods vary, but even as groups seek to protect their
separate identity by boundary maintenance, they are also impelled to seek
links by which they can establish a relationship to the rest of society.

SUMMARY

Earlier scholars argued over the inherent superiority of competition, cooperation, and conflict; sociologists today study the manner in which these
and other social processes contribute to social life. These processes are found
in all societies, although there is great variation in emphasis. *Cooperation* may
be personal or impersonal, deliberate or symbiotic in character. Primary groups
demand highly personalized cooperation; secondary-group cooperation is
found in many organized social groups as well as in a network of economic
relationships which use the motive of individual gain to draw men into essentially cooperative activities.

Competition serves the function of allocating scarce rewards among the competitors. It has the additional function of stimulating both individual and group activity in a manner to increase the total productivity of the competitors, but it also discourages the further efforts of those who regularly fail. Experimental studies show that both cooperation and competition are related to the values of the culture. When the culture legitimizes competition, a competitive system often, but not always, increases the rate of productive activity while quality of work often suffers. Competition is unstable and frequently yields either to cooperation or to conflict.

Conflict develops when attention shifts from the contest itself to an effort to eliminate rivals. Group conflict may take place even when the members of the groups involved lack any personal animosity toward members of the opposing factions. Social conflict is frequently costly and disruptive, but it also has integrative functions. Conflict helps to define issues and bring about a new equilibrium of contending forces. It also promotes unity within the group and may lead to expanding alliances with other groups. Conflict may be ended in several ways. Conflicts may be *displaced* and the aggression directed at a new enemy. Conflicts may sometimes be ended or avoided through an *institutionalized release* of hostilities and aggressions through mock combat, festival and orgy, and other emotional outlets. Conflicts may be relieved, at least temporarily, through *accommodation*, which takes several forms. *Superordination* consists in establishing uncontested rule over a weaker group. *Compromise* involves a limited surrender by all groups in order to end or avoid conflict. *Conciliators, mediators,* and *arbitrators* often aid in arranging compromises. Where compromise is unacceptable yet agreement not absolutely necessary, groups may use *toleration* as an alternative to conflict. Finally, when two groups have become *assimilated,* so that they share a common culture and common goals, they normally disappear as separate groups unless some visible identification remains as a focus for conflict.

Boundary maintenance is the process of preserving lines of distinction between groups and applies to every action which marks one as either "in" or "out" of a specific group. *Systemic linkage* denotes the process by which groups avoid isolation while maintaining their separate identities.

QUESTIONS AND PROJECTS

1. Are cooperation, competition, and conflict natural, instinctive, or automatic human responses, or must they be culturally acquired?

2. Why do you think the consumer cooperative has had such limited success in the United States?

3. What examples of impersonal or symbiotic cooperation can be observed on the campus?

4. Discuss this proposition: "It is man's nature to want more than his fellows; competition is therefore firmly rooted in human instinct."

5. Under what conditions is competition an encouragement? When does it inhibit effort?

6. Why does competition often turn into conflict? Does social conflict always involve physical violence?

7. To what extent do friendly personal relations and mutual understanding serve to prevent conflict?

8. How is knowledge of the effects of conflict upon group solidarity sometimes used in international relations? In labor-management relations?

9. When homesteaders invaded the land of the cat-tlemen, conflict developed. Was there any practical possibility of avoiding that conflict?

10. Do decent and humane people ever take part in atrocities? Why? How would most Americans, had they been socialized in Germany, have felt about the mas-sacre of 6 million Jews?

11. Why is accommodation always an unstable ar-rangement? What happens when the power balance shifts?

12. Why could not toleration have been used to avoid the Civil War, the present integration conflicts, or the cold war?

13. Why does assimilation not always bring social ac-ceptance and the end of conflict?

14. What boundary lines are maintained between those associated with a college and other residents of the local community? What types of systemic linkage exist between them?

15. What effect will the modernization of the garb of Roman Catholic nuns have on their group cohesion? Would the same comments apply to distinctive uni-forms for students in girls' schools?

16. Find an example of a major disagreement on the campus or in a community. Trace the history of this controversy to the achievement of some accommo-dation pattern which resolved the crisis. What type of accommodation developed?

SUGGESTED READINGS

ALLPORT, GORDON W.: *ABC's of Scapegoating*, Anti-defamation League of B'nai B'rith, New York, 1948. A concise pamphlet describing and analyzing the scapegoating process.

BOGARDUS, EMORY S.: "The Long Trail of Cooperation," *Sociology and Social Research*, 31:54–62, Septem-ber, 1946. A natural history of the process of co-operation.

*COSER, LEWIS A: *The Functions of Social Conflict*, The Free Press of Glencoe, New York, 1956. A study of the conflict process by a sociologist who believes it has functional values. (90681 Free P)

DODSON, DAN W.: "The Creative Role of Conflict Re-examined," *Journal of Intergroup Relations*, 1:5–12, Winter, 1959–1960. A presentation of the thesis that conflict may have useful consequences.

*GORDON, MILTON M.: *Assimilation in American Life*, Oxford University Press, Fair Lawn, N.J., 1964. A sociological analysis of current trends in the assimi-lation process together with a typography of various categories of assimilation which goes beyond as-similation as a cultural process. (Ox)

INTERNATIONAL SOCIOLOGICAL ASSOCIATION, IN COLLABO-RATION WITH JESSIE BERNARD, T. H. PEAR, RAYMOND ARON, AND ROBERT C. ANGELL: *The Nature of Conflict*, UNESCO, Paris, 1957. A sociological study of the conflict process, mainly with reference to war and international relations.

LIPPIT, RONALD: "The Process of Utilization of Social Research to Improve Social Practice," *American Journal of Orthopsychiatry*, 35:663–669, 1965. Re-printed in modified form in ARTHUR B. SHOSTAK, *So-ciology in Action*, Dorsey Press, Homewood, Illinois, 1966, pp. 276–280. Discusses the relation of social research to social processes.

MACK, RAYMOND W.: "The Components of Social Con-flict," *Social Problems*, 12:388–397, Spring, 1965. An eloquent statement from a sociologist who holds that conflict arises inevitably from the nature of social life, while boundary maintenance is a con-tinuous social process.

PARK, ROBERT E., AND E. W. BURGESS: *Introduction to the Science of Sociology*, 2d ed., The University of Chicago Press, Chicago, 1924, chaps. 4–6, 8–11. The classic discussion of the social processes.

PARK, ROBERT E., AND H. A. MILLER: *Old World Traits Transplanted*, Harper & Row, Publishers, Incorpo-rated, New York, 1921. A classic treatment of the assimilation process.

SHERIF, MUZAFER, AND CAROLYN SHERIF: *Groups in Har-mony and Tension*, Harper & Row, Publishers, In-corporated, New York, 1953. A research study of how different group structures promote cooperation and antagonism at a boys' camp.

*SIMMEL, GEORG: *Conflict*, translated by Reinhard Ben-dix, The Free Press of Glencoe, New York, 1955. A pioneer German sociologist's classic treatment of the functional nature of conflict. (92884 Free P)

YOUNG, PAULINE V.: *The Pilgrims of Russian Town*, The University of Chicago Press, Chicago, 1932. A highly readable account of the assimilation process.

SOCIAL POWER

I was assigned by a national magazine to do a story on the [Talmadge–George] campaign, but I soon discovered there wasn't going to be one. One of Senator George's supporters explained the situation to me:

"We used to re-elect the Senator every six years by getting in touch with about 100 of the right people in Georgia. When we did it this time, we discovered that those people had swung to Herman [Talmadge]. All that remains is for us to figure out who is going to give the bad news to Senator George." (George E. McMillan, Look, July 5, 1960, p. 25.)

$\mathbb{S}$OCIAL POWER and power contests provide much of the drama of modern life. Every political campaign and every congressional debate is an exercise in the use of power. Every newspaper contains dozens of examples. Nearly every novel has a power contest of some sort as its theme. What is power and how it is manipulated?

THE NATURE OF SOCIAL POWER

Although social power has been variously defined by Weber [1946], Simmel [1959], Bierstedt [1950], Goldhamer and Shils [1939], Parsons [1963], and others, all definitions carry the idea of control over others. Power might be formally defined as the *ability to control the actions of other people, regardless of their wishes.* Power has at least two components: *authority* and *influence.*

Authority is *an established right to make decisions and order the actions of others.* Sociologists have discussed the various types of authority. Weber, for example [1946, pp. 196–252], sees three main types of authority: (1) *bureaucratic authority,* resting on formal office or rank (general, foreman, civil service officer); (2) *traditionalist authority,* resting on a belief in sacred norms and traditions which one must obey (husband, father, prince, priest); and (3) *charismatic authority,* the authority of an extraordinary person who is obeyed because of his charisma—his image of remarkable wisdom, saintliness, or invincibility (Christ, Joan of Arc, Napoleon, Franklin D. Roosevelt, Hitler).

Influence is *the ability to affect the decisions and actions of others beyond any authority to do so.* The professor has authority to command certain work assignments and to assign grades; he has no authority to compel students to accept his opinions, but possibly he can influence them to do so. Influence rests partly upon respect, prestige, and affection and partly upon one's control over "facilities" which affect others. A newspaper publisher can be a valuable friend or a dangerous enemy; the corporation executive, school superintendent, or high-ranking army officer can speed or slow down one's promotions; a member of the local aristocracy has "contacts" which can open many doors for a favored protégé. Great influence generally rests upon some combination of engaging personal qualities and a position from which one can affect the destiny of other people.

Authority and influence interact in reinforcing the position of the powerful; or one may undercut the other in reducing a person's power. Brim [1954] found that mothers who attributed high prestige to the role of doctors were more likely to follow the doctor's advice. Strodtbeck [1951] studied authority roles in the family by setting up situations in which the members have a difference of opinion and by then recording the interaction. He found that Navajo wives won 46 arguments to their husbands' 34, while Mormon wives lost 29 to 42. These figures show the differing roles of authority and influence of wives in the two cultures.

Social power is easier to define than to measure. Sociologists have used three different approaches in an attempt to locate and measure social power [Rossi, 1957]. First, there is *potential power*—the power which is assumed to go with certain positions or situations in the community. The mayor presumably has more power than the city-hall janitor, and the chamber of commerce more than the teacher's club. Second, there is *reputed power*—the power ascribed to certain persons and groups by those who know the community. Reputed power is determined by asking the question, "Who really runs things in this town?" of a number of people who know the town well. Finally, there is *actual power*, as shown by observation of the decision-making process in operation. Observation of a power struggle as it takes place, with a detailed account of who did what and when, may reveal who is really in control of the situation.

Power has many degrees and forms, ranging from the tantrums of the small child to the armed mobilization of a great nation. This chapter will explore social power of four sorts: that of powerful individuals who are said to form an elite, of organized groups, of unorganized masses, and of law.

POWER OF THE ELITE

The power elite is composed of men whose positions enable them to transcend the ordinary environments of ordinary men and women; they are in positions to make decisions having major consequences. . . . For they are in command of the major hierarchies and organizations of modern society. They rule the big corporations. They run the machinery of the state and claim its prerogatives. They direct the military establishment. They occupy the strategic command posts of the social structure in which are now centered the effective means of the power and the wealth and the celebrity which they enjoy.

C. Wright Mills, *The Power Elite*, Oxford University Press, Fair Lawn, N.J., 1956, pp. 3–4.

Every complex society has a quite small number of persons who are believed to have great power. Such a controlling group is called an *elite*. Membership in the elite is often inherited, but in some societies it may be acquired. Its bases vary. In ancient China, the elite was headed by the scholars who were experts in the Confucian classics, plus the large landowners and military leaders. In medieval Europe the elite was composed of the higher clergy and the landowning nobility. After the industrial revolution these elite were increasingly displaced by the business entrepreneurs whose rapidly growing wealth gained them entree into the elite group. In Soviet Russia, where the possessions of the landlords and the businessmen were confiscated and the clergy largely deprived of influence, a new elite has apparently arisen composed of the artists, intellectuals, and top bureaucrats. In England when one speaks of "the Establishment," he refers to a few thousand persons of wealth and influence, mostly of noble or gentle birth, and educated mainly at Eton or Harrow and at Oxford or Cambridge.

The wealthy as an elite One of the best-known efforts to describe an American elite is Ferdinand Lundberg's study [1937] of "America's 60 Families." Lundberg assumed that wealth brings power, usually exercised indirectly. While members of the sixty wealthiest families occasionally occupy important posts, most of their influence is wielded through their ability to appoint and control those who actually fill the offices. This power of the purse places business managers, politicians, college presidents, and bishops under the sway of the holders of great wealth. Corporations are controlled through the ownership of stock; contributions and benefactions keep the foundations, churches, and universities under control. Occasionally the great families quarrel, but through intermarriage and close social contact they usually develop a common viewpoint and act as a more or less unified group. Thus, according to Lundberg, wealth rules.

This picture, which may have been approximately true at the end of the nineteenth century, is almost certainly less true today. Great wealth today is often invested in many scattered investments and administered by professional experts rather than by the owners themselves. Political parties and philanthropic organizations are steadily growing less dependent upon a few large contributors as they cultivate a mass of small contributors.

A more recent study of American wealth by *Fortune* magazine located 155 Americans worth $50 million or more, and estimated that there were about another hundred whom it failed to locate [Smith, 1957]. As one indication that these persons were powerful, this study noted that Philadelphia pursued a vigorous program of urban renewal while Boston for a time continued to decay; they attributed this contrast to a difference in attitude on the part of the two cities' millionaires. No doubt wealthy persons have disproportionate power; but the exact degree of this power is not easy to determine.

The executive elite Another theory of the American elite concludes that strategic position rather than personal wealth is the prime source of power [Burnham, 1941; Mills, 1956]. According to this view, the structure of our society is based on a complex division of labor which must be coordinated by a corps of expert managers. These highly paid executives are responsible for the smooth functioning of wealth-producing organizations, but they are not usually the principal owners of the enterprises they manage. Similarly, although they are responsible for supervising the services of scientists and technicians, they are not usually scientists themselves. Their skill lies in mastering the handling of organizations which channel the contributions of many different types of individuals toward a common goal. So strategic is their position that they often control the groups of which they are the nominal servants. Thus the typical great corporation is managed by a group of executives who own only a tiny fraction of the corporation's stock. While theoretically controlled by the stockholders who elect them, the managers tend in practice to become a self-perpetuating group whose actual control is unchallenged by stockholders as long as the flow of dividends is uninterrupted. Likewise, the most successful university president or foundation director is one who is able to "handle" his board of directors.

Executive skills are regarded as relatively independent of the context in which they operate; very different organizations may require the same type of coordination. With a few exceptions, executive skill is transferable. The same individual

With a few exceptions, executive skill is transferable.

may rotate among responsible positions in military, political, industrial, or educational institutions. Governments often "draft" corporate executives for top executive posts, and business recruits many of its executives from government or university people. These executives associate together, move from one field to another, and generally select their own successors.

The executive elite have undoubted authority in the detailed control of their enterprises, while their influence is buttressed both by their strategic position and by personality traits which have caused them to be respected. Their power, however, is restricted by limitations on their right to determine policy and the requirement that they operate within institutional norms. The "rubber stamp" board of trustees may quickly dump an executive when a business starts to lose money, a school arouses public criticism, or a church suffers a fall in membership. Similarly, the Secretary of Defense may be able to make major decisions about the composition of the armed forces and their weapons, but he lacks the authority to determine foreign policy with its consequences of peace or war, no matter how much influence he may be able to exert.

Mills views the corporation as either the base from which the executive elite originate or the goal toward which they are moving. He feels that their power means that society becomes dominated by men primarily committed to a view of life expressed by a prominent executive in the immortal words, "What's good for General Motors is good for the country."[1] Mills makes a strong case for the theory that executives who have had similar training, association, and outlook are often found in positions which involve decision making. There is no doubt that a professional managerial class has developed in the United States [Newcomber, 1956]. But many social scientists argue that the case for a ruling elite with a virtual monopoly of social power has not been proved [Rossi, 1956; Reissman, 1956; Dahl, 1958; Bell, 1958]. These social scientists prefer to work in the more restricted field of local community studies and observational studies of the decison-making process, feeling that by accumulating a number of studies of these kinds they can eventually build a theory of power with a convincing factual foundation.

The community influentials In recent years several sociologists have attempted to identify the people with unusual influence in particular American communities.[2] The usual technique is to select a group of people presumed to be well acquainted with a community and ask them for a list of the persons who are influential in that community. The people on the list are then interviewed in an attempt to narrow the field to a small number who appear to have the greatest power in community decision making. The final list is loaded with corporation executives, wealthy individuals of established social standing who are active in civic affairs, and lawyers associated with business interests. Politicians are seldom mentioned unless they are also prominent businessmen. Other professionals such as physicians,

[1] C. Wright Mills, *The Power Elite*, Oxford University Press, Fair Lawn, N.J., 1956, p. 168. For the context of Charles Wilson's statement, see "Conflict of Interest," *Time*, Jan. 26, 1953, p. 70.
[2] The major pioneer work in this field is Floyd Hunter, *Community Power Structure*, The University of North Carolina Press, Chapel Hill, N.C., 1953. An excellent brief summary and analysis of these studies is found in Richard A. Schermerhorn, *Society and Power*, Random House, Inc., New York, 1961, pp. 88–92. A comparison of community influentials in a Mexican and a nearby American city is found in William H. Form and Delbert C. Miller, *Industry, Labor, and the Community*, Harper & Row, Publishers, Incorporated, New York, 1960, pp. 554–572.

Table 17   Occupation of community influentials in Lansing, Michigan

Occupation	Number	Per cent
Executives		
Subtotal	14	36
Automobile manufacturing	3	8
Other manufacturing	4	10
Banks	3	8
Department stores	2	5
Labor unions	2	5
Proprietors		
Subtotal	17	44
Real Estate	6	16
Construction	2	5
Communication	2	5
Others	7	18
Professionals		
Subtotal	8	20
Lawyers	3	8
Educators	2	5
Clergy	2	5
Doctor of medicine	1	2
Total	39	100

SOURCE: William H. Form and Warren L. Sauer, *Community Influentials in a Middle-sized City.* Institute for Community Development, Michigan State University, East Lansing, Mich., 1960, p. 3.

ministers, and educators form a tiny fraction of the total number of leaders and are usually classified toward the bottom of the list on a ranking of comparative influence. Labor leaders, mentioned in some communities and ignored in others, never form a substantial proportion of the community influentials.

The community influentials are thought to be the top of a power pyramid which determines whether any given project will receive community support. In some communities the survey evidence suggests that the fate of all major community proposals depends on the reaction of the same small group of influentials. Other communities may contain several power pyramids, including different individuals who are effective in different areas. The support of one group might be vital for a hospital-fund drive, of another group for passing a school-bond issue, and of still another group for the success of an urban redevelopment program [McKee, 1953].

Community power appears to be exercised through determining the policies of community organizations. Organizational activity is a time-consuming process, and influentials often feel they have to struggle in order to limit their community participation so that they will have some time available for attention to their own businesses. The following description of the community participation of an "influential" in Lansing, Michigan is similar to that found in other cities:

On the average he now belongs to more than thirteen organizations: 3.9 business organizations, 2.4 professional organizations, 2.9 civic and welfare organizations, 0.8 service organizations and 3.5 social organizations. He has held the top appointive or elected offices in almost all of the organizations in which he has become actively involved. Almost all of the leaders belong to a common core of organizations: the Chamber of Commerce, Rotary, Country Club, a leading church, and the Community Chest.

William H. Form and Warren L. Sauer, *Community Influentials in a Middle-sized City*, Institute for Community Development, Michigan State University, East Lansing, Mich., 1960, p. 4.

The actual leadership offices in voluntary organizations are more likely to be held by those who are in the process of reaching the status of "community influentials" than by those who have already arrived. The established leader is apt to operate by remote control through junior executives who perform the endless chores of office holding. The established influential however keeps in touch with developments and may take office himself when some type of

Table 18 Participation by 39 Lansing influentials in local organizations

Civic organizations	Number actively involved	Number holding officerships		
		Past	Present	Total
Community Chest	*18*	*17*	*6*	*23*
Hospital boards	*12*	*3*	*11*	*14*
Downtown Development Council	*9*	*–*	*2*	*2*
YMCA	*7*	*7*	*2*	*9*
Hospital Expansion Fund	*5*	*4*	*4*	*8*
Michigan United Fund	*5*	*2*	*4*	*6*
PTA	*5*	*3*	*1*	*4*
Business				
Chamber of Commerce	*34*	*18*	*5*	*23*
Downtown Businessmen's Association	*9*	*5*	*1*	*6*
Commercial clubs	*6*	*3*	*–*	*3*
Service				
Rotary	*19*	*14*	*2*	*16*
Kiwanis	*7*	*5*	*2*	*7*
Social				
Country Club	*22*	*4*	*3*	*7*
Masons	*19*	*19*	*2*	*21*
Elks	*7*	*1*	*–*	*1*
City Club	*15*	*6*	*–*	*6*
American Legion	*8*	*3*	*–*	*3*

SOURCE: William H. Form and Warren L. Sauer, *Community Influentials in a Middle-sized City*, Institute for Community Development, Michigan State University, East Lansing, Mich., 1960, p. 4.

emergency seems to demand top-level leadership. His advice is sought on matters considered important, and even when not holding organizational office he is able to exercise a veto power on projects he considers of doubtful merit. New programs have a good chance of success when the influentials lend their support. Fund-raising drives usually get a major portion of their total from small contributors, but influentials add the large gifts that make the difference between success and partial failure, while their endorsement sets a good example of civic virtue.

With occasional exceptions, the community influentials are seldom office holders in local government and consider this kind of activity not very attractive. The influentials recognize the importance of government but dread the prospect of controversies that may be "bad for business" and shrink from direct involvement in "dirty" politics [Hunter, 1953, pp. 151–170; Form and Sauer, 1960, p. 11]. The community influentials are interested in seeing that government provides the services needed by business without either burdensome regulation or excessive taxation. In addition, as civic leaders they feel that good schools, reliable police protection, efficient public health services, and adequate sewage and water resources help to maintain a community which can attract both customers and employees.

In spite of their limited political participation, community influentials affect the policies of government through campaign contributions and through maintaining a liaison wih office holders. When the community influentials are agreed among themselves, they can usually persuade local government and community groups to act as they wish. Yet the community influentials appear to be more powerful in some types of situations than in others. In some cases organized groups appear to be powerful only when their aims are supported by the community elite. In other cases the balance is reversed, and the community elite are helpless unless organized groups are firmly in agreement. Rossi summarizes this situation in the following statement:

Who has power over whom? Perhaps the clearest distinction here is between the two areas of community life—local government and the voluntary community associations. For local government officials who are ultimately brought before the bar of public opinion on election days, the leaders of solidary [highly unified] groups normally on their side carry the most weight. Insofar as wealth and the mass media are seen as potential influencers of public opinion they too are powerful. Within the voluntary community associations which depend largely on the bounty of large contributors, wealth and its control play the major role.

Another distinction must be drawn as to types of issues. An issue which divides the community (or which poentially might divide the community) can be moved to a decision point only by solidary groups. I have in mind in this connection such issues as integration in public housing or public schools. Projects which can be achieved without striking deeply at the gains of one particular group are perhaps best moved by the elite of wealth and status. Thus the best way to get a hospital drive underway is to get together a group of prominent citizens, but the best way to get an FEPC [Fair Employment Practices Commission] ordinance is to prove that some significant part of the electorate is for it.

Peter H. Rossi, "Theory, Research and Practice in Community Organization," in Charles R. Adrian, Peter H. Rossi, Robert A. Dahl, and Lloyd Rodwin, *Social Science and Community Action*, Institute for Community Development, Michigan State University, East Lansing, Mich., 1960, p. 13.

The community influentials undoubtedly feel that they are far more success-fully in control of things at the local than at the state or national level [Form and Sauer, 1960, p. 11]. Their complaints about the "unfavorable business climate" in Washington and the state capital are frequent and bitter. Even the great businesses they run are subject to changes beyond their control. A decrease in demand or the shift of public interest from one product to another may ruin an industry which completely dominates the local scene. Many busi-ness establishments are minor parts of national corporations, and vital deci-sions are made by those living in other communities. Local politicians, labor leaders, and association executives are easier to deal with than those on the national scene who are responsible to a larger group. Even if one grants the theory that the executive type has major influence on the national scene, this does not necessarily strengthen the position of the community influentials. National leaders who come from the same general social background as the community leaders may still disregard their opinions on specific matters. The community is inextricably linked to the larger world, and a group apparently powerful in the locality may find its influence checkmated by decisions made elsewhere. In many communities the most powerful influentials may be the officers of absentee-owned corporations. They announce decisions meaning life or death for the community, but these decisions have been made elsewhere by corporate managers who may have little concern for the welfare of this community [Pellegren and Coates, 1956]. Thus the true power in many com-munities lies outside, and is not with their own leaders.

ORGANIZATIONAL POWER

The struggle for power often appears to be largely a contest between organi-zations. The John Birch Society attempts to elect conservative candidates to public office, while the Americans for Democratic Action supports liberals. The AFL-CIO calls for a higher minimum wage, and the National Chamber of Commerce assails high wages as the cause of inflation. The Teamster's Union demands that railroads be prohibited from "piggyback" shipments of trucks, and the railroad association urges higher taxes on truck operations. All these and many other items in the daily press suggest that the power of highly or-ganized groups is checked only by the opposition of other groups.

Sources of organizational power   **Wealth, numbers, and specialized facilities**   The obvious advantage of organi-zation is that it brings together the efforts of a large number of people along with a great deal of wealth. When an organization represents millions of veter-ans, church members, unionized workers, businessmen, farmers, or any other groups, it has at least a potential claim to speak for a considerable fraction of the population. An organization can accumulate a large treasury from the dues and small contributions of many members. By joining together, even the poor and unknown may gain some of the attributes of power often attributed to the elite.

The specialized facilities of the organization also increase its influence. The individual, far from any seat of government, may make his views known through the activities of the organizational lobbyist, who is constantly in con-tact with those who make government decisions. The special magazines or pamphlets put out by the organization help to keep the membership informed, while newspaper advertisements and radio and television programs carry the organization's program to the general public.

Coordinated membership response   The major source of organizational power lies in the ability to enable many people to take *planned, concerted action* to affect social decisions. In a democracy this action may be accomplished by organizing blocs of voters who will cast their ballots in a way designed to assist organizational objectives. Even a small group may have some political influence if it will vote as a bloc. Many elections are decided by small margins, and a shift of 1 or 2 per cent in votes may mean the difference between victory and defeat. If a comparatively small group can organize a united bloc of voters, it may be effective.

Organizations often launch a campaign in which each member is urged to write, wire, or see his congressman. A flood of several thousand individually worded letters from his constituents has a sobering effect upon the most daring congressman. The American Medical Association has occasionally sought to have each congressman approached by his own personal physician in support of the association's legislative objectives. The effectiveness of such efforts is hard to determine. Apparently, if a measure is earnestly sought by a small but determined group, and if no active or organized opposition appears, its passage is generally assured. Where there is organized opposition, a more prolonged power contest usually follows.

Sometimes a group fails to gain its objectives through political action, or perhaps it may be blocked from using political action, as are Negroes in some parts of the American South. Such groups may seek to exert power through some form of coercion—either through force or through nonviolent coercion. Both forms may be used either to overthrow a government or to gain some more limited objective.

Forceful coercion is normally the monopoly of government; yet history is filled with armed revolts against the established government. The Communist and Fascist parties have frankly planned to use violence as a means of gaining government control and have done so in Spain, Italy, Russia, and China, to name only the most prominent examples. In the United States the most dramatic use of armed coercion (except for our own Revolution) appeared with the Ku Klux Klan after the Civil War, when hooded Klansmen terrorized those who favored greater rights for Negroes [Brown, 1902, chap. 4; Horn, 1939].

Nonviolent coercion in the form of strikes, lockouts, and boycotts is almost an institutionalized part of the social system of many countries. India provided the most dramatic example of the use of nonviolent coercion as a means of overthrowing a governmental regime, when Mahatma Gandhi used this method of combating the English colonial rule. Even the Indian struggle is not purely an instance of nonviolent coercion, since the Indian Nationalists made use of their strength in the legislature to embarrass the British, and in spite of Gandhi's pleas, riots occurred sporadically. Nevertheless the massive campaign of nonviolent coercion appears to have been the major influence in making the English position untenable.

Power contests between labor unions and employers may involve all three types of coordinated group action—the organization of blocs of voters to influence government policy, nonviolent coercion through economic pressure, and occasional use of violence. Nonviolent coercion through economic pressure generally uses either the withdrawal of labor or the withdrawal of work opportunities. The employer is using nonviolent coercion through economic pressure when he threatens to close his factory or move it to another location, or remains in the same location and replaces his workers with more docile ("loyal") employees. The union may attempt nonviolent coercion through economic pressure on the employer by calling a strike and cutting off his labor supply or by calling for a boycott of his products. Violence sometimes occurs when the employer breaks up picket lines or when the union seeks to prevent strikebreakers from taking over their jobs.

Disputes over racial integration have used all three of these methods, but with less emphasis on violence than upon political manipulation and nonviolent coercion. The White Citizens' Councils sought to prevent race integration and to discourage Negro voting by "lawful" means [Martin, 1957]. They disclaimed violence and charged that the violence was the inevitable result of their opponents' attempts to change racial patterns. The White Citizens' Councils in some Southern areas invoked severe economic penalties upon all, white or Negro, who sought to aid the cause of school integration. If the person was a worker, he lost his job; if a tenant, he was evicted. If he was a storekeeper, his store was boycotted; his banker called his loans; his insurance agency canceled his insurance; and his wholesale supply houses cut off his supplies [Gamarekian, 1957; Cater, 1956]. In one community where a few Negroes registered to vote in 1956, there was an immediate rash of cross burnings, fire bombs, and threatening night phone calls. Soon all Negroes but one had removed their names from the voting lists, while the one defiant Negro "was forced to leave the county."[3] Where they were strongly organized, the White Citizens' Councils succeeded in making it impossible for any supporter of school integration to make a living in the community.

The use of nonviolent coercion by integrationist groups has usually been directed against the segregating policies of business concerns. The "sit-in" and "stand-in" demonstrations at lunch counters and theatre ticket offices prevent these concerns from serving any customers as long as they refuse to serve Negroes on an integrated basis. Sometimes pressure has been exerted simply by the withdrawal of Negro patronage. The most famous case of this type is probably the Montgomery, Alabama bus controversy, in which Negroes refused to use the bus system so long as segregated seating was enforced [King, 1958]. In some Northern cities Negroes have used the threat of a public boycott to persuade local businesses and industries to employ more Negroes in better jobs [Lees, 1961].

Nonviolent coercion sometimes rests as heavily upon moral pressure as upon economic pressure. The Negro sit-in demonstrators—almost invariably quiet, well-dressed, and orderly, allowed themselves to be insulted, spat upon, and even savagely beaten without making any reply or protest. A group which supports its claims by offering itself for suffering without fighting back makes a powerfully moving spectacle! Thus a Negro minority has sometimes shamed a white majority into opening its lunch counters to them.

While the moral basis of nonviolent resistance makes it especially effective, it is difficult to indoctrinate large numbers of people in the attitudes essential to

[3] See "Liberty in Peril," *Time*, Sept. 15, 1961, p. 24.

its use. Like Gandhi, Martin Luther King was never able to persuade all the discontented Negroes that nonviolence is a suitable way to express their protest. During the mid-1960's, many Negroes lost faith in nonviolence and began expressing their frustration and anger in an orgy of rioting and looting which, by the summer of 1967, had become a nightly occurrence.

As compared with force and violence, nonviolence is less costly in life, property, and bitterness. It is a difficult technique to use because of the constant temptation to turn to violence—especially in response to violence from the opposition. Its success has come in areas where the opposition has been unwilling or unable to use all-out force, perhaps because of economic costs, because of problems of conscience, or because of fear of an unfavorable public reaction. Whether it would be effective against an utterly ruthless opponent is doubtful.

Factors affecting group power **Size and organizational power** While large groups are not always effective, a large membership does give them a large power potential. The lethargy and inertia of many large groups continue only so long as society is friendly to their basic values. Members of Protestant churches are notoriously reluctant to follow the lead of their clergy on many matters [Glock and Ringer, 1956], but raised a mighty opposition when President Truman's proposal to send an ambassador to the Vatican appeared to threaten their traditional concept of separation of church and state. Veterans are relatively indifferent to the supernationalistic policies often adopted by their organizations, but if our elaborate system of veterans' benefits and bonuses were seriously threatened, the organizations representing twenty million veterans would become marvelously energetic! Large organizations become highly active and overwhelmingly powerful when their vital interests are threatened.

Cohesiveness and action orientation Solidary groups which can unite their members in a given program have a great advantage over loosely structured organizations which must seek agreement through an education and discussion process and may seldom be able to count on a concerted response from their members.

Large religious groups, veterans' organizations, and political parties usually include individuals with a wide variety of views. Members do not consider themselves bound by the actions of governing bodies of such groups and may ignore or even oppose official views of the organization. By contrast, small organizations in which the leadership can make decisions binding on the members may have an influence greater than their size would indicate. This is borne out in a rather striking fashion by the success of real estate boards in determining the action of municipal government. The typical board of realtors requires its members to list all properties for sale, splitting the commission between the firm making the listing and the firm completing the sale. The board of realtors also receives a proportion of the commissions on listed property which gives it a source of income apart from its membership assessments. The board normally has an executive committee with power to make policy decisions binding on all the members. A recalcitrant member can be suspended, which means that he is not allowed to make any sales from the board list during his suspension although other firms may sell off his listings.

Such an organization has power much greater than its limited size and the intermediate social status of its members would indicate. In several cities the board of realtors, although seldom regarded as a power organization or pressure group, has been highly effective in influencing community decision making. In one Midwestern city of about 250 thousand population the board of realtors first defeated a school-bond issue which was supported in a spirited campaign by a great many of the civic organizations; then two years later the board reversed its stand and helped carry to victory a bond issue larger than the one originally rejected. In a public housing campaign in this city, the board of realtors persuaded the voters to reverse a unanimous city commission by referendum although the housing proposal adopted by the commission had the support of both political parties, both daily newspapers, the council of churches, and many social welfare organizations, labor unions, and leading citizens [Bouma, 1962a, 1962b]. Soon after, a nearby city repeated this experience in almost identical detail [Bouma, 1962c].

While other power factors are also involved the board of realtors is a prime example of the power potential of small, cohesive, disciplined organizations.

Perceived role as a power factor   The members of an organization have an image of what kinds of activities are proper for the organization, and this image limits the areas in which it can exercise power. Labor union members will usually support their leadership in wage negotiations even to the point of costly strikes, but have repeatedly shown that their union leaders cannot dictate their voting behavior [Marshall, 1961]. If union leaders could really "deliver" the votes of the membership, their political power would be enormously increased. Most church members expect the church to "stay out of politics," and occasional church efforts to control voting behavior have generally failed. A good example was found in Puerto Rico in 1960, where Archbishop Davis attacked the incumbent administration on birth control and other issues and organized a Catholic party in opposition. Puerto Rico is about 85 per cent Catholic, and the church leaders threatened to excommunicate anyone supporting the administration; yet the administration was overwhelmingly reelected while the Catholic party got less than 10 per cent of the votes [*U.S. News and World Report*, 1960].

Perceived role.

For many years teachers' organizations were handicapped in seeking salary increases because their members' perception of the role of a professional organization kept them from threatening to strike. [Stiehm, 1961]. In recent years the members' perceived role of their organization has changed and teachers' organizations are beginning to use conventional strike tactics in seeking economic gains. Whether or not collective bargining really boosts employees' compensation above the level they would otherwise receive is a moot question on which economists disagree [Ross, 1947, Schultz and Meyers, 1950]. From our viewpoint, however, the essential point is that the teachers' perceived role of their organization limited the tactics it could use in power struggles.

The power of an organization is also limited by the role assigned to it by the community. To many people the chamber of commerce is an organization dedicated to community welfare, while labor unions are considered selfish and "too powerful." The chamber of commerce is expected to speak out on taxes and other political issues, but the unions are scolded for doing the same thing. Businessmen in government are applauded; labor officials in government are feared; and college professors in government are often ridiculed. Many consider it proper for medical associations to resist outside pressures for changes in medical practice, but think it arrogant for teachers' organizations to resist outside pressures for changes in teaching methods. Thus the public's perceived role of an organization or group limits its social power by determining the public support its actions will receive.

Organizational alliances Some of the advantages of large size may be won if several smaller groups join in united action. This alliance is simplified when the organizations involved are led by interlocking directorates. Most of the directors of corporations and community organizations also hold several other directorships in other corporations or organizations. Today the board of directors of the City National Bank hold a director's meeting, tomorrow three of them meet again at the community chest luncheon, and the next day one is elected to the official board of the First Methodist Church, and so on. Thus an overlapping network of membership links the organizations together, making for easy cooperation and vesting control of many organizations in a very small group of persons.

An alliance between entirely separate groups may be forged when their interests converge. The socialized-medicine controversies of recent years have found the American Medical Association allied with the chamber of commerce, the National Association of Manufacturers, the American Farm Bureau Federation, and many other organizations in opposing certain medical-care proposals, while many labor unions, public health and welfare organizations, and social-work organizations have been united in support. An alliance between farm organizations and business organizations has helped to persuade many state legislatures to pass "right to work" laws which outlaw the closed shop. Labor organizations have sometimes attempted to form an alliance with farm organizations, but without much success. Farm organizations seem to feel a greater convergence of interest with business than with labor, especially as farming itself is becoming more commercialized.

Countervailing power The opposite tendency of organized groups—to oppose each other rather than to cooperate—has been given the name of *countervailing power* [Galbraith, 1952]. This theory states that the exercise of great power by one organized group soon inspires an opposing power. Other groups may organize for effective opposition, or they may persuade the government to intervene. In the past, large-scale business enterprise eventually resulted in the appearance of the large labor union, and exploitation of farmers by milling interests and other middlemen produced the farm cooperatives. Large buyers such as chain stores limit the power of large manufacturers to set prices, while in turn the voluntary chains (associations of independently owned stores) enable the independent retailer to compete with the chain stores. Thus the power of one economic group is balanced by the power of another and none can entirely dominate the economy. While the concept of countervailance is most often applied to economic groups, this game of reciprocal checkmate tends to be true of all groups in society. The tendency of great power to inspire the organization of opposing power usually keeps any one group from gaining complete control.

SOCIAL POWER OF UNORGANIZED MASSES

Mass man in mass society In the folk society the individual lives in a world of rather small, highly integrated local groups whose behavior is closely governed by custom and tradition. In the mass society one's life is increasingly dominated by large, impersonal, secondary groups. Social change is rapid, and custom and tradition provide no sure guide to behavior. In the mass society few people can be leaders. The important decisions are often made by a handful of leaders gathered in the great metropolitan centers. For example, no more than a few dozen people will actually share in deciding whether steel prices shall be increased next year. Not only are most people cut off from any direct share in such decision making; they are not even able to understand the basis on which industrial and governmental decisions are made. It is true that newspapers and newscasts bring reports of what has happened, along with an interpretation offered to justify these decisions. But the mass media cannot provide a real forum with a chance for interaction between audience and speaker, or any way for the masses to share in the actual making of most important decisions.

Under ancient despotisms, decisions were made by a few leaders, but these decisions were based upon a traditional morality and custom which the masses could understand and support. The actions of the ancient despot reflected the social values learned in the family and the church and reinforced by the general moral consensus of the community. Today the masses no longer live in a traditional society and are no longer embedded in a protective coating of time-honored customs and institutions. Instead, our "mass man" lives in an era in which change is the norm, in which older customs cannot be trusted, and in which changes that he has no part in bringing about may transform his life for better or for worse. Men live in communities of people like themselves, as isolated fragments of a varied and complex world. Lacking an opportunity for understanding, they inevitably substitute stereotyped images for social analysis and fads for tradition. In these circumstances the mass media become primarily a route of escape rather than enlightenment.

The student should recall that in describing groups and associations the text distinguished between *gemeinschaft* and *gesellschaft* societal influences. The gemeinschaft social relationships were of a personal, traditional type that applied to the entire society. The gesellschaft scrapped tradition in favor of a realistic (hard-boiled), impersonal, and highly specialized approach to various aspects of life. While the gesellschaft frees society from older restraints, it also cuts the roots of traditional culture and transforms the individual into the "mass man," helplessly and unknowingly swept along by current fads and fancies.

We once had faith that public education and the universal right to vote would prepare the ordinary man to become involved in the public issues of the day and to exercise his influence in a society geared to meet his problems. To some extent, this has happened. Politicians, educators, labor leaders, and business advertisers all gear their appeal to mass consumption. The appeal, however, is usually for the passive acceptance of decisions already made, not an invitation to share in making them. Both the world of political action and that of participation in voluntary associations are closed to the average mass man. Usually he votes, if at all, only in the highly publicized presidential elections. Either he belongs to no voluntary association or he is a nominal member who attends few meetings, has only a vague idea of the purposes and problems of the group, and feels himself cut off from the inner circle who really run things.

The expression From this discussion of mass society, it might appear that mass man is totally
of mass power powerless to affect his destiny. Individually, possibly yes. But collectively, no! The unorganized masses can exert a decisive power over social developments through several avenues.

The power of mass markets   In a democratic society the masses exert influence through their choices of what goods to buy, what papers to read, what television programs to watch, and so on. This power is not unlimited, for the consumer is susceptible to some degree of manipulation, as motivation research has demonstrated [Packard, 1957]. But in a competitive market the consumer's preferences are rarely disregarded for very long. Courting his favor may produce a gaudy vulgarity in product design and shoddy escapism in television programs, but it unquestionably attests to the power of the mass market.

Mass veto power through noncooperation   Some decisions can become effective only through mass cooperation. Public health programs, mass-immunization campaigns, and voluntary blood banks are successful only if a great many people cooperate. The American civil-defense effort limped through over a decade of monumental public indifference. In many places a regional shift of labor would be economically sensible, as in many coal-mining regions where mechanization of mines and declining coal markets have produced much permanent unemployment; but any plans for their economic rehabilitation must begin with the fact that the miners simply don't want to move [Francois, 1961]. Wherever a decision cannot be effective without mass cooperation, the veto power of the masses must be considered.

Direct political power of masses   In a democracy the ultimate power of the masses rests in their franchise to "throw the rascals out." Sometimes, it is true, this power is empty because both candidates hold the same values and serve the same interests. But whenever there is widespread mass discontent with the way things are going in a democracy, some party or candidate will appeal to this discontent, focus it on certain issues, and propose changes. Deep mass discontent almost guarantees change; either a new party pledged to change replaces the old, or the old party introduces changes as the price of continued power. The elite cannot always veto changes sought by the masses. The reforms of the New Deal era, established over the opposition of most of the elite, attest to the power of the skillfully focused discontent of the masses.

In a democracy the masses can compel changes opposed by the elite or veto changes sought by the elite. The history of fluoridation controversies provide an example of mass veto of elite decisions. The addition of small amounts of fluoride to the water supply is an effective and apparently harmless method of greatly reducing tooth decay [Muhler and Hine, 1959]. Virtually every responsible scientific organization in the country has endorsed it, including the American Dental Association, the American Public Health Association, the American Medical Association, and many others. The scientific consensus is so complete that, according to one noted nutritionist, ". . . those who continue to oppose it are misinformed, stupid, or dishonest."[4] But in most cities where fluoridation was proposed, a bitter controversy developed. Opponents charged that it was a Communist plot to poison the water and an invasion of personal freedom and attributed a variety of preposterous evils to it. As soon as the announced date for the beginning of fluoridation had passed in this author's home town of Kalamazoo, the water department began receiving complaints that the water tasted bad, smelled foul, and caused headaches, nausea, and other ills, although, because of some mechanical difficulties, the actual addition of fluoride did not begin until several weeks later. In a majority of the cities where fluoridation was decided by popular vote, it was defeated, and the spread of fluoridation had virtually ceased by the end of the 1950s [McNeil, 1957; Attwood, 1958]. By the middle 1960s, however, fluoridation apparently had lost its appeal as a rallying point for discontented citizens, and elections began to be more favorable; yet mass opposition had delayed its introduction in many cities for nearly a generation.

The rejection of fluoridation was a clear-cut victory of the masses over the elite, since the voters were rejecting the decisions of their administrative officials, the authority of science, and the leadership of most of their community influentials. Research studies found that opposition centered among the less-educated and lower-income citizens [McNeil, 1957; Plaut, 1959; Mausner and Mausner, 1955]. A tabulation of communities voting on fluoridation showed that the greater the proportion of people voting, the greater was the possibility that the measure would be defeated. The correlation with the large turnout implies that the fluoridation issue drew to the polls many voters who are chronically uninterested in, or distrustful of government. A large number of poorly educated, lower-class people seem to be chronically distrustful of government, suspicious of science and intellectuals, and resentful of the dominant role of the elite. When some issue such as fluoridation or a school bond election offers a focus for their discontents, they unhesitatingly bury the decision makers in a flood of opposition votes. [Thompson and Horton, 1960].

[4] Frederick J. Stare, Chairman, Department of Nutrition, Harvard University, before Florida Dietetic Association; reported by Associated Press, Nov. 11, 1961.

Another striking example of mass veto of elite decisions occurred in Kala-mazoo, Michigan, one of the first cities to install a downtown mall. In 1963 the city commission presented for voter approval an urban redevelopment pro-gram, financed largely by Federal funds. For once, the Chamber of Commerce, the Board of Realtors, and the labor unions were on the same side, united to support the project along with the Council of Churches and many other organi-zations. No local organization opposed the proposal. Of several dozen com-munity influentials, only one announced opposition. The newspaper lent edi-torial support and generous news coverage. Advocates launched an intensive informational campaign to build popular support. No organized opposition whatever appeared, although one city commissioner opposed the program. The newspaper carried letters to the editor on both sides. The only opposition pub-licity was an ungrammatical, abusive handbill distributed the night before election. With no organized opposition and the local power system solidly in support, the program's passage seemed assured. Yet it was defeated by a 3 to 2 majority [Kalamazoo *Gazette*, July and August, 1963]. Obviously, the power elite, even when in almost unanimous agreement, cannot dictate all decisions.

Important as the power of veto may be, it does not altogether dispel the picture of the lowest income group of society as one which is essentially with-out the power to affect decisions concerning it. Alinsky [1965] argues that the poor can utilize power and must be able to do so if their position is to be ameliorated. (Alinsky is not a professional sociologist but a skillful organizer who attempts to promote the organization of poor people in slum neighbor-hoods for political action). He argues that the deliberate organization of the poor, stressing whatever grievances are most keenly felt, can lead to positive action. Through demonstrations, boycotts, and bloc voting, the poor can be-come one of the pressure groups in the community. As they achieve power, they will be able to prevent exploitation, to formulate positive programs for their own welfare, and replace a helpless apathy with a sense of being able to control their environment. Although Alinsky-type programs seem to have been effective in some localities, there is disagreement concerning their value. Some hold that organizing efforts of this type simply hamper cooperation between different groups without leading to effective participation by the poor. Others would argue that the poor should be assimilated in middle-class groups rather than attempting to develop organizations of their own. Whatever the merits of his organizing techniques, Alinsky has pointed up the disparity of power and the virtual exclusion of a large part of the population from positive decision making in community life.

Who, then, holds the reins of power in our society? No single group, for power is of several kinds and is diffused among many groups. The paradox of power in the twentieth century is that although our society is largely controlled by highly organized groups dominated by an elite leadership, this leadership may be blocked by the action of normally unorganized and apathetic masses of men whose basic attitudes toward life are often sharply different from those of the influentials who normally set the pace. Even this pace-setting function of the elite is restricted by the need to draw in the participation of the masses as consumers, workers, and participants in large-scale programs affecting public health and welfare. The gloomy predictions of a society doomed to mediocrity by the power of the most ignorant have not been altogether borne out, but no student of social power can ignore the role of those who seldom sit in the seats of the mighty.

THE SOCIOLOGY OF LAW

Law as legitimized power   Power may be either legitimate, that is, socially sanctioned, or illegitimate. The power of the underworld crime syndicates [Moynihan, 1961] is very real and very great, although not legitimate. Neither law nor our approved value system authorizes the acts of crime syndicates. Power is legitimate when it is sanctioned by society, and legal authority represents the formal legitimization of power. Most sociologists seem to agree with Roscoe Pound's definition of law as "social control through the systematic application of the force of politically organized society."[5] But this force is not always applied directly, in the form of the club-wielding policeman. As Hertzler [1961, p. 421] comments, ". . . the law in effect structures the power (superordinate-subordinate) relationships in the society; it maintains the status quo and protects the various strata against each other, both in governmental and non-governmental organizations and relationships."

The law "structures power relationships" by stating who may do what to whom. Before the passing of the National Labor Relations Act in 1935, employers were legally entitled to fire and blacklist employees who joined unions. This law established workers' legal right to join unions and prohibited employers from penalizing workers for union activity. While this law was not (and is not) fully enforced in all areas, it has greatly aided unions in organizing workers and was largely responsible for the great growth of union power from 1935 to 1945. By 1947, union power had grown enough to disturb many people. The somewhat restrictive Taft-Hartley Act was passed, and many state legislatures passed "right to work" laws which outlawed the closed shop. These laws hampered unions' organizing efforts and slowed the growth of union membership. In this way law "structures the power relationships" of a society and legitimizes the power of those whose power has the society's sanctions.

Law as expression of the mores   As was stated in our chapter on social control, law is a means of enforcing the mores in a complex, secondary-group society where informal group controls are less effective. Some laws are morally neutral and merely seek to establish a dependable procedure for doing something, such as, for example, writing an enforceable contract. But a great many laws deal with right and wrong behavior as determined by the values and experience of the society.

When a law expresses the moral consensus of the society, it will be effectively enforced. Comparatively few people in our society are murdered or forcibly raped. It is true that many murderers and rapists go unpunished, but their acquittal is largely due to the technical difficulties of legally establishing guilt "beyond all reasonable doubt." A law is effectively enforced when violations are comparatively infrequent and known violators may reasonably expect to be punished.

[5] Roscoe Pound, in George Gurvitch and Wilbert E. Moore, *Twentieth Century Sociology*, Philosophical Library, Inc., New York, 1945, p. 300.

When a law is backed by no firm moral consensus, effective enforcement is less likely. The classic illustration is the Eighteenth Amendment, which prohibited the manufacture, sale, or transportation of alcoholic beverages in the United States. Whether this law reflected the mores of the majority of citizens at that time has been debated. Certainly there was no moral consensus. Many people considered good liquor a part of the good life and soon located a source of supply. Laws against gambling and prostitution are other examples of poorly enforced laws which are supported by no clear moral consensus.

It is sometimes stated that a law *cannot* be enforced unless backed by a clear moral consensus. This generalization is not necessarily true, for it overlooks the great variation in the types of situations in which laws may be applied. Laws regulating gambling can be enforced only through the detailed supervision of the individual actions of a large number of people. On the other hand, laws requiring manufacturers to install safety equipment in automobiles can be enforced with comparative ease. Even though a law may have majority support, if this majority is apathetic and if enforcement requires tremendous individual supervision, the prospects for its enforcement are doubtful at best. But when the people supporting the law are keenly interested in its enforcement and when this can be done through inspection at a limited number of checkpoints, then even laws which do not rest on a clear consensus may be effective.

Law as molder of the mores In a changing society the mores are constantly changing. Law is one of the forces which change the mores. The law states the approved moral code and makes social policy; thus it functions as an educator [Litwak, 1956]. It is not always necessary to wait for a moral consenus before passing a law; the enactment and enforcement of the law help to create a moral consensus. Child labor laws and compulsory school attendance laws were passed at a time when there was by no means a moral consensus to support them. A considerable fraction of the people sharply disagreed. But important pressure groups, including labor unions and some business groups, found it to their economic advantage to support these laws. Today virtually all are agreed that full-time child labor is bad and that compulsory school attendance is good. Law has helped to create a moral consensus where none existed.

Today law is being used effectively to change the mores dealing with race relations in the United States. Many people recite the cliché, "You can't legislate against prejudice," ignoring the fact that it is discrimination, not prejudice, which is the subject of legislative concern. Most Americans may be unaware that, to a great extent, "social patterns of segregation were created by law, and not the other way around."[6] Negroes and whites in the prewar South were not generally segregated; they lived in close intimacy, although without equality. The Civil War and Reconstruction destroyed the traditional racial arrangements. Some years later, "Jim Crow" laws were passed, requiring the separation of the races in railroads, waiting rooms, theaters, and other public accommodations [Woodward, 1957]. Law imposed upon all people a pattern of segregation which had not existed in the past and was not yet being uniformly practiced. At the present moment, law is being used to impose the

[6] Jack Greenberg, *Race Relations and American Law*, Columbia University Press, New York, 1959, p. 5. See also Comer Vann Woodward, *The Strange Career of Jim Crow*, Oxford University Press, Fair Lawn, N.J., 1957.

practice of strict segregation, called "apartheid," upon the white and colored people of the Union of South Africa [Nakasa, 1961].

Within recent years, a number of United States Supreme Court decisions have overthrown many state segregation laws and have interpreted the Constitution to forbid many kinds of segregation practices. In addition, many types of discrimination and segregation are now prohibited by national civil rights acts as well as by legislation passed by many states and municipalities. Segregation, established with the help of law, is now being destroyed with the help of law. Segregation will not be ended easily or quickly, but the trend is unmistakable.

Under what conditions does law succeed in molding the mores? First, the law must operate with, and not against, the forces of change in the society. Attempts to stem the tide of change by law are foredoomed to failure. American marriage and divorce laws in the first two-thirds of the twentieth century have steadily grown more stringent and restrictive; yet the divorce rate has continued to rise. Law failed to prevent increasing divorce in a society whose values were growing increasingly tolerant of divorce.

When law is in harmony with the processes of change, it accelerates and institutionalizes changes. Compulsory segregation laws played an important role in establishing patterns of segregation in the South after the end of legal slavery created a desire for some other means of keeping Negroes under white control. They were thus in harmony with the trends of the time. Today it is the other way around. Discoveries by natural and social science have destroyed the intellectual respectability of theories of innate white superiority. Economic changes have made segregation increasingly costly and wasteful. The trend of change today is toward a greater equality of rights, opportunities, and rewards for Negro citizens. Antidiscrimination laws and court rulings are, therefore, working with the direction of social change in our society.

Second, if a law is to have any effect upon the mores, it must be actively enforced. In some Northern states, laws forbidding discrimination in restaurants and public accommodations were unenforced for many years. Negroes were too intimidated or apathetic to demand enforcement, and apparently few whites were interested. Most law enforcement begins when a citizen makes a complaint to the police or prosecutor, charging someone with a specific violation of law. Unless someone signs a complaint and will testify in the court, the law may not be enforced. Today many Negroes and sympathetic whites are prepared to demand enforcement of antidiscriminatory legislation.

Whether a law will be obeyed will depend partly upon the costs and inconveniences of continued disobedience. As this is written, the white officials in many Southern communities are desegregating their schools, even though most of them are opposed to the measure. After years of opposition, it became clear to the responsible community leadership that they must either accept some degree of desegregation or abandon the public school system. Thus law can force people to act in opposition to some of their customs and mores by creating a situation where it is unbearably costly for them to do otherwise.

The effects of law upon attitudes, prejudices, and mores are indirect. Law cannot forbid a person to hold an attitude, but it can prevent him from carrying his attiude into action. Law can bring behavior changes and restructure the kinds of contacts groups have with each other, and these can in turn bring changes in attitudes and mores. That law functions indirectly to change mores

Law can prevent him from carrying his attitude into action.

is no longer a theory; it is now an established fact. We are, however, not yet certain of the exact circumstances under which a particular law or an administrative edict will change mores and practice in the desired direction, or will simply intensify opposition. The question cannot be answered without further research.

To sum up, law is powerless to change the mores of an entire people, or to reverse the direction of changes. But where the mores are conflicting, laws can mold conduct and eventually the mores. Laws can impose the behavior patterns of certain groups upon other groups in the society. Law is unenforceable if it is greatly in advance of, or greatly behind, the trends of change in the society, but law can somewhat accelerate or retard those changes in the mores which other changes in the society are encouraging.

SUMMARY

Power is the ability to control the actions of others; it includes *authority,* a recognized right to give orders to others, and *influence,* an ability to affect others' actions apart from authority. Influence rests both upon personal qualities and upon one's control over rewards which other desire.

The *power elite* includes those with great wealth, the top executives in business and other institutions and the community influentials. The degree to which a power elite actually rules in our society is a matter of dispute among social scientists.

Organizations wield great power, which stems from their ability to mobilize the wealth and specialized skills of a great many people in a coordinated program of action. The degree of an organization's power is affected by its size, its cohesiveness, its role as perceived by members and outsiders, its alliances with other organizations, and its countervailing opposition from other organizations and groups.

Unorganized masses possess a great and often unused power. Man may be individually powerless in mass society; yet as "mass man," he may be collectively decisive. Mass power is expressed through the mass market, which determines what products, designs, and entertainment forms shall predominate; it is expressed in the mass veto of elite decisions through mass non-cooperation; it is expressed directly through the voting power of the masses, who thus determine which social policies shall prevail.

Law is a major instrument of social power, for law legitimizes the use of force by certain groups for certain ends. Most laws are an expression of the moral consensus of the society. In a complex society, law enforcement supplements informal primary-group controls as a means of social control.

Law also molds the mores of a society. Law institutionalizes the mores of certain groups and imposes these mores upon the remainder of society. The power of the law to change the mores is not unlimited. Law cannot change mores or behavior in a direction opposed to the other forces of change in the direction in which they are already moving in response to other changes and pressures in the society. The effects of the law are indirect; by changing behavior and restructuring the contacts between groups, attitudes and mores are eventually modified. Law both expresses and makes social policy; it is both a conservative and a creative force in society.

QUESTIONS AND PROJECTS

1. Distinguish between influence and authority. Which is most characteristic of the dean of women in a college? Of a greatly admired university professor? Of an ex-President of the United States?

2. Is there a "power elite" among the student body on your campus? If so, upon what positions or characteristics is it based? Are there some reputed power structures which have little real power? Would these differ from campus to campus?

3. In your institution, what persons or groups do you believe would dominate the decision making in each of these issues: whether to drop intercollegiate athletics; whether to add a school of engineering to the institution; whether to dismiss a popular professor who has become "controversial"; whether to approve a student government charter sought by student leaders? Having formulated your answers, now answer the question: Who do you think really runs your institution?

4. Why do business executives apparently have greater community power than professionals?

5. Which do you think has shown the greater power to affect motion-picture content in the United States —the Catholic Church or the Protestant churches? Why?

6. Very often the policy statements of the official spokesmen for organized groups are not carried into action. What are some reasons for this inaction?

7. Do you know of any recent or current social changes which are undermining the power position of labor unions? Of farm organizations?

8. Must power be organized? Are there any ways for unorganized masses to express real power? Of all power expression in our society, how much is carried out by organizations?

9. What is meant by the statement that "law structures the power relationships" of a society? Can you think of any recent changes in power relationships which have been brought about (at least in part) by law?

10. What is the normal relationship between law and the mores in civilized societies? Is it ever possible to enforce a law which is not backed by a firm moral consensus?

11. Under what conditions can law change the mores? How greatly?

12. Make a brief study of campus influentials by the *reputed-power* approach. Query a few faculty members to see whether they perceive the campus power system in the same way as the students.

SUGGESTED READINGS

ADRIAN, CHARLES R., PETER H. ROSSI, ROBERT A. DAHL, AND LLOYD RODWIN: *Social Science and Community Action*, Michigan State University Press, East Lansing, Mich., 1960. A study of community power with special reference to community organization and the role of the planner.

BOUMA, DONALD H.: *Why Kalamozoo Voted No*, W. E. Upjohn Institute for Employment Research, Kalamazoo, Michigan, June, 1962; reprinted in MILTON H. BARRON, *Contemporary Society*, Dodd, Mead & Company, Inc., New York, 1964, pp. 353–383. Analysis of the effectiveness of a real estate board in a power struggle.

COLEMAN, JAMES S.: *Community Conflict*, The Free Press of Glencoe, New York, 1957. A brief, readable analysis of power conflicts in the community.

DEGRÉ, GERARD: "Freedom and Social Structure," *American Sociological Review*, 11:529–536, October, 1946; Bobbs-Merrill reprint S-70. Argues that a pluralistic basis of social power makes possible a maximum of freedom.

FORM, WILLIAM H., AND DELBERT C. MILLER: *Industry, Labor, and the Community*, Harper & Row, Publishers, Incorporated, New York, 1960. An analysis of community organizations and community influentials, with special attention to the role of organized labor.

HACKER, ANDREW: "Power To Do What?" in Irving Louis Horowitz, *The New Sociology*, Oxford University Press, Fair Lawn, N.J., 1964, pp. 134–147. Comments on the limits of the power of the managerial elite.

*HUNTER, FLOYD: *Community Power Structure: A Study of Decision-makers*, The University of North Carolina Press, Chapel Hill, N.C., 1953. A pioneering study of the organization of power in an American city. (A379-ANCH)

*MILLS, C. WRIGHT: *The Power Elite*, Oxford University Press, Fair Lawn, N.J., 1956. A persuasive development of the thesis that our society is run by a small group of power wielders. See also the critical review by Daniel Bell, "The Power Elite—Reconsidered," *American Journal of Sociology*, 64:238–250, November, 1958. (20-GB)

MOYNIHAN, DANIEL P.: "The Private Government of Crime," *Reporter*, July 6, 1961, pp. 14–20. A semi-popular article describing a nonlegitimized power structure.

*POLSBY, NELSON W.: *Community Power and Political Theory*, Yale University Press, New Haven, Conn., 1964. A trenchant critique of power studies based on social stratification; formulates an alternative theory based on "pluralist" assumptions. (Y-151-YALE)

SELZNIK, PHILLIP: "The Sociology of Law," in Robert K. Merton et al., *Sociology Today*, Basic Books, Inc., Publishers, New York, 1959, pp. 115–127. Deals with the contributions of sociological research to an understanding of legal processes.

*SCHERMERHORN, RICHARD A.: *Society and Power*, Random House, Inc., New York, 1961. A summary of theory and research on social power. (SS18-RH)

SRINIVAS, M. N.: "The Dominant Caste in Rampura," *American Anthropologist*, 61:1–16, February, 1959. A description of the exercise of power through caste dominance in an Indian village.

VANDERZANDEN, JAMES W.: "The Non-violent Resistance Movement Against Segregation," *American Journal of Sociology*, 68:544–550, March, 1963. An analysis of the appeal of nonviolent resistance as a weapon in the struggle against segregation.

"Law and Society," *Social Problems*, Supplementary Issue, vol. 13, Summer, 1965. Articles dealing with the use of sociological data in court decisions, the relation of jurisprudence to the sociology of law and social factors involved in different types of legal careers.

15

RACE AND ETHNIC
RELATIONS

It happened in an army camp in occupied Germany after World War II. She was a strikingly beautiful French girl who danced in an act in one of the local night clubs, and he was a sergeant in the United States Army. The sergeant and the girl wanted to get married, and I was one of several officers who had to interview them and pass on a report before headquarters would eventually give its approval or disapproval of the marriage. The couple had known each other for six months, a long period under wartime circumstances. The girl looked attractive and intelligent, and the local police had no unfavorable reports in her file. The sergeant had a good army record. He expected to be discharged soon and return to a job in a Pennsylvania factory. All marriages present hazards, and the GI-foreign bride combination has more than the average, but this couple both had good records, and ordinarily approval would have been routine except for one factor, and this one the army didn't officially recognize: He was Negro, and she was white.

After the initial introduction I interviewed the girl alone. With a rather brutal directness I probed for her awareness of racial prejudices and discrimination. It was not my assignment to stop the marriage, but I was afraid she might not realize how different the status of a wife in an interracial marriage in the United States might be as compared with the status of the girl friend of a member of the occupying army in a district where most of the troops were Negro.

For some time my questions got exactly nowhere. Her answers were in carefully guarded monosyllables which showed no realization that either her courtship or her marriage would be any different from those of thousands of other French-American couples. Finally, in typically feminine fashion, her composure gave way, and she burst into tears.

"I know what you mean," she said. "It's already happened to us here."

As I was transferred shortly afterwards, I never learned the final outcome. But in her pathetic confession, "I know what you mean," she revealed that she had discovered the barriers which they could never remove. (From the army experience of one of the authors.)

THIS INCIDENT highlights one of the many problems of intergroup relations in a changing world—interaction through which all the social processes are illustrated. In many countries throughout the world, colored and white are working together in industry, studying in school, deliberating in legislative bodies, worshiping in churches, and carrying on jointly all the many types of interaction which make up social life. In many cases, the terms of the interaction make no reference to race but only to individual abilities. Thus the colored man may be a general, and the white man a private, or vice versa; either may occupy a superordinate or a subordinate status without any implication of racial inferiority or superiority.

On the other hand, the social structure of many countries is largely determined by race. One's race largely controls the residential area, the governmental rights, the type of job and amount of compensation, the social groups in which one is accepted, the schools one can attend, and a host of other patterns of social interaction. Many group alignments are on the basis of function (what one does), such as labor unions or professional societies; or of interest, such as stamp collectors, athletic fans, music lovers, etc. But much of the world is still separated by what Giddings, an early American sociologist [1913, p. 17], called a "consciousness of kind." People who are "like us" we welcome; those who are "different" we often reject. The basis of similarity is some feeling of group identity, which may be based upon nationality, religious affiliation, economic status, language usage, or regional habitat, as well as race. Of all these criteria, race is one of those most widely used as a basis for group identity, and often "race relations" is considered a subject by itself.

THE CONCEPT OF RACE

"Race" is a troublesome concept, for it has no generally agreed meaning. In popular usage, "race" may mean all of mankind (the "human race"), a nationality (the "German race"), a color grouping (the "white race"), or even a group which is mixed in nearly all respects but socially designated as different (the "Jewish race"). Almost any kind of category of people may be called a "race."

Even social scientists have not fully agreed in defining the term [Hunt, 1951]. Some have defined a race as a group of people separated from other groups by a distinctive combination of physical characteristics. As will be seen later, this poses certain difficulties because of intermixing, overlapping, and the gradual shading of physical characteristics (e.g., skin color) along a continuum without definite separations. Therefore, a "race" is not a biologically distinct grouping of people, yet many people think and act as though it were. Race is a socially significant reality, for people attach great importance to one's assumed racial identity. The scientist's fondness for neat scientific precision must be tempered by his need to deal with a tremendously important social reality. Perhaps an acceptable definition might read: *a race is a group of people somewhat different from other groups in a combination of inherited physical characteristics, but race is also substantially determined by popular social definition.*

Some historic theories of race The ancient world was not much bothered by the question of race differences for the ancient world was not highly race-conscious. Slavery was not based on color, and the slave in pagan Rome had far brighter prospects than a slave in the American South. Intense race consciousness among European peoples did not develop until the colonial expansion, when white men needed a handy rationalization to justify their rule over nonwhite people. Then a succession of ingenious theories arose, all of which confirmed the white man's superiority and sanctified his rule.

One such theory, still widely held, is the theory of the Hamitic curse, holding that the Negroes are the sons of Ham, cursed by God to be servants [Genesis 9:18–25]. The Bible lays the curse upon Canaan, not upon Ham; and nowhere does the Bible say whom the Negroes are descended from; but these are biblical oversights which believers in this theory are happy to correct. When the work of Darwin popularized evolutionary theories, it was not long before such theories were applied to racial origins. These held that Negroes were either products of a separate evolution or were an intermediate offshoot, and therefore were a primitive, half-animal form of human being [Carroll, 1900]. A variety of geographic theories were given a racial twist; for example, the superior qualities of the white race were attributed to the climate it lives in. All these theories accomplished their purpose, which was to provide a plausible rationale for white rule at a time when science was unable to say much about race differences.

Most scientists today are agreed that all races are of one species, the product of a single evolution,[1] and all races are about equally "close" to the other animals. For example, the Negroes more closely resemble the apes in skin color, nose form, and facial slant; but the whites more closely resemble the apes in lip form, hair texture, and amount of body hair.

The contemporary view of race Scientists seek to classify races as groups of people with distinctive combinations of physical traits that set them off from other groups. Skin color is the principal trait used in classifying races, although hair color, hair texture, amount of body hair, eye fold, shape of nose and lips, head contour, and body build are also used.

How many races are there? No objectively correct number can be given. Whether there are three, six, or fifty races depends upon which physical features we consider significant and upon the degree of similarity in physical appearance we demand of the members of a race. Dobzhansky comments on this confusion:

> *Boyd has recognized five, and Coon, Garn, and Birdsell nine or thirty or thirty-two races. Does it follow that some of these classifications are necessarily wrong? No, all may be right; it should always be kept in mind that while race differences are objectively ascertainable facts, the number of races we choose to recognize is a matter of convenience.*

Theodosius Dobzhansky, *Mankind Evolving: The Evolution of the Human Species*, Yale University Press, New Haven, Conn., 1962, p. 266.

[1] For a dissenting view which advocates the theory of a multiple origin of races see C. S. Coon, *The Origin of Races*, Alfred A. Knopf, Inc., New York, 1962. For a critique of Coon's approach, see T. Dobzhansky, "The Origin of Races," *Scientific American*, 208:169–172, 1963.

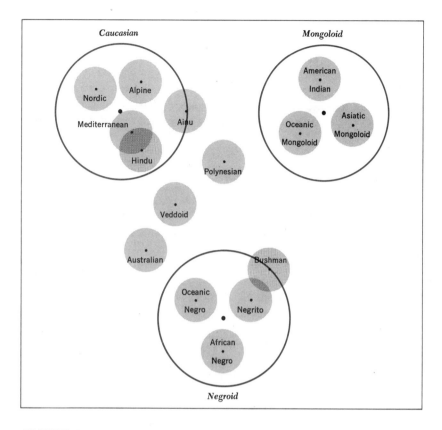

FIGURE 13 *The Races of Mankind.*

Distance between the centers of circles are representative of the degree of relationship.
SOURCE: A. L. Kroeber, *Anthropology,* Harcourt, Brace & World, Inc., New York, 1948, p. 10.

It is conventional to divide the human species into three main racial stocks—
the Mongoloid (yellow and brown), the Negroid (black), and the Caucasoid
(white). Most groups can be placed in one of these three categories, as is
shown in Figure 13. This figure also shows that the racial placement of some
groups is uncertain because their physical characteristics overlap. For example, the Asian Indians have Mongoloid skin color but Caucasoid facial features; the Ainu of Northern Japan have Caucasoid skin color and hair with
Mongoloid facial features. A further complication arises from the fact that the
races have been busily interbreeding for thousands of years so that nearly all
racial groups are considerably intermixed. Some groups, like the Jews, are not
properly racial at all yet form a definite social entity and are often treated as
though they were a race.

Physical anthropologists in searching for an objective basis for racial classification are now placing emphasis on genetic composition as indicated by blood
types. Currently, there is an attempt to combine blood-type data with more
easily observable differences such as color, stature, hair form, nasal index, etc.
Dobzhansky [1962], for instance, has suggested a tentative classification of
thirty-four racial groups which he hopes is neither so broad that it obscures
vital differences nor so numerous that it is unwieldy. Such research and

attempts at sound classifications may be expected to provide much useful information about the various branches of *homo sapiens*. The student should remember, however, that at the present time there is no generally accepted pattern of classification and that whenever one sees comment on "racial" differences, it is necessary to know what groups are involved. In the following sections of this chapter "racial" usually refers to "Negroid" and "Caucasian" and to members of these races found in the North American continent.

THE SCIENTIFIC VIEW OF RACE DIFFERENCES

It is clear that the races differ in some inherited physical characteristics. May they also vary in their inborn intellectual and emotional characteristics? This is a reasonable logical possibility. Is it a fact?

Physical race differences are unimportant   Physically, all races are approximately alike in every important characteristic. With a few exceptions (such as that a dark skin is useful under a tropical sun), the differences are ornamental, not functionally important. The physical differences within the human species are very modest compared with the differences within many species—dogs or horses, for example.

Intellectual and emotional race differences are hard to measure   Intellectual and emotional characteristics cannot be measured directly but must be inferred from some kind of performance. Here a difficulty arises. Many things can affect performance—native ability, experience, motivation, self-confidence, physical health, testing situation, and still others. The importance of any one of these factors can be measured accurately only if all others are held absolutely constant. How can comparative racial ability be measured? Only by comparing the performance of two racial groups where all these other factors are held constant. Does the evidence usually offered meet this test? Two kinds of evidence of racial inequality are usually offered: differential racial achievement and intelligence-test scores.

Differential racial achievements   If all races have equal innate abilities, why haven't they made equal achievements? This question is deceptively ethnocentric. We ask, "If they are as smart as we are, why don't they do what we do as well as we do it?" Meanwhile, another people may be asking the same question about us. Obviously, if we define achievement purely in terms of our culture's values, we can't lose.

Suppose achievement is defined as the building of a great civilization. Does this identify the superior races? Superior at what moment in history? By this test, the superior "races" 5,000 years ago would be the Egyptians and the Semitic peoples of Asia Minor; 3,000 years ago, these plus the Indians and the Chinese; 2,500 years ago, the Greeks and the Persians; 2,000 years ago, the Romans; and so it goes. Why, then, did the Nordic whites spend four-fifths of human history hovering about campfires and wiping their greasy fingers on their thighs? The cultural-achievement test of racial superiority works out most nicely if it is confined to the last thousand years of history.

But, one may ask, when have the Negroes built a great civilization? Doesn't their lack of creativity show inferiority? It is true that the Negroes built no very impressive civilization in the tropical jungles or arid grasslands where most Negroes lived. Neither did anybody else. It is also true that the Negroid peoples in Nubia and Ethiopia created states by 1000 B.C. which surpassed anything the Northwestern Europeans built until almost 2,000 years later. But the leading early civilizations were river-valley civilizations. Not until the development of modern technology was it possible to plant civilization in the tropical jungle, where its permanence is still uncertain. Negroes did, however, contribute to several civilizations which developed on the fringes of Africa, notably those of Carthage and Egypt. The great early civilizations arose in Egypt, Asia Minor, and Southern Asia. Some of their builders were, at least in part, Caucasian; others were entirely Mongolian. But all of them built great civilizations when our Anglo-Saxon ancestors were illiterate stone-age savages.

Cultural achievement is a product of many variables—geography and climate, contacts with other peoples, dominant values of the culture, the level of pre-existing technology, and, possibly, racial ability. Since we know no satisfactory way to hold these other variables constant, we have no scientific way to measure the factor of racial ability in cultural achievement.

A different sort of cultural achievement is a group's success in absorbing and using an advanced culture with which it comes into contact. By this test, the Nordic whites came off rather poorly. Falling heir to Roman civilization, they kicked it to pieces and sat on the remnants for hundreds of years. The nonwhite races of the world today, by comparison, are doing rather well.

Intelligence-test findings are inconclusive   Almost the only scientific attempts to measure comparative racial abilities have been through intelligence testing. There have been dozens, almost hundreds, of comparative studies of racial intelligence, usually Negro-white comparisons. Almost without exception they show a consistent degree of white superiority. The first large-scale test was run during World War I, when all servicemen took intelligence tests as part of army induction procedures. The average scores of whites were consistently higher than those of Negroes. Two qualifications, however, are important: Many individual Negroes had higher scores than many individual whites; and when the scores were broken down by states, Negroes in the top three Northern states had higher average scores than whites in the bottom three Southern states—as is shown in Table 19.

Why should Northern Negroes have made higher scores than Southern

Table 19   Southern whites and Northern Negroes by states: Army recruits, World War I

	Whites		Negroes	
State	Median score		State	Median score
Mississippi	41.25		New York	45.02
Kentucky	41.50		Illinois	47.35
Arkansas	41.55		Ohio	49.50

SOURCE: Otto Klineberg, "What Psychological Tests Show," in Barnhard J. Stern and Allain Locke (eds.), *When Peoples Meet*, Progressive Education Association, New York, 1942, p. 449.

whites? Selective migration—a tendency for the superior Negroes to migrate northward—is a possible answer, but the evidence for the tendency is not very convincing and certainly would not provide a complete explanation [Klineberg, 1935; Shuey, 1958, chap. 9]. A more probable explanation is that these Negro groups came from a more favorable environment, and that this advantage was reflected in their performance on intelligence tests. The average white man in these Southern states lived a poverty-stricken life in an area with poor schools and little social stimulation of any kind. The Northern Negroes, although subject to many types of discrimination, probably had better schools and a more intellectually stimulating environment than many of the Southern whites.

Nearly all intelligence-test studies which compare unselected groups of whites and Negroes show the whites to be superior; yet some Negro groups are superior to some white groups. Among the intelligence-test studies, almost all heavily Catholic groups make rather low average scores [Klineberg, 1944, p. 35]. Does this mean that Catholics have less native intelligence than Protestants? The heavily Catholic groups tested were from urban slum areas, densely populated by immigrants of southern European background; thus, these children were a disadvantaged group. The lowest test scores of all have been made by the isolated mountain people of the Southern highlands, the hillbillies, who are entirely Protestant, and are the most nearly pure Anglo-Saxons in the country. It is clear that we cannot predict a group's test score from its religion or racial origin, but we can make a quite accurate prediction of a group's intelligence-test score if we know its cultural environment.

This relationship of score to environment should be no surprise, once we recognize that the intelligence test is misnamed. *Intelligence tests do not measure intelligence; they measure intellectual performance.* The two differ widely; intelligence is inherited, but intellectual performance is affected by many variables of experience. When the intelligence test is used to compare two persons of similar background, motivation, learning experience, health, and familiarity with tests and test situations, it will quite reliably select the one with greater inborn intelligence. When it is used to compare the intelligence of persons or groups who differ in these other respects, the intelligence test is worse than useless, for it gives false measurements. Most Negroes are from a lower-class background. Among the factors which keep their test scores low are poor health, parental indifference to tests and learning, an educationally impoverished home background, and often a poor school adjustment—the same factors which handicap most lower-class white children. Added to these are some special handicaps imposed by race—a drummed-in sense of racial inferiority, and frequently an uncertain rapport with a white teacher or test administrator.

We cannot say how white and Negro achievements would compare under conditions of equal opportunity and reward, for nowhere are they fully equal. Not until white and

Equal abilities of all races.

Negro have competed under conditions which are equal in all respects—and for two or three generations of time so that the legacy of past discrimination and failure is forgotten—only then can we make a final judgment as to their respective racial abilities. Meanwhile, practically all social scientists are prepared to assume that all races have a potential capacity equal to the demands of our society, as is indicated in this resolution of the American Anthropological Association:

The American Anthropological Association repudiates statements now appearing in the United States that Negroes are biologically and in innate mental ability inferior to whites, and reaffirms the fact that there is no scientifically established evidence to justify the exclusion of any race from the rights guaranteed by the Constitution of the United States. The basic principle of equality of opportunity and equality before the law are compatible with all that is known about human biology. All races possess the abilities needed to participate fully in the democratic way of life and in modern technological civilization.

Resolution unanimously adopted by the Council of Fellows of the American Anthropological Association, Nov. 17, 1961.

But not all are prepared to accept this conclusion of science. For example, former Alabama Governor John Patterson in 1962 allocated $3,000 from his emergency funds to prove "scientifically" that the Negro is mentally inferior.[2]

Group differences in behavior are learned   Sometimes the "all men are alike" theme is distorted into a caricature of the facts. It is true that all groups appear to be alike in their inherited capacities. It is also true that groups differ greatly in their learned behavior. It is a fact that, as compared with whites in the United States, Negroes *average* lower in income, education, and stability of work habits; Negroes have higher rates of crime and delinquency, of venereal disease, illegitimacy, desertion, and practically every other unflattering index. The bitter resistance to school integration is based, in part, upon the fact that a large proportion of Negro children lack middle-class standards of either personal conduct or academic achievement.

How should we interpret such facts? To some, they serve as an excuse for a continued denial of equal opportunity to Negroes. The more perceptive observer sees that these unflattering facts are the *products* of unequal opportunity and will persist as long as opportunities and rewards are unequal. The perceptive observer also notes that averages do not apply to individuals; many Negroes rank far above many whites in achievement.

The social scientist recognizes that many *very real* group differences exist in personality, behavior, and achievement. There is no convincing evidence that any of these differences are rooted in anything inborn; in fact, the evidence strongly indicates that all or nearly all *major group differences in personality, behavior, and achievement are entirely learned;* they are rooted not in heredity, but in group tradition, opportunity, and reward. One aspect of this situation is summed up in the concept of the "self-fulfilling prophecy," discussed earlier on page 138. The supposedly impartial observer notes that Negroes have a more unfavorable record than whites in many kinds of social pathology, so he

[2] Reported in *Civil Liberties* (monthly newsletter of the American Civil Liberties Union), February, 1962.

acquiesces in a system whereby Negroes have inferior housing, more limited schooling, and more restricted job opportunities, thus producing the very results he had predicted. Why, then, do Negroes excel in music, dancing, and athletics? Not because of any special ability, but because these fields are more open to Negroes. Why do Jews pursue trade and avoid farming? For over a thousand years, trade was the only occupation gentiles would let them engage in. If scientists wish to understand special behavior traits of any group, they do not study the group's heredity; they study the conditions under which the group has lived and worked and interacted with other groups throughout its history.

Group averages tell nothing about individuals   On almost any uncontrolled comparison of whites and Negroes in the United States, Negroes will show a consistent inferiority. Many Negroes, however, will rank above many whites. This fact raises some interesting policy questions. For example, when Dallas, Texas, gave a "readiness-for-learning" test to its first-grade pupils, it found the following distribution:

Readiness for learning

Per cent	Negro	White
In below-average grouping	74	31
In average grouping	18	32
In above-average grouping	8	37

SOURCE: A. D. Albright, "What are Standards?" *Southern School News*, June, 1958, p. 1.

The above table and many similar pupil comparisons clearly show the average present *academic* superiority of white pupils. It also shows that many Negroes were above many whites, since 31 per cent of the whites were placed below-average, while 26 per cent of the Negroes were average or above. If these children are divided according to race for school experience, nearly one-third of the whites will receive certain experiences which are denied to the one-fourth of the Negroes whose "readiness for learning" is greater. Racial discrimination involves not only "the unequal treatment of equals"; it always goes beyond this to deny to the superior Negro the privileges enjoyed by the inferior white. Just how to reconcile this practice with the democratic ethos is a persistent problem for the supporters of a caste society.

To summarize the scientific facts about race differences, we may say that all theories of *inborn* race differences in ability, personality, or behavior are unsubstantiated by scientific evidence. While these characteristics cannot be exactly measured, it appears that all major groups are alike in their average inheritance of everything that is important for social behavior or learning. Any average differences in innate abilities, if they exist, are very small, are clouded by great overlapping, and are insignificant in effect when compared with differences in learning opportunity. There are, however, great differences in the present average behavior and personality of racial and other groups, but these differences are largely or entirely due to group differences in tradition, opportunity, and reward. Wherever the total behavior conditions are alike, behavior eventually becomes alike.

PATTERNS OF ETHNIC RELATIONSHIPS

We often hear people speak of the "Jewish race" or the "German race." In so doing they misuse the term. These peoples are not races; yet they are often thought of and treated as races. Sociologists use the term *ethnic group* to refer to any kind of group, racial or otherwise, which is socially differentiated to an important degree and has developed its own subculture [Gordon, 1964, p. 27]. In other words, an ethnic group is one recognized by society and by itself as a definite group. Although the distinction is associated with a particular set of ancestors, its identifying marks may be language, religion, relationship to a geographic locale, nationality, physical appearance, or any combination of these. The term is properly applied whenever the group differences are considered socially significant enough to set off the group clearly from others. Thus in the United States the name "Catholic" by itself would not be considered an ethnic label, but "French Canadian Catholic" would call up an image of a group with a definite character both in its own eyes and in those of the rest of society. Although we find some pattern of ethnic arrangements in every complex society, we find also a great variety in the way different groups have arranged to live together. We shall look at these briefly under the headings "Racist Patterns" and "Equalitarian Patterns." The term *racist* refers to a society which is frankly dominated by one group; *equalitarian* refers to a society in which an effort is made to treat all groups more equally. The following analysis is taken in part from Berry [1958, chaps. 7–12].

Some racist patterns of ethnic relationship In spite of some moves toward equalitarian intergroup living, the main trend of the twentieth century has been toward racist solutions of intergroup problems. Never in the world's history has there been so much mass slaughter, expulsion of minorities, and division of territory along ethnic lines as in the period of the last fifty years.

Annihilation Looking at the most grim of the racist solutions, we find that history's greatest annihilation was carried out by a highly civilized Christian nation. Between 1933 and 1945, the Nazis marched more than 5 million European Jews into the gas chambers with a systematic efficiency. Other cataclysms of history may have taken more lives, but we have no other example of such deliberate, premeditated mass slaughter carried out as a calculated government policy. Another recent instance of mass slaughter occurred in the Hindu-Moslem dispute in India in 1948, a conflict which involved practically all the techniques of racist procedure.

Until recent years annihilation or near-annihilation was the price primitive peoples often paid for their contact with those from an advanced technological culture. To some extent the annihilation occurred through deliberate slaughter, following the American pioneer philosophy that "the only good Indian is a dead

Indian." Usually though, group decline was a result of more indirect effects of culture contact. These included the greater deadliness of tribal wars with the introduction of firearms, the spread of diseases such as tuberculosis, syphilis, and smallpox, limitations of the food supply through the loss of lands, and the disorganization of society through the ravages of alcohol and the weakening of tribal authority. Sometimes disease was deliberately used to decimate a native people. A native would be caught and held in a white settlement until he developed measles, whooping cough, or some such disease; then he would be released to join his people, who were highly susceptible to the new disease. Often one-half or three-fourths of them would die within a few weeks.

One example of complete annihilation took place in Tasmania, an island south of Australia in which the aboriginal population was completely wiped out by English settlers, some of whom hunted the natives for sport and for dog meat [Murdock, 1936, pp. 16–18]. The Maoris in New Zealand who are now fairly well accepted and have amalgamated to some extent with the whites, dropped from a population estimated at 200,000 in 1800 to 40,000 in 1897 [Winiata, 1958]. In the United States the Indians declined from an estimated population of 1½ to 2 million at the time of the Pilgrims to less than 400,000 [Kallen, 1958]. Even in Hawaii, which the Westerners entered in a relatively benign manner, the number of Hawaiians of native stock dropped from 300,000 in 1778 to 57,000 in 1872 [Berry, 1958, p. 163].

The prospects of native peoples are now changing. The reduction of disease through mass immunization promises to swell their numbers higher than before contact with the white man. This new demographic development is a mixed blessing, since it may be impossible for a society with a traditional culture to sustain an unchecked population increase in the limited territory available.

Expulsion and partition   The idea that a nation should be composed of those who share a similar ethnic background has been especially popular in recent years. A mass shifting of population has resulted from an effort to make political boundary lines coincide with ethnic groupings—a shift which has frequently upset the patterns of centuries. People whose families have lived in certain areas for hundreds of years suddenly find themselves declared undesirable aliens and are forced to move to a land which to them is new, strange, and terrifying, even though it may be populated by persons of the same race, nationality, or creed.

An early example of this practice is told in Longfellow's *Evangeline*, a story based on the forcible removal of a colony of French settlers from Nova Scotia. Other examples would include the expulsion of Greeks from Turkey and of Turks from Greece, the partition of the land of Palestine into a Jewish state and an Arab state, the division of Ireland under which the heavily Protestant area around Belfast remains a part of the British Empire while the Catholic part of Ireland is an independent country, and the partition of India between Moslems and Hindus. Proof that no group is secure against the effects of such a policy is seen in the fate of the Germans living outside the boundaries of Germany. Czechoslovakia, Poland, Yugoslavia, Bulgaria, Rumania, and Hungary all feared that the presence of a German minority might some day lead to claims on their territory by another strong German government. The answer to this problem seemed simple—eliminate the minority from the territory. Consequently over 10 million Germans were ordered to leave areas in Central and Eastern Europe where their families had lived for centuries. It is very possible that in the near future white minorities will be expelled from parts of Africa.

During World War II both Russia and the United States forced ethnic groups to move from one part of the country to other areas. The Russians broke up the semiautonomous Volga German Republic and transported its inhabitants to Siberia; the United States placed thousands of West Coast Japanese in detention camps located hundreds of miles from their homes. Little is known of the ultimate fate of these Volga Germans whose ancestors had been invited to Russia by Peter the Great. The United States eventually reversed its policy and allowed the Japanese to live where they wished. Incidentally, although we justified the Japanese detention on the grounds of national security, a far larger concentration of Japanese in Hawaii seems to have been entirely loyal to the United States, and American soldiers of Japanese ancestry gave a good account of themselves in the final years of the war.

The effort to eliminate an ethnic group either through slaughter or through attempts to destroy its culture is called *genocide,* a practice which is now outlawed by the United Nations Convention on Genocide. This agreement is a significant step in intergroup relations, but its force is considerably weakened by the fact that at this writing the United States has not ratified this convention.

Segregation and discrimination   Another type of racist solution, which is less brutal than those just described, is even more widespread. In a great many countries the attitude toward the members of subordinate groups is that they should be allowed to function only in a way that serves the interest of the dominant group; in other words, *discrimination.* The essence of discrimination in this sense is *a practice that treats equal people unequally,* in that members of different ethnic groups do not have the same opportunities to compete for social rewards. Discrimination means that the duty of the subordinates is simply to do the work which the dominants are either unable or unwilling to perform.

The practice of *segregation* implies that contacts between the subordinates and the dominant group will be confined to those which are essential for the direction of the subordinates in their labors. Subordinates may come into intimate contact with the dominant group as household servants or as laborers in farm and industry. However, purely social contacts are greatly restricted, or if possible, altogether eliminated. If people eat together or sit down together, the association implies equality and tends to undermine the basic assumptions which underlie the system of discrimination. Intimacy but not equality of contact is permitted; dominant and subordinate may meet in bed as master and concubine, but not as husband and wife.

The segregation-discrimination pattern is probably most perfectly developed in the traditional caste society of India, in which the occupations that people may perform are carefully defined, intermarriage is taboo, and separation is the rule in most social relations. In terms of deliberate government policy, segregation and discrimination have been carried furthest by the Union of South Africa. Under the banner of apartheid, this country has sought to reverse the slight progress of earlier years toward integration and to separate the races absolutely except for employment, where jobs and pay are determined by color with whites getting favored treatment. Some logical consequences of this system are that white men never work under the direction of colored men, that colored men receive less money than white men when they are employed in the same capacity, and that service and educational facilities for colored people are separate from those used by white people.

For many years the United States was committed to segregation and discrimination, with several states enforcing such policies by state laws. Currently the Federal government and many state and local governments are working toward integration, but in many respects, American Negroes remain as fully segregated as ever.

Colonialism and discrimination   At one time nearly half of the world's population and territory was included in the colonial empires of a few great powers. When this situation was at its height, the social, political, and economic dominance of the white man was frankly recognized. Perhaps a few native puppets might be kept in luxurious impotence; the rest of the native inhabitants could serve in menial positions or minor clerical occupations but could never hope to be given important executive posts. They might live in or near the houses of whites as servants, but strictly residential dwellings were usually segregated—the Europeans living in a compound cut off from the rest of the population. Native women might serve as mistresses for white men, but legal marriage was rare. The system was somewhat modified in practice by the need to use native personnel in the development of the country. This led to the limited training of a number of natives and to the opening of opportunities in higher education for a few (much more so in some colonies, such as British India, than in some others, such as the Belgian Congo). Eventually, as colonialism began to retreat, the social barriers of discrimination and segregation also tended to be eased; greater political power was granted to the native populations and social relationships reached more nearly a level of equality. This process has culminated in many countries in the end of foreign rule and the creation of independent governments.

With the coming of independence the tendency is to reverse the process of segregation and discrimination. Thus, the Europeans who once were dominant were, in some cases, forced out of the country. Most of the Dutch were compelled to leave Indonesia, while those who remained soon found that their activities were definitely restricted and their status changed from that of dominance to one of bare toleration. Europeans were shut out of many lines of business activity, and even missionaries and educators now find that their work takes place under the critical supervision of native governments.

Some equalitarian patterns of ethnic relationship   **Integration**   Perhaps the classic example of the integration of the disparate groups into a common society is seen in the assimilation of European immigrants in the United States. Such immigrants came from a number of national cultures with a variety of languages, customs, dietary habits, family patterns, and general attitudes toward life. The first reaction of immigrants was usually to settle in ethnic colonies, either in small towns—sometimes given a European name—or in urban neighborhoods which became known as "little" Poland, Greece, or Italy. Often they viewed the United States as a temporary haven where they might stay until an unfriendly political regime in their European homeland had disappeared or until they had accumulated enough money to retire in comfort in their homelands. Many immigrants did spend their entire period of sojourn in ethnic colonies surrounded by fellow nationals, and a considerable number were able to return to Europe as they had planned [Saloutos, 1956]. The majority of immigrants, however, remained in the United States, and either they or their descendants moved out of the ethnic colonies as their assimilation progressed to such an extent that their European background became only a faint memory.

While European immigrants quickly became integrated in a common society, Americans whose racial features set them off from the Caucasians have not found assimilation so easy. The prevailing pattern in America has been the integration of Caucasian immigrants and the segregation of other groups.

In actual practice most colored Americans are still living under conditions of discrimination and segregation. The trend toward integration should be seen against a general pattern in which privileges taken for granted by whites are often denied to other citizens. Housing and employment are unequally available to ethnic groups, and in spite of some change, most Negro children are still attending segregated schools. The trend toward integration is undeniable, but many further changes will be required if the integration of colored citizens is to be accepted as the standard pattern of American life.

Cultural pluralism The standard example of cultural pluralism is Switzerland, a country which maintains a high degree of national unity although it has no national language and is religiously divided. In Switzerland, Protestants and Catholics have been able to live agreeably under the same government, while speaking German, French, or Italian. Since the Swiss citizen does not feel that either his religious loyalty or his ethnic identification is threatened by other Swiss, he is free to give a complete allegiance to the Swiss nation as a common government which allows for the tolerance of distinctly different cultural groups. Canada, with the division between the French and the English, and Belgium, with a division between the French- and the Flemish-speaking population, are other examples of cultural pluralism (not, however, without some instances of interethnic conflict). The different groups who make up a pluralistic society in these nations frequently engage in a struggle for influence, but the essential idea is that national patriotism does not require cultural uniformity, and that differences of nationality, religion, language, or even race do not preclude loyalty to a common national government.

Cultural pluralism does not seem to attract the newly independent nations of Asia and Africa, although many of them have established governments in areas including a number of language and tribal groups which never before in history were recognized as one nation. Instead of assuring the various groups of their cultural autonomy, the usual trend has been a drive toward uniformity. This includes the establishment of a national language and a general push toward a high degree of cultural unity in following the patterns of the dominant group.

The United States has also been cool toward the concept of cultural pluralism as applied to racial and nationality groups, where most Americans have preferred either integration or discrimination and segregation as a solution. Indians constitute practically the only large racial group in the United States which has expressed some desire for treatment along the lines of cultural pluralism. Their preference may be explained by the fact that Indians were here before the arrival of Europeans and in spite of considerable pressure have been able to maintain some degree of cultural identity.

Our religious divisions are one area of intergroup relations where some observers [Herberg, 1960] believe cultural pluralism is an essential and valuable feature of American life. For other ethnic groups, it may be that cultural pluralism is only a transitional stage. Gordon [1964, pp. 243–245] argues that one has to accept and have pride in the group of his origin before he is ready to accept assimilation into the larger society. Thus immigrants and their children may gain a sense of security and identity when encouraged to talk about the contributions which their ethnic cultures have made to American society. Similarly, Negro students may profit from knowing that Africa has been an historic crossroads of civilization, not merely the locale of primitive tribes.

Although integration has been espoused by most American Negro leaders, policies similar to cultural pluralism have a persistent appeal. With the advent of legal desegregation, the appeal of these pluralistic policies has been reinforced by the realization that many Negroes have difficulty entering the mainstream of American society at a favorable level. Since middle-class status is often seen as "white middle-class," the Black Muslims and some other "black power" advocates recommend that Negroes work within racial lines and build their own society. Such a policy is handicapped by the impracticality of economic isolation and by the fact that the Negroes, unlike nationality groups, lack distinctive language or religious cultural patterns. On the other hand, it is promoted by the continued blocking of equal Negro participation in American society. "Black Nationalism" is stimulated by white hatred and rejection; it is weakened by evidence that Negroes can find acceptance and success in the total society.[3]

Amalgamation While assimilation refers to a blending of two cultures, the term *amalgamation* means a biological interbreeding of two peoples of distinct

The Saxon invasion of the sixth century soon produced the Anglo-Saxon type.

physical appearance until they become one stock. Although distinct physical types have seldom entirely disappeared, enough interbreeding has taken place so that it is difficult to find any large group of individuals who form a "pure" racial type.

England has practiced amalgamation on a grand scale. The Saxon invasion of the sixth century soon produced the Anglo-Saxon type, to be

---

[3] For a sympathetic portrait of "black power" see Lerone Bennett, Jr., "Stokely Carmichael, Architect of Black Power," *Ebony*, September, 1966, pp. 25–32. Probably the opposite point of view is best expressed in Martin Luther King, *Stride Toward Freedom: The Montgomery Story*, Harper & Row, Publishers, Incorporated, New York, 1958. See also, Martin Luther King, "Martin Luther King Defines 'Black Power'." *New York Times Magazine*, June 11, 1967, pp. 26ff.

Per cent of Negro marriages involving whites, in Michigan, 1953–1963

Year	1953	1954	1955	1956	1957	1958	1959	1960	1961	1962	1963
Percentage	0.75	0.78	0.80	0.89	0.76	0.94	1.01	1.01	1.13	1.20	1.56

SOURCE: David M. Heer, "Negro-White Marriage in the United States," *Journal of Marriage and Family Living*, 28:265, August, 1966.

blended again with the Normans in the eleventh century. Hawaii includes the descendants of the original inhabitants of the islands, plus a large number of Caucasian settlers, even larger numbers of Chinese, Japanese, and Filipinos, along with a sizeable group of Koreans. All these have intermarried quite freely, the highest rates being in groups which have more males than females. White and colored intermarriage is common, and many of the leading families of the islands trace back their ancestry to a union of early European or American traders with the Hawaiian nobility.

In the United States the conditions of slavery favored the amalgamation of white and Negro. Although intermarriage was illegal in the Southern states, concubinage was widespread. Sexual access by white males to Negro females was usually regarded as one of the privileges of the caste system. The system emphasized the dominant position of the white male, since he was in a position to possess Negro females at will and to prohibit such relationships between Negro males and white females. Mere association with white females, however willing, would subject a Negro male to charges of rape, and hundreds of Negro men have been lynched or legally executed on this charge. No white man has been lynched for a similar offense against a Negro woman, and only in recent years have white men been legally prosecuted for raping Negro women.

Amalgamation in the United States has greatly declined during the past century, for a variety of reasons: the end of slavery, the decline of the plantation, the diminishing number of white households with Negro servants, the rising status of Negroes, and a growing white disapproval of interracial sex contacts. But while extramarital amalgamation has declined, has interracial marriage increased? The limited evidence on this question is mixed and inconclusive. Hawaii for many years has had a fairly high rate of intermarriage, involving white and colored, as well as marriage between members of various oriental groups. In other parts of the United States the interracial marriage rate has fluctuated at a relatively low level, and no definite trend is discernible. In Boston, one of the few places where records are available over a period of time, an average of 3.9 per cent of all Negro marriages between 1914 and 1938 involved a white partner, while between 1900 and 1904, mixed marriages accounted for 13.6 per cent of all Negro marriages [Simpson and Yinger, 1965, p. 371]. Some current figures in other localities indicate a slight increase in such marriages, but the rate is still low, both absolutely and in comparison with some previous periods. National figures are not obtainable since many states keep no records by race. Data for Michigan might give some indication of current trends, since Michigan has a rather high degree of racial integration in education and employment.

Whether there will eventually be a blending of the races is by no means certain. At present, it is estimated that 21 per cent of the Americans classified as white have some American Negro ancestry, with about 155,000 Negroes moving into the white category between 1941–1950; nearly three-fourths of our Negroes have some white ancestry [Stuckert, 1958; Burma, 1946]. In all societies the choice of mates is affected by forces which make for endogamy and by counterforces working for exogamy. At present the marriage rate in the United States between those of different European stocks as well as between Protestant and Catholic is high, whereas the rate of Jewish-gentile intermarriage is low and that between colored and white is still lower. Legal equality along with increased contact between members of different races may bring a high rate of intermarriage. It is possible, however, that our great-great-great-grandchildren may be bound by our preferences in mate selection about as tightly as we are bound by those of our great-great-great-grandfathers. So many factors are involved that it is extremely difficult to predict future intermarriage trends.

MINORITY REACTIONS TO DOMINANT GROUPS

The patterns of ethnic relations which a society follows are mainly those imposed by the dominant group. Therefore, if ethnic relations become a problem, the dominant ethnic group has created it. American whites have not been lynched by Negroes; gentiles have not been led to gas chambers by Jews; and Asian and African nationals have not been legislated out of business by the overseas Chinese and Indians. Since the most powerful group in a society dictates the patterns of the society, it would be more correct to speak of a white problem than a colored problem, or of a majority problem than a minority problem. Yet the minority groups are not entirely passive. Each group plays a role in the interaction. What are some of the minority responses?

Submissive manipulation   Flattery is the historic weapon of the weak. Harriet Beecher Stowe's *Uncle Tom's Cabin* shows a submissive Negro slave whose adjustment was characterized by faithfulness to his master and deference to white people in general. Through dogged loyalty, flattery, and submissiveness he assumed that he would gain his white master's favor and protection. To many whites, such a Negro is a "good nigger"; that is, he accepts his caste position. But other Negroes may contemptuously call him an "Uncle Tom." In a period when discriminatory patterns are completely dominant, the Uncle Tom posture will help the subordinates to gain the favor of the dominants and also enable them to become acquainted with the culture of a technologically advanced group. As acculturation proceeds to reduce the cultural differences between the two groups, the Uncle Tom posture fades. The subordinates become less willing to assume the role, while the dominants grow less omnipotent in their ability to dispense penalties and rewards.

Marginal adaptation   Marginal adaptation is an effort to cultivate fields where the majority offers the least resistance. Booker T. Washington, a prominent Negro leader in the period between 1880 and 1910, urged that Negroes should seek to develop their skills in agriculture and craftsmanship. He promoted vocational education as a step in this direction. The success of his program, however, has been limited by technological trends and white resistance. Mechanization of agriculture and industry restricted the number of people who could make a livelihood as artisans, while both farmers and craftsmen were hostile to Negro competition. Negroes were welcomed as unskilled laborers or field hands but found resistance when they attempted to become independent farmers or highly skilled artisans.

Various groups have sought adaptation as marginal trading peoples through finding business opportunities neglected by the majority. This has been true of Jews, overseas Indians and Chinese, Syrians, Armenians and some Arab traders. Such business is often profitable, but the minority group's initial success in this adaptation has often aroused the resentment of the majority group, which replies by instituting various forms of discrimination against successful minorities.

In general, the effort of a minority to find an outlet in fields neglected by the majority group is successful only when the field is highly specialized and the minority group is small in numbers. Thus a small number of American Chinese have found a role in hand laundries and in the souvenir shops and restaurants of Chinatowns, and gypsies have been successful as fortune tellers and carnival operators; but no large ethnic group has been able to find an economic niche where it could escape discrimination.

Withdrawal and self-segregation

Withdrawal has been most characteristic of small religious groups such as the Amish, who deliberately limit their interaction with the rest of society; but it may be found to some extent in other types of groups as well. One mark of this tendency is the development of colonies in which an ethnic group sponsors schools, churches, social agencies, and recreational establishments catering primarily to an ethnic clientele. While particular institutions of this type, such as national or racial churches may persist for many years, it is difficult for the group to maintain the cohesion needed to resist the impact of the larger society. Over a period of time members of such groups find themselves increasingly involved with outsiders and tend to become absorbed in the general community, if they are not readily identifiable by their physical characteristics. As they become aware of the opportunities in the society, they discover that often the best economic openings are in businesses serving the general community, the most attractive houses are outside of the ethnic area, and the education best adapted to social mobility is found in schools not dominated by the ethnic group. Unless the ethnic colony is held together by a strong religious tie and is either replenished by a constant supply of new members or bitterly ostracized by the rest of society, it does not last very long.

This type of segregation does offer a small number of careers which are protected from the competition of outsiders. Ethnic schools, churches, and newspapers afford a chance for the employment of clergymen, teachers, and journalists, and the political power of an ethnic bloc may also guarantee a few government jobs. Business such as mortuary establishments, insurance companies, and restaurants may cater to a market ignored by concerns operated for the general society. Such segregated opportunities are necessarily limited in scope, and while they may provide an outlet for a few members of the ethnic colony, they cannot meet the economic aspirations of very many.

The oppression When one is treated in a special manner because of his ethnic identity he can-
psychosis not easily separate this treatment from the things that happen for other reasons. A member of a minority group may develop a tendency to imagine discrimination even when it is absent. The personal antagonisms normal to any
type of social life thus become group antagonisms, and every failure or frustration is attributed to discrimination, regardless of the real facts of the situation.
Since an inability to distinguish a real from an imaginary environment is a part
of many mental illnesses, this behavior in its extreme form may be considered
a type of psychosis. Kardiner and Oversey [1951] traced the patterns of behavior discovered in Negroes under psychoanalytic treatment and concluded
that ethnic discrimination is often a factor in serious mental illness, since it
produces tensions which some individuals are unable to resolve.

Reactions to ethnic status which do not actually lead to mental illness may
still prevent the individual from becoming fully socialized. Juvenile delinquency, excessive gambling, drug addiction, and alcoholism may also represent a flight from ethnic discrimination into activities that offer temporary
escape from the confines of a segregated existence. Ethnic barriers are usually
less rigid in the underworld, and narcotics and alcohol offer a temporary release from problems. The amount of such activity in any minority group may be
either higher or lower than the general average, depending on a variety of circumstances, but individuals in such groups sometimes find that antisocial
behavior is an easy type of reaction to a society which they feel has rejected
them.

Group self-hatred Group self-hatred is another reaction which militates against the maintenance
of mental equilibrium. Since the subordinates are a part of the total society, it
is difficult for them to reject unfavorable stereotypes that are a part of the
general culture. When the Negro infers from almost everything that he reads,
sees, hears, and experiences that he is inferior, he can hardly resist believing
that he is. The phenomenon of Jewish anti-Semitism is well known, and some
degree of similar feeling is hard for members of any minority group to escape.
Since society rejects the individual because of the alleged shortcomings of his
group, he naturally concludes that the cause of his trouble is not the dominant
group enforcing discrimination but the subordinates whose alleged unfavorable
traits apparently justify this discrimination. Some people who have internalized
this reaction are able to escape by "passing." The light-complexioned Negro
may become "white"; the Jew or the immigrant may change his name and
associate only with members of the dominant group.

For most people either marks of physical identification or close ties with the
group make "passing" impossible. Enforced identification with a group he
considers inferior makes it difficult for the individual to accept himself. Just
as respect for parents aids a person in establishing self-respect, so respect for
the group with which he is identified helps to establish the self-esteem necessary if one is to develop a secure personality. A rather striking example of this
process was recounted to one of the authors by a social worker in Hawaii in
connection with the local Filipino population. Filipinos were the last group to
enter Hawaii in large numbers and held the poorest-paying jobs. Their status
difficulties found expression in an attempt by Filipino children to deny their
national origin and call themselves Japanese or Chinese, since these groups

held a higher status in Hawaii. With the coming of independence for the Philippines in 1946 their attitude changed. Now they were identified with one of the first Asian colonial countries to gain independence, and their homeland occupied a prominent place in world affairs. They began to identify themselves as Filipino and, having reason to be proud of their ancestry, could accept it and enter into the process of assimilation without anxiety.

Nativism   A quite opposite type of reaction is found in the rejection of the culture of the dominant group and a zealous dedication to minority cultural patterns. Nativistic reactions have appeared in many parts of the world. The American Indians in the period around 1888 developed a "ghost dance" which symbolized the rejection of the white man's world and a futile attempt to revolt against those who had been forcing the Indians into subjection [Berry, 1958, pp. 501–502]. In 1918 Marcus Garvey organized the Universal Negro Improvement Association, whose aim was to lead American Negroes back to Africa. He attracted many followers, but his schemes foundered and eventually he was sent to prison on a charge of using the mails to defraud [Cronon, 1955]. Currently the Black Muslims and some other Black Power militants are preaching black supremacy and racial separation to American Negroes [see Chapter 20].

A very different type of group, the racist Southern whites, might also be classed as nativistic since their attempts to block national efforts toward racial integration led to a states-rights movement with a vigorous rejection of all non-Southern influence. Nativistic movements elsewhere would include the emphasis on "negritude" in central Africa [Balandier, 1955], the Dar Ul Islam movement in Indonesia, which strives to reject all Western influences and make Indonesia into a Moslem state [*Economist*, 1956], and a great variety of similar movements in many countries.

Nativistic movements often arouse a strong emotional response, but the conditions of life in the modern world make their chances of success rather dubious. In a time when the process of industrialization is forcing all groups to certain common cultural adjustments, any group will find it impossible to turn its back on the rest of the world. Isolation and a return to the past will not solve the problems of today.

Riots and   Most lynching forays, riots, and pogroms have been emotional outbreaks of a
violence   majority group bent on demonstrating that its superior position is not confined within legal bounds and that it can attack minorities with impunity. However, the emotional satisfaction of violence is not confined to majorities, for minorities also relish the catharsis which violence provides. Such violence does not need a definite aim and may not even be directed at those most responsible for minority oppression. Thus, most of the rioting in American cities since 1964 took place within Negro districts, and property destruction was done either to Negro-owned property or to other property serving Negroes, so that one result was an increase in property insurance rates and police surveillance, making life more difficult than before the riots took place. Similarly the riots were not related to specific demands, and the incidents which triggered the violence were often mere pretexts rather than obvious wrongs.

What did the rioters gain then? Sometimes the violence aroused community concern which resulted in improvement programs, although this was countered by a "white backlash" which often increased resistance to any kind of civil rights progress. More to the point, the riots provided an immediate sense of power to those who felt society had ignored and mistreated them. Tomorrow they might resume their misery in the ghetto, but tonight they could burn, attack, and pillage in ways that arouse fear in an entire city. Sporadic violence by a minority does very little, if anything, to improve their lot, but until the situation is drastically changed, such violence is apt to be a part of the price society pays for the frustration of minority citizens.

Movements of reform and revolt While the nativistic movements attempt to reestablish the supremacy of a dying culture, most of the current minority protest movements are an effort to secure for this minority group an acceptable status in the modern world. A number of reform and revolt movements are discussed in Chapter 20 of this text.

HOW DO ETHNIC PATTERNS CHANGE?

Individual attitudes and community behavior Since ethnic patterns are based upon prejudices, is it not useless to attack patterns of segregation and discrimination before prejudices are reduced? Until quite recently, even the social scientists shared the popular belief that "you can't legislate against prejudice." Like other people, we believed that those who wish to change ethnic relations must rely upon education and persuasion; then when persons have formed more tolerant attitudes, their actions will change and discrimination will disappear.

Social scientists now realize that these beliefs are based upon false assumptions. First, prejudice is not the cause of discrimination; it is far more nearly true to say that discrimination is the cause of prejudice. Discrimination separates groups so that they have only the inequality-type of contacts which create and feed prejudice. Second, we now know that our actions are not primarily determined by our individual attitudes. Current research indicates that probably the reverse is true—that our actions are determined by the pressures of groups of which we are a part and that our attitudes are largely determined by our group actions. This is to say that, over a period of time, our attitudes conform to the kind of action required by the community in which we live.

An example of this process is found in the experience of Washington, D.C., in connection with the desegregation of swimming pools in 1948. These swimming pools had been operated by the Department of the Interior on a segregated basis. The department had been criticized for allowing segregation and in considering a change of policy asked several experts their opinions. The usual verdict was that a separation of activities of this type was deeply embedded in the mores of the Southern whites and Negroes of Washington, D.C., and that an attempt to change to integrated swimming pools would lead to disaster. One expert differed. He pointed out that the individual attitudes of Washingtonians were less important than the group pressures they faced. The individuals who followed discriminatory patterns believed that in so doing they were conforming to what was expected of a good citizen. If this pattern could be changed, he believed that integration would proceed without disorder. He reasoned that in this case the essential focus was simply the attitude of the

Department of the Interior, and the actions of the police department. If the Department of the Interior indicated firmly and definitely that a policy had been decided upon, and if the police refused to allow any gangs or mobs to form and threaten the swimmers, he felt that integration would succeed. In the implementation of this policy he stressed to the police the fact that they were a professional group charged with preserving the law rather than a collection of individuals acting out their own attitudes. When the swimming pools were opened, a few gangs of white youths gathered in a threatening manner but were quickly dispersed, and after a few days integrated swimming became an accepted pattern [Lohman and Reitzes, 1952].

Some of the implications of this approach may be seen in another example, found in a study of an integrated teamsters' local union [Rose, 1952]. The union had strongly stressed the idea of integration and had insisted that equal opportunities be given to the drivers regardless of race. Interviewers found that the great majority of white teamsters recognized and supported the policy of employment integration. But when they were asked their opinion about integrated housing, the white teamsters expressed a high degree of opposition. Judged by the standard of racial tolerance, these two attitudes seem to be inconsistent. Looked at from the standpoint of group patterns, however, the inconsistency disappears. The teamsters were members of a union which felt that following a policy of employment integration was vital to the success of the union; as union members they had been indoctrinated with this policy, and they supported it. They were also residents of neighborhoods which supported the practice of housing segregation, and as conventional members of the community they accepted community values. In both circumstances the teamsters were responding to the patterns of group expectations, and in neither case could their actions be attributed to purely personal attitudes.

Important as personal attitudes are, they do not exist in isolation. A campaign designed to diminish prejudice is more effective when it is tied to a definite attack on discrimination, just as a campaign of racial intolerance is more effective when linked to a specific pattern of segregation. The community patterns of ethnic behavior are somewhat influenced by personal attitudes, but they are more directly shaped by the public and private groups able to control crucial decisions. The real estate board deciding whether or not it is "ethical" to promote integrated housing, the labor union which may seek either to exclude or to integrate, the corporation setting its promotion "ceiling" for Negroes, the school board drawing school-district boundaries and hiring teachers, the courts in reaching decisions, and the legislative bodies passing laws which treat different ethnic groups in either an equal or a discriminatory fashion— these and countless other groups set the pattern of the community. If individuals who feel strongly about ethnic relations are able to influence group policy, their attitudes will have some effect. Otherwise their individual feelings will have little influence on the development of ethnic relationships [Blumer, 1956].

An example of institutional integration   The experience of the United States Armed Forces provides a case study of the impact of individual attitudes as compared with organized patterns of relationships. Until the end of World War II the Army assumed that since soldiers came to military service with the attitudes they had acquired in a segregated civilian society, the Armed Forces had no choice but to follow a similar policy. By the end of the war there had been some experimentation in mixing Negro platoons in white companies, and by 1953 complete integration was the announced policy of all branches of the Armed forces.

In addition to a feeling that segregation was inconsistent with equal treatment of citizens, the change was stimulated by military considerations. Negroes in segregated units had performed very poorly in World Wars I and II, with many problems of discipline, low morale, riots, and frictions of all sorts [Lee, 1966]. In addition, since the average educational background of Negro soldiers was less than that of the whites, it was difficult to get the distribution of training in Negro units which the Army felt was essential. After much hesitation, the military authorities decided that integration should be the official policy, and this policy met the test of combat conditions in Korea. A team of social scientists was sent to Korea to assess the effects of integration under the title, "Project Clear." The following brief summary of their findings contains observations that may apply to many types of integration.

Negroes performed well under integration.

In general, combat-experienced officers held that Negro soldiers, though their performance in all-Negro unit was judged to be poor, became good soldiers in integrated units and that their presence had no adverse effects on the performance of hitherto all-white fighting teams (II, 26; IV, 119–121).

Whites who were exposed to integration tended to accept it.

Men in mixed units, overseas and in the United States, were consistently more favorable to mixing than were men in comparable segregated units. Those who had seen integration in action agreed that it works; those who had no basis for judging were in general agreement that it would not work (I, 10; II, 26).

Firm action by authorities helped integration.

Integration took place most smoothly in the Army, where individual troop commanders moved to implement the policy enthusiastically and decisively (I, 11).

Integration operated best in "army" situations.

When a series of interracial contact situations was considered, tensions regarding integration that did appear increased as these behaviors ran from public behavior (use of post buses) to private behavior (use of dance halls). Since other evidence made it clear that Army efficiency would be served by integration, this information proved the basis for time-phasing policy changes (II, 28–9).

Group identification overcame defects of segregated Negro units.

In segregated units Negro soldiers often exhibit the failings charged to them; in integrated units they approach the performance level of white soldiers. Resisting suggestions of incompetence becomes a big point for Negroes in mixed units; apparently the forces of competition that spur Negroes to perform well also spur white soldiers and thus create a bonus for integration (IV, 7, 123).

Condensed from Paul B. Foreman, "The Implications of Project Clear," *Phylon*, 16:263–274, September, 1955.

This fact that the shift to integration was made with unexpectedly little difficulty in the Armed Forces does not prove that it can be accomplished with equal ease in other social situations. Groups without the authoritarian power structure of the Armed Forces might have greater difficulty in making and implementing such a policy decision. It does indicate that once a firm group decision has been made and it is clear that it will be decisively carried out, individuals will tend to fall in line regardless of personal opinions. Rather than being decided on the basis of either individual attitudes or of some overall principle, the pattern of ethnic relationships is set by the action of the power structure which is able to operate effectively in a particular group. This does not necessarily mean that any particular pattern of ethnic relations is inevitable in the future. What it does indicate is that patterns of ethnic relationships can be deliberately chosen and imposed to a far greater degree than many people realize.

Technology changes the social structure Today all patterns of intergroup relationship are subject to controversy. While many persons and groups share in the debate, the real causes of change in intergroup relations may be the social changes—in population, in technology, in cultural values—which set the stage for our intergroup relations. For example, the invention of the cotton gin made large-scale cotton plantations profitable and created a need for a large supply of cheap, docile labor. The cotton gin ended all Southern discussion of whether slavery was desirable. More recently, the mechanization of Southern agriculture has replaced unskilled labor with mechanical slaves. Many of the rural Negroes moved to the city or to the North; they escaped from the paternalistic supervision of the planter and escaped also from some of the patterns of discrimination which could be rigidly enforced only in a rural setting where the white master knew everything that his colored hands were doing.

A caste society is best perfected in a static, unchanging system of relationships, sanctified by universally understood traditions. A growing, rapidly changing, dynamic society makes ancient caste rules quite unworkable; for example, a Brahmin in Calcutta today would soon starve if he ate only food upon which the shadow of no untouchable had fallen. A rapidly changing society tends either to reshuffle or to bypass crusty aristocracies and assign the important new tasks and rewards according to individual merit rather than inherited privilege.

FACTORS DETERMINING ETHNIC PATTERNS

Relationships between ethnic groups are seldom static for very long, although the causes of change are often complex and intertwined. Many attempts have been made to construct an ethnic-relations cycle of stages through

The "queer" people.

which such relationships will pass [Bogardus, 1930; Brown, 1934; Park, 1949; Glick, 1955]. Usually such cycles mention a stage of initial discovery in which the chief interest of the groups in each other is one of novelty or curiosity, followed by casual trading contacts which in turn result in friction leading to conflict. Conflict results in the defeat of the technologically backward group, which then undergoes a period of subordination until it has learned enough of the culture of the super-ordinate power to free itself from domination. Cycle theory emphasizes the changing character of ethnic relationships and does give a rough idea of developments which may be expected. However, the relationships which they describe are so complex and the potential patterns of ethnic relationships are so varied that cycle theory has only a very limited predictive value.

Ethnic relationships are subject to change because ethnic groups are continually engaged in the types of interaction described in the chapter on social processes. This interaction is constant, but the circumstances and the relative power of different groups is in a constant state of change. For instance, individuals from different ethnic groups are in a continuous state of competition, but the competition changes when a stable rural society enters a period of industrialization. Two major factors influence ethnic interaction. One is deliberate, planned change in the structure of society, which we will label *enacted* change, and the other is the gradual movement of society, unplanned and nondirected, which we will label *crescive* change. *Crescive* is defined in the dictionary as "increasing" or "growing" and implies change that develops out of the existing order without conscious design.

Enacted change

Occasionally governments or other social institutions decree certain patterns of relationships which have a far-reaching effect. The legalization of slavery is one such enacted measure which set the relative status of ethnic groups in extremely rigid form.

The legal definition of slaves in the United States as "property," while they were legally "persons" in Central and South America had great effects on their status. Central and South American slaves had certain rights guaranteed by law (to marry, hold property, buy their freedom, and others), but since property has no rights against its owners, slaves in the United States had no legal rights whatever [Silberman, 1964, chap. 4].

The acceptance of the idea of caste in Hindu religion is another type of enactment with persistent consequences. In the United States, the decision that the public lands would be reserved for homesteaders in 160-acre units prevented the rise of an agrarian landlord-tenant system in the West. Similarly the passing of a restrictive immigration act cut down support for cultural pluralism by limiting the number of immigrants to a number which could be assimilated with relative ease. After the Civil War, the "Jim Crow" laws of the Southern states made racial segregation legally mandatory in that area.

Currently, one of the leading types of enacted change is represented by the civil rights laws passed by the national Congress as well as by many of the individual states. These laws prohibit or restrict many types of racial segregation and discrimination. Civil rights laws have made many changes in American society, but no one would claim that they are completely effective. The limits of the effectiveness are very largely set by crescive changes which may work either for or against the aims of the law.

Crescive change

Most change in our society is not enacted by any legislature or the board of trustees of any organization but comes about without deliberate planning. No plan or decree is responsible for urbanization. No deliberative group brought forth the cotton gin which created a demand for cheap labor, or the mechanical cotton picker which later made this kind of cheap labor unnecessary. Nor did any legislative body produce the shift in scientific opinion which made a racist interpretation of human conduct untenable.

Policies of integration are favored by the general expansion of education, which makes it easier for members of a submerged minority to prepare themselves for social mobility. Conversely, they are hampered by the drift away from unskilled manual labor, which means that only the man with training is able to find a good job. Legislation can outlaw discrimination in employment, but this is of limited effect unless minority members are qualified for competition on a merit basis.

Enacted legislation has pretty well eliminated deliberate educational segregation in many areas, but *de facto* segregation continues to exist and may even expand because segregated housing produces segregated schools. Segregation in housing flourishes because a rapid Negro migration to the cities produces a massive demand for Negro housing, which means that integrated housing is often only a transitional phase until Negro demand takes up all the housing in districts open to Negro occupancy.

In the Union of South Africa industrial development and the consequent demand for labor works against apartheid legislation enacted to push the non-white population into rural areas. In India the caste system has survived onslaughts against it, in part, because the castes have become a political force in claiming group preference from government bodies. In the United States a rising income for Negroes has caused business firms to treat Negro customers with greater courtesy rather than in the demeaning fashion demanded by the traditional racial etiquette. Similarly the Negro movement to the cities makes political leaders more sensitive to the wishes of a constituency in which the "minority" grows larger.

These examples and many more indicate that crescive development may either accelerate or retard enacted programs of change in ethnic relations. This does not mean that ethnic relations are determined by the unconscious processes of history which man is powerless to control. Rather it means that to be effective, enacted change must be in harmony with the relevant trends in society. If industrial changes are in process, we must consider how these changes will affect the present and prospective situation of members of ethnic groups. If population is moving from the farm to the city and we desire residential integration, then positive steps must be taken to make the central city more attractive to the majority and also to enable racial minorities to enter the suburbs. If limited education or unstable family life prevent the minority from acquiring the skills and attitudes consonant with social mobility, then steps can be taken to stabilize family life and improve the schools. In other words, effective enacted change must do more than simply endorse a desirable pattern of ethnic relationships. It must either relate the enacted change to crescive development or seek to change the course of this development.

SUMMARY

Race differences are biologically trivial but culturally most important. Scientists are agreed that all racial groups probably inherit the same amounts and kinds of abilities, and that all differences in group personality, behavior, or achievements seem to be due to differences in learning situations. Intergroup relationships are broader than race, and the term *ethnic* is used to designate socially significant lines of group demarcation.

Ethnic relationships involve both cooperation and conflict between distinctive social groups, which often exist inside the same national boundaries. Bloody persecution, violent revolution, rigid and exploitative segregation, and a fragmenting of political units along ethnic lines have been the principal trends of ethnic relationships in the twentieth century. Other trends include cultural pluralism, which emphasizes the rights of societies rather than of individuals, and integration, which ignores group identification in favor of individual rights. Minority reactions to domination include submissive adjustment, marginal adaptation, withdrawal and self-segregation, the oppression psychosis, group self-hatred, nativism, protest movements, escape through antisocial conduct, and "passing" into the majority group.

Although great emotion may accompany ethnic attitudes, the actual pattern of behavior is found to be dependent on group pressure, while individual behavior usually conforms to community pressures. Community behavior patterns are not always consistent with widespread ethnic attitudes, and the community that supports integrated behavior in one sphere such as employment may support segregated practices in another such as housing. Amalgamation has been practiced on a large scale in the past but seems to be decreasing at the present time. Cycles of ethnic relationships interpret behavior of the past but are of limited value in predicting future trends.

Factors affecting the course of ethnic relationships include *enacted* change set in motion by deliberate decision of organized groups and *crescive* changes, which occur through the unplanned growth and development of society.

QUESTIONS AND PROJECTS

1. Why is the term *ethnic* used in preference to *race* throughout most of this discussion?

2. Is the world tending toward greater contact and cooperation between members of different ethnic groups or toward segregation and conflict?

3. Why do Negroes and Indians differ in their concepts of the treatment they wish to receive in the United States?

4. Is education the best way to change racial patterns?

5. Which occupational group has done more to change the pattern of ethnic relations—engineers or government officials?

6. Distinguish between segregation and cultural pluralism.

7. If all ethnic discrimination were ended would all groups produce equal proportions of highly successful men?

8. Many criticisms were made of the conduct of Negro units in World War II. Is this an argument for or against integration in the Armed Forces?

9. Has amalgamation been greatest in a discriminatory or an egalitarian situation?

10. What is the interrelationship between enacted and crescive change in promoting changes in ethnic relationships?

11. Read Richard Wright's *Black Boy*, Harper & Row, Publishers, Incorporated, New York, 1945. How do you think Richard's socialization was affected by race? Why did he become intensely ambitious?

12. Write a brief essay on what you would expect to happen if you were a Negro traveling through the American South. Then compare this estimate with the account of John H. Griffin, *Black Like Me*, Houghton Mifflin Company, Boston, 1961.

13. If both Negroes and whites attend your institution, how are they housed? Separate dormitories, separate dormitory sections, or integrated? Are room-mates assigned at random, or are Negroes paired as roommates? What can be said for and against each arrangement?

SUGGESTED READINGS

CAHNMAN, WERNER J.: "Socio-economic Causes of Anti-Semitism," *Social Problems,* 5:21–29, July, 1957. An analysis of the reactions to Jews as a marginal trading people.

CAMPBELL, EARNEST Q. (ED.): "Analysis of Race Relations in Current Perspective," *Sociological Inquiry,* 35 (1), Winter, 1965. A series of articles by various writers dealing with the civil rights movement.

CLARK, KENNETH: *Dark Ghetto,* Harper & Row, Publishers, Incorporated, New York, 1965. A lucid presentation of some aspects of lower-class Negro culture based on an analysis of an antipoverty program in Harlem.

DAVIDSON, BASIL: *Old Africa Rediscovered: The Story of Africa's Forgotten Past,* Victor Gollancz, Ltd., London, 1965. A balanced account of ancient African civilizations, which neither consigns the continent to barbarism nor erects a romantic façade on a basis of dubious historical evidence.

*GLAZER, NATHAN, AND DANIEL P. MOYNIHAN: *Beyond the Melting Pot,* Harvard University Press, Cambridge, Mass., 1963. A description of the interaction of ethnic groups in New York City. (MIT 13-MIT)

GLENN, NORVAL D., AND LEONARD BROOM: *Transformation of the Negro American,* Harper & Row Publishers, Incorporated, New York, 1965. Adaptation required by Negroes to enter the mainstream of American life.

HEER, DAVID M.: "Negro-White Marriage in the United States," *Journal of Marriage and the Family,* 28:265, August, 1966. Analysis of interracial marriage trends in recent years.

*HERBERG, WILL: *Protestant, Catholic, Jew,* Doubleday & Company, Inc., Garden City, N. Y., 1960. A treatment of religious identity as a form of cultural pluralism replacing nationalism. (A195-Anch)

LA FARGE, OLIVER: "The Enduring Indian," *Scientific American,* 202:37–45, February, 1960. A lucid presentation of major issues in American Indian adjustment.

LOHMAN, JOSEPH D., AND DELBERT C. REITZES: "Notes on Race Relations in a Mass Society," *American Journal of Sociology,* 58:240–246, November, 1952; Bobbs-Merrill reprint S-178. A classic presentation of the view that situational pressures rather than attitudes determine ethnic patterns.

NICHOLS, LEE: *Breakthrough on the Color Front,* Random House, Inc., New York, 1954. A popular discussion of the successful integration of the armed services.

RAINWATER, LEE, AND WILLIAM L. YANCEY: "Black Families and the White House," *Trans-action,* 3:6–11, July-August, 1966. A popular presentation of the controversy accompanying the Moynihan report which pointed to family disorganization as a basic cause of Negro difficulty.

ROSTOW, EUGENE V.: "Our Worst Wartime Mistake," *Harper's Magazine,* September, 1945, pp. 193–201. Discusses our wartime treatment of Japanese Americans.

SENIOR, CLARENCE: *Strangers—Then Neighbors,* Anti-Defamation League, New York, 1961. A brief analysis of the Puerto Rican in the United States.

WILLIAMS, ROBIN M., JR.: with JOHN P. DEAN AND EDWARD A. SUCHMAN: *Strangers Next Door,* Prentice-Hall, Inc., Englewood Cliffs, N. J., 1964. A readable account of several continuing research studies in racial and ethnic relations.

*WOODWARD, C. VANN: *The Strange Career of Jim Crow,* Oxford University Press, Fair Lawn, N.J., 1957. Students who take it for granted that segregation has always been a Southern tradition will be surprised to learn that it was not firmly established until after 1900. (6-GB)

I was there [at an address by Senator Joseph McCarthy] with a young lady, and we'd resolved that it would be the height of unwisdom to make any comment because the atmosphere at the conclusion of the meeting would undoubtedly be charged with tension. . . . We stood by and watched this particular performance.

Then a man next to me said, "Oh, I know that Wilbur Jerger [who had made anti-McCarthy comments]. He's a teacher in the Valley and a yid." To this the young lady with me said, "Well, he's got a right to speak." And then all my resolutions flew out the window. I said, "Yes, he's got a right to speak." And I said, "Everyone has a right to speak." And he said, "If you think everyone has a right to speak, you must be a Red." And I said, "Well, if believing that everyone has a right to speak makes me a Red, then I'm a Red!"

That was probably a very silly thing to have said, but I was defiant and this led to a call on his part, "Here's a Red, here's a Red, here's a Red." Well, from every direction they came. I was pretty terrified and looked about frantically for a wall or a fence—something to which I could put my back and at least fight in one direction. I was rendered completely inarticulate and frightened by the horde converging upon me. I felt that I was surrounded in every direction. There must have been a hundred people in the group that came around me. They were throwing punches. And I was trying to protect the young lady, whose arms were catching the blows, and holding her with one arm and swinging the other as well as I could. . . .

The battle went on, it may have been a minute, it may have been two minutes—it would be absolutely impossible for me to estimate its duration. It seemed like hours while looking up at the fear-crazed faces of these people—elderly people for the most part. . . .

As they went on for, as I say, a minute or two, a young fellow came up. He must have been 18 or 19, tall, I think almost 7 feet tall. . . . He approached the group and said, "We don't want any violence on this church property. Violence on church property won't help our cause. We don't want violence on church property." This had an almost magical effect upon the group. The whole group dissolved just as rapidly as it had gathered. . . .

Then this young fellow came up to me and said, "Man, you're a fool. I'm not with these people. I'm here for the same purpose that you are, but I have better sense than to make any remark at all before these people. . . . You could have been killed." And without even stopping to take his name or thank him, because I certainly wasn't in possession of my faculties, I just let him go. (Quoted in Ralph H. Turner and Lewis M. Killian, *Collective Behavior*, Prentice-Hall, Inc., Englewood Cliffs, N.J., 1957, pp. 149–150.)

16

COLLECTIVE BEHAVIOR

HIS IS AN example of collective behavior—an audience, momentarily a mob, finally calmed through a strategic leadership appeal. No topic in sociology is more fascinating than the study of collective behavior. Unfortunately, it is not easy to study scientifically. Mobs, riots, and panics do not often occur under the calm gaze of a visiting sociologist. Deliberately to provoke one, however studious our intent, would put us in jail. Besides, just how would a sociologist conduct an interview in the midst of a mob or panic? We are limited to eyewitness accounts by observers and participants, to police records, newspaper accounts and other scattered data. Seldom can we locate a statistically adequate sample of participants for systematic study. A number of ingenious attempts have been made to duplicate crowd conditions of behavior in a laboratory for purposes of research, but relatively few types of crowd behavior can be so reproduced. Even with these limitations we have a good deal of descriptive information, together with some empirical research, from which we have developed certain insights into the various forms of collective behavior.

NATURE OF COLLECTIVE BEHAVIOR

All sociologists talk about "collective behavior," but few attempt to define it. When they do, the definitions are not very helpful, Smelser's definition— "mobilization on the basis of a belief which redefines social action" [Smelser, 1963, p. 8] is as good as any but perhaps not very meaningful to most students. It is less formal but more understandable to say that collective behavior includes such topics as crowds, mobs, panics, crazes, mass hysteria, fads, fashions, propaganda, public opinion, social movements, and revolutions. The last two of these topics will be treated in a later chapter.

In a sense, all social interaction is "collective behavior," but that usage would make the term meaningless. We shall limit it to social behavior which is (1) *episodic*, that is, takes place in occasional episodes rather than regularly or routinely; (2) *unstructured*, in that there are no set rules or procedures to follow; (3) usually *unpredictable*, in that the direction and outcome of the behavior cannot be foretold, and (4) usually *irrational*, guided by unreasoning beliefs, hopes, fears, or hatreds. Not all forms of collective behavior perfectly fit this description, but they approach it fairly closely.

There are no fully satisfactory theoretical formulations of collective behavior. Perhaps this catch-all term includes so many kinds of behavior that no framework of theory can encompass them. One of the most provocative analyses is that of Smelser [1963, chap. 1], who lists the determinants of collective behavior as:

1. Structural conduciveness. Financial panics and fashion crazes do not plague simple, traditional societies. An urbanized society is more prone to mass phenomena than a scattered rural population. The rootless, anonymous, transient members of a highly mobile society are more given to extremes of behavior than those in a settled folk society.

2. Structural strain. Deprivation and fears of deprivation lie at the base of much collective behavior. The sting of injustice—real or fancied—prompts many to extreme action. Impoverished classes, oppressed minorities, groups whose hard-won gains are threatened, even privileged groups who fear the loss of their privileges—all these are candidates for extreme behavior.

3. *Growth and spread of a generalized belief.*   Before any collective action, there must be a belief among the actors which identifies the source of the threat, the route of escape, or the avenue to fulfillment.

4. *Precipitating factors.*   Some dramatic event, or a report thereof, sets the stage for action. A cry of "police brutality" in a racially tense neighborhood may touch off a riot. One person starting to run may precipitate a panic.

5. *Mobilization for action.*   All that remains now is for action to begin.

6. *Operation of social control.*   At any of the above points, the cycle can be interrupted by leadership, police power, propaganda, legislative and government policy changes, and other social controls.

CROWD BEHAVIOR

A crowd is a *temporary collection of people reacting together to stimuli.* A busload of passengers, each buried in his own daydreams, is not a crowd; let the driver announce that he wishes to stop for a few drinks, and they promptly form a crowd.

Unlike most other groups, a crowd is temporary. Its members rarely know one another. Most forms of crowd behavior are unstructured with no rules, no traditions, no formal controls, no designated leaders, no established patterns for the members to follow. Crowd behavior may appear to be spontaneous and utterly unpredictable, but as we shall see, crowd behavior is not purely a matter of chance or impulse. Crowd behavior is a part of the culture. The kinds of crowds that form and the things a crowd will do and will not do differ from one culture to another. Crowd behavior can be analyzed and understood, and to some extent predicted and controlled.

Some characteristics of crowd behavior   **Anonymity**   Crowds are anonymous, both because they are large and because they are temporary. The size of the group and the nature of the interaction remove the sense of individuality from the members, even when they recognize acquaintances. They do not pay attention to other members as individuals and do not feel that they themselves are being singled out as individuals. Thus the restraints of a member of a crowd are reduced, and he is free to indulge in behavior which he would ordinarily control, because moral responsibility has been shifted from him to the group.

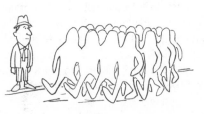

Crowds are anonymous.

At least one study [Festinger et al., 1952] claims to have confirmed these mechanisms through laboratory experimentation. Members of crowds seldom confess to any feeling of guilt after sharing in even the most outrageous atrocities, and this shift of moral responsibility to the group is part of the explanation.

Impersonality   Group behavior is typically impersonal. The soldier bears no personal grudge against the enemy soldier he shoots, nor does it matter that the opposing football player is a personal friend. The impersonality of crowd behavior is revealed in race riots where one member of the enemy race is as good or bad as another.

We drove around for a long time. We saw a lot of colored people, but they were in bunches. We didn't want any of that. We wanted some guy all by himself. We saw one at Mack Avenue.

Aldo drove past him and then said, "Gimme that gun." I handed it over to him and he turned around and come back. We were about 15 feet from the man when Aldo pulled up, almost stopped and shot. The man fell and we blew.

We didn't know him. He wasn't bothering us. But other people were fighting and killing and we felt like it, too.

Alfred M. Lee and Norman D. Humphrey, *Race Riot,* Holt, Rinehart and Winston, Inc., New York, 1943, p. 38.

It should be no surprise that peaceful passersby are attacked in race riots. If the other *group* is the enemy, then *any* member of the group is automatically a victim. When FLN terrorists in Algeria tossed a grenade, killing a guest in a hotel, Europeans surged into the streets and lynched the first two Moslems they found [*Time,* Aug. 11, 1961]. But if the group setting for behavior is destroyed, then the behavior changes. For example, in the Chicago race riot of 1919, one Negro outdistanced all but one of his assailants so that the two became separated from their groups and began to interact as individuals, whereupon they quit fighting [Chicago Commission, 1922, p. 22]. Removed from their groups, they realized that fighting was pointless. Group behavior is impersonal; when interaction becomes personal, it ceases to be group behavior and changes in nature.

Suggestibility   Since crowd situations are normally unstructured, there are no designated leaders and no recognized behavior patterns for the members to carry out. Furthermore their individual responsibility has been shifted to the group. Often the situation itself is confused and chaotic. In such a state of affairs, people act readily and uncritically upon suggestion, especially if the suggestion is made in a decisive, authoritative manner. The "unpredictability" of crowds is just another way of saying that crowds are highly suggestible [Lang and Lang, 1961, pp. 221–225].

Social contagion   The most dramatic feature of crowd behavior is the emotional buildup which crowd members give to one another. This communication of feeling is most impressive in mobs and riots, but is found in orderly crowds as well. The first one or two cheers at a pep rally normally fall flat; not until we hear the deep swell of voices around us will we cheer very lustily. Every professional speaker or entertainer knows that an audience thinly scattered over a large auditorium will be unresponsive. A well-filled smaller hall is far better. Above all, they must be seated closely together, without many empty seats separating them. Every revivalist tries to move the audience down front so that they are close to him, and solidly packed, before he starts. The phenomenon he seeks has sometimes been called by the cumbersome title *interactional amplification* although the term *social contagion* is simpler. This is the process whereby the members of a crowd stimulate and respond to one another and thereby increase their emotional intensity and responsiveness.

Contagion is increased by "milling" and "rhythm." The crowd, if unseated, may push and surge back and forth, carrying individuals along with it. The crowd may break into rhythmic clapping or shouting, with successive waves of sound carrying members to higher peaks of excitement. All these processes help to explain why crowd behavior sometimes goes farther than most of the members intended. Persons who came intending to be only onlookers get caught up in the process and find themselves joining in. Sometimes the interaction reaches the riot level, complete with injuries and destruction of property.

Social contagion helps to explain the great suggestibility of a crowd, once it is tuned up for action. A person reading in solitude a hilarious scene from a popular comedy will not find it nearly so funny as when he sees it as a member of an audience. The "claque," a small organized group that starts and leads the applause for a star at the right moment, is a familiar fixture in the European opera house. Since our own actions are reinforced by the action of others, it takes only a few to start a wave of laughter or applause.

When a crowd becomes emotionally aroused, it needs emotional release and may act upon the first suggested action which is in line with its impulses. Lynching mobs are not always concerned about which Negro they lynch; if the intended victim escapes, they may lynch any Negro who is handy. In Omaha in 1919, when the mayor refused to surrender a lynch victim, the mob attempted to lynch the mayor and very nearly succeeded [*Literary Digest*, Oct. 11, 1919]. In a Texas town in 1930, the victim was hidden in the vault of the courthouse; the mob burned the courthouse, then followed by wrecking the Negro part of town [Cantril, 1941, pp. 97–110]. The Civil War draft riots in New York City began as protests against the draft, but soon became full-fledged anti-Negro riots. Any suggested action, if it is in line with the established impulses and antagonisms of the members, is likely to be acted on by an emotionally aroused crowd [Lang and Lang, chap. 8].

These characteristics of crowd behavior explain why the crowd is more than a collection of individuals. Each individual member is to some degree different in the crowd from the person he is when alone. As Allport [in Lindzey, 1954, vol. 1, p. 28] remarks, "It used to be said in Germany that there is no such thing as a 'single Nazi.' Only with the support of a group does the peculiar subservience to the leader and his ideology take possession of the individual." We can never fully understand crowd behavior unless we understand that the crowd, like all groups, is more than merely a collection of individuals.

A crowd in action can be a terrifying thing. A factual account of everything said and done by an aggressive mob would be unprintable. To cite just one example, lynching victims were frequently burned alive, or slowly strangled, and sometimes emasculated as well as being subjected to other inexpressible tortures [Raper, 1933, pp. 6–7, 144]. People will apparently do anything when caught up in the crowd. Is this true?

Limitations on crowd behavior However irrational and unrestrained it may appear, crowd behavior is limited by at least four considerations: (1) the emotional needs of the members; (2) the mores of the members; (3) the leadership of the crowd; (4) the external controls over the crowd.

Emotional needs of members Crowd behavior expresses the emotional needs, resentments, and prejudices of the members. People who lead bored,

A crowd does only those things that most of its members would like to do.

monotonous lives, like the medieval European peasants, needed an occasional witch-burning to break the monotony of their lives. People who fear deprivation, like our second-generation immigrants who have struggled from the slum to a better neighborhood and who fear that Negro residents will "ruin" the neighborhood, need an outlet for their fears and anxieties. In a crowd situation people may do things they ordinarily would not do, but a crowd does only those things that most of its members *would like to do*. The emotional stimulus and protection of the crowd enables its members to express the impulses, hostilities, aggressions, and rages which they are restrained from expressing in calmer moments. Many of us, for example, like to break things, but we must restrain the impulse. In a riot men shed restraints and can tear things up without guilt feelings. If blocked from its first objective, a mob generally shifts to another. The substitute, however, still represents the hated victim, or fulfills the frustrated wish.

Homogeneous audiences are the most responsive. Having the same interests and viewpoints, the members respond enthusiastically to the speaker. The political rally attracts mainly the party faithful. Its function is similar to that of a pep meeting before a football game—to arouse enthusiasm and dedication to the team. A crowd is most likely to take aggressive action when its members share a common set of prejudices and hostilities. Persons who do not share these feelings are likely to edge backward to the fringes, while the core of the crowd is made up of like-minded members.

Analysis of members of race riots (based upon eyewitness accounts and upon police records of arrested members) shows that the active participants tend to be young, unmarried, lower-class, and economically insecure [Wada and Davies, 1957]. A great many of them already had police records for other offenses [Lee and Humphrey, 1943, pp. 80–88]. The participants therefore are likely to be persons with few responsibilities, many frustrations, and violent race prejudices. They have bitter class hostilities, reject middle-class values, and resent being lectured at and pushed around by authorities representing the middle-class world. They happily join in any riot available, and a race riot is especially satisfying.

Mores of the members Crowd behavior is limited by the mores of its members. The crowd rarely if ever does anything which does not claim a measure of moral approval. Lynchings did not occur in areas where the mores of most people strongly condemned them. Lynchings took place only where a large proportion of the people felt that a lynching was morally justified, even necessary, under certain circumstances. The members of the lynching party normally considered themselves public benefactors, not guilty law breakers. Even the lynching party, then, was expressing, rather than violating, the mores of the members and probably the dominant mores of the region. We note, furthermore, that while the victim might have been killed, burned, and mutilated, he was never crucified, nor was his body ever eaten. The crowd's mores did not support these actions.

It is true that a crowd member may confess later that he shared in acts he realizes were morally wrong. Each person, like each group, holds a number of mutually inconsistent moral views, and at a given moment one or another of them is operative. At the time it may seem very "right" that a self-appointed delegation of students should revenge past insults by painting indelicate epigrams on the walls of a rival institution; later, in the dean's office, it is equally clear that the act was destructive, illegal, and ungentlemanly. Our mores teach us that we should be loyal to family, friends, and fellow workers, and should do nothing that injures other people. When a strike is called in a vital industry, such as railroad transportation or telephone communication, should the worker loyally support his striking fellows and thereby inconvenience and possibly injure the public, or should he stay on the job and thereby injure his fellows? Rarely in a behavior situation does the individual have only *one* applicable moral judgment. Which of one's several sets of mores will operate in a particular situation will depend largely upon the group pressures surrounding him at that moment.

The function of the crowd is not to paralyze the moral judgments of its members; the function of the crowd is to isolate and neutralize some of one's moral judgments, so that certain others can find unrestrained expression. Thus a crowd is doing only those things for which the mores of the participants give considerable approval.

Crowd leadership   The leadership profoundly affects the intensity and direction of crowd behavior. Given a collection of frustrated, resentful people, a skillful demagogue can convert them into a vengeful mob and direct their aggression at any "enemy" who is included among their antagonisms. Likewise, a leader can sometimes calm or divert a crowd by a strategic suggestion or command. In the illustration which opens this chapter, the young man stopped a mob by reminding them that they were on church property. These people were church members, and this reminder called into operation some mores which they had forgotten.

Since most crowd behavior is unstructured, with no designated leaders, leadership is "up for grabs." Anyone may be able to assume leadership by simply calling out suggestions and commands. The most unlikely persons sometime assume leadership. In the panic of the *Lusitania* ship disaster, it was an eighteen-year-old boy under whose direction a few lifeboats were successfully filled and launched [LaPiere, 1938, p. 459]. In many crowd situations, the members, frustrated by confusion and uncertainty, *want* to be directed, and the first person who starts giving clear orders in an authoritative manner is likely to be followed. An impressive appearance is helpful, but the assured manner of one who knows what he is doing is essential. Let us see specifically what the crowd leader does.

1. The leader must establish rapport.   By *rapport,* we mean a responsive trusting attentiveness such as any really successful speaker gets from his audience. This author recalls observing a war-bond rally of workers in a large factory. A visiting dignitary first gave a speech which was a model of good speech construction and delivery, spoken in Harvard accents. It was received with polite applause. Then the plant manager began by holding out two ham-like paws and saying, "You guys see these hands? They didn't get that way pushing a pencil. They pushed a wheelbarrow for four years, and then they operated a drill press and a turret lathe and just about every damn machine in this place." With these few words, he established rapport. He spoke their language. Rapport is most easily established by a leader who has the same background as the members. He senses their wants, recognizes their antagonisms, speaks their language, and can predict their reactions.

2. The leader builds emotional tensions. For some types of crowds (mobs, riots, some audiences) he builds up their emotional tensions by an impassioned reminder of their problems and grievances. The revivalist convicts the sinners of their sins; the leader of the lynching mob arouses the men to defend the purity of their wives and daughters; the cheerleader focuses all history on the outcome of tomorrow's game. In some kinds of crowds (the panic, some audiences) the leader need not arouse emotional tension, for it already exists; he passes directly to the next function.

3. The leader suggests action to release the tension. The revivalist calls for repentance; the cheerleader demands victory and lights the bonfire; the riot leader cries, "Burn, baby, burn!"

4. The leader justifies the suggested action. Seldom does a crowd respond instantly to suggestion (except perhaps in panic behavior). Generally the leader makes some effort to justify the suggestion. The revivalist pictures the new life of release from sin; the lynch leader warns, "It'll be *your* daughter next!" The repetition of the suggestion and its justifications permits social contagion to continue to operate, so that tension continues to mount and the need for release of tension continues to grow.

Leadership can function either to stimulate or to restrain a crowd, or to direct activity from one objective to another. Leadership is, therefore, one of the limiting factors in crowd behavior.

External controls Most mob behavior occurs in the summertime when people are normally standing around and gathering in large outdoor assemblies. Cold weather discourages mobs; so do hard thundershowers. Mob behavior is rare on army posts, where military discipline can be invoked to maintain order. Servicemen must release their tensions off the post—and do so at intervals!

The principal external controls on crowd behavior, however, are those exerted by the police. There are practically no instances of persons being lynched in spite of a really determined effort of law-enforcement officials to prevent the lynching. Most lynchings were preceded by either the open connivance of law-enforcement officials, or by their merely token resistance. The virtual disappearance of lynching in recent years stems in large part, not from any lack of persons who would enjoy a lynching, but from the determination of law-enforcement officials to prevent lynchings. Today, shootings and "disappearances" have replaced the classic lynchings.

Within recent years police have learned a great deal about the management of crowds. A sociologist, Joseph D. Lohman [1947], has prepared a widely used handbook on the handling of potential riot situations, which summarizes in simple language what social science has learned about ways of directing crowd behavior. Among the procedures used in preventing small incidents from developing into riots are: (1) preventing crowd formation by promptly arresting and carrying off noisy troublemakers and ordering the onlookers to move on; (2) meeting threatened disorder with an impressive *show of force,* bringing enough police and equipment into the area so that a *use* of force is unnecessary; (3) isolating a riot area by throwing a police cordon around it and allowing people to leave but not to enter the area; (4) diminishing a crowd by directing the persons on the fringes to "break up and go home," thus stripping the crowd down to its core and depriving the core of its mass support; (5) emphasis in police training on the officer's duty to maintain the peace, so that the officer's own prejudices do not lead him into the fatal error of ignoring attacks on those whom he doesn't like.

With very few exceptions, serious riots are evidence of police failure. Recent school-integration disorders are an example. Where local police and public officials let it be known that no disorders will be tolerated, disorders are rare. Smelser [1963, pp. 261–268] cites many cases where hesitation and indecision of police and other officials, or even their open sympathizing with the rioters, has aided in riot development.

Some exceptions must be made to the proposition that police can control crowds if they wish. Small cities have no police reserves that can be shifted from place to place in an emergency. Police in a college town, outnumbered a hundred to one, may be unable to handle a student body on a rampage. A local festival or celebration may bring people into a locality in numbers beyond the capacity of the police to control. Some of the recent riots in Negro areas of many American cities defied the most determined efforts at police control [*Life*, Aug. 27, 1965, pp. 20–34; Cohen and Murphy, 1966]. Under most circumstances, however, mobs and riots in American society are symptoms of police failure.

Some forms of crowd behavior   **The audience**   An audience is a crowd with interest centered on stimuli outside themselves. The stimuli are mainly one-way. With the movie, radio, or TV audience, the stimuli are entirely one-way. Every instructor, however, realizes that any performer before a "live" audience is affected by the audience reaction. Dollard tells how he was stimulated by the responsive audience in a lower-class Southern Negro church which he was invited to address:

It was all I had expected and more too. Not familiar enough with the Bible to choose an opportune text, I talked about my own state, described the country through which I had passed in coming south, spoke of the beauty of their land, and expressed my pleasure at being allowed to participate in their exercises. Helped by appreciative murmurs which began slowly and softly and became louder and fuller as I went on, I felt a great sense of elation, an increased fluency, and a vastly expanded confidence in speaking. There was no doubt that the audience was with me, was determined to aid me in every way. I went on. . . .

The crowd had enabled me to talk to them much more sincerely than I thought I knew how to do; the continuous surge of affirmation was a highly elating experience. For once I did not feel that I was merely beating a sodden audience with words or striving for cold intellectual communication. . . .

Mine was a miserable performance compared to the many Negro preachers I have seen striding the platform like confident panthers; but it was exactly the intensive collective participation that I had imagined it might be. No less wth the speaker than with the audience there is a sense of losing the limitations of self and of unconscious powers rising to meet the unbound, unconscious forces of the group.

John Dollard, *Caste and Class in a Southern Town*, Yale University Press, New Haven, Conn., 1937, pp. 242–243.

Within an audience, then, there may be significant two-way stimulus and response, even though the audience situation discourages the communication. There is also a certain amount of communication between members, as they cheer, applaud, boo, whisper, mutter, doze, or snore. Social contagion still operates, usually at a more subdued level than in other crowds—highly subdued at a sedate church service, more freely expressive at a political rally or a sports event. Audiences may become unruly and may even become converted into a mob, as in the instance opening this chapter.

The mob A mob is an emotionally aroused crowd taking aggressive action. There are several types of mobs, differing in important respects.

1. The lynching mob. Lynchings were once popular in the South and the West, although they have occurred in all parts of the country. Unlike the riot, a lynching is a peculiarly American institution, rare in other parts of the world. It is a part of the vigilante tradition, wherein a self-appointed group of citizens seeks to preserve public order by punishing culprits. The nineteenth-century victims were both white and Negro; twentieth-century victims became predominantly Negro; 1,795 American Negroes and 195 whites have been lynched since 1900.

Lynchings were not all alike. Raper [1933, pp. 55ff.] and Cantril [1941, pp. 93–110] have distinguished between what they call the Bourbon and the proletarian lynching. The Bourbon lynching took place in Deep South areas of heavy Negro population. Rigid segregation prevented direct competition between whites and Negroes, and the "poor whites" were less likely to see the Negroes as a threat or to harbor a general bitterness toward Negroes than in some other areas. A lynching was considered a deserved punishment of a specific person for a specific offense. It was carried out by leading citizens (or with their encouragement) and without serious interference from law-enforcement officials. The mob was small and orderly, as though conducting a legal execution. Other Negroes were not molested, nor was Negro property destroyed.

The proletarian lynching took place where Negroes were less numerous and their status less exactly defined. There was more direct competition between Negroes and poor whites and much more poor-white hostility against Negroes in general. The lynching was an outburst of white antagonism against the Negro group; its object was to punish the race, not just an individual. The lynching mob was large and emotional, made up mainly of poor whites, who were unconcerned with whether the victim was guilty or whether they had the right person. The lynching was generally accompanied by torture and mutilation and often followed by mistreatment of other Negroes and destruction of Negro property. Community reaction tended to vary with social class; upper-class members and community leaders disapproved; lower-class members justified the lynching as necessary to keep the Negroes in "their place." A lynching, then, may be a pseudolegal execution by community leaders, an impassioned emotional outburst of deprived whites against the Negro race, or some combination of both. In either case the individual lyncher is supported by the crowd in taking an action which is basically in accord with his mores.

Lynching today has virtually ceased; only six persons (one white and five Negroes) were lynched during the 1950s. Although now replaced by other techniques of intimidation or punishment, lynching remains of interest to social scientists as a dramatic form of group behavior.

2. *The riot.* A riot is a violently aggressive, destructive mob. It may be a race riot, in which members of two races indiscriminately hunt down and beat or kill one another, as in Chicago in 1919 [Chicago Commission, 1922] or in Detroit in 1941 [Lee and Humphrey, 1943]. One study [Lieberson and Silverman, 1965] of many race riots finds that they are usually precipitated by a report of a dramatic violence by one race against the other—rape, murder, assault, police brutality—in communities where local government and leadership have been unresponsive to racial problems. It may be a religious riot, as that between the Hindus and the Moslems in India in 1947 [Duncan, 1947; McGinty, 1947]. It may be a nationality riot, like that between American servicemen and Mexicans in Los Angeles in 1943, or the so-called "zoot-suit" riot [Turner and Surace, 1956], or the many mob actions against European immigrants in the United States during the nineteenth and early twentieth centuries [Higham, 1955]. Race, religion, or nationality—no matter what the cause, the crowd behavior is much the same. A group is disliked because it is different; or it serves as a convenient scapegoat; or it is hated because it threatens competition. With suitable stimulating incidents and without effective police discouragement, persons who are individually frustrated and insecure start action; it builds and grows; the attacked group strikes back, and the riot is under way.

There are other kinds of riots. The protest riot, common in colonial countries, has the object of dramatizing grievances and wringing concessions from the governing powers. The Negro riots in many American cities beginning in 1965 were not conventional race riots—not primarily a clash between races—but protest riots. A decade of civil rights "victories" had brought few gains to lower-class Negroes who remained outside the "affluent society." While skilled and educated Negroes were gaining, lower-class Negroes were falling steadily farther behind, growing more frustrated than ever. Usually precipitated by reports of police brutality (often untrue), large-scale violence, burning, and looting exploded across the country [Moynihan 1965; Good, 1965; Cleghorn, 1966; Blauner, 1966; Cohen and Murphy, 1966; Johnson, 1967; Rustin, 1967; Stern, 1967; *Ebony*, special issue, Aug. 1967]. Any riot provides the individual with the support of the crowd and a release from moral responsibility, so that he may express any impulse which seizes him. Most riots include all these elements—flaunting of authority, attack upon disliked groups, and looting and wrecking of property, especially property belonging to the hated group.

Some recent campus riots, notably at Berkeley, California, in 1964 and 1965, caused many Americans to wonder what our students were coming to! As riots go, these student demonstrations were pretty tame affairs, involving only a small fraction of the students plus some nonstudents who hung around the larger campuses. Student disorders are, of course, as old as the university. A wave in the 1880s hit many colleges, with Amherst's rebellion led by Calvin Coolidge and (later Chief Justice) Harlan Fiske Stone (after Stone was thrown out of another college for demonstrating) [Feuer, 1966]. The nineteenth-century student rebellions were against arbitrary and authoritarian college administrations. The recent ones seem to be a student reaction against the impersonality of the vast multiuniversity, where the student is reduced to a number on an IBM card [Raskin, 1965; Lipset and Seabury, 1965].

3. *The orgy.*   A revelous crowd which transgresses the normal mores is an orgy. Like other mobs, the orgy serves to release tensions; but where the riot is mad with anger, the orgy is mad with joy. One cannot have an orgy by oneself; revelry must be shared or it falls flat. But a very creditable orgy may be promoted by anywhere from a handful of persons to a crowd of thousands. Exactly where "decent recreation" leaves off and the orgy begins is, perhaps, a value judgment. But to be effective in the release of tension, the orgy must involve behavior which exceeds the ordinary daily restraints and inhibitions.

In the orgy we see the factors which operate in all crowd behavior—leadership, social contagion, suggestibility, and transfer of moral responsibility to the group. Since it takes time for these forces to begin to operate, the party takes a while to get going. Before long, inhibitions are diluted, and interaction becomes less restrained. Thus many a motel party, after-the-game celebration, or convention get-together winds up as an orgy.

All societies create frustrations in their members, and all societies provide in some way for the release of tensions. In many societies the orgy is an institutionalized way for members to release their accumulated tensions. A great many primitive societies had periodic festivals or holidays in which ceremonial and orgiastic behavior were combined. Games, feasting, drinking, orgiastic dancing, and the suspension of some of the sex taboos were common features of primitive festivals. Among the Incas, for example,

Holidays might last for a day or for a week; there might be public dancing, such as when hundreds of radiantly clothed "Chosen Women" danced with Huaschar's chain; there could be games and sports; there was always drinking, of a sort one writer calls "approved license." For the Indian [Inca] was expected to get drunk, which he did, quaffing immense quantities of fermented chicha; for ritual drunkenness was as essential to a good festival as agricultural discipline to a good harvest.

Games at the festivals differed from those played by the Indian boy. . . . On the day fixed for the [December] feast, men and girls came to a predetermined place among the ripened fruit gardens, whose ripening they were to celebrate. Men and women were completely naked. At a given signal they started on a race, upon which bets were placed, toward some hill at a distance. Each man that overtook any women in the race "enjoyed her on the spot."

Victor W. VonHagen, *Realm of the Incas*, Mentor Books, New American Library of World Literature, Inc., New York, 1957, pp. 96–97. From the series, *The Ancient Sun Kingdoms of the Americas*, The World Publishing Company, Cleveland.

Students of revelry have assumed that the greater the accumulated tensions, the greater the temptation to find release through orgy. Casual observation would seem to support this thesis. Whenever men are isolated from female company and subjected to harsh discipline, monotonous work, and unsatisfactory living conditions for long periods of time, most of them promptly go on a spree at the first opportunity. Army camps, naval stations, construction camps, lumber camps, and mining camps are classic examples. Presumably, the greater the frustrations and tensions, the more riotous the release. Ernie Pyle [1943, p. 3], the perceptive war correspondent, observed that infantry men often endured mud, rain, and dirt, and continuous chaos and uncertainty even as to where they would eat and sleep, whereas sailors ordinarily had clean clothes, good food, and a ship to call home. He then remarked that ". . . sailors didn't cuss as much or as foully as soldiers. They didn't bust loose as riotously when they hit town." One writer describes the emotional needs and outlets of the men who built the Hoover Dam during the early 1930s:

To men who have pushed concrete fifteen days, or nights, with no more emotional outlet than a pool table can absorb, Las Vegas becomes a natural and compelling magnet. The liquor is vile and no one trusts the wheels; but all drink and play furiously. It is payday, and it matters not what the night of the week. Where Sunday and Christmas are days like any others, traditional Saturday-night revels lose all significance. By ten-thirty things are well under way. By two everyone is drunk and begging for more. Rooms, as large as small auditoriums, are packed to bursting with sweating inebriates fighting for the edge of the gambling tables.
Theo White, "Building the Big Dam," *Harper's Magazine*, June, 1935, p. 118.

Today the automobile and the mobile home have largely destroyed the isolation of the construction camp, lumber camp, or mining camp, and the orgy has largely faded from their fringes. What no amount of moralizing could do, changing technology has accomplished. The armed services have attempted to make military life more comfortable and less frustrating, and the row of taverns, gambling places, and houses of prostitution in the nearest town may have shortened, but not entirely disappeared.

American society has many approved forms of recreation—dancing, movie-going, participation sports, spectator sports, and many others—which doubtless serve to release tensions. Our society has not, however, institutionalized the orgy as a legitimate release. In primitive societies, the orgy is a relatively safe outlet. In a nonmechanical society, drunkenness which is limited to an occasional socially designated experience is comparatively harmless. In a society with a consanguine family system, collective property ownership, and a serene unconcern with exact biological paternity, an occasional period of sexual license creates no problems. But in our society the price of an orgy may be a painful accident, a costly fire, or a scandalous pregnancy. Our society's inability to provide safe, harmless orgies, however, also carries a price tag. In a society which produces a great many tensions within individuals, these tensions must find release in one way or another. Blocking one dangerous outlet does not guarantee that the substitute outlet will be less offensive. LaPiere comments:

That the cause of the drunken spree lies in social circumstances which demand an occasional escape, rather than, as moralists assume, in the commercial provision of opportunities for such indulgence, is illustrated by the history of an attempt to check the week-end sprees of English industrial workers. Motivated, no doubt, by the best of intentions, the stringent closing of the "pubs" in the depressing East End of London some years ago had, however, such unanticipated consequences that it was soon found advisable to remove the harsh restrictions. Withholding alcohol from workers who were accustomed to a week-end drunk reduced drunkenness and disorderly conduct, but it caused a striking increase in the frequency of wife beating, murder, and suicide.

Richard LaPiere, *Collective Behavior*, McGraw-Hill Book Company, Inc., New York, 1938, p. 484.

The persistent question of how to reconcile our appetite for revelry with our need for individual safety and social order is not likely to be settled in the foreseeable future.

4. The panic.   A panic is "a collective flight based on a hysterical belief" [Smelser, 1963, p. 131]. A panic involves the same elements of crowd behavior, blossoming suddenly under the stress of crisis. We have done little empirical research on panic, since we dare not produce panics to order for study. There are, however, many descriptive accounts and theoretical formulations [Strauss, 1944; Foreman, 1953; Smelser, 1963]. Panic appears to be most likely to seize a group which is fatigued by prolonged stress, although many panics have spread through perfectly relaxed groups. Smelser [1963, chap. 6] sees panic as likely when people feel in great danger with a very limited escape route; where there are ample escape routes, or no escape route whatever, panic is unlikely. Wherever they occur, a perceived crisis produces fear, uncertainty, confusion, and a lack of decisive leadership. The role of leadership is crucial in panic prevention, for panic spreads when members lose faith in organized, cooperative effort, and each takes individual defensive action [Mintz, 1951]. In a burning building, one person shouting "Fire!" or "Let me out!" may be enough to start a panic. When a crowd is leaving in orderly manner, if there is any interruption—if someone stumbles and momentarily blocks the aisle—somebody may break out of line in a dash and touch off a panic.

In panic prevention, a leader does at least two things: He organizes the crowd so that cooperative activity can proceed, and he relieves uncertainty by specific directions and reassurances. Marshall [1947, p. 130] has pointed out that when an army unit is under heavy fire, if the unit leader says, "Let's get out of here!" panic is likely; but if he says, "Follow me to that fence," panic is improbable. Once panic has spread, it generally continues until the crisis is past or the members are exhausted (or dead). Panic prevention depends upon a leader's assumption of authoritative direction quickly enough to organize cooperative action before some individual panics and touches off mass panic.

SOME OTHER FORMS OF COLLECTIVE BEHAVIOR

Crowds are temporary collections of people at a single point in space and time. There are other forms of collective behavior which are more prolonged and not limited to a single collection of people or a single point in space. The term *panic* is sometimes applied to business crises, extending over weeks or months and covering wide areas, as in the stock market panic of September and October, 1929. The panic situation is basically the same: a perceived threat (financial ruin) and a limited escape route (sell quickly!). Some of the more prolonged and extended forms of collective behavior are examined below.

The rumor   A rumor is a rapidly spreading report unsubstantiated by authenticated fact. It may be spread by mass media or by word-of-mouth. Much of our casual conversation consists of rumor mongering. Every topic, from our neighbor's morals to the fate of the nation, attracts interesting and disturbing rumors. Whenever there is social strain, rumors flourish. Wherever accurate and complete facts on a matter of public concern are not available or are not believed, rumors abound. Since rumors can ruin reputations, discredit causes, and undermine morale, the manipulation of rumor is a common propaganda device.

In the definitive work on rumor, Allport and Postman [1947, p. 46] point out that a great amount of rumor mongering springs from nothing more complicated than the desire for interesting conversation and the enjoyment of a salacious or unusual tidbit. A person is most likely, however, to believe and spread a rumor *if it will justify his dislikes or relieve his emotional tensions.* People who dislike Republicans, hate Negroes, or fear Communists will remember and repeat damaging rumors about these groups. The rumor changes continuously as it spreads, for people unconsciously distort it into the form that most perfectly supports their antagonisms. People uncritically accept and believe a rumor if it fits in with their pattern of beliefs and dislikes, or if it provides an emotionally satisfying explanation of phenomena. Thus many bitter critics of the Roosevelt administration readily believed and repeated rumors to the effect that wartime rationing was unnecessary (rumors that warehouses and gasoline storage tanks were overflowing, that the government was wasting or destroying vast quantities, and so on). Such rumors were emotionally satisfying to critics of the rationing program, and justified the black-marketing of the many people who violated rationing restrictions [Clinard, 1952].

The fad or fashion   A fad is a trivial, short-lived variation in speech, decoration, or behavior. As this is written, the phrase, "Sorry about that," and the practice of wearing no socks are "in" on the campus. Both will probably have passed by the time this manuscript fights its way through editors and publishers to the campus bookstores.

The fad apparently originates in the desire to gain and maintain status by being different, by being a leader, and dies out when it is no longer novel. Bogardus [1950, pp. 305–309] studied 2,702 fads over many years, finding that most of them deal with superficial accessories and gewgaws. They typically grow rapidly, have a two- or three-month plateau, and then decline, although some last longer, and a few become permanent parts of the culture.

Fashions are like fads, but change more slowly and are less trivial. Fashions reflect the dominant interests and motives of a society at a particular time. In the eighteenth century, elaborate clothing reflected an ornate and decorative upper-class culture, and the confining styles of the Victorian era reflected Victorian prudishness [Flugel, 1930]. Today's trend toward informality of dress harmonizes with our increasingly informal patterns of social life.

Fashion choices and changes are not entirely irrational, but meet various social needs as defined by social class, age and sex group, and other group affiliation. Fashion consciousness aids the middle-class social climber, and a distinct mode of dress fills the early teen-ager's need to "belong" in a private world not run by adults [Barber and Tobel, 1953]. Fashion changes may be deliberately manipulated by the apparel industry, but only to a limited degree, for there is evidence that consumers will not passively accept everything labeled "fashionable" [Jack and Schiffer, 1948; Lang and Lang, 1961, chap. 15].

The craze Where the panic is a rush away from a perceived threat, the craze is a rush toward some satisfaction. As Smelser observes [1963, chap. 7], the craze may be superficial (fads in jewelry) or serious (war crazes, nomination of a president); it may be economic (speculative boom), political (bandwagons), expressive (dance steps), religious (revivals), to mention only a few types. Flagpole sitting, dance marathons, monopoly games, jigsaw puzzles, canasta, and chain letters have all had their moments.

The craze differs from the fad in that it becomes an obsession for its followers. Many crazes involve some kind of get-rich-quick scheme. The Holland tulip craze of 1634 bid up the price of tulip bulbs until their value exceeded their weight in gold. The Florida land boom of the 1920s pushed land prices to levels fantastically beyond any sound economic valuation. In the craze, the individual gets caught up in a crowdlike hysteria and loses his caution. Speculators sell to one another at climbing prices until some bad news pricks the bubble or until so many susceptible persons have joined that no new money is entering the market; then confidence falters, and the market collapses in a frenzy to unload holdings [Mackay, 1932].

Since the craze is taken over by only a small fraction of the population and is a time-consuming preoccupation, it inevitably wears itself out quite quickly, soon to be replaced by another for those who are susceptible.

Mass hysteria This is some form of irrational, compulsive behavior which spreads among people. It can be a brief crowd phenomena, as when a wave of uncontrollable twitching spread through a Louisiana high school [Schuler and Parenton, 1943]. The *New York Times* [Sept. 14, 1952] reports that at a Mississippi football game, 165 teen-aged girls in a cheering section became excited and "fainted like flies." Or mass hysteria may extend beyond a single collection of people at a single moment in time. In one town, dozens of people over several weeks reported being attacked by a "phantom anesthetist" who sprayed them with an unknown drug which caused paralysis and other symptoms [Johnson, 1945]. The Salem witchcraft trials are an interesting historical example of mass hysteria [Starkey, 1949]. Recent waves of flying-saucer reports, together with an elaborate pseudoscientific literature on flying saucers, are a more modern example of mass hysteria [Hackett, 1948; Gardner, 1957, chap. 5]. From an analysis of the reports, it can be suspected that flying-saucer reports were the main cause of flying-saucer reports; that is, publicity about flying saucers was dependably followed by a series of new "sightings." While such mass delusions are interesting phenomena, we have not studied them closely enough to permit more than educated guesses as to why some people succumb while others resist. It is, of course, a scientific possibility that some of the "unidentified flying objects" are from outer space. As stated earlier, a negative proposition (e.g., "there are no flying saucers") is impossible to prove; but the evidence for them, at present, is not highly convincing.

Do we, then, have fully satisfactory explanations for collective behavior? Not entirely. All the forms of collective behavior herein discussed arise from some form of frustration or discontent. All serve to release tensions and provide some form of wish-fulfillment. We can venture some forecasts of when and where the more extreme forms of collective behavior are likely to appear and have some knowledge of how they may be controlled. With further study, we should know more.

PUBLICS AND PUBLIC OPINION

A public is a scattered group of people who share an interest in a particular topic. Many publics exist in a complex society. We have a baseball public, a theater public, an opera public, a movie public, a foreign-trade public, an investments public, a political-affairs public, and so on. Wherever an issue or activity appears, about which a number of persons have become interested, have formed opinions, and perhaps have argued, we have a public. The term *the public* is a favorite of the journalist or politician. Since no topic actually interests *everyone,* the term may be technically incorrect. When used, it is a synonym for "the people," or for "practically everybody."

The members of a public are not gathered together like the members of a crowd. Each member of a public can communicate directly with only a handful of the other members. A public is reached mainly through the mass media. The titles of many magazines reveal the public for which each is published—*House and Garden, Field and Stream, Guns and Ammo, Western Horsemen, Cats' Magazine, U.S. Camera, Stamps, Motor Trend, The Theater, Workbench, Audio, National Geographic Magazine, Holiday, Pacific Affairs,* and hundreds more. Since the members of a public can communicate effectively only through such mass media, it follows that those who control the media have considerable power to influence the opinions of that public.

Publics are created by cultural complexity. In a simple culture with many universals and few alternatives or specialties, there would be few if any publics. A complex culture offers many alternatives and specialties, and produces many interest groups with rival axes to grind. For example, one interest group wishes to keep our national parks in their unspoiled condition with a minimum of development; another group wants to develop them into recreation centers with resorts, airstrips, and ski lifts; still other groups wish to hunt the game, log the timber, mine the minerals, graze the grassland, or dam the streams in the parks. Such interest clashes multiply as a culture becomes more complex.

Few issues arise in a simple, stable culture; that is, few situations develop which cannot be handled by following the traditional folkways and mores of the society. But in a complex, changing culture, issues are constantly arising. In other words, situations are constantly developing which our traditional folkways and mores either will not handle at all, or will handle only in a way that leaves some groups dissatisfied. For example, "Should atomic tests, necessary for atomic development, be continued at the risk of possible injury to the health of the world's people?'' Tradition gives no clear answer. Or, ''Who should pay the costs when workers are displaced through automation?'' The traditional answer is, ''The worker himself''; but since many people consider this solution too cruel, an issue of ''What shall we do about technological unemployment?'' is created.

In these ways a complex changing culture creates a great many publics, each concerned with an activity, interest, or issue. As the members of a public consider the issue, and form opinions concerning it, *public opinion* is developed.

Public opinion refers to the opinions held by a public upon an issue.   Strictly speaking, the term should perhaps be *public opinions,* since several opinions are normally held by the members of a public; but the term *public opinion* is commonly used to refer to all the differing opinions held by the members of a public. The term is also often used to refer to the opinions of *the* public—of everybody—including those who have no interest and no definite opinions on the issue. These various connotations leave the exact meaning of the term a little confused; its meaning must be inferred from its context.

Dimensions of public opinion   Public opinion has at least three dimensions. *Direction* simply states whether an opinion is for or against a proposed course of action. A count of the ''yes'' and ''no,'' or the ''approve'' and ''disapprove'' opinions measures the direction of opinion. *Intensity* refers to the strength with which an opinion is held. ''Yes'' may mean, ''Yes, absolutely, whatever the costs,'' or it may mean, ''Yes, I guess so''! *Integration* refers to the way an opinion is tied in with one's total set of beliefs and values. Is this opinion an expression of a man's general outlook or an exception to it? For example, Mr. Smith favors national health insurance (sometimes called ''socialized medicine'') because he favors a welfare state wherein the government provides many social services to its citizens. Mr. Jones, less enthusiastic about the welfare state, supports national health insurance because after some study he believes that it is the only practical way to organize health services. Mr. Brown, strongly opposed to the welfare state, supports national health insurance because he dislikes physicians and wants to see their heads knocked together. Mr. Black supports it because his union tells him it is good. While identical in direction and perhaps intensity, these four opinions are basically quite different because of the way they relate to the mental context of their holders. The opinion which is well integrated with one's total value system is less susceptible to persuasion than the opinion which is divorced from or inconsistent with one's general system of beliefs and values.

Measurement of public opinion   The leaders of a group or a nation cannot lead wisely unless they know which way the people are willing to be led. The public-opinion poll is a recent invention for finding out what people are thinking. A poll is simple in concept but difficult to carry out because, as is shown above, an opinion is a rather complicated phenomenon. The pollsters prepare a set of questions on an issue, seeking to phrase the questions in such a way that the wording does not prejudice the informant's answer. Then these questions are offered to a small number of people (from a few hundred to a few thousand) so that each group or class in the total population is represented in the sample in its correct proportion. If all these preliminary arrangements are made without serious error, opinion is measured quite accurately. The Gallup Poll, for example, has predicted the vote on recent elections with an average error of less than 2 per cent [Gallup, 1957]. But there are many pitfalls in public-opinion polling which a pollster must guard against if he is to attain this level of accuracy. One of the greatest is the tendency of people to state firm opinions on issues which they know nothing about, have not thought about, and really have no opinion upon. In 1959 a Los Angeles newspaperman asked a number of people the question, "Do you think the Mann Act deters or helps the cause of organized labor?" About one person in eight knew what the Mann Act was (it forbids the interstate transportation of women for immoral purposes) and realized that the question was unanswerable. But of the remainder who admitted that they knew nothing of the Mann Act, about one-half expressed decided opinions about its effects. If the "opinions" of people who know nothing about an issue are included, a poll is not very accurate. Other pitfalls surround the wording of questions, the selection of the sample, and the weighing or interpreting of responses [Parten, 1950; Selltiz et al., 1959; Phillips, 1966]. Polling is no job for amateurs!

Manipulation of public opinion   The main emphasis in public-opinion research has been upon ways of manipulating public opinion [Albig, 1957]. *Propaganda* includes all efforts to persuade people to a point of view upon an issue; everything from Sunday school lessons to billboards are propaganda; advertising, sales promotion, and fund-raising drives are prime examples. The usual distinction between education and propaganda is that education seeks to cultivate one's ability to make discriminating judgments, while propaganda seeks to persuade one to the undiscriminating acceptance of a ready-made judgment. In practice, education often includes a good deal of propaganda. Teachers sometimes propagandize for their own opinions; interest groups seek to get their own propaganda, disguised as "educational materials," into the school; society virtually forces the school to propagandize for the approved moral and patriotic values. To draw a clear distinction between education and propaganda is not always possible. And it should be repeated that propaganda is not necessarily "bad"; it is merely a term applied to *all* attempts to influence other peoples' opinions and actions. Most students, beginning perhaps with a ninth-grade course in civics, have seen descriptions of the techniques of propaganda in textbook after textbook. We shall not repeat them here. Good descriptions of propaganda techniques are easily available, should the student wish to consult them [Lee and Lee, 1939; Doob, 1948; Lasswell, 1933, 1951].

Does the propagandist get the greatest opinion change when his propaganda diverges greatly, or only slightly, from the opinions already held by the receivers? Some research studies find that when the degree of divergence from the original opinion is greater, so is the opinion change; other studies reach the opposite conclusion. Whittaker [1964] reconciles these contradictory findings, saying that when the issue is one upon which the receivers hold intense opinions with a deep personal involvement, opinion change diminishes as dissonance increases. Too great a dissonance even produces a "boomerang" effect; that is, the receiver rejects the propaganda with an even stronger loyalty to his original opinions. But when the issue is one on which the receiver has no intense opinions or deep personal involvement, increasing dissonance produces increased opinion change. For each receiver, there is an "optimal discrepancy" which will produce a maximum opinion change.

Goebbels' principles of propaganda:
As deduced from Goebbels' war diaries by Leonard W. Doob

1.   *Propagandists must have accurate information on current war developments and current public opinion.*

2.   *All propaganda must be planned and directed by a single authority.*

3.   *The propaganda consequences of a military or government policy must be considered in planning these policies.*

4.   *Propaganda must have an effect upon the enemy's policies and actions.*

5.   *Significant news material must be available for a propaganda campaign.*

6.   *To be effective, propaganda must be interesting, and be carried through popular media like movies and radio.*

7.   *Believability, rather than truth or falsity, should determine whether an item is used.*

8.   *Enemy propaganda should be answered only if it is proving to be effective, and can be convincingly answered; otherwise it should be ignored.*

9.   *Censorship should be used to suppress news which will not be believed, or which will create anxieties and damage morale.*

10.   *Enemy propaganda may be quoted whenever useful.*

11.   *Propaganda may be "planted" so that it seems to come from unofficial sources.*

12.   *Propaganda is more effective when associated with national heroes.*

13.   *Propaganda must be carefully timed.*

14.   *Propaganda must label people and events with distinctive phrases or slogans.*

15.   *Propaganda on the home front must not raise false hopes which will be dashed by future events.*

16.   *Propaganda on the home front must create an optimum anxiety level—some, but not too much, anxiety is beneficial.*

17.   *Propaganda on the home front must diminish the impact of frustrations.*

18.   *Propaganda must aid the displacement of aggressions by specifying the targets for hatred.*

Adapted by special permission from Leonard W. Doob, "Goebbels' Principles of Propaganda," *Public Opinion Quarterly*, 14:419–442, Fall, 1950.

Limits of propaganda   If the powers of propaganda were unlimited, the side with the most money and the best public relations agency would always win. Since this does not always happen, the power of propaganda must be limited in various ways.

1. Competing propagandas are probably the greatest limitation. Where the state has a monopoly of propaganda, as in totalitarian states, a citizen can hardly find any facts to use in arriving at opinions other than the officially approved ones. With a monopoly of propaganda, a propagandist can suppress and manufacture facts, and no effective rebuttal is possible. The mere *exist-*

Competing propaganda exerts a restraining influence.

ence of competing propagandas in a democratic state exerts a restraining influence both upon the propagandist and upon his receiver.

2. The credibility of the propagandist in the eyes of the receivers limits what they will accept. When his "facts" and opinions diverge from theirs, this creates tensions which the receiver can relieve either by changing his opinions or by downgrading the propagandist [Aronson et al., 1963]. Credibility is reduced where the propagandist is obviously grinding his own ax, so propaganda is often conducted under the name of a noble-sounding organization (Fundamental Freedoms Foundation, Tax Equality Association, Homeowners' Association) which conceals the selfish interests of the propagandists.

3. The sophistication of the receiver limits the effects of propaganda. In general, those who are well educated or well informed on the issue are less affected by propaganda than the poorly educated and the poorly informed.

4. The beliefs and values of the recipient limit the propaganda he will believe. Many people are fond of picturing themselves as open-minded, discriminating analysts of competing propagandas, but they are usually reacting mechanically to slogans and catchwords. Most people accept uncritically any propaganda which fits in with their established attitudes and values, and usually reject, equally uncritically, any which conflicts. For this reason, a propagandist rarely tries to change the basic attitudes of his recipients; instead, he tries to get them to accept his definition of the issue, in terms of their attitudes. For example, a propagandist for civil rights legislation would not try to change white attitudes toward Negroes; instead, he would try to identify civil rights legislation with their belief in democracy and fair play and point out how racial turmoil hurts business and discourages new industry. The propagandist against civil rights legislation rarely attacks democracy or fair play, or even attacks Negroes; he pictures civil rights legislation as a Communist-inspired scheme to stir up trouble, or as a bureaucratic assault upon states' rights and personal liberties. Communist propaganda has been ineffective in the United States because its pictures of the villainous businessman, the "oppressive" church, and a "proletariat" middle class simply struck no responsive note in the basic images, attitudes, and values of the American people.

5. Cultural trends limit the effectiveness of propaganda. A cultural trend is not stopped by propaganda. For this reason, all "back to the simple life," "away with materialism," and "women's place is in the home" propagandas are doomed to futility. Propaganda may accelerate or retard a cultural trend, reinforce or weaken a value. But it is doubtful if propaganda in a democratic society can either initiate or halt a cultural trend, destroy a well-established value, or instill a new value which the culture is not already developing.

Psychological warfare

There is nothing new in the use of propaganda as a military weapon; only the great modern emphasis upon psychological warfare is new. Entirely too much was expected of psychological warfare in World War II. Propaganda intended to undermine the morale of the enemy had little effect, either upon enemy civilians or military units, so long as their primary-group structures remained intact. Not until disruption of primary-group life was accomplished through separation, loss of communication, loss of leadership, interruptions of food and medical supplies, and other disruptions—not until then did morale and organized resistance crumble. Apparently psychological warfare has little effect upon an efficiently operating enemy; its main effect is to hasten the disintegration of the enemy after superior military force has begun his defeat [Shils and Janowitz, 1948].

The United States and the Soviet Union are both engaged in worldwide propaganda programs whose effects cannot be accurately predicted. The short-run effects of such propaganda campaigns seem to lie in ". . . providing people with a rationale for their existing convictions rather than in changing their attitudes" [Bogart, 1957]. The long-run effects of a sustained propaganda program may be greater, since it may gradually build up a body of factual information among its recipients and thus effect gradual changes of attitude and opinion. This, at least, is the hope that motivates our "Voice of America" broadcasts.

SUMMARY

Collective behavior is a characteristic of complex cultures and is usually absent in simple societies. A crowd is a temporary gathering of people who are acting together. Crowd behavior is characterized by: (1) anonymity—the individual loses his customary restraints and sense of personal responsibility; (2) impersonality—only the group affiliation of the person is important; (3) suggestibility—crowd members act uncritically upon suggestions; (4) social contagion—crowd members build up one another's emotional involvement. Crowd behavior is limited, however, by: (1) the emotional needs and attitudes of the members; (2) the mores of the members, who rarely do anything which is not condoned by certain of their mores; (3) crowd leaders, who must establish rapport, build emotional tensions, suggest action to relieve these tensions and justify this action; and (4) external controls, mainly the police, who can usually control crowd behavior if they wish to and are properly trained.

Crowd behavior takes many forms. The *audience* is largely, but not entirely a one-way crowd responding to a single stimulus. The *mob* is a crowd in violent action. The *lynching mob* is an extralegal device for the enforcement of local mores, and takes different forms according to the local setting. The *riot* is a violently aggressive mob whose members are generally releasing accumulated hostilities against other groups. The *orgy* is a good-natured mob enjoying itself, through uninhibited indulgence. The *panic* is a mob in sudden, disorganized flight from danger. Some other forms of collective behavior include *rumors, fads and fashions, crazes,* and outbreaks of *mass hysteria.*

A complex, rapidly changing society creates many *publics,* each of which is a group of people who share a particular interest. The various opinions of the members of the public that is concerned with an issue, together with the more casual views of those persons who are not much concerned with the issue, are loosely lumped together under the term, *public opinion.* Individual opinions differ in direction, in intensity, and in integration, or the way they tie in with the rest of one's thinking. Consequently, it is difficult to "add up" individual opinions and measure the sum of public opinion, but professional pollsters have developed techniques which can measure opinion with considerable accuracy.

Practically every interest group today is trying to manipulate public opinion so that propaganda, often called "public relations," is one of our largest businesses. Propaganda may be less powerful than it sometimes appears to be, for its effects are limited by competing propagandas, by the credibility of the propagandists, by the sophistication of its receivers, by the established beliefs and values of the receivers, and by the existing trends within the culture. Psychological warfare attempts to use propaganda to weaken an enemy and to project a favorable image of one's own country upon the world's people.

QUESTIONS AND PROJECTS

1. When we say that crowd behavior is "unstructured," what do we mean? Of what importance is its unstructured character?

2. Why do mob members seldom feel guilty about their mob actions?

3. Are there any situations in our culture which contain elements of the institutionalized orgy?

4. Should we fully institutionalize the orgy in American society? What benefits might accrue? What difficulties would arise?

5. What caused the recent student disorders at Berkeley and elsewhere? Are students generally becoming more restless, or less restless? Why?

6. Do you think you are immune to panic? To crazes? To mass hysteria? What makes you think so?

7. Can you think of any propaganda efforts or causes which have failed in the United States because they conflicted with our cultural values? With prevailing cultural trends?

8. Write up a description of a campus pep rally as an example of crowd behavior.

9. Try an experiment in rumor. Select a rumor (consulting with your instructor in finding a harmless rumor) and set it going by a specified number of tellings. Then record the time, frequency, and form in which it "comes back" to you as it spreads over the campus.

10. Recall and describe a crowd situation in which the behavior lagged dispiritedly for a time. Show how each of the characteristics of crowd behavior came into operation and kindled a proper enthusiasm in the members.

11. Prepare a list of aggressive actions which you think you could engage in if placed in a suitably encouraging crowd situation. Prepare a list of actions in which you think you could not possibly share, no matter what the crowd situation. Give your reasons for each listing.

12. Run a campus public-opinion poll on a fictitious proposition such as "Do you favor or oppose the Hill-Wallerton proposal to pay college students a salary according to their point averages? See how many will admit that they do not know of the proposal, and how many state firm opinions on it.

SUGGESTED READINGS

ALLPORT, GORDON W., AND LEO POSTMAN: *The Psychology of Rumor*, Holt, Rinehart and Winston, Inc., New York, 1947; or "The Basic Psychology of Rumor," in WILBUR SCHRAMM (ED.): *The Process and Effects of Mass Communication*, The University of Illinois Press, Urbana, Ill., 1955, pp. 141–155. How and why rumors appear and circulate.

BROWN, ROGER W.: "Mass Phenomena," in GARDNER LINDZEY (ED.), *Handbook of Social Psychology*, Addison-Wesley Publishing Company, Inc., Reading, Mass., 1954, vol. 2, chap. 23. A comprehensive summary of research and scientific viewpoint on many of the topics treated in this chapter.

*CANTRIL, HADLEY, *The Psychology of Social Movements*, John Wiley & Sons, Inc., New York, 1963, chap. 4, "The Lynching Mob." A vivid description of two lynchings, analyzed in terms of the people who performed them. (Sci Ed)

KATZ, DANIEL, DORWIN CARTWRIGHT, SAMUEL ELDERSVELD, AND ALFRED MCCLUNG LEE (EDS.), *Public Opinion and Propaganda,* Holt, Rinehart and Winston, Inc., New York, 1954. A collection of readings covering many aspects of public opinion and propaganda.

LANG, KURT, AND GLADYS ENGEL LANG: *Collective Dynamics,* Thomas Y. Crowell Company, New York, 1961. A textbook on collective behavior, with interesting chapters on rumor, panic, crowd behavior, fashion, public opinion, and other topics covered in this chapter.

LEE, ALFRED MCCLUNG, AND NORMAN D. HUMPHREY: *Race Riot,* Holt, Rinehart and Winston, Inc., New York, 1943. A description and analysis of the Detroit race riot of 1941.

*LIPSET, SEYMOUR M., AND SHELDON S. WOLIN (EDS.): *The Berkeley Student Revolt,* Anchor Books, Doubleday & Company, Inc., Garden City, N.Y., 1965. A collection of essays about this student disorder. For a brief account, see SEYMOUR M. LIPSET AND PAUL SEABURY, "Lesson of Berkeley: Question of Student Political Activities," *Reporter,* Jan. 28, 1965, pp. 36–40. (A486-Anch)

SMELSER, NEIL J.: *Theory of Collective Behavior,* The Free Press of Glencoe, New York, 1963. Attempts to develop and apply a theoretical framework for analyzing collective behavior.

TURNER, RALPH H., AND LEWIS M. KILLIAN: *Collective Behavior,* Prentice-Hall, Inc., Englewood Cliffs, N.J., 1957, chaps. 3–13. An interestingly written textbook, about half of which is devoted to the topics covered in this chapter.

WHITE, THEO: "Building the Big Dam," *Harper's Magazine,* June, 1935, pp. 112–121. An entertaining explanation of how and why construction-camp workers used to go on payday sprees.

Five

HUMAN ECOLOGY

Part Five studies the way people and institutions are distributed in space, and the way they relate to the physical environment they occupy. Chapter 17, "Population," considers the factors in population change, migration, and population composition. Chapter 18, "The Community," studies rural and urban communities and the emergence of a world-wide urban culture.

POPULATION

Since the end of World War II the rate of population increase has continued to accelerate and has reached a level of about 1.7 per cent per year. . . . At the rate of world population increase for the period 1800–1850, for example, the present population would double in 135 years; at the 1900–1950 rate, in 67 years; at the postwar rate, in only 42 years.

Projection of the post-World War II rate of increase gives a population of one person per square foot of the land surface of the earth in less than 800 years. (Philip M. Hauser, *Population Perspectives*, Rutgers University Press, New Brunswick, N.J., 1960, p. 7.)

|H|UMAN ECOLOGY is the study of men's interrelationships with their physical environments. More simply, it is the study of how people and institutions are located in space. It includes both the study of population (demography) and the study of community and regional organization.

Demographers are interested in both the size and the composition of a population. A small population with large natural resources and extensive territory will have limited economic growth and urban development. A dense population with limited natural resources will have difficulty in maintaining a high standard of living. On the other hand, a growing population offers increasing markets for housing, food, and similar commodities, whereas a declining population may reduce market demand. Sometimes a population will vary from the usual sex and age distribution with certain predictable social consequences. A population with a large number of children and old people leaves a smaller proportion of people in productive labor to support them. If the sex ratio is markedly unequal, then many people will be unable to marry and may seek companionship outside of the normal family relationships. In many ways, population statistics are reflected in the social life of a people.

Population has been relatively stable throughout most of history. In the first 1,650 years after the birth of Christ, world population a little more than doubled. In the next 125 years it doubled again. By the year 2000, it is expected to double in only 27 years. World population now grows in about six years by as many persons as it grew in the first 1,650 years following the birth of Christ. The earth could support a population somewhere between 7.5 billion and 50 billion, depending upon whose estimate we accept; the higher figure, however, assumes that our technology will be able to produce the "things" we need from rocks, sea, and air, and that we shall be willing to live on food from "algae farms and yeast factories." At present rates of growth, we shall reach this 50 billion figure in less than 200 years.

One demographer [Knibbs, 1928, p. 49] has estimated that if the offspring from a single couple were to grow at the rate of 1 per cent a year for 10,000 years, it would take 248,293,000 billion earths to hold the bodies of all these people. Yet our present rate of world population increase is 1.7 per cent, and is expected to go as high as 2.6 per cent by the year 2000 [United Nations, 1958]. Even now, India is growing at an annual rate of 2 per cent, and Ceylon, Taiwan, the Philippines, Mexico, and some other areas are growing at a rate

One person per square foot of land surface in less than 800 years.

of over 3 per cent. Obviously, such rates of population growth are a recent phenomenon and are certain, *one way or another*, to be temporary. Eventually either the birth rate will drop to replacement levels or the death rate will rise to eliminate the population the world is unable to support. Since no one advocates death as an answer to population problems, attention has been concentrated on reducing the birth rate. But birth rates have seldom responded to large-scale efforts at change either up or down, and the success of such efforts in the underdeveloped countries is by no means certain. So far only the Japanese have been substantially successful in deliberate national efforts to reduce the birth rate.

DEMOGRAPHIC CONCEPTS

In order to study population questions, one must understand the very definite meanings of demographic concepts. Birth and death rates, for instance, are terms frequently used in demographic discussion. Usually they refer to the *crude* rate, which is the number of births or deaths per thousand people per year. Crude birth and death rates do give a picture of population trends, but they may be misleading because births and deaths are greatly affected by the age structure of the population. A population in which a large proportion of people are relatively old would show a high crude death rate even though health levels were very high. Similarly, a population with a high proportion of either the very old or the very young would have a low crude birth rate even though the women of childbearing age were producing children at close to their biological potential. To allow for this factor of age we frequently use *age specific* rates, which give birth or death rates for specific age levels. *Standardized birth rates* are those in which the actual age distribution of females in a population has been weighted to give the birth rate which would have resulted if the age distribution had been that of a presumably "standard" population. In this way two populations with different age and sex distributions can be compared so as to distinguish differences which arise from age and sex distribution from those due to other factors.

The influence of age distribution on the crude birth rate can be seen in the hypothetical example detailed in Table 20. The two towns in the table have identical age specific birth rates, but because of differences in age distribution, the crude birth rates are 26 and 14.

Sex distribution is also of interest to the demographer, for it affects the crude birth rate as well as many other social phenomena. Thus we speak of the *sex ratio,* which is the number of males per 100 females. A sex ratio of 100 indicates that the two sexes are found in equal number, one of 110 that there are 110 men to 100 women, and one of 90 that there are 90 men to 100 women.

Table 20   Hypothetical Birth Rates

| Age category | Jonesville | | | Plainville | | |
	No. of persons	Age specific birth rate	No. of births	No. of persons	Age specific birth rate	No. of births
Young	*100*	*10*	*1*	*400*	*10*	*4*
Middle-aged	*800*	*30*	*24*	*200*	*30*	*6*
Old	*100*	*10*	*1*	*400*	*10*	*4*
			26			*14*

SOURCE: Adapted from Everett K. Wilson, *Sociology,* Dorsey Press, Homewood, Illinois, 1966, p. 311.

Demographers often speak of *life expectancy*. This usually refers to the number of years of life the average infant may expect at birth, but it may also be age specific—for example, life expectancy at age 60 (average additional years of life to be expected after reaching an age of 60).

Insurance companies, for instance, use actuarial tables indicating the life expectancy at any given age. Life expectancy should be distinguished from *life span*, which refers to the length of life possible for a species. In the last century life expectancy at birth has increased greatly, while there is no evidence that our life span has changed at all.

The very elementary concepts which we have just described represent only a few of the tools used in demographic analysis, but they are probably adequate for an introductory treatment of the subject. Knowledge of the techniques of population-trend analysis is essential to those who plan business, governmental, religious, or educational programs, and many students may wish, eventually, to pursue specialized courses in this field.

CHANGING POPULATION COMPOSITION

The composition of a population affects its social life. Washington, D.C., with its droves of female clerical workers, St. Petersburg with its retired people, and Columbus, Georgia, with nearby Fort Benning—these cities are different, in part, because of differences in the age, sex, and occupational composition of the population whose needs they fill.

As shown in Table 21, the age composition of the United States has been

Table 21   The changing age composition of the American population

| | Dependents per 100 persons of working age (20–64) | | |
Year	Young and old	Young only (under 20)	Old only (over 64)
Census			
1820	*153*	*146*	*7*
1850	*123*	*117*	*6*
1900	*94*	*86*	*8*
1940	*71*	*59*	*12*
Estimate			
1950	*72*	*58*	*14*
Projection			
1960	*91*	*74*	*17*
1970	*98*	*80*	*18*
1980	*104*	*85*	*19*

SOURCE: Slightly adapted from Philip M. Hauser, *Population Perspectives*, Rutgers University Press, New Brunswick, N.J., 1960, p. 71.

constantly changing. A high birth rate means that children will compose a large fraction of the total population and old people a relatively small fraction. The long-term decline in our birth rate, lasting until the 1930s, reduced the children's share of our population and increased the proportion of the aged. Meanwhile, a very slight extension of the life expectancy of the aged further increased the proportion of the aged. Then, in the 1930s the birth rate started back up, climbing from 16 births per 1,000 in 1935 to 27 in 1947; then it hovered around 24 during the 1950s, and fell to 18 by 1967. This again increased the proportion of children, while the proportion of aged continued to rise.

We must remember that it is primarily changes in the birth rate, not in the death rate, which have changed the proportion of the aged in our population. This point is widely misunderstood by people who confuse *life span* with *life expectancy.* As stated earlier the life span measures the time which fortunate people live until carried off by "old age"; life expectancy is the mean number of years of life remaining at any given age. Life expectancy at birth has doubled in the last century and a half; life expectancy at age sixty has increased only a couple of years. In other words, infants today are far more likely to reach the age of sixty than infants a century ago, but people who have reached sixty today have only two more years of life remaining than those who reached sixty a century ago. Stated still differently, more people live to be old today, but old people today do not live much longer than old people used to live, as shown in Figure 14.

So life span and death rates have had only a minor part in the increasing proportion of the aged. But if the number of children in a population is increased, the *proportion* of the aged in the population is reduced. The rapid present growth in the proportion of the aged is due to the fact that those now approaching old age were born during the period of high birth rates, while those now approaching middle age were born during a period of lower birth rates. If the birth rate should remain stable over a long period of time, the proportion of the people at each age level would stabilize, and we should then have what demographers call a "normal" or "standard" population distribution.

Since 1940 the United States has seen two major changes in population composition: a rise in the proportion of the young compared with the level prevailing in 1900 and an increase of one-third in the proportion of the aged. These changes have caused both an increase of interest in the study of problems of the aged and major crises in many school districts as they engage in a frantic expansion to meet increased numbers of children.

The American marriage and birth rates were swelled for many years by the effect of immigration, which brought in many people of childbearing age. The American population grew rapidly, partly because so large a proportion of the people were in this age bracket. Immigration has now declined, but we are noticing a population bulge because the offspring born in the World War II baby boom are now of marriageable age themselves. Thus, even if the number of children per family should fall, we should still have a high number of births because the number of people in the childbearing age groups is large in comparison with the rest of the population.

Changes in population composition have many social consequences. A

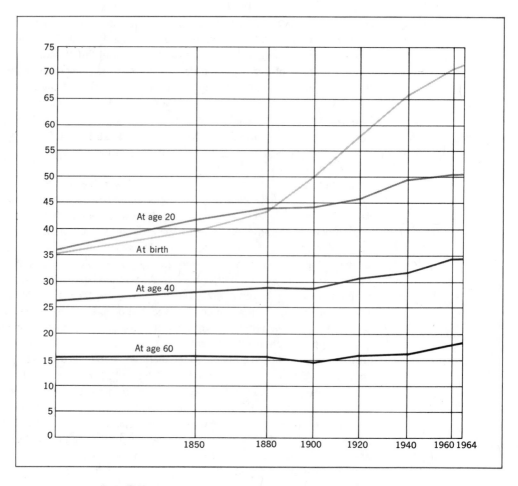

FIGURE 14 *Life Expectancy at Various Ages in the United States: 1789–1964.*
SOURCE: *Statistical Abstracts of the United States, Historical Statistics of the United States.*

change in the ratio of dependents to workers has great economic impact. It affects employment, living standards, and price levels. The proportion of the aged has important economic and political consequences, such as the drive for more generous pension plans, the promotion of health and welfare services for old people, and experimentation with retirement communities, recreational programs, and other services for the aged. Possibly the greater influence of our older citizens may reinforce a conservative trend as they try to slow the course of social change.

The scientific study of the aged is claiming increased attention. *Geriatrics* is a branch of medicine which studies old age and its diseases; *gerontology* is a more inclusive field embracing the entire study of the aged and their problems. In a society with a growing proportion of old people, who are living in a society which is less comfortable for the aged than a rural society used to be—in such a society, gerontology is a rapidly growing discipline. One fact alone—the fact that men by 1975 can expect three times as many years of retirement as men at the turn of this century (Figure 15) makes gerontology an important field of study.

Important as these effects have been in the United States, they are dwarfed by comparison with the impact of changing population composition in the underdeveloped countries. A sharp reduction in the death rate in these coun- tries, mainly in infancy and early childhood, has allowed a rapid population increase, which is reflected in a very high proportion of the population under fifteen years of age. In these countries the ratio of children under fifteen to total population varies from 35 to 50 per cent, while in most western countries the ratio varies between 20 and 30 percent.

This means that the poorest countries are also those with the largest propor- tion of children to raise and the smallest proportion of people of working age to support them. Education, for instance, is a major expense as all of the world's countries endeavor to produce a trained citizenry. The developing countries, however, often have twice as large a proportion of school-age chil- dren as the industrialized nations. Or, to put the matter another way, they could double the educational expenditures per child with no increase in the school budget if their population composition was the same as that of Western Europe.

One of the long-run consequences of a severe war is alteration of the pop- ulation composition. The population picture in Berlin, Germany, in 1910 was similar to that of an American city, and the population pyramid for that year indicates a fairly "normal" age and sex distribution. In 1945, however, the German population as a whole had an estimated "surplus" of 8 million women of childbearing age, meaning that many German women at this time had no

FIGURE 15 *By 1975, Men Age 60 Can Expect Three Times as Many Years of Retirement as in 1900.*

SOURCE: 1961 White House Conference on Aging, Chart Book, Federal Council on Aging, Government Printing Office, Washington, D.C., 1961, p. 50.

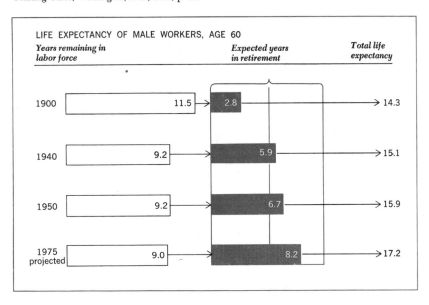

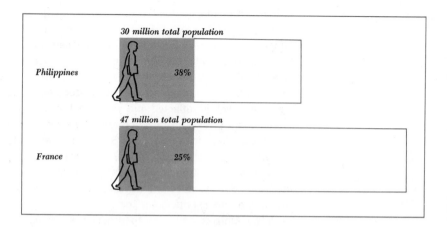

FIGURE 16   *Effect of Population Composition on Proportion of School-age Children.*

In the Philippines 38 per cent of a population of 30 million fall between the ages of 5 and 19, giving the Philippines the same number of school-age children as France, with 25 per cent of a population of 47 million falling between the ages of 5 and 19 (1963).

SOURCE: *Demographic Yearbook,* 1964, The United Nations, New York, 1964.

FIGURE 17   *A Population Pyramid Shows the Age and Sex Distribution of a Population.*

These two pyramids show the age and sex composition of Berlin in 1910 and 1945. In 1910, Berlin was growing rapidly through the migration of young adults, showing as a huge bulge above age 20. In 1945, the pyramid shows the scars of two wars, with a relative shortage of men at all ages between 20 and 65, and a spectacular shortage of infants.

SOURCE: Reproduced by permission from Gustav Stalper's "Germany's Biological Destruction," *Fortune,* 37:93, May, 1948.

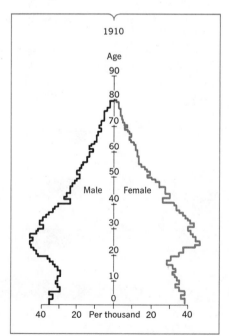
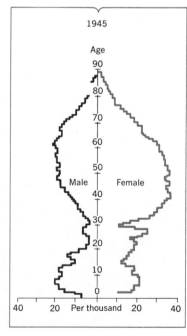

chance for marriage. Two world wars killed millions of Germans, and the fact that most of these casualties were men of marriageable age means that these wartime losses will alter the composition of German population for many years.

Changes in population composition are less dramatic than the recent spectacular spurts of population growth, but they are both the cause and the result of major changes in a society. Hence the demographer is constantly concerned with ascertaining changes in the sex ratio, the age composition, and the movement of population both within and between countries. Although the demographer makes use of the concept of a "standard" population, no actual society ever attains a completely normal population distribution. Social change is the rule rather than the exception, and most social changes, directly or indirectly, affect population composition.

MIGRATION

The ancestors of the American Indians are thought to have come to the North American continent over a landbridge from Asia some time in the remote past. All other Americans trace their ancestry to relatively recent migrants. From the time of the Pilgrim fathers, some 30 million immigrants, mostly from Europe, settled in this country and changed it from a wilderness of food gatherers and hunters to the flourishing nation we know today. International immigration is now less important than in previous years, but a tremendous movement within the country leads to a constant redistribution of population.

Push, pull,
and channels
The forces affecting migration may be grouped under three headings: (1) push, (2) pull, and (3) channels. *Push* relates to unfavorable conditions in the homeland which make people want to leave. In the 1840s a potato famine in Ireland made the United States seem attractive to many Irishmen, and the failure of the Revolution of 1848 caused many Germans to seek their fortunes in a land where immigrants were asked no questions about political beliefs. Sometimes the push comes from a catastrophe, sometimes from economic stagnation and lack of opportunity, sometimes from political or religious persecution. Today the shifts of national boundary lines after World War II and the rise of intolerant political movements, especially communism, have made life in their native lands intolerable for many people. At the time of the International Refugee Year, 1960, it was estimated that 15 million people had been forced to leave their ancestral homes and had not yet found a permanent place of residence [*New York Times*, Jan. 26, 1959, p. 5].

Pull refers to the attractive features in the country receiving immigrants. Immigration proceeds toward the area of greater opportunities, as these are perceived by the individual. This perception is a cultural definition

Except for the American Indians, they are all the descendants of immigrants.

and not necessarily an objectively valid judgment. It is not the overall opportunity for economic development which is decisive, but the ease with which the
individual can move into a situation with relatively little cultural readjustment.
Alaska, for instance, is much more sparsely settled than California or New
York and may have greater potential economic opportunities. Yet dozens of
immigrants move to these states for every one who enters Alaska simply because they seek an opportunity to make a living in an area where they believe
they will be comfortable. Very few people seem to want the hardy life of the
raw frontier. Indonesians continue to move into heavily populated Java, although sparsely peopled Sumatra asks for settlers. In some parts of Central
and South Amerca, good—but remote—land lies unused, while people flock into
the miserable shanty-town slums which climb the hills outside the major cities.
Possibly this picture may be changed by the growth of industrialization
which brings both jobs and cultural amenities to the more isolated areas. Likewise, extraordinary opportunity for gain, such as a gold discovery or the presence of rich agricultural land with easy access to markets, may exert a powerful pull. Frequently though, the migration to areas of supposedly rich potential
is slow until "social overhead"—towns, schools, medical resources, roads, and
stable governments—has been provided. An area becomes attractive when
the handicaps of a different environment seem less significant than the opportunity for more rapid social mobility in a direction that does not seem to
threaten traditional cultural standards.

Channels refer to the means of movement from one area to another. They
include the availability of transportation, of information, of help in overcoming
financial obstacles, and the presence or absence of barriers in both the homeland and the receiving country. The twentieth century has seen the development of marvelous means of transport accompanied by severe restrictions
on immigration. Physically it was never easier to move from one country to
another.

Socially or politically, people find it harder to make such a move now than
they did in the nineteenth century. Then they could ordinarily move about
without restrictions of any kind. Even passports were seldom required. Today
we take it for granted that countries will select the type and number of immigrants they wish to receive and that individuals will be unable to move unless some governmental bureau has given permission. Among the early immigrants to America were prostitutes, prisoners from penal colonies, illiterates,
adherents of radical political movements, the diseased and the physically de-
formed, none of whom would be admitted today. Indeed, it is certain that many
of the early migrants whose memory is now enshrined by the Daughters of the
American Revolution and similar organizations would not be able to qualify for
entry under our present laws.

International migration

Increasing population and a developing nationalism have combined to make
governments wish to restrict immigration to the type of immigrants they feel
the national culture can most easily assimilate and to the number the nation
can easily absorb into its economy. In the United States we exclude those with
physical defects and certain other personal disqualifications. Until 1968 we
also set a quota for each country, based upon our population composition in
1920 and designed to favor the Northwestern European nations. We will
normally admit no more than 170,000 immigrants from outside the Western

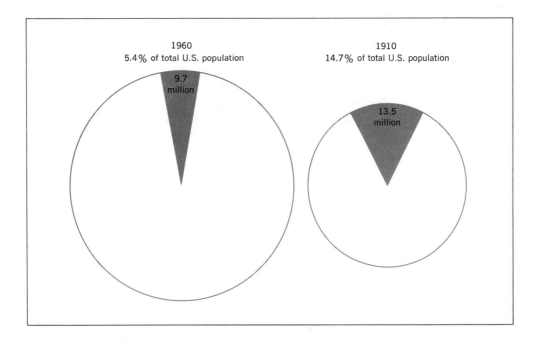

FIGURE 18   *Foreign-born Population of the United States: 1910 and 1960.*
SOURCE: For 1910, U.S. Bureau of the Census, *Historical Statistics of the United States,* 1789–1945, Washington, D.C., 1949, p. 30. Data for 1960 from U.S. Census of Population.

hemisphere. While some additional immigration was allowed as an emergency measure to help displaced persons after World War II, the net effect of the United States immigration policy since 1921 has been to make immigration relatively unimportant as far as the size and composition of the American population is concerned.

Most of the world has followed immigration policies similar to those of the United States. The countries friendliest to immigration are those like Brazil, Canada, and Australia which are considered underpopulated and welcome additional immigrants as a means of developing their resources. Since Australia and Canada restrict Oriental and African immigration, even those countries cannot be described as having a completely open immigration policy.

Characteristics of immigrants to the United States.

Before 1890, were predominantly	After 1890, were predominantly
From Northwestern Europe	*From Central, Southern, and Eastern Europe*
Protestant	*Catholic*
Literate	*Illiterate*
Skilled or semiskilled	*Unskilled or peasant*
Accustomed to democracy	*Accustomed to authoritarian government*
Scattered in settlement	*Bunched in urban areas*
Easily assimilated	*Uneasily accommodated*

Does the above table suggest some reasons why immigration became viewed as a "problem" after the turn of the century?

Internal Although international migration is subject to increasing restrictions, a con-
migration siderable shift of people is constantly going on within nations. In a normal
year, one American family in five will move. In times past the American industrial labor force was recruited from European migrants and the agricultural
force from African slaves and, until recently, from temporary Mexican migrants.
Now that slavery has been ended and immigration reduced, the need for labor
is met by movement of the American population. The past forty years have
seen millions of people moving to the cities of the West and the East from the
agricultural areas of the South and the Middle West; they have seen, too, a
considerable movement of Puerto Ricans to the mainland.

While this internal migration is different in form from that crossing international boundary lines, the processes of the two shifts are much the same.
The movement into a new region changes the population composition, provides
new labor, and introduces a group of people ignorant of the prevailing folkways, who have to make their adjustment to a strange cultural setting. Southern whites and Negroes along with Puerto Ricans and others thus make many
of the same contributions and experience many of the same problems as did
the European immigrants of an earlier day.

SOCIAL AND CULTURAL ASPECTS OF POPULATION CHANGE

What causes a change in the rate of population growth? There is no evidence
that groups differ in their biological capacity to reproduce and to survive, or
that this capacity changes from time to time. One scholar [de Castro, 1952]
has advanced the theory that hunger and poor diet produce a rise in the reproductive capacity as the species struggles to survive. Critics have noted
that his evidence is contradictory and inconclusive, and that he confuses the
actual birth rate with biological capacity to reproduce and survive [Fairchild,
1952]. Research on birth rates concerns both *fecundity*, the biological capacity
to reproduce, and *fertility*, the actual rate of reproduction. Fecundity varies
greatly between individuals, but we have no evidence of major differences
between large population groups. In every population some individuals are
either sterile or have limited fecundity, but distribution of such persons is
relatively constant. Fertility is based on fecundity, but no group reproduces
at its biological maximum. Since our biological capacity to reproduce appears
to be constant, social and cultural factors must explain most variations in
birth and death rates.

Changes in Throughout most of history, both birth and death rates have been high, with
death rates only a small rate of natural increase. In the Bronze Age of ancient Greece,
expectation of life at birth was an estimated 18 years. By the opening of the
nineteenth century it had doubled to about 36 years. A century and a half
later it has doubled again, now standing at 70 years in the United States
(specifically, 67.7 for white males, 74.6 for white females, 61.1 for nonwhite
males, and 67.2 for nonwhite females in 1964). Between 1900 and 1967, our
death rate fell by almost one-half, from 17.2 to 9.5 deaths per 1,000 people.
What has caused such a sharp decline?

Table 22 Wife's age at marriage and fertility

Children per 100 wives by age 44	Age at marriage							
	Under 17	17–19	20–22	23–25	26–28	29–31	32–34	35 +
Catholic couples	394	351	331	227	191	165	—°	—°
Protestant couples	366	276	207	169	129	69	72	34

° Too few cases to be reliable.
SOURCE: Pascal K. Whelpton and Clyde V. Kiser, "Social and Psychological Factors Affecting Fertility," *Milbank Memorial Fund Quarterly*, 21:232, 233, July, 1943. This study covers a sample of white families in Indianapolis, Ind.

A great many factors, stretching backwards for hundreds of years, have contributed to the drop in the death rate. Improved transportation made it possible to transport a food surplus and to alleviate a local famine. Improvements in food preservation made it possible to preserve a food surplus. The growth of nationalism brought political institutions which were better able to cope with local crop failures and threatened famines. But medicine, sanitary engineering, and public-health measures were mainly responsible for the dramatic drops of the past century. After Pasteur and the germ theory of disease, many epidemic diseases quickly yielded to preventive measures. Pure food and water supply routed others. In the Western countries today, the great killers of the past—smallpox, cholera, diphtheria, typhoid, and scarlet fever—have become so rare that it is hard to find cases for medical students to observe.

The decline in the death rate began about 1750 in England and France and generally preceded any decline in the birth rate. A country with a falling death rate and a stationary birth rate will show an explosive rate of population increase. This is what explains the rapid population growth of recent centuries.

Age at marriage and marriage rate One factor in the birth rate is the proportion of people who get married and the ages at which they marry. A study of fertility in Indianapolis finds that women married under the age of seventeen have twice as many children as do women married at the age of twenty-six to twenty-eight (shown in Table 22). Early marriage not only increases the number of years for childbearing; early marriage is also associated with lower social-class background, together with attitudes and practices which favor large families.

The proportion of people who never marry varies greatly with different social conditions. In this connection, a comparison of the United States with Ireland is revealing. In 1955 the birth rate was 21.2 in Ireland compared with 24.6 in the United States. The Irish simply don't marry as much, or as early, as the Americans.

The 1946 census showed that of all those [Irish] over thirty-five years of age, 46.6 of the men and 29.5 percent of the women in rural areas were unmarried; and 33.7 percent of the men and 34.8 percent of the women in urban areas. In the whole country more than two-thirds of the men between the ages of 20 and 44 were still

*single. The average marriage age for men is 35 and for women 29. About one fourth
of the population never marries at all, compared to about one tenth in England.*

Kevin Devlin, quoted in Paul Blanchard, *The Irish and Catholic Power*, Beacon Press, Boston, 1953,
p. 142.

Yet Ireland is one of the rather poor, largely agricultural countries which usually have a high birth rate, and in addition, the laws of the country prohibit
divorce and discourage the sale of contraceptives. Marriage is a serious business with no escape clause, and birth control is not seriously considered by
most of the Irish families. Therefore many of the Irish either marry late or
not at all; the culture promotes fertility within marriage but discourages marriage itself. The net population growth is less than in countries like the United
States which encourage both marriage and birth control.

The marriage rate is also related to the age and sex composition of the
population. One would assume that usually the number of both sexes is approximately equal and that the age distribution is "normal"; but actually this
is seldom true. In the United States female workers are attracted to well-
established urban areas; Washington, D.C., in 1960 had a sex ratio of 88.3
(that is, 100 females for every 88.3 males). Areas of recent settlement attract
more men; Alaska had a sex ratio of 132.3. Such unbalanced sex ratios reduce
the marriage rate.

The recent American increase in the number of marriages in general and of
early marriages in particular has been one of the unexpected developments
of the last half century. People had often assumed that while marriage was a
practical necessity in the rural setting, the city encouraged bachelorhood.
They also assumed that in an agricultural society men could and should marry
early, whereas in an urban society marriage would have to be postponed in

Table 23 *Proportion of persons married and median
age at first marriage in the United States, 1890 to 1960*

| Year | Proportion married, 14 years old and older, standardized for age | | Median age at first marriage | |
	Male, per cent	Female, per cent	Male	Female
1890	61.2	59.4	26.1	22.0
1900	59.9	58.7	25.9	21.9
1910	60.4	60.1	25.1	21.6
1920	61.3	60.4	24.6	21.2
1930	62.1	61.2	24.3	21.3
1940	62.8	61.0	24.3	21.6
1950	68.0	66.1	22.8	20.3
1955	69.3	67.4	22.6	20.2
1960	70.0	67.8	22.8	20.3
1965	67.9	63.9	22.8	20.6

SOURCE: Department of Commerce, Bureau of the Census, *U.S. Census of
Population*, vol. 2, part 1, *Current Population Reports*, series P–20, nos.
96 & 105.

order to gain an education. Again the rural society was associated with a system in which the work of women was largely restricted to the home, and it was
assumed that as women became "emancipated" from restriction to a domestic
life, they would postpone or avoid marriage for the sake of a career.

None of these assumptions has been borne out. Feminine emancipation,
urbanization, and increased education have all been accompanied by a rush to
the altar. It remains true that urban people and college-educated people still
marry later than rural and less-educated people. But *every* group is marrying
earlier than formerly. This general tendency toward earlier marriage has more
than canceled the effects of increasing urbanization and education. Why, in
the face of so many "logical" reasons for postponing marriage, has the age
at marriage fallen so sharply? We are uncertain. Perhaps it is a natural consequence of the fact that parents permit and often encourage children to start
"dating" and "going steady" at earlier ages than formerly. Perhaps it illustrates a growing unwillingness of young people to follow the deferred gratification pattern and is an expression of the buy-now-pay-later attitude which
characterizes a growing sector of our economy. At any rate, the fact of earlier
marriage is indisputable, and one consequence is accelerated population
growth.

Cultural norms Since both governments and churches are often concerned about the birth
and family rate, one might assume that the controlling cultural norms are of a political
limitation or religious character. Rulers of expanding countries usually oppose birth
control and urge a high birth rate as the basis of military strength. On different grounds, the Roman Catholic clergy has been reluctant to approve the
use of contraception and, until recent years, has tended to minimize the seri-
ousness of population pressure. The Protestant clergy tend to accept contraception as a legitimate aspect of social adjustment. The governments of
some overpopulated countries encourage birth control as necessary for population stabilization.

The evidence to date indicates that, with the previously cited exception of
Japan, neither governments nor churches have been able to effect much
change in the birth rate. Hitler and Mussolini had little success in the effort
to stimulate a higher birth rate, and most of the current government efforts
to reduce population increases have had disappointing results. Likewise, the
endorsement of birth control by the Protestant clergy has had little effect in
areas where the general social milieu favors large families, and the strictures
of the Catholic clergy have not prevented a falling birth rate among urban
Catholics. Currently [1967] a Papal commission has been considering a possible revision of the Catholic stand on contraception. For a number of years,
however, the Catholic clergy have discouraged the use of any means of birth
control except the rhythm method, one which is less effective than other
techniques. Thus an analysis of the reproductive patterns of Catholics affords
a case study of the effectiveness of the efforts of a religious group to influence
family limitation practices. One rather striking example is found in a study
of birth rates in the city of Hamtramck, a municipality entirely surrounded by
the city of Detroit. Hamtramck, from the period 1920 to 1955, was about 90
per cent Polish Catholic in population. In 1920, when most of the residents
were newly arrived immigrants of rural peasant background, the birth rate was

Table 24   Religion and births, selected cities, 1950

City	Percentage of population Catholic	Children per 100 women, 15 to 49 years old, standardized for age, 1950
San Francisco	*67*	*302*
Atlanta	*6*	*318*
Boston	*59*	*338*
Denver	*35*	*367*
New Orleans	*73*	*373*
Birmingham	*8*	*374*

SOURCE: Wilson H. Grabill, Clyde V. Kiser, and Pascal K. Whelpton, *The Fertility of American Women*, John Wiley & Sons, Inc., New York, 1958, pp. 93–94.

97 per cent above that of surrounding Detroit, which had about a 50:50 Catholic-Protestant ratio. The Polish immigrants, however, quickly changed their family patterns. In 1930 the Hamtramck birth rate was only 18 per cent higher than that of Detroit; in 1940 it was 3 per cent lower; and by 1950 it was 13 per cent lower. The authors of the report [Mayer and Marx, 1957] conclude, after interviewing a sample of the residents, that this change in the birth rate was accomplished by the widespread use of contraception.

Hamtramck may be an extreme example of the spread of a secularizing type of influence which nullified the effect of Catholic teachings, but similar conclusions would be drawn from an analysis of the data in Table 24. Here you will notice that some cities with a heavily Catholic population had lower birth rates than others which were predominantly Protestant.

To be seen in its true perspective, religion would have to be recognized as one of many parts of a cultural complex which determines whether or not families adopt birth-control practices. It is difficult to establish the relative influence of religious teaching, since even with the most rigorous controls, observers can almost never find groups of people who are entirely comparable except in their religious affiliation. Three careful attempts to determine the role of religion, two in the United States mainland and the other in Puerto Rico, have given contradictory results.

The Indianapolis study [Whelpton and Kiser, 1943] excluded both Negroes and foreign-born, and sought to compare the birth rate of white Protestants and Catholics of comparable economic status. The results indicated a higher birth rate for Catholics. A later study [Freedman et al., 1961] which again controlled other socioeconomic variables, concluded that Catholics have a substantially higher birth rate than *similarly situated* Protestant Americans. True, the *overall* Catholic birth rate is very close to that of non-Catholics, as is shown in Table 25, and this is partly because ". . . young Catholic women appear to have adopted the family planning practices of the general population to such an extent that their age-standardized fertility measure in 1957 was only 1 per cent above that of the nation" [Bogue, 1959, p. 696].

In Puerto Rico a survey [Hill et al., 1959] made to evaluate the efforts of public-health clinics to spread contraceptive practice did not find that religious objections were a significant barrier. In fact, Catholics who regularly attended

Table 25   Number of children ever born per 1,000 women, married and husband present, by religion, 1957

Religion	Women 15 to 44 years old		Women 45 years old and over	Ratio to nation	
	Per 1,000 women	Per 1,000 women standardized for age		Women 15–44 standardized for age	Women 45 years old and over
Total U.S.	2,218	2,188	2,798	1.00	1.00
Protestant	2,220	2,206	2,753	1.01	0.98
Baptist	2,359	2,381	3,275	1.09	1.11
Lutheran	2,013	1,967	2,382	0.90	0.85
Methodist	2,155	2,115	2,638	0.97	0.94
Presbyterian	2,001	1,922	2,188	0.88	0.78
Other Prot.	2,237	2,234	2,702	1.02	0.97
Roman Catholic	2,282	2,210	3,056	1.01	1.09
Jewish	1,749	°	2,218	0.79	0.79
Other, none, and not reported	2,069	2,075	2,674	0.95	0.96

° Standardized rate not computed where there are fewer than 150,000 women in several component 5-year age groups.
SOURCE: Department of Commerce, Bureau of the Census, *Current Population Reports*, series P-20. Table as presented in Donald J. Bogue, *The Population of the United States*, The Free Press of Glencoe, New York, 1959, p. 696.

mass were more apt to use contraceptives consistently than either Protestants or the less faithful Catholics. The Puerto Rican Catholics and Protestants were somewhat comparable groups, since they were similar in education and in rural and urban residence and shared a fairly homogeneous cultural background.

Perhaps American Catholicism exercises greater control than Puerto Rican Catholicism; we do not yet have really conclusive evidence. A few religious groups whose faith is closely related to their general culture, such as the Amish and the Hutterites, show a consistently high birth rate. For large groups whose members are not knit in a closely controlled culture, such as Protestants and Catholics, one can only say that their birth rate tends to follow general social trends; the religious factor is difficult to isolate from other variables.

Social status and the birth rate The folk proverb that the "rich get richer and the poor get babies" describes fairly correctly the relationship between social status and the birth rate. In general, a low birth rate is more characteristic of urbanized, well-educated, and high-income groups, and a high birth rate is more apt to be found among rural, poorly educated, and low-income groups. Groups in which these characteristics are mixed usually have intermediate fertility rates.

The planning attitude and family limitation In rural areas a large family has labor value. In the modern city child labor is prohibited, and each additional child adds to the family expenses without increasing its income. Supposedly, in the city only the wealthier couples could afford large families, whereas the poor would find a large family a difficult burden. Such reasoning assumes that both the poor and the more well-to-do have the same tendency to plan their lives. In the discussion of the deferred gratification pattern in the chapter on social mobility, we found that planning was not a typical lower-class pattern. Instead of trying to control his environment, the lower-class person is apt to consider himself a creature of fate, subject to forces beyond his control. He does not budget his income, pursue long-term educational goals, or manipulate occupational opportunities. If the rest of his life is subject to chance, why then should he take pains to control the number of his children? Conversely, the middle-class person is quite well aware that the cost of a large family may make his financial goals unattainable, and he uses contraception to control the number of offspring.

Birth rates in the United States since 1945 show a trend which may modify this pattern, since there has been a sharp increase in the birth rate among urbanized, college-educated couples. Their birth rates are still somewhat below those of the uneducated and rural groups, but are well above the rates

FIGURE 19 *Occupation of Husbands and Fertility. Number of Children per Wife Aged 35–39 in 1955.*

SOURCE: Based on data from U.S. sampling survey of 2,700 families in 1955 from Ronald Freedman, et al., *Family Planning, Sterility and Population Growth*, McGraw-Hill Book Company, New York, 1959, pp. 306–307.

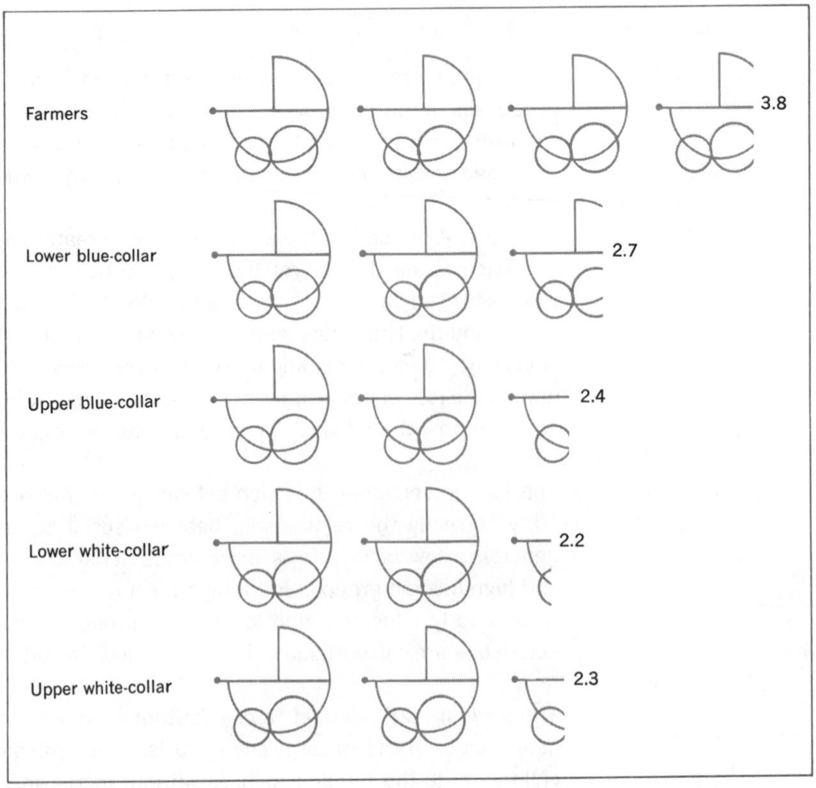

Farmers	3.8
Lower blue-collar	2.7
Upper blue-collar	2.4
Lower white-collar	2.2
Upper white-collar	2.3

required to replace themselves. There is no evidence that the urbanized, college-educated couples have abandoned family planning or birth control; they are simply planning larger families and thus contributing to the population explosion. The United States now has a birth rate which, although in considerable part planned, is high enough to produce the largest population increase per decade that the country has ever known.

Family limitation was known among the upper-class families of Greece, Rome, and some other classical civilizations and in some primitive societies, but only recently has family limitation become common in the Western world. It arose as an urbanized middle class saw a chance for economic advancement through the control of their environment and gradually shifted from a fatalistic to a planning approach. As time passed, the planned family pattern has gradually been diffused to lower-income groups and rural areas. While the process has been accompanied by controversy, the spread of birth control seems due rather to cultural changes that prompted the adoption of the planning process than to the actual success of birth-control propaganda.

National planning and family limitation From the preceding discussion it appears that neither religious nor government institutions have been very successful in the effort to influence family size when their definition of the situation did not correspond to that of the bulk of the population. In general, the residents of a rural folk society have been indifferent to the activities of free birth-control clinics, and an urbanized middle class has resisted efforts of church and state to increase its fertility. Currently, the governments of many nations in the underdeveloped areas consider the unchecked population increase a major problem. They are considering government efforts to persuade their people to adopt practices of family limitation, and in the case of India, Puerto Rico, and Japan have set up free or inexpensive birth-control clinics along with propaganda in favor of the use of contraception.

In all cases the efforts to popularize contraception have been less than completely successful. India also tried to promote the use of the rhythm method in one province, again with disappointing results [*Newsweek*, Mar. 2, 1959]. All these experiments dealt with people who were either rural peasants or had recently emerged from that status. Some of these people showed a degree of interest in family limitation, but few followed a consistent pattern in the use of contraceptive practices. Apparently this type of birth control is congenial to a well-educated, urban, middle-class group but is contrary to the cultural norms of other types of population. In fifty to a hundred years' time the people in overpopulated areas may acquire a culture consistent with this type of family plan-

In general the residents of a rural folk society have been indifferent.

ning, but by then the population explosion may have reached unmanageable dimensions.

Something about the dynamics of population control may be learned from the Japanese experience. The Japanese population grew from 56 million in 1920 to 73 million in 1940. This increase alone would have populated Japan with 114 persons per square mile, a density exceeded by only twelve of the United States. Defeat in war and the loss of an expanding empire made population pressure even more unmanageable. Following World War II, the government encouraged population restriction through legalized abortion and contraception. By 1953, it was estimated that about one-half of all conceptions were ended by abortion [Muramatsu, 1960]. The Japanese birth rate fell from 34.3 in 1947 to 17.2 in 1957, almost exactly by one-half. This is the most precipitous intentional decline in a nation's birth rate known to history. The principal means has been abortion, but some Japanese sentiment favors a shift of emphasis to contraception and female sterilization as more desirable techniques.

Several favorable situations help to explain why Japan is the only nation which has been highly successful in restricting its population growth. Unlike countries like India, the government encountered no great general reluctance. The Japanese traditional family system was more concerned with the well-being of the heir than with large numbers of offspring. Abortion and infanticide had long been occasional practices. Neither of the dominant religions, Buddhism and Shintoism, objects to family planning. Japan is an urban industrial country with an efficient governmental bureaucracy and a literate population. All these circumstances made the task far simpler than in a country like India with widespread illiteracy, primitive village life, some religious hostility to family planning, and a different emphasis in the familistic system. In such a setting the average village Indian lacks either the means or the motivation for family planning. Just one anecdote will tell something of the problem facing family planners in many underdeveloped areas. In one district the literacy barrier was surmounted by a large poster showing a three-child native family in comfortable surroundings, contrasted with another larger family amid squalor. But the reaction was unexpected. Instead of admiring the greater comfort of the small family, the observers murmured, "That poor family—only three children!" Even so, the practice of contraception is spreading in India, and some observers are optimistic over the prospects of effective population control [Agarwala, 1960].

Puerto Rico has used the public-health services to make contraception available to its people, but like India and Japan, has had only limited success with this technique. Students of the situation report that contraception is often tried but seldom adopted as a lasting practice and consequently has had little effect on the birth rate. They also report that sterilization has become amazingly popular, although it is not officially encouraged; and many who want the operation may have difficulty in obtaining it [Hill et al., 1959, pp. 178–181]. In India, where attempts to popularize contraception have not been very successful, a small but growing interest in sterilization is reported [Evans, 1961].

From the results of the attempts to popularize family limitation in Japan, Puerto Rico, and India one would conclude that the adoption of contraception is not so much a matter of governmental or religious policy as of cultural adjustment. The regular practice of contraception appears a logical step to an urbanized middle-class group but is difficult for other parts of the population. A peasant population beginning to think of a higher standard of living may have some desire to limit the number of children but has not acquired the acceptance of a planned life essential to the consistent carrying out of contraceptive practices. Sociologists studying the birth-control program in Puerto Rico believe that a program stressing group discussion and aimed at overcoming cultural difficulties, for example, lack of communication between man and wife, might lead to a successful use of contraception [Hill et al., 1959, pp. 365–389]. Such a program is difficult to carry out because of the expense, the shortage of skilled personnel, and the possibility of opposition from elements of the community opposed to a birth-control program. It would seem more likely that effective population control in underdeveloped areas would depend upon either the official acceptance of methods such as abortion or sterilization which do not require a change in usual family habits, or upon the development of much simpler and more effective means of contraception than are now widely available.

To achieve effective family limitation, either a means of birth control must be developed which is consistent with the culture or the culture must be altered to provide encouragement for consistent planning. To some extent both developments are occurring. Increased urbanization and education are changing the culture of traditional peasant populations in a manner consistent with the adoption of consistent planning practices. On the other hand, research is constantly being carried on toward the perfection of methods which require only one decision rather than daily planning. One such method, the Lippes loop, an intrauterine device which can remain in place for months at a time, has already been developed, and other methods may be found in the future. Eventually the combination of general cultural change and technical progress in contraception should provide effective methods of family limitation. The question is whether effective family limitation can be achieved before population increase becomes completely unmanageable.

Future population pressure Urbanization and industrialization in Western countries have had twin effects upon population growth. The development of urbanization and industrialization was accompanied by changes in mediine and sanitation that produced a rapid drop in death rates and a great population growth. But urbanization and industrialization also unleashed forces which eventually led to a reduction of the birth rate. We have thus shifted from a society with high birth and death rates to a society with low death rates and medium birth rates, but with a higher rate of population growth than can possibly be sustained over any long time.

The non-Western world is now in the earlier stages of this demographic transition. Death rates have been plunging precipitously as non-Western lands gained epidemic control in the post-World War II years. For example, the death rate in Ceylon fell by one-half in a single decade [Morgan, 1956]. In such countries a rapidly falling death rate and an approximately stationary birth rate give a rate of population growth which soon becomes unmanageable. The pressure of numbers may lead to effective means of population restraint or to an aggressively expansionist military policy. Some forty years ago, Thompson [1929] stated that population pressure was encouraging Japan's march toward war,

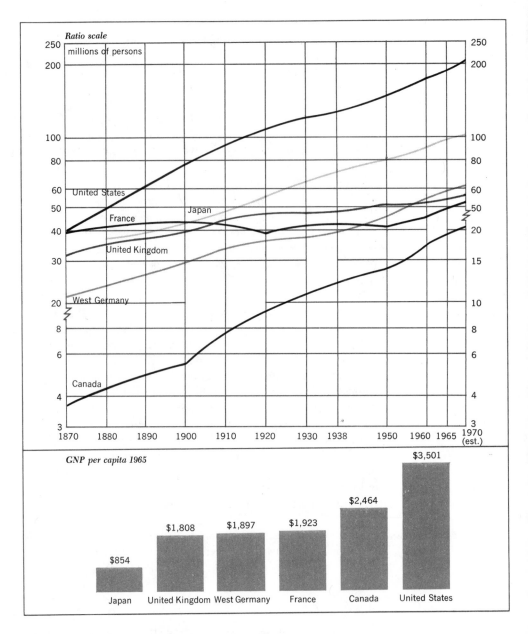

FIGURE 20   *Trends in Population.*

SOURCE: National Industrial Conference Board.

and suggested ways of averting this consequence. His suggestions were not followed, and we all know the outcome. Will China and India repeat this story? Possibly so. Only they might be less likely to lose [Organski and Organski, 1962].

The argument about population pressure still swirls around the ideas of the Rev. Thomas R. Malthus, an English clergyman whose *Essay on Population* in

1798 called the world's attention to this topic. Malthus believed that the essential reason for poverty was the pressure of population growth on the world's resources. He reasoned that the effects of natural fertility were held in check only by such negative forces as famine, war, and pestilence. Thus, whenever an improvement in the arts yielded an economic surplus, these products would soon be consumed by an expanding population. Malthus did not deny the possibility of increasing industrial and agricultural production, but he believed that the increase would be unable to keep up with population growth, and expressed his belief that population tends to multiply in geometric ratio (2, 4, 8, 16, etc.) while production can only increase in an arithmetic ratio (1, 2, 3, 4, etc.). Each increase in population becomes a basis for a further increase in the next generation, but each increase in the yield from an acre of land is not a basis for a still further increase the following season. Instead, having boosted the yield this year, producers will find it harder, not easier, to boost the yield still higher next year. Thus, people increase through multiplication whereas the food supply increases only by addition and is constantly being outrun by the growth of population. Malthus urged later marriage as a means of keeping down the birth rate, but he was pessimistic about the chance that this policy would be followed. He saw no practical possibility of averting hunger, famine, and pestilence. Organized charity and relief would only enable a few more to survive today so that they might starve tomorrow. Because of these gloomy predictions of Malthus, economics became known as the "dismal science."

In the 1920s it was popular to believe that the events of the preceding century had disproved the Malthusian hypotheses. The world had seen the greatest population growth in its history, and at the same time the standard of living had improved rather than declined. Why did Malthus's gloomy predictions fail to materialize? One reason is that Malthus failed to foresee the widespread use of improved methods of contraception. The contraceptive devices of his day were so crude and inefficient that he and other writers paid little or no attention to them. Another reason was that Malthus could not be expected to foresee the magnitude of the industrial and agricultural revolution of the nineteenth and twentieth centuries. Great new land areas in North and South America and Australia were brought under cultivation. Improvements in agriculture rapidly boosted output per acre. For a time, birth rates in the Western world were falling so rapidly and production was rising so rapidly that Malthus began to sound like a gloomy scold instead of a gifted thinker.

Recently, however, Malthus has been restored to fashion by scholars known as the "neo-Malthusian school." The Western nations, while using family planning, now seem to be planning and raising families much larger than can possibly be maintained for very many generations. Pressure upon our water resources is already acute in some parts of the United States, and further pressures may be anticipated as our population figures continue to soar. Granted that the United States can provide a high standard of living for 250 million people, can we provide it for 400 million, or a billion, or 10 billion?

But it is the underdeveloped areas of the world that offer the best illustrations of Malthus's chilling predictions. Here the "revolution of rising expectations" meets the population explosion. In these areas death control has been sensationally effective; birth control is difficult to popularize; and the expansion of agricultural and industrial production is a slow and complex process. In spite

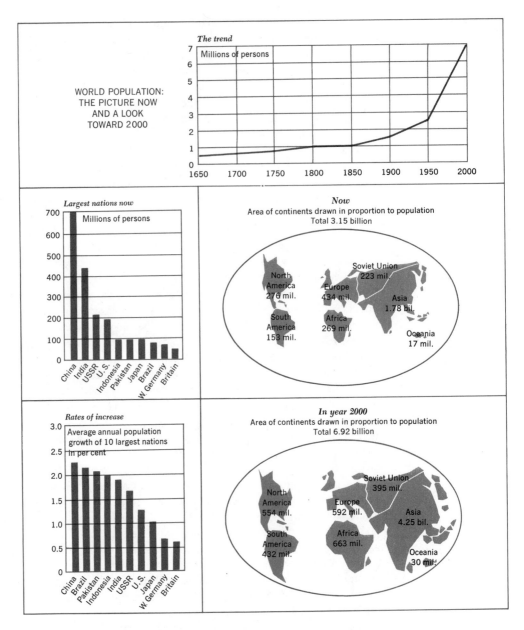

FIGURE 21   *World Population: 1963 and 2000.*

SOURCE: *New York Times,* Dec. 22, 1963, sec. 4, p. 8. © 1963 by the New York Times Company. Reprinted by permission.

of considerable improvement, production in these areas has done little more than keep up with the population increase, and in some places has actually fallen behind population growth. In spite of herculean efforts, the gap between the per capita income of the industrialized and the underdeveloped areas continues to increase [Myrdal, 1957, pp. 4–5].

Whether an unchecked population growth can take place in even the next fifty years without a deterioration in living standards is still debatable. Possibly economic developments in Asia and Africa will speed up, once the basic equipment of a modern society has been established. Possibly new scientific developments may multiply our productivity. But even if we might escape a Malthusian doom, some people are asking if this kind of struggle is really worthwhile. Rapid population growth carries a price tag of many kinds. One scholar [A. Miller, 1960] claims to have evidence that rapid population growth

FIGURE 22   *The Race between People and Food.*

SOURCE: *State of Food and Agriculture, 1965,* Food and Agricultural Organization of the United Nations, Rome, 1965, p. 17.

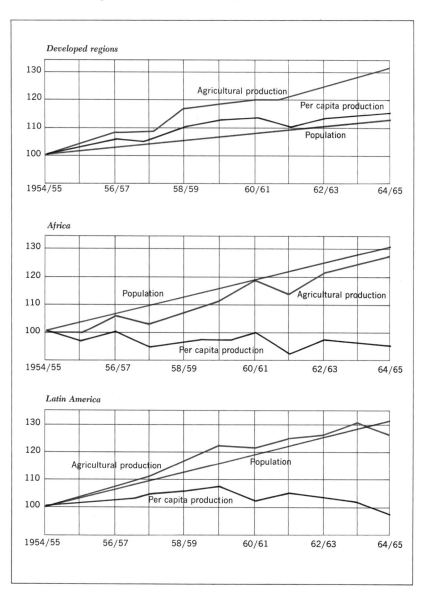

requires an increase in government controls of many kinds, promotes the bureaucratization of society, and reduces the range of individual liberties. Already in England, that historic citadel of individual liberty, the state will take away a farmer's land (with compensation) if he does not farm it efficiently; the national interest cannot allow a landowner the luxury of inefficient land use. In the Netherlands one is not permitted to build a one-story house; the land cannot be spared. Individual liberty is a luxury which is gradually sacrificed as population pressure grows intense. How much of it should be sacrificed in order to feed more people? Landis frames the issue in this manner:

Certainly individualized Western man has reached the point where he is unwilling to devote his full energies to food supply. The dream of luxuries, of leisure which comes from having plenty, has motivated him to cross oceans in quest of spices, and has led him to penetrate nature's deep secrets with microscope and telescope. He will not willingly settle for a life motivated primarily by a struggle for appeasement of hunger. He can hardly conceive of the fact that millions live on that level already.

The world now supports around 2.4 billion people. It perhaps could sustain a maximum of somewhere between 5 and 10 billion, but to do so would require a maximum of free migration between continents and nations and the exertion of all human effort toward producing the maximum of food. Is man willing to devote all his energies to feeding the world, as will be required in a hundred to a hundred fifty years, assuming present rates of population growth?

Paul H. Landis, "Is There Room for the Next 1,000,000,000 People?", *The Clearing House*, 28:140–141, November, 1953.

SUMMARY

Demography is concerned with the age and sex composition of the population, its movement, both within and across national frontiers, and its rate of growth.

The age and sex composition of a population affects its social life in many ways. Changes in age composition are due mainly to changes in birth and death rates and are presently increasing the proportions of both aged and children in many populations. The increased proportion of youth is a major handicap to underdeveloped countries since it increases educational costs while reducing the proportion of the population in productive labor. The permanent rise of a rather large group of old people has prompted the rise of geriatrics and gerontology, disciplines devoted to the problems of the aged.

Migration is affected by the *push* given to people by unsatisfactory conditions at home, by the *pull* of attractive opportunities elsewhere, and by the *channels* or means through which they are able to migrate. The United States received a constant stream of immigrants until the enactment of restrictive legislation in 1921. Since then immigration has been restricted not only by the United States but also by many other countries. Most migration today is internal, especially from farm to city within a country. Political dislocations have produced record numbers of refugees, but although transportation is easy, social restrictions make refugee resettlement more difficult than ever before.

In the past three centuries a nearly stable world population has exploded into fantastic growth. Effective death control has cut the death rate in nearly all areas of the world, while only in some areas has the birth rate fallen appreciably, and in scarcely any has it fallen enough to restore a historic stability of population.

A society's birth rate is largely a result of the average age at marriage, the proportion of people who marry, and their use or nonuse of birth control. Malthus dismissed the idea of the effectiveness of contraception and predicted inevitable overpopulation and misery unless people controlled population growth by postponing marriage. The rapid colonial expansion and industrial and agricultural development of the nineteenth century delayed the fulfillment of Malthus's predictions, but they now appear likely to be fulfilled in at least some parts of the world. Family planning is being used in some areas, but many cultural barriers impede its acceptance in the areas where the most unmanageable population explosions are likely to occur. Effective family planning apparently requires either a cultural base which the undeveloped societies may not have until after they have developed an urban industrial civilization, or the development of contraceptive techniques which do not involve constant planning.

QUESTIONS AND PROJECTS

1. What has been the rate of population growth throughout most of history? Why have world rates of population growth changed recently? How long will present rates of growth continue?

2. What factors other than birth control affect the rate of reproduction?

3. At the present time the prosperity of some areas of the world might be favorably affected by population increase. Evaluate the prospects of migration from overpopulated areas to those considered underpopulated.

4. What were the ideas of Malthus? Do you feel that the passage of time has outdated or confirmed these ideas? Why or why not?

5. Is it true that the countries of Asia, Africa, and Latin America are now undergoing a population cycle similar to that experienced by the United States and Western Europe at an earlier date?

6. How would you explain the tendency of inhabitants of underdeveloped areas to react more favorably to the use of sterilization and abortion than to contraception?

7. What are the factors which limit the ability of governmental or religious institutions to influence the birth rate?

8. How would you explain the tendency toward an excess of females in American cities and an excess of males in the rural districts?

9. What is meant by "push," "pull," and "channels" in connection with immigration?

10. In recent years the United States has had an increase in the proportion of both children and aged in the overall population. What effects would you expect this change in population to have in social and economic relationships?

11. Using the most recent Statistical Abstract of the United States, compare the population growth of your state with others. What factors would appear to affect the relative position of your state? What adjustments do you feel your state will be required to make to meet the needs indicated by population changes?

12. Using the *United Nations Demographic Yearbook*, compare birth and death rates in the Philippines, India, and Mexico with those in Great Britain, France, and the United States. What conclusions would you draw about the probable future of population growth in these countries?

SUGGESTED READINGS

DAVIS, KINGSLEY: "The Unpredicted Pattern of Population Change," *Annals of the American Academy of Political and Social Science,* 305:53–59, May, 1956. A concise analysis of population trends in underdeveloped areas.

FAGLEY, RICHARD M.: *The Population Explosion and Christian Responsibility,* Oxford University Press, Fair Lawn, N.J., 1960. Family limitation in the light of Christian ethics.

FREEDMAN, RONALD: "Planned Family and American Population Growth," *Antioch Review,* 17:31–44, Spring, 1957. Treats the paradoxical combination of widespread family planning and rapid population growth.

*HANDLIN, OSCAR: *The Newcomers,* Harvard University Press, Cambridge, Mass., 1959. A comparison of Puerto Rican adjustment in New York City with that of previous immigrants. (A283-Anch)

HAUSER, PHILIP M.: *Population Perspectives,* Rutgers University Press, New Brunswick, N.J., 1960. A scholarly popularization of consequences of rapid population growth.

*HILL, REUBEN, J. MAYONE STYCOS, AND KURT W. BACK: *The Family and Population Control,* The University of North Carolina Press, Chapel Hill, N.C., 1959. An intensive analysis of the Puerto Rican effort to popularize birth control. (B-24-C & UPS)

HUNT, CHESTER L.: "Female Occupational Roles and Urban Sex Ratios in the United States, Japan and the Philippines," *Social Forces,* 43:407–417, March, 1965. Analyzes why Japanese urban sex ratios differ from those in the Philippines and the United States.

MAYER, ALBERT J., AND SUE MARX: "Social Change, Religion and the Birth Rate," *American Journal of Sociology,* 62:383–390, January, 1957. A discussion of the trend toward the adoption of birth control in Hamtramck, Michigan.

MORRIS, JUDY K.: "Professor Malthus and His Essay," *Population Bulletin,* 22:7–27, February, 1966. Background and current relevance of the Malthusian theory.

RAINWATER, LEE: *And the Poor Get Children,* Quadrangle Books, Chicago, 1960. A report on the fertility patterns of the poor, based on intensive interviews.

REEDER, LEO G., AND GOTETI B. KRISHNAMURTY: "Family Planning in Rural India: A Problem in Social Change," *Social Problems,* 12:212–223, Fall, 1964. Relates a study of the fertility of a sample of Indian high school teachers to a general theory of social change.

SPENGLER, JOSEPH J.: "Population and Economic Growth," in Ronald Freedman (ed.), *Population: The Vital Revolution,* Doubleday & Company, Inc., Garden City, N.Y., 1964, pp. 56–69. The relationship of population to economic development.

SPIEGELMAN, MORTIMER: "Mortality Trends and Prospects and Their Implications," *The Annals of the American Academy of Political and Social Science,* 315:25–33, March, 1958. A comparison of the mortality experience of the United States and Canada since 1900.

TAEUBER, IRENE B.: *The Population of Japan,* Princeton University Press, Princeton, N.J., 1958. A definitive treatment of population trends in Japan.

18

RURAL AND URBAN COMMUNITIES

. . . if the anonymity New York grants us is a problem, it is also a blessing. In small towns it is natural and easy to be passing friendly with everyone nearby, and in small towns it works. But in New York there are too many people nearby. Just try to imagine walking down Madison Avenue and being friendly to everyone you meet there! Not only would you never get where you were going, but you would be making a nuisance of yourself to thousands of people with their own errands to run. The very multitude of people makes it necessary for us to stare through and beyond one another.

. . . were I living in an apartment house, I would not care to know who lives above me, below me, or in the next apartment on either side. I want to choose my friends: I do not care to have them thrust upon me by the rental agent. And I do not want people dropping in to borrow whatever people borrow, nor to chitchat whatever neighbors chitchat . . .

It can be lonely at times inside that anonymity, but let a small-town friendliness echo through those canyons and the future would be chaos forever, bumper to bumper and nose to nose from here to infinity. (John Ciardi, "Manner of Speaking," *Saturday Review*, Feb. 12, 1966, pp. 16–17.)

HE SOCIAL LIFE people lead is affected by the kind of community in which they live. The community is as old as man—or even older, for our subhuman ancestors probably shared a community life. *A community is a local grouping within which people carry out a full round of life activities.* Defined in greater detail [Jonassen, 1959, p. 20; Hillery, 1955], a community includes (1) a grouping of people, (2) within a geographic area, (3) with a division of labor into specialized and interdependent functions, (4) with a common culture and a social system which organizes their activities, (5) whose members are conscious of their unity and of belonging to the community, and (6) who can act collectively in an organized manner. The community is a relatively self-sufficient local area within which all or nearly all aspects of the culture can be experienced. The term is sometimes loosely used to describe other groups or subcultures—the "community of scholars," the "artistic community," or the "community of nations," for example—but these are not the usual sociological uses of the term.

It has been traditional to classify communities as rural or urban, depending upon whether their populations were small and agricultural, or larger and industrial or commercial. The classification was never entirely satisfactory, for it made no provision for the fishing village, the mining camp, the trading post, or many other special types of communities. Today the growth of the suburb and the urbanization of rural life makes the rural-urban dichotomy still less perfect, but the terms continue to be used for lack of better ones.

THE RURAL COMMUNITY

The physical and social conditions of urban and rural life are different. Consequently there are differences in the personality and behavior of urban and rural people. These differences have provided endless source material for the novelist and the playwright, and continue to interest the sociologist.

The folk society Some sociologists have seen the concept of the folk society as a close parallel to rural life. This concept is somewhat reminiscent of the *gemeinschaft* described in Chapter 8. Redfield describes the folk society:

> *Such a society is small, isolated, nonliterate and homogeneous with a strong sense of group solidarity. The ways of living are conventionalized into that coherent system which we call a "culture." Behavior is traditional, spontaneous, uncritical and personal; there is no legislation or habit of experiment and reflection for intellectual ends. Kinship, its relationships and institutions, are the type categories of experience and the familial group is the unit of action. The sacred prevails over the secular; the economy is one of status rather than of the market.*
>
> Robert Redfield, "The Folk Society," *American Journal of Sociology*, 52:293–308, January, 1947. Copyright, 1947 by The University of Chicago. For criticism and discussion of the folk-society concept, see Oscar Lewis, *Life in a Mexican Village*, The University of Illinois Press, Urbana, Ill., 1951; Horace Miner, "The Folk-Urban Continuum," *American Sociological Review*, 17:529–537, October, 1952.

The folk society is most perfectly illustrated by the primitive agricultural society—tradition-bound, informal, homogeneous, and unchanging. Its opposite is the mass society—large, impersonal, changing, and dominated by secondary contacts and mass communication processes—reminiscent of the *gesellschaft*. Much of the discussion of rural-urban differences is in terms of folk society-mass society contrasts.

Today, however, rural life is losing its folk-society flavor. What are the traditional features of rural life and how are they changing?

Traditional characteristics of rural life   Rural communities are not all alike. Edwards [1959] distinguishes at least five types of rural communities: the town-country community with farms scattered about a village center; the open-country community without any village center; the village community, whose subtypes include the fishing village, the mining village, and the mill village; the line village, with farm homes strung along the road at the ends of long, narrow farms; and the plantation. Yet certain characteristics are common to nearly all kinds of rural communities.

Isolation   Perhaps the most conspicuous feature of American rural life in times past was its isolation. Throughout much of the world, rural people are clustered in villages. In the United States, the isolated homestead became the usual pattern of rural settlement, a pattern that was productively more efficient but socially isolating. Not only was the local group isolated from other groups but each family was isolated from other families. With a thinly scattered population, personal contacts were few. Each contact involved the preception of an individual as a complete person, not simply as a functionary. There were few impersonal contacts in folk or rural societies—no anonymous bus drivers, ticket sellers, grocery clerks, or policemen. Nearly every contact was with an acquaintance who must be treated, not only in terms of his economic function, but also in terms of his total personality and all the many facets of his status in the community.

The hospitality pattern of the American frontier, wherein the traveler was welcome to spend the night at almost any farmhouse, was a practical response both to frontier needs—where else would the traveler stay?—and to frontier loneliness. The traveler brought news, contact with the outside world, and a break in monotony. He was almost always welcome. Even today the hospitality pattern survives under conditions of extreme isolation. On the Alaska Highway the mores of the region require one to offer assistance to any stranded motorist; he may actually die if assistance is not given. The hospitality pattern is a perfect illustration of how customs and mores arise in response to social needs and change as these needs change.

Homogeneity   Taken as a whole, American settlers were a quite heterogeneous lot. But within a given locality, the settlers were likely to be quite homogeneous in ethnic and cultural background. They showed a strong tendency to follow earlier migrants from their home communities, so that the settlers from a particular country and district tended to be clustered into rather homogeneous settlements. This homogeneity, together with the comparative isolation of settlements from one another, helped to encourage the conservatism, traditionalism, and ethnocentrism of American rural communities.

Agricultural employment   Nearly all were farmers or hired hands, while even the minister, doctor, teacher, and storekeeper were deeply involved in an agricultural way of life. The agricultural practices were highly traditional, allowing very little experimentation or trial and error. All faced common problems, performed common tasks, and shared a common helplessness before the awesome natural forces which man cannot control.

Subsistence economy   The traditional American homestead tried to produce nearly everything it consumed. The bulging smokehouse, the well-stocked fruit cellar, and the shelves sagging with home-canned goods were a source of pride to the farm family. In a rapidly expanding economy with a chronic shortage of money and credit, a subsistence-and-barter economy was a socially useful adaptation. Thrift was an honored value, and conspicuous consumption was seen as an urban vice. A farmer's status was measured by his lands, his herds, his barns, his crops, and the inheritance he could pass on to his children—and not by the name of his tailor or interior decorator.

Living within a subsistence rather than a market economy, rural people were inclined to be suspicious of intellectuality and "booklearning." The farmer was most likely to see a piece of paper when some "city slicker" was trying to do him out of something. Distrust of city people and disapproval of urban life was a predictable rural attitude.

These are some of the influences which shaped American rural personality. Hospitable and cooperative, conservative and religious, hard-working and thrifty, ethnocentric and intolerant—these characteristics were products of the physical and social conditions of rural life in America. Today these conditions have vastly changed. And so has the social behavior of rural people.

The rural revolution   **Reduced isolation**   Two generations ago the isolation of rural life could be measured by the contrast between the styles shown in the Sears, Roebuck catalog and those on the pages of a metropolitan newspaper. Today the styles are the same. The automobile and good roads have wrought a transformation of rural and village life which is difficult for the present generation of students to appreciate. Thousands of small villages have ceased to be true communities, as good roads have carried their trade, their storekeepers, their professional men, and their recreation to a nearby city. If close enough to the city, they have become suburbs; if too distant, they have become the half-empty shells of decaying houses and aging people, as are so many of the villages of America today. Transportation, plus the press, movies, radio, and television have ended the social isolation of rural America. The true provincial today may be the urban slum dweller, who may spend years without venturing be-

The true "provincial" today may be the urban slum-dweller.

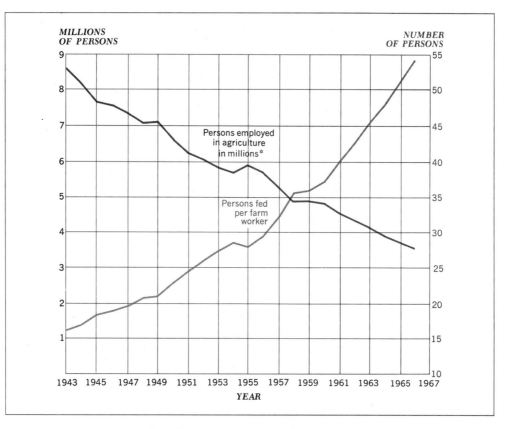

FIGURE 23   *The Agricultural Revolution in the United States.*

° Full-time agricultural workers, plus part-time workers equated to full-time basis.

SOURCE: *Statistical Abstracts of the United States,* various dates.

yond his own set of canyons, or possibly the suburbanite living within the walls of his one-class, one-age-group, lily-white neighborhood.

Commercialization and rationalization of agriculture   Without a revolution in agricultural productivity, there could have been little urban growth. In 1790 it required the surplus of nine farm families to support one urban family; today nineteen nonfarm families are supported by each farm family. Farming used to be a way of life calling for no special knowledge beyond that which one absorbed unavoidably as he grew up. Today farming is a highly complex operation demanding substantial capital, specialized knowledge, rapid changes in productive technology, and continuous market analysis. The "average" American farm represents an investment of $40,000 in land and buildings (1959), and this "average" includes many which are too small or ill-equipped to be efficient. This investment is rising rapidly. Most of the new harvesting machines for harvesting cherries, oranges, celery and other crops cost from $20,000 to $40,000 each. Today's successful farm has become a roofless factory, using a variety of managerial skills comparable to those needed for many another business, and more often described as "agribusiness."

As farming has grown more demanding, the number of farm families has fallen precipitously—from 6.7 million and 22 per cent of all American families in 1935 to 2.4 million and 6.0 per cent of all families in 1964. The tenant farmer and sharecropper have practically disappeared, their number falling from 2,770,000 in 1930 to 380,000 in 1959. Meanwhile the average size of farms has steadily increased from 174 acres in 1940 to 350 acres in 1965 and is expected to reach 700 acres by 1980 [*Business Week*, Dec. 3, 1966, p. 164]. These trends are still continuing at a rapid rate and would proceed even faster if they were not retarded by political programs intended to aid marginal farmers. Fewer than half of our farms produce 85 per cent of our farm produce, and they could easily produce the remaining 15 per cent if farm production were not deliberately restricted.

Because of changes in agricultural technology, the farm population is rapidly shrinking. In 1790 the rural (farm and nonfarm) residents comprised 94.8 per cent of the population. By 1920, when "farm" and "rural nonfarm" people were first separated in the census, farm people constituted 30.1 per cent of the population; in 1965, only 6.4 per cent, and they are still diminishing in number. We were once a nation of farmers. Today farmers are becoming one of the smallest of our major occupational groups. At present more than 1 million of our farm families are unnecessary and could leave the farm tomorrow without ever being missed. These are our "farm poor"—farmers with too little land, equipment, and capital, or too little energy or managerial skill to farm very profitably. One-fourth of our farms produce less than $5,000 of farm produce per year (and this is gross produce, not net income after expenses). One-third of our farms are part-time or post-retirement operations. These farms contribute little to our national farm product and do not provide a decent living to their operators. Yet an estimated three-fifths of the farm poor are too old, too handicapped, or too uneducated to transfer to other occupations, even if offered job training [Burchinal and Siff, 1964]. They steadily disappear from farming through retirement and rarely through transfer to other employment. As they retire, their lands are added to other farms. Thus the number of farmers shrinks, while the average size of farms increases. As the farm has become part of a market economy, the attitudes appropriate to a subsistence economy have languished. Thrift, as an absolute value, seen as *good* in and of itself, is also a useful practice in a subsistence economy. In a market economy it becomes an anachronism. Farm people today appear to have as avid an appetite for new cars and color television sets as urbanites. After all, values grow out of the experience of the group. In a subsistence economy of limited productivity, where there is rarely enough of anything, especially money, the elevation of thrift to an absolute value is practical and sensible. With the development of a highly productive market economy, thrift becomes pointless as an end in itself. Instead, reasonable thrift becomes a means to an end, for example, the saving of money on inessentials in order to afford the major purchase of a home or a new car. This and many other value changes have accompanied the technological revolution in American agriculture.

Urbanization of rural life   It is no longer possible to identify a rural rustic by his outmoded dress or bucolic manner. All the historic rural-urban differences are shrinking. To a high degree, rural life is becoming urbanized, as historically urban patterns have spread into rural areas. Taylor and Jones [1964] speak of the "urbanized social organization" of contemporary America, and every rural sociology textbook reflects this urbanization of rural life [Rogers, 1960; Copp, 1964]. This development is somewhat uneven. Rural areas closer to large cities and those where agriculture is most highly rationalized and commercialized show the highest degree of urbanization; more isolated areas and areas where farming practices are more traditional show fewer urban influences. But everywhere, the steady urbanization of rural society is evident.

There are many examples of urbanization. The electric pump and the septic tank have brought urban plumbing to the rural home. The rural birth rate has been dropping closer to the urban birth rate—77 per cent higher in 1940, 40 per cent higher in 1950, and 34 per cent higher in 1960. Our population in 1960 was classified as 69.8 per cent urban (living in communities of over 2,500), 8.7 per cent rural farm, and 21.5 per cent rural nonfarm. Not all, but many of these rural nonfarm people are urban commuters, who become a powerful urbanizing influence upon rural life. In many urban fringe areas, people are divided between farm and nonfarm employment, and any classification of such areas as either rural or urban is arbitrary. Recently the rather clumsy term *rurban* has been coined for these mixed areas which are neither urban nor rural. The term has not become very popular; but the phenomenon of the mixed urban-rural area is important, for this is a rapidly growing form of community in America.

THE URBAN COMMUNITY

The development In order for the primitive Stone Age village to overshoot its few dozen house-
of cities holds and expand to a size of several hundred thousand, it had to have a food surplus, a water supply, and a transportation system. Since a river valley provided all three, the first large cities arose six or seven thousand years ago in the valleys of the Nile, the Tigris, and the Euphrates. Surplus food to support an urban population was abundant in the fertile valley, and the slow-flowing rivers provided simple transportation. Although most ancient cities remained tiny by modern standards, a few reached a size of several hundred thousand, complete with problems of water supply, sewage disposal, and traffic congestion.

The growth of cities unleashed revolutionary changes. The primitive village was a folk society, organized on a kinship basis and guided by customary procedures. The large city brought: (1) a division of labor into many specialized occupations; (2) social organization based upon occupation and social class rather than kinship; (3) formal government institutions based on territory rather than family; (4) a system of trade and commerce; (5) means of communication and record keeping; and (6) rational technology. Obviously the large city could not arise until the culture had made a number of necessary inventions; at the same time, the development of the city proved a great stimulus to the making and improving of such inventions as carts and barges, ditches and aqueducts, writing, number systems, governmental bureaucracies, and many others.

Cities are of many kinds—temple cities, political capitals, resort cities, industrial cities, trading centers, and others. Most large cities are diversified, carrying on all of these functions. An early sociologist, Cooley [1894], noted that cities tend to grow wherever there is a "break" in transportation so that goods must be unloaded and reloaded for transshipment. Port cities like London, Montreal, and New Orleans are located up a navigable river at the point where large ocean vessels can go no further. Denver lies at the foot of a mountain range, Pittsburgh at the confluence of two rivers. Modern resort cities like Las Vegas may violate this rule, but the break-in-transportation theory still serves to explain the location of most cities.

In the Western world, urbanization has accompanied industrialization. Commercial and industrial development provided an urban "pull"; changing agricultural technology and high rural birth rates combined to provide a rural surplus of people. In many undeveloped countries today, however, urbanization is rushing along without a proportionate industrial development. Even with little prospect of finding jobs or housing, peasants over much of the world are deserting the village and flocking into the city. In Indonesia, for example, the population of the cities has doubled every ten to fifteen years without proportionate increase in either urban industrial output or in agricultural productivity. The results seem to be an intensification of every type of problem:

Since the war the supplies of food to the cities of Java have diminished at the same time as the number of city people to be fed has increased. . . . The result is that much of the food consumed in the cities is now brought from abroad. . . . A city whose physical structure was designed for half a million is now the home of about six times that number. . . . There is a free movement of population and so the erection of housing facilities in the cities, improvement of roads, introduction of subsidized bus service—in short any alleviation of the discomforts of city life—will operate, along with subsidized rice, to draw people from the crowded countryside. . . . Efforts of town planning and house construction are frustrated; people are drawn to the cities faster than decent places for them to live can be found.

Nathan Keyfitz, "The Ecology of Indonesian Cities," *American Journal of Sociology*, 66:348–354, January, 1961. Copyright, 1961, by The University of Chicago.

Whether this type of urban growth is functional or dysfunctional in terms of economic development is still open to debate. On the surface, growth in excess of the contribution made by the city would seem to be a parasitic drain on the countryside which distorts the economy of the entire nation. On the other hand, the very presence of a large urban population brings increased pressure for rapid economic development. The rural unemployed are often ignored; the urban mobs demand that something be done. Like other aspects of social life, the growth of cities may not be perfectly synchronized with changes in the rest of society. Regardless of the troubles and dislocations which may develop, the future course of civilization, even in the less-developed countries, is undoubtedly toward rapidly increasing urbanization.

The ecological pattern of cities Cities may look as though they just happened—grew without plan or design. It is true that urban growth does not proceed according to a prearranged design; but neither is the growth entirely haphazard. Cities have structure, that is, there is some reason for the arrangement of their parts. Several sociologists have sought to discover the underlying pattern according to which a modern city develops.

Patterns of urban design   Burgess's *concentric zone pattern,* shown in Figure 24, is one such attempt. Based upon his studies of Chicago in the early 1920s, it shows a central business district at the center, surrounded by a slum, consisting of old buildings which are gradually being replaced by the expansion of the business district. This in turn is surrounded by zones of successively better-class residences.

Do real cities resemble the Burgess pattern? Each American city has a central business district, partly or entirely surrounded by a slum. This surrounding zone contains the oldest buildings in the city, undesirable because of decay, dirt, and congestion. Housing quality tends to improve as one moves outward from this slum, and much of the choice residential area is located in the suburbs. However, these zones are not unbroken bands surrounding the city, nor are they circular in shape. Instead, the various grades of residence are rather irregularly distributed and often concentrated on one side of the city.

FIGURE 24   *The Concentric Circle Pattern: Zones of Chicago.*
SOURCE: R. E. Park and E. W. Burgess, *The City,* The University of Chicago Press, Chicago, 1925, p. 55.

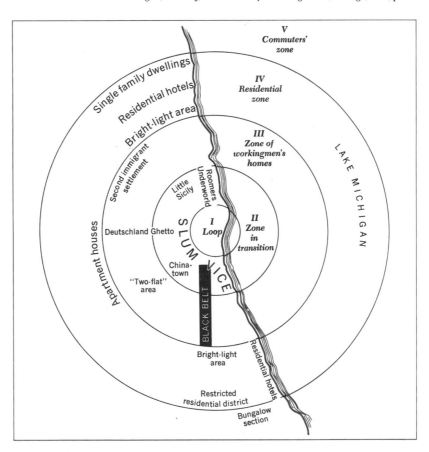

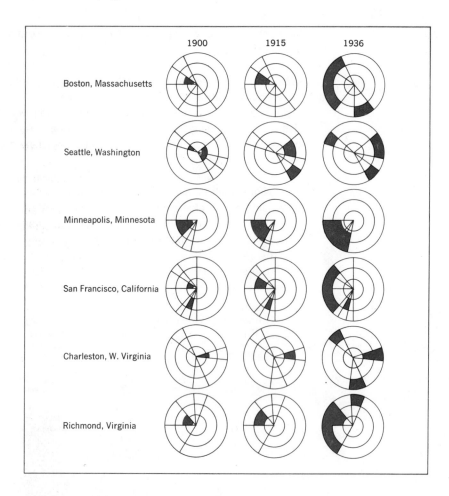

FIGURE 25 *Changes in the Location of Fashionable Residences.*

This graph illustrates Hoyt's sector theory. The solid red spaces show how the fashionable residential areas shifted outward from the city center between 1900 and 1936.

SOURCE: Homer Hoyt, *The Structure and Growth of Residential Neighborhoods in American Cities,* Federal Housing Administration, Washington, D.C., 1939, p. 115.

This observation led Hoyt [1933] to frame his *sector theory of city growth,* holding that a particular kind of land use tends to locate and remain in a particular sector of the city. Figure 25 shows how this theory is borne out in several American cities over several decades. Thus industry tends to locate in one sector, upperclass housing in an opposite sector, and working-class housing in intermediate sectors; then as time passes, each of these sectors simply expands outward until some change in topography breaks up the pattern.

The *multinuclear theory* [Harris and Ullman, 1945] holds that a number of centers—business, shopping, manufacturing—and residential areas become located early in a city's history. Topography, cost and historical accident all enter into these early choices. These concentrations tend to survive and fix the pattern of later city growth. Larger cities, which usually represent the growing together of once separate villages or communities, provide multiple nuclei. These three patterns are shown in comparison in Figure 26.

Still another pattern can be recognized—one so simple that it has not been dignified by being called a theory. It relates topography to land use. Railroads tend to follow the river bottom; heavy industry locates along the railroad; upper-class residence seeks the highlands; and the intermediate levels of housing are scattered in between.

The existence of alternative theories shows that none of them is entirely satisfactory. None of them is perfectly illustrated by any American city, and cities outside the United States will fit still less perfectly. Each is a theoretical pattern which real cities more or less perfectly resemble. Since most American cities do show some resemblance to one of these patterns, the theories are helpful in revealing their prevailing structure.

City structure today is being revolutionized by transportation. In most cities the central business district has ceased to expand, as the commercial growth leapfrogs to the suburban shopping centers. A growing ring of decay is left surrounding the business district, as it no longer razes its fringe as it expands.

FIGURE 26   *Three Patterns of City Structure.*

Generalizations of internal structure of cities. The concentric-zone pattern is a generalization for all cities. The arrangement of the sectors in the sector theory varies from city to city. The diagram for multiple nuclei represents one possible pattern among innumerable variations.

SOURCE: C. D. Harris and E. L. Ullman, "The Nature of Cities," *The Annals,* 242:13, November, 1945.

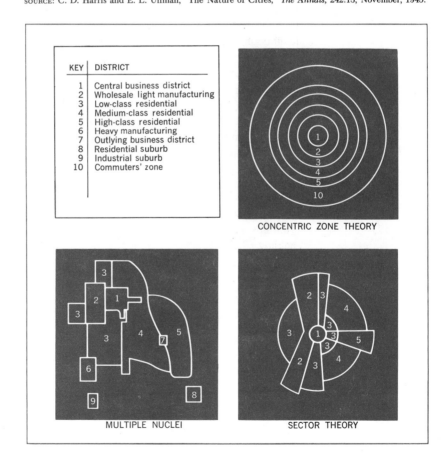

KEY	DISTRICT
1	Central business district
2	Wholesale light manufacturing
3	Low-class residential
4	Medium-class residential
5	High-class residential
6	Heavy manufacturing
7	Outlying business district
8	Residential suburb
9	Industrial suburb
10	Commuters' zone

CONCENTRIC ZONE THEORY

MULTIPLE NUCLEI

SECTOR THEORY

An aging and decaying central city is soon trapped by declining tax sources and mounting tax expenditures. This is the basic reason why nearly every city in the country is busily engaged in urban renewal programs which are both criticized [Jacobs, 1961; Greer, 1965] and defended [Weaver, 1964].

Metropolitan areas and suburbs   Modern transportation is responsible for the suburb and the metropolitan area. A "standard metropolitan statistical area" is defined by the census as a county or group of counties containing at least one city or a pair of "twin cities" with over 50,000 people. Adjacent counties are included if they are metropolitan in character, as measured by certain criteria. In 1965, some 65 per cent of the nation's population lived in our 212 metropolitan areas, and this figure is expected to rise to at least 70 per cent by 1975.

The suburb is the fastest growing part of America. Between 1950 and 1960 the suburbs of our metropolitan areas grew by 49 per cent, while our rural population was shrinking 0.8 per cent and the central cities were growing by only 10.6 per cent. In 58 of the metropolitan areas, the central city actually *lost* population between 1950 and 1960, and a comparable loss was experienced by nearly all the major cities. Nearly two-thirds of the entire nation's growth for the decade took place in the suburbs of these 212 metropolitan areas.

This explosion of the suburbs is a part of what has recently come to be known as *urban sprawl*. Vast strip cities are developing along our superhighways. A continuous urbanized area is developing from Boston to Baltimore, another from Buffalo to Detroit, across Michigan and on through Chicago around to Milwaukee, and many others. These strip cities fit no traditional pattern of city structure. In time, new theoretical constructs will be developed to describe them. Urban sprawl and strip cities bring a host of problems with them [Whyte, 1958]. The existing structures of township, city, and county government are quite inadequate to organize this developing urban monstrosity. With over 1,400 separate political units in the New York metropolitan area, each with its vested interests to defend, any coherent overall planning becomes almost an impossibility. Some observers believe that the problems of these metropolitan areas are so difficult that they will not be solved, and that the largest metropolitan areas will go into a relative decline [Vernon, 1960]. Some other observers believe that bold planning *can* solve the problems of urban sprawl and urban blight [Jacobs, 1961; Gruen, 1964; Abrams, 1965]. Urban sprawl is not exclusively an American problem; it is taking place all over the world,

Any coherent overall planning becomes almost an impossibility.

even in the Soviet Union, despite official efforts to stem the growth of the larger cities [Anderson, 1966]. Urban growth proceeds for much the same reasons and has much the same consequences everywhere in the world.

Changing racial structure   In every large American city the white people are fleeing to the suburbs while Negroes fill up the spaces they leave. Negroes are effectively excluded from the suburbs of most American cities. Wherever statistics show Negro suburban growth, it is generally found to be in industrial satellite towns, or occasionally in segregated Negro suburbs, not in typical residential suburbs. Between 1940 and 1950, while the white population of all central cities was increasing by 3.7 per cent, Negro population grew by 67.8 per cent. In Chicago, Negroes comprised 8 per cent of the population in 1940, 19 per cent in 1957, and are expected to reach 33 per cent by 1970. Non-

FIGURE 27   *The Changing Face of Chicago.*

Chicago has the second-largest Negro population of any city in the United States—813,000 at the 1960 census count, or three times as many as it had in 1940. Negroes now represent about 23 per cent of the city's total population. The pattern of change in Chicago typifies that of most Northern cities which have had a large Negro influx. In 1940, when Chicago had only 277,700 Negroes (8 per cent of total population), the great bulk lived in a long, narrow ghetto south of the Loop, the city's central business district. There were very few Negroes (i.e., fewer than 5 per cent) in 814 of the city's 935 census tracts. The 66 tracts that were 80 per cent or more Negro contained 86 per cent of the city's total Negro population. Chicago has remained a highly segregated city, despite the enormous increase in Negro population. Census tracts with 80 per cent or more Negroes now contain 80 per cent of the city's Negro population (tracts with 40 to 80 per cent Negroes hold another 12 per cent), while tracts with fewer than 5 per cent Negroes hold 89 per cent of the city's white population. But now there 152 tracts that are 80 to 100 per cent Negro, compared to 66 in 1940.

The growth in Negro residence has occurred largely by expanding the old Negro ghetto into the adjoining areas rather than by settling new areas. (See right-hand map.) The expansion of the Negro ghetto has produced some improvement in the quality of Negro housing, however, conditions that white middle-class people call "blight" represent to Negroes a great improvement in housing standards. SOURCE: Charles E. Silberman, "The City and the Negro," *Fortune*, 65:91, March, 1962.

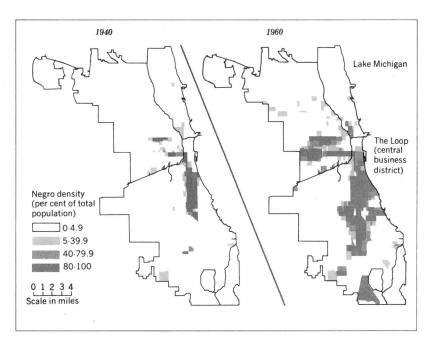

whites in New York City composed 6 per cent in 1940 and 13 per cent in 1957, while by 1970, Negroes and Puerto Ricans are expected to make up 45 per cent of the population of Manhattan and nearly one-third of the entire city [Grodzins, 1958, pp. 1–3]. Washington, D.C., in 1960 was 55 per cent Negro, higher than either Birmingham or Atlanta [Sharp and Schnore, 1962].

Such population shifts have many consequences. Negroes have lower average incomes but generally must pay higher prices than whites for comparable housing [Laurenti, 1960]. This discrimination brings overcrowding, congestion, and neighborhood deterioration to Negro areas, even though individual Negroes take as good or better care of property than *comparable class levels* of whites. But the sheer pressure of numbers ensures that the changing racial composition of the central city will bring a spreading of slums and their associated problems. The prospective political consequences of a Negro-dominated central city and a white suburb are interesting. Perhaps the traditional suburban dislike for annexation may change, as white suburbs annex themselves to the city in order to prevent city domination by Negroes. Or, conversely, perhaps the suburbs will resist annexation in order to remain publicly separate from Negroes. Of course, the ending of housing segregation would end these problems, for then Negroes would be distributed over the area according to their income and preference. While housing segregation is under spirited attack, white resistance to housing desegregation is intense, and housing segregation will probably not decline quickly enough to avert these problems.

Urban ecological processes   Change is continuous in the American city. The means through which the distribution of people and institutions change are known as *ecological processes.* To understand them we must begin with the *natural area,* a collection of people and activities which are drawn together in mutual interdependence within a limited area. The single-men's district of flophouses and cheap hotels, cheap restaurants, pawn shops, burlesque shows, taverns and missions, all catering to the needs of low-income homeless men, is an example of a natural area. Other natural areas include the department-store section, the entertainment area, the communities of recent immigrants, the rooming-house district, the college students' residential area, the warehouse district, and many others. Natural areas are unplanned. They arise from the free choices of individuals. Persons having similar needs and preferences are drawn together into an area where these are most easily fulfilled, and their association creates a natural area.

The *neighborhood,* unlike the natural area, may be either planned or unplanned. A neighborhood is an area where people neighbor, and not all areas are neighborhoods. There is very little neighboring in some areas, such as the rooming-house district, and more neighboring in the ethnic communities and family-residence areas. Some urban neighborhoods are consciously planned, with housing, communication, shopping, and recreation facilities deliberately arranged to encourage neighboring. More often the neighborhood is an unplanned product of people's need for social relations. Neighboring is greatest in family-residence areas where people face common problems of child rearing and crabgrass fighting. Neighborhoods and natural areas are constantly being formed, dissolved, and relocated through the urban ecological processes of *concentration, centralization, decentralization, segregation,* and *invasion* [Lee, 1955].

Concentration is the tendency for people and institutions to gather where conditions are favorable. It produces the growth of cities. *Centralization* is the clustering together of the economic and service functions within the city. People come together to work, to play, to shop, then return to other areas to live. The shopping district, the factory district, and the entertainment district are empty of people for a part of each day or night. The central business district is a prime example of centralization. *Decentralization* describes the tendency of people and organizations to desert the center of the city for outlying areas where congestion is less and land values are lower. The automobile and motor truck and electric power have greatly encouraged residential, commercial, and industrial decentralization—a tendency which greatly complicates the task of anyone who seeks to diagram the pattern of the city.

Segregation refers to the concentration of certain types of people or organizations within a particular area. The "Gold Coast," the ghetto, and the black belt are examples, along with the hotel and banking districts, the theater district, and "used-car row." Segregation may be either voluntary or involuntary. Most immigrant groups voluntarily segregated themselves, for life was more comfortable this way. The ghetto in the large American cities was partly voluntary and partly involuntary [Wirth, 1928]. The black belt is an example of involuntary segregation, as realtor practices, the threat of violence, and "neighborhood improvement associations" limit Negro residence to a restricted Negro area [Abrams, 1955; Grier and Grier, 1960].

Invasion takes place when a new kind of people, organization, or activity enters an area. Residential areas may be invaded by business; a business area may be invaded by a new kind of business; residents of a different class level or ethnic group may move into a residential area. Generally the invasion is of a higher-status area by a lower-status group or activity. This direction of invasion is a normal outcome of the process of city growth and of aging. A once-exclusive residential area of homes which are no longer fashionable is invaded by people a class level below the present occupants. A generation later the same area may be invaded by persons still another level lower, or by Negroes, or by secondhand stores and other business houses. Occasionally the direction is reversed. Many large cities today contain some areas where dilapidated housing is being renovated or rebuilt into an upper-class residential area. Many upper-income people have fled to the suburbs because attractive new housing is located there. Many would like to remain close to the city's center if satisfactory housing is available. Some areas have therefore traveled the complete cycle of upper-class residence to slum to upper-class residence. In all likelihood, the cycle will now be repeated.

Stages in the invasion cycle.   Several sociologists have sought to define the several stages of an invasion cycle [McKenzie, 1925, p. 25; Gibbard, 1938, pp. 206–207; Lee, 1955, pp. 257–260]. The *initial* stage brings a small number of people into the area and may not even be noticed for a time. When the old occupants become aware of an invasion, a *reaction* stage begins, whose intensity depends upon the cultural and racial characteristics of the invaders, the attitudes of the old residents, and the neighborhood solidarity. Opposition is most likely when the invaders are Negroes. A common device is the "civic," "protective," or "neighborhood-improvement" association. This organization seeks to prevent residents from selling or renting to the invaders, and to discourage the invaders from seeking to buy or rent in the area. Such associations are most effective when most of the homes are owned by their occupants. If the reaction fails to stop the invaders, then the *general influx* stage soon follows. When there are enough of the newcomers to make the old residents unwilling to remain, the "tip point" has been reached, and the old residents rapidly abandon the area to the newcomers. The *climax* is the complete replacement of the old residents with newcomers or with commercial or institutional land use. The final stage is *succession,* in which the area may remain in a disorganized and chaotic state, or may become well-organized around its new residents or land use.

This invasion cycle is continuously in operation in every American city. The processes of growth and aging make it inevitable. It is a costly process—costly in terms of human frustration and economic waste—but no one has suggested a practical alternative. Zoning is not an alternative—it is simply a technique for making invasion and succession more deliberate and orderly.

Incidentally, the Negro invasion is a perfect illustration of how the culture creates social conflicts. The Negro population of our major cities has been exploding, largely through the urban migration of Negroes. As Negroes are excluded from most new subdivisions, they can find room to live only by invading older white residential areas. If there were no discrimination, Negroes would scatter themselves over the community according to income and preference, as other ethnic groups have eventually done. But because there *is* discrimination, Negroes are continuously desperate for a place to live. Many whites would not object to a sprinkling of Negroes in their neighborhood but will not live in a predominantly Negro district. Fearing a mass Negro invasion, they try to keep out all Negroes. Their effort restricts Negro housing and makes a mass invasion more likely to follow an initial influx. Thus whites' attempts to keep Negroes out ensure that when they do come to many neighborhoods, they will come in an overwhelming tide. This is another example of the self-fulfilling prophesy. The prediction that the first Negro family will bring a flood of Negroes causes white people to act in ways which guarantee exactly this result [Wolf, 1957]. Of all possible ways of providing housing for a growing urban Negro population, we seem to have hit upon the most inefficient and painful.

It is through these ecological processes that the city continues to change. City planners today are trying to control and direct the processes in order to make them less wasteful and painful. It is too early to tell how successful they will be.

Urban life and personality The city has been a source of endless inspiration to artists and writers, as in this example:

> For Manila is a city like all cities—changeless and changing. Giving and taking back. Harsh and yet tender as a child's caress. And unlike other cities, it is the east and the west meeting at last. It is the Malay and the Latin. The American and the Chinese. . . . The city of the strident voice and the brick and cement jungles,

and the city with the hidden lullabies and the warm hand. Cankered by ugliness and evil, spiked with violence and sudden death, it has its moments of breathless beauty and primal innocence. And if a man could see his way clear through to the very core of the city, he might yet apprehend the final meaning which could be the germ of his fulfillment.

Vicente Rivera, Jr., "This is Manila," *Sunday Times Magazine* (Manila), Nov. 20, 1953, pp. 9–10.

Even though poetic rather than sociological, this description still carries a sense of the heterogeneity and contrast of the city. What are the dominant characteristics of the city, and how do they shape urban life and personality?

Speed and tension   The city is always in a hurry. Work and play are timed by the clock as we proceed from deadline to deadline. Lunches become business appointments, or the busy executive eats lunch at his desk, barking commands between bites, while even the most humble worker must catch the bus and punch the time clock. Genuine relaxation is impossible for many urbanites, and a vacation is merely a change of scene for equally tightly scheduled activities.

A vacation is merely a change of scene for equally tightly scheduled activities.

Anonymity   The sheer pressure of numbers makes for anonymity. Of course there are groups within which the urbanite is known as a person, but much of his routine life is spent in the anonymous crowd—the *Lonely Crowd* of David Riesman [1950]. The heterogeneity of city life, with its mixture of people of all races, creeds, classes, occupations, and ethnic origins heightens this sense of anonymity. Different interests separate people from any intimate acquaintance with others whom they meet in passing. Lee remarks:

Anonymity is a loss of identity in a city teeming with millions. Many urbanites live in a social void, or vacuum in which institutional norms are not effective in controlling or regulating their social behavior. Although they are aware of the existence of many institutional organizations and many people around them, they do not feel a sense of belongingness to any one group or community. Socially, they are poor in the midst of plenty.

Rose Hum Lee, *The City,* J. B. Lippincott Company, Philadelphia, 1955, p. 454.

In the rooming-house areas and "skid rows" are the extremes of urban anonymity—the forgotten men and women of obscure past and uncertain future. They exist outside the pale of organized conventional living, their lives centered in the rooming- or flophouse, the cheap tavern, and perhaps the rescue mission. Here the deviants may cluster and pursue their deviation with a minimum of interference. They are the defeated refuse of our social system, resigned, and often contented with a social role which demands little and offers little.

Social distance   City people are physically crowded but socially distant. Social distance is a product of anonymity, impersonality, and heterogeneity. Ethnic differences are one form of heterogeneity, dividing people into groups which often dislike or disdain one another. But occupational differences may be even more important sources of social distance. Unlike the agricultural community, the city has no common occupational focus which serves as a common interest for urbanites. Workers may follow any one of thousands of different occupations and have little understanding of, or interest in other lines of work. The varieties of work attract men with a great range of education, skills, training, and temperament. This diversity of interests, backgrounds, and economic levels means that a man learns to reveal only the side of his personality which the other person can be expected to understand. This constant masking of one's true feelings adds up to a great lack of understanding. The great city which multiplies contacts also produces loneliness. From this loneliness a man often flees into a frantic effort to accommodate himself to changing popular tastes in order to prove to his blasé neighbors that he really "belongs" and thus merits at least a segment of their attention. The city is a place of outward conformity and inner reservations, of "front" and conspicuous consumption, of "keeping up with the Joneses." When people cannot know us for what we are, they must judge us by what they see. Hence the great importance of the well-tailored appearance, the impressive car, the occupational title, and the "good" address.

Most routine social contacts in the city are impersonal, segmented, and correct. Formal politeness takes the place of genuine friendliness. The telephone and the printed checklist make it possible to contact people impersonally when necessary while keeping them at a distance. Urbanites become nigh-dwellers, not neighbors. Apartment dwellers may live for years without any acquaintance with many of the other occupants. In the absence of spontaneous, informal social interaction, a sort of social cleavage serves to restrict social interaction to that which is formal and correct. The ability of urbanites to look past or through people without seeing them is quite disconcerting to many rural visitors.

Regimentation   The pressure of numbers requires that urban life be highly regimented. Traffic lights control the flow of traffic; elevators and escalators move on schedule. The city dweller learns to work by the clock, under close supervision, often following the letter of his instructions without any effort to understand what he is doing or why. Changes in his routine are decreed from above and must be coordinated by the electronic computer, which places each human robot in the right spot at the right time performing the right function. Even recreation for children is organized, and the harried housewife races to get Junior to his club at 4:15 so that he will be on time for the period of "free play." Such control is sometimes irksome, but the true city dweller has learned to accept the idea that most of life is according to plan and to justify his subservience to regulation on the ground of efficiency.

What results do these conditions of urban life have on personality? Very little actual research has been done on this question, although it has attracted a great deal of sociological speculation. Sociologists suspect that urban life produces greater emotional tension and insecurity than does rural life, and some empirical evidence supports this conclusion. The rates of mental illness are higher in the city than in rural areas. It is, however, not clear whether the city causes more mental disorder, attracts the maladjusted person to the city, or merely locates and diagnoses more accurately the extent of mental illness in the population. One well-controlled study, however, finds that farm and small-town children show a higher level of personal adjustment than urban children, with greater self-reliance, a greater sense of personal worth, and fewer feelings of nonbelonging [Magnus, 1948]. Although insecurity and rejection are entirely possible in a rural setting, the heterogeneous and anonymous nature of the city probably increases insecurity and the sense of nonbelonging.

Segmentation of personality is a necessary technique for coping with the multiple human contacts of an urban area. Most routine urban contacts are of secondary-group rather than primary-group nature. Most contacts are instrumental; that is, we use another person as a necessary functionary to fulfill our purposes. We do not ordinarily interact with entire persons, but with people in terms of their formal roles as mailmen, bus drivers, elevator operators, salespersons, and other functionaries. We thus interact with only a segment of the person, not with the whole person. Such casual, superficial, short-lived relations with segments of people constitute a large part of the urbanite's social contacts, in contrast to the rural dweller, who has relatively fewer contacts with anyone whom he does not know well or with whom he fails to interact as a complete person [Sorokin and Zimmerman, 1929, pp. 48–58]. Even the superficial camaraderie with the taxicab driver is not genuine informal social interaction, but is a standardized part of the service [Davis, 1959].

The worldwide Is there an urban culture which is shared by cities everywhere, or are these
urban culture conditions of urban life and personality unique to the Western World? The descriptions of cities and city life read a good deal the same wherever the cities are located. This description of South Asian cities is not greatly different from descriptions of Chicago, Paris, or Buenos Aires.

> . . . *huge mausoleums of coal, smoke, iron and steel, of dirt and squalor, of overcrowding, of cooly-lines, and human warehouses. Long hours, low wages, bad housing, woman and child labor, infant mortality, accidents, high rents, poor sanitation, prostitution, gambling, racing, dope, dance halls, cabarets and night clubs were features of all the cities. The noise corroded the nerves of the city dwellers while absence of neighborhood restricted their contacts with each other.*
>
> Kewal Motwani, "The Impact of Modern Technology on the Social Structure of South Asia," *International Social Science Bulletin*, Winter, 1951, p. 787.

One sociologist sought to answer the question by studying a city which had as little Western influence as any he could locate, Timbuctoo in northern Africa. In his words:

> *Briefly the theoretical implications of the Timbuctoo data are that lack of isolation, marked population density and heterogeneity seem to be accompanied by disorganization, secularization and impersonalization even in the absence of western influence. The market economy appears as the system which makes possible the basic ecological conditions, holds the diverse cultural elements together and mediates most relationships among them.*
>
> Horace Miner, "The Folk-Urban Continuum," *American Sociological Review*, 17:531, 1952.

The presence of diversity in Timbuctoo was found to work both for and against the development of an urban type of culture. In so far as it crowded together people from different backgrounds, it promoted a segmented, impersonal type of adjustment. However, within the subgroups of the city a more familistic, traditional, folk-society brand of social life prevailed. It has also prevailed in immigrant colonies in North American cities. A recent report on Egyptian urbanization finds that the migrant from rural areas settles in homogeneous districts with his own village mates and maintains many of his traditional behavior patterns [Abu-Lughod, 1961].

In other words, an urban culture operates in a roughly similar fashion wherever urbanization has taken place. Regardless of the cultural setting, urbanization brings certain inescapable social consequences—population density, anonymity, impersonality, regimentation, segmentation of personality. Urban people are recognizably different from country people the world over. At the same time, subcommunities within all larger cities retain a culture with some elements of the folk society. These are products of urban migration and presumably will endure as long as the city is fed by a constant stream of migrants from rural areas. The higher rural birth rate and the shrinking need for rural labor as farming grows more efficient, make it likely that this migration will endure for some time.

The antiurban bias Ever since their earliest appearance, cities have been viewed with suspicion by rural peoples. The Old Testament prophets were rural men, denouncing the sins and vices of the wicked cities. Jefferson despised cities and felt that only a nation of freeholding farmers could possibly remain a democracy. Even many city people share the antiurban bias, which sees the city as a center of sin and crime, of trickery and hypocrisy, of political corruption, of frivolity and superficiality, and of vexing problems of all sorts. Meanwhile the country is assumed to be a haven of simple honesty and rugged integrity where good things grow and God's own people dwell. The antiurban bias is revealed in the widespread assumption that the country or small town is a better place to raise children, that farming and raising food is more noble than other work, that "grass roots democracy" is more genuine and rural voters more trustworthy, and that rural life and rural people are simply "better" in nearly every way. Even social research follows the antiurban bias. Most urban research shows what a mess the city is in, while funded research on rural life is generally screened to avoid any data which would challenge the assumption that "the rural community is a good place to live" [Olson, 1964].

All of these assumptions are dubious, and many of them are demonstratably false. Urban and rural life are *different,* but whether one is better than the other is a question of values. The "goodness of life" in a community cannot be measured until we agree on what measures to use. If high health levels, average incomes, educational levels, and many social amenities are the values chosen, then city life is better. If a quiet, less complicated life far from the maddening throng is preferred, then the country has the edge. Obviously, this is a philosophical question, not a scientific question, and it should be remembered that the assumption of rural (or urban) superiority represents a bias, not a fact.

URBAN AND RURAL CONVERGENCE

Much of the foregoing discussion is already becoming outdated. We have mentioned the urbanization of rural life and the suburban movement. Urban-rural differences of all sorts are rapidly shrinking in the Western world, and in time this will probably be true of the rest of the world. The suburb is the most rapidly growing part of America, and the suburban family is tending to become the "normal" family as we conceive it. This family is intermediate in size between the rural and urban families, and as compared with the urban family, is more strongly integrated around kinship ties; parental and sibling roles are strengthened, and the family is more active in voluntary organizations and community life [Jaco and Belknap, 1953]. The problems of community organization are increasingly those of the suburb and its relation to the central city. Suburban America *is* America.

The rural-urban distinction has already become secondary to the occupational distinction in importance [Stewart, 1958; Dewey, 1960]. The distinctive rural pattern of life is more closely linked to an agricultural occupation than to mere residence in a rural area. A recent study of rural-urban differences in interpersonal relations found that farm people differed considerably from urban residents, while there was comparatively little difference between urban and rural nonfarm people [Reiss, 1959]. Clearly, occupation has become more important than rural or urban residence as a clue to one's personality and way of life.

Nor should it be assumed that urbanization *necessarily* brings anomie, disorganization, and a lack of informal primary-group relationships. Earlier observers of urbanism were impressed by these features of urban life [Park et al., 1925; Sorokin and Zimmerman, 1929]. But either the observers exaggerated these characteristics, or urbanites have changed. Some recent studies have found that anomie is no more widespread in highly urbanized than in less highly urbanized areas [Greer and Kube, 1959]. As urbanism increases, neighboring and participation in formal organizations decline, but primary-group relationships within kinship and friendship groups increase. When rural people migrate to the city, they do not enter a social vacuum but rely heavily upon relatives for social interaction [Blumberg and Bell, 1959]. Instead of the extended family declining in importance with urbanization, research finds that the extended family is an even more important unit in large cities than in rural areas [Key, 1961]. Apparently as urbanism increases and people tend to become anonymous members of the community, they rely more heavily upon close friends and relatives for intimate response, identity, and a sense of belonging. The rise of the proportion of secondary contacts with urbanism implies no absolute weakening of primary-group life.

Community integration and planning Today all American communities—urban, rural, or suburban—are more nearly alike than ever before. Locality has ceased to be an effective basis for grouping. Special interest has largely replaced locality as the basis for grouping. Locality groups are too diversified to have very much in common. But special interests of all kinds—occupational, recreational, religious, promotional—unite people who may have little in common except this special interest. As one enthusiast testifies: "The friendships and pleasures I owe to collecting! The people you get to know! Book collectors are nocturnal people; they love to sit up and talk, and they're always good fun."[1] Such unity as survives in the modern community comes largely from the interlocking membership of many such special-interest groups.

In rural America, where locality and occupation once converged to give a common way of life to most people, it was not difficult to maintain an integrated community and an effective system of social control. Today it is more difficult. While the primary group survives in the city, it no longer functions as a very effective community control. Whether it is possible for the primary group to be an effective social control in the modern city is debatable [Tannenbaum, 1948; Riemer, 1959]. Angell [1947; 1951] in his study of the integration of American cities took a low crime rate and a high proportion of contributors to the community chest as indexes of community integration. He concluded that cities with an ethnically homogeneous population and a low rate of geographic mobility had a higher degree of moral integration. While geographic mobility will probably continue, ethnic heterogeneity will decline as present immigrant groups become fully assimilated. There is therefore some prospect that community integration may grow more complete as time passes.

City planning is today the recommended antidote for urban problems. Practically every city has a city-planning board, although often it does little but decide upon the location of highways and public buildings. Any comprehensive planning is certain to meet opposition from many vested interests. Yet without comprehensive planning and execution of these plans, the American city faces accelerating decay. Slums are spreading faster than they are being cleared. Uncoordinated, piecemeal development of the urban fringe and of the "strip" cities is certain to mean great waste and agonizing future problems. Sewers, water mains, and expressways, built *after* many homes and buildings are constructed, will require expensive demolition. One suburb will wind up with lots of children to educate; while another suburb will have the industrial properties which make up the tax base needed to finance good schools. Certain areas will begin to have costly floods when the development of adjacent areas alters the watershed. Quiet residential areas will become noisy thoroughfares because of developments in adjacent areas. Problems like these are the fruit of uncoordinated, unplanned regional development. There are, as yet, few planning authorities with power to make, let alone enforce the execution of plans for an entire metropolitan area. Eventually, after the problems have become intolerable and most of the mistakes have already been made, we shall probably create the plans. One sociologist a few years ago outlined the problem in these terms:

If the cities, and especially their decaying centers are to be brought up even to a tolerable standard of life, they must be reconstructed by the square mile instead of the individual house or the city block. . . . Despite the blight which has crept outward from the heart of cities, there are in the blighted areas billions of wealth in the form of physical utilities to be salvaged by making these centers habitable and attractive for human living. . . . We have the beginnings of a new house-

---

[1] Donald F. Hyde, quoted in *The New Yorker*, Mar. 22, 1958, p. 25.

building industry and we can develop further the prefabrication of houses, the assembling of land, and the financing of community building all of which are still in embryo. We do not start with a clean slate. We shall not have the opportunity to build new cities as we did a century ago, but we shall have an unprecedented opportunity to reconstruct with new materials and new methods the old cities which were created in response to conditions which have ceased to exist.

Louis Wirth, "Life in the City," in Leon Carnovsky and Lowell Martin, *The Library in the Community,* The University of Chicago Press, Chicago, 1944, pp. 21–22. Copyright, 1944, by The University of Chicago.

This statement emphasizes the physical reconstruction of buildings; but other problems are attracting equal attention. They include the provision of adequate public facilities such as recreation centers, public-health units, and schools; the necessary supplies of clean air, light, and water along with provisions for sewage disposal; the guidance and control of the restless youth of our cities; and finally the overwhelming problem of urban traffic. In some cases the unit of planning is an urban neighborhood, whereas other problems may demand state, regional, or even national attention. Urban renewal programs are now a fixture of nearly every large American city. Congress in 1966 authorized a "model cities" program, administered by the Model Cities Administration of the Department of Housing and Urban Development. This is intended to show, in a few cities, what a coordinated attack on a city's multiple problems could accomplish.

Cities are as old as recorded history, but only within the lifetime of living men have we begun to live in an urban society. And only within the memory of today's college undergraduates have we begun seriously to consider how man can organize an urban society for his comfort and contentment.

SUMMARY

A community is an area within which all a group's life activities can be carried on. Rural and urban people are different because the physical and social conditions of life are different in urban and rural communities. The traditional rural community tended to be a folk society. Its isolation, homogeneity, agricultural occupation, and subsistence economy all tended to develop people who were thrifty, hard-working, conservative, and ethnocentric. Changing technology has brought a rural revolution, with reduced isolation, commercialized large-scale farming, and a way of life very similar in many respects to urban patterns.

Cities become possible when an agricultural surplus develops, together with improved means of transportation, and tend to locate at "breaks" in transportation. Attempts to explain the ecological pattern of American cities have produced the concentric zone, sector, and multiple-nuclei theories, none of which any city perfectly fits but which all cities somewhat corroborate. The most significant current developments in city structure are the suburb and the metropolitan area, which now account for most of our current population growth. As whites flee to the suburbs, the central city becomes increasingly Negro, thereby aggravating certain racial and political problems of the city.

The city is a conglomeration of natural areas, constantly forming and shifting through the ecological processes of concentration, centralization, decentralization, segregation, and invasion. The invasion cycle has several stages: the initial influx, reaction, general influx, climax, and succession.

Urban life and personality are affected by the physical and social conditions of urban living—speed and tension, anonymity, social distance, and regimentation. These conditions produce impersonality, insecurity, and segmentation of personality, which appear to be universal characteristics of urbanization all over the world. The widespread assumption that these differences make rural life and rural people "better" is known as the antiurban bias. Today, urban and rural differences are rapidly shrinking in the Western world and will eventually do so elsewhere. The rural-urban distinction is already less important than occupational classification as a clue to one's personality and way of life. Yet our increasingly urban world is beset by problems of community integration and organization, and community planning is a growing concern in our urban society.

QUESTIONS AND PROJECTS

1. Why did prehistoric man build no cities?

2. To what extent does the folk society survive in rural America today? Where and why has it most completely disappeared from rural America?

3. How are the personality characteristics of rural and urban people a product of their physical and social conditions of life? What sort of problems are faced by rural migrants to the city?

4. What has produced the rural revolution? What has this done to rural-urban differences?

5. Are there rural slums? What produces them? How do they resemble and differ from urban slums?

6. Why has "conspicuous consumption" been more of an urban than a rural pattern? Is this relation changing today? How or why?

7. A few sociologists have objected to the phrase "urbanization of rural life" to describe current changes. Are there any respects in which urban life is being "ruralized"? Contrast the relative amounts of diffusion in each direction.

8. Why has it been easier to integrate the small rural community than the large city? Is there any reasonable prospect of greater community integration for urban areas?

9. Read Edward T. Chase, "Jam on the Côte d'Azur," *Reporter*, Sept. 28, 1961, pp. 44–46, or Wilfred Owen, *Cities in the Motor Age,* The Viking Press, Inc., New York, 1959. Then prepare your answer to the question: Are automobiles an asset or a blight upon the modern city?

10. Take the city you know best and apply each of the three theories of city structure. Which fits it best? How well does the theory describe the actual arrangement of this city?

11. Trace the stages of the invasion cycle for an area of the city you know best. Try to date each stage. How long did each stage last and how long did the entire cycle require? Was it a happy period?

12. What factual data can you find to measure the "goodness" of life in rural and urban society? What values are used in this evaluation?

SUGGESTED READINGS

ABRAMS, CHARLES: *The City is the Frontier*, Harper & Row, Publishers, Incorporated, New York, 1965. A readable analysis of urban planning, housing, and urban renewal.

ALLEN, FREDRICK LEWIS: "The Big Change in Suburbia," *Harper's Magazine*, June, 1954, pp. 21–28, July, 1954, pp. 47–53. Some social effects of the mass-produced suburbs.

BELL, WENDELL, AND MARION D. BOAT: "Urban Neighborhoods and Informal Social Relations," *American Journal of Sociology*, 62:391–398, January, 1957; Bobbs-Merrill reprint S-14. Research data on the extent and intimacy of neighborhood contacts in the urban milieu.

CHASE, EDWARD T.: "Jam on the Côte d'Azur," *Reporter*, Sept. 28, 1961, pp. 44–46. A popularly written article on traffic problems in European and American cities.

*CONANT, JAMES BRYANT: *Slums and Suburbs*, McGraw-Hill Book Company, New York, 1961. Contrasts the effects of slum and suburb on the functioning of the school. (P2421-Sig)

*GREER, SCOTT: *Urban Renewal and American Cities*, The Bobbs-Merrill Company, Inc., Indianapolis, 1965. A critique of urban renewal and a call for a different approach. (Bobbs)

GRUEN, VICTOR: *The Heart of Our Cities*, Simon and Schuster, Inc., New York, 1964. Discussion of urban redevelopment by America's best-known urban planner.

*JACOBS, JANE: *The Death and Life of Great Amercan Cities*, Random House, Inc., New York, 1961. An attack on current city planning and a call for a new approach. (V-241-Vin)

MARTINDALE, DON: "Prefatory Remarks: The Theory of the City," introduction to Max Weber, *The City*, The Free Press of Glencoe, New York, 1958. A penetrating review of sociological theory on the city.

ROGERS, EVERETT M.: *Social Change in Rural Society*, Appleton-Century-Crofts, New York, 1960. A textbook in rural sociology, with emphasis upon rural social change.

SUSSMAN, MARVIN B. (ED.): *Community Structure and Analysis*, Thomas Y. Crowell Company, New York, 1959. A series of articles summarizing recent research and its relation to community problems.

TAYLOR, MILLER LEE, AND A. R. JONES: *Rural Life and Urbanized Society*. Oxford University Press, Fair Lawn, N.J., 1964. A description of how rural society is becoming urbanized.

*WHYTE, WILLIAM H., JR.: *The Organization Man*, Simon and Schuster, Inc., New York, 1956. An impressionistic description of life in a Chicago suburb. (A117-Anch)

WIRTH, LOUIS W.: "Urbanism as a Way of Life," *American Journal of Sociology*, 44:1–25, July, 1938; Bobbs-Merrill reprint S-320. A classic essay describing urban life and personality.

Six

SOCIAL CHANGE AND SOCIAL POLICY

Part Six deals with change and man's efforts to effect change. Chapter 19, "Social and Cultural Change," discusses the forces which encourage and resist change and the social consequences of change when it is accomplished. Chapter 20, "Social Movements," describes some more or less organized efforts of people to promote changes they desire or to resist changes they deplore.

SOCIAL AND CULTURAL CHANGE

Homouda Awadan's nights have been restless recently, mainly because his cow no longer sleeps in the same room with him.

Awadan is one of 2,000 peasants moved last summer from overpopulated mud-hut villages into Ibis, a modern village with brick houses, electric lighting, running water and special pens for cattle.

The operation is sponsored by the U.S. Point Four program and the Egyptian Agriculture Department.

Life in the modern village has posed many problems to the fellaheen [peasants], many of whom came from villages that have seen little change since the days of the pharaohs.

All his life Awadan has slept with his cow, his chief work animal and provider of milk, yogurt and white cheese. Keeping the animal inside the house kept his floor littered with animal refuse, but Awadan could not take a chance on the beast being stolen.

"For the past three nights I have been waking in the middle of the night to check on my cow down in the village," said Awadan, still not used to the separation from his most treasured possession.

Awadan often yearns for the uncomplicated life of the mud village, but he remembers the five acres of land the government gave him and decides to stay. He never owned land before. He had to rent it from a big landowner.

Sheikh Rashad, director of the co-operative union at Ibis village, said it took much convincing to move the fellaheen into the model village. They are not inclined to move, no matter how crowded, he said.

In spite of all preparations, unexpected situations arose, Rashad said. Stacks of dry wood soon began appearing on top of the houses, similar to the mud villages, he added. At Ibis they had special storage rooms for wood, but the fellaheen would not use them. (Associated Press, Nov. 9, 1959.)

ALL CULTURES are constantly changing—some rapidly and some very slowly. Even when it tries to do so, no society succeeds in exactly copying and transmitting the culture of its ancestors. This fluidity is most easily illustrated by language changes. English has changed so greatly that most students have their troubles with Shakespeare and are hopelessly lost in Chaucer. In 1755 Samuel Johnson published his dictionary in the hope that it would stabilize word meanings and stop language changes, but soon he confessed that he had failed. Social change is continuous and irresistible. Only its speed and direction vary.

There is a distinction between *social change*—changes in the social structure and social relationships of the society—and *cultural change*—changes in the culture of a society. Some social changes might include changes in the age distribution, average educational level, or birth rate of a population; or the decline of informality and personal neighborliness as people shift from village to city; or the change in the relationship between workers and employers when unions become organized; or the change of the husband from the boss to a partner in today's democratic family. Cultural changes might include such things as the invention and popularization of the automobile, the addition of new words to our language, changing concepts of propriety and morality, new forms of music, art, or dance, or the general trend towards sex equality. Yet the concepts overlap. The trend towards sex equality involves both a changing set of cultural norms concerning male-female roles, and some changing social relationships as well. Nearly all important changes involve both social and cultural aspects. In practice, therefore, the distinction is seldom a very important one, and the two terms are often used interchangeably.

There is an important distinction between social change and progress. The term *progress* carries a value judgment. Progress means change in a desirable direction. Desirable as measured by whose values? Are faster automobiles, increased leisure, rising standards of living, and growing acceptance of divorce and birth control desirable or not? Not even all Americans are agreed, and the Pakistani or Masai will be still more skeptical. Since progress is an evaluative term, social scientists prefer the neutrally descriptive term *social change*.

PROCESSES OF SOCIAL CHANGE

Discovery A discovery is *a shared human perception of a fact or relationship which already exists.* Man discovered the principle of the lever, the circulation of the blood, and the conditioned reflex. A discovery is an addition to mankind's store of verified knowledge.

A discovery becomes a factor in social change only when it is put to use. A discovery may become part of the background of knowledge which people use in evaluating their present practices. Thus the recent discoveries of physiology and psychology that males and females are very much alike in their intellectual capacities did not *compel* men to alter the status of women; but the discoveries made the nineteenth-century patriarch look ridiculous and certainly diluted men's determination to preserve traditional male dominance.

When new knowledge is used to develop new technology, vast changes generally follow. The ancient Greeks knew about the power of steam, and before A.D. 100 Hero of Alexandria had built a small steam engine as a toy, but steam power produced no social changes until it was put to serious use nearly 2,000 years later. Discoveries become a factor in social change when new knowledge is put to new uses.

Invention An *invention* is often defined as *a new combination or a new use of old ideas* of the culture. Thus George Selden in 1895 combined a liquid-gas engine, a liquid-gas tank, a running-gear mechanism, an intermediate clutch, a driving shaft, and a carriage body, and patented this contraption as an automobile. None of these ideas were new; the only novelty was the combined use of them. The Selden patent was attacked and eventually revoked by the courts on the ground that he did not originate the idea of combining these items.

Inventions may be classified as *material* inventions, such as the bow and arrow, telephone, or airplane, and *social* inventions, such as the alphabet, constitutional government, or contract bridge. In each case, old elements are used, combined, and improved for a new application. Invention is thus a continuing process, with each new invention the last in a long series of preceding inventions and discoveries. In a popularly written book, Burlingame [1947] has analyzed a number of familiar inventions, showing how each began hundreds or thousands of years ago and passed through dozens of preliminary inventions and intermediate stages. Invention is not strictly an individual matter; it is a social process involving an endless series of modifications, improvements, and recombinations. As Gillin [1948, pp. 158–163] has pointed out, each invention may be new in *form, function,* and *meaning.* "Form" refers to the shape of the new object or the actions of the new behavior trait; "function" refers to what the invention does; "meaning" refers to the long-range consequences of its use. To these three, we might also add that an invention may be new in *principle,* that is, in the basic scientific law upon which it is based.

The jet engine and the piston engine use the same principle (expansion of burning gases) but differ in form (one uses expanding gases directly for thrust, the other to push a piston in a cylinder). The steam engine and the piston gasoline engine are similar in form but differ in principle (one creates expanding gases by boiling water, the other by burning gasoline). The bow and arrow differ in both principle and form from the primitive spear but have the same function and meaning. The wheeled cart was new in all respects (in principle, since the load was carried by wheel and axle instead of being dragged or packed; in form, since it was new in design; in function, since it carried both people and possessions; in meaning, since it made large-scale, long-distance overland transport possible). Very few inventions are new in all four respects.

The term, *innovation,* has sometimes been used to include both discoveries and inventions [Barnett, 1953, pp. 7–8]. In either case, something new has been added to the culture.

Diffusion Even the most inventive society invents only a modest proportion of its innovations. Most of the social changes in all known societies have developed through *diffusion, the spread of culture traits from group to group.* Diffusion operates both within societies and between societies. Jazz originated among Negro musicians of New Orleans and became diffused to other groups within the society. Later it spread to other societies and has now been diffused throughout the civilized world.

Diffusion takes place whenever societies come into contact. Societies may seek to prevent diffusion by forbidding contact, as did the Old Testament Hebrews:

When the Lord thy God shall bring thee into the land whither thou goest to possess it, and hath cast out many nations before thee . . . thou shalt smite them and utterly destroy them; thou shalt make no covenant with them, nor shew mercy unto them; neither shalt thou make marriages with them. . . . For they will turn away thy son from following me, that they may serve other gods. . . . But . . . ye shall destroy their altars, and break down their images, and cut down their groves, and burn their graven images with fire.
Deuteronomy 7:1–5.

Like most efforts to prevent intercultural contacts, this prohibition failed. The Old Testament tells how the Hebrews persisted in mingling and intermarrying with the surrounding tribes, adopting bits of their cultures in the process. Whenever cultures come into contact, some exchange of culture traits always takes place.

Most of the content of any complex culture has been diffused from other societies. Ralph Linton has written a famous passage which tells how the 100 per cent American has actually borrowed most of his culture from other societies.

Our solid American Citizen awakens in a bed built on a pattern which originated in the Near East but which was modified in Northern Europe before it was transmitted to America. He throws back covers made from cotton, domesticated in India, or linen, domesticated in the Near East, or silk, the use of which was discovered in China. All of these materials have been spun and woven by processes invented in the Near East. He slips into his moccasins, invented by the Indians of the Eastern woodlands, and goes to the bathroom, whose fixtures are a mixture of European and American inventions, both of recent date. He takes off his pajamas, a garment invented in India, and washes with soap invented by the ancient Gauls. He then shaves, a masochistic rite which seems to have been·derived from either Sumer or Ancient Egypt.

Returning to the bedroom, he removes his clothes from a chair of Southern European type and proceeds to dress. He puts on garments whose form originally derived from the skin clothing of the nomads of the Asiatic steppes, puts on shoes made from skins tanned by a process invented in ancient Egypt and cut to a pattern derived from the classical civilizations of the Mediterranean, and ties around his neck a strip of bright-colored cloth which is a vestigial survival of the shoulder shawls worn by seventeenth century Croatians. Before going out for breakfast he glances through the window, made of glass invented in Egypt, and if it is raining puts on overshoes made of rubber discovered by the Central American Indians and takes an umbrella, invented in southeastern Asia. Upon his head he puts a hat made of felt, a material invented in the Asiatic steppes.

On his way to breakfast he stops to buy a paper, paying for it with coins, an ancient Lydian invention. At the restaurant a whole new series of borrowed ele-

ments confronts him. His plate is made of a form of pottery invented in China. His knife is of steel, an alloy first made in southern India, his fork a medieval Italian invention, and his spoon a derivative of a Roman original. He begins breakfast with an orange, from the eastern Mediterranean, a cantaloupe from Persia, or perhaps a piece of African watermelon. With this he has coffee, an Abyssinian plant, with cream and sugar. Both the domestication of cows and the idea of milking them originated in the Near East, while sugar was first made in India. After his fruit and first coffee he goes on to waffles, cakes made by a Scandinavian technique from wheat domesticated in Asia Minor. Over these he pours maple syrup, invented by the Indians of the Eastern woodlands. As a side dish he may have the egg of a species of bird domesticated in Indo-China, or thin strips of the flesh of an animal domesticated in Eastern Asia which have been salted and smoked by a process developed in northern Europe.

When our friend has finished eating he settles back to smoke, an American Indian habit, consuming a plant domesticated in Brazil in either a pipe, derived from the Indians of Virginia, or a cigarette, derived from Mexico. If he is hardy enough he may even attempt a cigar, transmitted to us from the Antilles by way of Spain. While smoking he reads the news of the day, imprinted in characters invented by the ancient Semites upon a material invented in China by a process invented in Germany. As he absorbs the accounts of foreign troubles he will, if he is a good conservative citizen, thank a Hebrew deity in an Indo-European language that he is a 100 per cent American.

Ralph Linton, *The Study of Man*, Appleton-Century-Crofts, New York, 1936, pp. 326–327.

Diffusion is always a two-way process. Europeans gave horses, firearms, Christianity, and whisky to the Indians, in exchange for corn, potatoes, tobacco, and the canoe. Yet the exchange is often lopsided. When two cultures come into contact, the simpler one generally borrows more traits than the more complex, and low-status groups generally borrow more than high-status groups. Slave groups generally absorb the culture of their masters, while their own is largely forgotten.

Diffusion is a selective process. A group accepts some culture traits from a neighbor, at the same time rejecting others. We accepted much of the Indian's food but rejected his religion. Indians quickly accepted the white man's horse but long rejected the white man's cow.

Diffusion generally involves some modification of the borrowed element. As noted earlier, each cultural trait has *principle, form, function,* and *meaning.* Any or all of these may change when a trait is diffused. When Europeans adopted Indian tobacco, they smoked it in a pipe somewhat like the Indian pipe, thus preserving the form, although they also added other forms—cigarettes, chewing tobacco, and snuff. But they entirely changed function and meaning. Indians smoked tobacco as a ceremonial ritual; Europeans used it first as a medicine, and later

Most of the content of any complex culture has been diffused from other societies.

for personal gratification and sociability. The outward forms of Christianity have been diffused more readily than the functions and meanings. In missionary areas many converts have accepted the forms of Christian worship while retaining many of their traditional supernatural beliefs and practices. Non-Western peoples have put tin cans and other Western artifacts to a variety of uses, both utilitarian and aesthetic. American colonists accepted maize (corn) from the Indians unchanged; it traveled to Europe, where it was used as food for animals but not for people; it was then diffused to West Africa, where it became a favorite food and even an offering to the gods. Endless examples could be cited to show how traits are nearly always modified as they are diffused.

FACTORS IN THE RATE OF CHANGE

Discovery, invention, and diffusion are processes of change. But what causes them to happen? We cannot answer this question without first examining the meaning of the term *cause*. A cause is sometimes defined as a condition which is *both necessary and sufficient* to produce a predictable effect. It is necessary in that we never have this effect without this cause, and sufficient in that this cause, alone, always produces this effect. Thus defined, very few causes have been established in social science. Does drunkenness cause divorce? Many long-suffering souls put up with a drunken mate, while others divorce mates who are bone dry. Obviously, drunkenness is neither a necessary nor a sufficient condition to produce a divorce. Most causation in social science is multiple—that is, a number of factors interact in producing a result. What factors interact in producing a social change?

First of all, we note that the factors in social change are predominantly social and cultural, not biological or geographic. Not everyone accepts this view. Some people would attribute the rise and fall of great civilizations to changes in the biological characteristics of nations. Often these theories have a racial twist; a great civilization is said to arise from a vigorous, creative race, and falls when the race mixes with lesser breeds and dilutes its genius. According to an opposite version, a great burst of creativity follows a fortunate intermixture of races and dies out as the hybrid strain runs out. Most scientists reject all such theories. There is no convincing scientific evidence that any race differs from any other race in its biological basis for human learning, or that man's biology has changed during the last twenty-five thousand years or so. During the period of recorded history, man's biological attributes appear to have been a constant, not a variable, in his behavior.

Physical environment   Changes in the physical environment are quite rare, but very compelling when they happen. The desert wastes of North Africa were once green and well populated. Climates change, soil erodes, and lakes gradually turn into swamps and finally plains. Although social life is greatly affected by these changes, they usually come about so very slowly that the changes in social life may be largely unnoticed. True, man may speed up these changes through his land use; he can accelerate or retard soil erosion through conservation practices. But in this instance, the causes are still social and cultural, for it is the actions of men which set in motion these environmental changes.

Much more common in human history is a change of a group's physical environment through migration. Especially in primitive societies, whose members are very directly dependent upon their physical environment, migration to a different environment brings major changes in culture. Civilized man can more easily transport his culture and practice it in a new and different environment. The British colonial in the jungle outpost often persisted in taking afternoon tea and dressing for dinner. Yet no one would suggest that he was unaffected by the jungle environment; even civilized man's culture is affected by a change of physical environment.

Population changes   Any major change in size or distribution of a people always produces major social changes. When a thinly settled frontier fills up with people, the hospitality pattern declines, secondary-group relations multiply, institutional structures grow more elaborate, and many other changes occur. A rapidly growing population must either migrate or improve its productive techniques. Great historic migrations and conquests—the Huns, the Vikings, and many others—have arisen from the pressure of a growing population upon limited resources. Migration itself encourages change, for it brings a group into a new environment, subjects it to new social contacts, and confronts it with new problems. No major population change leaves the culture unchanged.

Isolation and   Societies located at world crossroads have always been centers of change.
contact   Since most new traits come through diffusion, those societies in closest contact with other societies are likely to change most rapidly. In ancient times of overland transport, the land bridge connecting Asia, Africa, and Europe was the center of civilizing change. Later, sailing vessels shifted the center to the fringes of the Mediterranean Sea, and still later to the northwest coast of Europe. Areas of highest intercultural contact are the centers of change.

Conversely, isolated areas are centers of stability, conservatism, and resistance to change. Almost without exception, the most primitive tribes have been those who were the most isolated, like the polar Eskimos or the Aranda of Central Australia. Even among civilized peoples, isolation brings cultural stability. The most "backward" American groups have, at least until recently, been found in the inaccessible hills and valleys of the Appalachians [Sherman and Henry, 1933].

Leyburn [1935] has shown how European groups who migrated to remote, isolated frontiers often retained many elements of their native culture long after they had been discarded by their parent society. Thus by the nineteenth century, the social life of the Boers in the Transvaal resembled the life of the late seventeenth-century Dutch more than that of their contemporaries in the Netherlands. Isolation invariably retards social change.

Structure of society   The structure of a society affects its rate of change in subtle and not immedi-
and culture   ately apparent ways. A society which vests great authority in the very old people, as classical China did for centuries, is likely to be conservative and stable. A society which stresses conformity and trains the individual to be highly responsive to the group, such as the Zuñi, is less receptive to change than a society like the Ileo who are highly individualistic and tolerate considerable cultural variability [Ottenberg, 1959]. When a culture is very highly inte-

grated, so that each element is tightly interwoven with all the others in a mutually interdependent system, change is difficult and costly. Among a number of Nilotic African peoples, such as the Pakot, Masai, and Kipsizis, the culture is integrated around the cattle complex. Cattle are not only a means of subsistence; they are also a necessity for bride purchase, a measure of status, and an object of intense affection [Schneider, 1959]. Such a system is strongly resistant to social change. But when the culture is less highly integrated, so that work, play, family, religion, and other activities are less dependent upon one another, change is easier and more frequent. A tightly structured society, wherein every person's roles, duties, privileges, and obligations are precisely and rigidly defined, is less given to changes than a more loosely structured society wherein roles, lines of authority, privileges, and obligations are more open to individual rearrangement.

The structure of American society is highly conducive to social change. Our individualism, our lack of rigid social stratification, our relatively high proportion of achieved statuses, and our institutionalization of research all encourage rapid social change. Today tens of thousands of workers are systematically employed in finding new discoveries and inventions. This exploration is something new in the world's history. Our dazzling and sometimes upsetting rate of change is one consequence.

Attitudes and values To us change seems normal, and most Westerners pride themselves upon being progressive and up to date. By contrast, the Trobriand Islanders off the coast of New Guinea have no concept of change, and do not even have any words in their language to express or describe change [Lee, 1959a, pp. 89–104]. When Westerners tried to explain the concept of change, the Islanders could not understand what they were talking about. Societies obviously differ greatly in their general attitude toward change. A people who revere the past, worship their ancestors, honor and obey their elders, and are preoccupied with traditions and rituals will change slowly and unwillingly. When a culture has been relatively static for a long time, the people are likely to assume that it should remain so indefinitely. They are intensely and unconsciously ethnocentric; they assume that their customs and techniques are correct and everlasting. A possible change is unlikely even to be seriously considered. Change, then, occurs mainly when it is too gradual to be noticed.

A changing society has a different attitude toward change, and this attitude is both cause and effect of the changes already taking place. Changing societies are aware of social change. They are somewhat skeptical and critical of some parts of their traditional culture and will consider and experiment with innovations. Such attitudes powerfully stimulate the proposal and acceptance of changes.

Different groups within a society may show differing receptivity to change. Every changing society has its liberals and its conservatives. The Amish subculture in the United States has been notably resistant to change of every kind except, sometimes, in farming techniques. And a group may be highly receptive to change of one kind but highly resistant to changes of other kinds. Thus we can enter many churches of strikingly "modern" architecture and hear a sermon basically unchanged since the days of Luther.

Attitudes and values affect both the amount and the direction of social change. The ancient Greeks made great contributions to art and learning but little to technology. Work was done by slaves; to concern oneself with a slave's work was no proper task for a Greek scholar. No society has been equally dynamic in all aspects, and its values determine in which area—art, music, warfare, technology, philosophy, or religion—it will be inventive.

Perceived needs A society's rate and direction of change are greatly affected by the needs its members perceive. "Needs" are subjective; they are real if people feel that they are real. According to our values, half the world needs to discard ancient systems of land holding and consolidate tiny, scattered parcels into more efficient units. But unless people feel such a need, nothing changes; only the perceived needs of a society count.

Some practical inventions languish until the society discovers or develops a need for them. The zipper fastener was invented in 1891 but ignored for a quarter century. The pneumatic tire was invented and patented by Thompson in 1845 but was ignored until the popularity of the bicycle created an awareness of need for it; then it was reinvented by Dunlop in 1888.

It is often stated that changing conditions create new needs—genuine, objective needs, not just subjectively "felt" needs. Thus, urbanization created a need for sanitary engineering; the modern factory system created a need for labor unions; and the high-speed automobile created a need for superhighways. The concept of cultural lag implies that changes in one part of the culture create a need for adaptive changes in related parts of the culture.

It is doubtless true that failure to recognize an objective need may have unpleasant consequences. For centuries, sickness and death was the price of man's failure to recognize that urban growth made sanitary engineering a necessity. A more recent failure to recognize that death control creates a need for birth control has brought half the world to the brink of starvation. All this does not alter the fact that it is only those "needs" which are perceived as necessary which stimulate innovation and social change.

Necessity, however, is no guarantee that the needed invention or discovery will be made. At present, we need a cure for cancer, a reliable missile defense, and an effctive protection against radioactivity. There is no certainty that we shall develop any of these. Necessity may be the mother of invention, but invention also needs a father—a cultural base to provide the necessary supporting knowledge and technique.

The cultural base The cave man could make exceedingly few material inventions, for he had very little to work with. Even the bow and arrow combines a number of inventions and techniques—notching the bow ends, tying the bowstring, hafting and pointing the arrow, plus the idea and technique of shooting it. Not until these components were invented was it possible to invent the bow and arrow. By the *cultural base*, we mean *the accumulation of knowledge and technique* available to the inventor. As the cultural base grows, an increasing number of inventions and discoveries become possible. The invention of the geared wheel provided a component which has been used in hundreds of inventions. The discovery of electromagnetism and the invention of the vacuum tube provided necessary components for hundreds of more recent inventions.

It is highly probable that imaginative persons will put these items together.

Unless the cultural base provides the necessary preceding inventions and discoveries, an invention cannot be completed. Leonardo da Vinci in the late fifteenth century sketched many machines which were entirely workable in principle and detail, but the technology of his day was incapable of building them. His drawings for the aerial bomb, hydraulic pump, air-conditioning unit, helicopter, machine gun, military tank, and many others were clear and workable, but the fifteenth century lacked the advanced metals, the fuels, the lubricants, and the technical skills necessary to carry his brilliant ideas into practical reality. Many inventive ideas have had to wait until the supporting gaps in knowledge and technique were filled in.

When all the supporting knowledge has been developed, the appearance of an invention or discovery becomes almost a certainty. In fact, it is quite common for an invention or discovery to be made independently by several persons at about the same time. Ogburn [1950, pp. 90–102], a sociologist who specialized in the study of social change, listed 148 such inventions and discoveries, ranging from the discovery of sun spots, independently discovered by Galileo, Fabricius, Scheiner, and Harriott, all in 1611, to the invention of the airplane by Langley (1893–1897), Wright (1895–1901), and perhaps others. In fact, disputes over who was first with an invention or a scientific discovery are common and sometimes acrimonious [Merton, 1957c]. When the cultural base provides all the supporting items of knowledge, it is very probable that one or more imaginative persons will put these items together for a new invention or discovery.

The great importance of the cultural base is seen in the principle of *cross-fertilization* and the *exponential principle.* By cross-fertilization we mean that discoveries and inventions in one field became useful in an entirely different field. Pasteur's germ theory of disease grew out of his efforts to tell France's vintners why their wine turned sour. The vacuum tube, and later the transistor, developed for radio, made possible the electronic computer, which now aids research in nearly everything from astronomy to zoology. Certain radioactive materials, by-products of the search for more deadly weapons, are now invaluable in medical diagnosis, therapy, and research. We cannot predict in what remote fields of knowledge a new discovery or invention may prove useful.

The exponential principle simply states that as the cultural base grows, its possible uses tend to grow in a geometric ratio. To illustrate: If we have only two chemicals in a laboratory, only one combination (of two or more) is possible; with three chemicals, four combinations are possible (A-B-C, A-B, A-C, and B-C); with four chemicals, ten combinations; with five chemicals, twenty-five, and so on. As the size of the cultural base grows by addition, the possible combinations of these elements grow by multiplication. This helps to explain today's high rate of discovery and invention. A vast accumulation of scientific technical knowledge is shared by all the civilized societies, and from this base new inventions and discoveries flow in a rising tide.

RESISTANCE TO AND ACCEPTANCE OF SOCIAL CHANGE

Not all proposed innovations are accepted by the society. A process of *selective acceptance* operates as some innovations are accepted instantly and some only after long delay; some are rejected entirely; and others are accepted in part. Thus we accepted completely the Indian's corn, accepted and modified his tobacco, accepted in a very small, highly modified way his totemic clans (Boy Scout "beaver" and "wolverine" patrols), and totally rejected his religion. Acceptance of innovations is never automatic and is always selective according to a number of considerations.

Specific attitudes and values   Aside from its general attitude toward change, each society has many specific attitudes and values which cling to its objects and activities. When government agents introduced hybrid corn to the Spanish American farmers of the Rio Grande Valley a few years ago, they readily adopted it because of its superior yield; but within three years, they had all returned to the old corn. They didn't like the hybrid corn because it didn't make good tortillas [Apodaca, 1952]. People's established likes and dislikes are important factors in social change.

If an object has a purely utilitarian value—that is, if it is valued because of what it will *do*—change may be accepted quite readily. Thus a recent study [Fliegel and Kivlin, 1966] of the acceptance of new farm practices by American farmers finds that those which are perceived as most profitable and least risky are most readily accepted. If something is valued intrinsically—valued for itself, aside from what it will do—change is less readily accepted. To the American farmer, cattle are a source of income, to be bred, culled, and butchered whenever most profitable. But to many of the Nilotic peoples of Africa, cattle represent intrinsic values. The owner recognizes and loves each cow. To slaughter one would be like killing one of the family. A Pakot with a hundred cattle is rich and respected; one with only a dozen is poor; while the man with no cattle is ignored as though he were dead. Efforts of colonial officials to get such peoples to manage their herds "rationally"—to cull their herds, breed only the best, and stop overgrazing their lands—have generally failed.

The average American, who usually takes a coldly rational, thoroughly unsentimental view of economic activities, finds it hard to appreciate the sentiments and values of non-Western peoples. He is irritated by the Biaga of Central India, who refused to give up their primitive digging sticks for the far superior moldboard plow. Why? The Biaga loved the earth as a kindly and generous mother; they would gently help her with the digging stick to bring forth her yield, but could not bring themselves to cut her "with knives" [Elwin, 1939, pp. 106–107]. The American is annoyed by the Ettwah Indians' unwillingness to adopt green manuring (plowing under a crop of green sanhemp as fertilizer). But to this Indian, "green manuring involves a very cruel act of plowing under the sanhemp leaf and stalk before they are ripe. This act involves violence." [Mayer, 1958, p. 209.] Yet is there any basic difference between these illustrations and an American's refusal to eat horse meat because it conflicts with his values? What is the basic difference between the Cambodian farmer who rejects fertilizer because it is an interference with nature and the many Americans who reject contraception because it is an interference with nature? How about those American groups who reject divorce, or alcoholic beverages, or movies, or card playing because these would conflict with their values? To each of us, it seems entirely logical and right to reject any innovation that conflicts with our mores or values; when another group does likewise, their refusal often impresses us as stubborn ignorance. Such is ethnocentrism!

Demonstrability of innovations An innovation is most quickly accepted when its usefulness can be easily demonstrated. The American Indians eagerly accepted the white man's gun, but still have not fully accepted the white man's medicine, whose superiority is less easily demonstrated. Many inventions are so inefficient in their earlier stages that general acceptance is delayed until they are perfected. During the automobile's first three decades of development, public scorn was expressed by the derisive advice to "get a horse!" Early imperfections delay, but rarely prevent, the eventual acceptance of workable inventions.

Some innovations can be demonstrated quite easily, on a small scale; others cannot be demonstrated without costly, large-scale trials. Most mechanical inventions can usually be tested in a few hours or days, and at modest cost. Most social inventions such as universal suffrage, free love, or world government are not easily tried out in the laboratory or testing bureau. Many social inventions can be tested only through a long-term trial, involving at least an entire society. We hesitate to adopt an innovation until we have been shown how it works; yet we can determine the practical value of most social inventions only by adopting them. This dilemma slows their acceptance.

Compatibility with existing culture Innovations are most readily accepted when they fit in nicely with the existing culture. The horse fitted easily into the hunting culture of the Apache, as it enabled them to do better what they were already doing. Not all innovations mesh so well. Innovations may be incompatible with the existing culture in at least three ways.

First, *the innovation may conflict with existing patterns.* In some parts of Asia and Africa, Islam now appears to be spreading faster than Christianity, perhaps because Christianity conflicts with native polygamy while Islam does not. We have already pointed out how it would be difficult for American society to institutionalize premarital sex experience. Not only does it conflict with some of our mores and sentiments; it also conflicts with our family structure and our property institutions, neither of which makes any very satisfactory provision for children born out of wedlock.

When an innovation conflicts with existing culture patterns, there are at least three possible outcomes: (1) It may be rejected, just as most Americans have rejected communism; (2) it may be accepted, and the conflicting cultural traits may be adjusted to it, as we have altered our child-labor practices to permit compulsory public education; (3) it may be accepted and its conflict with the existing culture may be concealed and evaded by rationalization, as in those areas (including France and five of the United States) where contraceptives are freely sold for "prevention of disease," in spite of the fact that their sale is forbidden by law. While not always decisive, conflict with the existing culture discourages acceptance of an innovation.

Second, *the innovation may call for new patterns not present in the culture.* The American Indians had no patterns of animal husbandry into which the cow could be fitted. When they were first given cows by government agents, they hunted them as game animals. A society generally tries to use an innovation in old, familiar ways. When this fails, the society must develop new ways of making effective use of the new element. Thus we have disguised each new building material to make it look like an old, familiar material. Early concrete blocks were faced like rough-finished stone; asphalt and asbestos shingles were finished to look like brick or wood; aluminum siding is still made to look like wood. Then, after some years, each of these materials begins to be used in designs and ways which make full use of its own properties and possibilities. Most innovations call for some new patterns in the culture, and it takes time to develop them.

Third, *some innovations are substitutive, not additive,* and these are less readily accepted. It is easier to accept innovations which can be added to the culture without requiring the immediate discard of some familiar trait complex. American baseball, jazz, and the "western" movie have been diffused throughout most of the world. Each could be added to almost any kind of culture without requiring the surrender of any native traits. But the approximate equality of the sexes, democracy, and rational business enterprise have been diffused more slowly; each requires the surrender of traditional values and practices. Wherever the nature of the choice is such that one cannot have *both* the new and the old, the acceptance of the new is usually delayed.

Costs of change

Change is nearly always costly. Not only does change disrupt the existing culture and destroy cherished sentiments and values, but it also involves some specific costs.

Technical difficulties of change   Very few innovations can simply be added to the existing culture; most innovations require some modification of the existing culture. England's monetary system (pence, shillings, and pounds) is a clumsy nuisance as compared with a decimal monetary system like ours, while the American system of weights and measures is clearly inferior to the European metric system. Why have such clumsy systems been retained for so long? Because the changeover is so difficult. England's switch to a decimal currency in 1967 proved to be far more complicated than simply learning a new system. Changes in cash registers, coin machines, bookkeeping records, standardized merchandise sizes, and arguments over pound fractions were all involved. Learning the metric system would be very simple, but the task of making and stocking everything from window frames to nuts and bolts in both size ranges for a half century or so is overwhelming. Railroads would be more efficient if the tracks were a foot or two farther apart to permit wider cars; but the cost of rebuilding the tracks and replacing the rolling stock is prohibitive. Our city streets are far too narrow for today's traffic, but street widening is unbearably costly after the streets are lined with skyscrapers. New inventions and improved machines often make present machinery obsolete and destroy the market for technical skills which workmen have spent years in developing.

Vested interests and social change   The costs of social change are never evenly distributed. The industry which is made obsolete and the workmen whose skill is made unmarketable are forced to bear the costs of technical progress, while others enjoy the improved products. Those to whom the *status* *quo* is profitable are said to have a *vested interest*. Communities with an army post or navy yard nearby find that all this government money is good for business, so these communities have a vested interest in retaining these military establishments. Students attending state universities have a vested interest in tax-supported higher education. Nearly everyone has some vested interests— from the rich with their tax-exempt bonds to the poor with their welfare checks.

Most social changes carry a threat, real or imaginary, to some vested interests who then oppose these changes. Examples are almost endless. In 1579 the Council of Danzig, acting in response to pressure from weavers, ordered the strangulation of the inventor of an improved weaving machine; and the spinsters of Blackburn, England, invaded Hargreaves's home to destroy his spinning jennies [Stern, 1937]. The early railroads were opposed by landowners who didn't want their lands cut up, and by canal owners and toll-road companies; and then in turn the railroads became vigorous opponents of the automobile and helped to block construction of the St. Lawrence Seaway. In 1922, the major automobile manufacturers launched a massive advertising campaign against four-wheel brakes, claiming that they would injure passengers, damage tires, and cause cars to overturn. Employer opposition to the organization of labor unions was long and bitter, and still continues in the Deep South and on the factory farms of the Southwest [Bendiner, 1961], while many unions resort to "featherbedding" in the effort to retain jobs made unnecessary by technical change. The radio industry bottled up FM radio as long as possible, and more recently the television industry and the motion-picture-theatre operators have done their best to block pay television. Each group is an ardent advocate of progress in general, but seldom at the expense of its own vested interests.

Vested interests, however, appear as promoters of change whenever they believe the proposed change will be profitable to them. American corporations spend billions of dollars each year to develop new products which they can sell profitably. Many business groups in the Great Lakes area energetically supported the St. Lawrence Seaway proposal. Such government enterprises are normally denounced as socialism by vested interests which are not enriched thereby, while those vested interests whom the proposal benefits will find other terms to describe it. (Apparently, *socialism* operates when the government spends money to benefit *you*, not me!) Business interests have sought and obtained many kinds of government regulation and "interference" when it seemed in their interest to do so. Labor unions have been most eloquent supporters of laws to limit child labor. The great Chicago fire of 1871 showed the weakness of competing private fire-fighting companies, and, more important, imposed such heavy losses upon fire insurance companies that they threw their support behind the proposal for tax-supported municipal fire departments. Many social reforms have finally been secured, after long agitation, because powerful vested interests came to redefine their interests and decided that the reform would benefit them.

Role of the change agent   Who proposes a change and how does he go about it? The identity of the originator greatly affects acceptance or rejection. Any proposal of the Communist Party in the United States is doomed to certain defeat. Opponents of all sorts of proposals often label them Communist in order to defeat them. Innovations which are first adopted by persons at the top of the prestige scale and power system are likely to filter downward quite rapidly; those first adopted by low-status persons are likely to percolate upward more slowly, if at all.

Successful change agents often seek to make the change appear innocuous by identifying it with familiar cultural elements. King Ibn Saud introduced radio and telephone to Saudi Arabia by quoting the Koran over them. Franklin D. Roosevelt's leadership rested partly upon his ability to describe significant reforms in terms of homespun American sentiments and values.

The change agent must know the culture in which he works. When American officials sought to combat communism through posters contrasting pictures of great religious leaders with those of Communist leaders, the campaign failed among the Moslem Indonesians, who felt it irreverent and offensive to display a picture of Mohammed. Government attempts to settle Navajo Indians as individual families on irrigated land were unsuccessful, for the Navajo were accustomed to work land cooperatively along extended kinship lines. An amusing illustration of how ignorance and ethnocentrism handicapped a change agent is found in Micronesia, where an American labor relations expert sought to recruit Palauan workers for a mining operation. He first demanded to see the "chief"—a request which posed a problem since they had no chief in their social structure. Finally they produced a person with whom the American expert sought to establish rapport by throwing an arm around his shoulders and laughingly tousling his hair. In Palauan culture this was an indignity roughly equivalent, in our culture, to opening a man's fly in public [Useem, 1952]. Needless to add, this expert was not very successful.

Sometimes a change agent succeeds in promoting a change, only to find that the results are an unhappy surprise. In one South African area the Western workers noticed that the native mothers were exhausted by nursing their babies for two years; they successfully introduced bottle feeding. The innovation had the effect of evading the native taboo upon sexual relations during lactation, so that instead of bearing a child every three or four years, the women now bore a child every year or so, and were more exhausted than ever [Lee, 1959b]. Change agents must thoroughly understand the interrelations of the culture if they are to be able to predict the consequences of a particular change. At this moment, when thousands of American representatives are functioning as change agents in nearly every underdeveloped country of the world, we might remind ourselves of the necessity for change agents to be observant students of the society they wish to help, if they are to avoid unhappy consequences.

The efforts of the change agent are not always appreciated. The inventor is often ridiculed; the missionary may be eaten; and the agitator or reformer is usually persecuted. Radicals are likely to be popular only after they are dead, and organizations (like the Daughters of the American Revolution) dedicated to the memory of dead revolutionists have no fondness for live ones. Those who are seeking to change the segregated racial patterns of the American South may become heroes tomorrow, but they must be prepared to face jail and physical violence today. The recent record of a prominent Negro minister is revealing:

Christmas, 1956, Shuttleworth home bombed and completely demolished; winter 1957, Bethel Baptist Church dynamited by racists; late 1957, Shuttleworth and

wife mobbed, beaten, and stabbed; jailed eight times—four times during the Freedom Rides; sued for three million dollars by state officials of Alabama; automobile and personal property sold at public auction; driver's license revoked for a whole year; three Shuttleworth children illegally arrested and beaten in Gadsden (Alabama) . . . is currently involved in twenty-seven criminal and civil actions.
SCLC Newsletter (Southern Christian Leadership Conference), September, 1961.

Change agents are often hated and despised, especially when they attack attitudes and values which other people cherish.

The deviant as change agent   Many change agents are deviants of some sort. The nonconformist may unwittingly launch a new fashion, speech form, or dance step. Inventors are people who love to tinker; they are more excited by the challenge of a new idea than by the possibility of riches [Barnett, 1953, pp. 150–156]. Social reformers are necessarily people who are disenchanted with some aspect of the *status quo*. Without deviants, there would be many fewer social changes.

SOCIAL AND PERSONAL DISORGANIZATION

Social effects of discovery and invention   No social change leaves the rest of the culture entirely unaffected. Even an "additive" innovation draws time and interest away from other elements of the culture. Some innovations are shattering in their impact. When the missionaries passed out steel axes to the Yir Yoront of Australia, the gift appeared to be an innocuous gesture, but the stone ax was so tightly integrated into the culture that a chain reaction of disruption spread through the social structure [Sharp, 1952]. The stone ax was a symbol of adult masculinity. It might be lent to women and to youths, and the lines of ax borrowing were very important features of the social organization. When superior steel axes were passed out indiscriminately, and owned by women and youths, the symbol of authority was so undermined that authority itself became clouded, relations were confused, and reciprocal obligations became uncertain. The stone for the axes was quarried far to the south, and traded northward along trade routes through an established system of trading partners, who also shared in important ceremonials. With the substitution of the steel ax, trading relationships languished, and this rich ceremonial sharing was lost. Deep and serious disturbance of Yir Yoront culture is traced to the single innovation of the steel ax. The illustration is dramatic; but have the effects of the automobile or the radio upon American culture been less far-reaching? Ogburn [1933, pp. 153–156] has compiled a list of 150 social changes which he attributes to the radio; and television has brought still more.

Ogburn distinguishes three forms of the social effects of invention. (1) *Dispersion, or the multiple effects of a single mechanical invention,* is illustrated by the many effects of the radio, or by the automobile, which shortens travel time, supports a huge manufacturing and servicing industry, provides a market for vast quantities of gasoline and oil, steel, glass, leather, and other materials, requires a massive road-building program, alters courtship and recreational behavior, promotes suburbs and shopping centers, and has many other consequences. (2) *Succession, or the derivative social effects of a single invention,* means that an invention produces changes, which in turn produce further changes, and so on. The invention of the cotton gin (*a*) simplified cotton processing and made cotton more profitable; this result (*b*) encouraged the planting of more cotton; and the planting (*c*) required more slaves; the increase in slavery and growing Southern dependence upon cotton export (*d*) helped to provoke the Civil War, which (*e*) greatly stimulated the growth of large-scale industry and business monopoly; these in turn (*f*) encouraged antitrust laws and labor unions; and the chain still continues. While these developments were not entirely due to the cotton gin, it helped to produce them all. (3) *Convergence, or the coming together of several influences of different inventions,* may be variously illustrated. The six-shooter, barbed-wire fencing, and the windmill facilitated the settlement of the great American plains. The automobile, the electric pump, and the septic tank made the modern suburb possible. Nuclear warheads, intercontinental missiles, and radar detection systems have, in the opinion of many military theorists, made total war obsolete.

Much has been written about the social effects of invention. It does not matter whether the new trait has been invented within the society or diffused into it; the social effects are equally great from either method. Explosives, invented by the Chinese and used only for fireworks, were diffused to the West and led to the invention of firearms. Guns "made all men the same size" and ended the power advantage of the horsed knight in armor; cannons ended the relative impregnability of the medieval castle and strengthened the king at the expense of the provincial nobility. A diffused trait often finds a society quite unable to cope with it successfully. For example, primitive societies which brew their own alcoholic beverages generally have cultural controls over its use, but primitive societies which have received alcohol from white men have had no such controls, and the effects have been generally devastating [Horton, 1943]. To cite one instance, the Eskimo of St. Lawrence Island, when first introduced to alcohol, promptly went on a month-long drunk and missed the annual walrus migration; the following winter most of them died of starvation [Nelson, 1899]. Innovations, whether invented or diffused, can be equally disruptive.

Unequal rates of change   Since a culture is interrelated, changes in one aspect of the culture invariably affect other aspects of the culture. Eventually the affected traits will be adapted to this change, but only after some time has passed. This time interval between the arrival of a change and the completion of the adaptations it prompts is called *cultural lag,* a concept developed by Ogburn [1922, pp. 200–213]. As an illustration, he pointed out that about 1870, workers in large numbers began entering factories where they were often injured in unavoidable accidents. But not until another half century had passed did most states get around to enacting Workmen's Compensation laws. In this instance, the cultural lag was about fifty years.

A cultural lag exists wherever any aspect of the culture lags behind another aspect to which it is related. Probably the most pervasive form of cultural lag in present Western societies is the lag of institutions behind changing technology. For example, in most states the size of a county was based upon the distance one could travel to the county seat and return in the same day; despite improved transportation, the county unit still remains at its old size, inefficient for many of its functions. The metropolitan city sprawls over a hodgepodge of many different state, county, city, and township units, so that efficient area planning, government, and law enforcement become an im-possibility. At least a half century ago, advancing technology had tied the civilized world into an interdependent whole; but it took a second world war to jolt the United States out of its complacent isolationism. For a full century, urbanization and industrialization were destroying the possibility for the indi-vidual worker to ensure the security of his family by depending upon himself, his relatives, and his neighbors; yet only after the Great Depression of the 1930s dramatized this fact did we establish social security, unemployment insurance, and other welfare measures.

Some cultural lags involve the lag of one part of the material culture behind a related part of the material culture. A quarter century after cars are built to cruise at high speeds, we get started on a superhighway system. Most air-ports are too small to accommodate the latest types of aircraft. For a quarter century after we replaced the horse with the automobile, we continued to build the garage out behind the house, back where the smelly stables used to go. Sometimes the material culture lags behind changes in the nonmaterial culture. For example, educational research has long since discovered that movable classroom furniture aids in organizing learning activities; yet thousands of classrooms still have inflexible rows of desks screwed to the floor. Finally, one aspect of the nonmaterial culture may lag behind other related aspects of nonmaterial culture. For example, millions of dollars are spent on quack practitioners and patent medicines which medical science has repeatedly shown to be useless, while dozens of communities reject measures like fluoridation which science has shown to be effective and harmless.

The concept of cultural lag applies to differing rates of change *within* a society, not to rates of change between societies. It describes the disharmony between related parts of a single culture, produced through unequal rates of change. Cultural lags are most numerous in a rapidly changing culture. They are symptoms, not of a backward society, but of a highly dynamic and increasingly complex society. But even if all people were wise, objective, and adaptable, they would still need some time to discover what adaptations a new change would require, and more time to work out and complete those adaptations. Most of us, however, are pretty ignorant about matters outside our specialty, are prejudiced and swayed by vested interests, and are not nearly so adaptable as we like to imagine. Cultural lags are numerous and persistent.

Social change and social problems   A social problem is a condition which many people consider undesirable and want to correct. A perfectly integrated society would have no social problems, for all institutions and behavior would be neatly harmonized and defined as acceptable by the values of the society. A changing society inevitably develops problems. Either conditions themselves change and become unacceptable (population growth, soil erosion, and deforestation create a conservation problem), or the society's changing values define an old condition as no longer tolerable (child labor, poverty, or lack of education). Social problems are part of the price of social change. The detailed analysis of social problems, however, belongs in another textbook and another course.

Social and As has been repeatedly suggested in this chapter, all new elements disrupt
personal the existing culture to some extent. If a culture is well organized, with all
disorganization its traits and institutions fitting closely together, change in any one of them will disorganize this arrangement.

When a culture becomes highly disorganized, the people's sense of security, morale, and purpose in life is damaged. When people are confused and uncertain, so that their behavior is also inconsistent, hesitant, and contradictory, they are described as *personally disorganized*. If their disorganization proceeds until they lose their sense of purpose in life and become resigned and apathetic, we describe them as *demoralized*. They have lost their morale, and often their behavior controls are lost as well. A demoralized people is likely to suffer population decline, through a lowered birth rate, a higher death rate, or both. The capacity of a thoroughly demoralized people simply to die out has attracted the attention of a number of anthropologists [Rivers, 1922; Maher, 1961].

The extermination of the buffalo had such effects upon the American Indians of the Great Plains [Wissler, 1938; Lesser, 1933; Sandoz, 1954, chap. 15]. The buffalo provided food, clothing, and shelter; in all, over fifty separate parts of the buffalo carcass were used by the Indians. The buffalo hunt provided the principal object of the Indian's religious ceremonials, the goal of his maturing, and a road to status and recognition. His other avenue to status —warfare—was also dependent upon an ample supply of dried buffalo meat. When the government exterminated the buffalo in order to pacify the Indians, it demoralized them as well. The integrating and status-giving functions of the war party and the buffalo hunt were lost. Religious ceremonials were now empty and meaningless. The hunting economy was totally destroyed, and the Indians lived, and sometimes starved, on government handouts. The traditional goals and values which gave zest and meaning to life were now unavailable, and to substitute the white man's goals and values was an almost impossible task of learning. In the few instances where Indians did successfully adopt the white man's economy, this, too, was soon destroyed by the white man's hunger for the Indians' land [Collier, 1947, pp. 199–219; Foreman, 1932]. Suffering from the destruction of their own culture, denied access to the white man's culture, ravaged by the white man's diseases, and corrupted by his alcohol, many Indian tribes became deeply demoralized. Depopulation was almost universal, and only in recent decades has Indian population begun to rebuild. This story of devastatingly disruptive social change, disorganization of the culture, and personal disorganization and demoralization of the people has been repeated hundreds of times in the world's history.

Not all native peoples, however, have been demoralized by their contacts with Western societies. The Palauans of Micronesia have worked out an interdependent blend of traditional culture and Western commercialism. They happily drive trucks and pound typewriters to earn money to buy the traditional clan gifts, and use motor launches to carry their sweet potatoes to traditional festivals [Mead, 1955, p. 128]. Whether change disrupts a society to the point of demoralization depends upon the nature of the changes, the way they are introduced, and the structure of the society upon which they impinge.

Is change least painful when it comes slowly? Not necessarily. Since culture involves interrelations, it is generally easier to accept a cluster of related changes than to accept them one at a time. For example, if a primitive people acquires cotton clothes without soap, then filth and disease are predictable; if given clothes without irons and sewing machines, then they will be clothed in tatters. With mud floors to sit upon, and no place to store clothing and these other artifacts, filth and clutter are a certainty. But if all these elements —clothes, soap, irons, sewing machines, and floored houses with shelves and closets—are adopted together within a single generation, these changes can be made far more easily than if they are spaced over several generations.

Western cultural diffusion generally converts the native village into a depressing slum, not because the people adopt too many new traits but because they adopt too few. It may even be psychologically easier to make a lot of changes than a few. As Margaret Mead [1956, pp. 445–446] has observed, "A people who choose to practice a new technology or enter into drastically new kinds of economic relationships will do this more easily if they live in different houses, wear different clothes and eat different, or differently cooked, food." Much of the social disorganization which accompanies social change stems from the fact that a people who are willing to adopt new trait complexes are blocked from doing so. Sometimes they are blocked by their own limited resources and sometimes by the unwillingness of the dominant whites to admit them into full participation in Western civilization. The Mau Mau terrorism in Kenya was largely attributable to the frustration of the Kikuyu's intense desire to share in Western civilization [Bascom and Herskowitz (eds.), (1959), p. 4].

We need, therefore, to revise the notion that slow change is necessarily more comfortable than rapid change. In some situations, the rapid wholesale change of a way of life may be infinitely less disturbing than piecemeal changes, as Mead [1956, chap. 18] has shown in her study of the Manus, who have moved from the Stone Age into Western civilization in a single generation. The reason may be that slow change allows cultural lags to accumulate, not to be corrected until they become painful. Rapid change may actually produce fewer lags, because many of the related items of the culture may be changed at the same time.

Change has come with dazzling speed upon contemporary Western societies. Within a few short generations, the Western peoples have shifted from life in rural, agricultural, folk societies to life in an immensely complex urban, industrial, impersonal mass society. Are contemporary Western societies disorganized? Certainly! Cultural lags are numerous at every point. The school strains constantly to prepare children for a society which changes even before they become adult. The church carries a doctrine stated largely in the language and context of an agricultural society; much of it is irrelevant to the needs and problems of our impersonal, secondary-group world; yet the effort to restate its message in modern terms has riven the church into warring factions. A century ago husband and wife could each assume a quite clearly

Children in our society are socialized to anticipate and appreciate change.

defined role; today no bride can be at all sure what she will be expected to be and do in her marriage. Every level of government is struggling with tasks which few of our grandfathers would have guessed it would ever assume. Disputes over the privileges and responsibilities of corporations, unions, and other economic groups now occupy the center of the political arena. In this impersonal urban world of ours, although the traditional informal controls of the folk society are failing to regulate the behavior of individuals, we are still hunting for effective substitutes.

These are symptoms of social disorganization—failure of traditional controls, role confusions and uncertainties, conflicting moral codes, experimentation and change in institutional behavior. In such a disorganized society, people are affected. Many fail to internalize a coherent system of values and behavior controls. A smaller number become seriously disorganized, and grow so erratic and contradictory in behavior that they are diagnosed as mentally ill and in need of psychotherapy.

If our society is so badly disorganized, why are we not all mentally ill? Despite our accelerating rate of social change during the past century, we find no conclusive evidence that the amount of mental illness has significantly increased [Goldhamer and Marshall, 1953]. True, mental-hospital patients have multiplied, but this proves only that more persons receive hospital treatment, not that more are ill. The answer may be that a changing society may be able to develop personalities that are more adaptable to social change [Mead, 1947]. Children in our society are socialized to anticipate and appreciate change. The strain of change may be considerably reduced by a socialization which seeks to prepare persons to adapt themselves. Since adult roles are uncertain, we seek to socialize and educate children to function successfully in several roles, not just in one. Finally, we have developed social case work and psychiatry for persons who cannot work out an effective life pattern by themselves. All over the world today, the rate of social change is accelerating. Whether man can adapt himself as rapidly as his social life is changing is still a moot question.

The organization-disorganization-reorganization cycle What eventually happens to a society disorganized by social change? Some primitive societies died out, but most larger societies eventually succeed in reorganizing their culture to accommodate the social changes. The horse disorganized the Plains Indians' cultures; but very quickly the people adapted their culture to the changes the horse made possible. They developed new skills of caring for horses and making gear, developed a status system around horse ownership, and greatly increased their class distinctions. The Sioux and the Comanche changed from sedentary agriculturalists to nomadic hunters in a very dramatic example of a rapid and successful integration of a new culture complex. The hunting tribes like the Crow, Blackfeet, and Apache were able to hunt buffalo more effectively than before and transport a larger supply of preserved food. Their warfare became more mobile and more lethal. They developed an elaborate horse complex including at least 119 items [Ewers, 1955], and the richness and comfort of their lives was greatly increased.

The United States is now well into the process of reorganizing its culture to integrate the automobile. Garages are now attached to our houses. High-speed highway networks are under construction. Parking facilities are now planned and provided along with new public buildings. The layout of cities and suburbs and the location of schools and shopping areas are increasingly reflecting our dependence upon the automobile. Most of these developments have gained momentum only within the past decade—one-third of a century after the automobile became common—another instance of cultural lag.

When social changes arrive slowly, there is time to integrate one change before the next arrives. Today, however, all the major societies of the world and most of the minor societies are changing at a breakneck pace. Before one change can be integrated, a dozen more have arrived. *Change has now become the norm.* The static, integrated society which sociologists used to pose as a model, as a starting point for analysis, is only an intellectual construct, not a concrete reality. Used in this way—as a starting point for study—the model of the static society has some intellectual usefulness. But we must remember that, except for a few isolated bands of primitives, all societies are changing rapidly and that change is now the norm all over the world. Disorganization and reorganization are a continuous process all over the world. All major societies are in a race to see whether adaptive reorganization can proceed fast enough to avoid the accumulation of intolerable lags and irreconcilable social tensions.

SOCIAL PLANNING: CAN CHANGE BE DIRECTED?

It is possible to control and direct social changes so that they will be less painful and costly? Social scientists disagree. Some feel that social change is caused by social forces beyond man's effective control. For example, when the necessary supporting knowledge is developed, an invention will be made by someone, even if this invention is most troublesome to man. The atom bomb is an example. Although we fear it may destroy us, we go on advancing it because others will do so anyway. Could the Indian wars possibly have been avoided? The Indians had land we needed for our growing population, and our advance was certain to destroy the Indian's way of life. The many unnecessary brutal episodes were merely the symptoms, not the cause, of a conflict which was unavoidable, given these groups with their respective needs and cultural backgrounds. Practically any great social change can be thus described in terms of blind social forces, so that we conclude that what *did* happen was about the only thing that *could* happen in that situation.

Some other social scientists think that we can exert *some* influence over the course of social change. They believe that some degree of social planning is possible. *Social planning* is defined [Himes, 1954, p. 18] as "a conscious interactional process combining investigation, discussion, agreement, and action in order to achieve those conditions, relationships, and values that are regarded as desirable." More simply, social planning is an attempt at the intelligent direction of social change [Adams, 1950; Riemer, 1947]. Advocates point out that social planning is an old American tradition. When the framers of our Constitution rejected primogeniture (the European provision that the lands pass intact to the eldest son) and entail (the provision that prevents him from selling them), these American planners were seeking to construct a society of small, landowning farmers instead of a society of landed estates. This purpose was reinforced by the Homestead Act of 1862, which gave public lands in small parcels to individual farmers instead of selling it in large blocks to the highest bidders. Zoning ordinances, building codes, public education, and compulsory school-attendance laws are examples of social planning. Nearly every city now has its city-planning commission, and regional-planning commissions are a next step that many are advocating.

A critic of planning would contend that such planning efforts do not really change anything, but are merely a slightly more orderly way of carrying out changes that are inevitable anyway. The comment perhaps sums up the matter. Certainly, no social planning will prevent or reverse a change which present knowledge and long-time trends are creating. There is, for example, no way of returning to the "simple life," nor is it possible by planning to steer social change in a direction contrary to most people's wishes and values. The major social changes are probably uncontrollable, but social planning may be able to reduce the delays and costs of integrating them into the culture.

SUMMARY

All societies change continuously. New traits appear either through *discovery* and *invention*, or through *diffusion* from other societies.

The rate of social change varies enormously from society to society and from time to time. In rare instances, certain *geographic changes* produce great social change. More often, *migration* to a new environment brings changes in social life. *Changes in population size or composition* always produce social changes. Since *isolation* retards change and cross-cultural contacts promote change, physically or socially isolated groups show fewer changes. The *structure of the society and culture* affect change: a highly conformist, authoritarian society or a highly integrated culture is less prone to change than the individualistic, permissive society or the less highly integrated culture. A society's *attitudes and values* greatly encourage or retard change. The *perceived needs* of a people affect the speed and direction of change. Perhaps most important of all, the *cultural base* provides the foundation of knowledge and skill necessary to develop new elements; as the cultural base expands, the possibilities of new combinations multiply in an exponential manner, while knowledge in one area often cross-fertilizes other areas of development.

Not all innovations are accepted. The attitudes and values of a group determine what kind of innovations a group is likely to accept. If an innovation's usefulness can be demonstrated easily and cheaply, the proof is helpful; but many social inventions cannot be tested except through a complete acceptance. Compatible innovations are more readily accepted than those which clash with important features of the existing culture. Technical difficulties of fitting a change into the existing culture often cause great economic cost and personal inconvenience. Vested interests normally oppose change, but they occasionally discover that a proposed change is to their advantage. The change agent's ingenuity and social position affect his success in introducing changes. Unless the change agent knows the culture very well, he may fail in his efforts, because he generally miscalculates the consequences of his changes.

Social and personal disorganization are costs of social change. Discoveries and inventions, as well as diffused new traits and complexes, often set off a chain reaction of change disrupting to many aspects of the culture. The different parts of the culture, interrelated and interdependent though they are, do not change at the same rate of speed. The time interval between the appearance of a new trait and the completion of the adaptations it forces is called *cultural lag*. All rapidly changing societies have many cultural lags and are said to be somewhat disorganized. In a disorganized society, persons who may have greater difficulty in finding a comfortable behavior system, become themselves disorganized. When they lose hope of finding a rewarding way of conducting their lives and cease trying, they have become demoralized and may actually die out as a group. Changing societies are in a constant process of disorganization and reorganization since change is now the norm in all modern societies. In an effort to speed and simplify this process and reduce the costs and wastes of social change, social planning is increasingly being attempted. Social scientists are not agreed upon the degree of success to be expected from the direction of social change by social planning.

QUESTIONS AND PROJECTS

1. Why are social scientists hesitant to use the term *progress?*

2. Is knowledge of the diffusion process likely to reduce ethnocentrism?

3. Have any recent American attempts been made to prevent diffusion or to limit contacts of Americans with other cultures?

4. What are some of the change-promoting features of American society? What are some of its change-resisting features?

5. Is the rate of invention likely to continue rising, or to fall off? Why?

6. Is our fondness for European art inconsistent with our fear of certain European ideas?

7. Why will a person who insists upon the latest cars, fashions, and gadgets often be entirely satisfied with ancient social philosophies?

8. How many of those persons whom we now consider "great" were noncontroversial during their lives? How many achieved greatness by promoting changes and how many by preventing changes?

9. Is it possible for a change agent to promote a major change without arousing violent hostilities?

10. What are some recent social changes in our society which you consider undesirable? Some which you consider desirable? What values are you using in making these judgments?

11. Evaluate this statement: "The more successfully we progress, the fewer cultural lags and social problems we shall have."

12. Is our high divorce rate a symptom of social disorganization or reorganization? How about our rather widespread practice of premarital sex relations? The growing popularity of very youthful marriages?

13. If it is assumed that racial integration in the United States is desirable, would acceptance of integration be easier if we proceed slowly, step by step, or rapidly integrated all activities and services at the same time?

14. Can social planning ever change "human nature"? Must it, in order to succeed?

15. Read one of the following novels, which describe Americans operating as change agents in other societies, and explain the agents' successes or failures in that capacity: Ronald Hardy, *The Place of the Jackals;* Graham Greene, *The Quiet American;* James Ullman, *Windom's Way;* Kathryn Grondahl, *The Mango Season;* Margaret Landon, *Never Dies the Dream;* Thomas Streissguth, *Tigers in the House.*

SUGGESTED READINGS

ABRAHAMSON, JULIA: *A Neighborhood Finds Itself,* Harper & Row, Publishers, Incorporated, New York, 1959. An account of urban-renewal planning for a deteriorating Chicago neighborhood.

ADAMS, E. M.: "The Logic of Planning," *Social Forces,* 28:419–423, May, 1950. A brief outline of the principles of social planning in a democracy.

*BARNETT, H. G.: *Innovation: The Basis of Cultural Change,* McGraw-Hill Book Company, New York, 1953. An anthropologist's analysis of the development and acceptance of innovations. (03793-McGH)

*BASCOM, WILLIAM R., AND MELVILLE J. HERSKOVITS (EDS.): *Continuity and Change in African Cultures,* The University of Chicago Press, Chicago, 1959. Two essays—SIMON OTTENBERG, "Ibo Receptivity to Change" (pp. 130–143), and HAROLD K. SCHNEIDER, "Pakot Resistance to Change" (pp. 144–167)—seek to explain the opposite reactions of two societies to social change (P85-Phoen)

GILLIN, JOHN P.: *The Ways of Men,* Appleton-Century-Crofts, New York, 1948, chap. 25, "Conditions and Processes of Culture Change." A well-illustrated, systematic treatment of the factors involved in change and in its acceptance or rejection.

HIMES, JOSEPH S.: *Social Planning in America: A Dynamic Interpretation,* Doubleday & Company, Inc., Garden City, N.Y., 1954. A brief outline of principles and practices of social planning.

LEE, DOROTHY: "The Cultural Curtain," *Annals of the American Academy of Political and Social Science,* 323:120–128, May, 1959. An interesting article showing, with many illustrations, the need for change agents to understand the culture in which they promote change.

MAHER, ROBERT F.: *The New Men of Papua: A Study in Culture Change,* The University of Wisconsin Press, Madison, Wis., 1961. A primitive society, described several decades ago by anthropologists, is restudied to evaluate the impact of culture change.

*MEAD, MARGARET: *Cultural Patterns and Technical Change,* UNESCO, 1955; Mentor Books, New American Library of World Literature, Inc., New York, 1955. Studies the impact of modern technology on five traditional societies with discussion of how to proceed in bringing modern technology to traditional societies. (MT346-Ment)

*OGBURN, WILLIAM F.: *Social Change,* The Viking Press, Inc., New York, 1922. (8064-Delta-Dell)

OGBURN, WILLIAM F. (ED.): *Technology and International Relations,* The University of Chicago Press, Chicago, 1949.

OGBURN, WILLIAM F., WITH MEYER F. NIMKOFF: *Technology and The Changing Family,* Houghton Mifflin Company, Boston, 1955. The above series of books were written wholly or in part by the foremost sociological student of social change.

*SPICER, EDWARD H. (ED.): *Human Problems in Technological Change,* Russell Sage Foundation, New York, 1952. A casebook describing a number of societies where important changes were introduced, showing the process of adoption and the social consequences of these changes. (Sci Ed)

20

SOCIAL
MOVEMENTS

For a time after President Hoover took office, there were scant indications that prohibition was on the way out. Very much to the contrary, it appeared to be riding high, and the Protestant prelates who had delivered so many votes in the campaign seemed to be potent at the White House. The Anti-Saloon League and the two Methodist boards, all of which maintained offices virtually within the shadow of the Capitol, impressed observers as more powerful than ever. . . .

Despite the apparent confidence of the drys following the Hoover landslide, there were a few happenings that made them wonder. As early as 1926 both Illinois and New York had urged Congress overwhelmingly by referendum to amend the Eighteenth Amendment, Montana repealed its enforcement act, and Wisconsin voted heavily for 2.75 beer. . . . Then in 1928 Massachusetts instructed its senators to seek repeal of the Eighteenth Amendment, and Montana refused to re-enact its state dry law. The following year Wisconsin repealed its state law by a huge majority. . . . The cloud on the horizon seemed hardly bigger than the scriptural "man's hand," but it was there.

Throughout these years the cartoonists of the metropolitan press, the overwhelming bulk of which was implacably opposed to prohibition, dedicated their pens to the task of ridiculing the drys. "Prohibition" was usually depicted as a long-faced, long-nosed, cadaverous-looking individual with a battered high silk hat and a black umbrella. His facial expression was sour, if not cruel, and his demeanor repulsive. . . .

In the spring of 1930, [the Literary Digest] set out to get a cross-section of national sentiment on the dry law. When the results came in, they jarred the prohibitionists from head to toe. More than 4,800,000 ballots were returned to the Digest, and of these fewer than 1,500,000 were for retention of the Eighteenth Amendment. . . .

An agency that added much impetus to the movement was the Women's Organization for National Prohibition Reform. . . . It was an innovation to have an aggressive group of women working for elimination of the dry law, since the weight of organized womanhood had previously been thrown into the scales on the side of prohibition. . . .

Half a dozen states fell in line for repeal during the spring of 1933, all by huge majorities. . . . The thirty-sixth state, Utah, ratified repeal on December 5, and on that date the Eighteenth Amendment was superseded by the Twenty-first. . . . The long reign of the Anti-Saloon League had come to an end. (Virginius Dabney, *Dry Messiah: The Life of Bishop Cannon*, Alfred A. Knopf, Inc., New York, 1949, pp. 293–317.

$\mathbb{T}$HESE BITS of history describe the decline and fall of a once powerful social movement. What are social movements? Why do they appear? What are the conditions under which they succeed or fail?

NATURE AND DEFINITION OF SOCIAL MOVEMENTS

Early sociologists saw social movements as efforts to promote change. More recent sociologists view social movements as efforts either to promote or to resist change. For example, Turner and Killian [1957, p. 308] define a social movement as *"a collectivity acting with some continuity to promote or resist a change in the society or group of which it is a part."*

This definition covers a wide range of movements: religious movements like Moral Rearmament or Youth for Christ, reform movements like the Anti-Saloon League or the Planned Parenthood Federation, revolutionary movements like the Communist Party, and many others.

Social movements are not institutions. Social institutions are relatively permanent and stable elements of a culture, whereas social movements are highly dynamic and have an uncertain life span. Institutions hold institutional status; that is, nearly everyone regards them as necessary and valuable aspects of the culture. A social movement lacks institutional status, for vast numbers of people view it with indifference or hostility. If a movement gains general or nearly universal support, its work is done and its active life, as a movement, is over.

Social movements are also distinguished from associations. An association is generally a formal organization, with members, officers, and a written constitution. A social movement often comes to include one or more associations, but usually includes many supporters who are not members of these supporting associations, while some movements are almost totally unorganized. Furthermore, the association is typically engaged in carrying out the customary behavior of the society, while the social movement is concerned with some change in behavior forms. The fact that a movement which has reached the stage of formal organization may call itself the "so-and-so-association" should not blur the distinction between association and movement.

Social movements sometimes act as pressure groups, but most pressure groups are not social movements. Most pressure groups merely want the existing norms and values of the society to be interpreted to their benefit. But social movements are primarily and consciously concerned with promoting or resisting actual changes in these social norms and values. Occasionally, but only occasionally, do social movements function as pressure groups.

Sociologists and other social scientists are much interested in the scientific analysis of social movements. They study them in several ways, including: (1) participant-observer studies, in which the sociologist joins the movement to observe it from the inside [Lincoln, 1961]; (2) historical or longitudinal studies, combing published accounts, historical documents, newspaper files, and other sources [Edwards, 1927; Gusfield, 1955]; (3) comparative-membership studies, analyzing a sample of leaders or members (*a*) statistically, according to age, race, sex, occupation, education, and other characteristics in an effort to find out who joins and why [Lipset, 1950; Almond, 1954], or (b) through interviews and biographical accounts, in an effort to discover their common feelings and motives [Ernst and Loth, 1952]; (4) content analyses of a movement's statements and propaganda [Lasswell and Blumenstock, 1939].

SOCIAL SITUATIONS FAVORING SOCIAL MOVEMENTS

Social movements do not "just happen." They arise wherever social conditions are favorable, and these conditions will have produced many people who are ready and willing to promote them. What kinds of social conditions are favorable to the appearance and spread of social movements?

Cultural drifts   Gradual, broad, sweeping changes in values and behavior are constantly going on in all civilized societies today (and in most primitive societies as well). Such changes are called *cultural drifts*. The concept originated with Herskovits [1949, p. 581], who describes it as a process "where minor alterations slowly change the character and form of a way of life, but where the continuity of the event is apparent." In the course of a cultural drift most of the people develop new ideas of what society should be like and how society should treat them. The long development of a democratic society is an example of cultural drift. Some other recent examples include the emancipation of women, the accent on materialism, the changed attitude toward leisure and recreation, the higher evaluation of education, and a number of others.

Each cultural drift arises through the interaction of many causative factors. Each is far too extensive to be produced by any one social movement, although one or more movements may be involved in the change process. Cultural drifts thus often provide an opportunity for social movements to prod and hasten developments already under way. For the past century, a cultural drift has been running toward more nearly equal rights for all kinds of groups—age, sex, religious, political, racial, or ethnic. This cultural drift makes it almost a certainty that present social movements seeking social equality of Negroes with whites will eventually succeed, while present movements to resist such Negro gains will eventually fail. Thus do cultural drifts aid or doom a social movement.

Social   "I took away their despair," said Nasser to explain his devoted following in the
disorganization and   Arab world. Before a man can be a leader, there must be people ready to be
social movements   led. Few such people are found in stable, well-integrated societies. The members of a well-integrated society are generally complacent and secure, feel no discontent, and have no interest in change. They rarely join social movements. It is the changing society—simple or complex—in which social movements flourish.

A changing society is always to some extent disorganized. As we outlined in the last chapter, societies differ greatly in the speed with which they change and in the degree to which a particular change disorganizes the culture. Social disorganization brings confusion and uncertainty to a society's members, since their traditions no longer form a dependable guide to behavior. In a disorganized society, individuals tend to become rootless and anomic. Leo Srole has drawn up an anomie scale which reveals some of the characteristics of the anomic frame of mind. In ascending order of intensity, these characteristics are: (1) a feeling that the community leaders are indifferent to a man's needs; (2) a feeling that little can be accomplished in a society which he sees as basically unpredictable and disorderly; (3) a feeling that his life goals are slipping out of reach; (4) a general sense of futility; and (5) a conviction that he cannot count on his personal associates for social and psychological support [Merton, 1957a, pp. 164–169].

Another concept which describes the individual's imperfect integration with his society is the concept of *alienation.* This is more inclusive than anomie, for it includes the components of *powerlessness, normlessness,* and *social isolation* [Dean, 1961; Nettler, 1957]. It is, therefore, an almost complete emotional separation from the society.

Alienation and anomie become widespread states of mind in a disorganized society. Their symptoms are insecurity, confusion, restlessness, and suggestibility. Once-honored rules no longer seem binding and once-cherished goals no longer attainable, while no other rules or goals seem worth the effort. Such a confused and frustrated setting is ideal for the appearance and growth of social movements.

The spread of the Ghost Dance among the American Indians illustrates the relationship between social disorganization and social movements. This was a dance which, if performed properly, was supposed to bring the end of the white man and the return of the buffalo. It originated among the North Paiutes of Nevada and spread in two great waves in 1870 and 1890. However, it spread only among those peoples whose tribal life was seriously disrupted, mainly by the destruction of the buffalo [Lesser, 1933]. Each tribe participated in Ghost Dance ceremonials with an intensity roughly proportional to the amount of deprivation they suffered through the disruption of their tribal life [Nash, 1937]. The Sioux, flushed with recent victories and favorable treaties under Red Cloud, ignored the Ghost Dance in the 1870s; but by 1890, wretched and dispirited on a reservation, they eagerly adopted it. The Navaho, who remained prosperous and comfortable throughout this period, greeted the Ghost Dance with an amused and tolerant indifference; but when the Great Depression of the 1930s brought acute distress to the Navaho, aboriginal ceremonials had a remarkable revival [Kluckhohn, 1938].

Frustration and confusion, rather than poverty and misery, spawn social movements. People can be emotionally secure and contented at a miserable level of bare subsistence, *if* their value system defines this deprivation as a necessary and proper condition of life. Corruption, social inequality, and social injustice do not necessarily doom a social system. Many social systems have remained stable and unshakable for centuries, despite grinding poverty, rampant corruption, and gross exploitation. Such a social order can survive as long as most members can attain the goals they have been encouraged to pursue. Man is so pliable and educable that almost any kind of social system will appear good to him, if it has a fair degree of internal consistency and if he is properly socialized to live within it. Therefore, traditional societies are often highly stable until they once begin to change; once the traditional customs and values are questioned, the people may experience a tremendous inflation of wishes, sometimes called a "revolution of rising expectations." Revolutions are most likely to occur, not when a people are most miserable, but after things have begun to improve [Brinton, 1938, pp. 40–44; Street and Street, 1961]. What apparently happens is that, although people have begun to live better, their scale of wants expands so much more rapidly that they are more frustrated than ever. Revolutions and other uprisings are especially likely to break out after a downturn has interrupted a period of improvement, creating an intolerable gap between rising expectations and falling realizations [Davies, 1962].

Today most of the underdeveloped areas of the world are at a critical point of development. The traditional folk cultures are being disorganized at record speed. All over the world, the impoverished peoples are getting the notion that poverty, hunger, and illness are not necessary after all. They are beginning to long for bicycles, candy, pretty clothing, and all the other things that glitter along the slope of endlessly ascending desires. They hunger for these treasures but have little real understanding of what it takes to produce them. Therefore, even where people are beginning to get some of the things they covet, the satisfactions come with a tantalizing and unbearably frustrating slowness. A weakening of traditional and tribal controls generally accompanies this enormous inflation of desires. It will be a remarkable achievement if the underdeveloped areas are able to carry through an orderly program of economic and social development. Meanwhile, the population explosion in the underdeveloped countries, combined with limited rural opportunity, is sending hordes of peasant peoples to the cities, where they huddle in squalid suburban slums, built largely of packing crates and other junk materials. Uneducated and untrained, many are unemployed and often come to share the "culture of poverty" which Oscar Lewis has so eloquently described [1959, 1963*a*, 1963*b*, 1965, 1966]. Cut off from the extended family and village life which formerly made their poverty bearable, and unable to enter successfully into the urban culture, these rootless, alienated unfortunates are the potential shock troops for tomorrow's revolutionary movements.

Perceived social injustice Social injustice is not an objective social fact; it is a subjective value judgment. Is it just or unjust that one man should have ten times, or ten thousand times, as much wealth as another? This depends upon one's beliefs and values. In a number of countries the masses live in abject poverty while the rich live in Sybaritic splendor, pay virtually no taxes, and block all attempts at social reform. Is such a social system unjust? Most readers will probably think so; but whether a social system is unjust is irrelevant. It is when a social system is *perceived* as unjust by its members that they become frustrated and alienated. Perceived social injustice thus provides both a desire for change and a moral justification for breaking heads, if necessary, to get it.

The perception of social injustice is not limited to the miserable poor. Any group, at any status level, may come to feel itself the victim of social injustice. A wealthy class, firmly believing that its wealth and privileges are just and proper, may suffer an intense and righteous sense of injustice when faced with "confiscatory" taxes or land-reform policies intended to benefit the poor.

Whether such policies are "objectively" just is impossible to establish, since "justice" is a matter of values. But a *feeling* of social injustice provides fertile soil for social movements, equally among the rich, the poor, and the in-betweens.

PERSONAL SUSCEPTIBILITY TO SOCIAL MOVEMENTS

In a stable, well-integrated society with very few social tensions or alienated groups, there are few social movements and few people who are interested. Contented people rarely join social movements. Those who are at peace within themselves and with their society are likely to be fully absorbed in their own activities. They generally view social movements with either amusement, indifference, or hostility. But in a changing, continuously disorganized society, the fully contented person is a rarity. More people in such a society believe they perceive social injustice and become dissatisfied or alienated. It is the dissatisfied who build social movements. The frustrated and misplaced, the restless and rootless, those who putter in boredom, those who seethe with hostility, and those who are oppressed by the futility of their present lives—these are the material of which most social movements are built. Let us note some of the circumstances apparently associated with such states of mind.

Contented people rarely join social movements.

Mobility   People on the move have little chance to put down roots and become integrated into the life of the community. Their mobility not only weakens the community's control over them; it also deprives them of the emotional satisfactions of really belonging to the local group. California, whose population has doubled in less than a generation, seems to be, very naturally, the birthplace of more movements, cults, and sects than any other several states combined [McWilliams, 1946, chap. 14; 1949, chap. 10]; in low-mobility states like Vermont, an agitator can address his largest crowds in a whisper.

When mobility is forced upon people by changing circumstances, they are even more in need of a social movement as an emotional refuge. Cohn's [1957] study of European millennial movements in the Middle Ages found that millennial fantasies were strongest among the uprooted peasants who were forced off the land to become urban workers or beggars and unemployed. Mobility is almost invariably productive of social movements.

We should remember, of course, that this is a joint cause-and-effect situation. That is, many people are mobile because they are rootless, and many people are rootless because they are mobile. No matter what the circumstances, high-mobility groups generally provide more than their share of a movement's converts.

Marginality Persons who are not fully accepted and integrated into a group are termed *marginal*. A classic example is the immigrant, partly assimilated into two cultures and fully assimilated into neither. Our society has many marginal roles—the occupational group who consider themselves professionals but are not granted full professional status by the community; first- and second-generation immigrants who have become successful businessmen but are not accepted as equals in the business community; college instructors in automobile mechanics or other "trade school" subjects, who are patronized by the faculties of the liberal arts and sciences; successful upperclass Negroes who must be deferential to lower-class whites, and many others. Marginal persons are likely to feel uneasy and insecure, anxious for acceptance and resentful that it has been withheld. Stated differently, they are aware of a discrepancy between their self-image and the public image of them, and the inconsistency is frustrating.

Marginality often seems to produce overconformity, as is shown by the fierce patriotism of the newly naturalized citizen, the tireless zeal of the new religious convert, or the meticulous etiquette of the new-rich. But sometimes marginal people give up this search for acceptance and join an unpopular social movement, as though to say, "Here, at least, *someone* appreciates me!" In fact, much of the membership and leadership of many social movements seems to have come from marginal groups in society [Lasswell and Blumenstock, pp. 277–300]. This does not mean that only marginal people join movements. In the case of the Cooperative Commonwealth Federation, a socialist political movement in Saskatchewan, the established leaders among the farm people became active CCF members; yet among the town businessmen, mainly the marginal persons joined [Lipset, 1950]. Since the CCF reflected basic changes in the value system of rural Saskatchewan, the opinion leaders among the farmers were among the first to join. But since the movement did not reflect the dominant values of the business community, it attracted those businessmen whose marginal acceptance had prevented them from fully internalizing the values of the group.

Most movements draw many of their early members and leaders from the marginal persons and groups in the society. Marginal people are more susceptible because they are anxious for acceptance somewhere and are less firmly wedded to the norms and values of the groups which have only partly accepted them. But until a movement succeeds in also attracting the leaders and decision makers of the groups it aims at, it generally remains weak and ineffectual.

Social isolation Considerable research shows that persons and groups who are isolated from the community are more alienated and are more receptive to mass movements than groups whose status and work integrates them into the community. Kornhauser [1959, p. 159] says that ". . . free-lance intellectuals appear to be more disposed toward mass movements than intellectuals in corporate bodies, especially universities." The worker groups who are most receptive to social movements, especially to violent movements, are those whose work cuts them off from the larger society, such as miners, maritime workers, and longshoremen [Kornhauser, 1959, chap. 12]. Either because of geographical location or social structure, these workers have few social contacts with other groups in the society. They rarely belong to the mixed-membership voluntary associa-

tions which thrive among other groups. They have few opportunities to participate in the formal and informal life of the community; their ties to the established order are weak, and they are more easily mobilized to overthrow it.

Changing social No evidence shows that interest in social movements is more intense at one
status class level than another, but evidence does show that a *change* of status increases susceptibility. Upward mobility brings a person into new class groupings in which his position is marginal and where he is somewhat insecure. But
a loss of social status, or threatened loss, is still more unsettling. There is a
good deal of evidence that those who feel they are suffering downward mobility are abnormally hostile toward other groups and are more often violent
and authoritarian in their social attitudes [Kaufman, 1957; Srole, 1956;
Bettelheim and Janowitz, 195 , pp. 55ff.]. In Germany the farmers who voted
most heavily for Hitler between 1932 and 1934 were neither the rich nor the
poor, but were the commercial-type farmers who were most vulnerable to
market changes [Heberle, 1951, pp. 222–236; Loomis and Beagle, 1946]. In
other words, the farmers who feared that they might become poor turned Nazi
more regularly than did those who were already poor. But all the observers of
Nazism agree that the strongest support before the Nazis gained power came
from the lower-middle-class shopkeepers, tradesmen, and artisans who,
having lost their savings in the postwar inflation, were now being squeezed
between the gains of organized labor and the rationalization of production and
distribution by the big corporations and department stores [Fromm, 1941, pp.
211–216; Mannheim, 1940, pp. 102ff.; Gerth, 1940]. The same groups formed
the core of the French Poujadist movement in the 1950s, a tax-revolt movement centered among the small shopkeepers who were threatened by big-
business retailing [Heberle, 1956; Lipsedge, 1956]. The most violent reaction
to Martin Luther King's demonstration marches came in Northern upper-
working-class neighborhoods whose residents, often first- or second-generation immigrants, had clawed their way out of the slum and feared that Negro
residents would recreate the slum they had escaped [Giles, 1967]. A recent
study [Rother, 1967] of John Birch Society members found that, as compared
with a control group of nonmembers, the society members had experienced
far more mobility, mostly downward, and the study concluded by attributing
their political extremism to their status frustrations. Probably no development
is more certain to inspire a social movement than a perceived threat to the
economic security and social status of some segment of the society.

Lack of family ties The advice, "Marry and settle down," is not just a piece of rhetoric; it actually
happens. When a man gets a little home with a big mortgage and a wife busily
presenting him with new mouths to fill and feet to cover, he may lose his urge
to man the barricades! The more extremist and unpopular the movement, the
more strongly do family ties discourage one's participation. Activity in a social
movement is time-consuming and competes with family responsibilities.
Furthermore, a person with a warm, richly satisfying family life has no emotional need to find a cause to fill the emotional void in his life.

   Membership studies of social movements have generally found a dispropor-
tionate share of members who either have no families or are estranged from
their families. This is especially true with the more radical movements. Thus

Ernst and Loth's [1952, pp. 1–15] study of former American Communist Party members found that most of them joined the party during their late teens or early twenties, while still unmarried, and while engaged in bitter emancipation conflicts with their parents. During the 1930s, a youth with a strong emotional need to tell his devout-Baptist-Republican-businessman father, "You can't run *my* life!" often joined the Communist Party. Today, he can choose between the "New Left" and "turning on" as a "hippie."

For these reasons most revolutionary movements, from early Christianity to the Communist Party, have attacked the family. The Apostle Paul counseled Christians to remain single and undistracted if they were able to. One of the first moves of the new Communist government of China was to launch a vigorous, calculated attack upon the family, aiming to undermine family authority, sever the lines of family obligation, and transfer personal loyalties and emotional moorings from the family to the Communist Party [Chandrasekhar, 1959; Yang, 1959]. But a new regime, after it is firmly established, supports and uses the family as a conservative and stabilizing force. Thus the early Communist regime in Russia attacked the family, endorsed free love, ridiculed parental authority, and encouraged postcard divorce; in Russia today, parental authority is supported, divorce is exceedingly difficult, public morals are puritanical, and affectionate family life is officially encouraged [Alt and Alt, 1959; Kharchev, 1961]. There is no inconsistency in this about-face. It merely reveals a revolutionary movement at different stages in its career.

Personal In the preceding pages we have repeatedly hinted that the maladjusted are
maladjustment especially susceptible to social movements. Those who have failed to find a satisfying life role and a comfortable, secure status are very likely, consciously or unconsciously, to be shopping for something to bring purpose and meaning to their lives. In a perceptive discussion, Hoffer [1951, pp. 45–46] has distinguished the temporary from the permanent misfits. The temporary misfits are "people who have not found their place in life but still hope to find it." Adolescent youth, unemployed college graduates, demobilized veterans, and new immigrants are examples. Restless, frustrated, and fearful that opportunity may elude them, they are good fodder for movements but are not very dependable. As rapidly as the society can offer rewarding jobs and statuses to them, they are likely to lose interest in social movements. The permanent misfits are those who, because of limited talent or some impassable social barrier, are forever blocked from the role and status they crave. The unsuccessful artist or writer, the middle-aged craftsman whose trade is destroyed by automation and who must compete as an unskilled laborer, the educated native in a colony where natives are confined to manual labor—all are permanent misfits, since there is little prospect of their ever finding a life role and status rewarding enough to absorb their interests. They remain frustrated and in emotional need of something to fill the aching void in their lives.

Are social movements, then, only a refuge for the homeless failures and misfits of society? Do such people join a movement in a sort of emotional reflex, and not as an act of intellectual judgment? Yes, to some extent, Heberle [1951, p. 113] remarks, "The neurotic, maladjusted, unbalanced or psychopathic seem to be attracted not so much by the ideas [of a movement] as by the sense of oneness, of belonging, which appeases their feelings of insecurity, of helplessness, of isolation." Certainly there are both rational and nonrational factors in movement membership, and the nonrational factors are more important than we sometimes admit. Members of the more extreme movements often shift from one movement professing one set of beliefs to another movement professing an opposite set of beliefs with very little intellectual difficulty. Thus, "Hitler looked on the German Communists as potential National Socialists. . . . [Nazi] Captain Roehm boasted that he could turn the reddest Communist into a nationalist in four weeks. On the other hand, [Communist] Karl Radek looked on the Nazi Brown Shirts (S.A.) as a reserve for future Communist recruits" [Hoffer, 1951, p. 17]. Later history showed all these men to be correct. People join extremist movements to satisfy their emotional compulsions, and the rational programs of these movements are unimportant so long as the members' emotional yearnings are fulfilled.

Are the less extreme movements equally nonrational? Probably not. When a movement expresses a developing consensus of opinion among the more influential members of the society, as the temperance movement did in the nineteenth century [Gusfield, 1955], as the Cooperative Commonwealth Federation did in Saskatchewan [Lipset, 1950], or as the civil rights movement is doing today, such a movement attracts the responsible leaders of the community, not the misfits. Probably most of the members of a movement find some element of emotional compensation in their activity, as nearly all of us find it in our own behavior. But the evidence would not justify a conclusion that movements arise solely from the people's need to scratch their emotional itch.

All the above conditions help to prepare people who are receptive to the appeal of a social movement. The circumstances do not "cause" important mass movements. Unless there is deep and widespread social discontent, any movement growing purely from the misfits' hunger for a crusade will have no future. But when social unrest is intense and alienation and anomie become normal, then the homeless, the status cliff-hangers, and the misfits become the shock troops of mass movements which can set an entire nation on fire. The ultimate consequences depend upon the actions of the responsible leaders of the society. If they perceive social injustices in need of correction and social tensions in need of resolution, assume leadership, and channel this mass protest into constructive social reforms, the main features of the social system may be conserved. But if they seek to block social reforms passionately sought and long overdue, as did the eighteenth-century French or the early twentieth-century Russian aristocrats, they guarantee the eventual destruction of the social system.

TYPES OF SOCIAL MOVEMENTS

To classify social movements is not always easy, for sometimes a movement is intermediate or mixed in nature, or is different at different stages of its career. As always, the categories below are "ideal types," into which actual movements more or less perfectly fall.

Migratory At the close of the Civil War, about ten thousand Southerners left the country
movements rather than endure the Yankee Reconstruction and established colonies in Mexico and Brazil [Nunn, 1956; Ross and Kerner, 1958]. Sometimes discontent with present circumstances together with the lure of a greener distant

pasture leads large numbers of people to migrate. The mere fact that a lot of people migrate does not create a migratory social movement, nor is one created purely by the number of people who move, each for private and widely varied reasons. We have a migratory social movement when there is a common focus of discontent, a shared purpose or hope for the future, and a widely discussed and shared decision to move to a new location, regardless of whether they migrate as an organized group or as individuals and families. The northward migration of Southern Negroes began to assume the proportions of a social movement about the time of World War I and continues unabated. A more spectacular example is the Irish migration in which over 750,000 of the Irish people, already economically distressed and politically discontented, left their country in the five years following the great potato-crop failures beginning in 1845 [Morehouse, 1928]. The Zionist movement has had a long history, but only in recent years have Jews been able to migrate freely to Israel. History, especially recent history, is filled with migratory movements.

The refugees from East Germany: a recent migratory social movement   Since the Iron Curtain clanked down between the Communist and non-Communist worlds, more than four million East Germans have fled to the West. The migration continued for seventeen years, until their number equaled one-fourth of the present population of East Germany. This was the greatest voluntary mass migration in the recorded history of Europe [Gilroy, 1961; Bailey, 1961].

The push came from the dull gray monotony and the unyielding tyranny of the German Democratic Republic, tightly run by Walter Ulbrecht for his Russian masters. This "workers' paradise" was a nightmare of long working hours and endless shortages, of forced collectivization which the farmers hated, and worst of all, of the inability of parents to protect their children from Communist indoctrination. The pull came from the glowing freedom and burgeoning prosperity of West Germany, which failed to sink into the sodden depression so constantly predicted by the Communist theoreticians. The escape hatch was Berlin, whose Western sector contrasted with the Eastern as a four-color magazine advertisement contrasts with a sheet of faded newsprint. Residents and visitors in East Berlin could cross freely into West Berlin, and many made it a one-way trip. West Germany welcomed the refugees, most of whom brought youth, ambition, and valuable technical or professional skills. Soon they were holding good jobs, buying refrigerators and Volkswagens, and sending glowing letters to their friends back in the workers' paradise. So the migration continued, rising sharply whenever a political crisis aroused the fear that the escape hatch might slam shut.

The East German government tried desperately to persuade or intimidate its subjects into remaining, but the desertions continued. Not only were they politically embarrassing, but the flight of technical and professional skill was an unbearable drag upon the East German economy. Finally in the fall of 1961, this last chink in the Iron Curtain was plugged with the building of the Berlin wall, and unhappy East Germans had to begin looking for some other way to meet their frustrations. Some of them, at least, found a way. The suicide count in East Berlin rose from an average of one a day before the wall went up to nearly fifty a day by the end of 1961 [*Time*, Jan. 12, 1962, p. 28].

Expressive When people are bottled up within a confining social system from which they
movements cannot flee and which they feel powerless to change, the result generally is an
expressive social movement. In the expressive movement the individual comes
to terms with an unpleasant external reality *by modifying his reactions to that
reality*, not by modifying the external reality itself. Through some kind of
activity—dreams, visions, rituals, dances, games, or other forms of emotional
expression—he finds enough emotional release to make life bearable. Often
the expressive movement is millennial. Dozens of movements have helped
people to ignore a miserable present by fixing their gaze upon a glorious
millennium that is about to dawn.

Expressive movements are many and varied. The medieval flagellants sought
a release from their sense of sin and personal unworthiness (and possibly
gratified other compulsions) by masochistic orgies [Cohn, 1957, chap. 6]. A
modern religious movement like Youth for Christ, which concentrates upon
changing persons, not upon changing the society, is an expressive movement.
Whereas our angry young men of the 1930s joined reform or revolutionary
movements, many of them today become hippies and express their rejection
of conventional values by wearing beards and dirty clothing, avoiding baths,
and sitting on the floor, listening to nihilistic poetry.

The "new left" of the 1960s, mainly among American university students
and nonstudents [Luce, 1966; Cohen and Hale, 1966; Newfield, 1966] is
basically an expressive social movement rather than a revolutionary movement. It is largely negative, long on criticism of conservatives and liberals
alike and short on positive programs or constructive alternatives. It thus serves
more as a rallying point for the expression of alienation than as an organizing
focus for social action.

Some scholars would include crazes, fads, and fashions as expressive movements [Blumer, 1951, pp. 216–218], but the present writers consider them
too trivial to be social movements and have discussed them in Chapter 16,
"Collective Behavior."

The cargo cult: a contemporary expressive movement   The native peoples of
Melanesia, like most primitive peoples everywhere, considered the white man's
social system inferior to theirs but the white man's goods highly desirable.
They noted that the white men apparently did not work; only the natives
worked. Yet shiploads of wonderful cargo kept appearing over the horizon.
Since they already believed that the Europeans were spirits of their dead ancestors, sent to bring these things to them, it was only a small step to believe
in the myth that a vast cargo, temporarily diverted by the whites, would some
day arrive in ships and planes along with the spirits of their ancestors. The
cargo would arrive when they had successfully performed the proper rituals
and completed the right preparations to receive and store it. Then the whites
would be driven away, and the cargo would revert to its rightful owners. These
beliefs arose among various Melanesian peoples, becoming widespread in the
1920s. They led to a little violence in some places and to government attempts
at suppression, but the movement was mainly nonviolent. Faith was not
diminished by failure of the cargo to arrive, and cargo cults still remain active
in the area. Cargo cults are understandable as the response of people who have
developed an intense desire for European goods but have very limited means

for getting them. Like all millennial movements, they are the effort of a confused and frustrated people to make new adjustments to situations of social
crisis for which their traditional culture has no satisfactory answers [Worsley,
1957; Firth, 1955].

Utopian movements   Ever since Sir Thomas More wrote his *Utopia*, the term has meant a society
of such perfection that it can be found only in man's imagination. Many other
writers had a try at describing a perfect society, from Plato in his *Republic* to
Edward Bellamy in *Looking Backward*. Many attempts to create such a perfect
society were made in the eighteenth and nineteenth centuries when utopian
movements were popular [Davis, 1930, chap. 2]. Since these idealists were
never able to get an entire society to experiment with, the utopian movement
took the form of an attempt to create an ideal social system within a small
community of dedicated followers; later this system might expand to include
the entire society. Many of the utopian communities which were strongly religious survived longer because they did not have to "pay off" in personal
happiness or material well-being. The payoff was in following the will of God.
But other utopian communities, like Brook Farm and the Oneida Community,
were secular in ideology. They were based on a conception of man as basically
good, cooperative, and altruistic, needing only a favorable setting to unlock
these virtues. Most of the religious and all of the secular utopian movements
failed, either because of inner contradictions and impracticabilities or because
of conflict with the external society [Bestor, 1950; Halloway, 1951; Burton,
1939].

Communism is sometimes called utopian, because Communists visualize a
perfect society. But whereas utopians seek to build a perfect society on a small
scale, believing that then its perfection will attract others to copy it, Communists, on the other hand, teach that the movement cannot be fully successful until the entire world is forcibly converted. The Communist program is more
revolutionary than utopian.

The Kingdom of Father Divine: a contemporary utopian social movement
Utopian movements are no longer fashionable, possibly because the interdependence of modern society makes it more difficult for a perfectionist group
to isolate itself within its microcosm. Yet Father Divine conducted a utopian
movement, highly successful, among the impoverished Negroes of Harlem.
There were a number of "kingdoms"—assembly and residence halls, where
some followers lived and all gathered for feasts and meetings. The movement
was a limited or imperfect utopia, since the members were not fully isolated
from the outside world. Residents of the kingdom held outside jobs and contributed their entire savings, property, and earnings to Father Divine, who in
turn provided for their needs. Followers were urged to isolate themselves, in
so far as was possible, from the outside world, centering their interests and
activities in the kingdoms. Worldly habits such as smoking, drinking, and
gambling were forbidden, and there was no cohabitation within the kingdoms.
Husbands and wives separated, or more often only one joined, leaving children
and spouse. Assemblies consisted of lavish feasting, fervid testimonials, and
prolonged chanting and singing, which reached hysterical and delusional proportions, together with boundless adulation of Father Divine. The movement

was rigidly ruled by Father Divine, who tolerated no opposition or controversy and encouraged a confusion of his identity with that of God.

In exchange for the surrender of property, income, and worldly indulgences, the follower gained an escape from economic insecurities, a sense of meaning amid the chaotic jungle of a Negro slum, and a tremendous elevation of status. The kingdom gave the member a feeling of self-respect and fortified him to run the daily gauntlet of a segregated society. This largely explained the success of the movement [Parker, 1937; Cantril, 1941; Harris, 1953]. Since the movement was strongly focused upon the personality of Father Divine, some observers doubted that it would survive his death. It has survived and is still active, but the authors can locate no description of its present operation.

Reform movements The reform movement is an attempt to modify some parts of the society without completely transforming it. Reform movements are impossible in an authoritarian society whose rulers will tolerate no criticism. Reform movements can operate only in a democratic atmosphere where people have considerable freedom to criticize existing institutions and may secure changes in them when the majority wishes.

American history is crowded with reform movements—abolition, feminism, prohibition, and many others. In the past month one of your authors has received fund appeals from at least two dozen reform movements and organizations, all seeking some reform in American law or public practice—several seeking equal rights for Negroes, and one or more concerned with wildlife conservation, wilderness preservation, national parks' protection, birth control and population policy, sharecroppers, American Indians, nuclear policy, and one from the "Defenders of Furbearers," seeking to outlaw the "cruel" steel trap—besides several appeals from groups who wish to reform other parts of the world. Our democratic atmosphere, our Judeo-Christian values, and our tradition of voluntarism have combined to make reform movements a conspicuous feature of past and present American history.

The freedom riders: a recent reform movement In 1946 the Supreme Court of the United States ruled that segregated seating of passengers on interstate trains and buses was unconstitutional, and since then has held unconstitutional a number of state laws and city ordinances requiring segregation on intrastate buses. In 1960 it banned segregation in terminal facilities used by interstate passengers and in 1962 extended the ruling to cover local passengers as well. Yet segregated washrooms, waiting rooms, and dining facilities continued in bus terminals in many areas of the Deep South. In the summer of 1961 the Freedom Rides began. Mixed white and Negro groups began touring the South, entering segregated facilities as a group, and calmly submitting to arrest for violating state or local laws and ordinances. Within six months, more than 350 men and women had been jailed in several states for doing what the Supreme Court had solemnly declared they had a right to do. A number were beaten, a few narrowly escaped death, and at least one received permanently disabling injuries. The object of the movement was to focus national attention upon the persistence of a form of segregation already forbidden by law, and to mobilize public opinion against this segregation. To accomplish their purpose, the reformers chose the method of nonviolence, relying upon the moving spectacle of people voluntarily submitting to suffering in support of their principles. Some of the groups were organized by the Congress of Racial Equality, but others were independent and spontaneous [Peck, 1962; Farmer, 1961; Rostow, 1961; Maybee, 1961].

The technique of the Freedom Riders is not entirely new, having been used over a century ago in a partly successful attack upon segregated public facilities in the North [Litwak, 1961]. The modern revival of the Freedom Rides has proved even more effective. In September, 1961, the Interstate Commerce Commission issued regulations forbidding interstate carriers from using segregated terminal facilities, and the "white" and "colored" signs began coming down.

The Freedom Rides were a short-lived social movement for a limited reform. But they were only one expression of the general movement for equal rights for Negroes. The sit-in, wade-in, and walk-in demonstrations were similar expressions. The sit-ins began spontaneously among Negro youths, impatient at the slow pace of desegration. Organizations such as the Congress of Racial Equality and the Southern Christian Leadership Conference then moved to assume leadership of sit-ins and other similar demonstrations [Thompson, 1960; Fleming, 1960]. In all such actions a group of orderly, well-behaved Negroes, usually together with some whites, would enter a lunch counter, restaurant, bathing beach, or theater-ticket line, and wait patiently for service, submitting unresistingly to insult, indignity, and even violence. When arrested, they often refused bail and sat out their jail terms. This technique of nonviolent resistance has been highly successful in opening many public facilities to Negro patrons.

At this writing, the nonviolent resistance technique is being abandoned, possibly because it has achieved those goals for which it is effective. Nonviolent resistance is better suited to integrating a public service than a residential neighborhood. Furthermore, Negro patience has worn thin while white resistance has stiffened. Negro leadership is now sharply divided between moderate leaders who counsel nonviolence and legislative approaches and a new group of bitter and violent young revolutionaries.

Revolutionary movements

The revolutionary movement seeks to overthrow the existing social system and replace it with a greatly different one. Unlike the reformer who wants to correct some imperfections in the present social order, the revolutionist considers the system not worth saving. The reformer is, therefore, the revolutionist's worst enemy, for social reforms may drain off the discontent upon which the revolutionist wishes to build his revolution.

A democracy is poor soil for revolution. A revolutionary movement must be rooted in a tremendous social discontent; but in a democracy, social unrest generally leads to social reform, and reform indefinitely

A democracy is poor soil for revolutionary movements.

postpones the revolution. But where authoritarian government blocks the popular wish for reform, the reformer must then attack the government, and he becomes a revolutionist. Revolutionary movements flourish where reform is blocked so that the revolutionary movement is the people's only alternative to their present misery. It is no accident that the Communist party is weakest in the thoroughly democratic countries like the United States, England, and the Scandinavian countries, and is far stronger in countries with a tradition of repressive government, or where government is nominally democratic, yet is so structured as to be an ineffective instrument of the popular wish for reform. In France and Italy, many people despair of reform and turn to revolutionary parties [Cantril, 1958].

Edwards [1927] and Brinton [1938] have independently arrived at a practically identical sequence of stages which they believe to be typical of most successful revolutions: (1) an accumulation of deep unrest, stretching over many years; (2) the defection of the intellectuals, who grow increasingly critical of the *status quo;* (3)) the emergence of an economic incentive for revolt and a social myth or set of beliefs to justify it; (4) the revolutionary outbreak, aided by the hesitation and weakness of the ruling group; (5) the rule of the moderates, who soon fail to control the various groups among the revolutionists or to satisfy the aroused passions of the populace; (6) the rise of the radicals or extremists, who gain power and begin to exterminate all opposition; (7) the reign of terror; (8) the return to normality, as moderates regain power, consolidate the achievements of the revolution, and restore some aspects of the prerevolutionary society. This outline is based largely upon the French and Russian revolutions; the more recent Mexican revolution has followed this course fairly closely. How closely the Chinese and Cuban revolutions will follow the pattern remains to be seen.

The Negro Rebellion: a contemporary revolutionary movement   The civil rights gains since World War II were of direct benefit mainly to educated and well-trained Negroes. The great mass of the Negro poor gained little. Meanwhile, many social changes worked to their disadvantage. Automation destroyed many of the unskilled and semiskilled jobs, while creating new jobs which most Negroes were not prepared to fill. The migration of business, industry, and middle-class residence to the suburbs and countryside carried many jobs out where Negroes were unable to live. Public transport was steadily deteriorating, and increasing time-travel-cost was a barrier to Negro employment. Negro unemployment, measured as a ratio to white unemployment, rose steadily. In many ghettos, over a fourth the adults and half the youth were unemployed. Fed by the urban migration of Southern Negroes and the suburban migration of whites, the urban Negro ghetto grew steadily larger, more wretched, and more thoroughly isolated from white society. After 1965, civil rights legislation was being regularly defeated, and local open occupancy housing ordinances were regularly overturned at the polls. Poverty programs, announced with great hopes, were being cut back as the war in Vietnam expanded, where proportionately more Negroes than whites were dying. The great mass of Negroes felt left out of the affluent society, as they grew relatively poorer while others grew richer.

Beginning with the Watts (Los Angeles) riot in 1965, the Negro rebellion grew until by the summer of 1967, riots were almost a nightly occurrence. The calm counsels of Roy Wilkins (N.A.A.C.P.) and Martin Luther King were challenged by the bitter calls to violence from new leaders like H. Rap Brown, who said, "get you some guns" and "burn this town down if it does not meet Negro demands" [*New York Times,* July 28, 1967, p. 11]. The "First National Congress on Black Power" in 1967 found 1,100 participants unanimously voting for Negro boycotts of white business, churches, and sports competitions, paramilitary training for Negro youth, and Negro refusal of military service in Vietnam [*New York Times,* July 25, 1967, p. 1ff.]. Negroes are no longer united in seeking an integrated society, for in 1967 the more extremist leaders began calling for a separate Negro society with its own churches, businesses, and public officials [*New York Times,* August 1, 1967, p. 17].

The riots beginning in 1965 were not classic race riots. They were not primarily a clash between Negroes and whites, even though "get Whitey" was a common cry. They were basically a revolt of the Negro poor against the "establishment,"—against those, white and Negro, whom they felt were exploiting them. The main effort was to loot and burn, with Negro businesses attacked almost as readily as white businesses. Both white and Negro officers were pelted and shot at, for in the ghetto, the police are the hated symbol of the establishment. Police brutality and disrespect, while often exaggerated, were common enough to be a source of bitter resentment. These riots, usually initiated by Negro youths and later joined by others, were a spontaneous outburst of people who were seething with repressed anger. While no more than 10 per cent of the Negro population participated (and often much less), and many Negroes agonized over them, many other Negroes took a grim satisfaction in seeing "Whitey" and "Uncle Tom" get hurt. [*New York Times,* July 30, 1967, IV, p. 1; August 6, 1967, IV, p. 1; *Time,* July 31, 1967, pp. 15–21; August 4, 1967, pp. 12–19; *Life,* August 4, 1967, pp. 16–28].

The Negro rebellion is following the familiar course of revolutions—initial gains, interruption and slowdown, intolerable frustration, violence. As this is written (summer of 1967), it is a revolutionary movement in its excitement stage. It is spontaneous and unorganized, without a coherent ideology or program, showing little agreement on either goals or techniques, and bitterly opposed by many Negroes. Its future is impossible to predict. Your authors suspect that there will be many more riots through the later 1960's, and that they will spread more widely through the Southern cities. What they will accomplish remains to be determined.

Resistance movements   The revolutionary movement arises among people who are dissatisfied because social change is too slow. The resistance movement arises among those dissatisfied because change is too fast. The resistance movement is an effort to block a proposed change or to uproot a change already achieved. The Ku Klux Klan is perhaps our best-known resistance movement, organized in the South after the Civil War to keep Negroes "in their place" by terror and intimidation [Brown, 1902, part 4; Mecklin, 1924], and reborn in the North after World War I as a nativistic movement [VanderZanden, 1960; Alexander, 1965]. The nativistic movement is an attempt to protect the purity of the group and its culture from new or foreign intrusions [Higham, 1955]. The Native American party and the Know-Nothing movements of the 1830s and 1840s were anti-immigrant and anti-Catholic, and coincided with an increase of Irish and German immigration to the United States. As in most resistance movements, there was a large element of scapegoating in the focusing of frustrations arising from many sources upon the immigrant, who was blamed for practically all troubles.

In a democratic society, all periods of rapid change will stimulate resistance movements. The New Deal era of reform produced a large number of them [Schlesinger, 1960, vol. 3, chap. 1]. Some, like the Committee for Constitutional Government and the American Liberty League, were largely fund-collecting offices for the distribution of anti-New Deal propaganda. Others like the Silver Shirts, the Black Legion, and the Christian Americans were would-be mass movements which united opposition to New Deal reforms with anti-Semitism, isolationism, and antiforeign sentiments in a fascist-type organization [Lowenthal and Guterman, 1949; Carlson, 1943, 1946]. More recently the movement of extreme resistance to liberalism, internationalism, and welfare statism has come to be known as the "radical right" [Bell, 1963].

Over ninety resistance organizations appeared in the wake of the Supreme Court's school desegregation decision in 1954. The most successful was the White Citizens' Councils, which claimed 65 chapters and 80,000 members in Mississippi alone [VanderZanden, 1959; Routh and Anthony, 1957; Cater, 1956]. The councils applied economic sanctions to any person, white or Negro, who supported desegregation. The councils included many prominent politicians and business leaders, and were able to exert enough influence so that desegregation supporters were likely to be dismissed from their jobs, evicted from rented properties, have credit withdrawn, and suffer other economic penalties. Uncooperative businessmen might be boycotted by wholesalers and have their loans called and their insurance canceled. The White Citizens' Councils apparently succeeded, at least temporarily, for there was practically no school desegregation in large areas of the South where the councils were most active.

The John Birch Society: a contemporary resistance movement The John Birch Society is perhaps the most influential of the long list of organizations resisting most of the social reforms of the past half century [Barrett, 1961; Mosk and Jewel, 1961; Grove, 1961; Epstein and Forster, 1967; Buckley, 1966; Freedman, 1966]. The society was founded in December, 1958, by Robert Welch, Jr., a retired businessman who describes democracy as government by "mobocracy," and has branded ex-President Eisenhower as a "dedicated, conscious agent of the Communist conspiracy" (although some members think this is going a little "too far"). Mr. Welch's book, the *Blue Book of the John Birch Society* is a quite remarkable volume which tells how nearly all of America's recent leaders have been pro-Communist, and how even most of the anti-Communist organizations are secretly Communist. While avowedly anti-Communist, Mr. Welch and his followers concentrate mainly upon attacking American moderates like Mr. Eisenhower, Chief Justice Earl Warren, and the late Mrs. Eleanor Roosevelt. Mr. Welch's prime immediate objective is the impeachment of Chief Justice Warren. The movement thus falls into the standard pattern of recent American resistance movements in opposing social reforms by calling them Communistic.

The movement began to grow more rapidly after the press "exposed" it, showing that there were many people ready to join an organization with its purposes. Membership figures are secret but are known to include a number of present or former congressmen and other prominent persons. It expended over 5 million dollars in 1965, a figure exceeded among political organizations only by the Democratic and Republican parties [*The Progressive*, July, 1966, p. 7]. The organization is semisecret and under completely authoritarian control at all levels. Mr. Welch determines its policies, handles funds without the necessity of accounting for them to its members, and is authorized to expel members at his discretion. Activities are centered upon recruiting members and denouncing "pro-Communists." Techniques include infiltrating and assuming control if possible of political parties, PTAs, and other organizations, writing campaigns, and telephone harassment of the society's critics and opponents.

It is ironical that the structure and operation of the John Birch Society should so closely parallel that of the Communist Party it opposes. Both of them: (1) attack and discredit the nation's responsible leadership; (2) oppose foreign aid, the United Nations and international cooperation; (3) disdain civil rights, collective bargaining, and the social gospel of the churches; (4) organize "fronts" to conceal their operation; (5) use admittedly "dirty" tactics like disrupting peaceful public meetings; (6) are authoritarian and permit no dissent within the ranks. Most serious students of communism believe that organizations like the Birch Society are more of a help than a hindrance to the Communist movement. In a non-Communist country, the Communists seeks to block social reforms and to arouse suspicion and mistrust of the nation's leaders. Therefore it is no surprise that the Moscow *Literary Gazette* should remark, "Now the Communist movement has gained unexpectedly a new supporter. His name is Robert Welch" [Mosk and Jewel, 1961].

Meanwhile other resistance movements are currently active, such as the Christian Anti-Communist Crusade, the National Education Program, the Christian Crusade, and dozens of other organizations [Horton, 1961; Barth, 1961]. As some die, others are born. Wherever there is change and reform, people who are unhappy over them will organize in protest. Often these opponents use anti-Communism as a vehicle for their resentment, labeling as "Communist" everything and everybody they dislike. This group felt betrayed and abandoned when the Eisenhower administration failed to dismantle the New Deal. Movements like the John Birch Society and the Christian Anti-Communist Crusade are their response. All this does not, of course, mean that the members are insincere, or that they are secretly procommunist. It is an example of how groups may act in ways which have the effect of aiding, rather than harming, their opponents. And it illustrates how all extremist movements tend to develop similarities in structure and operation.

LIFE CYCLE OF SOCIAL MOVEMENTS

No two movements are exactly alike; yet different movements have much in common. Most completed movements pass through much the same set of four stages—of unrest, excitement, formalization, and institutionalization, first suggested by W. E. Gettys [Dawson and Gettys, 1934, pp. 708–709], who applied them to his study of the Methodist movement in England. A few accomplish their purpose without needing to enter the later stages.

The unrest stage All movements are rooted in social unrest. When people grow bored and restless, or develop a sense of social injustice, or when some change has disrupted an established way of life, they develop an unstable volatility which we call social unrest. When they confront situations that their traditional ideology cannot explain, they are frustrated. For example, the Great Depression of the thirties brought actual destitution to millions of workers who had been socialized to believe that there must be something wrong with a man who can't support his family. The emotional experience was shattering for most unemployed men, many of whom agonized painfully about accepting relief when it was offered. Social change, social disorganization, and social unrest are inseparable. This stage may be very prolonged, lasting as much as several generations.

The excitement stage Unrest is vague, generalized, and unfocused. When it becomes focused on certain conditions, and when certain "causes" of misery are identified so that proposals for action fill the air, the excitement stage has come. During this stage it is easy to gather an audience, and agitators seem to pop up everywhere. Many fledgling movements are launched, mostly to founder on the rocks of clumsy leadership or ineffective appeals. Sometimes a magnetic agitator, working on people whose needs have made them receptive, can rouse a huge following almost overnight. To convert such a mass into an effective movement requires a skillful organizer. The excitement stage is typically brief, leading quickly either to action or to a loss of interest.

The formalization stage Some of the migratory and expressive movements may be able to operate without formal organization, but those which seek to modify the society must become organized. An excited mass of followers will drift away unless their enthusiasms are ordered and directed. In the formalization stage, a chain of officers is worked out, fund raising is systematized, and the ideology of the movement is clarified. The ideology reminds people of their discontents, identifies the villains, states the movement's objectives, outlines the strategy and tactics for attaining the stated purposes, and provides the moral justification for all these actions. Formalization converts an excited mass into a disciplined membership and a vague cause into a practical enterprise. This, too, is a brief phase leading quickly into institutionalization.

The institutionalization stage Institutionalization eventually overtakes most movements if they last long enough. The movement crystallizes into a definite pattern, including traditions to uphold and possibly vested interests to defend. Efficient bureaucrats replace zealous agitators as leaders, and members feel themselves supporters of a worthy organization rather than campaigners in a sacrificial crusade. The acquisition of elaborate office suites or buildings (as by labor organizations in recent years) is evidence that the institutionalization of the movement is complete. This stage may last almost indefinitely.

The dissolution stage   Most scholars end the movement's cycle with the institutionalization stage. But this is not really the end, for different movements come to different conclusions. A movement may die at any stage in its career. Some movements achieve their objectives and then disappear, like the movement for women's suffrage. The officers of a movement which is killed through success may attempt to switch the movement to a new objective, as the National Foundation did after polio was conquered. Such a change of direction is rarely successful. Some movements, however, do undergo a transition in which the movement comes to pursue objectives quite different from the original ones. As an example, the Townsend movement for liberal old-age pensions lost most of its members when returning prosperity and the growth of other pension plans undercut its program, but the Townsend clubs survive as recreational groups which are only mildly interested in the pension plan [Messinger, 1955]. A movement may shrink into a sectlike band of followers, doggedly pursuing an objective which is probably forever unattainable, such as the prohibitionist movement embodied in the WCTU [Gusfield, 1955]. Some movements achieve full institutional status and make a contribution to the institutions of the society. This progress is illustrated by the many religious sects which have completed the transition into denominations.

Agitators seem to pop up everywhere.

APPRAISAL

Do social movements do more good than harm? That is like asking if wind does more good than harm. Social movements are one of the ways a society changes itself. The changes, though often painful, would not occur unless some social forces produced them.

Are the members emotionally sick people finding outlet for their compulsions, or are they generous humanitarians seeking to alleviate human suffering? Some of each! Some movements have more of one than of the other characteristic, but most movements have both, just as each person may have some of both within his own personality.

Will there be more new movements in the future? Certainly, for social movements are inseparable from social change. What kinds? This we cannot predict. Authoritarian society encourages migratory, expressive, and perhaps revolutionary movements. An optimistic era like the eighteenth century abounds in utopian and reform movements, while, as Stephan Runciman [1956, p. 14] notes, "a disillusioned age turns to religion, as an escape from the uncertainties of the world." We can be certain only that social movements will continue to express people's dissatisfaction with the society in which they find themselves.

SUMMARY

Social movements are collective attempts to promote or resist change, either in the society or in its members. Broad cultural drifts provide a favorable setting for social movements pushing in the same direction as the cultural drift. Social change and social disorganization produce the frustration, alienation, anomie, and confusion which make people more receptive to social movements. Perceived social injustice provides both the desire for change and the moral justification for a movement's actions. Mobility, marginality, social isolation, changing social status, lack of family ties, and personal maladjustments all tend to make persons more receptive.

Movements are of several types: *migratory*, wherein people physically flee a frustrating society; *expressive*, wherein they modify themselves rather than the society and find emotional outlet through expressive behavior; *utopian*, wherein a small band seeks to create a perfect society in miniature; *reform*, wherein a group seeks to persuade a democratic society to correct its imperfections; *revolutionary*, wherein people seek to replace an outworn social system with a new one; and *resistance*, wherein conservatives seek to block or uproot social changes they dislike.

Sociologists and historians seek to describe a "typical" life cycle which movements may approximate: an *unrest* stage of widespread but unfocused discontent; an *excitement* stage, during which discontent is increased and focused; a *formalization* stage, when mass excitement is organized into effective action; an *institutionalization* stage, when the movement crystallizes into a bureaucracy, and a *dissolution* stage, when an active movement receives one of several kinds of funerals. While not always rational and sometimes annoying, social movements help a democratic society to take up cultural lags and remain passably integrated.

QUESTIONS AND PROJECTS

1. How is a social movement distinguished from an institution, association, or pressure group?

2. How do cultural drifts affect social movements? Considering present cultural drifts, what do you think will be the eventual success of the prohibitionist movement? Of the John Birch Society? Of the effort to abolish discriminatory clauses in fraternity constitutions and rituals?

3. Why are social movements most likely to arise after a society begins to improve its material conditions rather than when it is in abject poverty?

4. Compared with other Western countries, has the United States had few or many social movements? Why?

5. What factors affect a person's receptivity to social movements?

6. Among the several types of social movements, which are the most numerous in present American society? Why?

7. Can you think of any social movements in the United States not mentioned in this chapter? In which classification would you place each?

8. What determines a person's decision to support one of several movements? Is it pure chance? The ideas and goals of the particular movement? The emotional needs it fills? Or what?

9. Is a movement likely to appeal to different kinds of people at different stages in its career? Why?

10. Some movements seem to attract mainly misfits and neurotics, while others attract the solid "respectables" of the community. Why? Sometimes a movement attracts the opinion leaders of one group and the misfits of another group. How do you explain this phenomenon?

11.   How do you explain the failure of the Communist Party to build a mass movement in the United States?

12.   Suppose you were a promoter, seeking a favorable area in which to launch a social movement. What statistics would you use in finding a receptive location?

13.   Do you know anyone who has a long history of involvement in "far-out" causes or movements? What kind of person is he? Do you know another person with a long activity in more moderate movements and organizations? How does he contrast with the other person?

14.   Take three or four students whom you know very well and estimate, according to the information in this chapter, the receptivity of each one to social movements. How about yourself? Are you a good or poor prospect for membership? In what kind of movement?

SUGGESTED READINGS

BARBER, BERNARD: "Acculturation and Messianic Movements," *American Sociological Review,* 6:663–669, October, 1941; Bobbs-Merrill reprint S-332. Shows how messianic movements arose among American Indian peoples as a reaction to the disorganization of their tribal life.

BLUMER, HERBERT: "Social Movements," in ALFRED M. LEE (ED.), *Principles of Sociology,* College Outline Series, Barnes & Noble, Inc., New York, 1955, pp. 199–220. A concise outline of the field of social movements.

GREEN, ARNOLD W., AND ELEANOR MELNICK: "What Has Happened to the Feminist Movement?" in ALVIN W. GOULDNER (ED.), *Studies in Leadership,* Harper & Row, Publishers, Incorporated, New York, 1950, pp. 277–302. A detailed account of how a movement has been affected by victory, defeat, and social change.

GREER, THOMAS H.: *American Social Reform Movements,* Prentice-Hall, Inc., Englewood Cliffs, N.J., 1949. An interesting historical account of reform movements in American history.

GUSFIELD, JOSEPH R.: "Social Structure and Moral Reform: A Study of the Women's Christian Temperance Union," *American Journal of Sociology,* 61: 221–232, November, 1955. A longitudinal leadership study of a social movement, relating a change in class composition of leaders to its loss of influence.

KORNHAUSER, WILLIAM: *The Politics of Mass Society,* The Free Press of Glencoe, New York, 1959, especially part 3, "Social Composition of Mass Movements." A readable analysis of social movements as a result of discontinuity and alienation in mass society.

LANG, KURT, AND GLADYS ENGEL LANG: *Collective Dynamics,* Thomas Y. Crowell Company, New York, 1961, chaps. 16, 17. Two detailed and perceptive chapters on social movements, in a textbook on collective behavior.

*LINCOLN, C. ERIC: *The Black Muslims in America,* Beacon Press, Boston, 1961. A participant-observer study of a contemporary Negro revolutionary movement by a Negro sociologist. (BP137-BEA)

*NEWFIELD, JACK: *A Prophetic Minority,* New American Library of World Literature, Inc., New York, 1966. A sympathetic analysis of the new student left in the U.S. (T3140-Sig)

SMELSER, NEIL J: *Theory of Collective Behavior,* The Free Press of Glencoe, New York, 1963, Chaps. 9, 10. A systematic theoretical analysis of social movements.

VANDERZANDEN, JAMES W., "The Klan Revival," *American Journal of Sociology,* 65:456–462, March, 1960; Bobbs-Merrill reprint S-299. A membership study of the revived Ku Klux Klan, showing social backgrounds and possible motivations of current members.

WORSLEY, PETER: *The Trumpet Shall Sound: A Study of "Cargo" Cults in Melanesia,* MacGibbon & Kee, London, 1957. Reviewed in *American Journal of Sociology,* 64:324–325, November, 1958. A comprehensive study of millennial cults in New Guinea.

BIBLIOGRAPHY

ABRAHAMSEN, DAVID: *Crime and the Human Mind,* Columbia University Press, New York, 1944.

ABRAMS, CHARLES: *Forbidden Neighbors: A Study of Prejudice in Housing,* Harper & Row, Publishers, Incorporated, New York, 1955.

ABRAMS, CHARLES: *The City is the Frontier,* Harper & Row, Publishers, Incorporated, New York, 1965.

ABU-LUGHOD, JANET: "Migrant Adjustment to City Life: The Egyptian Case," *American Journal of Sociology,* 65:22-32, 1961.

ADAMS, E. M.: "The Logic of Planning," *Social Forces,* 28:419-423, 1950.

ADAMS, SAMUEL HOPKINS: "The Juke Myth," *Saturday Review,* Apr. 2, 1955, pp. 13ff.

ADORNO, T. W., ELSE FRENKEL-BRUNSWICK, D. J. LEVINSON, AND R. N. SANFORD: *The Authoritarian Personality,* Harper & Row, Publishers, Incorporated, New York, 1950.

AGARWALA, S. N.: "Population Control in India: Progress and Prospects," *Law and Contemporary Problems,* 25:577-592, 1960.

ALBIG, WILLIAM: "Two Decades of Opinion Study: 1936-1956," *Public Opinion Quarterly,* 21:14-22, 1957.

ALBRIGHT, A. D.: "What Are Standards?" *Southern School News,* 4:1, 1958.

ALEXANDER, CHARLES C.: *The Ku Klux Klan in the Southwest,* University of Kentucky Press, Lexington, Kentucky, 1965.

ALINSKY, SAUL D., "The War on Poverty—Political Pornography," *Journal of Social Issues,* 21:41-47, Jan., 1965.

ALLEN, FREDRICK LEWIS: "The Big Change in Suburbia," *Harper's Magazine,* June, 1954, pp. 21-28; July, 1954, pp. 47-53.

ALLPORT, GORDON W.: *ABC's of Scapegoating,* Anti-Defamation League of B'nai B'rith, New York, 1948.

ALLPORT, GORDON W., J. S. BRUNER, AND E. M. JANDORF: "Personality under Social Catastrophe: Ninety Life-Histories of the Nazi Revolution," *Character and Personality,* 10:1-22, 1941.

ALLPORT, GORDON W., AND LEO POSTMAN: *The Psychology of Rumor,* Holt, Rinehart and Winston, Inc., New York, 1947.

ALLPORT, GORDON W., AND LEO F. POSTMAN: "The Basic Psychology of Rumor," *Transactions of the New York Academy of Sciences,* series 2, 8, pp. 61-81; reprinted in THEODORE M. NEWCOMB AND EUGENE L. HARTLEY, *Readings in Social Psychology,* Holt, Rinehart and Winston, Inc., New York, 1947, 1958, pp. 547-558, 54-65.

ALMOND, GABRIEL A., ET AL.: *The Appeals of Communism,* Princeton University Press, Princeton, N.J., 1954.

ALT, HERSCHEL, AND EDITH ALT: *Russia's Children,* Bookman Associates, Inc., New York, 1959.

ALTUS, W. D., AND T. T. TABEJIAN: "MMPI Correlates of the California E-F Scale," *Journal of Abnormal and Social Psychology,* 48:145-149, 1953.

America, Aug. 24, 1957, p. 518, "Rome and New Orleans."

ANDERSON, RAYMOND H.: "Soviet Urban Sprawl Defies Official Efforts to Curb the Growth of Cities," *New York Times,* Nov. 13, 1966, p. 122.

ANDERSON, SCARVIA B., ET AL.: *Social Studies in Secondary Schools: A Survey of Courses and Practices,* Princeton University Press, Princeton, N.J., 1964.

ANGELL, ROBERT C.: "Social Integration of American Cities," *American Sociological Review,* 12:335-342, 1947.

ANGELL, ROBERT C.: *The Moral Integration of American Cities,* special issue of *American Journal of Sociology,* no. 1, part 2, July, 1951.

APODACA, ANADETO: "Corn and Custom: The Introduction of Hybrid Corn to Spanish American Farmers in New Mexico," in EDWARD H. SPICER (ED.), *Human Problems in Technological Change,* Russell Sage Foundation, New York, 1952, pp. 35-39.

ARGYRIS, CHRIS: "We Must Make Work Worthwhile," *Life,* May 5, 1967, pp. 56ff.

ARNOLD, THURMAN: *The Folklore of Capitalism,* Yale University Press, New Haven, Conn., 1937.

ARONSON, ELLIOT, ET AL.: "Communicator Credibility and Communication Discrepancy as Determinants of Opinion Change," *Journal of Abnormal and Social Psychology,* 67:31-36, 1963.

ASCH, S. E.: "Effects of Group Pressure upon the Modification and Distortion of Judgments," in HEINZ GUETZKOW (ED.), *Groups, Leadership, and Men,* U.S. Office of Naval Research, Carnegie Press, Carnegie Institute of Technology, Pittsburgh, Pa., 1951.

ATTWOOD, WILLIAM: "The Fluoridation Controversy," *Look,* June 4, 1958, pp. 9–23.

AXELROD, MORRIS: "Urban Structure and Social Participation," *American Sociological Review,* 21:13–18, 1956.

BAILEY, GEORGE: "The Disappearing Satellite," *Reporter,* Mar. 16, 1961, pp. 20–23.

BAIN, READ: "Our Schizoid Culture," *Sociology and Social Research,* 19:266–276, 1935.

BAIN, READ: "The Self- and Other-words of a Child," *American Journal of Sociology,* 41:767–776, May, 1936.

BALANDIER, GEORGE: "Race Relations in West and Central Africa," in ANDREW W. LIND (ED.), *Race Relations in a World Perspective,* University of Hawaii Press, Honolulu, 1955.

BALES, ROBERT F.: "Small-group Theory and Research," in ROBERT K. MERTON, LEONARD BROOM, AND LEONARD S. COTTRELL, JR. (EDS.), *Sociology Today: Problems and Prospects,* Basic Books, Inc., Publishers, New York, 1959, pp. 293–308.

BALTZELL, E. DIGBY: *Philadelphia Gentlemen: The Making of a National Upper Class,* The Free Press of Glencoe, New York, 1958.

BARBER, BERNARD: *Social Stratification,* Harcourt, Brace & World, Inc., New York, 1957.

BARBER, BERNARD, AND LYLE S. TOBEL: "Fashion in Women's Clothes and the American Social System," *Social Forces,* 31:124–131, 1953.

BARLOW, ROBIN, ET AL.: *Economic Behavior of the Affluent,* Brookings Institution, Washington, D.C., 1966.

BARNES, C. A.: "A Statistical Study of the Freudian Theory of Levels of Psychosexual Development," *Genetic Psychology Monographs,* 45:105–174, 1952.

BARNES, HARRY ELMER: *An Introduction to the History of Sociology,* The University of Chicago Press, Chicago, 1948.

BARNETT, H. G.: *Innovation: The Basis of Social Change,* McGraw-Hill Book Company, New York, 1953.

BARRETT, GEORGE: "Close-up of the Birchers' Founder," *New York Times Magazine,* May 14, 1961, pp. 13ff.

BARTH, ALAN: "Report on the 'Rampageous Right.'" *New York Times Magazine,* Nov. 26, 1961, pp. 25ff.

BASCOM, WILLIAM R., AND MELVILLE J. HERSKOVITZ (EDS.): *Continuity and Change in African Cultures,* University of Chicago Press, Chicago, 1959.

BAVELAS, ALEX: "Communication Patterns in Task-oriented Groups," in DORWIN CARTWRIGHT AND ALVIN F. ZANDER (EDS.): *Group Dynamics,* Harper & Row, Publishers, Incorporated, New York, 1953, pp. 493–494.

BEARD, CHARLES, AND MARY BEARD: *The Rise of American Civilization,* The Macmillan Company, New York, 1930.

BECKER, HOWARD S.: *Outsiders,* The Free Press of Glencoe, New York, 1963.

BECKER, HOWARD S.: "Whose Side Are We On?", *Social Problems,* 14:239–247, Winter, 1967.

BEIN, A.: *Return to the Soil,* New York: Zionist Organization of America, New York, 1953.

BELL, DANIEL: "The Power Elite—Reconsidered," *American Journal of Sociology,* 64:238–250, 1958.

BELL, DANIEL (ED.): *The Radical Right: The New American Right, Expanded and Updated,* Doubleday & Company, Inc., Garden City, N.Y., 1963.

BELL, WENDELL, AND MARYANNE T. FORCE: "Urban Neighborhood Types and Participation in Voluntary Associations," *American Sociological Review,* 21:19–25, 1956.

BEN-DAVID, JOSEPH: "Scientific Productivity and Academic Organization," *American Sociological Review,* 25:828–843, 1960.

BENDINER, ROBERT: "What's Wrong in the House of Labor?" *Reporter,* 25:41–46, Oct. 12, 1961.

BENDIX, REINHARD, AND SEYMOUR M. LIPSET (EDS.): *Class, Status, and Power,* The Free Press of Glencoe, New York, 1953, 1966.

BENEDICT, RUTH: *Patterns of Culture,* Houghton Mifflin Company, Boston, 1934.

BENEDICT, RUTH: "Continuities and Discontinuities in Cultural Conditioning," *Psychiatry,* 1:161–167, 1938.

BERLE, ADOLF A., AND GARDINER C. MEANS: *The Modern Corporation and Private Property,* The Macmillan Company, New York, 1932.

BERNARD, JESSIE: "Autonomic and Decisive Competition," *The Sociological Quarterly,* 1:25–38, January, 1960.

BERNSTEIN, BASIL: "Elaborated and Restricted Codes: An Outline," *Sociological Inquiry,* 36:254–261, Spring, 1966.

BERNSTEIN, MOREY: *The Search for Bridey Murphy,* Doubleday & Company, Inc., Garden City, N.Y., 1956.

BERNSTEIN, WALTER: "The Cherubs Are Rumbling," *New Yorker,* Sept. 21, 1957, pp. 129–159.

BERRY, BREWTON: *Race and Ethnic Relations,* Houghton Mifflin Company, Boston, 1958.

BESTOR, ARTHUR E., JR.: *Backwoods Utopias: The Sectarian and Overnite Phases of Communitarian Socialism in America: 1663–1829,* University of Pennsylvania Press, Philadelphia, 1950.

BETTELHEIM, BRUNO, AND MORRIS JANOWITZ: *The Dynamics of Prejudice,* Harper & Row, Publishers, Incorporated, New York, 1950.

BETTELHEIM, BRUNO: "Does Communal Education Work? The Case of the Kibbutz," *Commentary*, 33:117–125, February, 1962; reprinted in EDWIN M. SCHUR (ED.), *The Family and the Sexual Revolution*, Indiana University Press, Bloomington, Ind., 1964, pp. 293–307.

BIDERMAN, ALBERT D.: "Social-Psychological Needs and 'Involuntary' Behavior as Illustrated by Compliance in Interrogation," *Sociometry*, 23:120–147, 1960.

BIDERMAN, ALBERT D.: *March To Calumny*, The Macmillan Company, New York, 1963.

BIERSTEDT, ROBERT A.: "An Analysis of Social Power," *American Sociological Review*, 15:730–738, December, 1950.

BIERSTEDT, ROBERT A.: *The Social Order*, McGraw-Hill Book Company, New York, 1963.

BLAU, PETER M.: *The Dynamics of Bureaucracy*, The University of Chicago Press, Chicago, 1955.

BLAUNER, ROBERT: "Whitewash over Watts," *Transaction*, 3:3–9, March-April, 1966.

BLIVEN, BRUCE: "The Revolution of the Joneses," *New York Times Magazine*, Oct. 9, 1960, pp. 28ff.

BLOOD, ROBERT A., AND DONALD M. WOLFE: *Husbands and Wives*, The Free Press of Glencoe, New York, 1960.

BLOODWORTH, DENNIS: "How Mao Rides the Dragon," *The Observer* (London), Sept. 11, 1966; reprinted in *Current*, October, 1966, pp. 48–50.

BLOOM, B. S.: "The Thought Process of Students in Discussion," in SIDNEY J. FRENCH (ED.), *Accent on Teaching*, Harper & Row, Publishers, Incorporated, New York, 1954.

BLUMBERG, LEONARD, AND ROBERT R. BELL: "Urban Migration and Kinship Ties," *Social Problems*, 6:328–333, Spring, 1959.

BLUMER, HERBERT: "Social Movements," in ALFRED M. LEE (ED.), *College Outline Series: Principles of Sociology*, Barnes & Noble, Inc., 1951, pp. 199–220.

BLUMER, HERBERT: "Social Science and the Desegregation Process," *Annals of the American Academy of Political and Social Sciences*, 304:137–143, 1956.

BOGARDUS, EMORY S.: "A Race Relations Cycle," *American Journal of Sociology*, 35:612–617, 1930.

BOGARDUS, EMORY S.: "The Long Trail of Cooperation," *Sociology and Social Research*, 31:54–62, 1946.

BOGARDUS, EMORY S.: *Sociology*, The Macmillan Company, New York, 1949.

BOGARDUS, EMORY S.: *Fundamentals of Social Psychology*, Appleton-Century-Crofts, New York, 1950.

BOGARDUS, EMORY S.: "Racial Distance Changes in the United States during the Past Thirty Years," *Sociology and Social Research*, 43:127–135, 1958.

BOGARDUS, EMORY S.: "Racial Reactions by Regions," *Sociology and Social Research*, 43:286–290, 1959.

BOGART, LEO: "Measuring the Effectiveness of an Overseas Information Campaign: A Case History," *Public Opinion Quarterly*, 21:475–498, 1957.

BOGART, LEO: *The Age of Television*, Frederick A. Praeger, Inc., New York, 1958.

BOGUE, DONALD J.: *The Population of the United States*, The Free Press of Glencoe, New York, 1959.

BOODISH, HYMAN M.: "Liberal Arts Training for Engineers and Scientists," *The Social Studies*, 48:31–33, 1957.

BOSSARD, JAMES H. S., AND W. P. SANGER: "The Large Family System," *American Sociological Review*, 17:3–91, February, 1952.

BOSSARD, JAMES H. S.: *The Sociology of Child Development*, Harper & Row, Publishers, Incorporated, New York, 1954.

BOULDING, KENNETH E.: "Protestantism's Lost Economic Gospel," *Christian Century*, 67:970–972, Aug. 16, 1950.

BOUMA, DONALD: "The Analysis of the Social Power Position of a Real Estate Board," *Social Problems*, 10:116–128, Fall, 1962 (a).

BOUMA, DONALD: "The Legitimation of the Social Power Position of a Real Estate Board," *American Journal of Economics and Sociology*, 21:383–392, October, 1962 (b).

BOUMA, DONALD: *Why Kalamazoo Voted No*, W. E. Upjohn Institute for Employment Research, Kalamazoo, Michigan, 1962 (c).

BOVARD, EVERETT W., JR.: "Group Structure and Perception," *Journal of Abnormal and Social Psychology*, 46:398–405, 1951.

BRADY, THOMAS F.: "French Worker-Priests Must Abandon Politics," *New York Times*, Jan. 31, 1954, sect. 4, p. 7.

BRIM, ORVILLE G., JR.: "The Acceptance of New Behavior in Child-rearing," *Human Relations*, 7:473–491, 1954.

BRINTON, CRANE: *The Anatomy of Revolution*," W. W. Norton & Company, Inc., New York, 1938.

BROWN, ROGER W.: "Determinants of the Relationship between Rigidity and Authoritarianism," *Journal of Abnormal and Social Psychology*, 48:469–475, 1953.

BROWN, WILLIAM G.: *The Lower South in American History*, The Macmillan Company, New York, 1902.

BROWN, WILLIAM O.: "Culture Contact and Race Conflict," in E. B. REUTER (ED.), *Race and Culture Contacts*, McGraw-Hill Book Company, New York, 1934.

BRUYN, SEVERYN T.: *The Human Perspective in Sociology: The Methodology of Participant Observation*, Prentice-Hall, Englewood Cliffs, N.J., 1966.

BUCKLEY, THOMAS: "When Good Birchers Get Together," *New York Times*, June 5, 1966, pp. 48ff.

BURCHINAL, LEE G., AND HILDA SIFF: "Rural Poverty," *Journal of Marriage and Family*, 26:399–405, November, 1964.

BUREAU OF LABOR STATISTICS: *Summary of the Report on Conditions of Women and Children Wage Earners in the United States*, Bulletin no. 175, Washington.

BURGESS, ERNEST W., AND LEONARD S. COTTRELL: *Predicting Success or Failure in Marriage*, Prentice-Hall, Inc., Englewood Cliffs, N.J., 1939.

BURGESS, ERNEST W., AND HARVEY J. LOCKE: *The Family: From Institution to Companionate*, American Book Company, New York, 1953.

BURGESS, ERNEST W., AND PAUL WALLIN: *Engagement and Marriage*, J. B. Lippincott Company, Philadelphia, 1953.

BURLINGAME, ROGER: *Inventors behind the Inventor*, Harcourt, Brace & World, Inc., 1947.

BURMA, JOHN H.: "The Measurement of Negro Passing," *American Journal of Sociology*, 52:18–22, 1946.

BURMA, JOHN H.: "Student Attitudes towards and Participation in Voluntary Organizations," *Sociology and Social Research*, 32:625–629, November, 1947.

BURNHAM, JAMES F.: *The Managerial Revolution*, The John Day Company, Inc., New York, 1941.

BURTON, KATHERINA: *Paradise Planters: The Story of Brook Farm*, David McKay Company, Inc., New York, 1939.

Business Week, "Sociologists Invade the Plant," Mar. 21, 1959, pp. 95ff.

CADY, JOHN F.: "Religion and Politics in Modern Burma," *Far Eastern Quarterly*, 12:149–162, 1953.

CAHNMAN, WERNER J.: "Socio-economic Causes of Anti-Semitism," *Social Problems*, 5:21–29, 1957.

CALVIN, A. D., AND WAYNE H. HOLTZMAN: "Adjustment to the Discrepancy between Self Concept and the Inferred Self," *Journal of Consulting Psychiatry*, 17:39–44, 1953.

CAMPBELL, DONALD T., AND THELMA H. MCCORMACK: "Military Experience and Attitudes toward Authority," *American Journal of Sociology*, 62:482–490, 1957.

CANTRIL, HADLEY: *The Psychology of Social Movements*, John Wiley & Sons, Inc., New York, 1941.

CANTRIL, HADLEY: "Identification with Social and Economic Class," *Journal of Abnormal and Social Psychology*, 38:74–80, 1943.

CANTRIL, HADLEY: *The Politics of Despair*, Basic Books, Inc., Publishers, New York, 1958.

CAPLOW, THEODORE: *The Academic Marketplace*, Basic Books, Inc., Publishers, New York, 1958.

CARLSON, J. R.: *Under Cover*, E. P. Dutton & Co., Inc., New York, 1943.

CARLSON, J. R.: *The Plotters*, E. P. Dutton & Co., Inc., New York, 1946.

CAROTHERS, J. C.: "A Study of Mental Derangement in Africans, and an Attempt to Explain its Peculiarities, More Especially in Relation to the African Attitude of Life," *Journal of Mental Science*, 93:548–597, 1947. Summarized in James C. Coleman, *Abnormal Psychology and Modern Life*, Scott, Foresman and Company, Chicago, 1956, pp. 256–259.

CARROLL, CHARLES: *The Negro a Beast, or, In the Image of God*, American Bible and Book House, St. Louis, 1900.

CARTWRIGHT, DORWIN, AND ALVIN F. ZANDER (EDS.): *Group Dynamics: Theory and Research*, Harper & Row, Publishers, Incorporated, New York, 1960.

CATER, DOUGLAS: "Civil War in Alabama's Citizens' Councils," *Reporter*, May 17, 1956, pp. 19–21.

CENTERS, RICHARD: *The Psychology of Social Classes*, Princeton University Press, Princeton, N.J., 1949.

CHAMBERS, ROSALIND C.: "A Study of Three Voluntary Organizations," in D. V. GLASS (ED.), *Social Mobility in Britain*, The Free Press of Glencoe, New York, 1954, pp. 384–406.

CHANDRASEKHAR, S.: "Mao's War with the Chinese Family," *New York Times Magazine*, May 17, 1959, pp. 21ff.

CHAPIN, F. STUART: "Research Studies of Extra-curricular Activities and Their Significance in Reflecting Social Change," *Journal of Educational Sociology*, 4:491–498, 1931.

CHAPIN, F. STUART: "Contemporary American Institutions," Harper & Row, Publishers, Incorporated, New York, 1935.

CHAPIN, F. STUART, AND JOHN E. TSOUDEROS: "Formalization, Observed in Ten Voluntary Associations: Concepts, Morphology, Process," *Social Forces*, 33:306–309, May, 1955.

CHAPIN, F. STUART, AND JOHN E. TSOUDEROS: "The Formalization Process in Voluntary Associations," *Social Forces*, 34:342–344, May, 1956.

CHASE, EDWARD T.: "Jam on the Côte d'Azur," *Reporter*, Sept. 28, 1961, pp. 44–46.

CHICAGO COMMISSION ON RACE RELATIONS: *The Negro in Chicago*, The University of Chicago Press, Chicago, 1922.

CHIDZERO, B. T. G.: "African Nationalism in East and Central Africa," *International Affairs*, 36:465–475, 1960.

CHINOY, ELY: "The Tradition of Opportunity and the Aspirations of Automobile Workers," *American Journal of Sociology*, 57:453–459, 1952.

CLAUSEN, CONNIE: *I Love You Honey, but the Season's Over*, Holt, Rinehart and Winston, Inc., New York, 1961.

CLEGHORN, REESE: "Allen of Atlanta Collides with Black Power and White Racism," *New York Times Magazine*, Oct. 16, 1966, pp. 32ff.

CLINARD, MARSHALL B.: *The Black Market: A Study in White Collar Crime*, Holt, Rinehart and Winston, Inc., New York, 1952.

CLINARD, MARSHALL B.: *Sociology of Deviant Behavior*, Holt, Rinehart and Winston, Inc., New York, 1963.

COHEN, ALBERT K.: *Delinquent Boys: The Culture of the Gang*, The Free Press of Glencoe, New York, 1955.

COHEN, JERRY, AND WILLIAM S. MURPHY: *Burn, Baby, Burn*, E. P. Dutton & Company, Inc., New York, 1966.

COHEN, MITCHELL, AND DENNIS HALE (EDS.): *The New Student Left*, Beacon Press, Boston, 1966.

COHN, NORMAN: *The Pursuit of the Millennium*, Essential Books, Fair Lawn, N.J., 1957.

COLEMAN, JAMES C.: *Abnormal Psychology and Modern Life*, Scott, Foresman and Company, Chicago, 1964.

COLEMAN, JAMES S.: *The Adolescent Society*, The Free Press of Glencoe, New York, 1961.

COLLIER, JOHN: *Indians of the Americas*, W. W. Norton & Company, Inc., New York, 1947.

CONANT, JAMES B.: *Slums and Suburbs: A Commentary on Schools in Metropolitan Areas*, McGraw-Hill Book Company, New York, 1961.

COOLEY, CHARLES HORTON: "The Theory of Transportation," *Publications of the American Economic Association*, vol. 9, no. 3, 1894.

COOLEY, CHARLES HORTON: *The Nature of Human Nature*, Charles Scribner's Sons, New York, 1902.

COOLEY, CHARLES HORTON: "A Study of the Early Use of Self Words by a Child," *Psychological Review*, 15:339–357, 1908.

COPP, JAMES H., (ED.): *Our Changing Rural Society: Perspectives and Trends*, The Department of Publications, State University of Iowa, Iowa City, Iowa, 1964.

COSER, LEWIS A.: *The Functions of Social Conflict*, The Free Press of Glencoe, New York, 1956.

COSER, LEWIS A., AND BERNARD ROSENBERG: *Sociological Theory*, The Macmillan Company, New York, 1957.

COUSINS, NORMAN: "Where Violence Begins," *Saturday Review*, Jan. 18, 1954, pp. 22ff.

CRONON, EDMUND D.: *Black Moses*, The University of Wisconsin Press, Madison, Wis., 1955.

DAHL, ROBERT A.: "A Critique of the Ruling Elite Model," *American Political Science Review*, 52:463–469, 1958.

DAI, BINGHAM: "Obsessive-Compulsive Disorders in Chinese Culture," *Social Problems*, 4:313–321, 1957.

DALE, EDWARD EVERETT: *The Range Cattle Industry*, University of Oklahoma Press, Norman, Okla., 1930.

DAVIDSON, BILL: "Combat Soldiers Fail to Shoot," *Colliers*, Nov. 8, 1952, pp. 16–18.

DAVIES, JAMES C.: "Toward a Theory of Revolution," *American Sociological Review*, 27:5–19, 1962.

DAVIS, ALLISON: "The Motivation of the Underprivileged Worker," in WILLIAM F. WHYTE (ED.), *Industry and Society*, McGraw-Hill Book Company, New York, 1946, 1946, pp. 84–106.

DAVIS, ALLISON, AND ROBERT J. HAVIGHURST: "Social Class and Color Differences in Child-rearing," *American Sociological Review*, 11:698–710, 1946.

DAVIS, ALLISON: *Social-class Influences on Learning*, Harvard University Press, Cambridge, Mass., 1952.

DAVIS, A. K.: "Bureaucratic Patterns in the Navy Officer Corps," *Social Forces*, 27:143–153, 1948.

DAVIS, FRED: "The Cabdriver and His Fare: Facets of a Fleeting Relationship," *American Journal of Sociology*, 65:158–165, 1959.

DAVIS, JEROME: *Contemporary Social Movements*, Appleton-Century-Crofts, New York, 1930.

DAVIS, KINGSLEY, AND WILBERT MOORE: "Some Principles of Stratification," *American Sociological Review*, 10:242–249, April, 1945.

DAVIS, KINGSLEY: *Human Society*, The Macmillan Company, New York, 1949.

DAVIS, KINGSLEY: "The Unpredicted Pattern of Population Change," *Annals of the American Academy of Political and Social Science*, 305:53–59, 1956.

DAWSON, CARL, AND W. E. GETTYS: *Introduction to Sociology*, The Ronald Press Company, New York, 1934, 1948.

DEAN, DWIGHT G.: "Alienation: Its Meaning and Measurement," *American Sociological Review*, 26:753–758, 1961.

DEASY, LEILA CALHOUN: "Socio-economic Status and Participation in the Poliomyelitis Vaccine Trial," *American Sociological Review*, 21:185–191, 1956.

DE CASTRO, JOSUÉ: *The Geography of Hunger*, Little, Brown and Company, Boston, 1952.

DEMERATH, N. J.: "Schizophrenia Among Primitives," *American Journal of Psychiatry*, 98:703–707, March, 1942.

DEMPSEY, DAVID: "What It's Like To Live with Genius," *New York Times Magazine*, Oct. 5, 1958, pp. 36ff.

DEUTSCH, MORTON: "An Experimental Study of the Effects of Cooperation and Competition upon Group Process," *Human Relations*, 2:199–231, 1949.

DEWEY, RICHARD: "The Rural-Urban Continuum: Real but Relatively Unimportant," *American Journal of Sociology*, 66:60–66, 1960.

DITTES, JAMES E., AND HAROLD H. KELLEY: "Effects of Different Conditions of Acceptance upon Conformity to Group Norms," *Journal of Abnormal and Social Psychology*, 53:100–107, 1956.

DJILAS, MILOVAN: *The New Class*, Frederick A. Praeger, Inc., New York, 1957.

DOBRINER, WILLIAM M. (ED.): *The Suburban Community*, G. P. Putnam's Sons, New York, 1958.

DODSON, DAN W.: "The Creative Role of Conflict Reexamined," *Journal of Intergroup Relations*, 1:5–12, 1959.

DOOB, LEONARD: *Propaganda*, Holt, Rinehart and Winston, Inc., New York, 1948.

DOTEN, DANA: *The Art of Bundling*, Farrar, Straus & Co., Inc., New York, 1938.

DOUVAN, ELIZABETH: "Employment and the Adolescent," in F. IVAN NYE, *The Employed Mother in America*, Rand McNally & Company, Chicago, 1963, pp. 142–164.

DRAPER, THEODORE: "The Psychology of Surrender," *Atlantic Monthly*, 176:62–65, 1945.

DRURY, ALLEN: *Advise and Consent*, Doubleday & Company, Inc., Garden City, N.Y., 1959.

DUBOIS, CORA: *The Peoples of Alor*, The University of Minnesota Press, Minneapolis, 1944.

DUNCAN, DAVID DOUGLAS: "In the Middle of an Indian Massacre," *Life*, Oct. 6, 1947, pp. 6ff.

DUNHAM, H. WARREN, AND S. KIRSON WEINBERG: *The Culture of the State Mental Hospital*, Wayne State University Press, Detroit, 1960.

DURKHEIM, EMILE (1897): *Le Suicide: étude de Sociologie*, F. Alcon, Paris, tr., J. A. SPAULDING AND G. SIMPSON, The Free Press of Glencoe, New York, 1951.

Economist, 181:59, 1956, "Rebels in Indonesia."

EDITORS OF *Wall Street Journal*: *The New Millionaires and How They Made Their Fortunes*, Bernard Geis Associates, New York, 1961.

EDWARDS, ALLEN A.: "Types of Rural Communities," in MARVIN B. SUSSMAN (ED.), *Community Structure and Analysis*, Thomas Crowell Company, New York, 1959.

EDWARDS, LYFORD P.: *The Natural History of Revolution*, The University of Chicago Press, Chicago, 1927.

EGGAN, DOROTHY: "The General Problem of Hopi Adjustment," *American Anthropologist*, 45:357–373, July, 1943.

EHRMANN, WINSTON: *Premarital Dating Behavior*, Holt, Rinehart and Winston, Inc., New York, 1959.

EKSTEIN, BENJAMIN R., AND ARNOLD FORSTER: *The Radical Right: Report on the John Birch Society and Its Allies*, Vintage Books, Random House, Inc., New York, 1967.

ELLIS, EVELYN: "Social Psychological Correlates of Upward Social Mobility among Unmarried Career Women," *American Sociological Review*, 17:558–563, 1952.

ELWIN, VARRIER: *The Biaga*, John Murray (Publishers), Ltd., London, 1939.

ERNST, MORRIS, AND DAVID LOTH: *Report on the American Communist*, Holt, Rinehart and Winston, Inc., New York, 1952.

ESSIEN-UDOM, E. U.: *Black Nationalism: A Search for an Identity in America*, The University of Chicago Press, Chicago, 1962.

ETZIONI, AMITAI (ED.): *Complex Organizations*, Holt, Rinehart and Winston, Inc., New York, 1961.

EULAN, HANS: "Identification with Class and Political Role Behavior," *Public Opinion Quarterly*, 20:515–529, 1956.

EVANS, ROWLAND, JR.: "India Experiments with Sterilization," *Harper's Magazine*, November, 1961, pp. 78–88.

EWERS, JOHN C.: *The Horse in the Blackfeet Culture*, Bureau of American Ethnology, Bulletin no. 159, Washington, 1955.

FAIRCHILD, HENRY PRATT (ED.): *Dictionary of Sociology*, Philosophical Library, Inc., New York, 1957.

FAIRCHILD, HENRY PRATT: Review of JOSUÉ DE CASTRO, *The Geography of Hunger*, in *Social Forces*, 31:82–84, 1952.

FANFANI, AMINTORE: *Catholicism, Protestantism and Capitalism*, Sheed & Ward, Inc., New York, 1955.

FARIS, R. E. L., "The Alleged Class System in the United States," *Research Studies of the State College of Washington*, Vol. 22, June, 1954.

FARMER, JAMES: "I Will Keep My Soul," *Progressive*, 25:21–22, November, 1961.

FELDMESSER, ROBERT A.: "The Persistence of Status Advantages in Soviet Russia," *American Journal of Sociology*, 59:19–27, 1953.

FESTINGER, L., A. PIPESTONE, AND T. NEWCOMB: "Some Consequences of Deindividuation in a Group," *Journal of Abnormal and Social Psychology*, 47:382–389, 1952.

FESTINGER, LEON, HENRY W. RIECKEN, AND STANLEY SCHACHTER: *When Prophecy Fails*, The University of Minnesota Press, Minneapolis, 1956.

FEUER, LEWIS S.: "The Risk is 'Juvenocracy,'" *New York Times Magazine*, Sept. 18, 1966, pp. 56ff.

FEY, HAROLD E.: "Let Us Possess the Land," *Christian Century*, 71:757–759, 1954.

FIRTH, RAYMOND: "The Theory of Cargo Cults: A Note on Tikopia," *Man*, 55:130–132, 1955.

FLEMING, HAROLD C.: "The Price of a Cup of Coffee," *Reporter*, May 12, 1960, pp. 25–26.

FLETCHER, JOSEPH F.: *Situation Ethics: The New Morality*, The Westminster Press, Philadelphia, 1966.

FLIEGEL, FREDERICK C., AND JOSEPH E. KIVLIN: "Attributes of Innovation as Factors in Diffusion," *American Journal of Sociology*, 72:235–248, November, 1966.

FLUGEL, J. C.: *The Psychology of Clothes*, The Hogarth Press, Ltd., London, 1930.

FOLSOM, JOSEPH K.: *The Family*, John Wiley & Sons, Inc., New York, 1943.

FOREMAN, GRANT: *Indian Removal*, University of Oklahoma Press, Norman, Okla., 1932.

FOREMAN, PAUL B.: "Panic Theory," *Sociology and Social Research*, 37:295–304, 1953.

FORM, WILLIAM, ET AL.: *Community in Disaster*, Harper & Row, Publishers, Incorporated, New York, 1958.

FORM, WILLIAM H., AND WARREN L. SAUER: *Community Influentials in a Middle-sized City*, Institute for Community Development, Michigan State University, East Lansing, Mich., 1960.

FORTUNE, R. F.: *The Sorcerers of Dobu*, E. P. Dutton & Co., Inc., New York, 1932.

Fortune, February, 1940, p. 21, "The People of the United States—A Self Portrait."

Fortune, February, 1950, p. 63, "The American Way of Life."

FOSKETT, JOHN M.: "Social Structure and Community Participation," *American Sociological Review*, 20:431–438, 1955.

FOX, ROBERT B.: "The Study of Filipino Society and Its Significance to Programs of Economic and Social Development," *Philippine Sociological Review*, 7:2–11, 1959.

FOX, RUTH: "The Alcoholic Spouse," in VICTOR W. EISENSTEIN (ED.), *Neurotic Interaction in Marriage*, Basic Books, Inc., New York, 1956, pp. 148–167.

FRAKES, MARGARET: "Folk Church in a Welfare State," *Christian Century*, 75:1020 (1958).

FRANCOIS, WILLIAM: "Where Poverty Is Permanent," *Reporter*, Apr. 17, 1961, pp. 38–39.

FREEDMAN, JANET: "The Birch Tree Grows," *Library Journal*, 91:625–628, Feb. 1, 1966.

FREEDMAN, RONALD, PASCAL K. WHELPTON, AND ARTHUR A. CAMPBELL: *Family Planning, Sterility, and Population Growth*, McGraw-Hill Book Company, New York, 1959.

FREEDMAN, RONALD, PASCAL K. WHELPTON, AND JOHN W. SMIT: "Socio-economic Factors in Religious Differentials in Fertility," *American Sociological Review*, 26:608–614, 1961.

FREEMAN, HOWARD E.: "Attitudes toward Mental Patients among Relatives of Former Patients," *American Sociological Review*, 26:59–66, 1961.

FREUD, SIGMUND: *Civilization and Its Discontents*, The Hogarth Press, Ltd., London, 1961.

FROMM, ERICH: *Escape From Freedom,* Holt, Rinehart and Winston, Inc., New York, 1941.

FROMM, ERICH: "Individual and Social Origins of Neurosis," *American Sociological Review*, 9:380–384, 1944.

FROMM, ERICH: *The Art of Loving*, Harper & Row, Publishers, Incorporated, New York, 1956.

FULLER, JOHN G.: "Trade Winds," *Saturday Review*, 45:12, Feb. 17, 1962.

GALBRAITH, JOHN KENNETH: *American Capitalism: The Concept of Countervailing Power*, Houghton Mifflin Company, Boston, 1952.

GALBRAITH, JOHN KENNETH: *The Affluent Society*, Houghton Mifflin Company, Boston, 1958.

GALLUP, GEORGE, AND S. F. RAE: *The Pulse of Democracy*, Simon and Schuster, Inc., New York, 1940.

GALLUP, GEORGE: "The Changing Climate for Public Opinion Research," *Public Opinion Quarterly*, 21:23–28, 1957.

GAMAREKIAN, EDWARD A.: "The Ugly Battle of Orangeburg," *Reporter*, Jan. 24, 1957, pp. 32–34.

GARDNER, MARTIN: *Fads and Fallacies in the Name of Science*, Dover Publications, Inc., New York, 1957.

GERBNER, GEORGE: "The Social Role of the Confessions Magazine," *Social Problems*, 6:29–40, 1958.

GERTH, HANS: "The Nazi Party: Its Leadership and Composition," *American Journal of Sociology*, 55:517–541, 1940.

GIBB, CECIL A., in GARDNER LINDZEY (ED.): *Handbook of Social Psychology*, Addison-Wesley Publishing Company, Inc., Reading, Mass., 1954, vol. 2, pp. 884–889.

GIBBARD, HAROLD: "Residential Succession: A Study in Human Ecology, unpublished Ph.D. dissertation, University of Michigan, 1938.

GIDDINGS, F. H.: *The Principles of Sociology*, The Macmillan Company, New York, 1913.

GILES, ROBERT H.: "How to Become a Target City," *The Reporter*, June 15, 1967, pp. 38–41.

GILLIN, JOHN L., AND JOHN P. GILLIN: *Cultural Sociology*, The Macmillan Company, New York, 1948.

GILLIN, JOHN P.: *The Ways of Men*, Appleton-Century-Crofts, New York, 1948.

GILROY, HARRY: "Flight from East Germany: The People," *New York Times*, Aug. 13, 1961, section 4, p. 4.

GIST, NOEL P.: "Caste Differentials in South India," *American Sociological Review*, 19:126–137, 1954.

GLICK, CLARENCE: "Social Roles and Types in Race Relations," in ANDREW W. LIND, *Race Relations in World Perspective*, University of Hawaii Press, Honolulu, 1955.

GLICK, PAUL C., AND EMANUEL LANDAU: "Age as a Factor in Marriage," *American Sociological Review*, 15: 517–529, 1950.

GLICK, PAUL C.: *American Families*, John Wiley & Sons, Inc., New York, 1957.

GLOCK, CHARLES Y., AND BENJAMIN B. RINGER: "Church Policy and the Attitudes of Ministers and Parishioners on Social Issues," *American Sociological Review*, 21:148–156, April, 1956.

GLUECK, SHELDON, AND ELEANOR GLUECK: *Predicting Juvenile Delinquency and Crime*, Harvard University Press, Cambridge, Mass., 1959.

GOFFMAN, ERVING: *Presentation of Self in Everyday Life*, Social Science Research Center, University of Edinburgh, 1956: reprinted by Anchor Books, Doubleday & Company, Inc., Garden City, N.Y., 1959.

GOLDHAMER, HERBERT, AND EDWARD A. SHILS: "Types of Power and Status," *American Journal of Sociology*, 45:171–182, September, 1939.

GOLDHAMER, HERBERT, AND ANDREW MARSHALL: *Psychosis and Civilization: Two Studies in the Frequency of Mental Illness*, The Free Press of Glencoe, New York, 1953.

GOLDNER, FRED H.: Review of Vance Packard, *The Pyramid Climbers, American Journal of Sociology*, 69: 197, September, 1963.

GOLDSTEIN, SIDNEY: "Migration and Occupational Mobility in Norristown, Pennsylvania," *American Sociological Review*, 20:402–408, 1955.

GOOD, PAUL: "Birmingham Two Years Later," *The Reporter*, Dec. 2, 1965, pp. 21–27.

GORDON, ALBERT ISAAC: *Intermarriage: Interfaith, Interracial, Interethnic*, Beacon Press, Boston, 1964.

GORDON, MILTON: *Social Class in American Society*, Duke University Press, Durham, N.C., 1958.

GREENWALD, HAROLD: *The Call Girl*, Ballantine Books, Inc., New York, 1959.

GREER, SCOTT: *Urban Renewal and America's Cities*, The Bobbs-Merrill Company, Inc., Indianapolis, 1965.

GREER, SCOTT, AND ELLA KUBE: "Urbanism and Social Structure: A Los Angeles Study," in MARVIN B. SUSSMAN (ED.), *Community Structure and Analysis*, Thomas Y. Crowell Company, New York, 1959.

GRIER, EUNICE, AND GEORGE GRIER: *Discrimination in Housing*, Anti-Defamation League, New York, 1960.

GRIFFIN, JOHN H.: *Black Like Me*, Houghton Mifflin Company, Boston, 1961.

GRODZINS, MORTON: *The Metropolitan Area as a Racial Problem*, University of Pittsburgh Press, Pittsburgh, Pa., 1958.

GROSS, EDWARD: "Some Functional Consequences of Primary Group Controls in Formal Work Organizations," *American Sociological Review*, 18:368–373, 1953.

GROVE, GENE: *Inside the John Birch Society*, Fawcett Publications, Inc., Greenwich, Conn., 1961.

GRUEN, VICTOR: *The Heart of Our Cities*, Simon and Schuster, Inc., New York, 1964.

GUSFIELD, JOSEPH R.: "Social Structure and Moral Reform: A Study of the Women's Christian Temperance Union," *American Journal of Sociology*, 56:221–232, 1955.

HACKER, ANDREW: "The Boy Who Doesn't Go to College," *New York Times Magazine*, June 24, 1962, pp. 11ff.

HACKETT, HERBERT: "The Flying Saucer," *Sociology and Social Research*, 32:869–873, 1948.

HAER, JOHN L.: "Predictive Utility of Five Indices of Social Stratification," *American Sociological Review*, 22:541–546, 1957.

HALLOWAY, MARK: *Heavens on Earth: Utopian Communities in America, 1680–1880*, Library Publishers, New York, 1951.

HARLOW, HARRY F., AND MARGARET K. HARLOW: "A Study of Animal Affection," *Natural History*, 70:48–55, 1961.

HARRIS, C. D., AND E. L. ULLMAN: "The Nature of Cities," *Annals of the American Academy*, 242:7–17, 1945.

HARRIS, LOUIS: "Election Polling and Research," *Public Opinion Quarterly*, 11:111, 1957.

HARRIS, SARA, WITH ASSISTANCE OF HARRIET CRITTENDEN: *Father Divine: Holy Husband*, Doubleday & Company, Inc., Garden City, N.Y., 1953.

HART, DONN V.: "The Philippine Cooperative Movement," *Far Eastern Survey*, 24:27–30, 1955.

HARVEY, JESSE: Unpublished doctoral dissertation, reported in *Science News Letter*, Dec. 5, 1953, p. 360.

HAVIGHURST, ROBERT J., AND ALLISON DAVIS: "A Comparison of the Chicago and Harvard Studies of Social Class Differences in Child-rearing," *American Sociological Review*, 20:438–442, 1955.

HAWLEY, AMOS H.: *Human Ecology: A Theory of Community Structure*, The Ronald Press Company, New York, 1950.

HEBERLE, RUDOLF: *Social Movements*, Appleton-Century-Crofts, New York, 1951.

HEBERLE, RUDOLF: Review of STANLEY HOFFMAN, *Le Mouvement Poujade* (Librairie Armand Colin, Paris), in *American Journal of Sociology*, 63:440–441, 1956.

HEGGEN, THOMAS, AND JOSHUA LOGAN: *Mister Roberts,* Random House, Inc., New York, 1948.

HERBERG, WILL: *Protestant, Catholic, Jew,* Doubleday & Company, Garden City, N.Y., 1960.

HERSKOVITZ, MELVILLE J.: *Man and His Works,* Alfred A. Knopf, Inc., New York, 1949.

HERTZLER, J. O.: *American Social Institutions,* Allyn and Bacon, Inc., Englewood Cliffs, N.J., 1961.

HERZOG, ELIZABETH: *Children of Working Mothers,* Children's Bureau Publication no. 382, U.S. Department of Health, Education, and Welfare, 1960.

HESS, ROBERT W., AND GERALD HANDEL: *Family Worlds,* The University of Chicago Press, Chicago, 1959.

HIGHAM, JOHN: *Strangers in the Land: Patterns of American Nativism, 1860–1925,* Rutgers University Press, New Brunswick, N.J., 1955.

HILL, REUBEN, J. MAYONE STYCOS, AND KURT W. BACK: *The Family and Population Control,* The University of North Carolina Press, Chapel Hill, N.C., 1959.

HILLERY, GEORGE A.: "Definitions of Community: Areas of Agreement," *Rural Sociology,* 20:111–123, 1955.

HIMES, JOSEPH S.: *Social Planning in America: A Dynamic Interpretation,* Doubleday & Company, Inc., Garden City, 1954.

HOCART, ARTHUR M.: *Caste: A Comparative Study,* Methuen & Co., Ltd., London, 1950.

HOEBEL, E. ADAMSON: *Man in the Primitive World,* McGraw-Hill Book Company, New York, 1949.

HOFFER, ERIC: *The True Believer,* Harper & Row, Publishers, Incorporated, New York, 1951.

HOFFMAN, LOIS W.: "Effects of Maternal Employment on Children," *Child Development,* 32:187–197, 1961.

HOFFMAN, LOIS W.: "Research Findings on the Effects of Maternal Employment on the Child," in F. IVAN NYE AND LOIS W. HOFFMAN (EDS.), *The Employed Mother in America,* Rand McNally & Company, Chicago, 1963, pp. 190–212.

HOLLINGSHEAD, AUGUST B.: *Elmtown's Youth,* John Wiley & Sons, New York, 1949.

HOLLINGSHEAD, AUGUST B., AND FREDRICH C. REDLICH: "Social Stratification and Psychiatric Disorders," *American Sociological Review,* 18:163–169, 1953.

HOLLINGSHEAD, AUGUST B., R. ELLIS, AND E. KIRBY: "Social Mobility and Mental Illness," *American Sociological Review,* 19:577–584, 1954.

HOLMES, J.G.: *In Primitive New Guinea,* G. P. Putnam's Sons, New York, 1924.

HOOTON, E. A.: *Crime and the Man,* Harvard University Press, Cambridge, Mass., 1939.

HOOVER, J. EDGAR: *Masters of Deceit,* Holt, Rinehart and Winston, Inc., New York, 1958.

HOPPER, JANICE A.: "Sociologists in the 1964 National Register of Scientific and Technical Personnel," *The American Sociologist,* 7:71–78, February, 1966.

HORN, STANLEY F.: *Invisible Empire,* Houghton Mifflin Company, Boston, 1939.

HORNEY, KAREN: *The Neurotic Personality of Our Time,* W. W. Norton & Company, Inc., New York, 1937.

HOROWITZ, IRVING LOUIS (ED.): *The New Sociology: Essays in Social Science and Social Theory in Honor of C. Wright Mills,* Oxford University Press, Fair Lawn, N.J., 1964.

HORTON, DONALD: "The Functions of Alcohol in Primitive Societies," *Quarterly Journal of Studies on Alcohol,* 4:293–303, 1943.

HORTON, PHILIP: "Revivalism on the Far Right," *Reporter,* July 20, 1961, pp. 25–29.

HOULT, THOMAS FORD: *The Sociology of Religion,* The Dryden Press, Inc., New York, 1958.

HOYT, HOMER: *One Hundred Years of Land Values in Chicago,* The University of Chicago Press, Chicago, 1933.

HUANG, L. J.: "Some Changing Patterns in the Communist Chinese Family," *Marriage and Family Living,* 23:137–146, May, 1961.

HUFF, DARRELL: *How To Lie with Statistics,* W. W. Norton & Company, Inc., New York, 1954.

HUNT, CHESTER L.: "The Treatment of 'Race' in Beginning Sociology Textbooks," *Sociology and Social Research,* 35:277–284, 1951.

HUNT, CHESTER L.: "Cultural Barriers to Point Four," *Antioch Review,* 14:159–167, Summer, 1954.

HUNT, CHESTER L.: "Moslem and Christian in the Philippines," *Pacific Affairs,* 28:331–350, 1955.

HUNT, CHESTER L.: "Ethnic Conflict in the Orient," *Journal of East Asiatic Studies,* 5:327–331, University of Manila, 1956.

HUNTER, FLOYD: *Community Power Structure,* The University of North Carolina Press, Chapel Hill, N.C., 1953.

HURLOCK, ELIZABETH B.: "The Use of Group Rivalry as an Incentive," *Journal of Abnormal and Social Psychology,* 22:278–290 (1927).

HUXLEY, ALDOUS: *Brave New World,* Doubleday & Company, Inc., Garden City, N.Y., 1932.

HUXLEY, ALDOUS: *Brave New World Revisited,* Harper & Row, Publishers, Incorporated, New York, 1958.

INKELES, ALEX: "Social Stratification and Mobility in the Soviet Union: 1940–1950," *American Sociological Review,* 15:465–479, 1950.

INKELES, ALEX: "Industrial Man: The Relation of Status

to Experience, Perception, and Value," *American Journal of Sociology*, 66:1–31, 1960.

INTERNATIONAL SOCIOLOGICAL ASSOCIATION, IN COLLABORATION WITH JESSIE BERNARD, T. H. PEAR, RAYMOND ARON, AND ROBERT C. ANGELL: *The Nature of Conflict*, UNESCO, Paris, 1957.

JACK, NANCY KOPLIN, AND BETTY SCHIFFER: "The Limits of Fashion Control," *American Sociological Review*, 13:730–738, 1948.

JACO, E. GARTLEY, AND IVAN BELKNAP: "Is a New Family Form Emerging in the Urban Fringe?" *American Sociological Review*, 18:551–557, 1953.

JACOB, K. K.: "Are Missionaries 'Western' Agents?" *Catholic World*, 184:449–451, 1957.

JACOBS, JANE: *The Death and Life of Great American Cities*, Random House, Inc., New York, 1961.

JOHNSON, DONALD M.: "The 'Phantom Anesthetist' of Mattoon: A Field Study of Mass Hysteria," *Journal of Abnormal and Social Psychology*, 40:175–186, 1945.

JOHNSON, THOMAS A.: "Black Power Parley Asks Olympic and Ring Boycott," *New York Times*, July 25, 1967, pp. 1ff.

JONASSEN, CHRISTEN T.: "Community Typology," in MARVIN B. SUSSMAN (ED.), *Community Structure and Analysis*, Thomas Y. Crowell Company, New York, 1959.

JONES, HOWARD W., AND WILLIAM W. SCOTT: *Hermaphroditism, Genital Abnormalities, and Related Endocrine Disorders*, The Williams & Wilkins Company, Baltimore, 1958.

JOST, HUDSON, AND LESTER W. SONTAG: "The Genetic Factor in Autonomic Nervous-system Function," *Psychosomatic Medicine*, 61:308–310, 1944.

KAHL, JOSEPH A.: "Educational and Occupational Aspirations of 'Common Man' Boys," *Harvard Educational Review*, 23:186–203, 1953.

KAHL, JOSEPH A., AND JAMES A. DAVIS: "A Comparison of Indexes of Socioeconomic Status," *American Sociological Review*, 20:317–325, 1955.

KAHL, JOSEPH A.: *The American Class Structure*, Holt, Rinehart and Winston, Inc., New York, 1957.

KALLEN, HORACE M.: "On Americanizing the American Indian," *Social Research*, 25:469–473, 1958.

KALLMAN, FRANZ J.: "The Genetic Theory of Schizophrenia," *American Journal of Psychiatry*, 103:309–322, November, 1946.

KANE, JOHN: *Catholic-Protestant Conflicts in America*, Henry Regnery Company, Chicago, 1955.

KANIN, EUGENE J., AND DAVID B. HOWARD: "Postmarital Consequences of Premarital Sex Adjustments," *American Sociological Review*, 23:557–562, October, 1958.

KAPLAN, BERT: *A Study of Rorschach Responses in Four Cultures*, Papers of the Peabody Museum of American Archeology and Ethnology, 42, no. 2, Harvard University, Cambridge, Mass., 1954.

KAPLAN, BERT, AND THOMAS F. A. PLAUT: *Personality in a Communal Society: An Analysis of the Mental Health of the Hutterites*, University of Kansas Press, Lawrence, Kan., 1956.

KARDINER, ABRAM, AND LIONEL OVERSEY: *The Mark of Oppression: A Psychosocial Study of the American Negro*, W. W. Norton & Company, Inc., New York, 1951.

KAUFMAN, WALTER C.: "Status, Authoritarianism, and Anti-Semitism," *American Journal of Sociology*, 52:379–382, 1957.

KEATS, JOHN: Review of WILFRED OWEN, *Cities in the Motor Age*, in *New York Times Book Review*, Mar. 1, 1959, p. 7.

KELLOGG, W. N., AND L. A. KELLOGG: *The Ape and the Child*, McGraw-Hill Book Company, New York, 1933.

KELMAN, HERBERT C.: "Deception in Social Research," *Trans-action*, 3:20–24, July-August, 1966.

KEPHART, W. M.: *Family, Society, and the Individual*, Houghton Mifflin Company, Boston, 1961.

KERCHER, LEONARD, VANT W. KEBKER, AND WILFRED C. LELAND, JR.: *Consumers' Cooperatives in the North Central States*, The University of Minnesota Press, Minneapolis, 1941.

KEY, WILLIAM H.: "Rural-Urban Differences and the Family," *Sociological Quarterly*, 2:49–56, 1961.

KEYS, ANCEL: "Experimental Induction of Neuropsychoses by Starvation," in Milbank Memorial Fund, *Biology of Mental Health and Disease*, Harper & Row, Publishers, Incorporated, New York, 1952, pp. 515–525.

KHARCHEV, A. G.: "The Nature of the Russian Family," *Voporosy Filosofia*, no. 1, translated and abridged in *Soviet Review*, 2:3–19, 1961.

KING, MARTIN LUTHER: *Stride toward Freedom: The Montgomery Story*, Harper & Row, Publishers, Incorporated, New York, 1958.

KINKEAD, EUGENE, *In Every War but One*, W. W. Norton & Company, Inc., New York, 1959.

KINSEY, ALFRED C., WARDELL B. POMEROY, AND CLYDE E. MARTIN: *Sexual Behavior in the Human Male*, W. B. Saunders Company, Philadelphia, 1948.

KINSEY, ALFRED C., ET AL.: *Sexual Behavior in the Human Female*, W. B. Saunders Company, Philadelphia, 1953.

KIRKENDALL, LESTER A.: *Premarital Intercourse and Interpersonal Relations*, Julian Press, New York, 1961.

KITAGAWA, JOSEPH M.: "Search for Self-identity: A Reflection on Religion and Nationalism in Asia," *Ecumenical Review*, 12:332–346, 1960.

KLINEBERG, OTTO: *Negro Intelligence and Selective Migration*, Columbia University Press, New York, 1935.

KLINEBERG, OTTO: *Characteristics of the American Negro*, Harper & Row Publishers, Incorporated, New York, 1944.

KLUCKHOHN, CLYDE: "Participation in Ceremonials in a Navaho Community," *American Anthropologist*, 40:359–369, 1938.

KLUCKHOHN, FLORENCE: "Dominant and Substitute Profiles of Cultural Orientation: Their Significance for an Analysis of Social Stratification," *Social Forces*, 28:376–393, 1950.

KNIBBS, GEORGE HANDLEY: *The Shadow of the World's Future: Or the Earth's Population Possibilities and Consequences of the Present Rate of Increase of the World's Inhabitants*, Ernest Benn, Ltd., London, 1928.

KOENIG, ROBERT P.: "An American Engineer Looks at British Coal," *Foreign Affairs*, 26:285–286, 1948.

KOLKO, GABRIEL: "Economic Mobility and Social Stratification," *American Journal of Sociology*, 63:30–38, 1957.

KOLKO, GABRIEL: *Wealth and Power in America*, Frederick A. Praeger, Inc., New York, 1962.

KOMAROVSKY, MIRRA: "Cultural Contradictions and Sex Roles," *American Journal of Sociology*, 52:184–189, 1946 (a).

KOMAROVSKY, MIRRA: "The Voluntary Associations of Urban Dwellers," *American Sociological Review*, 11:686–698, 1946 (b).

KORNHAUSER, ARTHUR: "Public Opinion and Social Class," *American Journal of Sociology*, 55:333–345, 1950.

KORNHAUSER, WILLIAM: *The Politics of Mass Society*, The Free Press of Glencoe, New York, 1959.

KRETSCHMER, ERNEST: *Physique and Character*, Harcourt, Brace & World, Inc., New York, 1925.

KROPOTKIN, PETER: *Mutual Aid*, Alfred A. Knopf, Inc., New York, 1925.

KROUT, MAURICE A.: *Introduction to Social Psychology*, Harper & Row, Publishers, Incorporated, New York, 1942.

KUHN, MANFORD H., AND THOMAS S. MCPARTLAND: "An Empirical Investigation of Self-attitudes," *American Sociological Review*, 19:68–75, February, 1954.

KUHN, MANFORD H.: "Self Attitudes by Age, Sex, and Professional Training," *Sociological Quarterly*, 1:39–55, January, 1960.

KUO, ZING YANG: "Genesis of Cat's Responses in Rats," *Journal of Comparative Psychology*, 11:1–35, 1931.

LABARRE, WESTON: "Professor Widjojo Goes to a Koktel Parti," *New York Times Magazine*, Dec. 9, 1956, pp. 17ff.

LANDER, BERNARD: *Toward an Understanding of Juvenile Deliquency*, Columbia University Press, New York, 1954.

LANDIS, PAUL H.: *Social Control*, J. B. Lippincott Company, Philadelphia, 1956.

LANDIS, PAUL H.: *Making the Most of Marriage*, New York: Appleton-Century-Crofts, New York, 1960.

LANG, KURT, AND GLADYS ENGEL LANG: *Collective Dynamics*, Thomas Y. Crowell Company, New York, 1961.

LANTZ, HERMAN R.: *People of Coal Town*, Columbia University Press, New York, 1958.

LAPIERE, RICHARD T., AND PAUL R. FARNSWORTH: *Social Psychology*, McGraw-Hill Book Company, New York, 1949.

LAPIERE, RICHARD T.: *A Theory of Social Control*, McGraw-Hill Book Company, New York, 1954.

LASSWELL, HAROLD D.: "Propaganda," *Encyclopaedia of the Social Sciences*, The Macmillan Company, New York, 1933, vol. 12, pp. 521–527.

LASSWELL, HAROLD D.: "The Strategy of Soviet Propaganda," *Proceedings of the Academy of Political Science*, 1951, vol. 24, pp. 214–226.

LASSWELL, HAROLD D., AND DOROTHY BLUMENSTOCK: *World Revolutionary Propaganda*, Alfred A. Knopf, Inc., New York, 1939.

LASSWELL, THOMAS E.: *Class and Stratum*, Houghton Mifflin, Boston, 1965.

LAURENTI, L. M.: *Property Values and Race*, University of California Press, Berkeley, Calif., 1960.

LAVA, HORACIO: "The Colonial Structure of the Philippine Economy," *Comment*, 2d quarter, 1958, pp. 42–55.

LAZARFELD, PAUL F., WILLIAM H. SEWELL, AND HAROLD L. WILENSKY: *The Uses of Sociology*, Basic Books, New York, 1967.

LAZERWITZ, BERNARD: "Religion and Social Structure in the United States," in LOUIS SCHNEIDER, *Religion, Culture and Society*, John Wiley & Sons, Inc., New York, 1964, pp. 426–435.

LEDERER, WILLIAM J., AND E. L. BURDICK: *The Ugly American*, W. W. Norton & Company, Inc., New York, 1958.

LEE, ALFRED M.: *Multivalent Man*, George Braziller, New York, 1966.

LEE, ALFRED M., AND ELIZABETH BRIANT LEE: *The Fine Art of Propaganda,* Harcourt, Brace & World, Inc., and the Institute for Propaganda Analysis, New York, 1939.

LEE, ALFRED M., AND NORMAN D. HUMPHREY: *Race Riot,* Holt, Rinehart and Winston, Inc., New York, 1943.

LEE, DOROTHY: "The Cultural Curtain," *Annals of the American Academy of Political and Social Science,* 323:120–128, 1959 (*b*).

LEE, DOROTHY: *Freedom and Culture,* Prentice-Hall, Inc., Englewood Cliffs, N.J., 1959 (*a*).

LEE, ROSE HUM: *The City,* J. B. Lippincott Company, Philadelphia, 1955.

LEE, ULYSSES G., JR.: *The Employment of Negro Troops,* Department of the Army, Office of the Chief of Military Operation, 1966.

LEES, HANNAH: "The Not-buying Power of Philadelphia's Negroes," *Reporter,* May 11, 1961, pp. 33–35.

LENSKI, GERHARD E.: "Trends in Intergenerational Mobility in the U.S.," *American Sociological Review,* 23:514–523, 1958.

LENSKI, GERHARD E.: *The Religious Factor,* Doubleday & Company, Inc., Garden City, N.Y., 1961.

LESSER, ALEXANDER: "Cultural Significance of the Ghost Dance," *American Anthropologist,* 35:108–115, 1933.

LEVY, MARION J.: *The Family Revolution in Modern China,* Harvard University Press, Cambridge, Mass., 1949.

LEWIS, MYRON F.: "Careers in Sociology," *School and College Placement,* 12:48–53, 1951.

LEWIS, OSCAR: *Five Families: Mexican Case Studies in the Culture of Poverty,* Basic Books, Inc., Publishers, New York, 1959.

LEWIS, OSCAR: *The Children of Sanchez: Autobiography of a Mexican Family,* Vintage Books, Random House, Inc., New York, 1963 (*a*).

LEWIS, OSCAR: *Life in a Mexican Village: Tepoztlan Revisited,* with drawings by Alberto Beltram, University of Illinois Press, Urbana, Ill., 1963 (*b*).

LEWIS, OSCAR: *Village Life in Northern India: Studies in a Delhi Village,* with the assistance of Victor Barnouw, Vintage Books, Random House, Inc., New York, 1965.

LEWIS, OSCAR: *La Vida: A Puerto Rican Family in the Culture of Poverty, San Juan and New York,* Random House, Inc., New York, 1966.

LEWIS, SINCLAIR: *Babbitt,* Harcourt, Brace & World, Inc., New York, 1922.

LEYBURN, JAMES G.: *Frontier Folkways,* Yale University Press, New Haven, Conn., 1935.

LIEBERSON, STANLEY, AND ARNOLD R. SILVERMAN: "Precipitants and Conditions of Race Riots," *American Sociological Review,* 30:887–898, December, 1965.

LINCOLN, C. ERIC: *The Black Muslims in America,* Beacon Press, Boston, 1961.

LINDESMITH, ALFRED E.: "Social Problems and Sociological Theory," *Social Problems,* 8:98–102, 1960.

LINDZEY, GARDNER (ED.): *Handbook of Social Psychology,* Addison-Wesley Publishing Company, Inc., Cambridge, Mass., 1954.

LINTON, RALPH: *The Study of Man,* Appleton-Century-Crofts, New York, 1936.

LIPSEDGE, M. S.: "The Poujade Movement," *Contemporary Review,* 189:83–88, 1956.

LIPSET, SEYMOUR M.: "Leadership and New Social Movements," in ALVIN W. GOULDNER (ED.), *Studies in Leadership,* Harper & Row, Publishers, Incorporated, New York, 1950, pp. 342–362.

LIPSET, SEYMOUR M.: "Vance Packard Discovers America," *Reporter,* July 9, 1959, pp. 32–33.

LIPSET, SEYMOUR M., AND PAUL SEABURY: "Lesson of Berkeley: Question of Student Political Activities," *The Reporter,* Jan. 28, 1965, pp. 36–40.

Literary Digest, Oct. 11, 1919, p. 16, "Omaha."

LITNER, JOHN: "The Financing of Corporations," in EDWARD S. MASON (ED.), *The Corporation in Modern Society,* Harvard University Press, Cambridge, Mass., 1959, chap. 9.

LITWAK, EUGENE: "Three Ways in Which Law Acts as a Means of Social Control: Punishment, Therapy, and Education," *Social Forces,* 34:217–223, 1956.

LITWAK, LEON F.: *North of Slavery,* The University of Chicago Press, Chicago, 1961.

LOHMAN, JOSEPH D.: *The Police and Minority Groups,* Chicago Park District, Chicago, 1947.

LOHMAN, JOSEPH D., AND DELBERT C. REITZES: "Note on Race Relations in Mass Society," *American Journal of Sociology,* 58:240–246, 1952.

LOMBROSO, CESARE: *Crime, Its Causes and Remedies,* tr. by H. P. Horton, Little, Brown and Company, Boston, 1912.

LOOMIS, ALBERTINE: *Grapes of Canaan,* Dodd, Mead & Company, Inc., New York, 1951.

LOOMIS, CHARLES P., AND J. ALLAN BEAGLE: "The Spread of German Nazism in Rural Areas," *American Sociological Review,* 11:724–734, 1946.

LOOMIS, CHARLES P., AND ZONA KEMP LOOMIS: *Modern Social Theories,* D. Van Nostrand Company, Inc., Princeton, N.J., 1961.

LOWENTHAL, LEO, AND NORBERT GUTERMAN: *Prophets of Deceit,* Harper & Row, Publishers, Incorporated, New York, 1949.

LOWIE, ROBERT H. *Are We Civilized?* Harcourt, Brace & World, Inc., New York, 1929.

LOWIE, ROBERT H.: *Introduction to Cultural Anthropology*, Holt, Rinehart and Winston, Inc., New York, 1940.

LUCE, PHILLIP ABBOTT: *The New Left*, David McKay Company, Inc., New York, 1966.

LUMLEY, FREDERICK E.: *Means of Social Control*, Century Company, New York, 1925.

LUNDBERG, FERDINAND: *America's Sixty Families*, Vanguard Press, Inc., New York, 1937.

LYNCH, FRANK: *Social Class in a Bicol Town*, Philippines Studies Program, University of Chicago, Chicago, 1959.

LYND, ROBERT S., AND HELEN M. LYND: *Middletown*, Harcourt, Brace & World, Inc., New York, 1929.

LYND, ROBERT S., AND HELEN M. LYND: *Middletown in Transition*, Harcourt, Brace & World, Inc., New York, 1937.

MCARTHUR, CHARLES: "Personality Differences between Upper-class Harvard Freshmen (private school graduates) and Middle-class Harvard Freshmen (public school graduates)," *Journal of Abnormal and Social Psychology*, 50:247–254, 1955.

MCCLOSKY, HERBERT, AND JOHN H. SCHAAR: "Psychological Dimensions of Anomy," *American Sociological Review*, 30:14–40, February, 1965.

MCCORMICK, THOMAS C., AND ROY G. FRANCES: *Methods of Research in the Behavioral Sciences*, Harper & Row, Publishers, Incorporated, New York, 1958.

MCDONALD, DONALD: *Opinion Polls: One of a Series of Interviews on the American Character*, Fund for the Republic, New York, 1962.

MCGINTY, ALICE B.: "India: A House Divided," *Current History*, 13:288–289, 1947.

MACK, RAYMOND W.: "The Components of Social Conflict," *Social Problems*, 12:394–397, Spring, 1965.

MACKAY, CHARLES: *Extraordinary Popular Delusions and the Madness of Crowds*, L. C. Page & Company, Boston, 1932.

MCKEE, JAMES B.: "Status and Power in the Industrial Community: A Comment on Drucker's Thesis," *American Journal of Sociology*, 58:364–370, 1953.

MCKENZIE, R. D.: "The Ecological Approach to the Study of the Human Community," in ROBERT E. PARK, E. W. BURGESS, AND R. D. MCKENZIE (EDS.), *The City*, The University of Chicago Press, Chicago, 1925, pp. 63–79.

MCMAHON, FRANCIS E.: "Protestant Disability in Spain," *Commonweal*, 52:177–178 (1950).

MCNEIL, DONALD R.: *The Fight for Fluoridation*, Oxford University Press, Fair Lawn, N.J., 1957.

MCWILLIAMS, CAREY: *Southern California Country*, Duell, Sloan & Pearce, New York, 1946.

MCWILLIAMS, CAREY: *California: The Great Exception*, Current Books, New York, 1949.

MAHER, ROBERT F.: *The New Man of Papua: A Study in Cultural Change*, The University of Wisconsin Press, Madison, Wis., 1961.

MALINOWSKI, BRONISLAW: *Crime and Custom in Savage Society*, Routledge & Kegan Paul, Ltd., London, 1926.

MANGUS, A. R.: "Personality Adjustment of Rural and Urban Children," *American Sociological Review*, 13:566–575, 1948.

MANIS, JEROME G., AND BERNARD N. MELTZER: "Attitude of Textile Workers to Class Structure," *American Journal of Sociology*, 60:30–35, 1954.

MANIS, JEROME G., AND BERNARD N. MELTZER: "Some Correlates of Class Consciousness among Textile Workers," *American Journal of Sociology*, 69:177–184, September, 1963.

MANNHEIM, KARL: *Man and Society in an Age of Reconstruction*, Harcourt, Brace & World, Inc., New York, 1940.

MARRIOTT, MCKIM (ED.): *Village India*, The University of Chicago Press, Chicago, 1955.

MARSHALL, RAY: "Labor in the South," *Antioch Review*, 21:80–95, 1961.

MARSHALL, S. L. A.: *Men Under Fire*, William Morrow and Company, Inc., New York, 1947.

MARTIN, JOHN BARTLOW: *The Deep South Says Never*, Ballantine Books, Inc., New York, 1957.

MARTY, MARTIN E.: "Sects and Cults," *The Annals of the American Academy of Political and Social Science*, 332:125–134, November, 1960.

MASTERS, WILLIAM H., AND VIRGINIA E. JOHNSON: *Human Sexual Response*, Little, Brown and Company, Boston, 1966.

MATTHEWS, HERBERT L.: *The Yoke and the Arrow*, George Braziller, Inc., New York, 1957.

MAUSNER, BERNARD, AND JUDITH MAUSNER: "A Study of the Anti-scientific Attitude," *Scientific American*, 192:35–39, 1955.

MAYBEE, C.: "Evolution of Non-violence," *Nation*, 193:78–81, 1961.

MAYER, ALBERT J., AND PHILIP HAUSER: "Class Differentials in Expectation of Life at Birth," *La Révue de l'Institute de Statistique*, 18:197–200, 1950; reprinted in REINHARD BENDIX AND SEYMOUR M. LIPSET (EDS.), *Class, Status, and Power*, The Free Press of Glencoe, New York, 1953, pp. 281–285.

MAYER, ALBERT J., AND THOMAS FORD HOULT: "Social Stratification and Combat Survival," *Social Forces*, 34:155–159, 1955.

MAYER, ALBERT J., AND SUE MARX: "Social Change, Religion and the Birth Rate," *American Journal of Sociology*, 62:383–390, 1957.

MAYER, ALBERT J., ET AL.: *Pilot Project: India*, University of California Press, Berkeley, Calif., 1958.

MEAD, GEORGE HERBERT: *Mind, Self and Society*, The University of Chicago Press, Chicago, 1934.

MEAD, MARGARET: *Cooperation and Conflict among Primitive Peoples,* McGraw-Hill Book Company, New York, 1937.

MEAD, MARGARET: "Administrative Contributions to Democratic Character Formation at the Adolescent Level," *Journal of the National Association of Deans of Women*, 4:51–57, January, 1941.

MEAD, MARGARET: "The Implications of Culture Change for Personality Development," *American Journal of Orthopsychiatry*, 17:633–646, 1947.

MEAD, MARGARET: *Cultural Patterns and Technical Change*, UNESCO, Mentor Books, New American Library of World Literature, Inc., New York, 1955.

MEAD, MARGARET: *New Lives for Old*, William Morrow and Company, Inc., New York, 1956.

MEAD, MARGARET, AND MARTHA WOLFENSTEIN (EDS.): *Childhood in Contemporary Cultures*, The University of Chicago Press, Chicago, 1955.

MECKLIN, JOHN H.: *The Ku Klux Klan*, Harcourt, Brace & World, Inc., New York, 1924.

MEEKER, MARCIA: "Status Aspirations and the Social Club," in W. LLOYD WARNER (ED.), *Democracy in Jonesville*, Harper & Row, Publishers, Incorporated, New York, 1949, pp. 130–148.

MERRILL, FRANCIS E.: "The Self and the Other: An Emerging Field of Social Problems," *Social Problems*, 4:200–207, January, 1957.

MERTON, ROBERT K.: "Social Structure and Anomie," *American Sociological Review*, 3:672–682, 1938.

MERTON, ROBERT K.: "Bureaucratic Structure and Personality," in *Social Theory and Social Structure*, The Free Press of Glencoe, New York, 1949, pp. 151–160.

MERTON, ROBERT K., ET AL. (EDS.): *Reader in Bureaucracy*, The Free Press of Glencoe, New York, 1952.

MERTON, ROBERT K.: *Social Theory and Social Structure*, The Free Press of Glencoe, New York, 1957 (a).

MERTON, ROBERT K.: "Manifest and Latent Functions: Toward a Codification of Functional Analysis in Sociology," in *Social Theory and Social Structure*, The Free Press of Glencoe, New York, 1957, pp. 19–84 (b).

MERTON, ROBERT K.: "Priorities in Scientific Discovery: A Chapter in the Sociology of Science," *American Sociological Review*, 22:635–659, December, 1957 (c).

MESSINGER, SHELDON L.: "Organizational Transforma-

tion: A Case Study of a Declining Social Movement," *American Sociological Review*, 20:3–10, 1955.

MICHELS, ROBERT: *Political Parties: A Sociological Study of the Oligarchical Tendencies in Modern Democracy*, tr. by Eden and Cedar Paul, The Free Press of Glencoe, New York, 1911.

MILLER, ARTHUR S.: "Some Observations on the Political Economy of Population Growth," *Law and Contemporary Problems*, 25:614–632, 1960.

MILLER, DANIEL C., GUY E. SWANSON, ET AL.: *Inner Conflict and Defense*, Holt, Rinehart and Winston, Inc., New York, 1960.

MILLER, HERMAN P.: *Rich Man–Poor Man*, Thomas Y. Crowell Company, New York, 1964, p. 36.

MILLER, S. M., AND ELLIOT G. MISHLER: "Social Class, Mental Illness, and American Psychiatry," *Milbank Memorial Fund Quarterly*, 37:174–199, 1959.

MILLER, S. M., AND FRANK RIESSMAN: "The Working Class Subculture: A New View," *Social Problems*, 9:86–97, Summer, 1961.

MILLER, WALTER B.: "Lower Class Culture as a Generating Milieu of Gang Delinquency," *Journal of Social Issues*, (3) 14:5–19, 1958.

MILLER, WALTER B.: "Implications of Lower-class Culture for Social Work," *Social Service Review*, 33:219–236, 1959.

MILLS, C. WRIGHT: *The Power Elite*, Oxford University Press, Fair Lawn, N.J., 1956.

MINER, HORACE: "Nacirema Culture," *American Anthropologist*, 58:503–507, 1956.

MINTZ, ALEXANDER: "Non-adaptive Group Behavior," *Journal of Abnormal and Social Psychology*, 46:150–158, 1951.

MIYAMOTO, S. FRANK, AND SANFORD M. DORNBUSCH: "A Test of Interactionist Hypothesis of Self-conception," *American Journal of Sociology*, 61:399–403, 1956.

MONROE, KEITH: "The New Gambling King and the Social Scientists," *Harper's Magazine*, January, 1962, pp. 35–41.

MONTAGUE, ASHLEY: *Man: His First Million Years*, Mentor Books, New American Library of World Literature, Inc., New York, 1958.

MOORE, W. E.: *Industrial Relations and the Social Order*, The Macmillan Company, New York, 1947.

MOREHOUSE, FRANCES: "The Irish Migration of the 'Forties,'" *American Historical Review*, 33:579–592, 1928.

MORENO, J. L.: "Psychodramatic Treatment of Marriage Problems," *Sociometry*, 3:2–23, 1940.

MORGAN, THEODORE: "The Economic Development of Ceylon," *Annals of the American Academy of Political and Social Science*, 305:92–100, 1956.

MORRIS, RAYMOND N.: "British and American Research

on Voluntary Associations: A Comparison," *Sociological Inquiry*, 35:186–200, Spring, 1965.

MOSK, STANLEY, AND HOWARD H. JEWEL: "The Birch Phenomenon Analyzed," *New York Times Magazine*, Aug. 20, 1961, pp. 12ff.

MOYNIHAN, DANIEL P.: "The Private Government of Crime," *Reporter*, July 6, 1961, pp. 14–20.

MOYNIHAN, DANIEL P.: "Behind Los Angeles: Jobless Negroes and the Boom," *The Reporter*, Sept. 9, 1965, p. 31.

MUHLER, JOSEPH CHARLES, AND MAYNARD K. HINE (EDS.): *Fluorine and Dental Health: The Pharmacology and Toxicology of Fluorine*, Indiana University Press, Bloomington, Ind., 1959.

MURAMATSU, MINORU: "Effect of Induced Abortion on the Reduction of Births in Japan," *Milbank Memorial Fund Quarterly*, 38:153–166, 1960.

MURDOCK, GEORGE P.: *Our Primitive Contemporaries*, The Macmillan Company, New York, 1936.

MURDOCK, GEORGE P.: *Social Structure*, The Macmillan Company, New York, 1949.

MURDOCK, GEORGE P.: "Sexual Behavior: A Comparative Anthropological Approach," *Journal of Social Hygiene*, 36:133–138, 1950.

MURPHY, GARDNER, LOIS MURPHY, AND THEODORE M. NEWCOMB: *Experimental Social Psychology*, Harper & Row, Publishers, Incorporated, New York, 1937.

MYERSON, ABRAHAM: *Social Psychology*, Prentice-Hall, Inc., Englewood Cliffs, N.J., 1934.

MYRDAL, GUNNAR: *An American Dilemma*, Harper & Row, Publishers, Incorporated, New York, 1944.

MYRDAL, GUNNAR: *Rich Lands and Poor*, Harper & Row, Publishers, Incorporated, New York, 1957.

NAKASA, NATHANIEL: "The Human Meaning of Apartheid," *New York Times Magazine*, Sept. 24, 1961, pp. 42ff.

NASH, PHILLEO: "The Place of Religious Revivalism . . ." in FRED EGGAN (ED.), *Social Anthropology of the North American Tribes*, The University of Chicago Press, Chicago, 1937.

NATIONAL EDUCATION ASSOCIATION: *Status and Trends of Education*, Washington, August, 1959.

NELSON, EDWARD W.: "The Eskimo about Bering Straits," *18th Annual Report, Bureau of American Ethnology*, Washington, 1899, part 1, pp. 268–270.

NETTLER, GWYNN: "A Measure of Alienation," *American Sociological Review*, 22:670–677, 1957.

NEWCOMBER, MABEL: *The Big Business Executive: The Factors That Made Him, 1900–1950*, Columbia University Press, New York, 1956.

NEWFIELD, JACK: *A Prophetic Minority*, New American Library of World Literature, Inc., New York, 1966.

Newsweek, Mar. 2, 1959, p. 40, "Tidal Wave of Humans."

New York Times, Apr. 24, 1960, sect. 4, p. 4, "Bias in Housing."

NICHOLS, LEE: *Breakthrough on the Color Front*, Random House, Inc., New York, 1954.

NIMKOFF, MEYER F., AND RUSSELL MIDDLETON: "Types of Family and Types of Economy," *American Journal of Sociology*, 66:215–225, 1960.

NISBET, ROBERT A.: "The Decline and Fall of Social Class," *Pacific Sociological Review*, 2:11–17, Spring, 1959.

NORTHCOTT, WILLIAM C.: "Christianity's Lost Continent," *Spectator*, 202:217, 1959.

NUNN, W. C.: *Escape From Reconstruction*, Leo Potishman Foundation, Ft. Worth, Tex., 1956.

NYE, F. IVAN: "Adolescent-Parent Adjustment: Age, Sex, Sibling Number, Broken Homes, and Employed Mothers as Variables," *Marriage and Family Living*, 14:327–332, November, 1952.

NYE, F. IVAN: *Family Relationships and Delinquent Behavior*, John Wiley & Sons, Inc., New York, 1958.

NYE, F. IVAN: "Maternal Employment and the Adjustment of Adolescent Children," *Marriage and Family Living*, 21:240–244, August, 1959.

NYE, F. IVAN, AND LOIS M. HOFFMAN: *The Employed Mother in America*, Rand McNally & Company, Chicago, 1963.

O'CONNOR, PATRICIA: "Intolerance of Ambiguity and Abstract Reasoning Ability," *Journal of Abnormal and Social Psychology*, 47:526–530, 1952.

ODUM, HOWARD W.: *Understanding Society*, The Macmillan Company, New York, 1947.

OGBURN, WILLIAM F.: *Social Change*, The Viking Press, Inc., New York, 1922, 1950.

OGBURN, WILLIAM F.: "The Influence of Invention and Discovery," in President's Research Committee on Social Trends, *Recent Social Trends*, McGraw-Hill Book Company, New York, 1933, pp. 122–166.

OGBURN, WILLIAM F.: "The Wolf Boy of Agra," *American Journal of Sociology*, 64:449–454, March, 1959.

OGBURN, WILLIAM F., AND MEYER F. NIMKOFF: *Technology and the Changing Family*, Houghton Mifflin Company, Boston, 1955.

O'KANE, LAWRENCE: "Negro Muslim Convicts Suing for Religious Rights in Prison," *New York Times*, Mar. 19, 1961, pp. 1ff.

OLSON, PHILIP: "Rural American Community Studies: The Survival of Public Ideology," *Human Organization*, 23:342–350, Winter, 1964–1965.

ORGANSKI, KATHERINE, AND A. F. K. ORGANSKI: *Population*

and World Power, Alfred A. Knopf, Inc., New York, 1962.

OTTENBERG, SIMON: "Ileo Receptivity to Change," in WILLIAM R. BASCOM AND MELVILLE J. HERSKOVITZ (EDS.), *Continuity and Change in African Cultures*, The University of Chicago Press, Chicago, 1959, pp. 130–143.

PACKARD, VANCE: *The Hidden Persuaders*, David McKay Company, Inc., New York, 1957.

PACKARD, VANCE: *The Status Seekers*, David McKay Company, Inc., New York, 1959.

PACKARD, VANCE: *The Pyramid Climbers*, McGraw-Hill Book Company, New York, 1962.

PARK, ROBERT E., AND ERNEST BURGESS: *Introduction to the Science of Sociology*, The University of Chicago Press, Chicago, 1921.

PARK, ROBERT E., AND H. A. MILLER: *Old World Traits Transplanted*, Harper & Row, Publishers, Incorporated, New York, 1921.

PARK, ROBERT E., E. W. BURGESS, AND R. D. MCKENZIE: *The City*, The University of Chicago Press, Chicago, 1925.

PARK, ROBERT E.: *Race and Culture*, The Free Press of Glencoe, New York, 1949.

PARKER, ROBERT A.: *The Incredible Messiah*, Little, Brown and Company, Boston, 1937.

PARKINSON, C. NORTHCOTE: *Parkinson's Law and Other Studies in Administration*, Houghton Mifflin Company, Boston, 1957.

PARSONS, TALCOTT: "Certain Primary Sources and Patterns of Aggression in the Social Structure of the Western World," *Psychiatry*, 10:167–181, 1947.

PARSONS, TALCOTT: *Essays in Sociological Theory*, The Free Press of Glencoe, New York, 1954.

PARSONS, TALCOTT: "On the Concept of Political Power," *Proceedings of the American Philosophical Society*, 107:232–262, June, 1963.

PARTEN, MILDRED: *Surveys, Polls, and Samples: Practical Procedures*, Harper & Row, Publishers, Incorporated, New York, 1950.

PASLEY, VIRGINIA: *21 Stayed*, Farrar, Straus & Co., New York, 1955.

PEARSON, KARL: *The Grammar of Science*, A. & C. Black, Ltd., London, 1900.

PECK, JAMES: *Freedom Ride*, Simon and Schuster, Inc., New York, 1962.

PELLEGREN, ROLAND J., AND CHARLES H. COATES: "Absentee-owned Corporations and Community Power Structure," *American Journal of Sociology*, 61:413–419, 1956.

PETERSEN, WILLIAM (ED.): *American Social Patterns*, Doubleday & Company, Inc., Garden City, N.Y., 1956.

PETERSEN, WILLIAM: Review of Vance Packard, *The Status Seekers, American Sociological Review*, 25:124–126, February, 1960.

PETERSEN, WILLIAM: *Population*, The Macmillan Company, New York, 1961.

PHILLIPS, BERNARD S.: *Social Research*, The Macmillan Company, New York, 1966.

PHILLIPS, DEREK L.: "Deferred Gratification in a College Setting: Some Gains and Costs," *Social Problems*, 13:333–343, Winter, 1966.

PLAUT, THOMAS F. A.: "Analysis of Voting Behavior on a Voting Referendum," *Public Opinion Quarterly*, 23:213–222, 1959.

PODALSKY, EDWARD: "The Sociopathic Alcoholic," *Quarterly Journal of Studies on Alcohol*, 21:292–297, June, 1960.

POPE, LISTON: "Religion and the Class Structure," *Annals of the American Academy*, 256:84–91, 1948.

PORTERFIELD, AUSTIN L.: *Youth in Trouble*, Leo Potishman Foundation, Fort Worth, Tex., 1946.

PROTHRO, E. TERRY: "Ethnocentrism and Anti-Negro Attitudes in the Deep South," *Journal of Abnormal and Social Psychology*, 47:104–108, January, 1952.

PYLE, ERNIE: *Brave Men*, Holt, Rinehart and Winston, Inc., New York, 1943.

QUEEN, STUART A., ROBERT W. HABERSTEIN, AND JOHN B. ADAMS: *The Family in Various Cultures*, J. B. Lippincott Company, Philadelphia, 1961.

RAO, P. KODANDRA: *Bi-lingualism for India*, W. O. Judge, Bengal, India, 1956.

RAPER, ARTHUR F.: *The Tragedy of Lynching*, The University of North Carolina Press, Chapel Hill, N.C., 1933.

RASKIN, A. H.: "Berkeley Affair," *New York Times Magazine*, Feb. 14, 1965, pp. 24ff.

RECKLESS, WALTER C., ET AL.: "The Good Boy in a High Delinquency Area," *Journal of Criminal Law, Criminology and Police Science*, 47:18–25, May-June, 1957.

REISS, ALBERT J., JR.: "Rural-Urban Status Differences in Interpersonal Contacts," *American Journal of Sociology*, 65:182–195, 1959.

REISS, IRA L.: *Pre-marital Sexual Standards in America*, The Free Press of Glencoe, New York, 1960.

REISSMAN, LEONARD: Review of C. WRIGHT MILLS, *The Power Elite, American Sociological Review*, 21:513–514, August, 1956.

REUSCH, JURGEN: "Social Technique, Social Status, and Social Change in Illness," in CLYDE KLUCKHOHN AND

HENRY A. MURRAY, WITH D. M. SCHIENDER (EDS.), *Personality in Nature, Society, and Culture*, 2d ed., Alfred A. Knopf, Inc., New York, 1953, pp. 123–136.

RIBBLE, MARGARET A.: *The Rights of Infants*, Columbia University Press, New York, 1943.

RIEMER, SVEND: "Social Planning and Social Organization," *American Journal of Sociology*, 52:508–516, 1947.

RIEMER, SVEND: "Urban Personality—Reconsidered," in MARVIN B. SUSSMAN (ED.), *Community Structure and Analysis*, Thomas Y. Crowell Company, New York, 1959, pp. 433–444.

RIESMAN, DAVID, WITH NATHAN GLAZER AND REUEL DENNEY: *The Lonely Crowd: A Study in the Changing American Character*, Yale University Press, New Haven, Conn., 1950.

RIVERS, W. H. R.: "On the Disappearance of Useful Arts," in *Festskrift Tillägnad Edward Westermarck*, Helsingfors, 1912, pp. 109–130; summarized in A. L. KROEBER, *Anthropology*, Harcourt, Brace & World, Inc., New York, 1949, p. 375.

RIVERS, W. H. R. (ED.): *Essays on the Depopulation of Melanesia*, Cambridge University Press, London, 1922.

ROBERTSON, HECTOR MONTEITH: *South Africa*, Duke University Press, Durham, N.C., 1957.

ROBINSON, H. A., F. C. REDLICH, AND J. K. MYERS: "Social Structure and Psychiatric Treatment," *American Journal of Orthopsychiatry*, 24:307–316, 1954.

ROEBUCK, JULIAN, AND S. LEE SPRAY: "The Cocktail Lounge: A Study in Heterosexual Relations in a Public Organization," *American Journal of Sociology*, 72:388–395, January, 1967.

ROETHLISBERGER, F. J.: *Management and Morale*, Harvard University Press, Cambridge, Mass., 1949.

ROETHLISBERGER, F. J., AND WILLIAM J. DICKSON: *Management and the Worker*, Harvard University Press, Cambridge, Mass., 1939.

ROGERS, EVERETT M.: *Social Change in Rural Society*, Appleton-Century-Crofts, New York, 1960.

ROGERS, LINDSAY: *The Pollsters*, Alfred A. Knopf, Inc., New York, 1949.

ROGOFF, NATALIE: *Recent Trends in Occupational Mobility*, The Free Press of Glencoe, New York, 1953 (a).

ROGOFF, NATALIE: "Social Stratification in France and the United States," *American Journal of Sociology*, 58:347–357, 1953 (b).

ROSE, ARNOLD: *Union Solidarity: The Internal Cohesion of a Union*, The University of Minnesota Press, Minneapolis, 1952.

ROSE, ARNOLD: *Theory and Method in the Social Sciences*, The University of Minnesota Press, Minneapolis, 1954.

ROSEN, BERNARD: "The Reference Group Approach to the Parental Factor in Attitude and Behavior Formation," *Social Forces*, 24:137–144, 1955 (a).

ROSEN, BERNARD: "Conflicting Group Membership: A Study of Parent-Peer Group Cross-Pressure," *American Sociological Review*, 20:155–161, 1955 (b).

ROSEN, BERNARD: "The Achievement Syndrome: A Psychocultural Dimension of Social Stratification," *American Sociological Review*, 21:203–211, 1956.

ROSS, ARTHUR: "Wage Determination and Collective Bargaining," *The American Economic Review*, 37:793–822, December, 1947.

ROSS, MADELINE, AND FRED KERNER: "Stars and Bars along the Amazon," *Reporter*, Sept. 18, 1958, pp. 34–36.

ROSSI, PETER H.: Review of C. WRIGHT MILLS, *The Power Elite*, *American Journal of Sociology*, 62:232–233, 1956.

ROSSI, PETER H.: "Community Decision Making," *Administrative Science Quarterly*, 1:415–443, 1957.

ROSTOW, EUGENE V.: "Our Worst Wartime Mistake," *Harper's Magazine*, September, 1945, pp. 193–201.

ROSTOW, EUGENE V., "Freedom Riders and the Future," *Reporter*, June 23, 1961, pp. 18–21.

ROTHER, IRA S.: "The Righteous Rightists," *Transaction*, 4:27–35, May, 1967.

ROUTH, FREDERICK B., AND PAUL ANTHONY: "Southern Resistance Forces," *Phylon*, 18:50–58, 1957.

ROY, DONALD: "Efficiency and 'The Fix'; Informal Intergroup Relations in a Piecework Machine Shop," *American Journal of Sociology*, 60:225–266, 1955.

RUNCIMAN, STEPHEN: *Byzantine Civilization*, Meridian Books, Inc., New York, 1956.

RUSTIN, BAYARD: "A Way Out of the Exploding Ghetto," *New York Times Magazine*, August 13, 1967, pp. 16ff.

RYAN, BRYCE F.: *Caste in Modern Ceylon*, Rutgers University Press, New Brunswick, N.J., 1953.

SAHLINS, MARSHALL D.: "Land Use and the Extended Family in Moala, Fiji," *American Anthropologist*, 59:449–462, 1957.

SALOUTOS, THEODORE: *They Remember America: The Story of the Repatriated Greek Americans*, University of California Press, Berkeley, Calif., 1956.

SANDERS, IRWIN T.: *Societies around the World*, Holt, Rinehart and Winston, Inc., New York, 1956.

SANDOZ, MARI: *The Buffalo Hunters*, Hastings House, Publishers, Inc., New York, 1954.

SCHACHTER, STANLEY: "Deviation, Rejection, and Communication," *Journal of Abnormal and Social Psychology,* 46:190–207, 1951.

SCHEIN, EDGAR H.: "Interpersonal Communication, Group Solidarity and Social Influence," *Sociometry,* 23:148–161, 1960.

SCHINDLER, JOHN A.: *How to Live 365 Days a Year,* Prentice-Hall, Inc., Englewood Cliffs, N.J., 1954.

SCHLESINGER, ARTHUR M., JR.: *The Age of Roosevelt,* vol. 3, *The Politics of Upheaval,* Houghton Mifflin Company, Boston, 1960.

SCHNEIDER, HAROLD K.: "Pakot Resistance to Change," in WILLIAM R. BASCOM AND MELVILLE J. HERSKOVITZ (EDS.), *Continuity and Change in African Cultures,* The University of Chicago Press, Chicago, 1959, pp. 144–167.

SCHNEIDER, LOUIS, AND SVERRE LYSGAARD: "The Deferred Gratification Pattern: A Preliminary Study," *American Sociological Review,* 18:142–194, 1953.

SCHULER, EDGAR A., AND V. J. PARENTON: "A Recent Epidemic of Hysteria in a Louisiana High School," *Journal of Social Psychology,* 17:221–235, 1943.

SCHULTZ, GEORGE, AND CHARLES MEYERS: "Union Demands and Unemployment," *The American Economic Review,* 40:362–380, June, 1950.

SCHUR, EDWIN M. (ED.): *The Family and the Sexual Revolution,* Indiana University Press, Bloomington, Ind., 1964.

SCOTT, J. C., JR.: "Membership and Participation in Voluntary Associations," *American Sociological Review,* 22:315–326, 1957.

SEARS, ROBERT R., ELEANOR E. MACOBY, AND HARRY LEVIN: *Patterns of Child Rearing,* Harper & Row, Publishers, Incorporated, New York, 1957.

SEBOLD, HANS: "Studying National Character through Comparative Content Analysis," *Social Forces,* 40:318–322, May, 1962.

SELLTIZ, CLAIRE, MARIE JAHODA, MORTON DEUTSCH, AND STUART A. COOK: *Research Methods in Social Relations,* Holt, Rinehart and Winston, Inc., New York, 1959.

SELZNICK, PHILIP: "An Approach to the Theory of Bureaucracy," *American Sociological Review,* 8:47–54, 1943.

SEWELL, WILLIAM H.: "Infant Training and the Personality of the Child," *American Journal of Sociology,* 58:150–159, 1952.

SHARP, HARRY, AND LEO F. SCHNORE: "The Changing Color Composition of Metropolitan Areas," *Land Economics,* 38:169–185, 1962.

SHARP, LAURISTON: "Steel Axes for Stone Age Australians," in EDWARD H. SPICER (ED.), *Human Problems in Technological Change,* Russell Sage Foundation, New York, 1952, pp. 69–90.

SHAW, CLIFFORD R., AND M. E. MOORE: *The Natural History of a Delinquent Career,* The University of Chicago Press, Chicago, 1931.

SHAW, CLIFFORD R., H. D. MCKAY, AND G. F. MCDONALD: *Brothers in Crime,* The University of Chicago Press, Chicago, 1938.

SHELDON, WILLIAM H., AND S. S. STEVENS: *The Varieties of Temperament,* Harper & Row, Publishers, Incorporated, New York, 1942.

SHELDON, WILLIAM H.: *Varieties of Delinquent Youth,* Harper & Row, Publishers, Incorporated, New York, 1949.

SHERIF, MUZAFER A.: "A Study of Some Social Factors in Perception," *Archives of Psychology,* no. 187, 1935.

SHERIF, MUZAFER, AND CAROLYN SHERIF: *Groups in Harmony and Tension,* Harper & Row, Publishers, Incorporated, New York, 1953.

SHERIF, MUZAFER: "Superordinate Goals in the Reduction of Intergroup Conflict, *American Journal of Sociology,* 63:349–356, 1958.

SHERMAN, MANDELL, AND THOMAS R. HENRY: *Hollow Folk,* Thomas Y. Crowell Company, New York, 1933.

SHILS, EDWARD A., AND MORRIS JANOWITZ: "Cohesion and Distintegration in the Wehrmacht in World War II," *Public Opinion Quarterly,* 12:280–315, 1948.

SHILS, EDWARD A.: "Primary Groups in the American Army," in ROBERT K. MERTON AND PAUL LAZARSFELD (EDS.), *Continuities in Social Research: Studies in the Scope and Method of the American Soldier,* The Free Press of Glencoe, New York, 1950.

SHORT, JAMES F., JR., AND FRED L. STRODTBECK: *Group Process and Gang Delinquency,* The University of Chicago Press, Chicago, 1965.

SHOSTAK, ARTHUR B. (ED.): *Sociology in Action: Case Studies in Social Problems and Directed Social Change,* Dorsey Press, Homewood, Illinois, 1966.

SHUEY, AUDREY M.: *The Testing of Negro Intelligence,* J. P. Bell Company, Lynchburg, Va., 1958.

SHUVAL, JUDITH L.: "Class and Ethnic Correlates of Casual Neighboring," *American Sociological Review,* 21:453–458, 1956.

SILBERMAN, CHARLES E.: *Crisis in Black and White,* Random House, Inc., New York, 1964.

SIMMEL, GEORG: *Conflict,* tr. by Reinhard Bendix, The Free Press of Glencoe, New York, 1955.

SIMMEL, GEORG: *Georg Simmel,* tr. and ed. by Kurt Wolff, Ohio State University Press, Columbus, Ohio, 1959.

SIMPSON, GEORGE E.: "Darwinism and Social Darwinism," *Antioch Review*, 19:33–46, 1959.

SIMPSON, GEORGE E., AND J. MILTON YINGER: *Racial and Cultural Minorities: An Analysis of Prejudice and Discrimination*, Harper & Row, Publishers, Incorporated, New York, 1965.

SINGH, J. A. L., AND ROBERT M. ZINGG: *Wolf-Children and Feral Men*, Harper & Row, Publishers, Incorporated, New York, 1942.

SJOBERG, GIDEON: "Are Social Classes in America Becoming More Rigid?" *American Sociological Review*, 16:775–783, 1951.

SMELSER, NEIL J.: *Theory of Collective Behavior*, The Free Press of Glencoe, New York, 1963.

SMITH, HARVEY L.: "Psychiatry: A Social Institution in Process," *Social Forces*, 33:310–317, 1955.

SMITH, RICHARD AUSTIN: "The Fifty-million-dollar Man," *Fortune*, November, 1957, pp. 176ff.

SMUTZ, ROBERT W.: *Women and Work in America*, Columbia University Press, New York, 1959.

SOROKIN, PITIRIM A., AND CARLE C. ZIMMERMAN: *Principles of Rural-Urban Sociology*, Holt, Rinehart and Winston, Inc., New York, 1929.

SPINDLER, GEORGE D., AND LOUISE SPINDLER: "American Indian Personality Types and Their Socio-Cultural Roots," *Annals of the American Academy of Political and Social Sciences*, 311:147–157, May, 1957.

SPIRO, MELFORD E.: "Culture and Personality: The Natural History of a False Dichotomy," *Psychiatry*, 14:19–46, 1951.

SPIRO, MELFORD E.: *Children of the Kibbutz*, Harvard University Press, Cambridge, Mass., 1958.

SPITZ, RENÉ: "Hospitalism," in *The Psychoanalytic Study of the Child*, vol. 1, International Universities Press, Inc., New York, 1945, pp. 53–74.

SPOCK, BENJAMIN: *The Pocket Book of Child Care*, Pocket Books, Inc., New York, 1945, 1957.

SROLE, LEO: "Social Integration and Certain Corollaries: An Exploratory Study," *American Sociological Review*, 21:709–716, 1956.

STARKEY, MARION L.: *The Devil in Massachusetts*, Alfred A. Knopf, Inc., New York, 1949.

STEIN, MAURICE, AND ARTHUR VIDICH: *Sociology on Trial*, Prentice-Hall, Inc., Englewood Cliffs, N.J., 1964.

STEINBECK, JOHN: *The Moon is Down*, The Viking Press, Inc., New York, 1942.

STERN, BERNHARD J.: "Resistance to the Adoption of Technological Inventions," in U.S. National Resources Committee, *Technological Trends and National Policy*, 1937, pp. 39–66.

STERN, SOL: "The Call of the Black Panthers," *New York Times Magazine*, August 7, 1967, pp. 10ff.

STEWART, CHARLES T., JR.: "The Rural-Urban Dichotomy: Concepts and Uses," *American Journal of Sociology*, 64:152–158, 1958.

STIEHM, JUDITH H.: "The Teacher's Millstone," *Progressive*, 25:23–25, July, 1961.

STOETZEL, JEAN: Cited in ALVA MYRDAL AND VIOLA KLEIN, *Women's Two Roles: Home and Work*, Routledge & Kegan Paul, Ltd., London, 1956.

STOLTZ, LOIS KEEK: "Effects of Maternal Employment upon Children: Evidence from Research," *Child Development*, 31:749–782, 1960.

STONE, CAROL: "Some Family Characteristics of Socially Active and Inactive Teenagers," *Family Life Coordinator*, 8:53–57, 1960.

STONEQUIST, EVERETT H.: *The Marginal Man*, Charles Scribner's Sons, New York, 1937.

STOUFFER, SAMUEL A., ET AL.: *Studies in the Social Psychology of World War II*, vol. 2, *The American Soldier: Combat and Aftermath*, Princeton University Press, Princeton, N.J., 1949.

STOUFFER, SAMUEL A.: *Communism, Conformity and Civil Liberties*, Doubleday & Company, Inc., Garden City, N.Y., 1955.

STRAUS, MURRAY A.: "Deferred Gratification, Social Class, and the Achievement Syndrome," *American Sociological Review*, 27:326–335, June, 1962.

STRAUSS, ANSELM L.: "The Literature on Panic," *Journal of Abnormal and Social Psychology*, 39:317–328, 1944.

STREET, PEGGY, AND PIERRE STREET: "In Iran, a New Group Challenges Us," *New York Times Magazine*, July 23, 1961, pp. 11ff.

STRODTBECK, FRED L.: "Husband-Wife Interaction over Revealed Differences," *American Sociological Review*, 16:468–473, 1951.

STRODTBECK, FRED L., AND A. PAUL HARE: "Bibliography of Small Group Research," *Sociometry*, 17:107–178, May, 1954.

STUCKERT, ROBERT P.: "African Ancestry of the White American Population," *Ohio Journal of Science*, 58:155–160, 1958.

SULLIVAN, WALTER: "Seeing Things," *New York Times Book Reviews*, Aug. 28, 1966, pp. 2ff.

SUMNER, WILLIAM GRAHAM: *Folkways*, 3d ed., Ginn and Company, Boston, 1960.

TANNENBAUM, JUDITH: "The Neighborhood: A Socio-psychological Analysis," *Journal of Land Economy*, 24:358–369, 1948.

TAYLOR, MILLER LEE, AND A. R. JONES: *Rural Life in Urbanized Society*, Oxford University Press, Fair Lawn, N.J., 1964.

TERMAN, LEWIS M.: *Psychological Factors in Marital Happiness*, McGraw-Hill Book Company, New York, 1938.

TERMAN, LEWIS M.: *Gifted Group at Midlife: 35 Years' Follow-up of the Superior Child*, Stanford University Press, Stanford, Calif., 1959.

THOMAS, W. I.: *The Unadjusted Girl*, Little, Brown and Company, Boston, 1923.

THOMAS, W. I., AND FLORIAN ZNANIECKI: *The Polish Peasant in Europe and America*, Alfred A. Knopf, Inc., New York, 1927.

THOMPSON, PHILIP A.: "American Negro Student Revolt," *Contemporary Review*, 198:613ff., 1960.

THOMPSON, VICTOR A.: *Modern Organizations*, Alfred A. Knopf, Inc., New York, 1961.

THOMPSON, WARREN S.: *Danger Spots in World Population*, Alfred A. Knopf, Inc., New York, 1929.

THOMPSON, WAYNE E., AND JOHN E. HORTON: "Political Alienation as a Force in Political Action," *Social Forces*, 38:190–195, March, 1960.

Time, Apr. 25, 1960, p. 25, "Grosse Pointe's Gross Points."

Time, Aug. 11, 1961, pp. 20–21, "What's Wrong?" (*a*).

Time, Mar. 31, 1961, p. 14, "Recruits behind Bars" (*b*).

Time, Jan. 19, 1962, p. 35, "Rebellion by the Rules."

TONNIES, FERDINAND: *Community and Society*, tr. and ed. by CHARLES A. LOOMIS, Michigan State University Press, East Lansing, Mich., 1957.

TUDDENHAM, READ D.: "The Influence of a Distorted Group Norm upon Judgments of Adults and Children," *Journal of Psychology*, 52:231–239, 1961.

TUMIN, MELVIN J.: "Some Principles of Stratification: A Critical Analysis," *American Sociological Review*, 18:387–394, August, 1953.

TUMIN, MELVIN J.: "Some Unapplauded Consequences of Social Mobility," *Social Forces*, 36:21–37, 1957.

TURNER, RALPH H.: "Role-taking, Role Standpoint, and Reference Group Behavior," *American Journal of Sociology*, 61:316–338, 1956.

TURNER, RALPH H., AND SAMUEL J. SURACE: "Zoot-suiters and Mexicans: Symbols in Crowd Behavior," *American Journal of Sociology*, 62:14–20, 1956.

TURNER, RALPH H., AND LEWIS M. KILLIAN: *Collective Behavior*, Prentice-Hall, Inc., Englewood Cliffs, N.J., 1957.

TURNER, THOMAS B.: "The Liberal Arts in Medical Education," *Association of American Colleges Bulletin*, 44:71–77, 1958.

TYLER, EDWARD: *Primitive Culture: Researches into the Development of Mythology, Philosophy, Religion, Language, Art and Custom*, vol. 1, John Murray (Publishers) Ltd., London, 1871.

UNITED NATIONS: *The Future Growth of World Population*, New York, 1958.

UNNI, K. P.: "Polyandry in Malabar," *Sociological Bulletin* (India), 7:62–79, 1958.

USEEM, JOHN: "South Sea Island Strike: Labor-Management Relations in the Carolina Islands, Micronesia," in EDWARD H. SPICER (ED.), *Human Problems in Technological Change*, Russell Sage Foundation, New York, 1952, pp. 149–164.

VAN DER KROEF, JUSTUS M.: "Some Head-hunting Traditions of Southern New Guinea," *American Anthropologist*, 54:221–235, April, 1952.

VAN DER KROEF, JUSTUS M.: "The Changing Class Structure in Indonesia," *American Sociological Review*, 21:138–148, 1956.

VANDERZANDEN, JAMES W.: "Resistance and Social Movements," *Social Forces*, 37:312–315, 1959.

VANDERZANDEN, JAMES W.: "The Klan Revival," *American Journal of Sociology*, 65:456–462, 1960.

VAUGHN, JAMES: "An Experimental Study of Competition," *Journal of Applied Psychology*, 20:1–15 (1956).

VELLA, CHARLES G.: "Italian Catholicism," *Catholic World*, 179:367–372 (1954).

VERNON, RAYMOND: *Metropolis 1985: An Interpretation of the Findings of the New York Metropolitan Study*, Harvard University Press, Cambridge, Mass., 1960.

VINE, MARGARET WILSON: *An Introduction to Sociological Theory*, David McKay Company, Inc., New York, 1959.

VON HENTIG, HANS: "Redhead and Outlaws," *Journal of Criminal Law and Criminology*, 38:1–6, May-June, 1947.

WADA, GEORGE, AND JAMES C. DAVIES: "Riots and Rioters," *Western Political Quarterly*, 10:864–874, 1957.

WAKEFIELD, DAN: "The Careful Conversion of the Nouveau Riche," *Esquire*, November, 1961, pp. 105ff.

WALLACE, A. F. C.: "The Modal Personality Structure of the Tuscarora Indians as Revealed by the Rorschach Test," *Bureau of American Ethnology*, Bulletin no. 150, 1952 (*a*).

WALLACE, A. F. C.: "Individual Differences and Cultural Uniformities," *American Sociological Review*, 17:747–750, 1952 (*b*).

WALLERSTEIN, JAMES S., AND CLEMENT J. WYLE: "Our Law-abiding Law Breakers," *National Probation*, pp. 107–112, March-April, 1947.

WARNER, LUCIEN: "A Survey of Psychological Opinion on E.S.P.," *Journal of Parapsychology*, 2:296–301, 1938.

WARNER, WELLMAN J.: "The Roles of the Sociologist," *Bulletin of the American Sociological Society* (now the American Sociological Association), September, 1951.

WARNER, W. LLOYD: "Murngin Warfare," *Oceania*, 1:457–494, 1931.

WARNER, W. LLOYD, AND PAUL S. LUNT: *The Social Life of a Modern Community*, Yale University Press, New Haven, Conn., 1941.

WARNER, W. LLOYD, AND PAUL S. LUNT: *The Status System of a Modern Community*, Yale University Press, New Haven, Conn., 1942.

WARNER, W. LLOYD, AND JAMES C. ABEGGLEN: *Big Business Leaders in America*, Harper & Row, Publishers, Incorporated, New York, 1955.

WARRINER, CHARLES K.: "The Nature and Functions of Official Morality," *American Journal of Sociology*, 54:165–168, 1958.

WEAVER, ROBERT C.: *The Urban Complex*, Doubleday & Company, Inc., Garden City, N.Y., 1964.

WEBER, MAX: *The Protestant Ethic and the Spirit of Capitalism*, tr. by TALCOTT PARSONS, George Allen & Unwin, Ltd., London, 1930.

WEBER, MAX: *From Max Weber: Essays in Sociology*, tr. and ed. by H. H. Gerth and C. Wright Mills, Oxford University Press, Fair Lawn, N.J., 1946.

WEINBERG, S. KIRSON: *Society and Personality Disorder*, Prentice-Hall, Inc., Englewood Cliffs, N.J., 1952.

WEINBERGER, ANDREW D.: "A Reappraisal of the Constitutionality of the Miscegenation Statutes," *Journal of Negro Education*, 26:435–446, 1957.

WELLMAN, PAUL L.: *The Trampling Herd*, Carrick and Evans, New York, 1939.

WEST, JAMES: *Plainville, U.S.A.*, Columbia University Press, New York, 1945.

WESTIE, FRANK R.: "Social Distance Scales: A Tool for the Study of Stratification," *Sociology and Social Research*, 43:251–258, 1959.

WHELPTON, PASCAL K., AND CLYDE V. KISER: "Social and Psychological Factors Affecting Fertility," *Milbank Memorial Fund Quarterly*, 21:221–280, 1943.

WHITE, LESLIE A.: "Culturological vs. Psychological Interpretations of Human Behavior," *American Sociological Review*, 12:686–698, 1947.

WHITTAKER, JAMES O.: "Cognitive Dissonance and the Effectiveness of Persuasive Communication," *Public Opinion Quarterly*, 28:547–555, Winter, 1964.

WHYTE, WILLIAM F.: *Street Corner Society*, The University of Chicago Press, Chicago, 1955.

WHYTE, WILLIAM H., JR.: "The Wives of Management," and "The Corporation and the Wife," *Fortune*, October, 1951, pp. 86–88ff.; and November, 1951, pp. 109–111ff.

WHYTE, WILLIAM H., JR.: "Urban Sprawl," in EDITORS OF *Fortune, The Exploding Metropolis*, Doubleday & Company, Inc., Garden City, N.Y., 1958, pp. 115–139.

WILDER, RUSSELL M.: "Experimental Induction of Psychoneuroses through Restriction of Intake of Thiamine," in Milbank Memorial Fund, *Biology of Mental Health and Disease*, Harper & Row, Publishers, Incorporated, New York, 1952, pp. 531–538.

WILENSKY, HAROLD, AND HUGH EDWARDS: "The Skidder," *American Sociological Review*, 24:215–231, 1959.

WILLIAMS, F. E.: *The Natives of the Purari Delta, Anthropological Report no. 5*, Port Moresby, Territory of Papua, 1924.

WILLIAMS, ROGER J.: *Biochemical Individuality*, John Wiley & Sons, Inc., New York, 1956.

WILSON, BRYAN R.: "The Pentacostalist Minister: Role Conflicts and States Considerations," *American Journal of Sociology*, 54:494–504, March, 1959.

WINIATA, M.: "Racial and Cultural Relations in New Zealand," *Phylon*, 19:286–296, 1958.

WINSLOW, CHARLES N.: "The Social Behavior of Cats," *Journal of Comparative Psychology*, 37:297–326, 1944.

WIRTH, LOUIS: *The Ghetto*, The University of Chicago Press, Chicago, 1928.

WIRTH, LOUIS: "Urbanism as a Way of Life," *American Journal of Sociology*, 44:1–25, 1938.

WISSLER, CLARK: "Depression and Revolt," *Natural History*, 41:108–112, 1938.

WITTFOGEL, KARL A.: *Oriental Despotism*, Yale University Press, New Haven, Conn., 1957.

WOLF, ELEANOR P.: "The Invasion-Succession Sequence as a Self-fulfilling Prophecy," *Journal of Social Issues*, 13:7–20, 1957.

WOLFE, DONALD M.: "Power and Authority in the Family," in DORWIN CARTWRIGHT (ED.), *Studies in Social Power*, Institute for Social Research, University of Michigan, Ann Arbor, Mich., 1959.

WOLFLE, DAEL, for the Commission on Human Resources and Advanced Training: *America's Resources of Specialized Talent*, Harper & Row, Publishers, Incorporated, New York, 1954.

WOMEN'S BUREAU: *Who Are the Working Mothers?* U.S. Department of Labor, Leaflet, no. 37, 1961.

WOOD, ROBERT C.: *Suburbia: Its People and Their Politics,* Houghton Mifflin Company, Boston, 1958.

WOODWARD, COMER VANN: *The Strange Career of Jim Crow,* Oxford University Press, Fair Lawn, N.J., 1957.

WORSLEY, PETER: *The Trumpet Shall Sound: A Study of "Cargo" Cults in Melanesia,* MacGibbon & Kee, London, 1957.

WORTHY, WILLIAM: "The Angriest Negroes," *Esquire,* Feb., 1961, pp. 102–105.

WRIGHT, CHARLES R., AND HERBERT H. HYMAN: "Voluntary Association Memberships," *American Sociological Review,* 23:284–294, 1958.

WRIGHT, GRACE S.: *Subject Offerings and Enrollments in Public Secondary Schools,* Government Printing Office, Washington, D.C., 1965.

YANG, C. K.: *The Chinese Family in the Communist Revolution,* The Technology Press of the Massachusetts Institute of Technology, Cambridge, Mass., 1959.

YINGER, J. MILTON: *Toward a Field Theory of Behavior,* McGraw-Hill Book Company, New York, 1965.

YOUNG, KIMBALL: *Isn't One Wife Enough? The Story of Mormon Polygamy,* Holt, Rinehart and Winston, Inc., New York, 1954.

YOUNG, LEONTINE: *Out of Wedlock,* McGraw-Hill Book Company, New York, 1954.

YOUNG, PAULINE V.: *The Pilgrims of Russian Town,* The University of Chicago Press, Chicago, 1932.

ZILBOORG, GREGORY: *Mind, Medicine, and Man,* Harcourt, Brace & World, Inc., New York, 1943.

ZORBAUGH, HARVEY: *The Gold Coast and the Slum,* The University of Chicago Press, Chicago, 1929.

GLOSSARY

ACCOMMODATION   Peaceful adjustment between hostile or competing groups; "antagonistic cooperation."

ACCULTURATION   Acquisition by a group or individual of the traits of another culture.

ACHIEVED ROLE OR STATUS   Role or status attained by individual choice or effort.

AFFINAL   Related by marriage as with a relative of spouse.

AGGREGATE   A gathering of people without conscious interaction.

ALTERNATIVES   A number of possibilities among which each member of a society must choose; e.g., to be married or single.

AMALGAMATION   Biological interbreeding of two or more peoples of distinct physical appearance until they become one stock.

ANOMIE   A situation in which a large number of persons lack integration with stable institutions, to the extent that they are left rootless and normless.

ANXIETY   Fear that is out of proportion to any objective stimulus.

APPLIED SCIENCE   Scientific methodology applied to the search for knowledge which will be useful in solving practical problems.

ASCRIBED ROLE OR STATUS   A role or status assigned without regard to individual preference, ability, or performance.

ASSIMILATION   Mutual cultural diffusion through which persons or groups come to share a common culture.

ASSOCIATION   A group with its own administrative structure, organized to pursue some common interest of its members.

ATTITUDE   A tendency to feel and act in a certain way.

AUTHORITY   An established right to order the actions of other people.

BUREAUCRACY   A pyramid of officials who conduct rationally the work of a large organization.

CASTE SYSTEM   A stratified social system in which social position is entirely determined by parentage, with no provision for achieved status.

CHARISMATIC LEADERSHIP   Type of leadership in which the personality and image of the leader give him great authority and influence.

CLIQUE   A small group of intimates with intense in-group feelings based on common sentiments and interests.

COMPARTMENTALIZATION   Process of attempting to isolate parts of the personality from each other so that the individual is unaware of value conflicts.

COMPETITION   Process of seeking to obtain a reward by surpassing all rivals.

CONCEPT   An idea or mental image that embodies generalized or common elements found in a number of specific cases.

CONFLICT   The effort to obtain rewards by eliminating or weakening the competitors.

CONJUGAL FAMILY   A married couple and their dependent children.

CONSANGUINE FAMILY   Extended clan of blood relatives with their mates and children.

CONTRACULTURE   A subculture not merely different from, but also in opposition to, the conventional behavior of the society; e.g., the delinquent subculture.

COOPERATION   Joint activity in pursuit of common goals or shared rewards.

CROWD   A temporary collection of people reacting together to stimuli.

CULTURAL INTEGRATION   The degree to which the traits, complexes, and institutions of a culture are harmoniously adjusted to one another.

CULTURAL PLURALISM   Toleration of cultural differences within a common society; allowing different groups to retain their distinctive cultures.

CULTURAL RELATIVISM   Concept that the function, meaning, and "desirability" of a trait depend upon its cultural setting.

CULTURAL TRAIT   Smallest unit of culture as perceived by a given observer.

CULTURE   Everything that is socially learned and shared by the members of a society; social heritage which the individual receives from the group; a system of behavior shared by members of a society.

CULTURE COMPLEX   A cluster of related traits organized around a particular activity; less elaborate and less important than an institution.

DEFERRED GRATIFICATION PATTERN   Postponement of present satisfactions for future rewards.

DEMOGRAPHY   Statistical study of population composition, distribution, and trends.

DEVIATION   Failure to conform to customary norms of a society.

DISCOVERY   A shared human perception of a fact or relationship which already exists.

DISCRIMINATION   A practice that treats equal people unequally; limiting opportunity or reward according to race, religion, or ethnic group.

ELITE   A small controlling group within a society.

ENDOGAMY   Requirement that mates be chosen within some specified group.

ETHNIC GROUP   A number of people with a common cultural heritage which sets them apart from others in a variety of social relationships.

ETHNOCENTRISM   Tendency of each group to take for granted the superiority of its own culture.

ETHOS   Unifying spirit running through various aspects of a culture.

EXOGAMY   Requirement that mates be selected outside some specified group.

FAMILY   A kinship grouping which provides for the rearing of children and for certain other human needs.

FERAL MAN   Individual supposedly reared apart from human society and hence imperfectly socialized.

FOLK SOCIETY   Small, isolated, often nonliterate, homogeneous society characterized by a high degree of group solidarity, traditionalism, and informal social control.

FOLKWAYS   Customary, normal, habitual behavior characteristic of the members of the group.

GEMEINSCHAFT   A society in which most relationships are either personal or traditional.

GESELLSCHAFT   A society based on contractual as contrasted with traditional relationships.

GHETTO   Any part of a city in which the population is restricted to a particular ethnic group; historically applied to a Jewish district, but today often applied to Negro districts.

GOALS   Attainments which our values define as worthy.

GROUP   An aggregate of people who have a consciousness of membership and of interaction.

GROUP DYNAMICS   The scientific study of the interaction within small groups.

HUMAN ECOLOGY   The study of man in relation to his physical environment; a study of how people and institutions are located in space.

HYPOTHESIS   Tentative, unverified statement of the relationship of known facts; a reasonable proposition worthy of scientific testing.

IDEOLOGY   A system of ideas which sanctions a set of norms.

IN-GROUP   A group with which one has a sense of identity or of belonging.

INFLUENCE   The ability to affect the decision and actions of others without any formal authority to do so.

INSTINCT   An inborn behavior pattern characteristic of all members of the species.

INSTITUTION   An organized cluster of folkways and mores centered around a major human activity; organized system of social relationships which embodies certain common values and procedures and meets certain basic needs of society.

INVENTION   A new combination or a new use of old ideas of the culture.

LATENT FUNCTIONS   Unintended effects of a policy or program.

LAW   Regulations enforced by coercive power which is either organized or sanctioned by the society; sometimes referred to as "stateways."

LOOKING-GLASS SELF   Perception of the self that one forms by interpreting the reactions of others to him.

MANIFEST FUNCTIONS   Professed objectives of institutions or associations.

MARGINAL MAN   Individual torn between two or more cultures; partly assimilated into each and fully assimilated into neither; often an immigrant.

MARRIAGE   The approved social pattern whereby two or more persons establish a family.

MEAN   Sum of all the items divided by the number of items; sometimes referred to as the "average."

MEDIAN   The midpoint in a series of items arranged according to size.

MODE   Value which appears most frequently in a series.

MONOGAMY   Marriage form permitting only one mate (at a time).

MORES   Strong ideas of right and wrong which require certain actions and forbid others.

NORM   A standard of behavior. Statistical norm is a measure of actual conduct; cultural norm states the expected behavior of the culture.

OPPRESSION PSYCHOSIS   Tendency for members of a group with a history of persecution to feel persecuted even in situations where they are not being mistreated.

PERSONALITY   The sum total of a person's behavior characteristics.

POLYANDRY   A form of polygamy in which one or more husbands share one wife.

POLYGAMY   A plurality of mates.

POLYGYNY   A form of polygamy in which one husband has two or more wives.

POSITION   The rank one holds in an hierarchial series.

POWER   The ability to control the actions of others, regardless of their wishes.

PRIMARY GROUP   Small group in which people come to know one another intimately as individual personalities; distinct from the impersonal, formal, utilitarian secondary group.

PRIMITIVE   Characteristic of small societies which are culturally homogeneous and relatively isolated, with fairly simple technological and economic organization. Such a society is usually, but not always, preliterate.

PUBLIC   A scattered group of people who share an interest in a particular topic.

PURE SCIENCE   Search for knowledge for its own sake without primary regard to its practical usefulness or consequences.

RACE   A group of people somewhat different from other people in a combination of inherited physical characteristics, but the meaning of the term is also substantially determined by popular social definition.

REFERENCE GROUP   Any group accepted as model or guide for our judgments and actions.

RITE OF PASSAGE   Any ritual which marks movement from one life stage to another, such as the ceremonies attending birth, death, puberty, or marriage.

ROLE   Behavior of one who holds a certain status.

SACRED SOCIETY   A society with a homogeneous set of folkways and unified moral values which are revered as sacred and eternal.

SCIENTIFIC METHODS   Methods of study which produce organized, verified knowledge.

SECONDARY GROUP   Group in which contacts are impersonal, segmental, and utilitarian, as distinct from the small, intimate, highly personal primary group.

SECULAR SOCIETY   Society with a diversity of folkways and mores; also any group in which religious influence is minimized.

SECULARIZATION   Movement from a sacred to a rationalistic, utilitarian, experimental viewpoint.

SEGREGATION   Separation of two or more groups based on a desire to avoid equal-status social contact.

SOCIAL CLASS   A stratum of persons of similar position in the social-status continuum.

SOCIAL CONTROL   Means and processes by which society secures its members' conformity to its norms and values.

SOCIAL DISTANCE   Degree of closeness to, or acceptance of, members of other groups.

SOCIAL MOBILITY   Movement from one class level to another. Synonymous with "vertical" mobility.

SOCIAL MOVEMENT   A collectivity acting with some continuity to promote or resist a change in the society or group of which it is a part.

SOCIAL ORDER   A system of people, relationships, and customs operating smoothly to accomplish a society's tasks.

SOCIAL PROCESSES   Repetitive forms of behavior which are commonly found in social life.

SOCIALIZATION   Process by which one internalizes the norms of his groups so that a distinct self emerges unique to this individual.

SOCIETY   A group of people who share a common culture.

SOCIOLOGY   Scientific study of man's social life.

SPECIALTIES   Traits and complexes shared by some, but not all, members of a society; e.g., baby nursing.

STATUS   Position of an individual in a group, or of a group in relation to other groups.

SUBCULTURE   A cluster of behavior patterns related to the general culture of a society and yet distinguishable from it; behavior patterns of a distinct group within the general society.

SYMBIOSIS (SOCIAL)   Mutual interdependence without conscious decision to cooperate.

SYMBOL   That which stands for something beyond its own immediate meaning; especially a specific object representing a more diffused, generalized, or abstract concept. The flag, the cross, and Uncle Sam are examples.

SYMBOLIC COMMUNICATION   Exchanging meanings through words and other symbols which have no meaning in themselves, but to which agreed meanings have become attached; distinguished from exchange of meanings through instinctive barks and growls.

UNIVERSALS   Cultural traits required of all members of a given society.

UTOPIA   A perfect society.

VALUES   Measures of goodness or desirability.

XENOCENTRISM   Rejection of the culture of one's own group.

Name Index